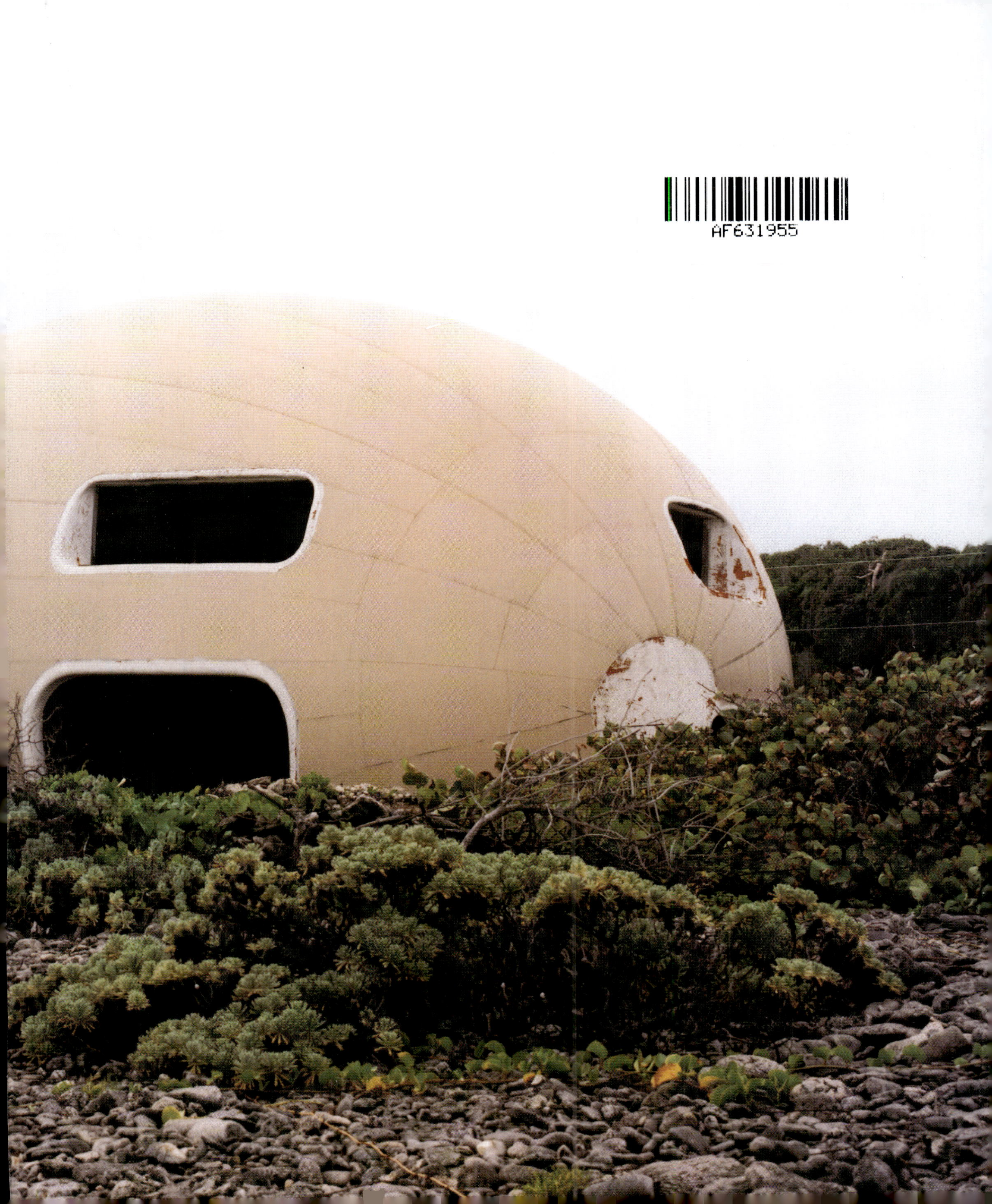

DIE PARKETT-REIHE MIT GEGENWARTSKÜNSTLERN / THE PARKETT SERIES WITH CONTEMPORARY ARTISTS

Book Series with contemporary artists in English and German, published three times a year. Each volume is created in collaboration with artists, who contribute an original work specially made for the readers of Parkett. The works are reproduced in the regular edition and available in a limited and signed Special Edition.

Buchreihe mit Gegenwartskünstlern in deutscher und englischer Sprache, erscheint dreimal im Jahr. Jeder Band entsteht mit Künstlern oder Künstlerinnen, die eigens für die Leser von Parkett einen Originalbeitrag gestalten. Diese Werke sind in der gesamten Auflage abgebildet und zusätzlich in einer limitierten und signierten Vorzugsausgabe erhältlich.

PARKETT NR. 63 ENTSTEHT IN COLLABORATION MIT • **TRACEY EMIN, WILLIAM KENTRIDGE, GREGOR SCHNEIDER** • WILL BE COLLABORATING ON PARKETT NO. 63

JAHRESABONNEMENT (DREI NUMMERN) / ANNUAL SUBSCRIPTION (THREE ISSUES) SFR. 116.– (SCHWEIZ), € 78 (BRD), € 82 (ÜBRIGES EUROPA), US$ 80 (USA AND CANADA ONLY)

ZWEI- UND DREIJAHRESABONNEMENTPREISE SIEHE GELBE BESTELLKARTE IM HEFT / FOR TWO & THREE YEAR RATES, PLEASE CONSULT YELLOW ORDER FORM.

Zürichsee Druckereien AG (Stäfa) Satz, Litho, Druck/Copy, Printing, Color Separations

PARKETT-VERLAG AG, ZÜRICH, SEPTEMBER 2001 PRINTED IN SWITZERLAND ISBN 3-907582-12-8 ISSN 0256-0917

Cover, front page & flap / Umschlag und Klappe: THOMAS DEMAND, TERRACE/TERRASSE, 1998, C-Print Diasec.

Inside cover page & flap / Innere Umschlagseite & Klappe: JOHN WESLEY, WOW! OOPS! OH BOY!, 1999, acrylic on canvas / Acryl auf Leinwand.

Inside cover page & page 1: TACITA DEAN, BUBBLE HOUSE, 1999, location photograph / Photo am Drehort.

Back cover / Rückseite: JOHN WESLEY, JOKE, 2000, acrylic on canvas, detail / SCHERZ, Acryl auf Leinwand, Ausschnitt.

PARKETT Zürich New York Frankfurt

Bice Curiger Chefredaktorin/Editor-in-Chief; **Jacqueline Burckhardt** Redaktorin/Senior Editor; **Cay Sophie Rabinowitz** Redaktorin USA/Senior Editor US; **Susanne Schmidt** Textredaktion und Produktion/Editing and Production; **Hanna Koller · Simone Eggstein · Trix Wetter** (beurlaubt/on temporary leave) Graphik/Design; **Catherine Schelbert** Englisches Lektorat/Editorial Assistant for English; **Claudia Meneghini Nevzadi** Korrektorat/Proof Reading; **Isabelle Hren** Graphikvolontariat/Design Trainee

Beatrice Fässler Vorzugsausgaben, Inserate/Special Editions, Advertising; **Brigitte Grüninger** Buchvertrieb, Administration/Distribution, Administration; **Mathias Arnold** Abonnemente/Subscriptions; **Ali Subotnick** Redaktionsassistenz, Vorzugsausgaben und Marketing USA/Assistant Editor, Editions and Marketing US; **Monika Condrea** Abonnemente USA/Subscriptions US; **Mariya Hoskins** Praktikantin USA/Intern US; **Adrian Koerfer** Deutsche Verlagsvertretung/German Representative

Jacqueline Burckhardt – Bice Curiger – Dieter von Graffenried Herausgeber/Parkett Board; **Jacqueline Burckhardt – Bice Curiger – Dieter von Graffenried – Walter Keller – Peter Blum** Gründer/Founders

Dieter von Graffenried Verleger/Publisher

www.parkettart.com

PARKETT-VERLAG AG, QUELLENSTRASSE 27, CH-8031 ZURICH, TEL. 41-1-271 81 40, FAX 41-1-272 43 01
PARKETT, NEW YORK, 155 AV. OF THE AMERICAS, N.Y. 10013, PHONE (212) 673-2660, FAX (212) 271-0704
PARKETT-VERLAG AG, TANNENWALDALLEE 17, D-61348 BAD HOMBURG, FAX 06172-937 444

Editorial

«Aus Freude an neuen Bekanntschaften hebt Gerda diese in die Höhe und Jörg photographiert sie.» So liest sich die Notiz zu den Photos von Gerda Steiner und Jörg Lenzlinger im Insert dieser Ausgabe, die in den Jahren 1998-1999 auf einer Weltreise entstanden sind. Es sind heitere Bilder von lachenden und staunenden Menschen, die kurz zuvor vom Boden gehoben worden sind. «Abheben» erscheint metaphorisch, und wir stellen fest: Eine einfache, kindliche, spontan mitreissende Aktion vermag über alle kulturellen Unterschiede und Konformitätsmarken hinweg zu beflügeln und zu entwaffnen.

In seiner Direktheit steht das Insert sicherlich im Kontrast zu den Collaborations mit John Wesley, Tacita Dean und Thomas Demand. Hier betreten wir das Reich des Rätsels, der Abwesenheit, der Erinnerungsräume, der Stellvertretung, der Künstlichkeit und Stilisierung. Und doch gilt auch hier das Stichwort Reise als mögliche verbindende Konstante, Reisen in Raum und Zeit. Mehr als zu den Menschen, führen diese zu Schauplätzen und mentalen Echoräumen. Verlassen und nur von Gespenstern bewohnt, heisst es manchmal. Oder es werden Vorstellungen von Objekten genährt, die Ominöses zu erzählen wüssten, wenn sie nur reden könnten.

Jemand meinte, die Parkett-Editionen dieses Bandes liessen an «Fernweh» denken. Tatsächlich sehen wir ein Boot mit zwei Männern auf dem See und eine zurückgelassene Figur am Ufer. Eine Postkarte, aus Afrika nach Zürich entsandt, hält den mythischen «rayon vert», das Phänomen des grünen Strahls fest, der bei ganz bestimmten, seltenen Konstellationen des Sonnenuntergangs am Meereshorizont aufleuchtet. Und schliesslich lässt auch die flugbereite Maschine, deren Tür einladend offen steht, an Fernreisen denken – erst wenn wir auf Grund des Streifenemblems erkennen, dass hier das Flugzeug des amerikanischen Präsidenten ab- oder vielmehr nachgebildet wurde, gelangen wir sozusagen auf den Boden der alltäglichen Tatsachen zurück.

Beim Schreiben dieser Zeilen ereilte uns die Nachricht vom Tode von Juan Muñoz, mit dem wir 1995 zusammengearbeitet haben. Wie eine merkwürdige Überblendung schiebt sich das Bild seiner Edition für Parkett Nr. 43 vor das innere Auge – jene zwei Gestalten, die eine auf dem Rücken der anderen hockend –, als wärs ein Photo aus unserem Insert. Doch Muñoz' Vision ist am andern Pol angesiedelt in Isolation, Zurückhaltung und einer um sich greifenden Stille. Vor allem: Das Bild ist jeweils nur kurze Zeit sichtbar, wenn ein flüchtiger Atemhauch sich über die Scheibe legt, ehe er sich wieder auflöst.

Bice Curiger

Editorial

"Delighted at making new friends, Gerda lifts them up and Jörg takes pictures of them." This comment accompanies the photographs in our Insert, taken by Gerda Steiner and Jörg Lenzlinger on their journey around the world in 1998–1999. They are light-hearted pictures of people laughing in surprise at having just been lifted off the ground. "Lifting" has metaphorical implications and we notice that a simple, childlike, infectiously spontaneous act rises above cultural difference and the marks of conformity—and does so with disarming ease.

The essentially unfiltered immediacy of the Insert stands in contrast to the work of our collaboration artists in this issue: John Wesley, Tacita Dean, and Thomas Demand. Here we enter realms of enigma, absence, memory, exchange, artificiality, and stylization. Yet a uniting constant might be found in the keyword, 'journey'. The artists' journeys through time and space do not take us to people but to events and places of mental reverberation. Deserted and inhabited only by ghosts is a phrase we have heard before. Or the idea is nurtured of objects with ominous stories to tell if only they could speak.

While working on this issue, someone remarked that the editions conjure a sense of wanderlust. We actually see a figure left behind on shore gazing at two men in a rowboat. A postcard sent to Zurich from Africa shows the mythical "rayon vert," the phenomenon of the green ray that joins the sunset on the ocean horizon upon the rare convergence of certain climatic conditions. And finally visions of faraway lands are evoked by the carrier, its hatch invitingly open prior to take-off. Not until we espy the emblem indicating that this is a picture or rather a reconstruction of the American President's Air Force One vehicle do we return to the solid terrain of everyday facts.

On writing these lines, we were overtaken by news of the death of Juan Muñoz, with whom we worked in 1995. Like a disquieting double exposure, the image of his edition for Parkett no. 43—those two figures, one of them carrying the other on his back—takes possession of one's inner eye, as if it were a photograph from this issue's Insert. But Muñoz's vision occupies the opposite pole in its isolation, reticence, and spreading silence. Above all, its visible life is ineluctably ephemeral, revealed only for the few seconds when the vapor of a breath has misted the glass.

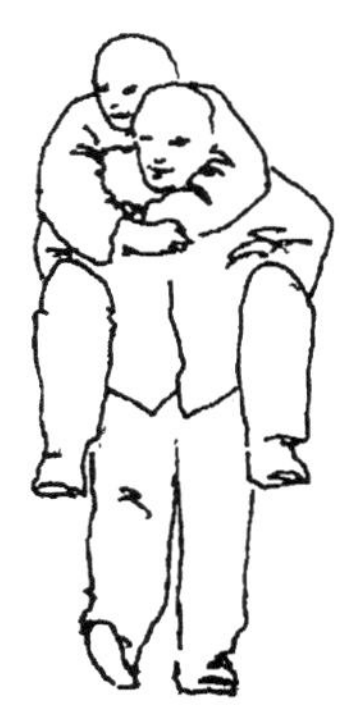

Bice Curiger

Household

PHILIP URSPRUNG

Wer im Frühling 1964 an der Cornell University in Ithaca, New York, studierte, hatte Gelegenheit, an einem aussergewöhnlichen Ereignis mitzuwirken. Allan Kaprow (geboren 1927) führte im Rahmen des Contemporary Arts Festival eines seiner spektakulärsten Happenings durch. Als Vorbereitung hatte er den Teilnehmern den Ablauf erläutert und drei Gruppen gebildet, Männer, Frauen und Volk. Am 3. Mai 1964 trafen sich alle auf einer Mülldeponie ausserhalb der Stadt. Unter dem Titel HOUSEHOLD spielten sie einen Tag lang Aktivitäten des häuslichen Lebens – Einrichten, Essen, Sex und Erholen. Am Morgen richteten sie sich ein. Die Männer bauten aus herumliegendem Sperrgut einen Turm, die Frauen ein Nest. Am Mittag zogen einige Studenten ein Autowrack im Schlepptau ins Lager. Die Beute wurde mit Marmelade eingerieben und Frauen, Männer und das Volk assen nacheinander. Nach dem Essen lockten die Frauen die Männer zu sich. Es kam zu einer Art Geschlechterkampf, auf dessen Höhepunkt sich alle die Oberhemden vom Leib rissen, sangen und das Auto in Brand steckten. Am späten Nachmittag fuhren zuerst die Frauen weg. Die Männer und das Volk rauchten noch eine Zigarette, bevor auch sie nach Hause gingen und das Happening beendet war.

HOUSEHOLD war, wie viele der seit 1959 von Kaprow und anderen Happeners wie Claes Oldenburg veranstalteten Happenings, eine Auftragsarbeit.[1] Kaprow schuf daher einen engen Bezug zum Ort und den Teilnehmern. Die Cornell University mit ihrer renommierten Architekturschule liegt in einem Park von Fredrick Law Olmsted, dem Landschaftsarchitekten des New Yorker Central Park. Ein architektonisches Motiv drängte sich also auf. Ausserdem war für die gerade dem Elternhaus entwachsenen Studenten das gemeinsame Haushalten in den nach Geschlechtern getrennten Studentenheimen sowie der Kontakt mit dem anderen Geschlecht zweifellos die einschneidendste Erfahrung. (Die Antibabypille war

PHILIP URSPRUNG ist Professor für Geschichte der Gegenwartskunst (Förderungsprofessur des Schweizerischen Nationalfonds) an der Eidgenössischen Technischen Hochschule Zürich. Von 1999 bis 2001 war er Gastprofessor an der Hochschule der Künste Berlin. Sein Buch *Grenzen der Kunst: Allan Kaprow und das Happening, Robert Smithson und die Land Art* erscheint 2001 bei Silke Schreiber, München.

Allan Kaprows Ökonomie

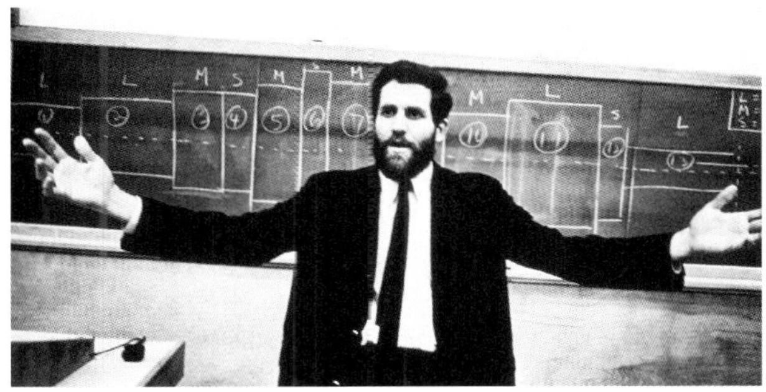

Allan Kaprow erläutert den Ablauf von HOUSEHOLD, Cornell University, Ithaca, New York, 2. Mai 1964 / Allan Kaprow, explaining the score of HOUSEHOLD. (PHOTO: SOL GOLDBERG)

im Mai 1960 freigegeben worden, und die puritanische amerikanische Gesellschaft stand am Beginn der *sexual liberation.*) Schliesslich regten sich in jenem Frühling an der Westküste auch die ersten Keime der Studentenrevolte, die den Generationenkonflikt der 60er Jahre markieren sollten. Kaprow selber hatte ironisch vom «pubertären» Charakter der Happenings gesprochen, die er als typisch für eine Gesellschaft auf dem Weg zu «kultureller Reife» bezeichnete.[2)]

Die umzäunte Deponie, eine Mischung aus Ruinenlandschaft und Spielplatz, fungierte als atmosphärischer Schauplatz von HOUSEHOLD – getreu der Devise des amerikanischen Philosophen John Dewey, dass das «Leben in einer Umgebung stattfindet, und zwar nicht nur in dieser, sondern wegen dieser».[3)] Deweys pragmatische Philosophie entsprach Kaprows Interesse an der individuellen Erfahrung. Tatsächlich sind die konkreten Erfahrungen der Teilnehmer, also die Vorfreude, die Fahrt an den ungewohnten Ort, der Gestank des Mülls, der süsse Geschmack von Erdbeermarmelade auf dem Metall des Autos, der beissende Rauch in den Augen, das Herumbalgen mit dem anderen Geschlecht etc. das eigentliche «Material» des Happenings. Diese Erfahrungen sind nicht vermittelbar, aber sie können in anderer Form wiederholt werden – Kaprow führte denn auch viele Happenings in mehreren Varianten auf – und sie sind für jedermann leicht nachvollziehbar.

Schrott und Haushaltgegenstände, die zum Bildrepertoire von Assemblage und Pop-Art gehörten, verwendete Kaprow hingegen bloss als Requisiten. Seine Haltung unterscheidet sich denn auch grundsätzlich vom damaligen Mainstream. Sie gleicht nur scheinbar jener Verwandlung des Alltäglichen zu Kunst, die die Kunstwelt Anfang der 60er Jahre faszinierte. Sei es im Werk von Marcel Duchamp, dem «Woolworth-Spiritualisten» (Robert Smithson)[4)], in Andy Warhols Idee der «Resteverwertungsphilosophie»[5)] oder Jean Tinguelys HOMAGE TO NEW YORK: A SELF-CONSTRUCTING AND SELF-DESTROYING WORK OF ART (1960). Diese Künstler operierten im Spannungsfeld von Kunst und Nicht-Kunst, beziehungsweise Hochkunst und Massenkultur und zielten auf die «Verklärung des Gewöhnlichen» (Arthur C. Danto). Für Kaprow hingegen war die Kunst kein Ort, wo die Wirklichkeit erhöht oder reflektiert wurde. Für ihn zählte nicht die Vermittlung zwischen Kunst und Leben, sondern allenfalls deren Konfrontation. Die genuin modernistische Frage nach dem Wesen der Kunst interessierte ihn nicht. In seinen Worten: «Die alten Unterscheidungen zwischen Kunst, Anti- oder Nichtkunst sind Pseudo-Unterscheidungen, die schlicht unsere Zeit vergeuden...»[6]

HOUSEHOLD nimmt aber auch dadurch eine Sonderstellung in der Kunstgeschichte ein, dass Kaprow die bei Happening und Performance übliche Trennung zwischen Akteuren und Zuschauern aufgehoben hatte. Er selber spielte ohnehin mit. Aber ausser dem Photographen der Lokalzeitung und einem Kameramann hatte HOUSEHOLD keine Zuschauer, sondern nur Mitwirkende. Der Unterschied zwischen aktivem Künstler und passivem Publikum, zwischen Produktion und Rezeption, zwischen Wirklichkeit und Repräsentation war aufgehoben. Kaprow hatte die traditionelle Ökonomie der Darstellung verändert und damit eine eingespielte Ökonomie der Bedeutung in Frage gestellt.

Die Kunstwelt hat ihm dies bis heute nicht verziehen. In einer Mischung aus Unbehagen und Genugtuung reduziert die Kritik Kaprows Happenings auf etwas, das verschwindet und sich damit gleichsam von selbst aus der Kunstgeschichte hinausschreibt. Sie verdrängt dabei die Tatsache, dass gerade die mittels Photographien und Text dokumentierten Happenings der Historiographie in besonderem Masse entgegenkommen und «vollständiger» beschreibbar sind als Skulptur und Malerei. Aber vielleicht muss sie dies verdrängen, denn Kaprows Kunst gefährdet auch das angestammte Privileg der Kritik, Bilder in Text zu übersetzen. Eine adäquate Beschreibung von HOUSEHOLD (mein eigener Text ist davon nicht ausgenommen) müsste seinerseits eine Art Happening sein.

Kaprow ging es nicht um den Prozess des Verschwindens. Wie auf den Müllhalden die Abfälle der Haushalte einer boomenden Konsumgesellschaft landeten, deren Produkte der *planned obsolescence* unterlagen, so hatten seiner Ansicht nach auch die Kunstwerke eine begrenzte Lebensdauer. Er wollte diese Fragilität und Kurzlebigkeit aber nicht sublimieren, also nicht das Verschwinden verewigen, sondern vielmehr artikulieren. Nicht die avantgardistische «Tradition des Neuen» (Harold Rosenberg), sondern das Re-Arrangieren des Bestehenden interessierte ihn. In HOUSEHOLD ist ihm dies vielleicht am schönsten gelungen. Denn in der Kunstgeschichte herrscht wie im Haushalt (griechisch: Ökonomie) ein fortwährendes Hin und Her zwischen Ordnung und Unordnung, Alt und Neu, Dauer und Moment. Dinge werden weggeworfen, verloren, gefunden, beschädigt und repariert. Die Kunstgeschichte ist wie ein Haushalt nie fertig, nie ordentlich. Mit HOUSEHOLD hat Kaprow dies nicht illustriert oder reflektiert, sondern performativ auf- und durchgeführt. Auch in der Kunstgeschichte werden die Dinge ständig weggeräumt und vergessen. Einige kann man später wieder hervorholen und neu gebrauchen. Es ist Zeit, dass dies mit dem Werk von Allan Kaprow geschieht.

1) Inez Garson, Deputy Director des Andrew Dickson White Museums, war Kurator des Happenings. (Freundliche Mitteilung von Sean Ulmer.) Unter den Teilnehmern fehlt eine prominente Figur: Gordon Matta (später Gordon Matta-Clark) studierte damals an der Cornell University Architektur, befand sich aber im Frühling 1964 in Paris. (Freundliche Mitteilung von Jane Crawford.) Das *score* von HOUSEHOLD sowie die Abbildungen sind publiziert in: Allan Kaprow, *Assemblage, Environments & Happenings*, Harry N. Abrams, New York 1966, S. 323–337. Eine gute Bibliographie enthält der Katalog *Experiments in the Everyday. Allan Kaprow and Robert Watts, Events, Objects, Documents*, hrsg. von Benjamin Buchloh und Judith Rodenbeck, Miriam and Ira D. Wallach Gallery, Columbia University in the City of New York, 1999. Ein von Jeff Kelley besorgtes Werkverzeichnis aller Happenings und Activities von Allan Kaprow ist unter dem Titel *Childplay* in Vorbereitung.

2) Allan Kaprow, «‹Happenings› in the New York Scene», in: *Art News* 60, Nr. 3, Mai 1961, S. 36–39, 58–62, wiederabgedruckt in: Allan Kaprow, *Essays on the Blurring of Art and Life*, hrsg. von Jeff Kelley, University of California Press, Berkeley 1993, S. 15–26; hier: S. 25.

3) John Dewey, *Kunst als Erfahrung*, übers. von Christa Velten, Suhrkamp, Frankfurt a. M. 1980, S. 21. Hervorhebung im engl. Original, *Art as Experience*, Minton, Balch & Company, New York 1934, S. 13.

4) «Robert Smithson über Duchamp, Interview mit Moira Roth» (1973), in: *Robert Smithson, Gesammelte Schriften*, hrsg. von Eva Schmidt und Kai Vöckler, Kunsthalle Wien, Walther König Verlag, Köln 2000, S. 309–311; hier: S. 310.

5) «Alles, was irgendwo übriggeblieben ist, hat irgendwie Witz.» Andy Warhol, *Die Philosophie des Andy Warhol. Von A bis B und zurück*, Knaur, München 1991, S. 93.

6) Allan Kaprow, «Communication Programming», in: Allan Kaprow, *Untitled Essay and other works*, Great Bear Pamphlet, New York 1967, S. 12. Übersetzung Philip Ursprung.

Allan Kaprow, *Household*

Ein Happening im Auftrag der Cornell University. Aufgeführt im Mai 1964. Es waren keine Zuschauer anwesend. Die Teilnehmer trafen sich im Vorfeld zu einer Besprechung des Happenings, in der auch die Rollen verteilt wurden.

Schauplatz:
Eine verlassene Müllhalde auf dem Land. Überall Abfallhaufen, von einigen steigt Rauch auf. Teile der Müllhalde mit altem, rotem Wellblech umzäunt. Der Rest von Bäumen umgeben.

Abfolge der Ereignisse:
I. 11 Uhr. Auf einem Abfallhaufen errichten Männer hölzernen Turm. Darum herum werden mit zerknüllter Dachpappe gekrönte Pfähle in den Boden gerammt.
Auf einem anderen Haufen bauen Frauen Nest aus jungen Bäumen und Schnüren. Um das Nest herum hängen sie an einer Wäscheleine alte Hemden auf.

II. 14 Uhr. Autos kommen an, ein rauchendes Wrack im Schlepptau, parken ausserhalb der Müllhalde.
Männer und Frauen arbeiten an Turm und Nest.

III. Volk kreist die Müllhalde ein, ausser Sichtweite, zwischen Bäumen und Blechzaun, wartet ab.
Frauen gehen ins Nest hinein und kreischen.
Männer stürzen sich auf das rauchende Wrack, rollen es in die Müllhalde, beschmieren es mit Erdbeermarmelade.

IV. Das Volk rund um die Müllhalde ruft: «He! He! He!»
Männer gehen zu den Frauen, ziehen Hemden an, kauern sich nieder und beobachten sie.
Ganz langsam kommt das Volk von rundum auf das Auto zu und ruft immer noch: «He! He!»
Frauen kreischen.

V. Frauen gehen zum Auto und lecken Marmelade.
Männer zerstören das Nest schreiend und fluchend.
Das näher kommende Volk beginnt sich allmählich vereinigend auf Töpfe zu trommeln und Polizeitrillerpfeifen zu blasen.

VI. Männer gehen zu den Frauen beim Wrack zurück, vertreiben sie, essen mit den Fingern Marmelade, pappen überall weisses Brot auf die klebrige Masse, essen es direkt mit dem Mund.
Frauen schreien die Männer an: «Schweinehunde! Schweinehunde!»
Volk rückt vor, trommelnd und pfeifend.

VII. Frauen zerstören Pfähle und Turm der Männer, lachen und schreien: «Seht her! Seht her!»
Männer essen Brot.
Volk rückt vor, trommelnd und pfeifend.

VIII. Frauen gehen zu den rauchenden Abfallhaufen, rufen den Männern in süssem Singsang zu: «Kommt doch, kommt!»
Männer strömen aus, ducken sich, um den Frauen aufzulauern.
Volk rückt vor, trommelnd und pfeifend.

IX. Frauen stürzen sich auf Männer, reissen ihnen die Hemden vom Leib und schmeissen sie in den rauchenden Müll, laufen zum Turmhaufen der Männer.
Männer wälzen sich laut lachend am Boden: «Ha! Ha! Ha! Ho! Ho!»
Volk rückt vor, trommelnd und pfeifend.

X. Frauen ziehen Blusen aus, schwenken sie über dem Kopf wie Taschentücher, jede ihre eigene Rock' n'Roll-Melodie singend und verträumt tanzend.
Männer schleudern rote Rauchbomben in den rauchenden Müllhaufen.
Das Volk umkreist das rauchende Marmeladen-Auto, verstummt, hockt sich hin, isst Marmeladenbrote.

XI. Männer gehen zum Wrack, nehmen vom Volk Vorschlaghämmer entgegen, heben einen Balken als Rammbock vom Boden auf, beginnen das Auto zu demolieren.
Frauen schauen aus einiger Entfernung zu und bejubeln jeden Schlag.
Das Volk isst schweigend und sieht zu.

XII. Männer bocken das Auto auf, nehmen die Räder ab, stecken es in Brand, setzen sich zum Zuschauen hin, zünden Zigaretten an.
Volk zündet Zigaretten an und sieht zu, wie das Auto verbrennt.
Frauen laufen aus der Mülldeponie hinaus, schwenken ihre Blusen und rufen fröhlich «Bye! Bye! G'bye! Bye!» Sie steigen in die Autos, fahren unentwegt hupend weg, bis sie nicht mehr zu hören sind.

XIII. Alle rauchen schweigend und schauen zu, bis das Auto ausgebrannt ist.
Dann gehen sie ruhig weg.

(Übersetzung: Wilma Parker)

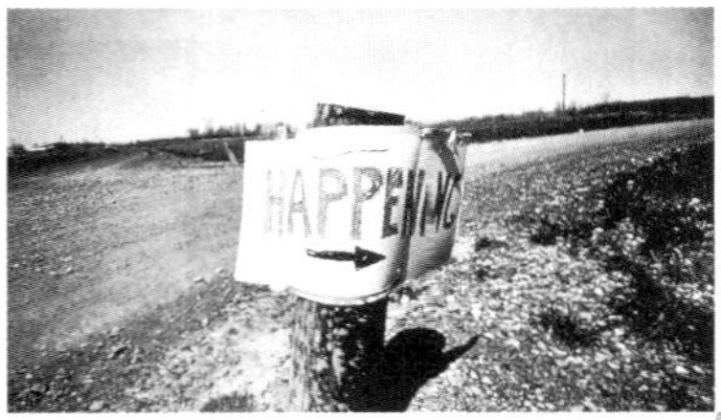

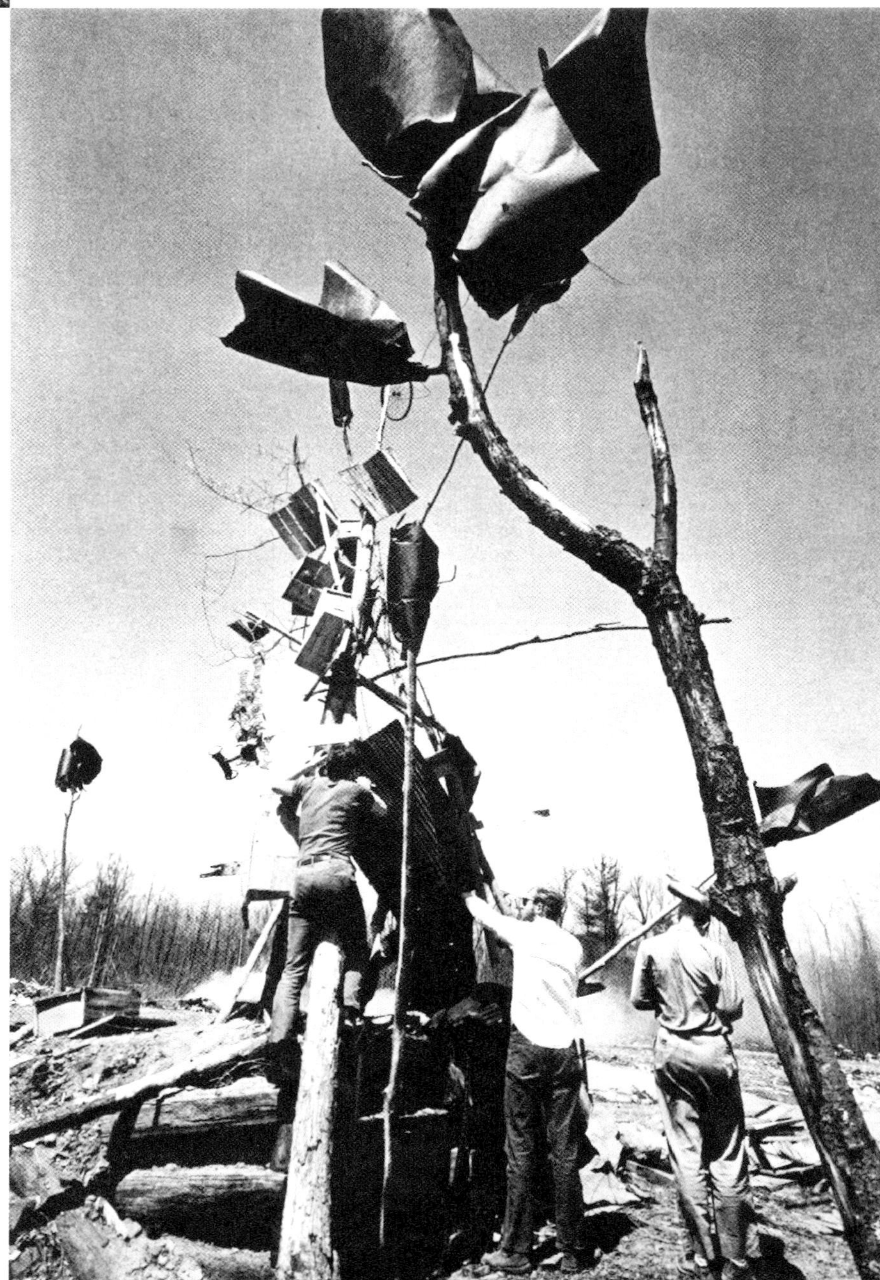

Seiten / Pages 10–14: ALLAN KAPROW, HOUSEHOLD, 1964.
(PHOTOS: SOL GOLDBERG)

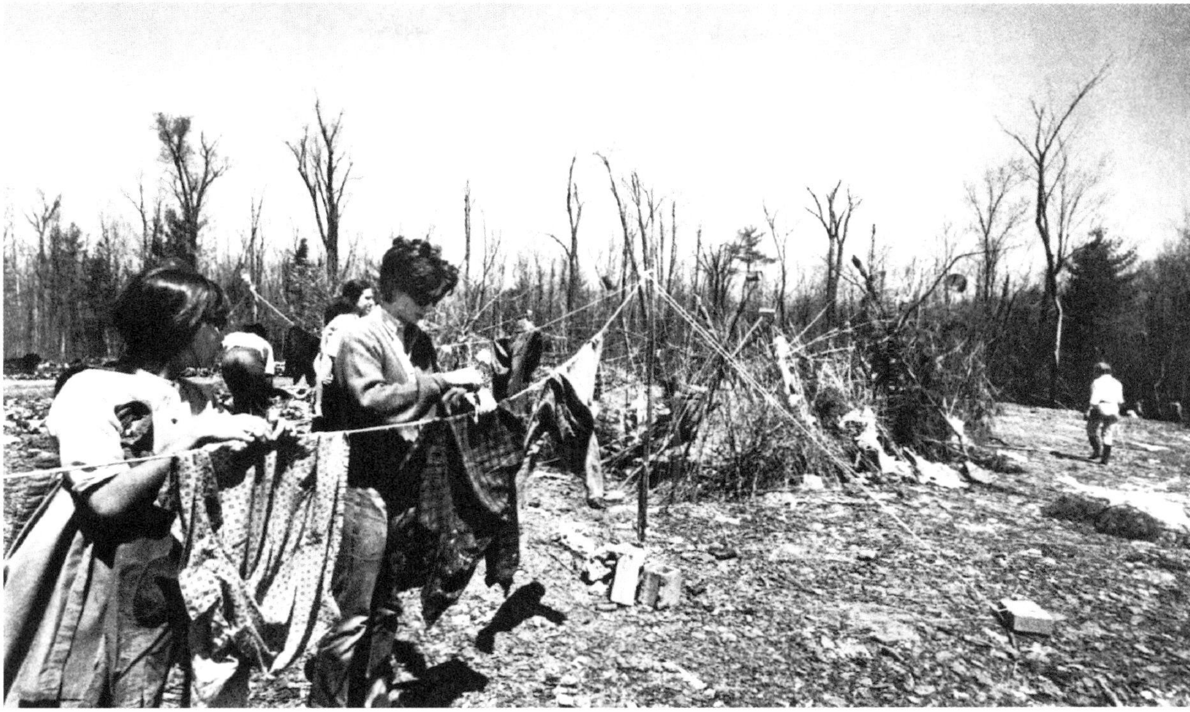

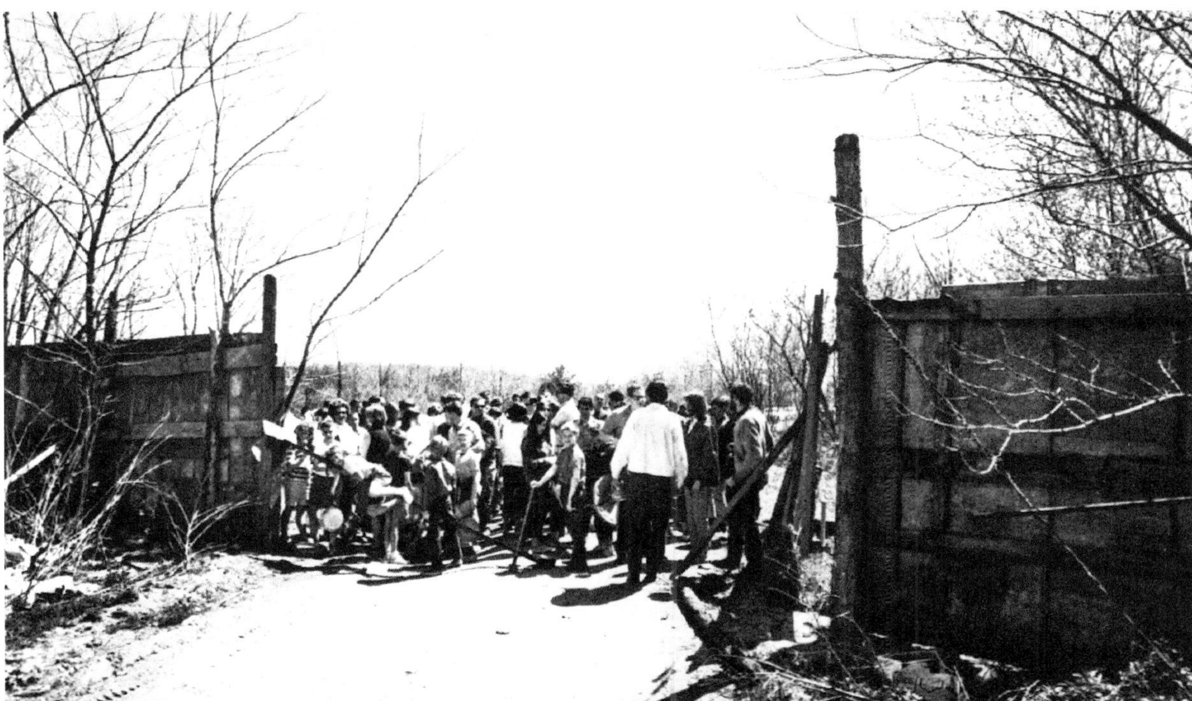

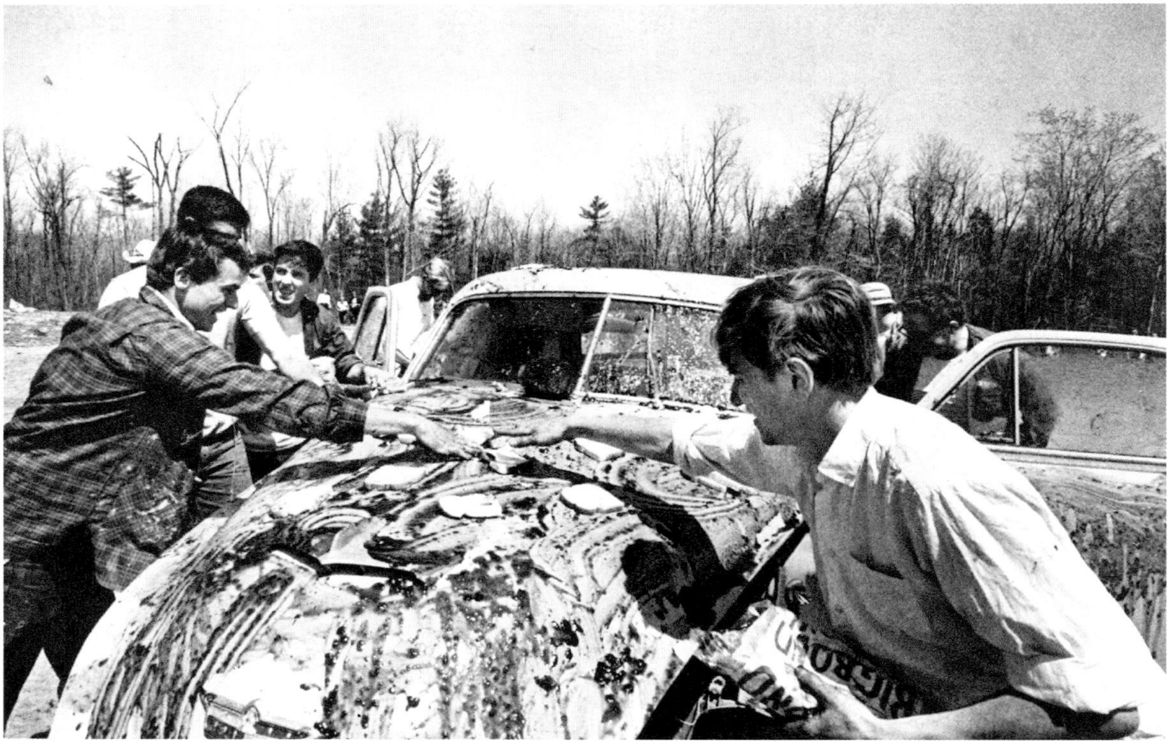

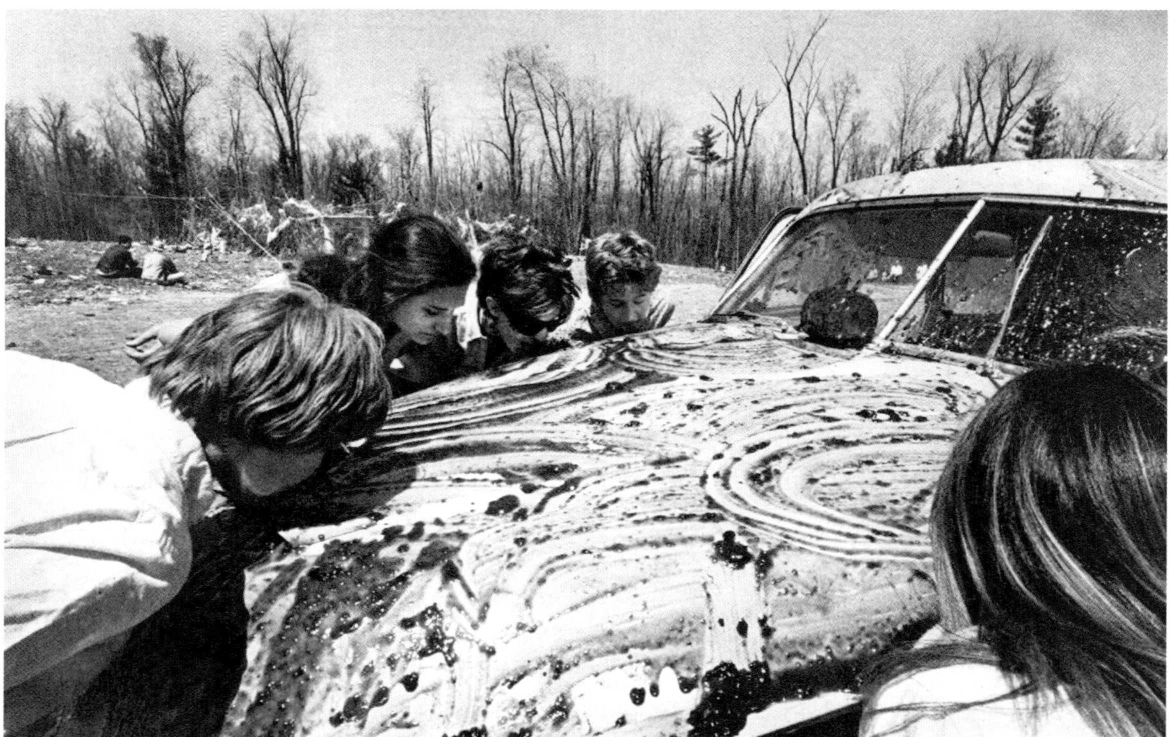

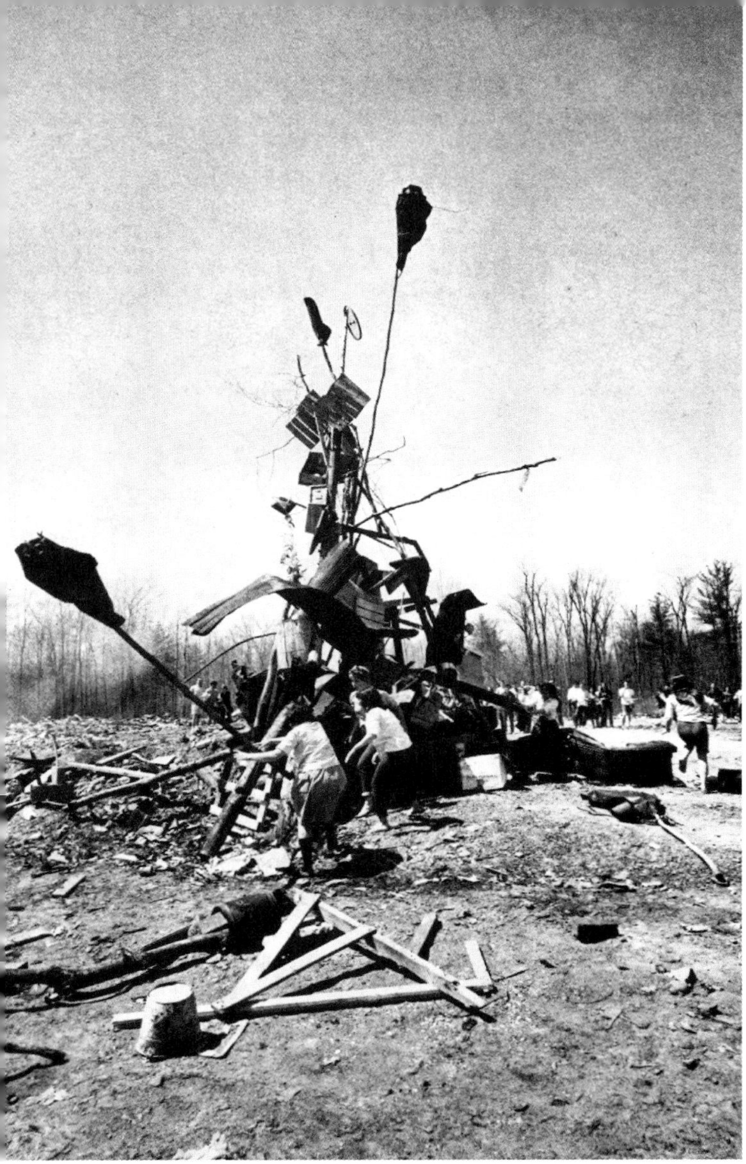

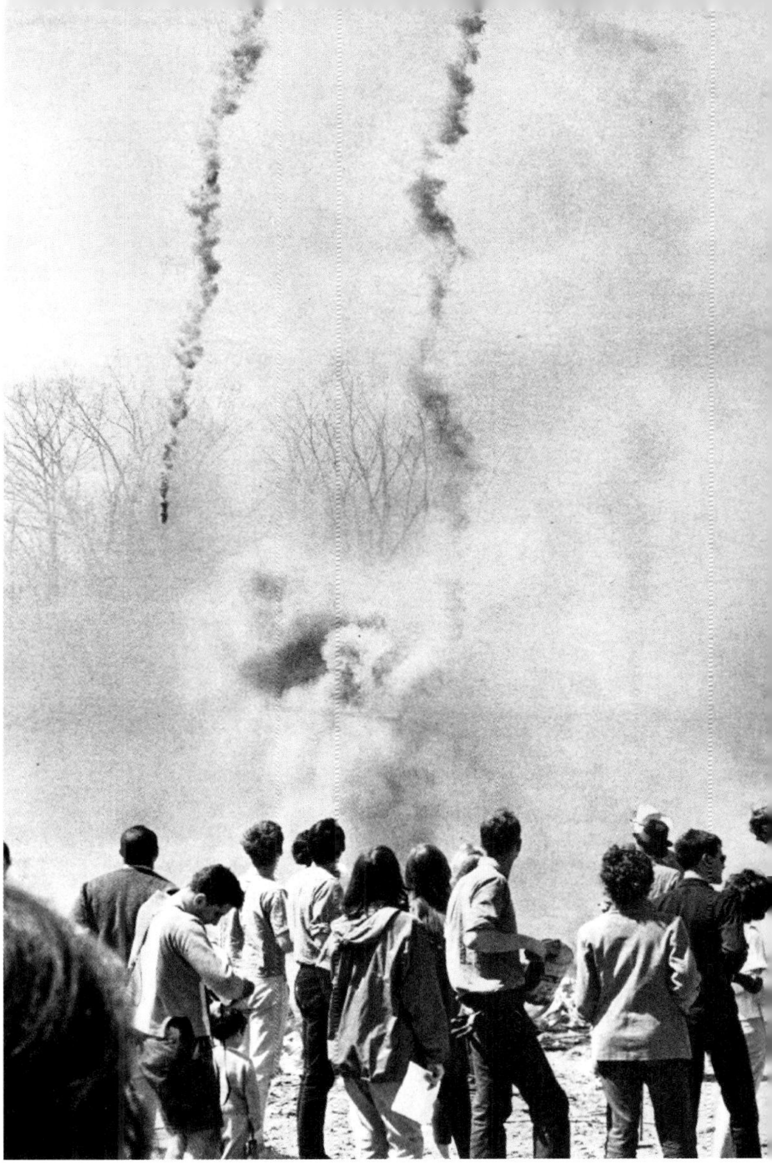

Seiten / Pages 10–14: ALLAN KAPROW, HOUSEHOLD, 1964.
(PHOTOS: SOL GOLDBERG)

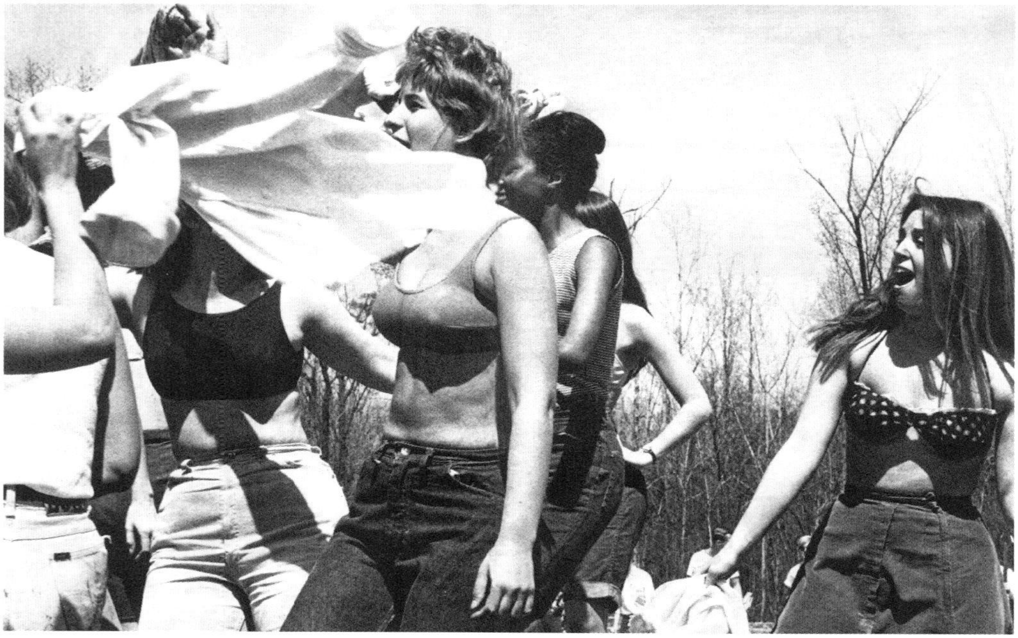

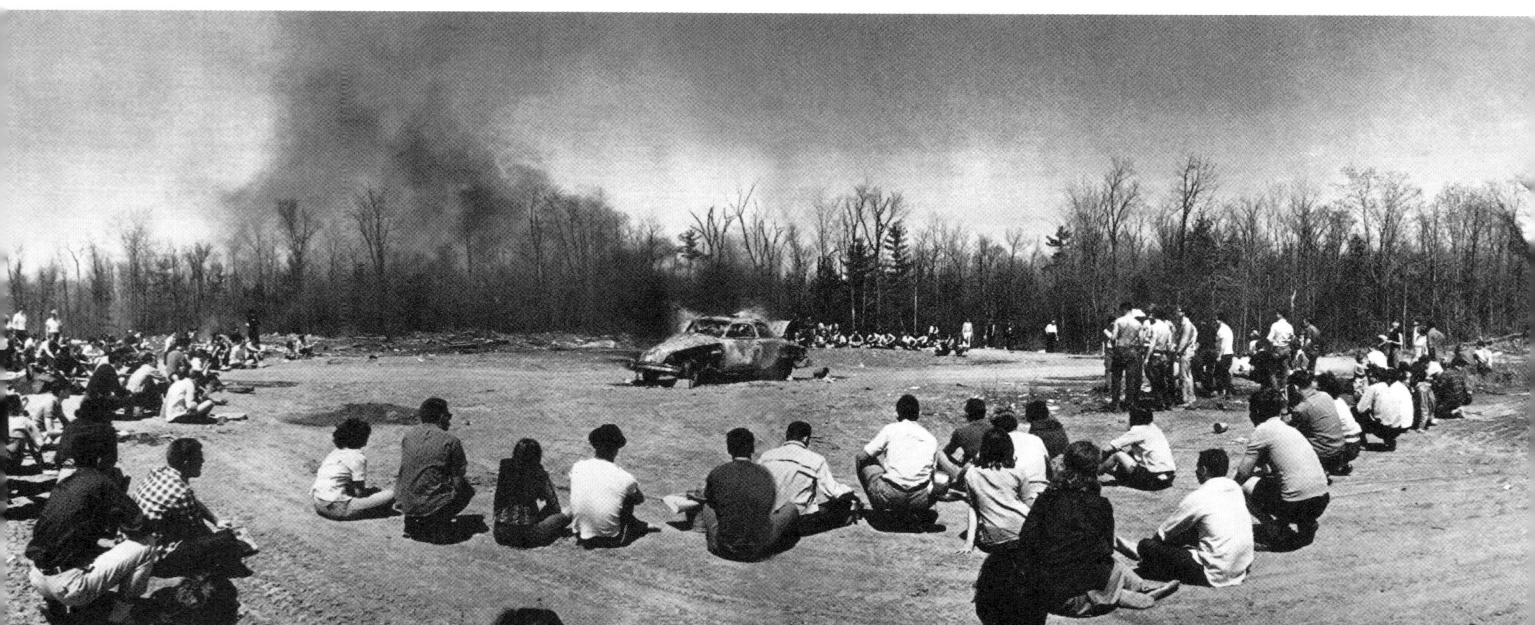

Allan Kaprow, *Household*

A Happening commissioned by Cornell University. Performed May 1964. There were no spectators at this event. Those taking part in it attended a preliminary meeting where the Happening was discussed and parts distributed.

Setting:
A lonesome dump out in the country. Trash heaps all around, some smoking. Parts of dump enclosed by old, red tin fence. Trees around rest of it.

Sequence of Events:
I. 11 A.M. Men build wooden tower on a trash mound. Poles topped with tarpaper clusters are struck around it.
Women build nest of saplings and strings on another mound.
Around the nest on a clothesline they hang old shirts.

II. 2 P.M. Cars arrive, towing smoking wreck, park outside dump, people get out.
Men and women work on tower and nest.

III. People circle dump, out of sight among trees and behind tin wall, wait.
Women go inside nest and screech.
Men go for smoking wreck, roll it into dump, cover it with strawberry jam.

IV. People's voices call "Hey! Hey! Hey!" all around dump.
Men go to women, put on shirts, squat down and watch them.
People very slowly start coming in toward car, still calling "Hey! Hey!"
Women screech.

V. Women go to car and lick jam.
Men destroy nest with shouts and cursing.
People, coming in, start to pound pots and blow police whistles in slow unison.

VI. Men return to women at wreck, yank them away, eat jam with fingers, slap white bread all over sticky stuff, eat with their mouths.
Women scream at men, "Bastards! Bastards!"
People advance, banging and whistling.

VII. Women destroy men's poles and tower, laughing, yelling "Watch this! Watch this!"
Men eat bread.
People advance, banging and whistling.

VIII. Women go to heaps of smoking trash, call sweet-songy come-ons to men.
Men fan out, creep low to ambush women.
People advance, banging and whistling.

IX. Women jump men, rip off shirts and fling them into smoking trash, run to men's tower mound.
Men roll on ground laughing loud: "Hee! Hee! Hee! Haw! Haw!"
People advance, banging and whistling.

X. Women take off blouses, wave them overhead like hankies, each singing own Rock'n'Roll tune and twisting dreamylike.
Men hurl red smoke flares into smoking trash heap.
People circle smoking jam-car, become silent, squat down, eat jam sandwiches.

XI. Men go to wreck, take sledge hammers from people, pick up battering log, begin to demolish car.
Women watch from a distance and cheer men for every smash.
People eat silently and watch.

XII. Men jack up car, remove wheels, set fire to it, sit down to watch, light up cigarettes.
People light up cigarettes, watch car burning.
Women run out of junkyard, waving blouses, gaily calling "Bye! Bye! G'bye! Bye!" They get into cars, drive away with horns blaring steadily till out of earshot.

XIII. Everyone smokes silently and watches car until it's burned up.
Then they leave quietly.

Household

PHILIP URSPRUNG

Anyone fortunate enough to be studying at Cornell University in Ithaca, New York, in spring 1964 could have been one of those who took part in an extraordinary event. Held during the Contemporary Arts Festival it was one of the most spectacular Happenings Allan Kaprow ever mounted. In his preparations for the event he explained the score to the participants and divided them into three groups: men, women, and people. On 3 May 1964, everyone gathered at a garbage dump outside the town. Taking 'household' as their theme, they spent a day acting out the daily round of domestic life—home-building, eating, having sex, and resting. In the morning they set up home. The men built a tower from the bits and pieces lying around, the women made a nest. At midday some students dragged a wrecked car into the camp. They smeared their booty with jam, and women, men, and people ate from it one after the other. Once they had eaten, the women enticed the men to come to them. This turned into something of a battle of the sexes: at its height everyone tore their shirts or tops off, sang, and set the car on fire. In the late afternoon the women drove away first. The men and the people smoked a last cigarette before they, too, went home and the Happening was over.

Like many of the Happenings put on since 1959 by Kaprow and others, like Claes Oldenburg, HOUSEHOLD was a commissioned work.[1)] Kaprow therefore linked the work closely to the place and the participants. Cornell University with its renowned School of Architecture is set in grounds designed by Fredrick Law Olmsted, the landscape architect responsible for Central Park in New York. An architectural motif thus seemed an obvious choice. In addition, the most crucial experiences for these Ivy League students who had just left home were undoubtedly keeping house together in the segregated dormitories and

---

PHILIP URSPRUNG is Professor for Contemporary Art History at the Eidgenössische Technische Hochschule Zurich. From 1999 to 2001 he was a guest professor at the Hochschule der Künste Berlin. His book, *Grenzen der Kunst: Allan Kaprow und das Happening, Robert Smithson und die Land Art* (Munich: Silke Schreiber), will be published this year.

Allan Kaprow's Economy

Allan Kaprow explaining the score of HOUSEHOLD to the participants, Cornell University, Ithaca, New York, 2 May 1964 / Allan Kaprow erläutert den Teilnehmern den Ablauf von HOUSEHOLD. (PHOTO: SOL GOLDBERG)

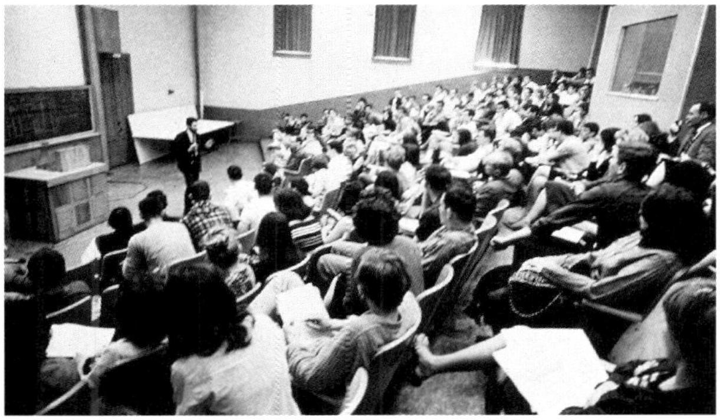

their contact with the opposite sex. (The contraceptive pill had been licensed in May 1960, and Puritan America was on the brink of sexual liberation.) Lastly, that spring the West Coast saw the first seeds of the student revolts that were to mark the generation conflict of the sixties. Kaprow himself had talked ironically of the adolescent character of the Happenings, which he saw as typical of a society on the road to "cultural maturity."[2]

The fenced-in garbage dump, a mixture of wasteland and playground, provided an atmospheric setting for HOUSEHOLD—in keeping with the maxim of the American philosopher John Dewey that "life goes on in an environment not merely in it but because of it."[3] Dewey's pragmatic philosophy suited Kaprow's interest in individual experience. The excited anticipation, the journey to the unaccustomed location, the stench of the rubbish, the sweet taste of the strawberry jam on the metal of the car, the acrid smoke in the participants' eyes, horsing around with the opposite sex—all this was, in fact, the 'material' of the Happening. These experiences cannot themselves be mediated but they can be repeated in a different form—Kaprow often staged his Happenings in several variations—and they can readily be imagined from descriptions of them.

Waste materials and household objects, which were very much part of the pictorial repertoire of Assemblage and Pop art, were no more than props in Kaprow's work. His approach was in fact fundamentally different from that of the mainstream. It only superficially related to the transformation of the everyday into art which so fascinated the art world in the early 1960s—be it in the work of Marcel Duchamp, the "spiritualist of Woolworth" (Robert Smithson),[4] in Andy Warhol's "philosophy of using leftovers,"[5] or Jean Tinguely's *Homage to New York: A Self-Constructing and Self-Destroying Work of Art* (1960). These artists were operating in the force-field between art and non-art, between high art and popular culture; they were trying to achieve the "transfiguration of the commonplace" (Arthur C. Danto). For Kaprow, on the other hand, art was not a place where reality could be heightened or reflected. In his view mediating between art and life did not count; if anything, there had to be a confrontation between the two. The truly modernist question as to the essence of art was of no interest to him. As he himself said: "Yesterday's distinctions between art, anti- or non-art are pseudo-distinctions which simply waste our time..."[6)]

But HOUSEHOLD also occupies a unique position in art history because in it Kaprow did away with the division between actors and audience that usually applied in Happenings and Performances. He himself naturally took part, and besides the photographer from the local newspaper and a cameraman, there were no spectators at HOUSEHOLD, just participants. The difference between active artist and passive public, between production and reception, between reality and representation was swept aside. Kaprow had changed the traditional economy of representation, thereby questioning the established economy of meaning.

To this day the art world has not forgiven him for this. Torn between disquiet and smug satisfaction, critics reduce Kaprow's Happenings to a phenomenon defined by its disappearance, which consequently writes itself out of art history as it were. In doing so the critics repress the fact that the Happenings, specifically by being documented in photographs and text, are particularly amenable to historiography and more 'fully' describable than sculpture and painting. But perhaps they have to repress this, since Kaprow's art is a threat to the time-honored privilege of critics to translate images into text. The only adequate description of HOUSEHOLD (and my own text is not exempt from these remarks) would have to be a form of Happening in its own right.

Kaprow was not concerned with the process of disappearance. Just as the domestic waste from a booming consumer society landed on the garbage dump—the detritus of planned obsolescence—so, too, Kaprow's works of art also had a limited lifespan. But he was not out to sublimate the fragile, short-lived nature of these works, that is to say his aim was not to immortalize their disappearance but rather to articulate it. It was not the avant-garde "tradition of the new" (Harold Rosenberg) but the rearrangement of the status quo that interested him. This he perhaps managed best in HOUSEHOLD. For in art history—as in any household (in Greek: economy)—things constantly shift between order and disorder, the old and the new, the long-term and the momentary. Things get thrown away, lost, found, damaged, and repaired. Like a household, art history is never finished, never tidy. In HOUSEHOLD Kaprow did not illustrate or reflect this fact, instead he used performance to present and to enact it. In art history things are also constantly being tidied away and forgotten. Some of these can be retrieved years later and put to use again: it is now time for precisely that to happen to Allan Kaprow's work.

(Translation: Fiona Elliott)

1) Inez Garson, Deputy Director of the Andrew Dickson White Museum was the curator of the Happening. (Information kindly supplied by Sean Ulmer.) There was one notable absence among the participants: Gordon R. Matta-Echaurren (later Gordon Matta-Clark) was studying architecture at Cornell from 1962 to 1968 but was in Paris during the fall semester of 1963 and the spring semester of 1964. He returned to Cornell in the fall of 1964. (Information kindly supplied by Jane Crawford and Elaine Engst.) The score of HOUSEHOLD and the photographs are published in: Allan Kaprow, *Assemblage, Environments & Happenings* (New York: Harry N. Abrams, 1966), pp. 323–337. A good biography is included in the catalogue *Experiments in the Everyday: Allan Kaprow and Robert Watts, Events, Objects, Documents*, ed. by Benjamin Buchloh and Judith Rodenbeck, Miriam and Ira D. Wallach Gallery (New York: Columbia University, 1999). A catalogue of all Allan Kaprow's Happenings and activities, entitled *Childplay*, is currently being prepared by Jeff Kelley.

2) Allan Kaprow, "'Happenings' in the New York Scene" in: *Art News* 60, no. 3, May 1961, pp. 36–39, 58–62, reprinted in: Allan Kaprow, *Essays on the Blurring of Art and Life*, ed. by Jeff Kelley (Berkeley: University of California Press, 1993), pp. 15–26, here: p. 25.

3) John Dewey, *Art as Experience* (New York: Minton, Balch & Company, 1934), p. 13.

4) "Robert Smithson on Duchamp, Interview with Moira Roth" in: *Artforum* 12, no. 2, October 1973, quoted after *Robert Smithson, The Collected Writings*, ed. by Jack Flam (Berkeley: University of California Press, 1996), pp. 310–312, here: p. 311.

5) "I always thought there was a lot of humor in leftovers." Andy Warhol, *The Philosophy of Andy Warhol from A to B and Back Again* (New York: Harcourt Brace Jovanovich, 1975), p. 93.

6) Allan Kaprow, "Communication Programming" in: Allan Kaprow, *Untitled Essay and other works* (New York: Great Bear Pamphlet, 1967), p. 12.

TACITA DEAN born 1965 in Canterbury, England, lives and works in London and Berlin (DAAD Künstlerprogramm) / geboren 1965 in Canterbury, England, lebt und arbeitet in London und Berlin (DAAD-Künstlerprogramm)

JOHN WESLEY born 1928 in Los Angeles, lives and works in New York / geboren 1928 in Los Angeles, lebt und arbeitet in New York.

THOMAS DEMAND geboren 1964 in München, lebt und arbeitet in Berlin / born 1964 in Munich, lives and works in Berlin.

TACITA

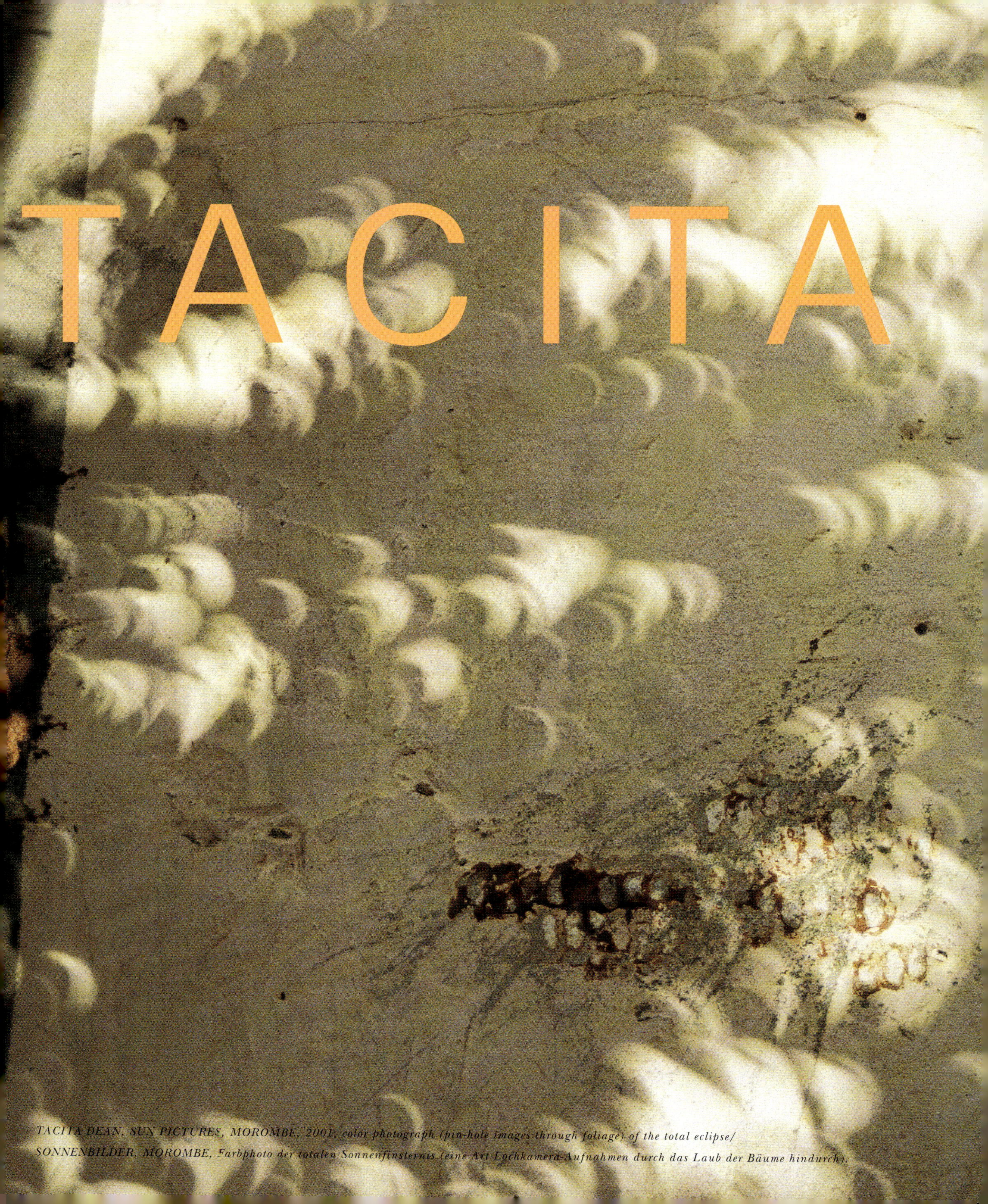

TACITA DEAN, SUN PICTURES, MOROMBE, 2001, color photograph (pin-hole images through foliage) of the total eclipse/ SONNENBILDER, MOROMBE, Farbphoto der totalen Sonnenfinsternis (eine Art Lochkamera-Aufnahmen durch das Laub der Bäume hindurch).

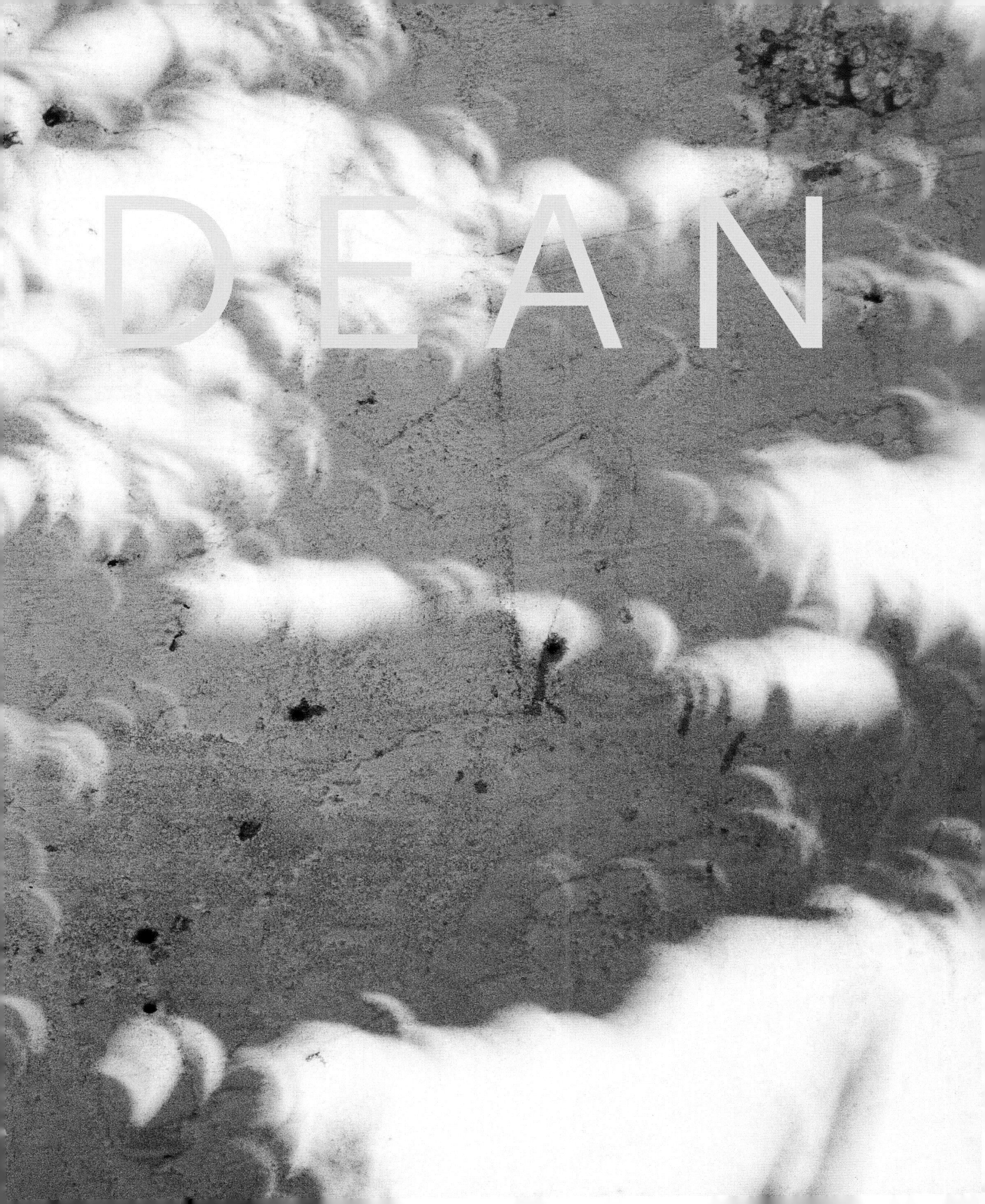
DEAN

JEREMY MILLAR

Genius Loci

In his new book, *Tracing Light*, David Alan Mellor refers to the seventeenth-century natural philosopher Jakob Böhme and his notion of the *Ungrund*—that is, the process by which light and dark have been split in order that they might approach a sublime state of divine corporeality.[1] Böhme's theory, which he first introduced in his 1612 treatise, *Aurora*, developed through his observations of ocular contrasts, gazing at the reflection of the sun in a darkened pewter plate, the darkness essential if the light was to be made manifest. After 1613, Böhme attempted to reconcile the medieval world of alchemy with the newly-emerging heliocentric cosmologies, and as such, perhaps we might see how he springs to mind when considering the work of Tacita Dean.

As Dean has written: *BANEWL was filmed entirely within the two hour and forty minute period of the total eclipse of the sun on 11 August 1999, and takes its title from a phonetic transcription of the Cornish pronunciation of the dairy farm's name, Burnewhall. Because the day was overcast, the film became less about the event and more about waiting for darkness to happen and then equally for the return of a normal sun. The clouds allowed us to experience this coincidence of cosmic time and scale on our own terms and in our own human time, measuring it against the movements of animals and the fine detailing of our natural world.*[2]

It is an extraordinary achievement that what could almost be considered a straightforward documentary account of the passage of time in a particular location—and Dean was very particular in the way that the shots we see are in a strict chronological sequence—can be transformed into something on such a grand philosophical scale, the base matter of the Cornish landscape transmutated into the precious metal of cosmic insight, and our place within the world. The alchemical echoes are further emphasized by the fact that all the sound on the film was made during post-production. Even the sound of cows chewing was made by foley artists.

TOTALITY (2000) was made at the same time, using a motion-tracking device on a film camera, which followed the sun across the sky, always keeping it at

---

JEREMY MILLAR is an artist and curator living in Whitstable, England.

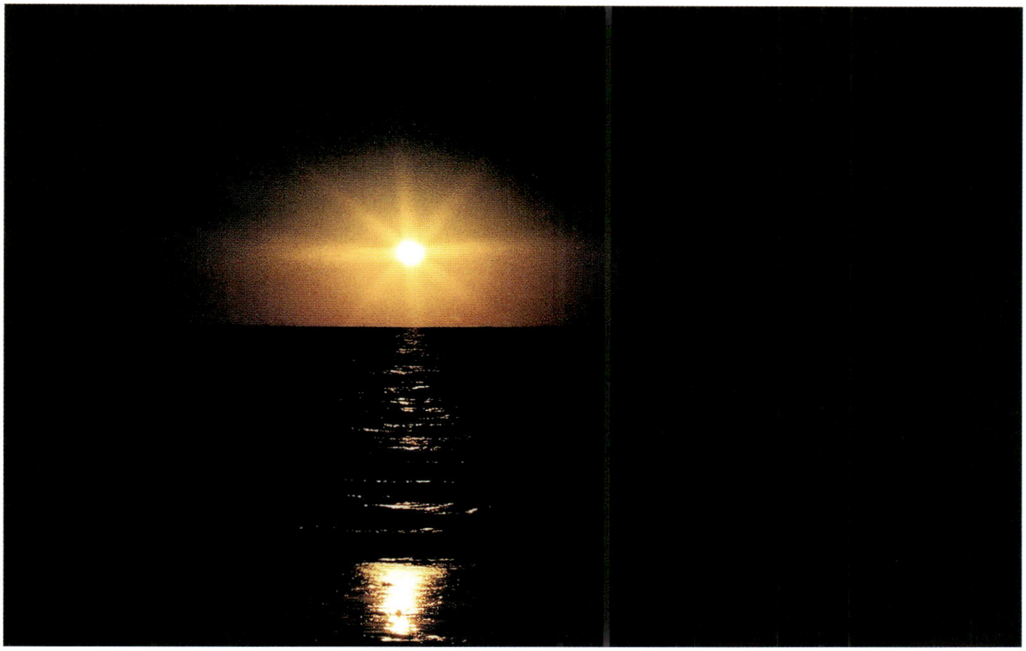

TACITA DEAN, TOTAL ECLIPSE, MOROMBE (BEFORE 4TH CONTACT), 2001, color photograph / TOTALE SONNENFINSTERNIS, MOROMBE (VOR DEM 4. KONTAKT), Farbphoto.

the center of the frame. It is only eleven minutes long and there is no sound, only the abstract vision of different tones and shades as the cloud-screened sun becomes covered, and then uncovered, by the moon. We are hypnotized by the grand, yet indistinct, movements above us. It is like witnessing the light at the Creation. Perhaps it is not so surprising, then, that at times the work might remind us of a color field painting, perhaps one by the American Barnett Newman, a man who viewed light as that which sets in motion the process of creation, change, and evolution. Perhaps we should not be surprised, therefore, that a large tripartite canvas left in Newman's studio after his death in August 1970, has been described as standing in the space "like a great lighthouse,"[3] one of Dean's more famous motifs.

A sense of being both in and outside of time and space is apparent elsewhere in Dean's work, in the short film SOUND MIRRORS (1999). As she notes, once more: *The sound mirrors were conceived during the First World War when the concept of an air attack became the new danger to national security. They were built between 1928 and 1930, at Denge, near Dungeness as well as at*

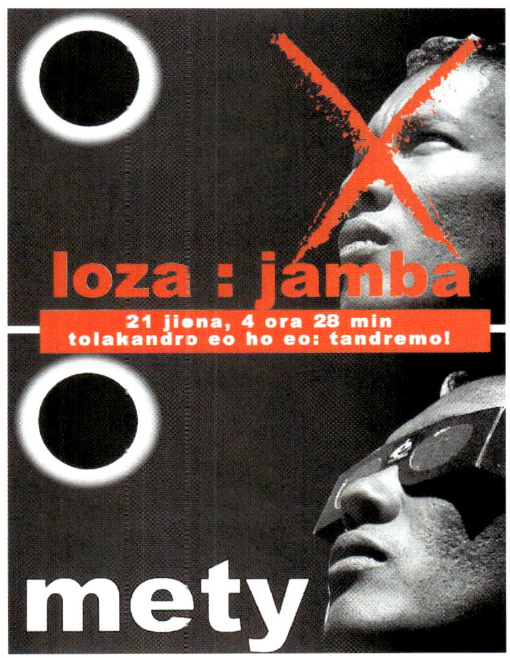

Eclipse Poster, Madagascar, 2001 / Sonnenfinsternis-Plakat in Madagaskar.

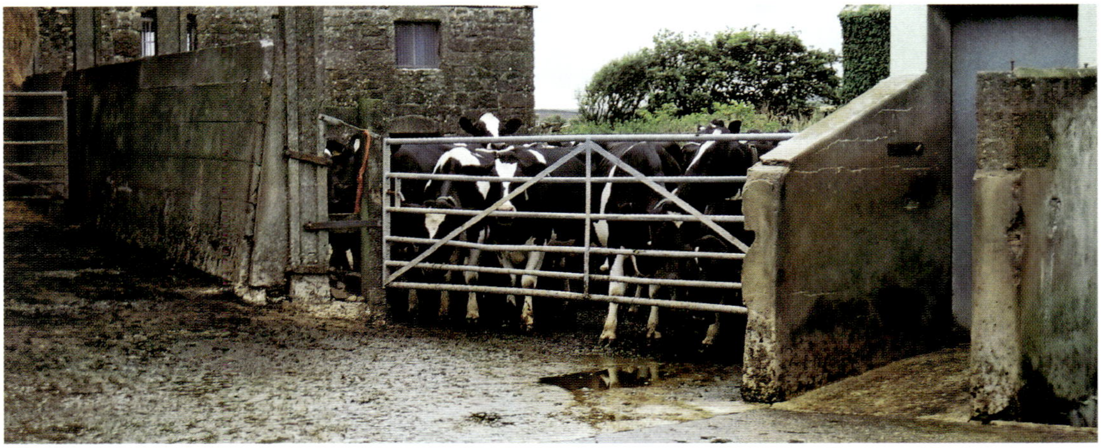

two other sites along the Kent coast, as huge listening devices designed to pick up the sound of approaching planes, but were quickly proved unreliable when they could not discriminate between a passing boat or local traffic and were then abandoned in favor of radar. However, the sound they continue to hear is extraordinary, and the soundtrack to this film is entirely recorded within the 200-foot mirror.[4)]

Perhaps with this film more than any other, we can discern Dean's interest in the writings of J.G. Ballard, a writer who "summons up a time when our everyday will be out of context; when our descendents will read votive meanings into our sports stadiums and race courses; when nothing will be understood by the totems of today."[5)] The film acts as a form of time-travel into an uncertain future, reminiscent, perhaps, of Chris Marker's extraordinary *La Jetée* (1962), incidentally one of Ballard's favorite films. They not only mark a present, which has passed, but also a future that cannot now exist. It is because of the authority of Dean's camera, and not despite it, that Dean's work might be seen as "fantastic." In this sense, perhaps we might also consider SOUND MIRRORS in relation to Andrei Tarkovsky's 1979 masterpiece *Stalker*, where arguably one of the most fantastic spaces in modern cinema was created within an abandoned hydro-electric power station in Estonia using no special effects beyond those of language and imaginative space. The appeal to memory, or the imaginative participation of the viewer, is also important in Dean's work and perhaps we might then find a comment from Tarkovsky's *Stalker* appropriate, where the eponymous guide into the forbidden Zone describes the strange place through which he is traveling:

The Zone is a highly complex system… of traps, as it were, and all of them are deadly. I don't know what happens here when we've gone… But people have only to appear for the whole thing to be triggered into motion. Our moods,

BANEWL, 1999, 16mm color anamorphic with optical sound (63 mins.), film stills / anamorphotischer 16mm-Farbfilm mit optischem Sound.

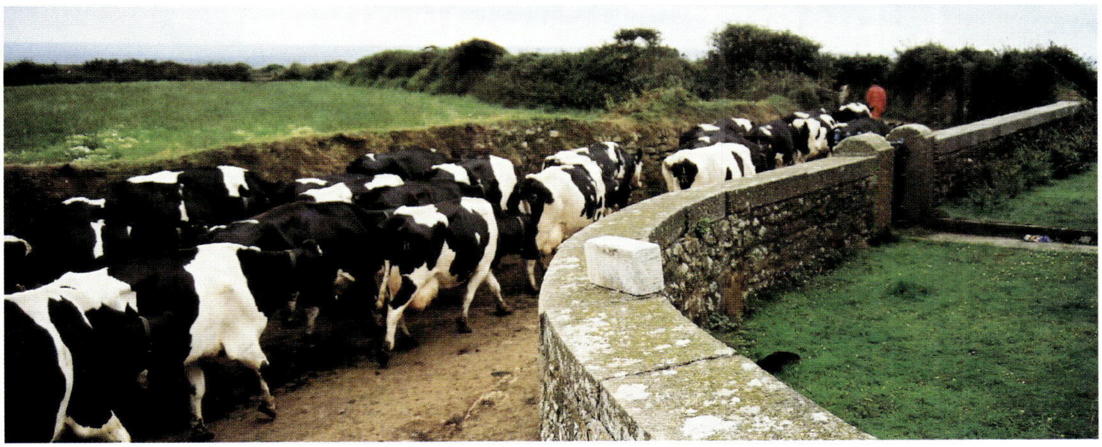

our thoughts, our emotions, our feelings can bring about change here. And we are in no condition to comprehend them. Old traps vanish, new ones take their place; the old safe places become impassable, and the route can either be plain and easy, or impossibly confusing. That's how the Zone is. It may even seem capricious. But in fact, at any moment it is exactly as we devise it, in our consciousness… everything that happens here depends on us, not on the Zone.[6)]

This relationship between the internal and external world is not simply that of the Romantics, where a personal emotional force was made manifest in the surrounding landscape, but perhaps something more modern, a schizophrenic response, where the boundary between the self and the environment thins, becomes porous, and ceases to exist.

A few years before the construction of the sound mirrors was begun, the painter Paul Nash moved with his wife to the nearby town of Dymchurch. A few years after the mirrors were completed, and shortly after his first visit to the stones at Avebury—a journey also made, nearly forty years later, by Robert Smithson—Nash completed a small painting, EQUIVALENTS FOR THE MEGALITHS (1935). The painting was on display in Tate Britain at the same time as Dean's recent exhibition there. The relationship between the works is remarkable, although unremarked upon. As Nash wrote:

If I were asked to describe this spirit I would say it is of the land: genius loci is indeed almost its conception. If its expression could be designated I would say it is almost entirely lyrical. Further, I dare not go: except to recount history and to stake my faith. Towards the end of the eighteenth century, William Blake, then, and often now, called a madman, perceived among many things, the hidden significance of the land he always called Albion. For him Albion possessed a great spiritual personality and he constantly inveighed against "Nature," the appearance of which he dis-

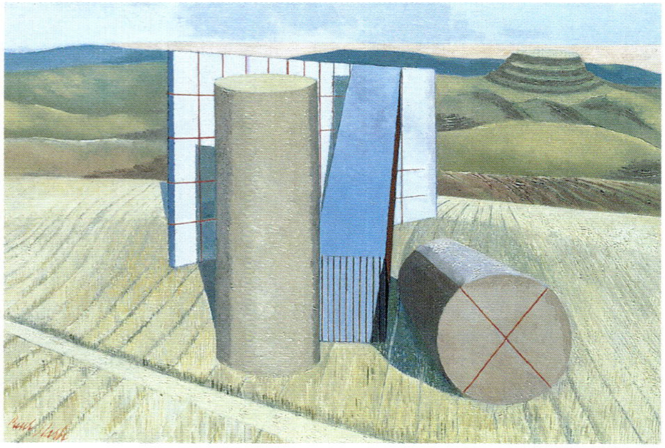

PAUL NASH, EQUIVALENTS FOR THE MEGALITHS, 1935, oil on canvas, 18 x 26" / ENTSPRECHUNGEN DER MEGALITHEN, Öl auf Leinwand, 45,7 x 66 cm. (PHOTO: TATE GALLERY, LONDON)

trusted as a false reality. At the same time, his work was immensely influenced by the country he lived in. His poetry literally came out of England. Blake's life was spent in seeking to discover symbols for what his "inward" eye perceived, but which, alas, his hand could seldom express. Turner, again, sought to break through the deceptive mirage, which he could depict with such ease, to a reality more real, in his imagination. In the same way, we, today, must find new symbols to express our reaction to environment.[7)]

What Dean shares with Nash (and Ballard, Marker, and Tarkovsky also) is a desire for "re-enchanting the land" with meaning, to use Nash's phrase, or to examine that point of overlap and coincidence between inner and outer spaces. Dean's work is always shaped by the environment in which it is made; yet it is as much about those things which have shaped the environment itself. Perhaps we might see this in Dean's most recent work, FERNSEHTURM (2001), a film made in a most symbolically charged environment, the revolving restaurant of the television tower in Alexanderplatz, a structure, like the sound mirrors, which is strangely out of time, at once futuristic and dated. (In fact, this sense is confirmed some way through the film when, in front of a rapidly bruising sky, the organist in the restaurant begins to play "The Blue Danube" and what is brought to mind is the graceful waltz of the space ships in Kubrick's *2001—A Space Odyssey*.) Because of the turning of the room, Tacita's camera remains fixed, and yet also in motion (like Kubrick's camera in the revolving space station), as the events unfold in front of her without her intervention. People move to their tables but do not sit, instead shielding their eyes, their arms outstretched, pointing. There are reflections upon the metal and glass, and we are reminded of the scenes Tacita filmed within the lighthouses, other radiating towers, which mark and frame their surroundings. A spotlight is turned on against a wall and, as the light begins to thicken outside, an electronic "Girl from Ipanema" accompanies the setting sun. As the world outside darkens and the interior becomes increasingly illuminated, the windows transform into mirrors and we become aware of the spectral visions of the diners, as they float above the city of Berlin, like the angels in Wim Wenders' *Wings of Desire* (1987). I'm reminded, finally, of someone recently mentioned, William Blake, and a description of one of his sketches, A VISION: THE INSPIRATION OF THE POET from about 1820:

The immense room is full of clear light which penetrates to all corners and leaves nothing undefined; yet the whole scene is charged with mystery and touched with remoteness, a loneliness, so intense that we feel it lies in the land "out of Space, out of Time" where, in the spacious and well-litten Chamber of the Mind, the Poet sits apart in the innermost Holy of Holies, the Shrine of the Imagination, writing wonderful words at Angelic dictation.[8)]

1) David Alan Mellor and Garry Fabian Miller, *Tracing Light* (Maidstone: PhotoWorks, 2001), p. 166.
2) *Tacita Dean*, Exhibition Guide (London: Tate Britain, 2001).
3) Thomas B. Hess, *Barnett Newman* (New York: Museum of Modern Art, 1971), p. 145, quoted in: Mellor and Miller, p. 165.
4) *Tacita Dean*, Exhibition Guide (London: Tate Britain, 2001).
5) Tacita Dean, *Teignmouth Electron* (London: Book Works, 1999), unpaginated.
6) Andrei Tarkovsky, *Collected Screenplays*, trans. William Powell and Natasha Synessios (London: Faber and Faber, 1999), p. 395.
7) Paul Nash, *Outline—An Autobiography and Other Writings* (London: 1949), quoted in: Peter Woodcock, *This Enchanted Isle* (Glastonbury: Gothic Image, 2000), pp. 18–19.
8) W. Graham Robertson, *The Blake Collection of W. Graham Robertson* (London: Faber and Faber, 1952), pp. 181–2, quoted in: Mellor and Miller, p. 173.

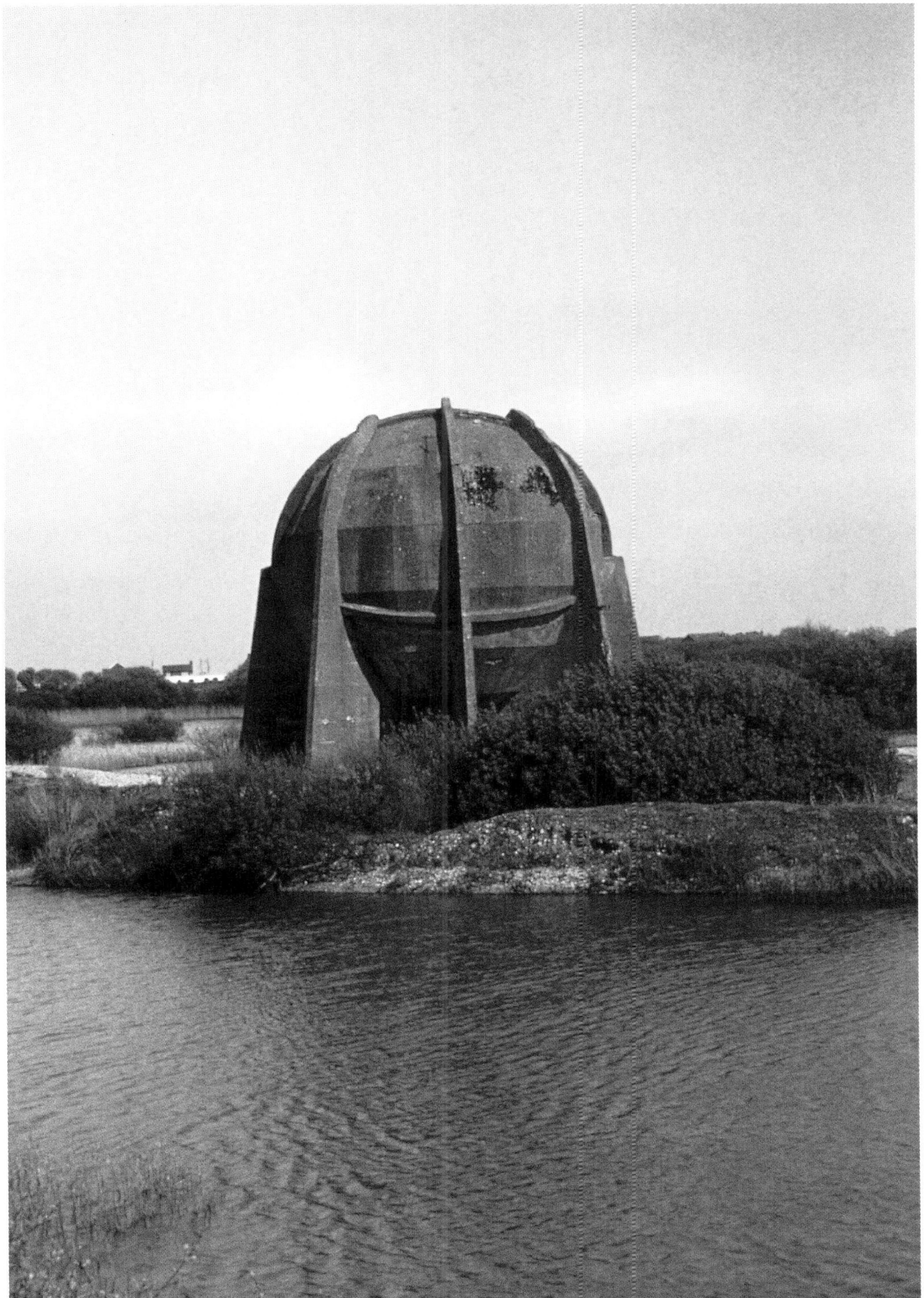

TACITA DEAN, SOUND MIRRORS, 1999, 16mm black and white film (7 mins.), location photograph /
SCHALLREFLEKTOREN, 16mm-Schwarzweissfilm (7 Min.), Photographie am Drehort.

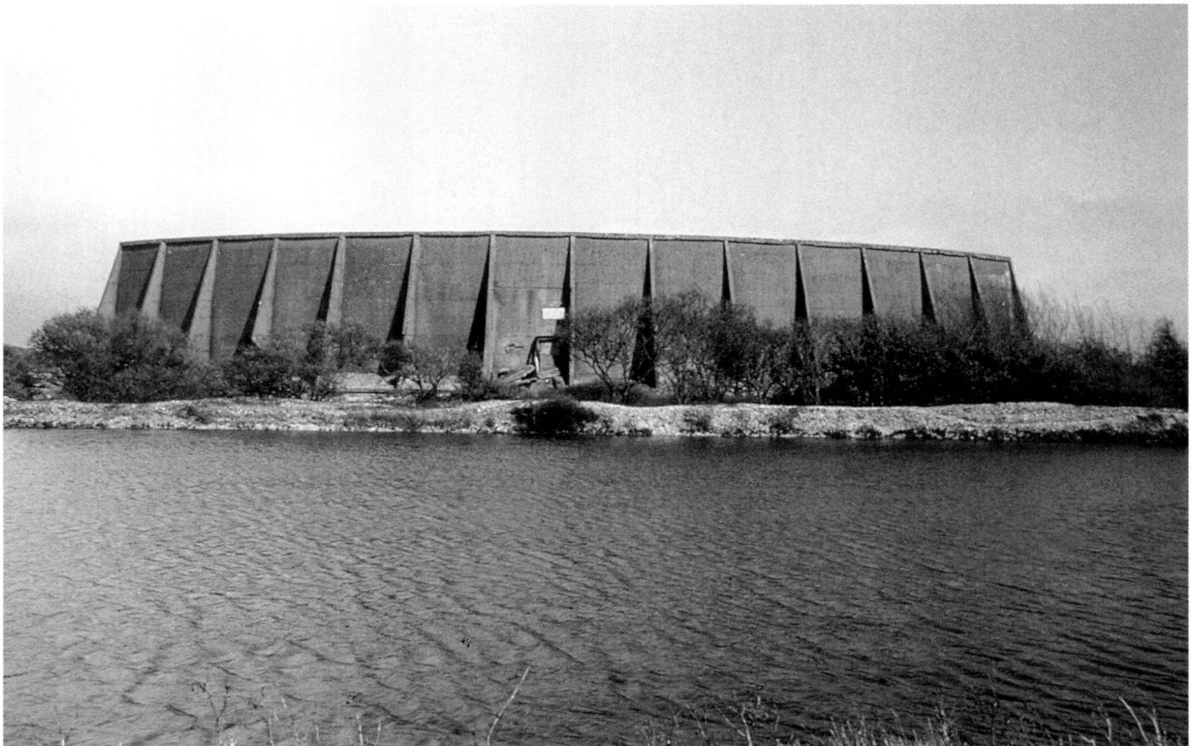

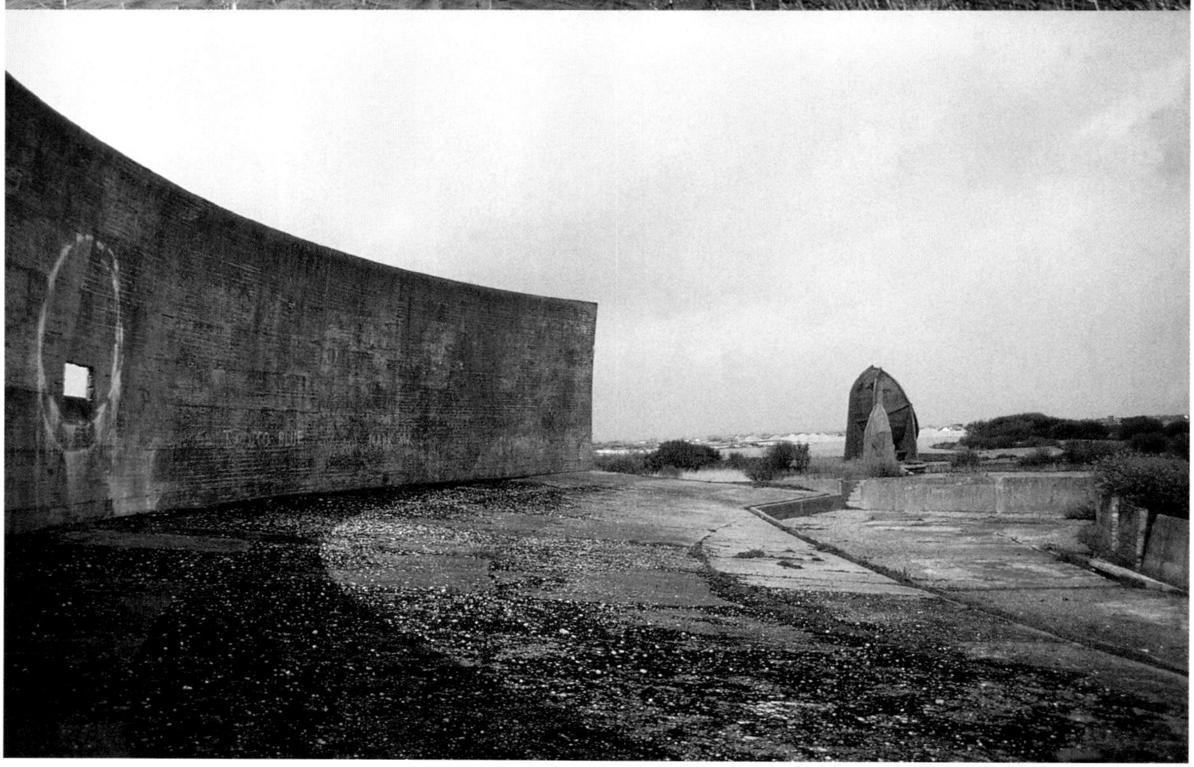

TACITA DEAN, SOUND MIRRORS, 1999, 16mm black and white film (7 mins.), location photograph / SCHALLREFLEKTOREN, 16mm-Schwarzweissfilm (7 Min.), Photo am Drehort.

JEREMY MILLAR

Genius Loci

In seinem neuen Buch, *Tracing Light*, erwähnt David Alan Mellor den Naturphilosophen Jakob Böhme, der im siebzehnten Jahrhundert lebte und den Begriff des «Ungrundes» prägte – zur Bezeichnung jenes Prozesses, der die Trennung von Licht und Finsternis in Gang setzt, so dass sie den erhabenen Zustand einer (be-)greifbaren, göttlichen Realität zu erreichen vermögen.[1] Böhme hatte seine Theorie, die er 1612 in der Abhandlung *Aurora oder Morgenröte im Aufgang* darlegte, anhand seiner Beobachtung der Kontrastwirkungen entwickelt, die bei der Spiegelung des Sonnenlichts auf einem dunklen Zinnteller auftraten, wobei sich das Dunkle als unerlässliche Voraussetzung für das Sichtbarwerden des Lichts erwies. Nach 1613 versuchte Böhme die mittelalterliche Welt der Alchemie mit den neu aufgekommenen heliozentrischen Kosmologien in Einklang zu bringen, und das ist wahrscheinlich der Grund, weshalb wir uns bei der Betrachtung von Tacita Deans Arbeiten an ihn erinnert fühlen.

JEREMY MILLAR ist Künstler und Kurator. Er lebt im englischen Whitstable.

Wie Dean schreibt, *ist BANEWL ausschliesslich während der 2 Stunden 40 Minuten dauernden, totalen Sonnenfinsternis vom 11. August 1999 gedreht worden. Der Titel des Films ist die phonetische Transkription der in Cornwall üblichen Aussprache des Namens des Milchwirtschaftshofs «Burnewhall». Da der Tag trübe war, zeigt der Film weniger das Ereignis als vielmehr das Warten auf die Dunkelheit und auf die Wiederkehr des normalen Sonnenlichts. Die Wolken liessen uns dieses Ereignis kosmischer Zeit- und Grössenordnung zu unseren Bedingungen und in unserer eigenen menschlichen Zeit miterleben, da sie ermöglichten, es mit den Bewegungen der Tiere und den feinen Details unserer natürlichen Umgebung in Beziehung zu setzen.*[2]

Es ist ausserordentlich, wenn eine Arbeit, die man beinah als simple Dokumentation des Verstreichens der Zeit an einem bestimmten Ort auffassen könnte – und Dean ist sorgfältig darauf bedacht, dass wir die Aufnahmen in streng chronologischer Folge zu sehen bekommen –, eine derartige philosophische Tragweite zu entwickeln vermag, dass die Ausgangsmaterie der Cornwall'schen Landschaft sich quasi in das edle Metall der kosmischen Erkenntnis verwan-

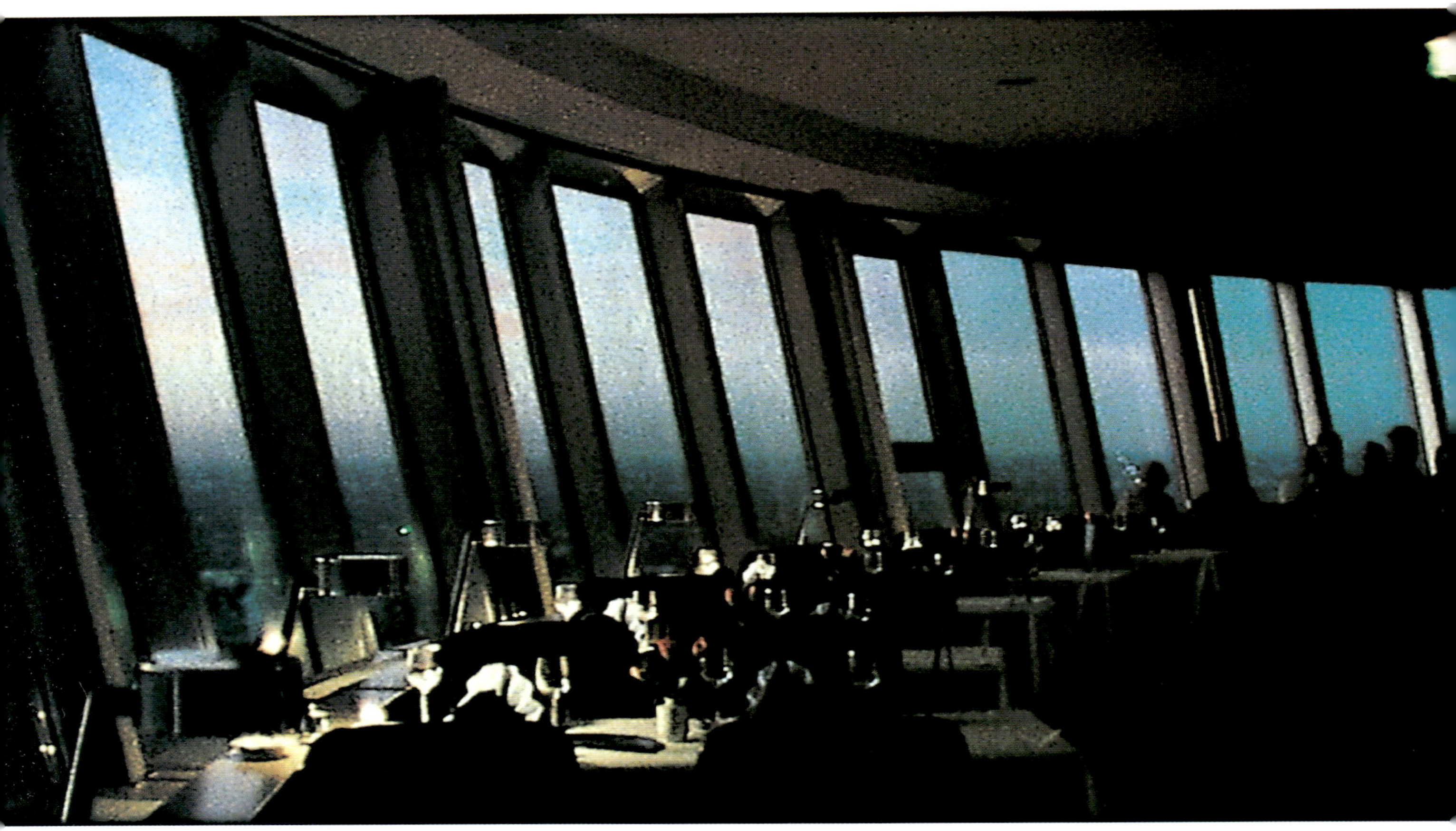

TACITA DEAN, FERNSEHTURM, 2001, 16mm color anamorphic with optical sound (44 mins.), film still / anamorphotischer 16mm-Farbfilm mit optischem Sound (44 Min.)

delt und unseren Platz in der Welt bezeichnet. Das Alchemistische wird zusätzlich noch durch die Tatsache unterstrichen, dass die gesamte Tonspur erst nach den Dreharbeiten hinzugefügt wurde. Selbst das Geräusch der wiederkäuenden Kühe wurde von Geräuschtechnikern beigesteuert.

TOTALITY (Totale Sonnenfinsternis, 2000) entstand zur selben Zeit. Dabei wurde eine speziell ausgerüstete Kamera verwendet, welche die Bewegung der Sonne am Himmel verfolgte und sie stets in der Mitte des Bildes hielt. Dieser Film dauert bloss elf Minuten und ist ohne Ton. Man sieht nur ein abstraktes Bild wechselnder Farbtöne und Schattierungen, während die hinter Wolken versteckte Sonne vom Mond verdeckt und allmählich wieder freigegeben wird. Der grandiose, aber nicht deutlich erkennbare Vorgang über uns wirkt hypnotisierend. Es ist, als sähen wir das Licht bei der Erschaffung der Welt. Vielleicht ist es deshalb nicht besonders überraschend, dass diese Arbeit mitunter an Farbfeldmalerei erinnert, etwa an Bilder des Amerikaners Barnett Newman, der das Licht als die Kraft betrachtete, die den Prozess aller Schöpfung, Veränderung und Entwicklung erst in Gang setzt. Darum mag uns auch die Aussage über das riesige dreiteilige Gemälde, das man nach Newmans Tod im August 1970 in seinem

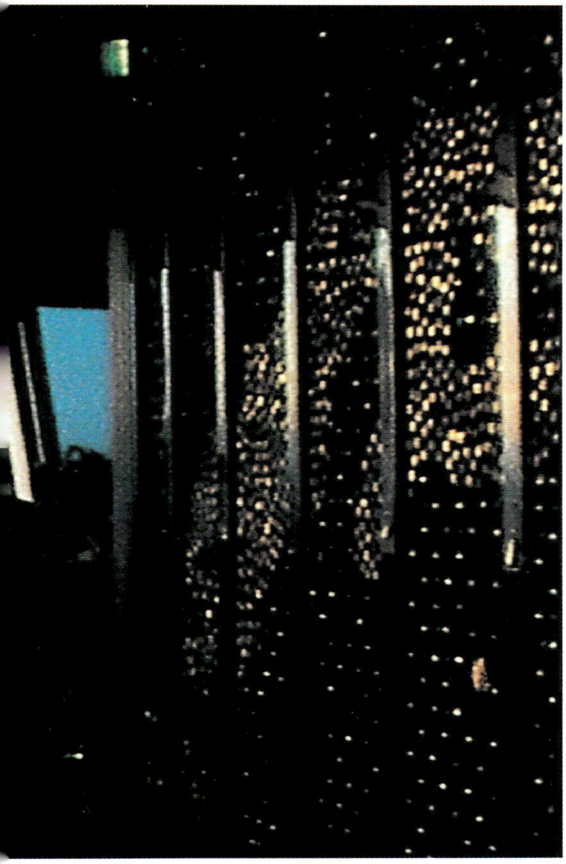

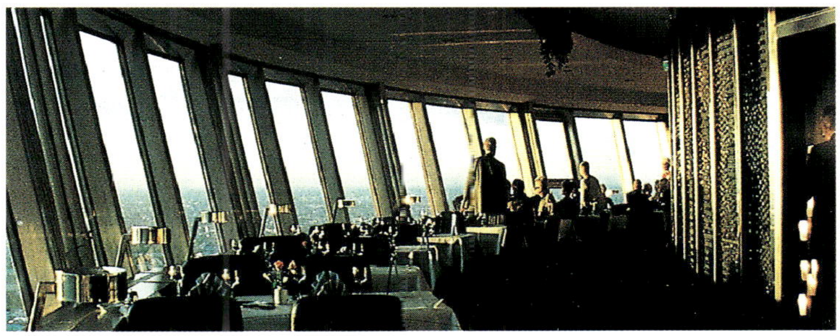

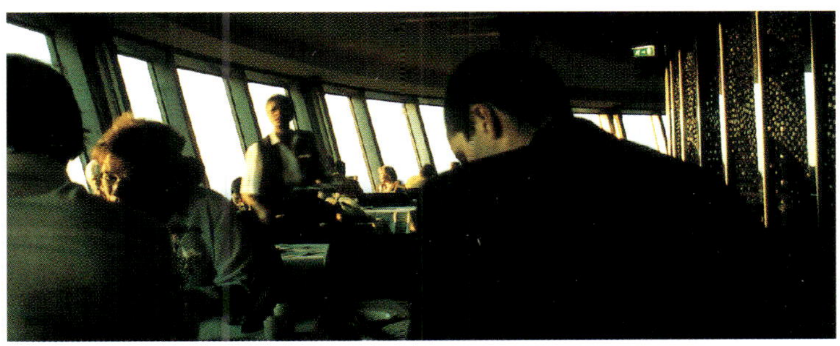

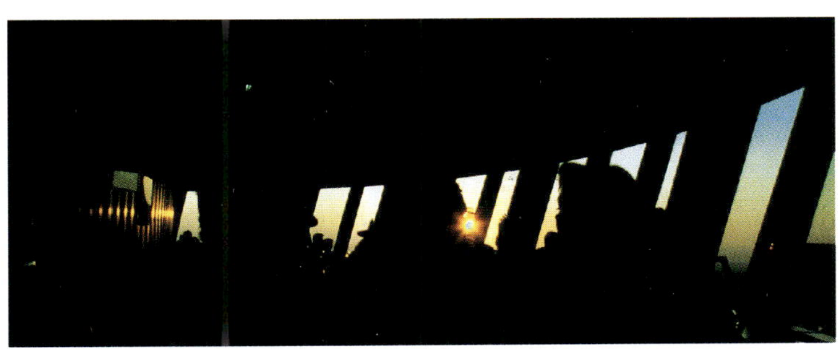

Top / Oben:
TACITA DEAN, FERNSEHTURM, 2001,
16mm color anamorphic with optical sound
(44 mins.), film still / anamorphotischer
16mm-Farbfilm mit optischem Sound (44 Min.)
Below / Darunter:
TACITA DEAN, location shots for FERNSEHTURM /
Photos am Drehort von FERNSEHTURM.

Atelier fand, nicht überraschen, nämlich: Es stehe im Raum «wie ein grosser Leuchtturm»,[3] wieder ein bekanntes Motiv von Dean.

Dem Gefühl, sich zugleich innerhalb und ausserhalb von Raum und Zeit zu befinden, begegnet man auch im Kurzfilm SOUND MIRRORS (Schallreflektoren, 1999). Dean schreibt dazu: *Die Schallreflektoren wurden während des Ersten Weltkriegs erfunden, als die Möglichkeit eines Luftangriffs zu einer neuen Gefahr für die nationale Sicherheit wurde. Sie wurden zwischen 1928 und 1930 in Denge, bei Dungeness und an zwei anderen Orten an der Küste von Kent aufgestellt, riesige Horchgeräte, die Motorengeräusche von näher kommenden Flugzeugen einfangen sollten. Nach kurzer Zeit stellte sich aber heraus, dass sie unzuverlässig waren, da sie die Geräusche von Flugzeugen, Booten und sonstigem Verkehr nicht voneinander unterscheiden konnten, so dass man sie durch Radar ersetzte. Dennoch sind die Klänge, die sie auch heute noch auffangen, etwas ganz Besonderes, und die gesamte Tonspur für diesen Film wurde innerhalb des 60-Meter-Reflektors aufgenommen.*[4]

Deutlicher noch als in anderen Filmen wird hier Deans Interesse für die Werke des Schriftstellers J.G. Ballard erkennbar, der «eine Zeit beschreibt, in der unser Alltag aus dem Rahmen fallen wird; in der unsere Nachfahren religiöse Bedeutungen in unsere Sportstadien und Rennbahnen hineininterpretieren werden und in der unsere heutigen Kultgegenstände unverständlich geworden sein werden».[5] Der Film ist eine Art Zeitreise in eine ungewisse Zukunft und erinnert etwas an Chris Markers ungewöhnliches Werk *La Jetée* (1962), übrigens einer von Ballards Lieblingsfilmen. Beide Filme zeigen nicht nur eine Gegenwart, die vorbei ist, sondern auch eine Zukunft, die es so noch nicht geben kann. Gerade wegen und nicht etwa trotz der Autorität von Deans Kamera könnte ihr Werk möglicherweise als «phantastisch» angesehen werden. Insofern könnte man SOUND MIRRORS vielleicht auch mit Andrej Tarkowskijs 1979 entstandenem Meisterwerk *Stalker* vergleichen, für den in einem verlassenen Wasserkraftwerk in Estland wohl einer der phantastischsten Räume des modernen Kinos geschaffen wurde, wobei neben Sprache und Vorstellungskraft keinerlei Spezialeffekte verwendet wurden. Auch in Deans Werk spielen Erinnerung und imaginative Beteiligung der Zuschauer eine wichtige Rolle. Da erscheint ein Ausschnitt aus Tarkowskijs *Stalker* ganz passend, in welchem der gleichnamige Protagonist, der Leute durch die verbotene Zone führt, das rätselhafte Gebiet beschreibt, durch das sie sich bewegen:

Die Zone ist ein äusserst komplexes System... gewissermassen mit Fallen ausgestattet, die alle tödlich sind. Ich weiss nicht, was geschieht, wenn wir weg sind... Aber die Leute müssen bloss herkommen, und das Ganze wird in Gang gesetzt. Unsere Stimmungen, unsere Gedanken, unsere Gefühle, unsere Empfindungen können hier Veränderungen bewirken. Und wir sind nicht in der Lage, das System zu begreifen. Alte Fallen verschwinden, neue tauchen auf; die alten ungefährlichen Orte werden unpassierbar, und der Weg kann entweder ganz einfach oder vollkommen verwirrend sein. So ist die Zone nun mal. Sie kann sogar launisch anmuten. Aber tatsächlich ist sie stets genau so, wie wir sie uns ausmalen... alles, was hier geschieht, hängt von uns ab und nicht von der Zone.[6]

Diese Beziehung zwischen Innen- und Aussenwelt ist nicht einfach die der Romantik, in der sich eine individuelle emotionale Kraft in der umgebenden Landschaft offenbart, sondern wohl etwas Moderneres, eine schizophrene Reaktion, bei der die Grenze zwischen Ich und Umwelt sich aufzulösen beginnt, durchlässig wird und schliesslich ganz verloren geht.

Ein paar Jahre ehe man mit dem Bau der Schallreflektoren begann, zog der Maler Paul Nash mit seiner Frau in die in jener Gegend gelegene Stadt Dymchurch. Ein paar Jahre nach der Fertigstellung der Reflektoren und kurz nach seinem ersten Besuch des Steinkreises von Avebury – den fast vierzig Jahre später auch Robert Smithson besuchen sollte – malte Nash das kleine Bild EQUIVALENTS FOR THE MEGALITHS (Entsprechungen der Megalithen, 1935). Das Bild war gleichzeitig mit Deans jüngster Ausstellung in der Tate Britain zu sehen. Der Bezug zwischen den Bildern ist bemerkenswert, wurde bisher jedoch nie erwähnt. Nash schrieb:

Müsste ich diesen Geist beschreiben, so würde ich sagen, dass er dem Land entspringt: Tatsächlich könnte man ihn beinahe als einen Genius Loci bezeichnen. Könnte sein Ausdruck benannt werden, so würde ich ihn als fast gänzlich lyrisch bezeichnen. Weiter wage ich nicht zu gehen: Ich gebe nur Geschichtliches wieder und bekenne mich zu meinem Glauben. Gegen Ende des achtzehnten Jahrhunderts er-

kannte William Blake – damals und oft auch heute als Verrückter bezeichnet – neben vielen anderen Dingen die verborgene Bedeutung des Landes, das er stets als Albion bezeichnete. Für ihn besass Albion einen grossartigen spirituellen Charakter, und er empörte sich ständig über «die Natur», deren Erscheinung er als falsche Realität ansah und ihr daher misstraute. Gleichzeitig war sein Schaffen sehr stark vom Land beeinflusst, in dem er lebte. Seine Dichtung kam im wahrsten Sinne des Wortes aus England. Blake suchte sein Leben lang nach Symbolen für das, was sein «inneres» Auge sah, seine Hand jedoch leider nur selten auszudrücken vermochte. Turner dagegen versuchte das Trugbild, das er mit so grosser Leichtigkeit wiedergeben konnte, zu durchbrechen und in seiner Phantasie zu einer realeren Wirklichkeit vorzudringen. So müssen auch wir heute neue Symbole finden, um unsere Reaktion auf die Umwelt zum Ausdruck zu bringen. [7)]

Dean teilt mit Nash (und Ballard, Marker und Tarkowskij) den Wunsch, «das Land» mit Bedeutung «neu zu verzaubern», wie Nash es ausdrückte, oder die Stelle zu untersuchen, wo Innen- und Aussenwelt zusammentreffen oder sich überschneiden. Deans Werke sind stets von der Umgebung geprägt, in der sie entstehen, doch geht es darin ebenso sehr um die Dinge, die diese Umgebung geprägt haben. Dies ist wohl auch in Deans neuestem Werk FERNSEHTURM (2001) erkennbar, einem Film, der an einem äusserst symbolträchtigen Ort, im Drehrestaurant des Fernsehturms auf dem Alexanderplatz, gedreht wurde, einem Bau, der sich wie die Schallreflekoren auf seltsame Weise ausserhalb der Zeit befindet – futuristisch und altmodisch zugleich. (Dieser Eindruck bestätigt sich denn auch während des Films, wenn der Organist des Restaurants vor einem sich rasch rötenden Himmel «An der schönen blauen Donau» zu spielen beginnt und uns dabei den anmutigen Walzer der Raumschiffe in Kubricks *2001 – A Space Odyssey* in Erinnerung ruft.) Da der Raum sich dreht, steht Tacitas Kamera still und ist dennoch in Bewegung (wie Kubricks Kamera in der sich drehenden Raumstation), so dass sich die Ereignisse vor ihren Augen, aber ohne ihr Zutun entwickeln. Die Leute begeben sich zu ihren Tischen, setzen sich aber nicht, sondern beschirmen die Augen und deuten mit ausgestreckten Armen auf die Umgebung. Auf Metall und Glas zeigen sich Spiegelungen, und wir fühlen uns an Deans in Leuchttürmen gedrehte Szenen erinnert, ebenfalls erhellte Türme, die ihre Umgebung prägen und in sich aufnehmen. Ein auf eine Wand gerichteter Scheinwerfer geht an und während das Licht draussen schwächer zu werden beginnt, wird die untergehende Sonne von elektronischen «Girl from Ipanema»-Klängen begleitet. Als die Welt draussen dunkler und der Innenraum immer heller wird, verwandeln sich die Fenster in Spiegel, und wir bemerken die geisterhaften Abbilder der Gäste, die über Berlin schweben wie die Engel in Wim Wenders' *Der Himmel über Berlin* (1987). Ich fühle mich schliesslich an den eben schon einmal erwähnten William Blake erinnert und an die Beschreibung seiner Skizze, A VISION: THE INSPIRATION OF THE POET (Eine Vision: die Inspiration des Dichters, ca. 1820):

Der riesige Raum ist von einem klaren Licht erfüllt, das in alle Winkel dringt und nichts im Ungewissen lässt; dennoch haftet der ganzen Szene etwas Geheimnisvolles und Unnahbares an, eine Einsamkeit, die so eindringlich ist, dass wir spüren, dass wir uns in einem Land «jenseits von Raum und Zeit» befinden, wo in der geräumigen und hell erleuchteten Kammer des Geistes der Dichter ganz allein im innersten Allerheiligsten, dem Schrein der Phantasie, sitzt und wunderbare Worte niederschreibt, die ihm von Engeln eingegeben werden. [8)]

(Übersetzung: Irene Aeberli)

1) David Alan Mellor und Garry Fabian Miller, *Tracing Light*, PhotoWorks, Maidstone 2001, S. 166.
2) *Tacita Dean*, Ausstellungskatalog, Tate Britain, London 2001.
3) Thomas B. Hess, *Barnett Newman*, Museum of Modern Art, New York 1971, S. 145; zitiert in Mellor und Miller, S. 165.
4) *Tacita Dean*, Ausstellungskatalog, Tate Britain, London 2001.
5) Tacita Dean, *Teignmouth Electron*, Book Works, London 1999, ohne Paginierung.
6) Andrei Tarkovsky, *Collected Screenplays*, Faber and Faber, London 1999, S. 395. (Hier aus dem Englischen übersetzt von I. Aeberli.)
7) Paul Nash, *Outline – An Autobiography and Other Writings*, London 1949; zitiert in: Peter Woodcock, *This Enchanted Isle*, Gothic Image, Glastonbury 2000, S. 18–19.
8) W. Graham Robertson, *The Blake Collection of W. Graham Robertson*, Faber and Faber, London 1952; zitiert in: Mellor und Miller, S. 173.

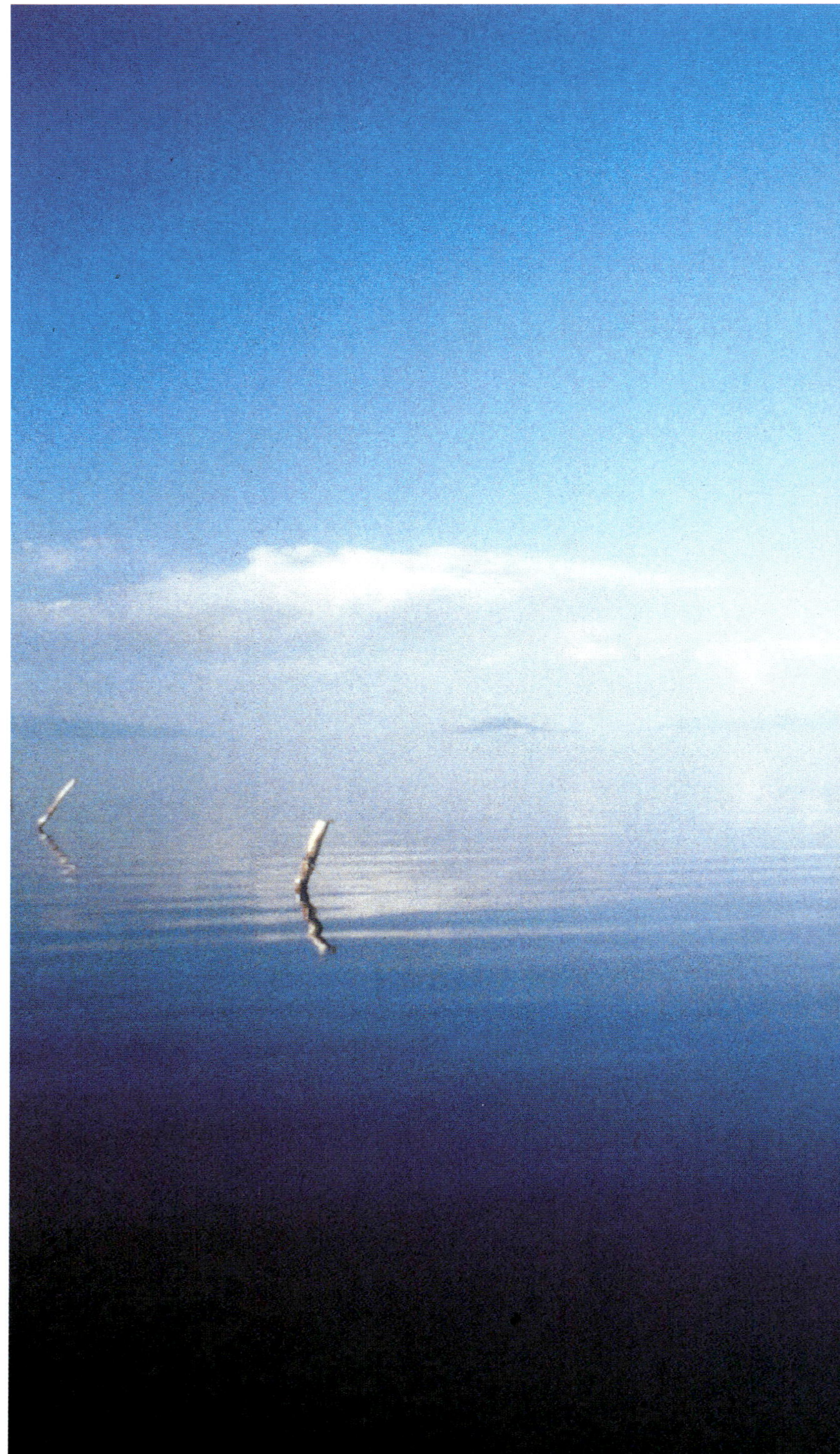

TACITA DEAN, ROZEL POINT, GREAT SALT LAKE, UTAH, 1997, slide projection / Diaprojektion.

SOUND AS DURATION IN THE FILMS OF TACITA DEAN

PAULA CARABELL

Anyone at all familiar with the work of Tacita Dean will know of her abiding fascination with the fateful journey of Donald Crowhurst.

In 1968, Donald Crowhurst entered the Sunday Times Golden Globe Race, the first contest to challenge a solitary individual to make a non-stop journey around the world. Crowhurst's hubris was extreme; he was an inexperienced sailor and his personal pride and feelings of civic responsibility lead to his tragic demise during the course of his journey. After the race had gotten underway, Crowhurst realized that he had taken on more than he could handle and the would-be hero, whose ship never reached beyond the Atlantic Ocean, began to radio in false locations rather than face the humiliation of failure. He eventually became totally disorientated and began to suffer from "time madness," which was common before the advent of longitude, when they discovered that by keeping Greenwich Mean Time aboard ship they could more accurately locate their position.[1)]

Crowhurst's inexperience may, in addition, have contributed to the resulting faulty equipment; his chronometer, the instrument that measures Greenwich Mean Time, was seriously flawed and he failed to wind it regularly to keep that rate of error constant. Unfortunately, the chronometer had become the center of his universe. It was an obsessive stronghold that, in the end, only further fostered his sense of disorientation until he became totally lost in time altogether and jumped overboard, taking his cherished chronometer with him.

For Dean, Crowhurst's experience serves as an emblem of time's potential deformation and signifies the possibility of total temporal malfunction. This conception of time as incalculable duration has impacted strongly on Dean's films. Rather than employing film as primarily a visual medium, her unusual emphasis on sound enables her fully to explore the notion of *durée*, the vicissitudes of lived time.

Dean's aim is to recreate Crowhurst's sense of temporal disorientation in the viewer by ignoring the conventions of cinematic unity, making clear the split between sound and image. The traditional cinematic apparatus fosters the fiction that both sound and image emanate from the screen, a homogenous space in which the observer is offered a false sense of plenitude. It has been suggested by some film theo-

PAULA CARABELL is an Art Historian and Independent Scholar currently living in London.

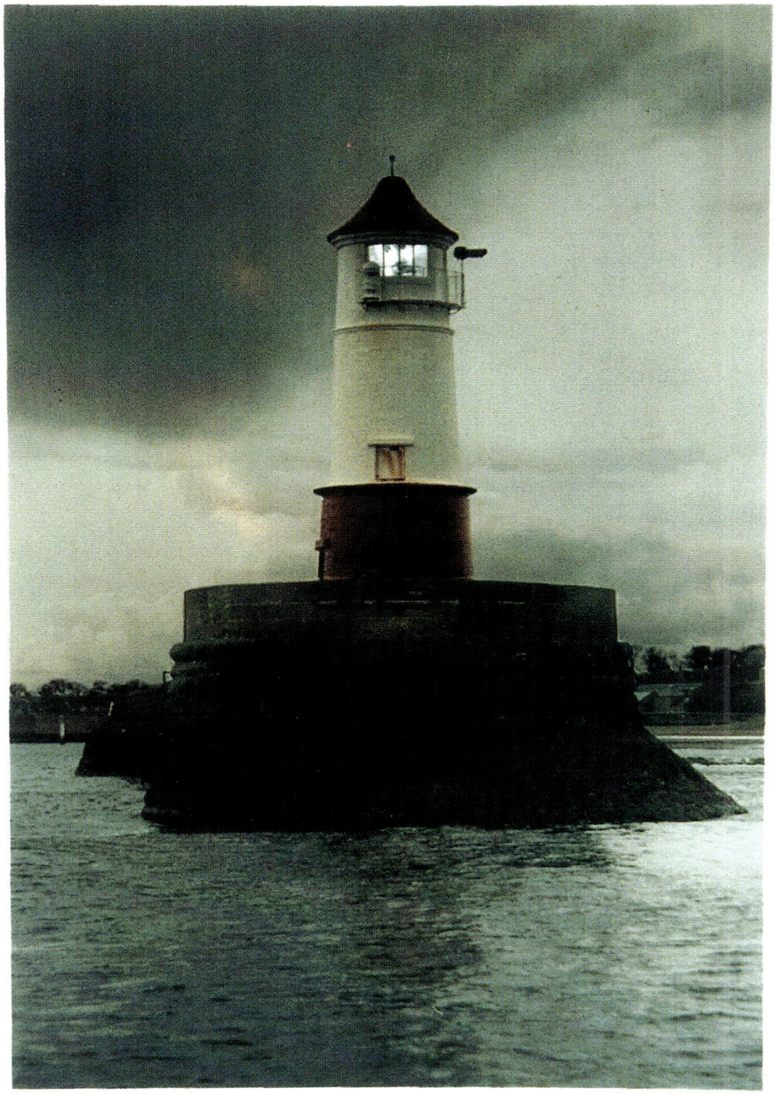

TACITA DEAN, BERWICK LIGHTHOUSE, 1996, dye-sublimation print /
DER LEUCHTTURM VON BERWICK, Thermosublimationsdruck.

rists that the cinematic image has always been constructed around the same principles as those employed in Renaissance painting, those of single-point perspective; this system not only serves to spatialize time but privileges the viewer and reinforces the illusion of a unified spatial field in which the observer finds herself the center.[2] Dean's goal is to deconstruct this fiction by destroying the synchronization between sound and image and by demasking the mechanisms of the cinematic process. Her films call into question the possibility of a privileged viewing subject by declaring the disembodied eye of the beholder a fictive construct that can only exist outside of temporal duration.

In both DISAPPEARANCE AT SEA (1996) and DISAPPEARANCE AT SEA II (1997), Dean invokes the theme of the lighthouse to serve as a direct reference to Crowhurst's fate and as a vehicle through which to explore the process of self-orientation/disorientation. DISAPPEARANCE AT SEA was filmed at the St. Abb's Head Lighthouse in Berwickshire, a structure, like any other lighthouse, devised to help the sailor calculate his course in relation to a final strip of land and to identify which bit of land. Through the illumination of the lighthouse's Fresnel lenses, we realize that night has fallen, the revolving lantern creating a geometry of reflection and refraction that fills the entire frame for most of the fourteen-minute film. The gaps between the rotations of light count out the passing moments, and yet also mesmerize the viewer to the extent that time can no longer be calculated; like Crowhurst, we experience our own version of "time madness."

In DISAPPEARANCE AT SEA II, the scene is reversed. The four-minute film was shot during the day at Longstone Lighthouse in the Farne Islands, Northumberland, and unlike the earlier work, the fascination of the lens plays no part in the scene. In-

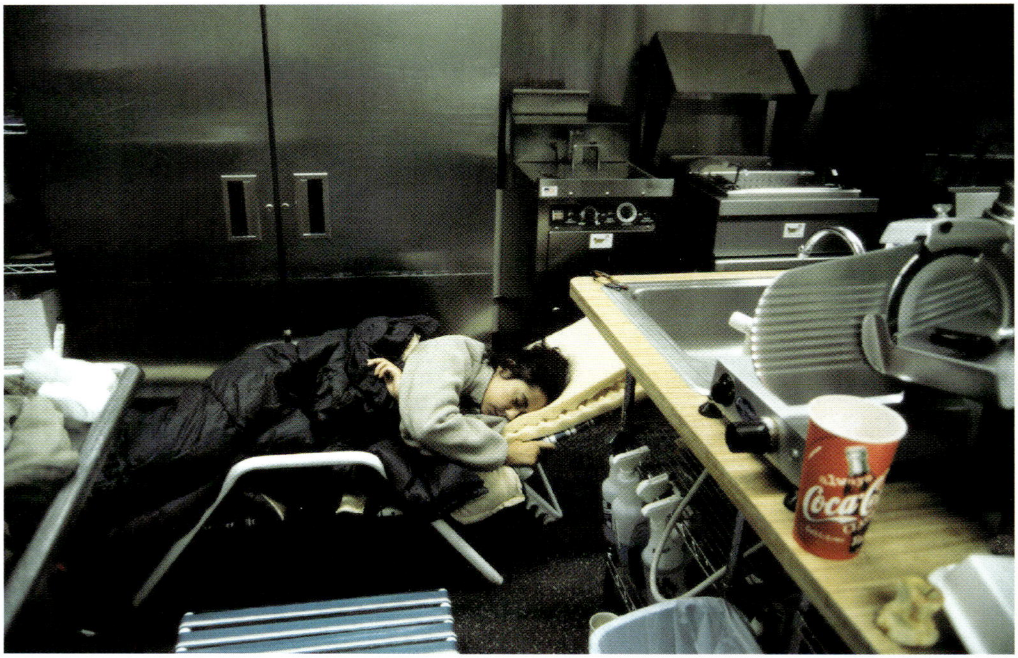

TACITA DEAN, DIXIE D'S SNACK BAR, HOONAH ALASKA,
EARLY HOURS OF THE MORNING, 1999–2000, color photograph, 35 3/8 x 39 3/8" /
FRÜHMORGENS IN DIXIE D'S SNACK BAR, HOONAH ALASKA, Farbphoto, 90 x 100 cm.
(PHOTO: MATTHEW HALE)

stead, the protective metal chevrons that form the outer shell of the lantern pass repeatedly before our eyes. Beyond these geometric shapes, we view the vast expanse of sea, the sea where Crowhurst met his death. Although the lantern remains in perpetual motion, Dean chose to employ a static camera, rather than one that might further suggest the object's endless rotation. Such a technique initially offers the viewers the illusion that they are circling a stationary object, surrogates for the camera's eye. This, then, is the empowered viewer of the Renaissance. In actuality, however, the beholder is given a restricted view, one controlled by an unseen, external force, the inability to see beyond that which is given, forming a disturbing actuality. The viewer finds herself, therefore, immobilized, trapped, mesmerized by the image, dismayed and disoriented by her lack of freedom and loss of control.[3]

Dean, alluding to such lacunae, has described her works within the context of missing narratives.[4] Within the majority of the films (including the two discussed here) there is no dialogue and so sound, rather than speech, takes on a heightened significance, ultimately forming a marker for that which has been lost. DISAPPEARANCE AT SEA, for example, is accompanied only by the grinding sound of the lighthouse mechanisms. After the screen has darkened the cry of seabirds can be heard in the darkness. In DISAPPEARANCE AT SEA II, we hear muted short-wave radio signals. Sounds of communication and life offer the promise of integration, the hope that we will retain our privileged status. That perhaps unlike Crowhurst we will find our way back to shore. But Dean's propensity for desynchronization destroys any possibility of the alluring fiction.

When Dean installs her cinematic work, she chooses to place the projector and screen within the same space, where the former stands prominently as a near intrusive, freestanding object. Its obvious workings make no secret that what we see on screen is pure illusion, while its presence also increasingly distracts us both visually and aurally. As the viewing benches are placed closer to the projector than to the screen, the clicking of the mechanism begins quickly to enter our consciousness, then to gain primacy over the illusion that what we see and hear emanates from the screen itself. The movement of the projector forms a parallel soundtrack, its own marking of time. This creates yet another decentering experience; splits exist between reality and illusion, sound and vision, the difference between what we see and what we hear. If we indeed look at Dean's films as installations, with screen, projector, and benches all forming part of a whole, what overtakes our consciousness is the clicking of the apparatus rather than the illusion of the cinematic image, for it is the sound of the projector as object that describes most clearly the passage of time.

Returning to the notion of duration, we see that Dean has adopted a cinematic ontology based on time rather than space, one that has much in common with the work of Henri Bergson who, in the late nineteenth century, strongly influenced such artists as Cézanne with his ideas on temporality.[5)] Reflecting on the topic of film, Bergson emphasizes the importance of sound and directs his comments against the primacy of vision. He equates vision with stasis, sound with movement and thus, temporality.[6)] Bergson insisted that sound, due to its innate fluidity, rather than image comes closest to the experience of temporal duration.[7)] The filmatic image may represent time, but it is merely a framed cross-section, one that ultimately negates the image's ability to express duration.

When asked, "What is the relation between sound and image in your work?" Dean answered, "My interest resides in this gap between the sound and the image... I require sound to have its own autonomy."[8)] Thus, in opposition to an approach to cinema in which the viewer experiences a sense of identification with the spectacle, Dean creates a mode of apprehension in which the observer feels at odds with what she sees. While on the one hand, Dean points out that the slowness of her films enables the viewer to explore a single frame, she is also concerned with making clear the discontinuities of the cinematic experience.[9)] The slightly disjointed relationship between sound and image, compounded by the clearly physical presence of the projector creates caesurae, which force the beholder to return to real-time, lived bodily experience rather than that of the cinematic. Sound serves as a decentering device that not only functions as the primary marker of duration, but most closely begins to approximate Donald Crowhurst's, "time madness," his loss of orientation, self, and life during his final journey at sea.

1) "Once Upon a Different Sort of Time: The Story of Donald Crowhurst" in: *Tacita Dean*, ex. cat. (Barcelona: Museu d'Art Contemporani de Barcelona, 2000), p. 39.

2) See, for example, Christian Metz, *The Imaginary Signifier: Psychoanalysis and the Cinema*, trans. Celia Britton, Annwyl Williams, Ben Brewster, and Andrew Guzetti (Bloomington, Indiana: Indiana University Press, 1982); André Bazin, *What is Cinema?*, vol. 1, trans. Hugh Grey (Berkeley: University of California Press, 1967); Jean Baudry, "Ideological Effects of the Basic Cinematographic Apparatus," *Film Quarterly*, 27, 2, Winter 1974–1975.

3) Jacques Lacan, *The Four Fundamental Concepts of Psycho-Analysis*, ed. by Jacques-Alain Miller, trans. Alan Sheridan (New York: Norton, 1978), p. 92.

4) "A Conversation with Tacita Dean" in: *Tacita Dean* (Barcelona: Museu d'Art Contemporani de Barcelona, 2000), p. 80.

5) Maurice Merleau-Ponty, "Cézanne's Doubt" in: *Sense and Non-sense*, trans. Hubert L. Dreyfus and Patricia A. Dreyfus (Evanston, IL: Northwestern University Press, 1964).

6) Martin Jay, *Downcast Eyes: The Denigration of Vision in Twentieth-Century French Thought* (Berkeley: University of California Press, 1993), p. 195.

7) Ibid., p. 197.

8) *Voice Over: Sound and Vision in Current Art* (London: The South Bank Centre, 1998), p. 19.

9) "A Conversation with Tacita Dean" in: *Tacita Dean* (Barcelona: Museu d'Art Contemporani de Barcelona, 2000), p. 92.

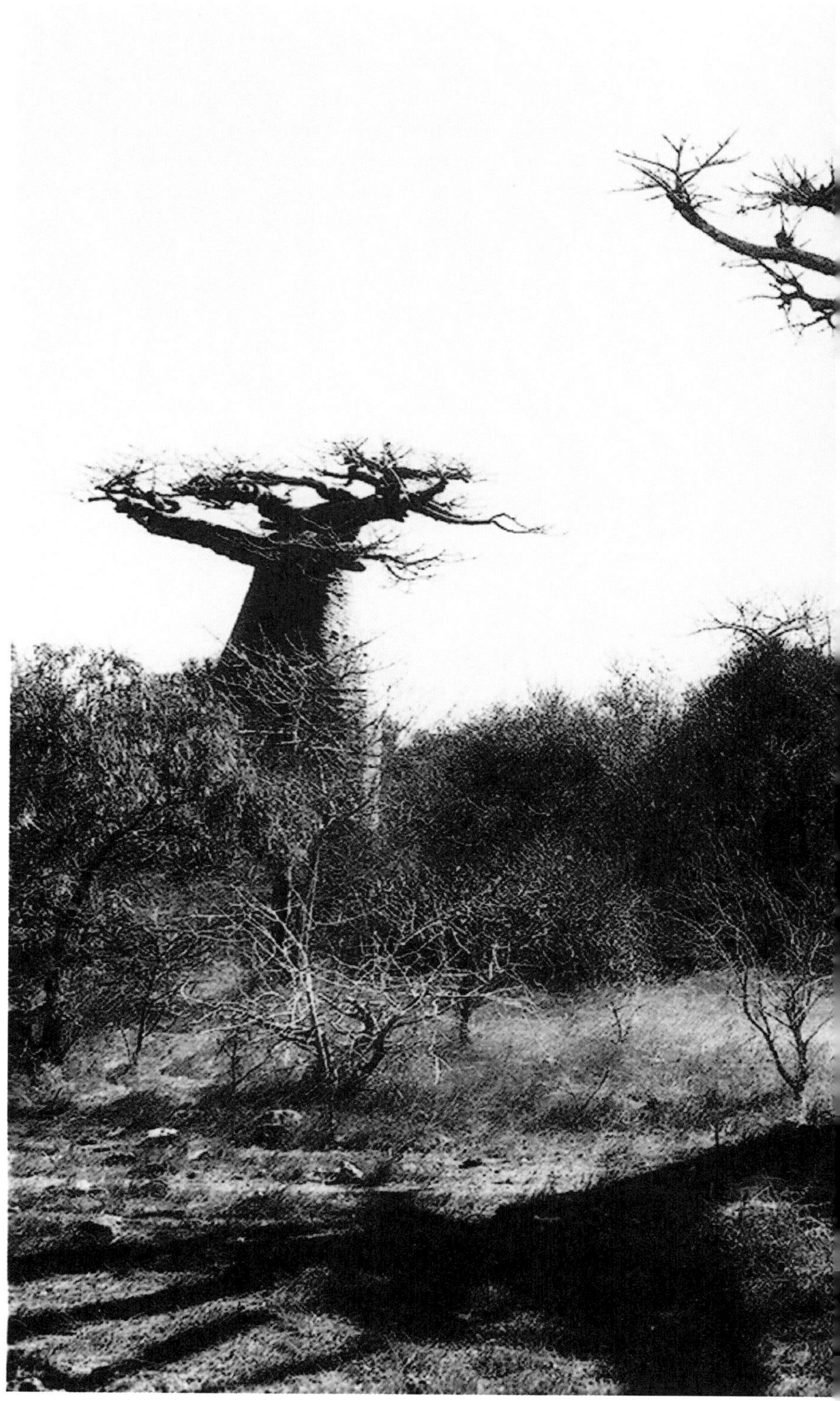

TACITA DEAN, BAOBAB, 2001, location photograph / Photo am Drehort.

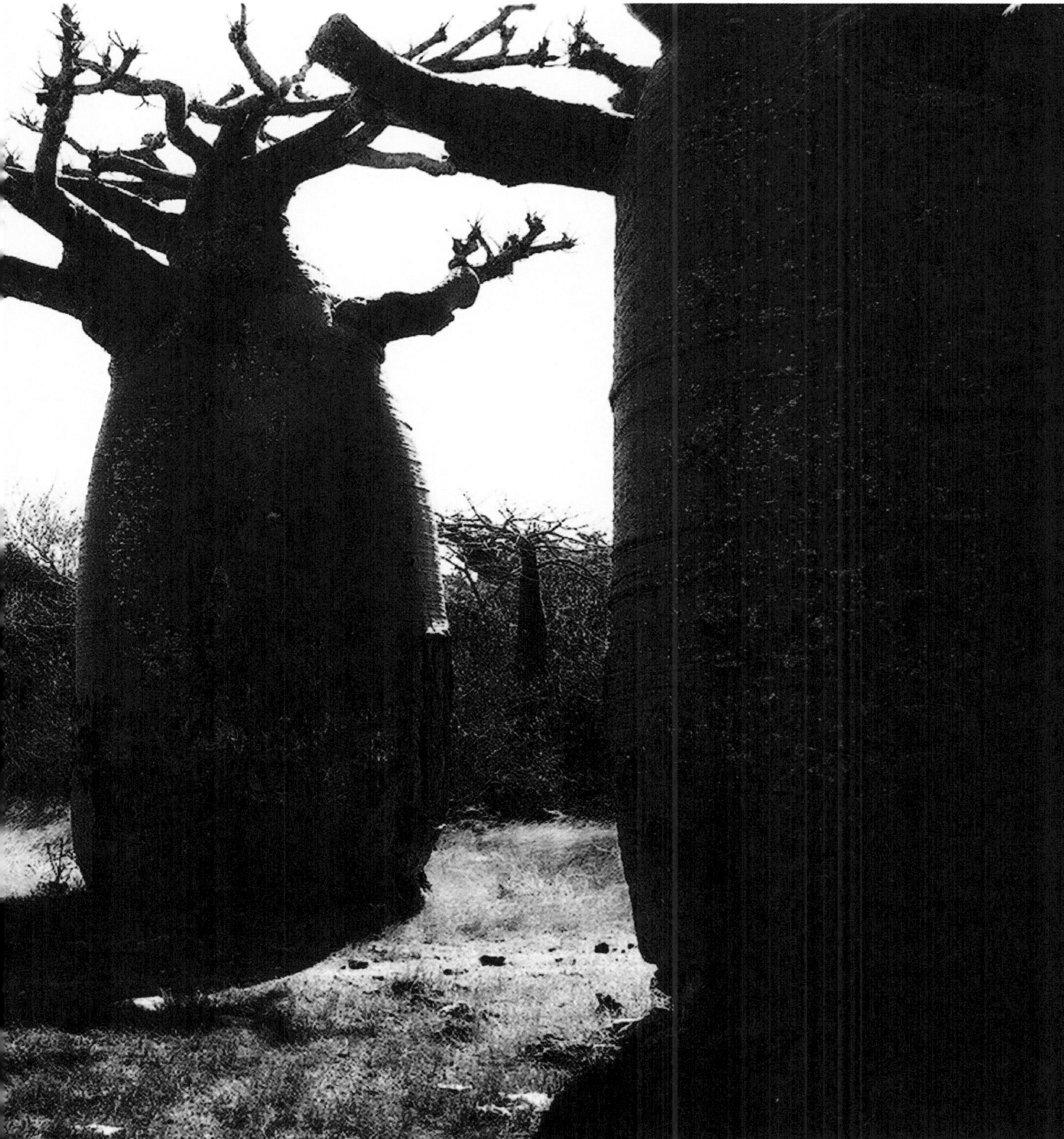

DER TON ALS DAUER IN DEN FILMEN VON TACITA DEAN

PAULA CARABELL

Wer mit Tacita Deans Arbeiten auch nur ein wenig vertraut ist, weiss, dass Donald Crowhursts Schicksalsfahrt sie schon lange fasziniert und beschäftigt.

1968 nahm Donald Crowhurst am *Sunday Times Golden Globe Race* teil, dem ersten Non-Stop-Wettsegeln rund um die Welt für Einhandsegler. Crowhursts Selbstüberschätzung war gigantisch: Er war ein unerfahrener Segler, dessen persönlicher Stolz und nationales Pflichtgefühl im Verlauf der Reise zu einem tragischen Ende führten. Nach Beginn des Rennens wurde Crowhurst klar, dass er sich übernommen hatte, und der Möchtegern-Held, dessen Boot nie über den Atlantischen Ozean hinausgelangte, begann lieber falsche Koordinaten auszusenden, statt der demütigenden Tatsache seines Scheiterns ins Gesicht zu sehen. Schliesslich verlor er die Orientierung und auch jedes Zeitgefühl, was auf hoher See vor Einführung der Längenmeridiane häufig vorgekommen war, bevor man entdeckte, dass durch Beibehaltung der Greenwicher Zeit die jeweilige Position genauer bestimmt werden konnte.[1)]

PAULA CARABELL ist Kunsthistorikerin und freie Wissenschaftlerin. Sie lebt in London.

Crowhursts Unerfahrenheit mag auch schuld sein an seiner mangelhaften Ausrüstung; sein Chronometer, das Instrument, welches die Greenwicher Zeit anzeigen sollte, war ernsthaft beschädigt und weil er ihn nicht regelmässig aufzog, versäumte er es, die Abweichung wenigstens konstant zu halten. Unglücklicherweise war dieser Chronometer zum Mittelpunkt seines Universums geworden. Wie besessen hielt er sich an diesem einen Strohhalm fest, was sein Gefühl der Desorientierung nur noch verstärkte, bis er Orientierung und Zeitgefühl ganz und gar verloren hatte und schliesslich samt seinem geliebten Chronometer über Bord ging.

Crowhursts Erfahrung dient Dean als Sinnbild einer möglichen Zeitdeformation und verweist auf die Möglichkeit der totalen zeitlichen Verwirrung. Diese Auffassung der Zeit als unberechenbare Dauer hat Deans Filme stark beeinflusst. Statt den Film in erster Linie als visuelles Medium einzusetzen, erlaubt ihr die unübliche Gewichtung des Tons, den Begriff der Dauer zu erforschen, das Wechselhafte der gelebten Zeit.

Deans Ziel ist es, im Betrachter Crowhursts Empfindung zeitlicher Orientierungslosigkeit zu erzeugen, indem sie die Konventionen der kinematischen Einheit ignoriert und die Kluft zwischen Bild und Ton deutlich macht. Die traditionelle Kinotechnik unterstützt die Illusion, dass Ton und Bild gleichermassen von der Leinwand her kommen, aus einem homogenen Raum, der dem Betrachter ein falsches Gefühl der Vollständigkeit vermittelt. Manche Filmtheoretiker sind der Meinung, dass sich das Filmbild schon immer nach denselben Prinzipien richtete wie die Renaissance-Malerei, nämlich jenen der Zentralperspektive; dieses System erlaubt nicht nur die Zeit räumlich darzustellen, sondern versetzt den Betrachter in eine privilegierte Position und verstärkt die Illusion eines einheitlichen Raumes, in dessen Zentrum der Betrachter oder die Betrachterin steht.[2] Dean zielt auf die Dekonstruktion dieser Fiktion, indem sie das synchrone Verhältnis von Bild und Ton aufbricht und die Mechanismen des filmischen Prozesses offen legt. Indem sie das körperlose Auge des Betrachters als fiktives Konstrukt entlarven, das nur unter Ausklammerung der zeitlichen Dauer bestehen kann, stellen ihre Filme die Möglichkeit des privilegierten Betrachtersubjekts überhaupt in Frage.

Sowohl in DISAPPEARENCE AT SEA (Verschwinden auf See, 1996) und DISAPPEARENCE AT SEA II (1997) setzt Dean das Leuchtturm-Thema als direkten Verweis auf Crowhursts Schicksal ein und als Vehikel zur Untersuchung des Prozesses unserer Orientierung bzw. Desorientierung. DISAPPEARENCE AT SEA wurde beim St. Abb's Head-Leuchtturm in Berwickshire gefilmt, einem Gebäude, das wie jeder andere Leuchtturm dazu gedacht ist, dem Seemann die Berechnung seines Kurses im Verhältnis zu einem letzten sichtbaren Landstrich sowie die Identifizierung dieses Landstrichs zu ermöglichen. Das Aufleuchten der Fresnel-Linsen im Leuchtturm zeigt an, dass es Nacht geworden ist, während die rotierende Lampe ein geometrisches Muster aus den Spiegelungen und Brechungen des Lichtstrahls erzeugt, welches das Blickfeld beinah den ganzen vierzehnminütigen Film hindurch ausfüllt. Die Pausen zwischen dem Wiederkehren des rotierenden Lichts geben den

TACITA DEAN, WALEED, OUR MINISTRY OF INFORMATION OFFICIAL, EARLY HOURS OF THE MORNING, 1999–2000, black and white photograph, 35 7/8 x 39 3/8" / WALEED, UNSER VERTRETER DES AMTS FÜR INFORMATIONEN, FRÜHMORGENS, Schwarzweissphoto, 90 x 100 cm.

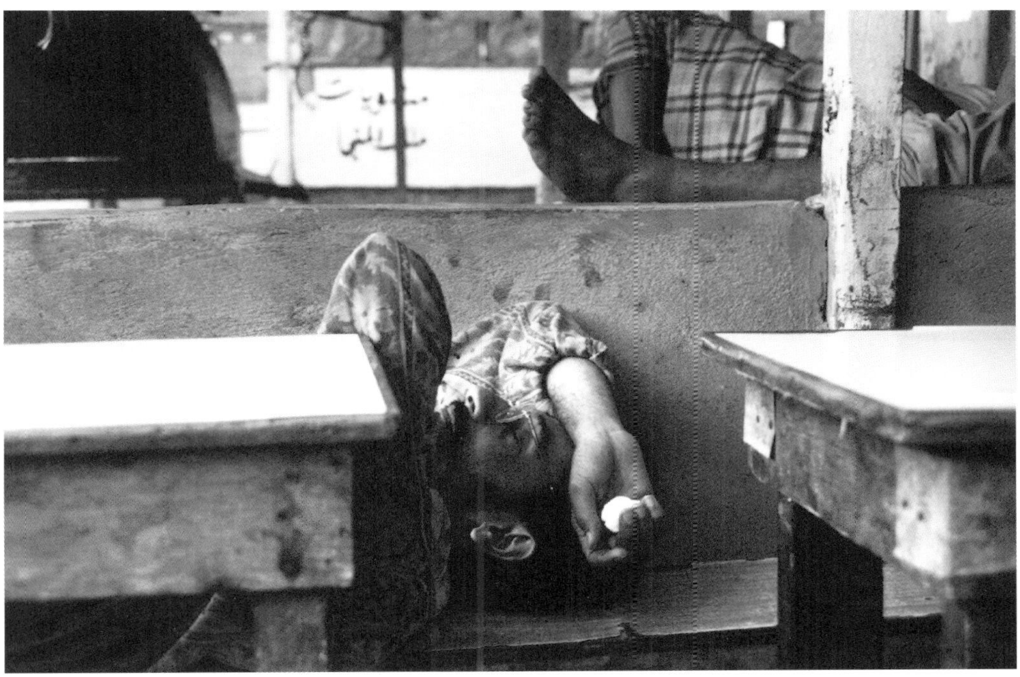

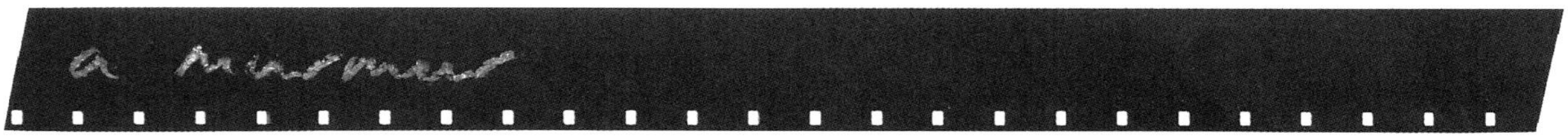

TACITA DEAN, A MURMUR (MAGNETIC), 1997, 16mm magnetic tape, chinagraph / EIN MURMELN (MAGNETISCH), 16mm-Magnetband, Wachskreidestift.

Takt der verstreichenden Zeit an, schlagen den Betrachter jedoch gleichzeitig derart in Bann, dass die Zeit gar nicht mehr berechenbar ist; wie Crowhurst erleben wir unsere eigene Form von Verlust des Zeitgefühls.

In DISAPPEARENCE AT SEA II ist die Situation gerade umgekehrt. Der vierminütige Film wurde bei Tag beim Longstone Lighthouse auf den Fame Islands in Northumberland gedreht, und die Faszination der Linse spielt hier keine Rolle. Stattdessen sehen wir wiederholt die metallenen Schutzgitter vorübergleiten, die das äussere Gehäuse der Lampe bilden. Jenseits dieser geometrischen Struktur sehen wir die ungeheure Weite des Meeres, jenes Meeres, in dem Crowhurst den Tod fand. Obwohl die Lampe immer in Bewegung bleibt, wählte Dean lieber eine stehende Kamera als eine, die die endlose Drehbewegung des Motivs noch unterstrichen hätte. Diese Technik vermittelt dem Betrachter gleich die Illusion, dass er ein unbewegliches Objekt umkreist und die Position des Kameraobjektivs einnimmt. Das entspräche dem allmächtigen Betrachter der Renaissance. Hier aber bietet sich dem Betrachter eine eingeschränkte Sicht, eine, die von einer unsichtbaren, äusseren Macht kontrolliert wird, und die Unfähigkeit, über das Dargebotene hinaus etwas zu erkennen, hat eine beunruhigende Aktualität. Die Betrachterin sieht sich also gefesselt, gefangen im Bann des Bildes und ist unangenehm berührt und verwirrt durch die fehlende Freiheit und den Kontrollverlust.[3)]

Dean hat in Aussagen über ihre Arbeiten in Anspielung auf solche Leerstellen das Fehlen narrativer Strukturen angesprochen.[4)] In den meisten Filmen (einschliesslich der beiden hier erwähnten) gibt es keinen Dialog, und so erhält der Ton gegenüber dem Gesprochenen grössere Bedeutung und wird schliesslich zu einem Hinweis auf das Verlorengegangene. DISAPPEARENCE AT SEA zum Beispiel wird nur vom schnarrenden Geräusch der Leuchtturmmechanik begleitet. In DISAPPEARENCE AT SEA II hören wir erstickte Kurzwellenfunksignale. Kommunikations- und Lebensgeräusche enthalten das Versprechen der Zugehörigkeit, die Hoffnung, dass wir unseren privilegierten Status behalten werden. Dass wir vielleicht, anders als Crowhurst, den Weg zurück an Land finden werden. Aber Deans Hang zum Desynchronisieren macht die Möglichkeit der so verlockenden Fiktion gleich zunichte.

Bei der Installation ihrer Filmarbeiten platziert Dean den Projektor immer im selben Raum mit der Leinwand, so dass er als gut sichtbares Objekt beinahe störend dasteht. Das offensichtliche Arbeiten des Apparates macht kein Hehl daraus, dass das, was wir auf der Leinwand sehen, eine Illusion ist, während uns seine unübersehbare Präsenz visuell und akustisch immer stärker ablenkt. Weil die Zuschauerbänke näher beim Projektor stehen als bei der Leinwand, nimmt das Klicken der Mechanik rasch von unserem Bewusstsein Besitz und verdrängt die Illusion, dass das, was wir sehen und hören, der Leinwand entspringt. Die Bewegungen des Projektors bilden einen parallelen Soundtrack und eine eigene

TACITA DEAN, A KISS (MAGNETIC), 1997, 16mm magnetic tape, chinagraph / EIN KUSS (MAGNETISCH), 16mm-Magnetband, Wachskreidestift.

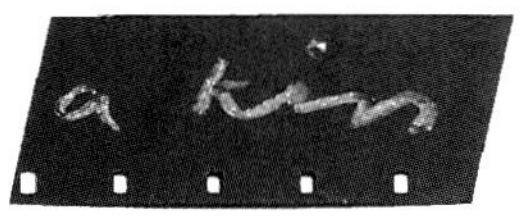

Zeitanzeige. Dadurch entsteht eine weitere dezentralisierende Erfahrung; es gibt eine Spaltung zwischen Realität und Illusion, Ton und Bild, eine Differenz zwischen dem, was wir sehen, und dem, was wir hören. Wenn wir Deans Filme als Installationen erleben, in denen Leinwand, Projektor und Bänke Teile eines Ganzen sind, so fesselt das Klicken des Apparates unser Bewusstsein mehr als die Illusion des Filmbildes, denn es ist das Geräusch des Projektors als Objekt, welches das Vergehen der Zeit am deutlichsten zum Ausdruck bringt.

Kehren wir zum Begriff der Dauer zurück, so sehen wir, dass sich Dean eine filmische Ontologie angeeignet hat, die mehr auf die Zeit als den Raum baut, eine, die Ähnlichkeit mit dem Denken von Henri Bergson hat, der im späten neunzehnten Jahrhundert Künstler wie Cézanne mit seinen Gedanken über die Zeit stark beeinflusst hat.[5] In seinen Gedanken zum Film unterstreicht Bergson die Bedeutung des Tons und wendet sich gegen die Vorherrschaft des Bildes. Er setzt das Bild gleich mit Stasis, den Ton dagegen mit Bewegung und daher mit Zeitlichkeit.[6] Bergson unterstrich immer wieder, dass der Ton durch seine fliessende Natur der Erfahrung der zeitlichen Dauer viel näher kommt als das Bild.[7] Das gefilmte Bild mag Zeit darstellen, aber es ist nur ein konstruierter Querschnitt, der letztlich die Fähigkeit des Bildes Dauer auszudrücken negiert.

Auf die Frage, in welchem Verhältnis Ton und Bild in ihrer Arbeit zueinander stünden, antwortete Tacita Dean: «Mein Interesse gilt der Kluft zwischen Bild und Ton... der Ton muss seine eigene Autonomie haben.»[8] Im Gegensatz zu einem Filmverständnis, bei dem der Betrachter ein Identifikationserlebnis hat, erzeugt Dean einen Spannungszustand, der den Betrachter dem, was er sieht, ratlos gegenüberstehen lässt. Während Dean einerseits unterstreicht, dass die Langsamkeit ihrer Filme dem Betrachter erlaube, das einzelne Bild zu erforschen, ist sie gleichzeitig darum bemüht, das Diskontinuierliche der filmischen Erfahrung deutlich hervorzukehren.[9] Die leichte Störung der Beziehung zwischen Ton und Bild in Gestalt der klaren physischen Präsenz des Projektors erzeugt Zäsuren, die den Betrachter zur Rückkehr in die reale Zeit zwingen und zu einer gelebten körperlichen Erfahrung anstelle des reinen Filmerlebnisses. Der Ton dient als dezentralisierendes Werkzeug, das nicht nur wichtigster Ausdruck der zeitlichen Dauer ist, sondern uns auch Donald Crowhursts Zeitwahnsinn näherbringt, seinem Verlust der Orientierung, seiner selbst und schliesslich seines Lebens im Lauf jener letzten Seereise.

(Übersetzung: Wilma Parker)

1) «Once Upon a Different Sort of Time: The Story of Donald Crowhurst», in: *Tacita Dean*, Ausstellungskatalog, Museu d'Art Contemporani de Barcelona, 2000, S. 39.
2) Siehe dazu zum Beispiel: Christian Metz, *Der imaginäre Signifikant: Psychoanalyse und Kino*, Nodus-Publ., Münster 2000; André Bazin, *Was ist Kino?*, Dumont, Köln 1975; Jean Baudry, «Ideological Effects of the Basic Cinematographic Apparatus», *Film Quarterly*, 27/2, Winter 1974/1975.
3) Jacques Lacan, *Die vier Grundbegriffe der Psychoanalyse (Das Seminar 11)*, hrsg. v. Jacques-Alain Miller, Walter Verlag, Olten 1978, S. 122.
4) «A Conversation with Tacita Dean», in: *Tacita Dean*, op. cit., S. 80.
5) Maurice Merleau-Ponty, «Der Zweifel Cézannes», in: *Sinn und Nicht-Sinn*, übers. v. Hans-Dieter Gondek, Fink, München 2000.
6) Martin Jay, *Downcast Eyes: The Denigration of Vision in Twentieth-Century French Thought*, University of California Press, Berkeley 1993, S. 195.
7) Ebenda, S. 197.
8) *Voice Over: Sound and Vision in Current Art*, The South Bank Centre, London 1998, S. 19.
9) «A Conversation with Tacita Dean», in: *Tacita Dean*, op. cit., S. 92.

DIETER SCHWARZ

Teignmouth Electron

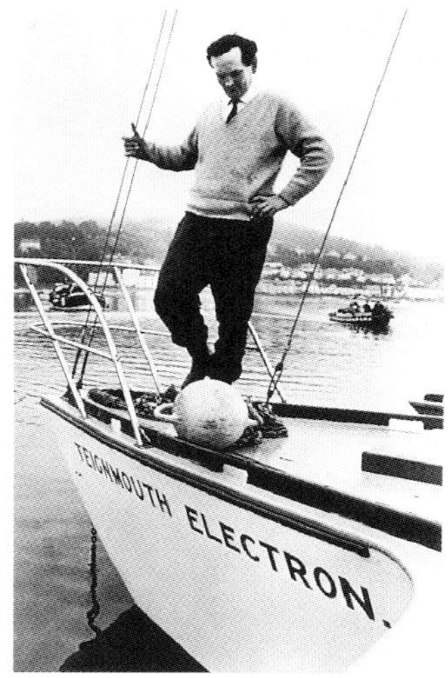

Postkarte mit der Legende / Postcard with caption: "Greetings from Teignmouth the Devon Resort chosen by Donald Crowhurst as the Home Port for his Triumphant around the World Yacht Race"

Tacita Dean hat uns durch ihr Werk die Figur von Donald Crowhurst nahe gebracht, das bizarre Schicksal eines Mannes, der sich entschloss, im Rahmen eines Wettbewerbs die Welt im Alleingang zu umsegeln, und der schliesslich über Bord ging. Dies wäre für sich genommen nur eine tragische Geschichte, kämen dazu nicht die besonderen Umstände, die ihn scheitern liessen, nämlich die durch finanzielle Bedrängnis geschürte Tollkühnheit, die ihn unzulänglich vorbereitet an Bord gehen liess, das Doppelspiel zwischen dem realen Umhertreiben seines Boots in der Sargassosee und der Übermittlung fiktiver Erfolge, schliesslich der Verlust der Orientierung und der Sprung über Bord mit dem Chronometer, dem Instrument, dessen Funktionieren die Position in Raum und Zeit zu bestimmen erlaubt. Eine vermeidbare und dennoch unausweichliche Katastrophe, Heldentum, das auf Waghalsigkeit und mutwilliger Täuschung beruht – wäre man nicht versucht, darin den Inbegriff des modernen Helden, des Künstlers, zu sehen? Doch von all dem weiss derjenige vorerst nichts, der Tacita Deans kurzen Film TEIGNMOUTH ELECTRON (2000) sieht, ausser er hätte bereits ihr gleichnamiges Buch durchgeblättert.[1)]

Im Film wird das Boot Teignmouth Electron, dessen Geschichte vorläufig am Strand der winzigen Karibikinsel Cayman Brac endet, besichtigt. Sicher vor den Gezeiten, liegt die vom Wetter mitgenommene, abgetakelte Bootshülse, die man zuerst aus der Distanz sieht, auf einem verlassenen Stück Land zwischen wucherndem Buschwerk und weggeschmissenen Bierdosen. Die Kamera nähert sich dem Boot; leicht auf die Seite geneigt, liegt der Rumpf auf dem Steuerruder und einem der äusseren Kiele des Trimarans auf; ausserhalb des Elements, wofür sie gebaut sind, wirken die Auslader schwerfällig. Von Seitenflächen und Planken blättert die Farbe ab; das ehemals seetüchtige Boot scheint gänzlich der Natur überlassen, seinem Ort und Gebrauch seit langem entrückt.

Der Blick auf das Meer durch die leeren Frontfenster der Kabine bleibt an einer Palme hängen, Inbegriff des von Marcel Broodthaers reinstituierten Dekors der Kunstfiktion. Oder ist es eine reale

---

DIETER SCHWARZ ist Direktor des Kunstmuseums Winterthur.

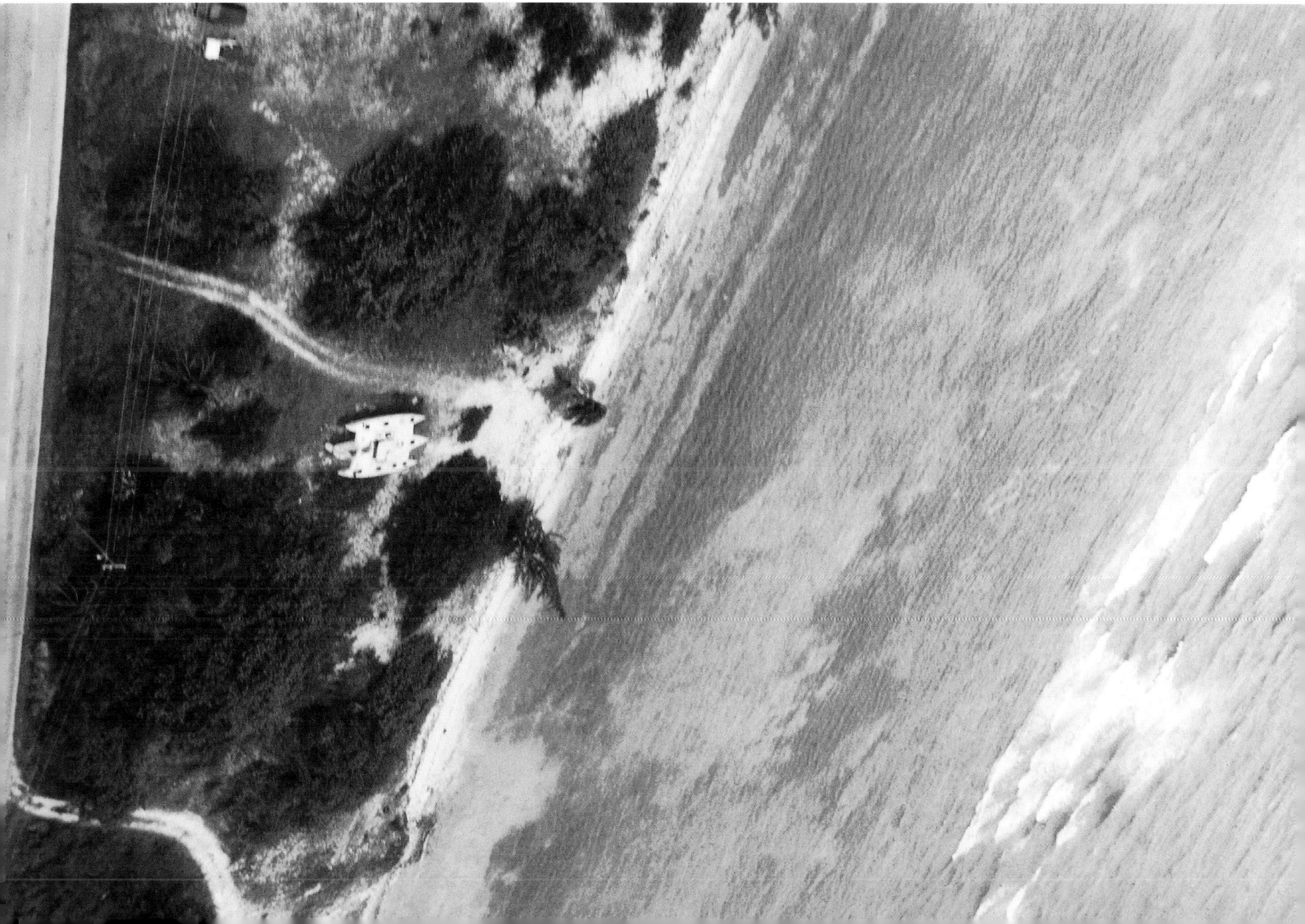

TACITA DEAN, TEIGNMOUTH ELECTRON, CAYMAN BRAC, 1999, black and white photograph, 39⅜ x 26" / Schwarzweissphoto, 100 x 66 cm.

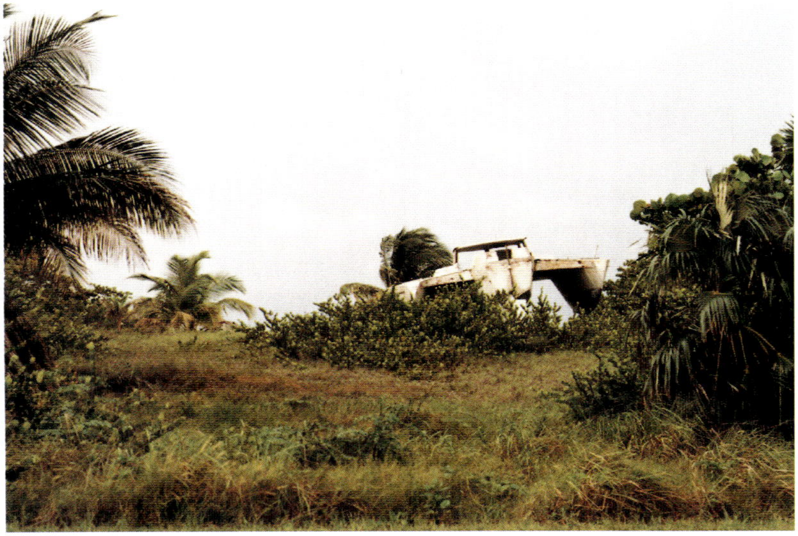

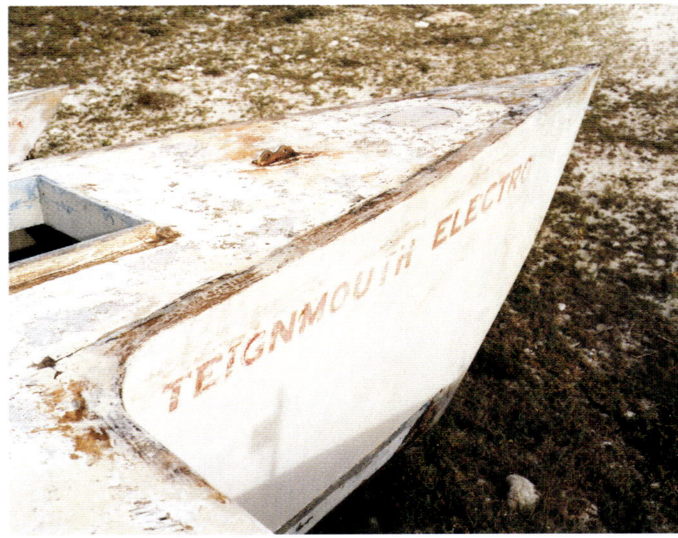

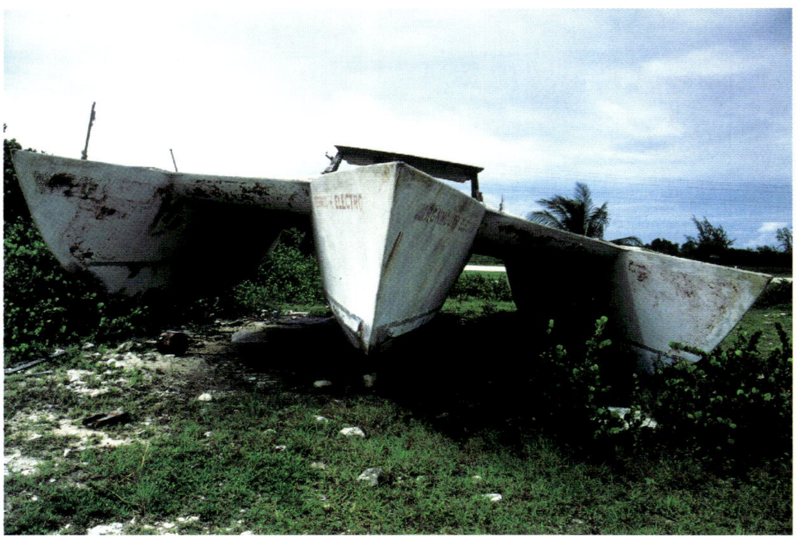

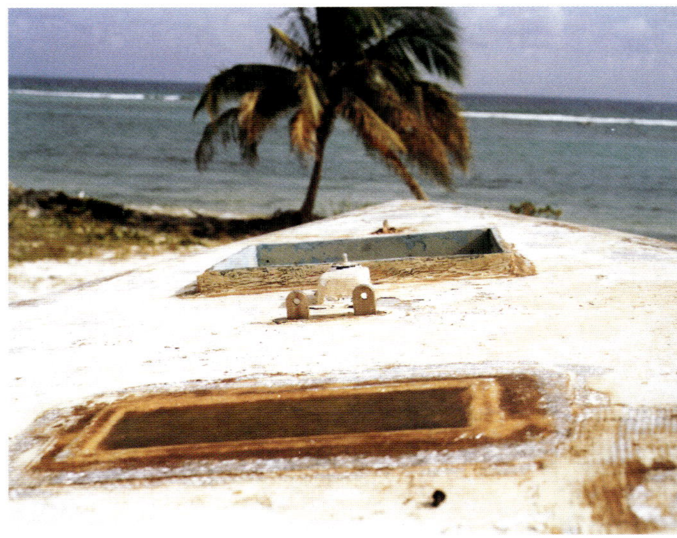

Top left / Oben links:

TACITA DEAN, TEIGNMOUTH ELECTRON, CAYMAN BRAC, 1999, color photograph, 44 x 51 1/5" / Farbphoto, 112 x 130 cm.

Other images / Übrige Bilder:

TACITA DEAN, TEIGNMOUTH ELECTRON, CAYMAN BRAC, 1999, color photographs from the book "Teignmouth Electron"/ Farbphotos aus dem Buch «Teignmouth Electron».

Page 49, top left / Seite 49 oben links:

TACITA DEAN, TEIGNMOUTH ELECTRON, 1999, 16mm color film with optical sound, film still / 16mm-Farbfilm mit optischem Soundtrack.

Other images / übrige Bilder:

TACITA DEAN, TEIGNMOUTH ELECTRON, CAYMAN BRAC, 1999, color photographs from the book "Teignmouth Electron"/ Farbphotos aus dem Buch «Teignmouth Electron».

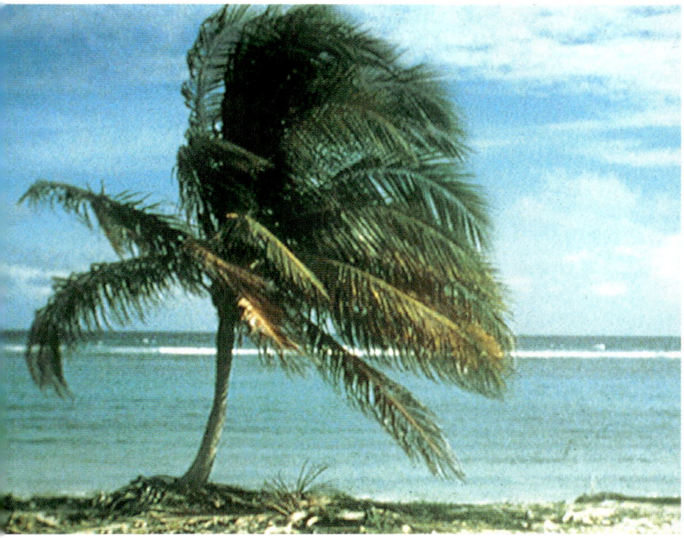

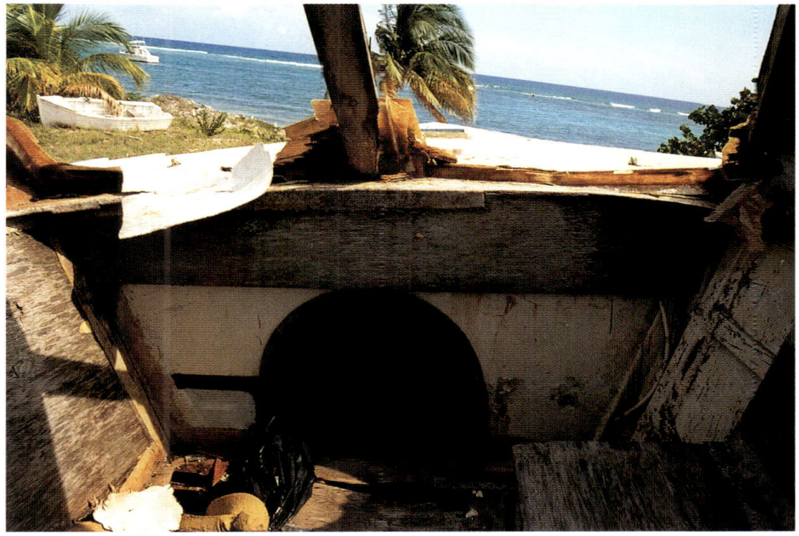

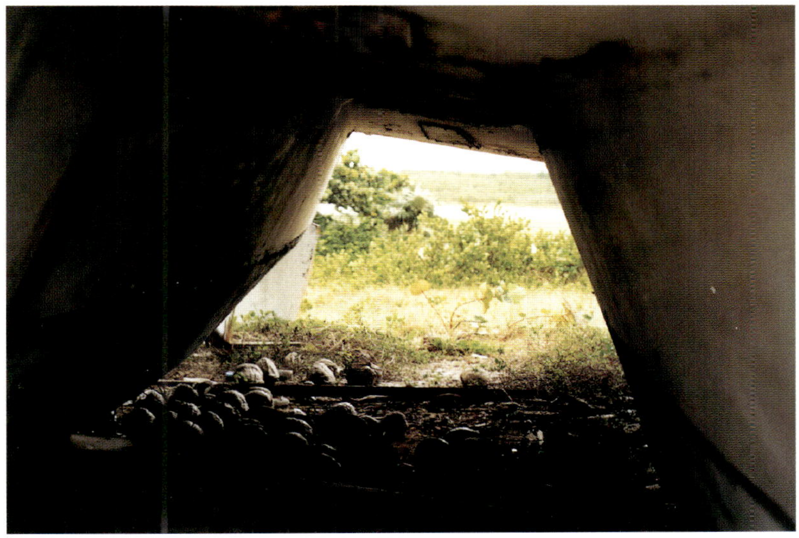

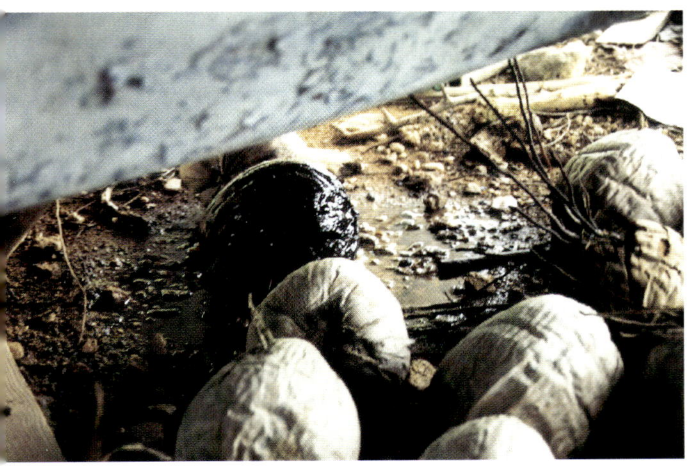

Szene? Wind fährt in die Blätter, Wasser tropft auf am Boden liegende Kokosnüsse. Dann nähert sich die Kamera dem Schriftzug, der an der Vorderseite des Boots aufgemalt ist, und fährt ihm langsam entlang, als ob sie das lesende Auge imitierte. Doch zu lesen ist nur der eigentümliche Name, Teignmouth Electron, der undeutliche Vorstellungen evoziert, für sich indes nichts bedeutet. Dieses Abtasten der Schrift, hervorgehoben allein schon durch die Bewegung der Kamera, die sonst meist Standbilder zeigt, ist einer der zentralen Momente des Films. Ein narratives Element, verkörpert durch die Schrift, tritt in die zeitlose Welt des ausser Gebrauch geratenen Boots. Besser würde man sagen, die nur auf sich selber verweisenden Schriftzeichen des Bootsnamens begegnen dem gestrandeten Material und messen sich in der Vorstellung des Betrachters damit – in Vergeblichkeit, Deplacierung, Frustration. Das Gelesene ist zwar lesbar, sprüht für einen Moment assoziative Funken und zerfällt wieder in Buchstaben; ebenso ist den Teilen des Schiffs alles abhanden gekommen, was sie mit ihrem Zweck verbunden hat. Bildlich kehren Schrift und Gebautes zurück in den Zustand der Entropie, in dem alle Anklänge an die Wörter einer Sprache, an die Regeln der Seefahrerkunst verhallen.

Während wir das Boot betrachtet haben, sind am Himmel Wolken aufgezogen, als ob ein Unwetter bevorstehen würde. Das umschlagende Wetter, Windgeräusche und die Schreie von Seevögeln auf der Tonspur sind uns aus der Natur zwar vertraut, erscheinen neben den Resten des Boots und dem verheissungsvollen Schriftzug jedoch nicht als dokumentarischer Hintergrund, sondern als anonyme, stimmungshafte Elemente, die mit seinem Schicksal verknüpft sind. Keine Symbole, keine Metaphern, nur sinnlose Dramatik, die den Betrachter von der sichtbaren Ruine auf die imminente Zerstörung jeder Ordnung verweist.

In dieser fragilen Idylle überlagert unversehens Motorengeräusch die Natur; am Himmel ist ein Flugzeug zu erkennen, das über der Insel eine weite Schleife ziehend aufsteigt. Erst ist das Flugzeug über dem Boot am Himmel zu sehen, dann folgt die Kamera der Bewegung des Flugzeugs, bis es ausserhalb ihrer Reichweite ist. Dieser Szene, die jäh in die Besichtigung einbricht, antwortet die letzte Einstellung des Films, die aus dem Innern eines startenden Flugzeugs aufgenommen ist. Durch das Fenster sieht man den Küstenstreifen, auf dem die Teignmouth Electron zu erkennen ist; die Kamera bleibt auf dem Wrack, bis es als weisser Punkt in der Tiefe verschwindet. Während das Bild weiterläuft, wird das laute Motorengeräusch, das die Illusion des Fliegens noch gesteigert hat, ausgeblendet, als ob sich schliesslich das verlassene Boot als reines Bild in der Erinnerung einprägen sollte. Während beim Blick nach oben zum Flugzeug am Himmel der Standort unverändert bleibt, ergreift die Schlusseinstellung den Betrachter mit einem Ruck und entführt ihn mit sich nach oben. Im Wechsel der Perspektiven von Stasis und Dynamik kreuzen sich zwei Möglichkeiten der kinematographischen Darstellung, die man als Beobachtung und Empathie benennen könnte. Während die Bewegung des Flugzeugs am Himmel auf das reale zerbrochene Wrack verweist, wächst im Moment des Verschwindens in der Ferne die imaginäre Präsenz der Teignmouth Electron.

Dies geschieht jedoch, ohne dass der Film tatsächlich eine narrative Ebene entwickelt oder dem Betrachter eine psychologische Perspektive auferlegt. Wenn der Moment des Erkennens der Schrift in seiner allegorischen Dimension beschrieben und wenn die Konfrontation von objektiver und subjektiver Bewegung als rhetorisches Element gewürdigt wurde, so basiert diese Lektüre auf der Organisation des Filmmaterials und nicht auf einer suggestiven Handlungsführung. Der Film besteht aus einer Anzahl von meist statischen Einstellungen unterschiedlicher Dauer, die mit Ausnahme der beschriebenen bewegten Bilder keine formale Steigerung erfahren. An Stelle des Spannungsbogens tritt die Vermittlung der Dauer eines bestimmten Bildes, die Erfahrung der Zeit, in der es stattfindet. Dabei gibt es keine äussere Begründung für die Dauer der einzelnen Bilder ausser der Ökonomie des Filmmaterials, das zur Verfügung stand. Auch die durch den Schnitt zusammengestellten Sequenzen suchen weder Konfrontation noch andere geläufige Floskeln, eher die Neutralität und Beruhigung der Abfolge der Bilder, die sich nicht über die Kontingenz der vereinzelten Teile von Wrack und Umgebung erhebt.

Wenn der Film auf seiner Materialität beharrt, so richtet er sich nicht in erster Linie auf Farbigkeit, Format, Bildkomposition, vielmehr auf die grundlegende Tatsache, dass ein aus belichteten Filmstreifen erzeugtes Bild jeweils eine bestimmte Dauer erhält. Diese Dauer misst sich sowohl in Sekunden wie in Zentimetern von Material, nicht anders als die Länge eines gezeichneten oder gemalten Strichs, die Schwere von Stein oder Stahl. An diese materielle Realität, mit der sie in ihrem Entstehungsprozess konfrontiert sind, erinnern alle Arbeiten von Tacita Dean. In MAGNETIC (1997), das in gewissem Sinne aus Zeichnungen mit Magnettonstreifen besteht, wie sie für die Filmvertonung verwendet werden, wird ein Ton als sichtbare Strecke von Magnetstreifen gezeigt, ohne dass man ihn hören könnte. Ob darauf nun vom Mund erzeugte Laute oder solche von Meervögeln aufgenommen sind, lässt sich erst auf einer zweiten Ebene feststellen: Sie besteht aus den Beschriftungen in Chinograph, welche die einzelnen Bänder identifizieren. Zugleich bleibt es Tacita Deans Geheimnis, ob die genannten Laute überhaupt auf den betreffenden Bändern registriert wurden oder ob es genügt, dass wir Länge und Beschriftung miteinander in imaginäre Beziehung setzen.

In DISAPPEARANCE AT SEA (Verschwinden auf See, 1996) gibt das Objekt des Films, ein Leuchtturm mit dem sich um seine Achse drehenden Scheinwerfer, in Verbindung mit der untergehenden Sonne eine einfache Struktur vor, welche die Organisation der Filmbilder in sieben längeren Sequenzen bestimmt. Auch Tacita Deans jüngster Film, FERNSEHTURM (2001), basiert auf der Drehbewegung um die eigene Achse, die das Restaurant auf dem Berliner Fernsehturm durchläuft. Kreisen und Statik, Ausblick in die Ferne und Blick auf das Zentrum, von dem die Bewegung ausgeht, sind Momente, die darin in Abfolge und Wiederholung deutlich zu unterscheiden sind und die in der Synthese sogar metaphorisch als Karussell des Lebens gelesen werden können. In TEIGNMOUTH ELECTRON besteht dagegen keine andere Vorgabe für die Organisation der Bilder als das Fehlen eines Zusammenhangs, die Deplacierung des vorgefundenen und betrachteten Objekts. Wonach kann sich demnach Dauer und Abfolge richten, wenn nicht nach den einzelnen Elementen des Wracks und der es umgebenden Natur, welche in das Blickfeld der Kamera geraten? So gilt, dass eines nach dem anderen gezeigt wird, bis etwas eintritt, was die Aufreihung unterbricht, bis dem Blick etwas Bestimmtes zufällt. Hier sind es die Beschriftung des Boots und das am Himmel aufsteigende Flugzeug, welche in die Kette der Bilder einbrechen und einen übergeordneten Zusammenhang andeuten. Es ist darüber hinaus auch der Fund eines zweiten Objekts am Strand von Cayman Brac, der vor der Fertigstellung verlassenen Ruine einer merkwürdigen Behausung, woraus ein zweiter Film resultierte, BUBBLE HOUSE (1999). Das hiess auch, aus dem für einen einzigen Film bestimmten Material einen zweiten zu drehen – jede Aufnahme des zweiten Films ist sozusagen vom ersten Projekt abgezweigt. BUBBLE HOUSE ist deshalb nicht nur aufgrund des Ortes seiner Entstehung ein Pendant zu TEIGNMOUTH ELECTRON, dieser Film ist sein reales Supplement.

In BUBBLE HOUSE findet sich die Szene mit dem Blick aus dem Panoramafenster des Hauses – ein cinemascopartiger Bildausschnitt innerhalb des Kamerabildes – auf das Meer, an dessen Horizont mit einem Mal ein Sturm aufzieht und auf die Küste zukommt, bis erste Regentropfen die Kamera erreichen. Obwohl das Bild statisch bleibt, trifft einen die aufkommende Bewegung, die sich am Licht des Himmels und auf den Wellen abzeichnet, so eindringlich wie das ins Bild geratene Flugzeug. Ohne einen Sinn zu verstehen, erkennt man, dass in diesem Moment der Film seine Bestimmung erreicht, die nicht die Eindeutigkeit einer Erzählung besitzt, sondern sich zwischen unauffindbarer Bedeutung und glücklichem Zufall bewegt. Sind dies nicht die beiden gegensätzlichen Bedingungen einer Reise, die Donald Crowhurst am letzten Tag seiner Reise in seinem Bordbuch tödlich fasziniert hatten? «MAX POSS ERROR», hielt er lakonisch fest, als er den abgelaufenen Chronometer neu einstellte. «It is finished – it is finished, IT IS THE MERCY», lautet der letzte Eintrag.[2]

1) Tacita Dean, *Teignmouth Electron*. Book Works in Zusammenarbeit mit dem National Maritime Museum, London 1999.
2) Ebenda.

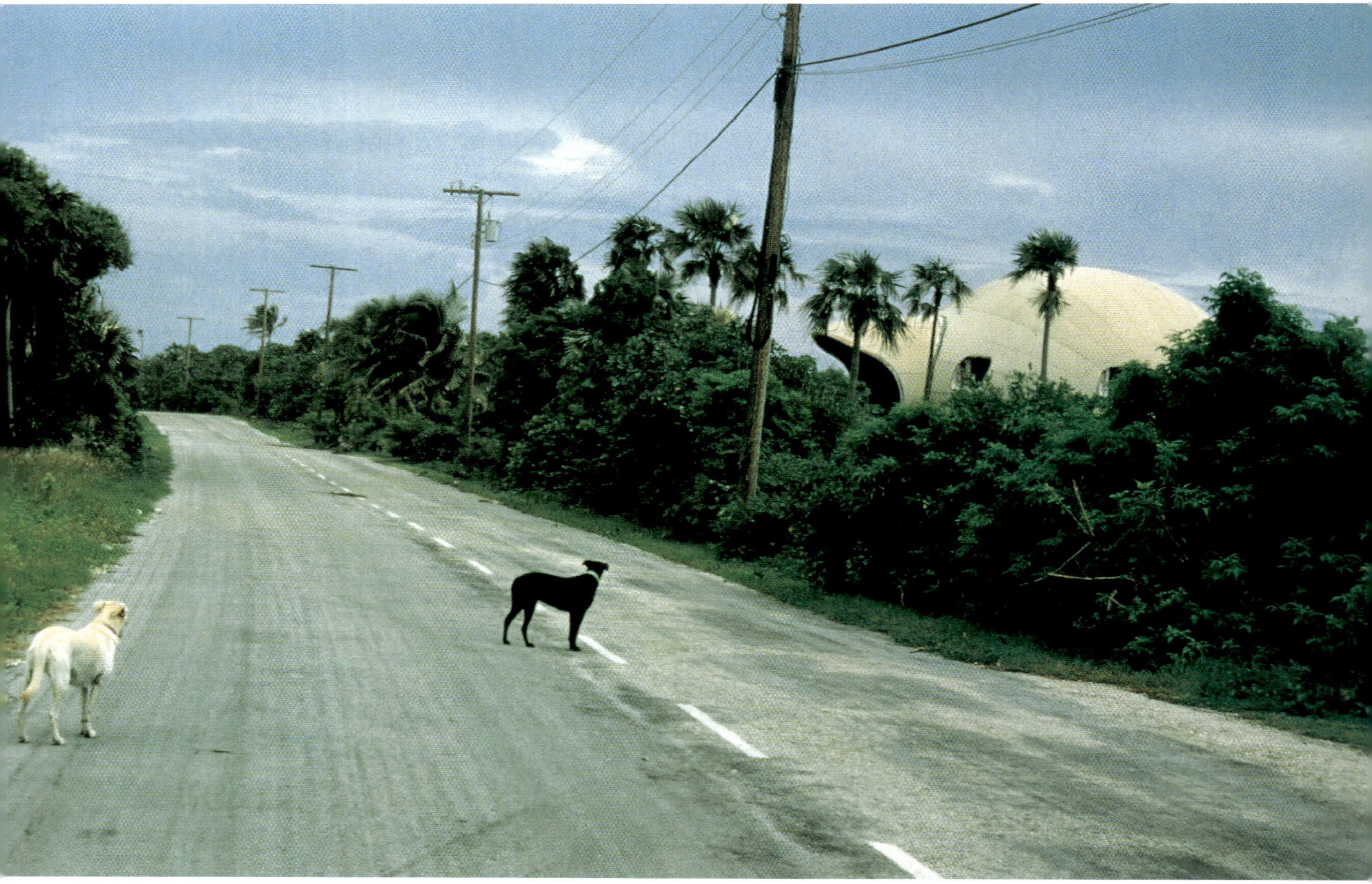

TACITA DEAN, BUBBLE HOUSE, 1999, color photograph, 23⅖ x 33" / Farbphoto, 59,5 x 84 cm.

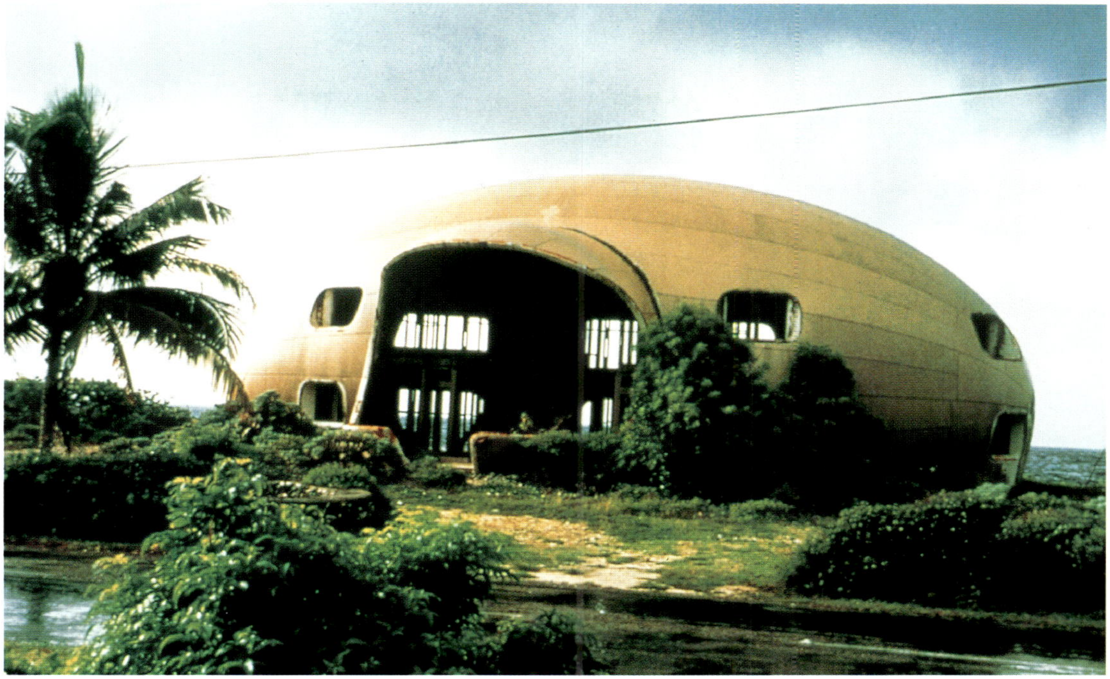

TACITA DEAN, BUBBLE HOUSE, 1999, color photograph, 39 x 58" / Farbphoto, 99 x 147,5 cm.

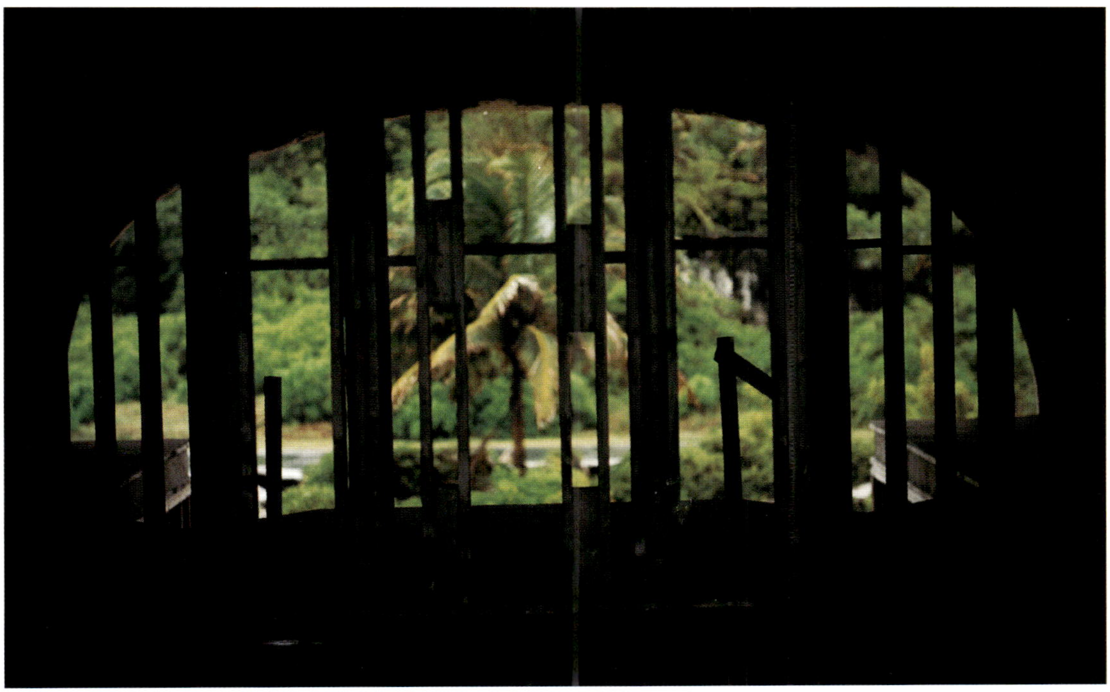

TACITA DEAN, BUBBLE HOUSE, CAYMAN BRAC, 1999, location photograph / Photographie am Drehort.

DIETER SCHWARZ

Teignmouth Electron

Through the work of Tacita Dean we learn something of the person of Donald Crowhurst and of the bizarre fate of a man who decided to enter a competition to circumnavigate the globe single-handedly, and who was ultimately lost overboard. In itself this would simply be a tragic story if it were not for the particular circumstances that led to his downfall, specifically the recklessness born of an acute lack of finances that impelled him to set sail inadequately prepared for the voyage, his reports of fictive successes when all the time his boat was in fact aimlessly drifting around the Sargasso Sea, his final disorientation, and the moment when he leapt overboard with his chronometer, the very instrument designed to determine one's position in space and time. A preventable yet inevitable catastrophe, heroism founded on foolhardiness and premeditated deception—might one not be tempted to see this as the epitome of the modern hero, of the artist? But those watching Tacita Dean's short film TEIGNMOUTH ELECTRON (2000) initially know nothing of all of that unless they have already leafed through her book of the same name.[1)]

The film examines the boat, the Teignmouth Electron, whose story comes to a temporary halt on the shores of the tiny Caribbean island, Cayman Brac. Well above the tideline, the dilapidated shell of the boat, bereft of its rigging, is first seen from a distance on a deserted stretch of land between sprawling scrub and discarded beer cans. The camera approaches the boat; tilted slightly to one side, the vessel is resting on its rudder and one of the outer keels of the trimaran; out of the element that they were built for, its hulls seem cumbersome. The paint is peeling from the sides and the deck; the once seaworthy yacht seems to be completely at the mercy of Nature, long since removed from its former environment and use.

The view of the ocean through the empty front windows of the cabin is interrupted by a palm tree: the archetype of Marcel Broodthaer's reinstated decor of the fiction of art. Or is this reality? Wind rustles through the leaves, water drips onto the coconuts lying on the ground. Then the camera closes in on the words painted on the bow of the boat, running slowly over them as though imitating the eye as it reads. But all we see is the odd name, Teignmouth Electron, vaguely associative but in itself meaningless. This letter by letter scrutiny—which already stands out from the rest of the film by the movement of the otherwise static camera—is one of the key moments in the film. A narrative element, embodied in the writing, enters the timeless world of this vessel that has fallen into disuse. Or, more precisely perhaps, the self-referential components of the yacht's name are seen in the light of the flotsam on the shore and measured against it in the viewer's mind—in their hopelessness, displacement, frustration. What we read is indeed legible, and ignites associative sparks for a brief moment, only to disintegrate into separate letters again; so, too, the different parts of the yacht have lost everything that connected them to their purpose. Before our eyes the writing and the boat's structure re-enter a state of entropy where any memories of words in a language and of the laws of the mariner's art fade away into nothingness.

While we have been looking at the boat, clouds have been gathering above as though a storm were brewing. The changing weather, the sound of the wind and the cries of seabirds on the soundtrack are all familiar from Nature but, in conjunction with the ruined yacht and the enigmatic writing, they seem less like a documentary background than anonymous, atmospheric elements connected to its fate.

DIETER SCHWARZ is Director of the Kunstmuseum Winterthur.

Not symbols, not metaphors, just a senseless drama that draws the viewer's attention from the sight of the wreck to the imminent destruction of order on all levels.

Suddenly the sound of an engine cuts across Nature in this fragile idyll; an airplane appears in the sky, climbing upwards as it describes a wide arc over the island. First the plane is seen in the sky above the boat, then the camera follows the path of the plane until it is out of range. This scene, which breaks abruptly into our scrutiny of the boat, is answered by the last shot of the film which is taken from inside a plane as it is leaving the ground. Through the window we see the coastline where the Teignmouth Electron is visible, the camera stays on the wreck until it is no more than a white speck far below. While the picture runs on, the loud engine noise which has heightened the illusion of flying is faded out, as though ultimately the abandoned boat is to stay in our minds purely as an image. While the camera position remained fixed as our gaze was drawn up to the plane in the sky, now the last shot takes sharp hold of viewers, spiriting them upwards with it. In the changing perspectives, the shift from static to dynamic, two possibilities of cinematographic representation intersect which could perhaps be defined as observation and empathy. While the movement of the plane in the sky points to the actual broken wreck as the Teignmouth Electron disappears in the distance, its imaginary presence grows ever stronger.

Yet this happens without the film in fact establishing a narrative thread or imposing a psychological perspective on the viewer. If it seems that the moment of recognizing the writing has been described here on a somewhat allegorical level and the confrontation of objective and subjective movement treated as a rhetorical element, then this reading is based on the way the material of the film is organized and not on an evocative plotline. The film consists of a number of generally static shots of various lengths, which—with the exception of the camera movement already mentioned—do not undergo any formal intensification. Instead of building-up tension the film focuses on the duration of each image, the sense of the time in which it takes place. At the same time there is no external reason for the duration of the individual images other than the amount of film material that was available. Moreover the images edited together neither rely on confrontation nor on any other conventions of editing used today; if anything they strive for neutrality and calm in sequences that do not go beyond the contingency of the isolated pieces of wreckage and their location.

While the film asserts its materiality, this is concerned less with the coloration, format, and pictorial composition than with the underlying fact that an image created by exposing a piece of film strip always has a particular duration. This duration may be measured in seconds or in centimeters of film material, just as one might measure the length of a drawn or painted line, or the weight of stone or steel. And all of Tacita Dean's works remind us of the material reality that they come up against during the course of their making. In MAGNETIC (1997), which consists in a certain sense of drawings made using magnetic sound tape of the kind used for film sound tracks, a sound is shown as a visible stretch of magnetic tape, without the sound itself being audible. Whether the recorded sounds are made by a human mouth or by seabirds can only be determined on a second level: namely by inscriptions in chinagraph identifying the individual tapes. At the same time Tacita Dean keeps secret whether the named sounds were indeed recorded on the relevant tapes or whether it is enough that in our imaginations we connect the length of the tape and the inscription.

In DISAPPEARANCE AT SEA (1996) the subject of the film—a lighthouse with its rotating light and the setting sun—presents a simple structure which determines the organization of the film's images into seven lengthy sequences. Tacita Dean's most recent film, FERNSEHTURM (2001), has a similarly rotating motif, the revolving restaurant on top of the TV tower in Berlin. Circular motion and stasis, the view into the distance and inwards to the center where the movement originates, are moments that can clearly be distinguished from each other in their motion and repetition and which, seen as a whole, can even be read metaphorically as an image of the carrousel of life. In TEIGNMOUTH ELECTRON, on the other hand, there is no other basis for the organization of the images than the absence of any wider context, the displacement of an object found and observed. What therefore should determine the duration and the sequence of the piece if not each individual element of the wreck and of Nature that enters the camera's field of vision? And so it is that they are shown, one after the other, until something happens to interrupt the sequence, until something distinctive comes into view. In this case it is the writing on the boat and the airplane climbing into the sky which break into the sequence of pictures and hint at an over-arching context. Moreover, the discovery of a second object on the shore of Cayman Brac—a strange, ruined house, abandoned before it was finished—led to a second film, BUBBLE HOUSE (1999). The material originally intended to be used in one film became two films with all the shots in the second film having been as it were diverted from the first film. BUBBLE HOUSE is thus not simply a companion piece to TEIGNMOUTH ELECTRON but an actual supplement to it.

In BUBBLE HOUSE the camera looks out through the panoramic window of the ruin—a cinemascope-like view within the actual frame—out over the ocean where a storm suddenly builds up on the horizon and approaches the coast until the first heavy drops of rain reach the camera. Although this image remains static, the viewer is struck by the incipient movement signaled by the changes in the light in the sky and on the waves—as vividly as by the plane that comes into view. Without being able to make sense of all this, one realizes that the film has reached its destination. It does not have the clarity of a narrative but operates instead somewhere between unfathomable meaning and happy chance. And were these not also the two contradictory conditions of a journey that had an ultimately fatal fascination for Donald Crowhurst, as noted in his ship's log on the last day of his voyage? "MAX POSS ERROR," he commented laconically, as he reset the chronometer that had run right down. "It is finished—it is finished, IT IS THE MERCY," reads his last entry.[2)]

(Translation: Fiona Elliott)

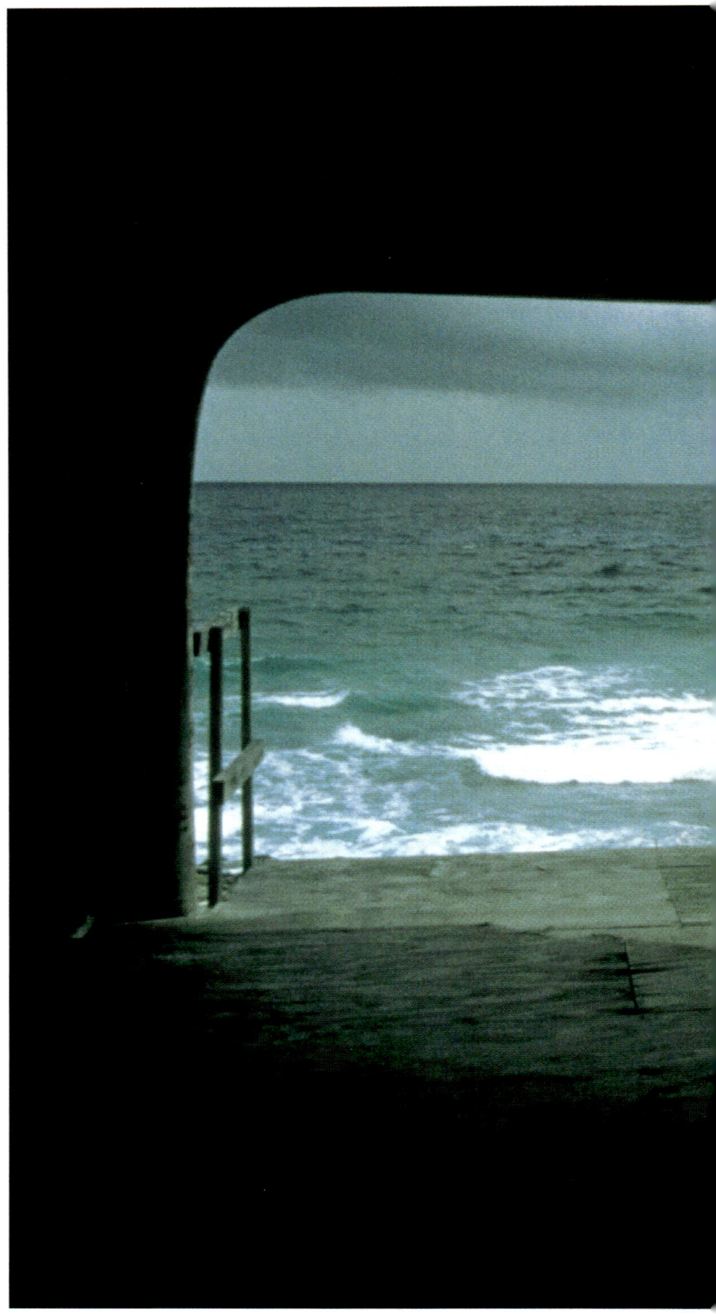

1) Tacita Dean, *Teignmouth Electron* (London: Book Works, in association with the National Maritime Museum, 1999).
2) Ibid.

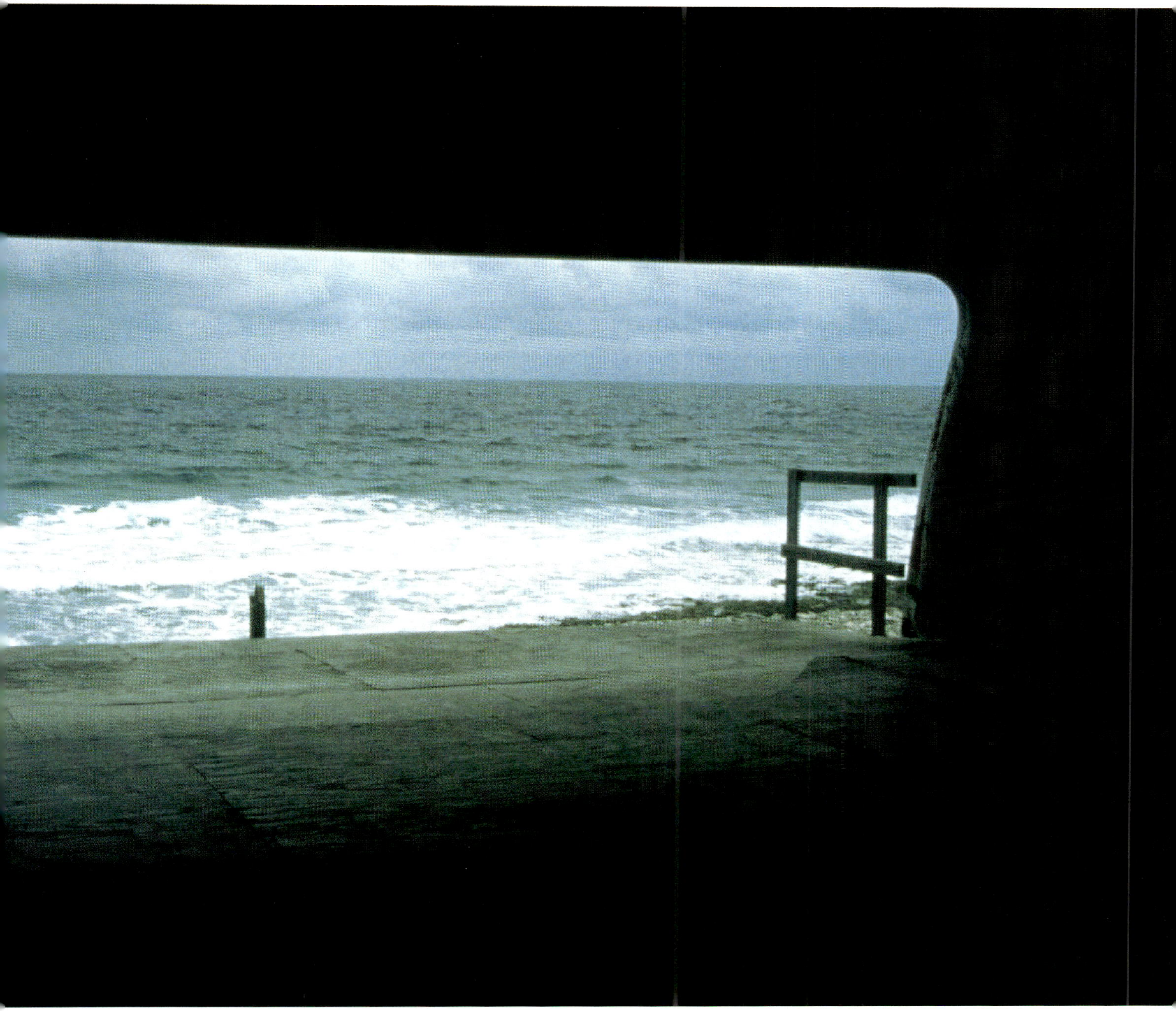

TACITA DEAN, BUBBLE HOUSE, 1999, color photograph, 23⅖ x 33" / Farbphoto, 59,5 x 84 cm.

EDITION FOR PARKETT

TACITA DEAN

THE GREEN RAY, 2001

Color postcard, 105 x 148,5 mm

Printed by Steidl Verlag, Göttingen, Germany

Edition of 100, signed, numbered, stamped,

and posted in Morombe, Western Madagascar.

The print run for this postcard is 1000.
The remaining cards have been distributed unsigned
among the few commercial outlets in Morombe,
where they will be sold as normal tourist postcards.

Farbpostkarte, 105 x 148,5 mm

Gedruckt bei Steidl Verlag, Göttingen

Auflage: 100, signiert, nummeriert, mit Poststempel

aufgegeben in Morombe, West-Madagaskar.

Die Druckauflage beträgt 1000 Exemplare.
Die überzähligen Karten wurden an die wenigen
Verkaufsstellen in Morombe verteilt, wo sie als normale
Ansichtskarten an Touristen verkauft werden.

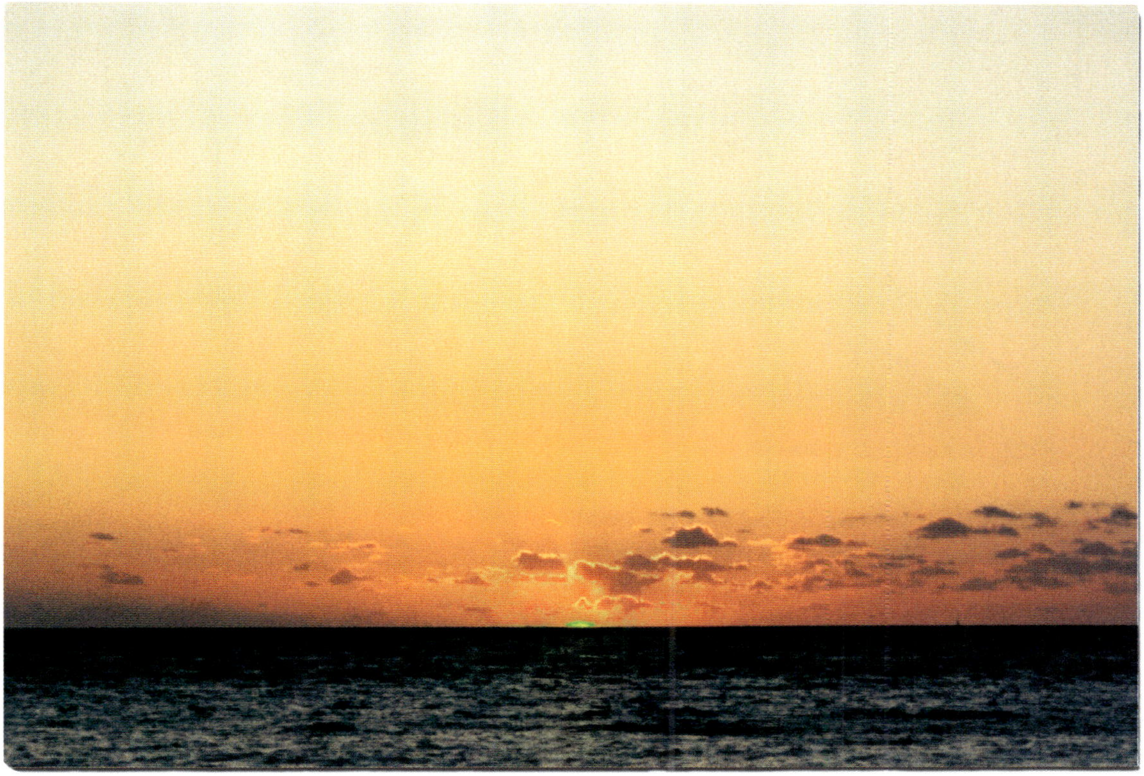

MADAGASCAR
Le rayon vert à Morombe

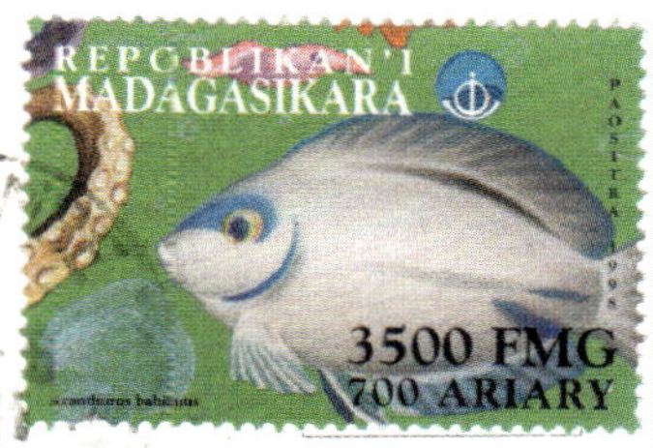

Edition for Parkett
No. 62
A/p I.
Tacita Dean
2001

Imprimée en Allemagne

Parkett – Verlag AG
Quellenstrasse 27
CH – 8031 ZURICH
SUISSE

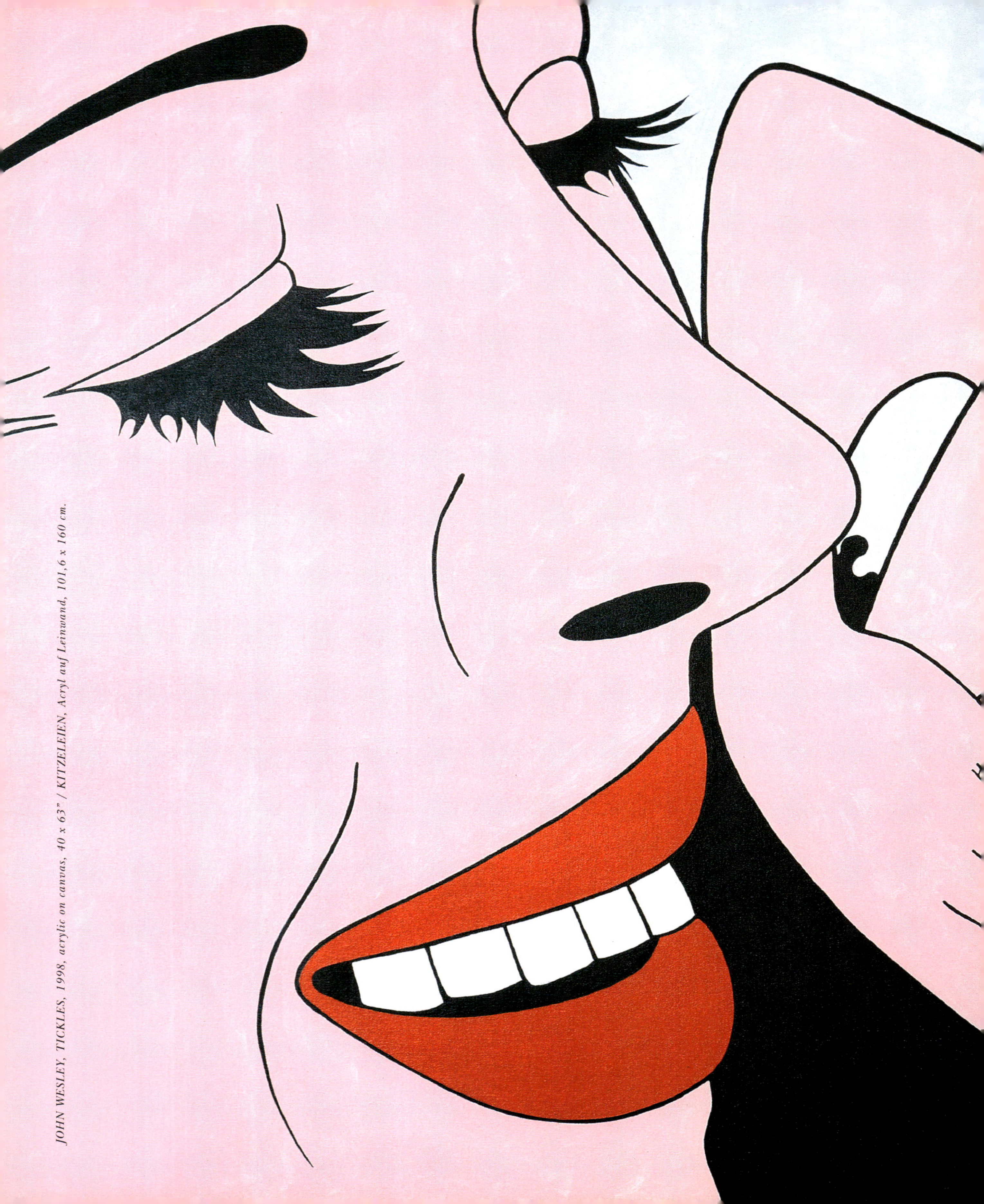

JOHN WESLEY, TICKLES, 1998, acrylic on canvas, 40 x 63" / KITZELEIEN, Acryl auf Leinwand, 101,6 x 160 cm.

JOHN WESLEY

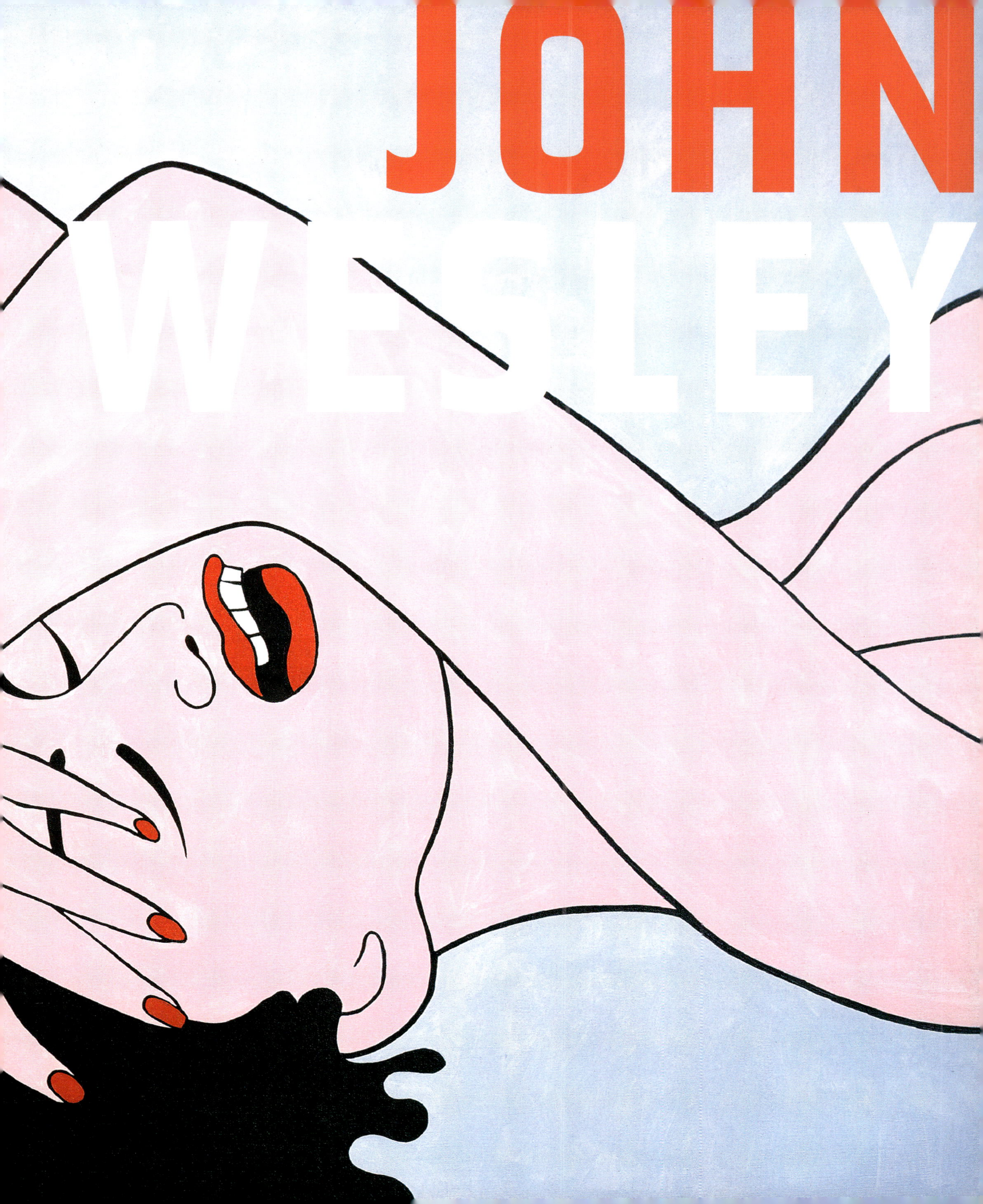

PASSIVE EXPRESSIVE

LINDA NORDEN

I could deliver the mail. I know the names of all the dogs.
- John Wesley[1]

John Wesley, who is also known as Jack, might well be described as the Henri Rousseau of his generation: a not-quite-pop, faux-primitive Californian he appeared on the New York scene fully formed circa 1960. His audacious rethinking of expressive, abstract-figurative painting intrigued and baffled even his closest colleagues, just as the French customs officer-turned-artist once intrigued Picasso and Braque.

According to a chronology compiled by Hannah Green, Wesley "began to paint regularly and think about art sometime during 1953," at the age of twenty-four, "while working as an illustrator for the Northrop Aircraft Corporation." This was not an advanced age at which to begin to paint, but it was late enough to allow others to treat Wesley as an innocent, albeit an inspired, sophisticated and charming innocent, with a secret or two. Even now, Wesley's enigmatic oeuvre and uncanny subject matter tend to lead his critics away from the painting in search of the man and his motive: "The question that immediately arises with any Wesley picture is not What does it mean?, but Why did the artist want to paint it?" wrote artist/critic Peter Plagens only a few years ago.[2]

"John Wesley: Love's Lust," the exhibition for which this essay was originally written, took its cue from a younger generation of artists, weaned on pixels and plastic princesses and less interested in the whys and wherefores of painting than in identifying new ways to make a picture; artists, that is, who look to Wesley for example. (It is this younger generation of painters—Carl Ostendarp, Paul Morrison, Monique Prieto, Laura Owens, Takashi Murakami, to name just a few—who seem to have most thoroughly examined Wesley's radical formal innovations; and they have done so in their art, rather than in writing.) Organized against the backdrop of last year's P. S. 1 Contemporary Art Center retrospective—Wesley's first in an American museum—the smaller Fogg Art Museum exhibition set out to ask not "Why does Wesley do what he does?" but "How does he do what he does?" And "Why John Wesley now?"

The most obvious answer to Wesley's newfound popularity is a heightened attention to the painting

LINDA NORDEN is Associate Curator of Contemporary Art at the Fogg Art Museum, where she organized the exhibition "John Wesley: Love's Lust," for which a version of this essay was originally written. The exhibition ran from January 20 – March 1, 2001.

itself. Wesley's painting looks like nothing else out there. And, while it has evolved significantly over the years, the most conspicuous characteristics of his work from the seventies on—its insistent flatness, powdered pastel palette, cartoon/cinematographic narratives, embrace of the sexually charged encounter, sophisticated anthropomorphism, and mannered drawing—have enormous appeal amid a digital revolution that has provoked yet another rethinking of the medium. Wesley's eccentric animation of familiar stereotypes, for example, foreshadows a current tendency to humanize cartoon characters. This talent expecially seems relevant to a generation for whom cartoon characters are more "real" in their expressive potential than either straight photographic reproductions or painted flesh. But Wesley's current cachet also reflects a widespread millennial hunger for evidence of emotion and a willingness to find it in unlikely encounters and characters of all sorts.

Struggling to assess John Wesley's first New York show in 1963, artist and critic Donald Judd described the paintings as "what some bumpkin made of appearances for some unartistic reason." But he added, "This is interesting."[3)]

Other critics, at a loss, located Wesley's painting somewhere between Pop art and Surrealism: his subjects looked familiar enough to seem appropriated, while their rendering and placement always worked to incite an unexpected but oddly compelling emotional response. It was clear that Wesley was up to something other than a straightforward co-opting of commercial iconography. He managed to picture the most banal of figures in the most embarrassing of poses and to make us believe that either he or his subjects were withholding something we needed, or wanted, to know.

Like most of the Pop artists, Wesley began painting against the gestural abstraction that had dominated the late forties and fifties. He found liberation, as did many others, in the work of Jasper Johns, especially in Johns' unprecedented treatment of his painting as object and sign. But where Johns intentionally chose subjects that functioned as "devices," allowing him to conflate the depicted image with the painting, Wesley constructed narrative tableaux that incorporated picture and frame. Even in such early

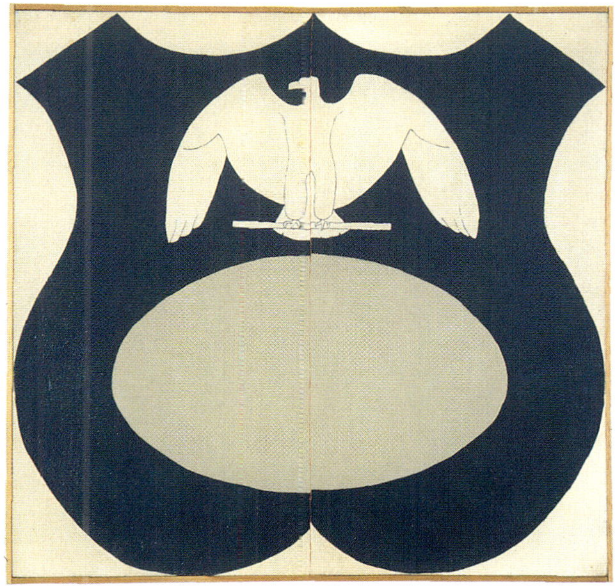

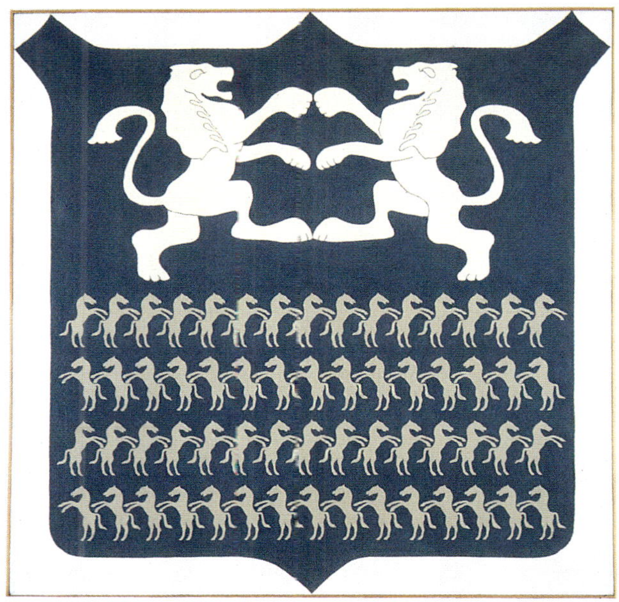

Top/Oben: JOHN WESLEY, AMERICAN EAGLE BADGE, 1962, Duco and oil on canvas, 24 x 24" / AMERIKANISCHES ADLERWAPPEN, Lackfarbe und Öl auf Leinwand, 61 x 61 cm.

Bottom/Unten: JOHN WESLEY, COAT OF ARMS, 1962, Duco and oil on canvas, 48 x 48" / WAPPENSCHILD, Lackfarbe und Öl auf Leinwand, 122 x 122 cm.

(ALL PHOTOS: FREDERICKS FREISER GALLERY, NEW YORK)

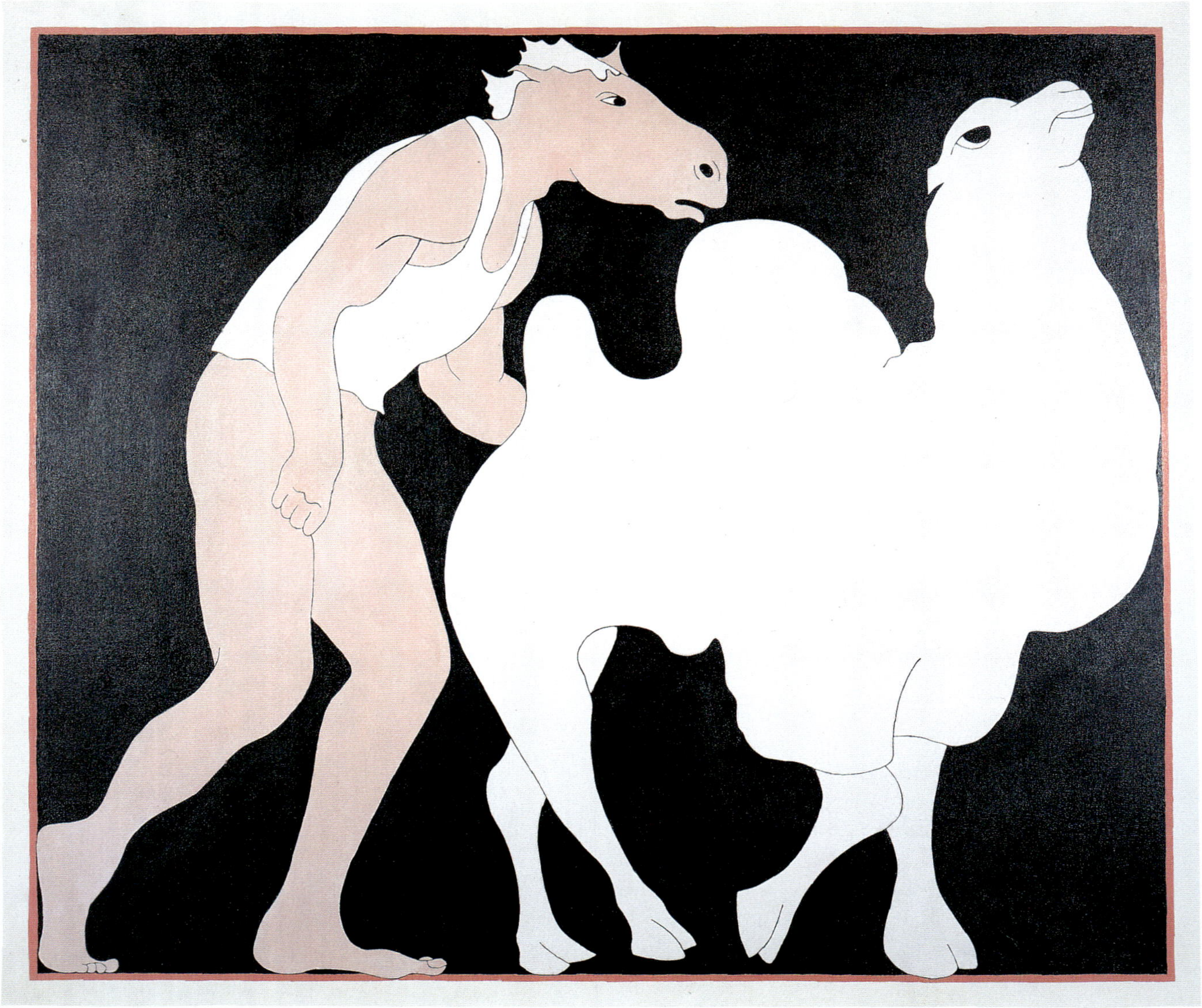

JOHN WESLEY, CAMEL, 1966, acrylic on canvas, 40½ x 46" / KAMEL, Acryl auf Leinwand, 102,9 x 116,8 cm.

works as his 1962 paintings DANCING FROGS AND WAITING SHARK, COAT OF ARMS, and AMERICAN EAGLE BADGE, which depict badge-shaped fields, there is action within the badges and a painted frame to contain it. Johns' devices functioned mechanically; they "made" his paintings. Wesley tends toward optical tricks, such as repetitive forms with subtle variations or ambiguous shapes that precipitate eye movement and posit multiple readings. He uses anthropomorphism in these early paintings the way a junior high school student uses double-entendre: Look closely at AMERICAN EAGLE BADGE or COAT OF ARMS and watch the badge become a body. "This," says Wesley, "is composition. Keep the eye on one locked device, limited by the edges."[4] Wesley's devices are not as literal as Johns' are, but they are just as deliberate. His paintings work on us without our knowing precisely what is operational. This may be what Judd was alluding to in that first review when he complained, "The only objection is theoretical, not critical. Wesley's method and Lichtenstein's, is somewhat the same as that of traditional painting; the form is relatively hidden. The guise here is not appearances, but what some bumpkin made of appearance for some unartistic reason. This is a big difference...a sort of meta-representation."[5]

Wesley's frames, decorated or plain, are probably his most conspicuous devices. They not only concentrate the action; they make us voyeurs without fully revealing just what it is we are witnessing. This is especially disconcerting when a body part presses up against the interior edges of the painted frame, as if Wesley had forced his figures into a too-tight container. In CAMEL (1966) for example, a ringletted centaur-in-reverse, thrusting the better part of his forearm into the humps of a haughty camel, seems to be pushing his foot against the frame for resistance; in BLUE BLANKET (2000) the errant elbow of an elderly Sumo wrestler embracing a blanketed woman jabs at the edge of the image plane and we almost feel him to be shooing us away. When a toe or a boot or a nipple actually exceeds the carefully demarcated field, as in TURKEYS (1965) or POPEYE (1973) or HOLD ME (2001), the impact can be viscerally erotic or violent or both, because it imposes onto the relatively passive act of looking the more invasive sense of touch. Few post-war artists have done as much to reconceive the painting as stage and window.

Wesley's early sixties paintings had a dated look—Judd read them as nineteenth-century—and the cast of characters they featured was not yet pegged to such familiar pop heroes and antiheroes as Popeye or the Bumsteads. Instead, Wesley perfected a cartoon style of his own, which relied on the stereotyping of animals as much as men, women, and children. The subversive anthropomorphism in such paintings as CAMEL or CADDY (1968) worked to intensify the bizarre, implausible scenarios he invented and gave him a certain latitude with which to broach such unseemly subjects as sex, lust, racial prejudice, and inexplicable violence, because it made his paintings as funny as they were outrageous. Posing a bare-skinned woman with a horny polar bear, as he did in TURKEYS, Wesley played out a quirky pun, then glossed it with the haptic sensation of skin against fur—his goofy take on the great Western tradition of dressed men and naked women. (For much of the sixties, Wesley was married to the artist Jo Baer, which adds another dimension to the pun.)

Wesley has said that toward the end of his extended stays in Conques, he would begin to covet creature comforts, such as a long enough bed, but that what he most missed was the TV. Among the gouaches that he painted in his small room there in 1978 is one called TELLY, which treats the window as a television screen. Less literally, Wesley's delight in television—a medium many of his generation found suspect—and his love of the movies and "funny papers"—may have helped him to soldier on as a painter in the early seventies, when most of the art world had declared that medium DOA.

Enlisting the world-weary Bumstead as both alter ego and surrogate for the father he lost at age six, Wesley transformed his earlier use of an interior frame into something with larger and more contemporary implications. His "Searching for Bumstead" paintings, begun in 1973 at the MacDowell Colony, replaced the tableaux with frames borrowed from the comic strip and traded his nineteenth-century decorative drawing style for one that selectively approximated the less rigid, more economical detailing of Bumstead's author. (Look, for example, at the use

Wesley makes of the short, paired, parallel strokes so ubiquitous in the comic: they mark out space, indicate reflection, and allude to all manner of decorative detail, as on the floor moldings.) Direct and intimate, these paintings enlarged Wesley's expressive scope beyond what he was able to convey through his humanized hounds and horses and bears. They also allowed him to move from hard-edge puns to something far more poignant, and to paint space as well as he did figures.

The "Bumstead" paintings—whether detailing scenes of domestic misunderstanding, zooming in on off-camera moments of bafflement or simply scanning empty halls and walls for private memories—are excruciatingly specific representations of the gulfs between feeling and comprehension and they garnered Wesley a new audience. Toward the end of the eighties, he also benefited from a mood change within feminist criticism and a more general interest in reading the objects of one's desire as "other." His willingness to implicate himself in the seductions he painted (beginning with his "Bumstead" series) and his ability to portray bewilderment in the face of life's lures without apology or explanation seemed a healthy alternative to the war between men and women. His pictures were smart, funny, startling, irreverently empathetic, and often heartbreaking—a welcome antidote to more laborious discourse.

In the exhibition "John Wesley: Love's Lust," several paintings featured a simple compositional technique that Wesley has repeatedly exploited: the isolation of two confronted figures. In his 1973 POPEYE, his 1976 MISSOURI COMPROMISE, and the more recent BLUE BLANKET, figures loom large and background detail has been nearly eliminated. Each uses a popular hero or figural type to convey a highly charged topical subject. Popeye shoots a blindfolded Wimpy in a painting that no one who lived through the Vietnam era can fail to relate to a famous wire photo of a point-blank street execution. Two white men posed as middle-aged politicians straining against their civility and captioned "Missouri Compromise" uncannily resemble Duke Ellington collaring his anxious manager. A nude and elderly Sumo wrestler gingerly embraces a blanketed young woman who eyes us with an inscrutably perturbed expression. These paintings are almost allegorical in their chain of associations, American history paintings that operate with the economy of a cartoon. But as Green, again, observed, "Jack never does anything obvious. His ideas come as the mind turns (like the globe) into darkness," and the turnings of the mind and eye and hand that produced these layered parables are worth pursuing.[6)]

The only indication that Popeye is Popeye, in POPEYE, for example, is the tiny tattooed anchor on the assassin's gun-wielding right hand. Wesley's painted Popeye is modeled on his son Ner. "What people need to know is that it always begins with a picture," says Wesley, referring, in this case, to his painting PRINCESS SACAJAWEA CROSSING THE SNAKE (1976), one of a series of "Bicentennial" paintings he prepared for his Robert Elkon exhibition of that year. "That one came from a picture of a gymnast, I think." But Wesley clearly responds to events as well as the pictures accompanying their stories. MISSOURI COMPROMISE, another of Wesley's "Bicentennial" paintings, was inspired by a newspaper photo and story about a mid-western politician who ran against JFK for the 1960 presidential nomination, a story that most of us would never have noticed. For reasons never explained, "Soapy" Williams, heir to a family soap fortune, was offered a diplomatic position in Africa shortly after Kennedy won the nomination. The photo, according to Wesley, pictured Williams with his arm around another politician. "He probably wasn't collaring the other guy in the news photo," Wesley added. "I probably brought them closer together." (Note the mixed message of the fat, embracing paw on the shoulder and the pincer-grip pull on the collar.) Wesley also subtly Africanized Williams' features. I asked him if he had seen the famous photo of Ellington arguing with his manager. He allowed that he might have, and pointing to the soon-to-be African ambassador's lips in his painting observed: "I made his lips bigger."

BLUE BLANKET, says Wesley, began with an image of the Sumo wrestler who opened the 1998 Summer

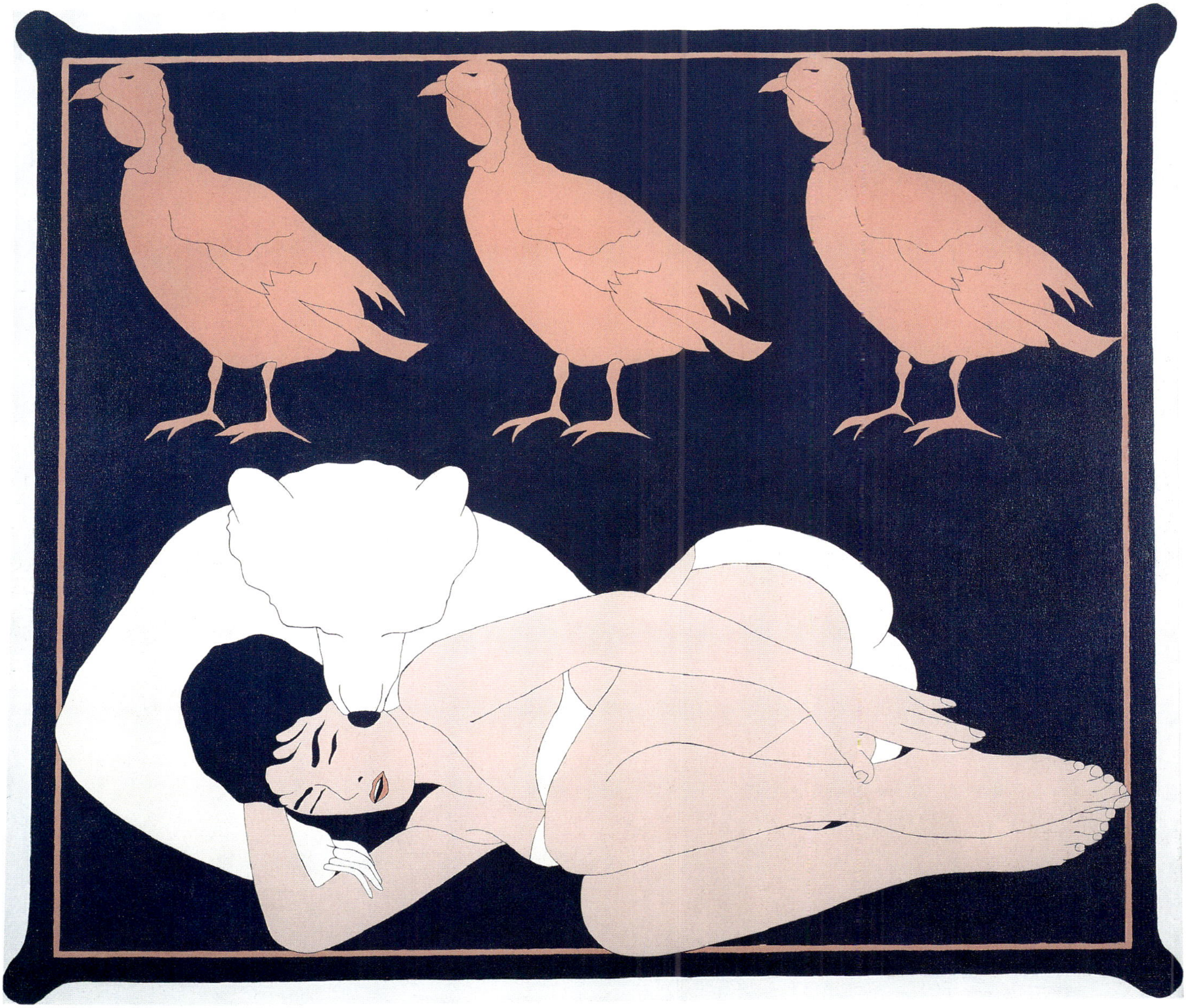

JOHN WESLEY, TURKEYS, 1965, acrylic on canvas, 46 x 52" / TRUTHÄHNE, Acryl auf Leinwand, 116,8 x 132 cm.

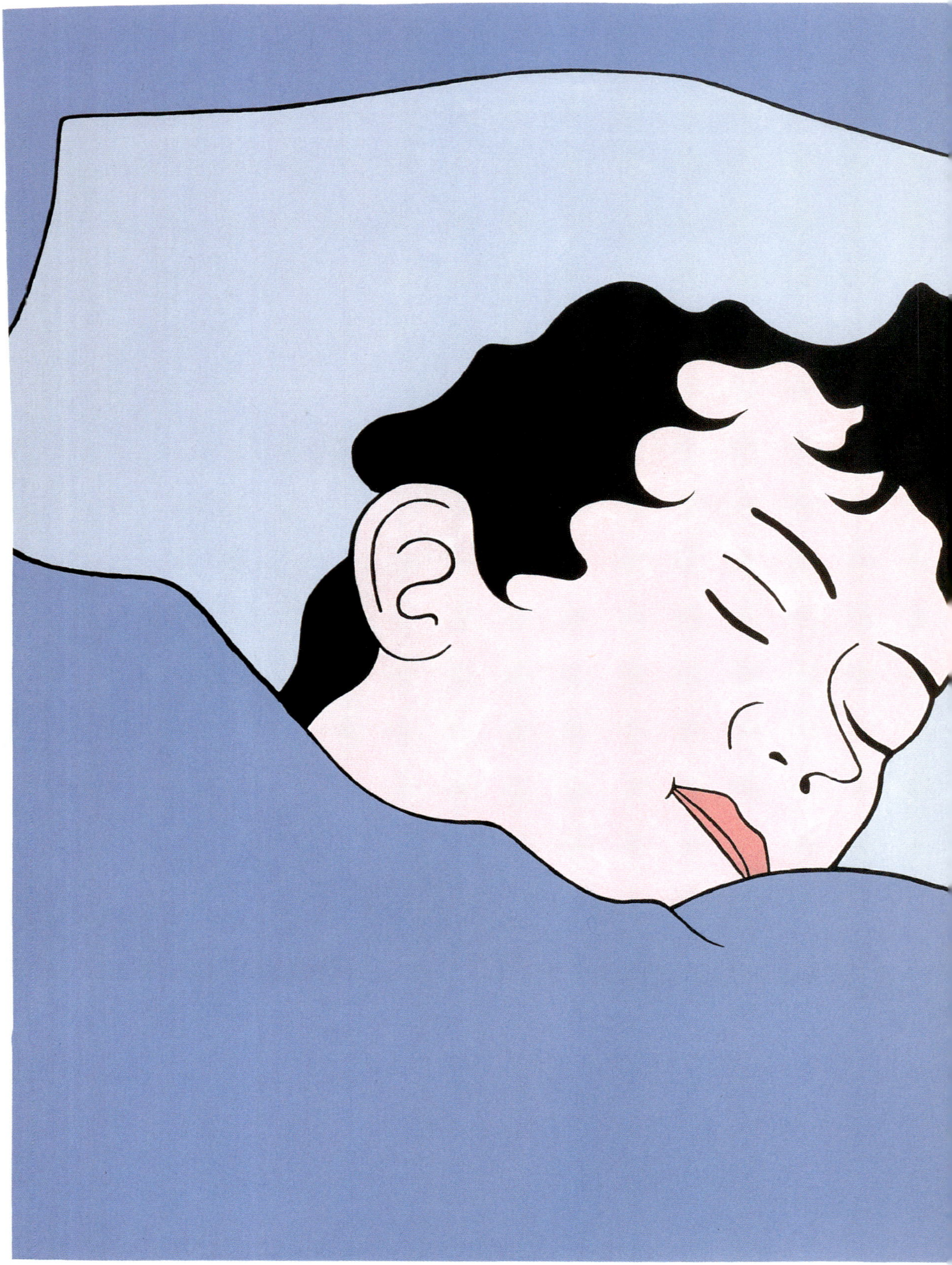

JOHN WESLEY, LAUTREC'S BED, 2000, acrylic on canvas, 42 x 66" / LAUTRECS BETT, Acryl auf Leinwand, 106,7 x 167,6 cm.

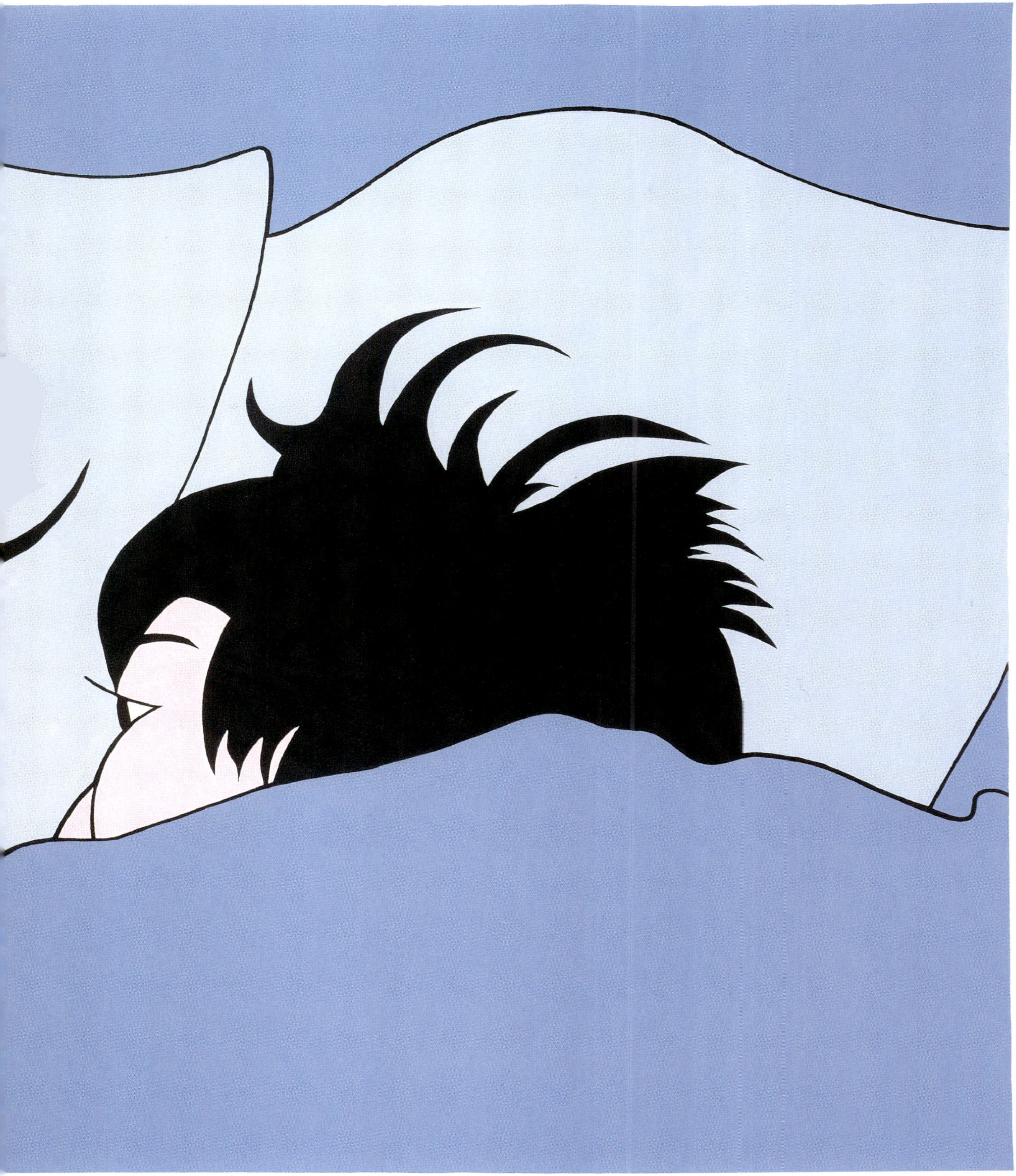

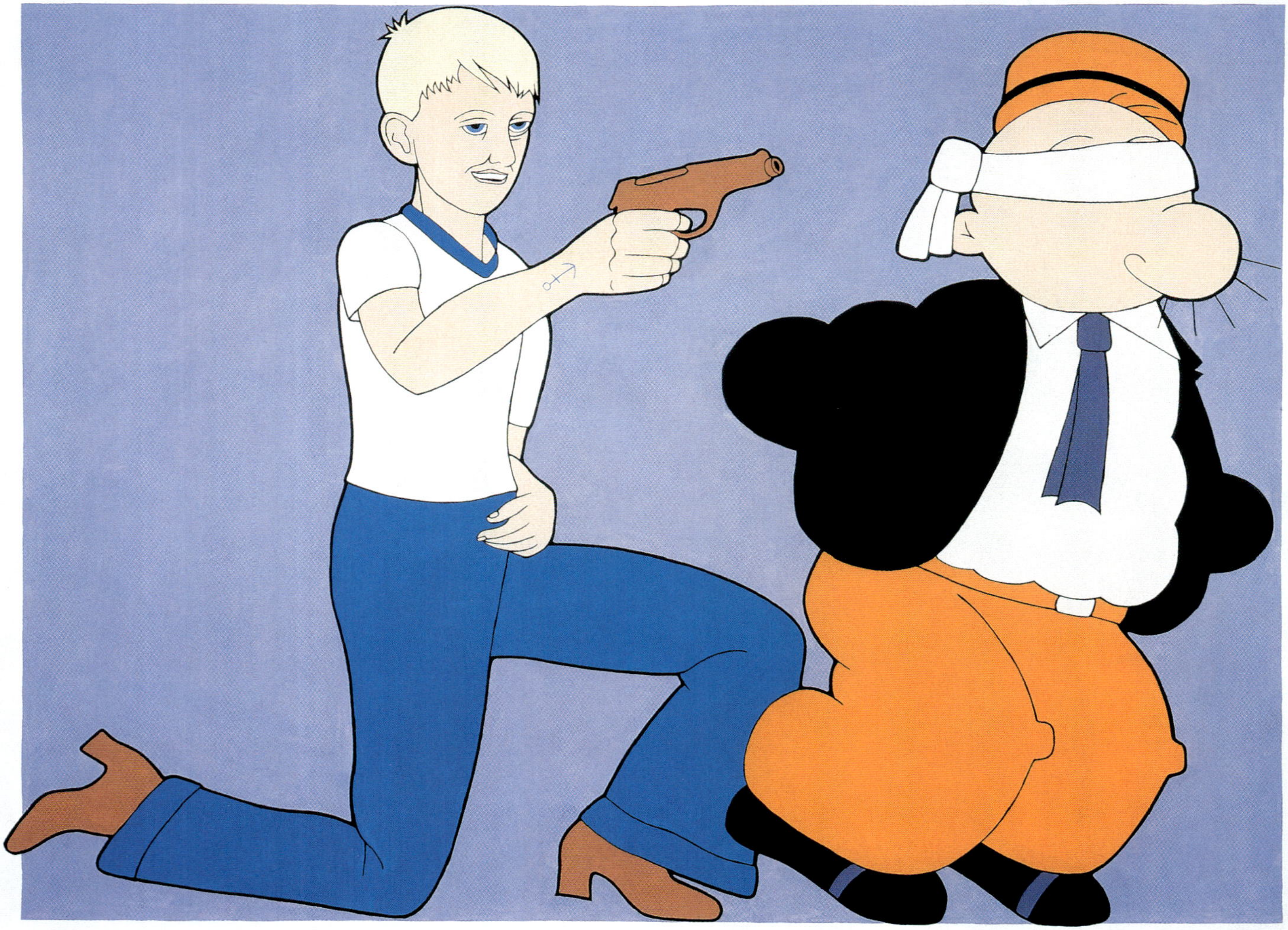

JOHN WESLEY, POPEYE, 1973, acrylic on canvas, 48 x 60" / Acryl auf Leinwand, 122 x 152,4 cm.

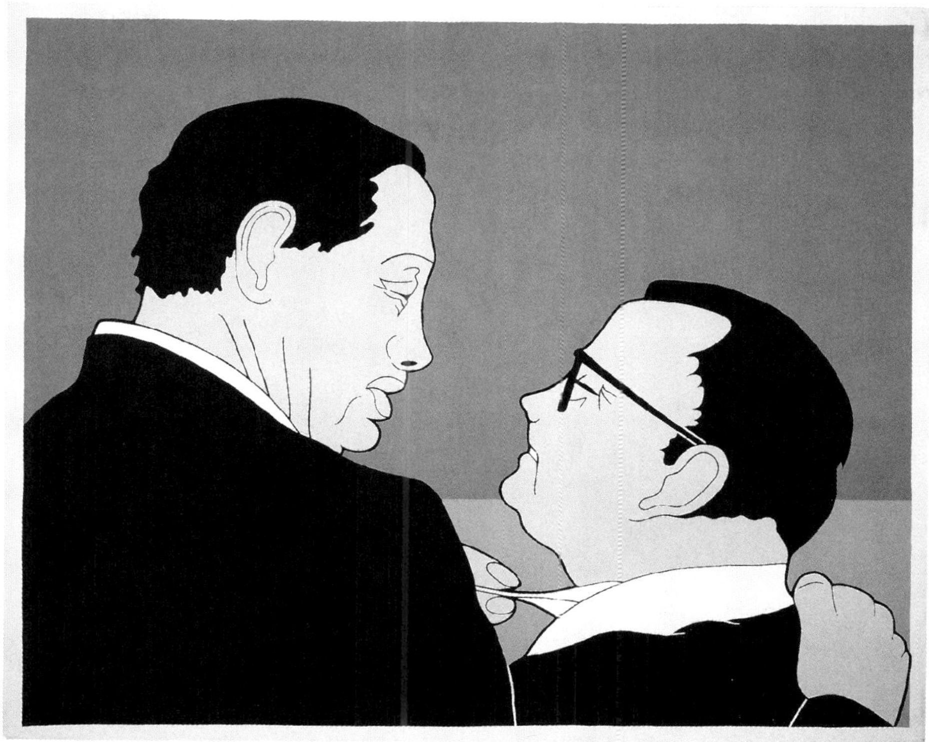

JOHN WESLEY, MISSOURI COMPROMISE, 1976, acrylic on canvas, 42 x 50" / MISSOURI-KOMPROMISS, Acryl auf Leinwand, 106,7 x 127 cm.

Olympics. Like a number of his recent paintings—UP DOGGY (2000) or YOUNG ARTIST USING HIS WIFE AS A MODEL (2000)—BLUE BLANKET is obliquely autobiographical. It would be hard to identify another contemporary male artist as preoccupied with his female subjects or as intelligent and earnest in his efforts to comprehend what the women that so intrigue him are feeling and thinking. (In searching for comparisons, only writers come to mind: Henry James, Armistead Maupin, John Casey.) Wesley's women always seem less befuddled and self-absorbed than his men do. It is the woman in BLUE BLANKET, for example, who catches our eye, assessing the situation, while registering a certain alarm at what she appears to have allowed. The wrestler, vulnerable and nude, is completely engrossed in his awkward embrace. Wesley further complicates the image by giving his wrestler feminine hands, rendering his allegory of an old man's lust, a *Beauty and the Beast* for our age of androgyny.

Wesley's working methods are as layered and responsive as the associations he manages to evoke. The second part of the Fogg exhibition was designed to suggest both studio and archive and to give some insight into his process. This section also included some of the traced drawings Wesley uses to compose his paintings and though he traces directly from sources such as magazine advertisements or newspaper photos, it becomes quickly apparent how little is fixed by this apparently mechanical means of reproduction. Wesley's stylized line immediately inflects his found imagery with expressive detail. Using tracing paper also allows him to reverse the orientation of figures and further complicate his compositions by selectively adjusting scale, or by cutting and taping figures from a found image, and compressing or expanding

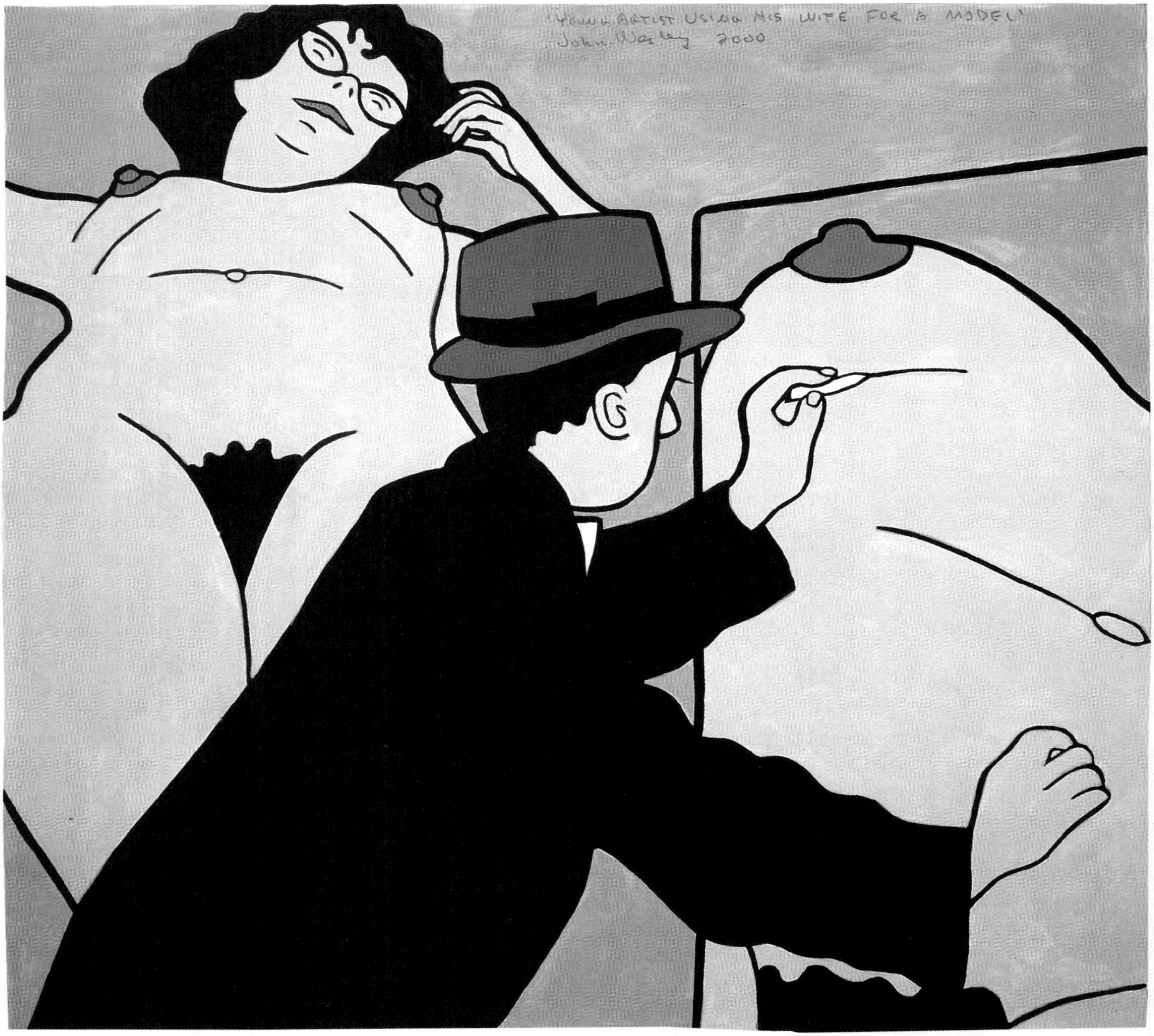

JOHN WESLEY, YOUNG ARTIST USING HIS WIFE AS MODEL, 2000, acrylic on paper, 16 x 17" /
JUNGER KÜNSTLER, DER SEINE FRAU ALS MODELL VERWENDET, Acryl auf Papier, 40,6 x 43,2 cm.

the spaces between them to modify their expressive impact, as he did in MISSOURI COMPROMISE and, more recently, in LAUTREC'S BED (2000). The tracing for Wesley's painting LAUTREC'S BED, for example, gives an indication of the extent to which his seemingly minor alterations up the expressive ante of his sources. (The tracing prefigures the painting in all details except color.) In this case, one can compare both the original Lautrec, which is delicately drawn and pastel pale, though no less transgressively erotic for its delicacy, and two recent paintings by Laura Owens based on the same Lautrec source. Where Owens takes over the harmonious color and patterning of the Lautrec (she changes the colors, but keeps them harmonious), as well as his barely differentiated androgynous lovers and sense of rumpled indolence, Wesley intensifies the image into a set of hard-edged oppositions. Without sacrificing any of the erotically charged androgyny, he nevertheless closes the eyes of one of the girls, whom he manages to make appear male, and draws "his" curls in more passive curves than the young girl who gazes at him, wide-eyed, from a few inches away on their pillows. "Her" hair stands up on her head in sharp spikes, an indication of her alertness. Asked by Klaus Biesenbach if this is literally a painting of Lautrec's bed, Wesley replied, "No. I lifted it off one of his paintings, his little girls in bed. I moved them a lot closer together in my picture."[7)]

Over the last ten years, Wesley has taken another turn in his paintings, opening spaces between figures, substituting distance for repetition, and conveying personality and mood less through facial expression than by refining and complicating an abstract, mannered line. Wesley's drawing has been mannered from the outset, but his line, conspicuous in waves and hair, has lately become more autonomous. The open spaces, as in BOYFRIENDS (1999) or WIND (2000), are often linked by nothing more than an unseen gaze or a sigh; like the empty rooms in Bumstead's home, they contribute to a sense of pathos. These newly emptied spaces also give Wesley a chance to lavish pure pigment on large areas of canvas and to play with the most minute of color adjustments, as he does in BLUE BLANKET and BOYFRIENDS or YOUNG ARTIST USING HIS WIFE AS A MODEL. For the first time, too, his brushstrokes are sometimes visible: never thick or agitated, but they are surprisingly present on surfaces that remain almost flat. "Surprisingly" because Wesley's opaque surfaces have become a kind of signature effect: the actions he contrives always seem to take place just beneath them.

Looking back, it seems as if Wesley never abandoned the expressionism his generation was so intent on jettisoning. Rather, he smuggled into flat paint and drawing the expressivity assumed to inhere in thick paint and gestural facture. The distance between his precisely mannered line and the aggressive gestural assaults with which Willem de Kooning conjured his women is almost immeasurably vast, as is the difference between Wesley's pop iconography and de Kooning's *ur*-woman. But Wesley's "passive" and mediated expression is no less intensely felt.

"Warhol's works of the early sixties," critic Peter Schjeldahl commented recently, "flag the moment when it was no longer possible to regard mass culture as a sphere of kitsch, remote from the values of serious folk."[8)] Wesley, one might say, extended Warhol's recognition to the realm of the domestic. But where Warhol humanized icons, simplifying them, Wesley humanized caricatures, making them more complex—revealing that Bumstead, like the Tin Man, had a heart and a libido and a temper. Wesley finds pathos in type and stereotype. The rest of us, it seems, have finally come round to the recognition that we, too, are loony, perverse, and full of dread and lust and wonder.

1) Hannah Green, *Little Saint* (New York: Random House, 2000), p. 27.
2) Peter Plagens, "John Wesley," *Artforum International*, New York, May 1998, pp. 140–141.
3) Donald Judd, "John Wesley," *Arts Magazine*, New York, April 1963, p. 50.
4) See Hannah Green, Excerpts from "A Journal in Praise of John Wesley," *The Unmuzzled Ox*, New York, Vol. II, No. 3, 1974, p. 46.
5) Judd, op. cit.
6) Green, op. cit.
7) Wesley is quoted by Klaus Biesenbach in: Alanna Heiss, *John Wesley: Paintings 1961–2000* (Long Island City, NY: P.S.1 Contemporary Art Center, 2000), p. 134.
8) Peter Schjeldahl, "Barbarians at the Gate: The Triumph of Picabia and Warhol in Two New Shows," *The New Yorker*, May 15, 2000, pp. 102–104.

PASSIVE AUSDRUCKSKRAFT

LINDA NORDEN

Ich könnte die Post austragen. Ich kenne die Namen aller Hunde.

- John Wesley[1)]

John Wesley, auch Jack genannt, könnte man durchaus als den Henri Rousseau seiner Generation verstehen: Kein eigentlicher Vertreter der Pop-Art, betritt er, ein pseudoprimitiver Kalifornier, um etwa 1960 völlig ausgereift die New Yorker Szene. Seine kühne, völlig neue Auffassung der abstrakten figürlichen Malerei faszinierte und verblüffte selbst seine vertrautesten Kollegen, so wie einst der zum Künstler avancierte französische Zollbeamte Picasso und Braque fasziniert hatte.

Einer von Green erstellten Chronologie zufolge begann Wesley «irgendwann im Jahr 1953 regelmässig zu malen und über Kunst nachzudenken», also im Alter von 24 Jahren, «während er als Illustrator für die Northrop Aircraft Corporation arbeitete». Das war zwar nicht alt für einen Anfang in der Malerei, aber es war immerhin so spät, dass die andern ihn als Naivling behandelten, wenn auch als einen zugegebenermassen begabten, gebildeten und bezaubernden Naivling, der durchaus über das eine oder andere Geheimnis verfügen mochte. Auch heute noch lassen sich die Kritiker durch das Rätselhafte von Wesleys Werk und durch seine unheimlichen Sujets dazu verleiten, nach dem Menschen und seinen Motiven zu fragen, statt sich mit den Bildern zu befassen: «Die Frage, die sich bei jedem Bild von Wesley sofort stellt, ist nicht, ‹Was bedeutet es?›, sondern, ‹Warum wollte der Künstler es malen?›», schrieb der Künstler und Kritiker Peter Plagens noch vor wenigen Jahren.[2)]

«John Wesley: Love's Lust», die Ausstellung, für die dieser Essay ursprünglich geschrieben wurde, nahm das Stichwort einer jüngeren Generation von Künstlern auf, die mit Pixeln und Plastikprinzessinnen aufgewachsen waren und sich weniger für das Warum und Wozu der Malerei interessierten als dafür, neue Methoden der Bilderzeugung zu finden; Künstler also, die sich, zum Beispiel, an Wesley orientieren. (Es ist diese jüngere Generation von Malern – Carl Ostendarp, Paul Morrison, Monique Prieto, Laura Owens, Takashi Murakami, um nur einige wenige zu nennen –, die Wesleys radikale formale Neuerungen am gründlichsten studiert hat; und sie haben es mit künstlerischen Mitteln getan und nicht schreibender Weise.) Vor dem Hintergrund der letztjährigen Retrospektive im P.S.1 Contemporary Art Center – Wesleys erster in einem amerikanischen Museum – setzte sich die kleinere

LINDA NORDEN ist Associate Curator für zeitgenössische Kunst am Fogg Art Museum, wo sie die Ausstellung «John Wesley: Love's Lust» organisierte, für die auch die erste Fassung dieses Essays ursprünglich entstand. Die Ausstellung dauerte vom 20. Januar bis 1. März 2001.

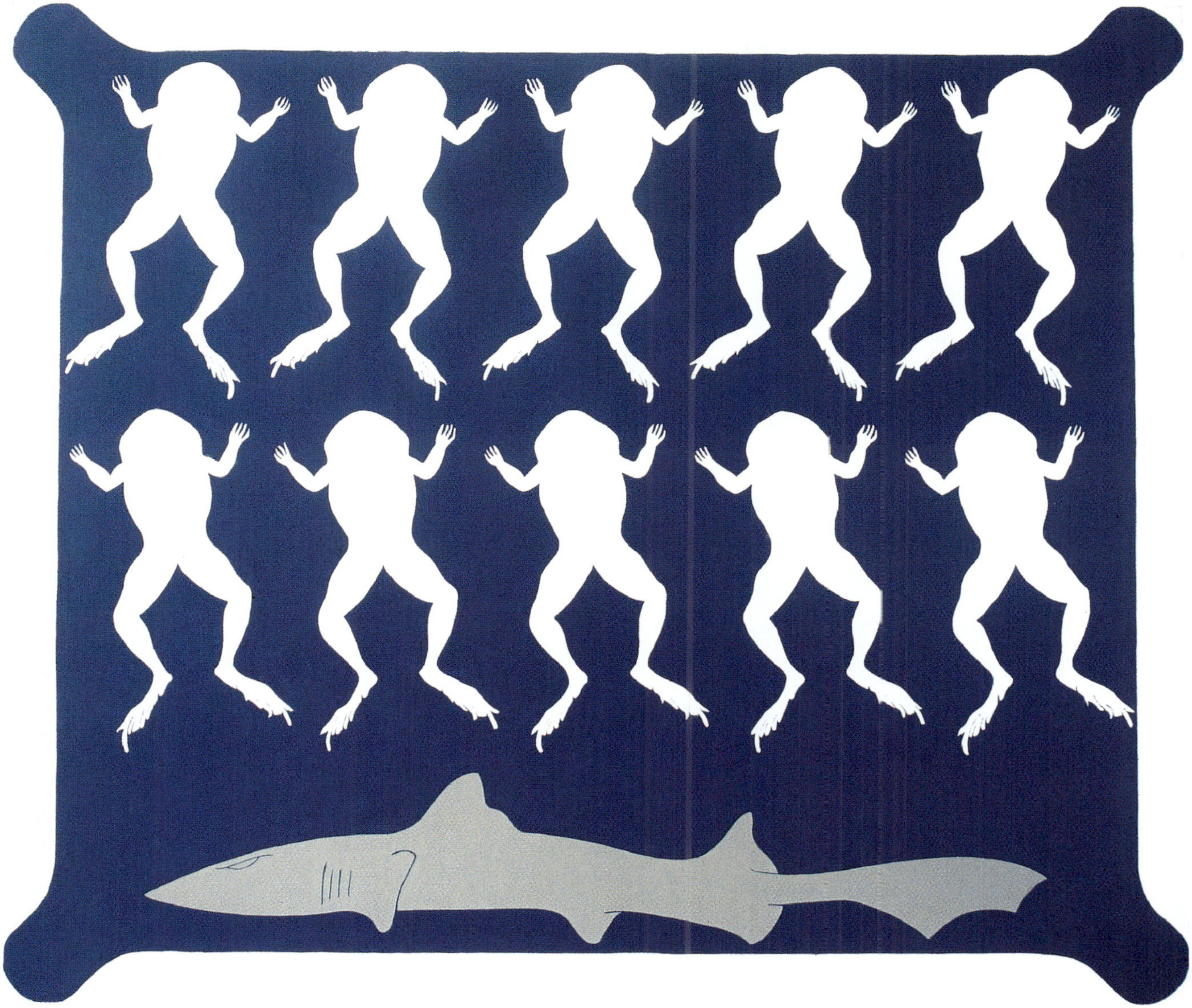

JOHN WESLEY, DANCING FROGS AND WAITING SHARK, 1962, Duco enamel and oil on canvas, 61 x 69" / TANZENDE FRÖSCHE UND WARTENDER HAI, Lackfarbe und Öl auf Leinwand, 155 x 175,3 cm.

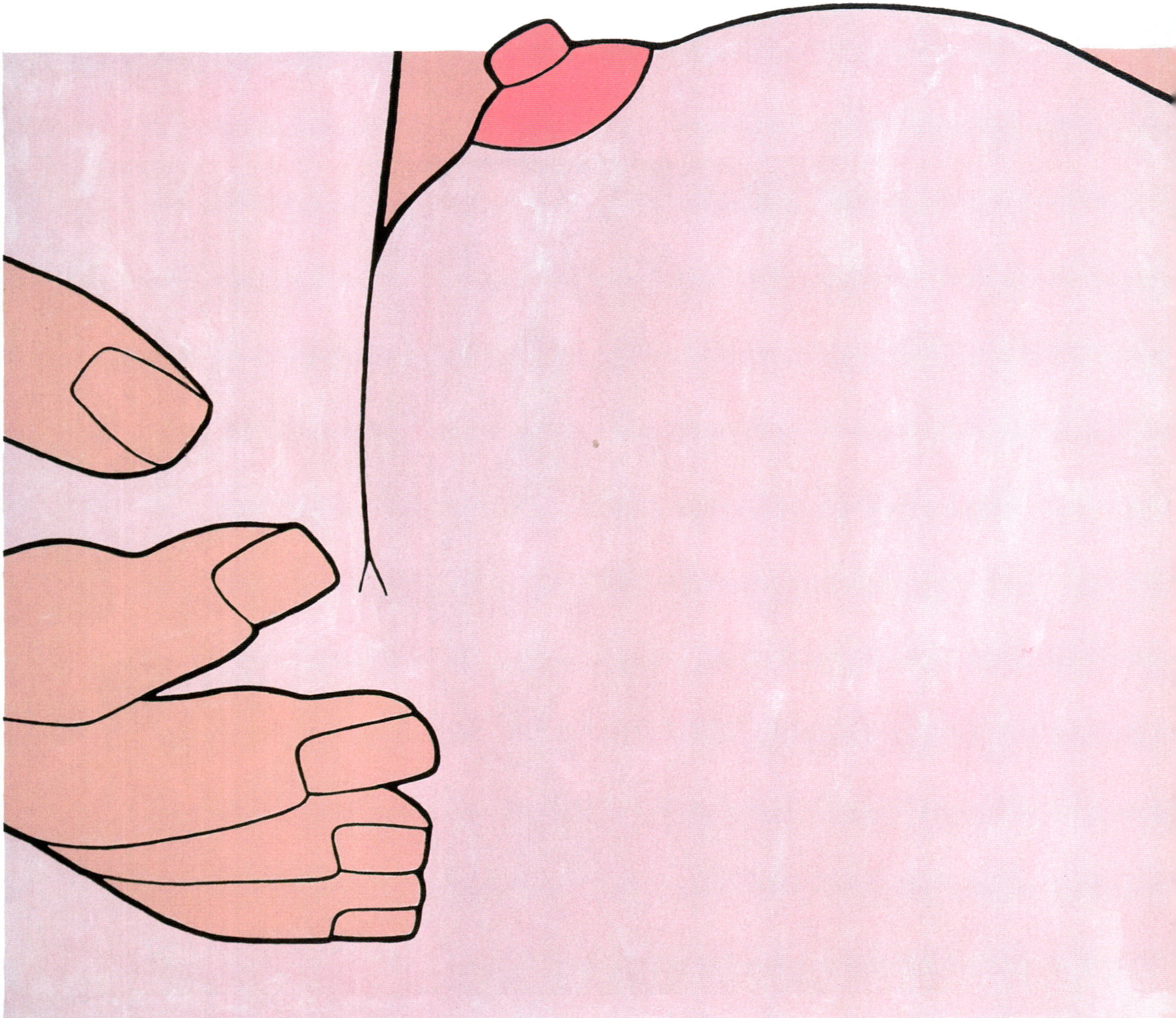

JOHN WESLEY, HOLD ME, 2001, acrylic on canvas, 30 x 67"/ UMARME MICH, Acryl auf Leinwand, 76,2 x 170,2 cm.

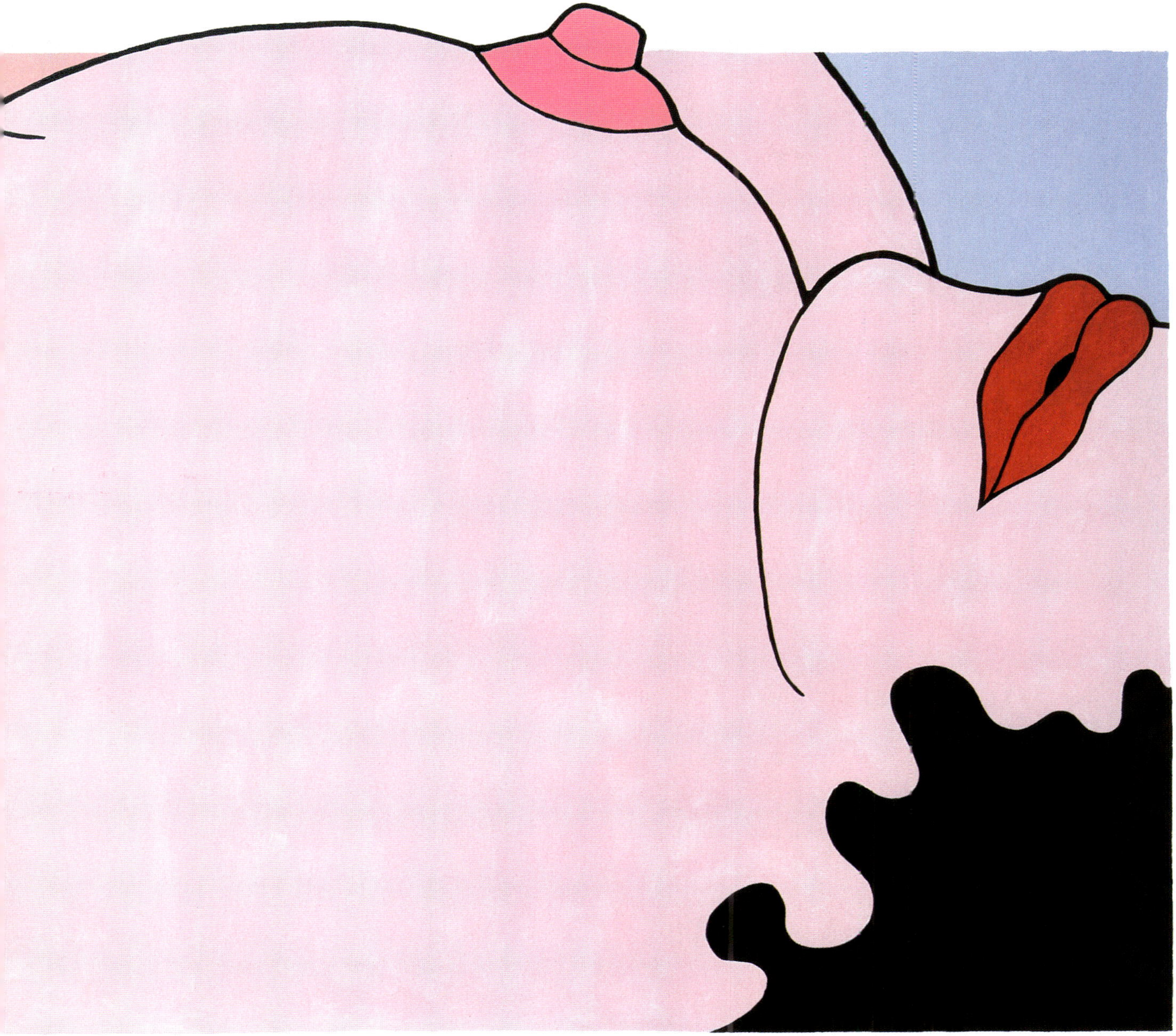

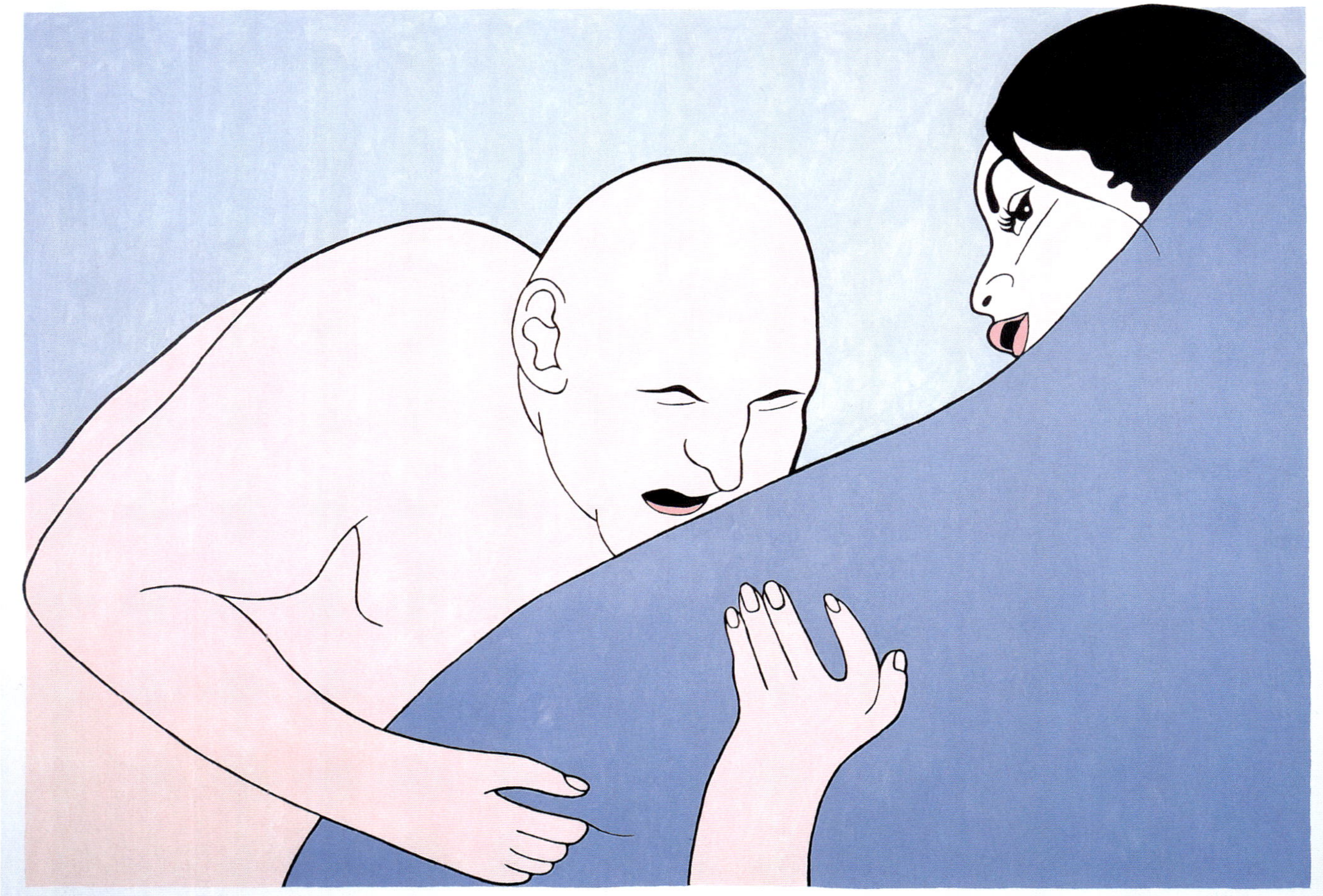

JOHN WESLEY, BLUE BLANKET, 2000, acrylic on canvas, 46 x 63¼" / BLAUE DECKE, Acryl auf Leinwand, 116,8 x 160,7 cm.

Ausstellung im Fogg Art Museum zum Ziel, nicht zu fragen «Warum tut Wesley, was er tut?», sondern vielmehr, «Wie tut er, was er tut?» und «Warum jetzt John Wesley?».

Die nächstliegende Erklärung für Wesleys neu gewonnene Popularität ist die momentan erhöhte Aufmerksamkeit für die Malerei überhaupt. Wesleys Malerei schaut aus wie nichts sonst weit und breit. Und obwohl sie sich über die Jahre stark verändert hat, üben die sofort ins Auge springenden typischen Merkmale seiner Werke seit den 70er Jahren – ihre hartnäckige Flachheit, die Farbpalette in Puderpastell, eine aus Cartoon oder Film entlehnte Thematik, eine Vorliebe für das sexuelle Spannungsverhältnis, ein raffinierter Anthropomorphismus sowie die manierierte Zeichnung – eine enorme Anziehungskraft aus, inmitten einer digitalen Revolution, die ein erneutes Überdenken des Mediums erfordert. Seine exzentrische Belebung vertrauter Stereotype greift dem heute aktuellen Hang zur Vermenschlichung von Cartoonfiguren vor. Dieses Talent scheint insbesondere für eine Generation wichtig zu sein, für die Cartoonfiguren über ein «realeres» Ausdruckspotenzial verfügen als direkte photographische Reproduktionen oder gemalte Körper. Aber Wesleys gegenwärtiges Prestige widerspiegelt auch das an der Jahrtausendwende verbreitete Bedürfnis nach sichtbaren Gefühlen und die Bereitschaft, diese in den unwahrscheinlichsten Begegnungen und Charakteren aller Art aufzuspüren.

Bei seinem Versuch einer Einschätzung von John Wesleys erster New Yorker Ausstellung im Jahr 1963 beschrieb der Künstler und Kritiker Donald Judd die Bilder als etwas, «was ein Tölpel aus irgendeinem unkünstlerischen Grund aus den Erscheinungen gemacht hat». Aber er fügte hinzu: «Das ist interessant.»[3)]

Andere, ratlose Kritiker ordneten Wesleys Malerei irgendwo zwischen Pop-Art und Surrealismus ein: Seine Sujets wirkten vertraut genug, um angemessen zu erscheinen, aber ihre Wiedergabe und Anordnung weckte immer wieder unerwartete, aber seltsamerweise auch unwiderstehliche Emotionen. Es war klar, dass Wesley anderes im Sinn hatte, als einfach die Bildsprache der Werbung zu übernehmen. Es gelang ihm, die banalsten Figuren in höchst beunruhigenden Posen darzustellen und uns glauben zu machen, dass er oder seine Sujets uns etwas Wichtiges vorenthielten, was wir unbedingt brauchten oder wissen wollten.

Wie die meisten Vertreter der Pop-Art malte Wesley zunächst gegen die gestische Abstraktion an, die die späten 40er und die 50er Jahre dominiert hatte. Wie viele andere fand er eine Befreiung im Werk von Jasper Johns, besonders in der absolut neuen Weise, wie Johns seine Malerei als Objekt und Zeichen verstand. Aber während Johns absichtlich Gegenstände wählte, die als «Instrumente» taugten und ihm erlaubten, das Abgebildete mit dem Bild eins werden zu lassen, konstruierte Wesley narrative Zusammenhänge, die Bild und Rahmen miteinander verbinden. Selbst in so frühen Werken wie DANCING FROGS AND WAITING SHARK (Tanzende Frösche und wartender Hai), COAT OF ARMS (Wappenschild) und AMERICAN EAGLE BADGE (Amerikanisches Adlerwappen), alle 1962, auf denen wappenförmige Flächen zu sehen sind, ereignet sich etwas innerhalb dieser Wappen und ein gemalter Rahmen umschliesst das Ganze. Johns' Instrumente funktionieren mechanisch; sie machen seine Bilder aus. Wesley bevorzugt dagegen optische Tricks, wie sich wiederholende Formen mit subtilen Variationen oder zweideutige Formen, die das Auge zur Bewegung zwingen und verschiedene Lesarten zulassen. In diesen frühen Bildern wirft Wesley mit Anthropomorphismen um sich wie ein pubertierender Schüler mit Zweideutigkeiten: Schauen Sie sich AMERICAN EAGLE BADGE oder COAT OF ARMS genau an und beobachten Sie, wie das Wappen sich in einen Körper verwandelt. «Das eben heisst Komposition», sagt Wesley, «das Auge mit einer geschlossenen, klar umgrenzten Form zu fesseln.»[4)] Wesley setzt seine Sinnbilder nicht derart wortgetreu ein wie Johns, aber ebenso bewusst. Seine Bilder wirken auf uns, ohne dass wir genau wüssten, was an ihnen diese Wirkung ausübt. Vielleicht ist es dies, worauf Judd in jener ersten Rezension anspielte, als er klagte: «Der einzige Einwand ist theoretisch, nicht kritisch. Wesleys Methode und auch die von Lichtenstein ist mehr oder weniger die der traditionellen Malerei; die Form ist relativ versteckt. Hier ist sie jedoch nicht hinter der Erscheinung verborgen, sondern hinter dem, was ein Tölpel aus irgendeinem unkünstlerischen Grund aus den Erscheinungen gemacht hat. Das ist ein grosser Unterschied… eine Art Meta-Darstellung.»[5)]

Wesleys Rahmen, mit oder ohne Verzierung, sind vielleicht sein auffallendstes Hilfsmittel. Sie erhöhen nicht nur den Konzentrationsgrad der Handlung, sie machen uns zu Voyeuren, ohne uns gänzlich zu enthüllen, wovon wir eigentlich Zeugen sind. Das ist besonders verwirrend, wenn ein Körperteil gegen die innere Kante des gemalten Rahmens stösst, als hätte Wesley seine Figuren in ein zu enges Gefäss gezwängt. In CAMEL (Kamel, 1966) etwa steckt ein umrahmter «verkehrter» Zentaur seinen Unterarm tief in den Rumpf eines überheblichen Kamels und scheint sich, um des besseren Widerstands willen, mit dem Fuss vom Rahmen abzustossen; in BLUE BLANKET (Blaue Decke, 2000) streift der freie Ellbogen eines ältlichen Sumo-Ringers, der eine in ein Leintuch gehüllte Frau umarmt, gegen den Rand der Bildfläche und wir gewinnen fast den Eindruck, er wolle uns wegscheuchen. Wenn eine Zehe, ein Stiefel oder eine Brustspitze tatsächlich aus dem sorgfältig umgrenzten Bereich hervortritt, wie in TURKEYS (Truthähne, 1965), POPEYE (1973) oder HOLD ME (Umarme mich, 2001), so wirkt das entweder zutiefst erotisch oder brutal oder beides, weil dabei der zupackendere Tastsinn zum relativ passiven Akt des Schauens hinzukommt. Wenige Künstler seit dem Krieg haben so viel zur Wiederentdeckung des Tafelbildes als Bühne und Fenster beigetragen.

Wesleys Bilder aus den frühen 60er Jahren wirkten altmodisch – Judd meinte, wie aus dem 19. Jahrhundert – und der Kreis der dargestellten Figuren konzentrierte sich noch nicht auf so vertraute Pop- und Antihelden wie Popeye oder die Bumsteads. Stattdessen pflegte und vervollkommnete Wesley einen eigenen Cartoon-Stil, der sich gleichermassen auf die stereotype Darstellung von Tieren wie von Männern, Frauen und Kindern stützte. Der subversive Anthropomorphismus von Bildern wie CAMEL oder CADDY (1968) verlieh den bizarren, unwahrscheinlichen Szenen noch grössere Intensität und gab dem Künstler die nötige Freiheit, auch heiklere Themen wie Sex, Lust, Rassismus und sinnlose Gewalt anzugehen, denn er liess seine Bilder ebenso witzig wie skandalös erscheinen. Wenn er eine nackte (b a r häutige) Frau mit einem geilen Polar b ä r e n zusammenbrachte, wie er das in TURKEYS tat, so war das ein verqueres Wortspiel, dem er dann noch den haptischen Gegensatz von Haut und Pelz gleichsam als Glosse hinzufügt – seine clowneske Version der langen westlichen Tradition von bekleideten Männern und nackten Frauen. (In den 60er Jahren war Wesley mit der Künstlerin Jo Baer verheiratet, was das Wortspiel noch um eine weitere Dimension bereichert.)

Wesley hat erzählt, dass er gegen das Ende seiner langen Aufenthalte in Conques begann, sich nach körperlichem Komfort zu sehnen, etwa nach einem Bett, das lang genug war, aber am meisten habe er den Fernseher vermisst. Unter den Gouachen, die er 1978 in seinem kleinen Raum dort malte, ist eine mit dem Titel TELLY, die so tut, als wäre das Fenster ein Fernsehbildschirm. Indirekt mag Wesleys Liebe zum Fernsehen – ein Medium, das viele seiner Generation verteufelt haben –, aber auch seine Vorliebe für Filme und Comic-Hefte ihm in den frühen 70er Jahren geholfen haben als Maler durchzuhalten, als die Malerei als Medium in einem grossen Teil der Kunstszene als «tot» galt.

Indem er den weltmüden Bumstead sowohl als Alter Ego wie als Ersatz für den mit sechs Jahren verlorenen Vater einsetzte, verwandelte Wesley seinen früheren Gebrauch eines inneren Rahmens in etwas Umfassenderes und Zeitgemässeres. Seine *Searching for Bumstead (Auf der Suche nach Bumstead)*-Serie, mit der er 1973 in der Mac Dowell Colony begann, ersetzte die Bilder mit den dem Comicstrip entliehenen Rahmen und gab den aus dem 19. Jahrhundert stammenden dekorativen Zeichenstil auf, zugunsten eines Stils, der sich selektiv dem weniger starren, in den Details sparsameren Stil von Bumsteads Schöpfer annäherte. (Man achte etwa auf Wesleys Verwendung der kurzen paarweisen Parallelstriche, die man überall im Comic antrifft: Sie umgrenzen einen Raum, deuten Lichtreflexionen an und stehen für allerlei dekorative Schnörkel, etwa auf Bodenbelägen.) Diese Bilder waren direkt und intim, und sie erweiterten Wesleys Ausdrucksmöglichkeiten gegenüber dem, was er mit seinen vermenschlichten Hunden, Pferden und Bären mitzuteilen vermochte. Sie erlaubten ihm auch von seinen bösen Witzen weg, zu einer viel wirksameren Ausdrucksweise zu gelangen und neben den Figuren auch den Raum zu malen.

Egal, ob die *Bumstead*-Bilder Szenen häuslicher Missverständnisse im Detail ausleuchten und kamerauntaugliche Momente der Verstörung gross ins Bild rücken, oder einfach leere Korridore und Wände nach persönlichen Spuren absuchen: Immer sind es peinlich genaue Darstellungen der Abgründe zwischen Gefühl und Verstand und sie gewannen Wesley ein neues Publikum. Gegen Ende der 80er Jahre profitierte er auch von einem Stimmungswechsel innerhalb der feministischen Kritik und von einem allgemeinen Interesse, im Objekt seiner Begierde «das jeweils Andere» zu sehen. Seine Bereitschaft, sich selbst von den gemalten Verführungsszenen (angefangen bei seiner *Bumstead*-Serie) nicht auszunehmen, und seine Fähigkeit, ohne jede Entschuldigung oder Erklärung die Verwirrung angesichts der Verlockungen des Lebens zu porträtieren, wirkte wie eine gesunde Alternative zum Geschlechterkampf. Seine Bilder waren gescheit, witzig, verstörend, einfühlsam bis zur Respektlosigkeit und

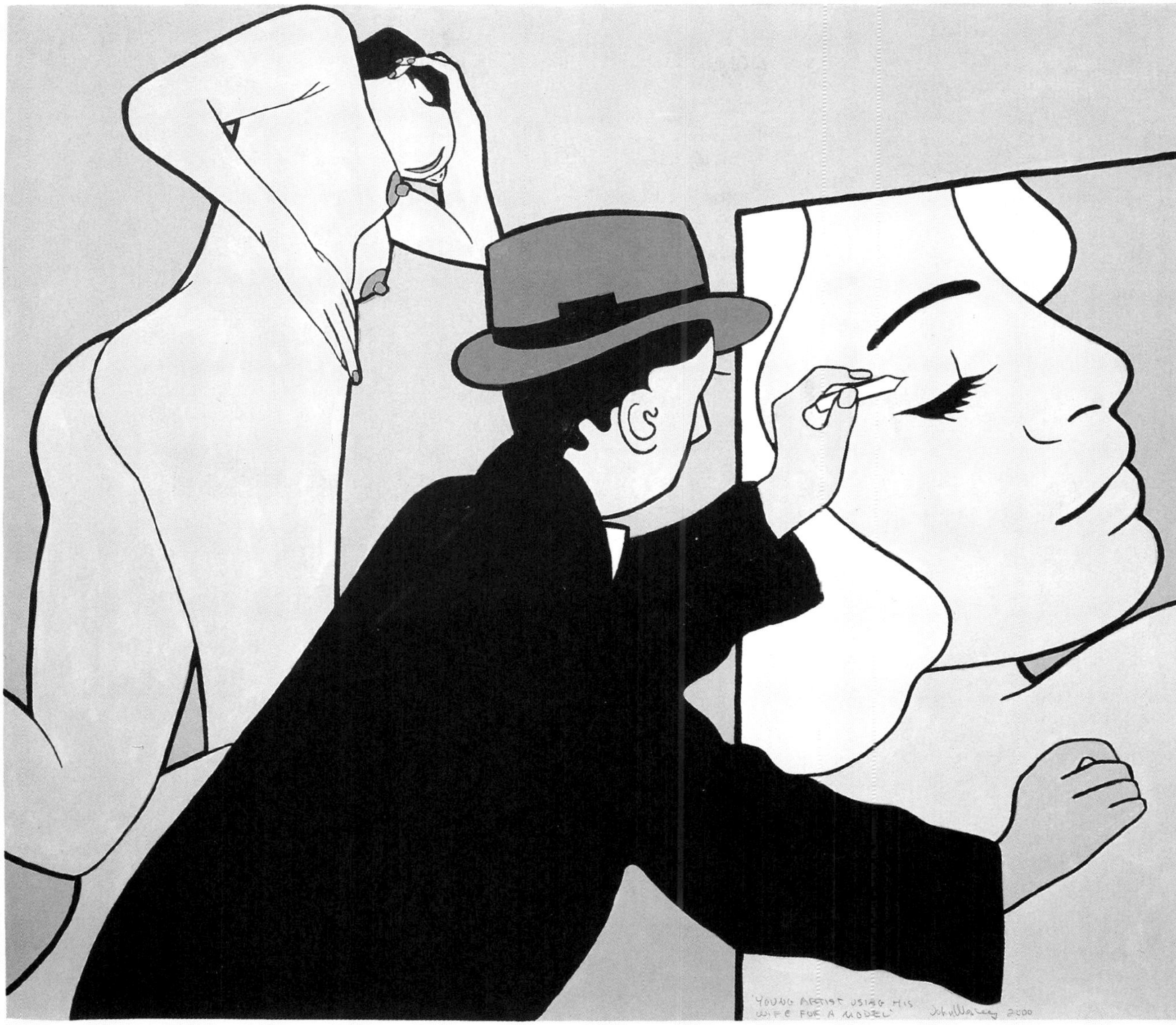

JOHN WESLEY, YOUNG ARTIST USING HIS WIFE AS MODEL, 2000, acrylic on paper, 22½ x 25" /
JUNGER KÜNSTLER, DER SEINE FRAU ALS MODELL VERWENDET, 57,2 x 63,5 cm.

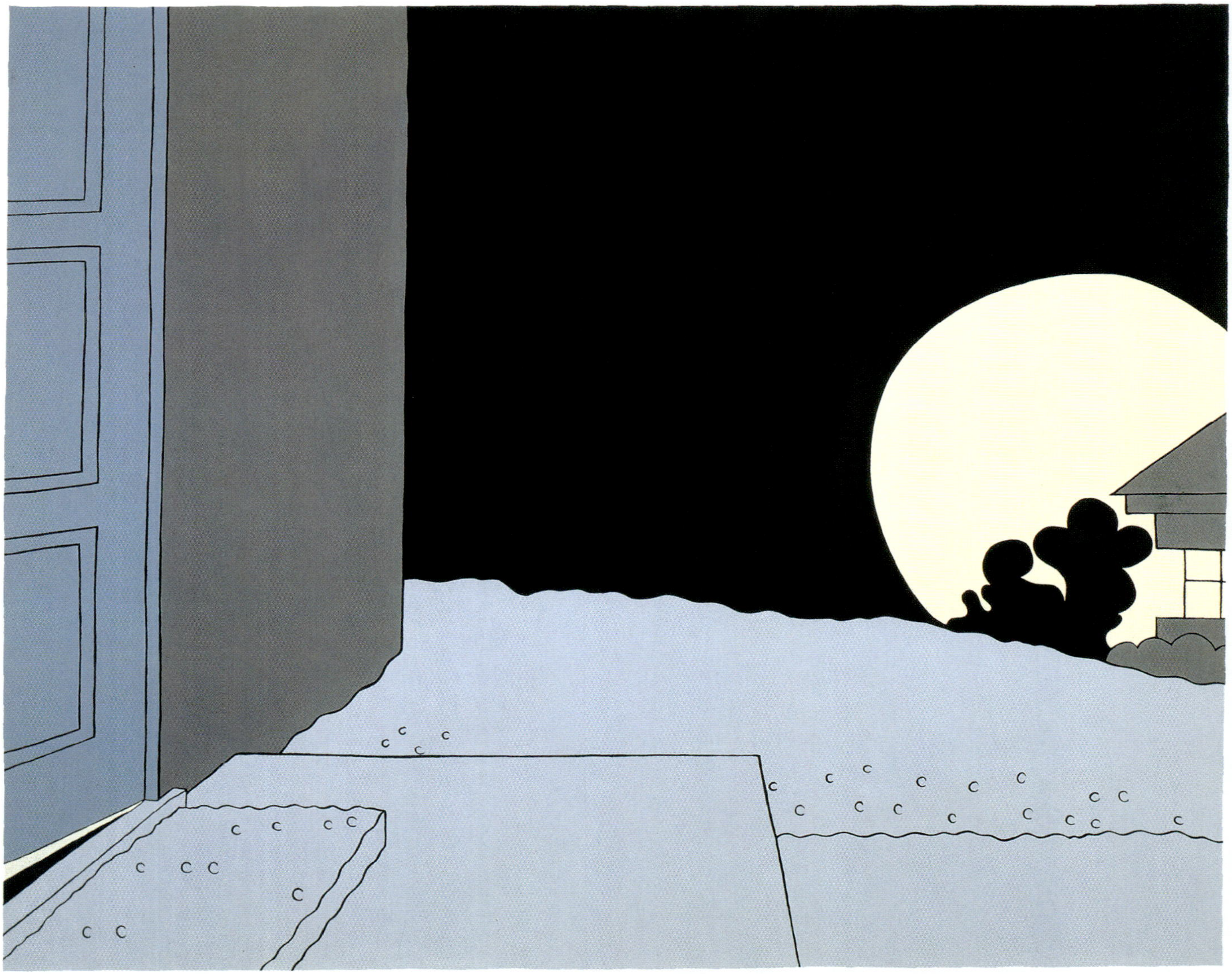

JOHN WESLEY, B'S STOOP, 1973, acrylic on canvas, 42 x 50" / B'S GEBEUGTE HALTUNG, Acryl auf Leinwand, 106,7 x 127 cm.

oft herzzerreissend – willkommene Medizin in einem anstrengenden Diskurs.

In der Ausstellung «John Wesley: Love's Lust» wiesen mehrere Bilder eine einfache Kompositionstechnik auf, die Wesley immer wieder angewandt hat: die Isolation zweier einander gegenüberstehender Figuren. In POPEYE (1973), MISSOURI COMPROMISE (1976) und dem neueren BLUE BLANKET (2000) sind die Figuren bedrohlich gross und die Details im Hintergrund fallen beinah ganz weg. Jedes dieser Bilder greift mittels eines populären Helden oder einer Kunstfigur eine heikle Thematik auf. In einem Bild, das jeder, der zur Zeit des Vietnamkriegs gelebt hat, unweigerlich mit dem berühmten Pressebild einer Hinrichtung auf offener Strasse in Verbindung bringen muss, schiesst Popeye auf einen hilflosen Menschen mit verbundenen Augen. In MISSOURI COMPROMISE erinnern die beiden weissen Männer in der Pose von Politikern mittleren Alters, die gegen ihre Höflichkeit ankämpfen, geradezu unheimlich an ein Bild von Duke Ellington, wie er seinen erschreckten Manager am Kragen packt. Ein nackter, schon älterer Sumo-Ringer umarmt behutsam eine in eine Decke gehüllte junge Frau, die uns mit unergründlich aufgewühlter Miene mustert. Angesichts der Kette von Assoziationen, die sie auslösen, sind diese Bilder schon fast allegorisch, amerikanische Historienmalerei, aber sparsam wie Cartoons. Doch wie Green wiederum bemerkte: «Jack tut nie das Naheliegende. Seine Ideen kommen, wenn der Verstand (wie die sich drehende Erde) in die Nacht eintaucht», und die Drehungen des Geistes, des Auges und der Hand, die diese vielschichtigen Parabeln hervorgebracht haben, sind es wert, dass man ihnen folgt.[6)]

So ist der einzige Hinweis darauf, dass Popeye in POPEYE wirklich Popeye ist, dieser winzige tätowierte Anker auf dem rechten Arm des Mörders, der auch die Schusswaffe hält. Wesleys gemalter Popeye hat seinen Sohn Ner zum Vorbild. «Was die Leute wissen müssen, ist, dass es immer mit einem Bild beginnt», sagt Wesley, diesmal in Bezug auf sein Bild PRINCESS SACAJAWEA CROSSING THE SNAKE (Prinzessin Sacajawea überquert den Snake-River, 1976), welches zu einer Serie von Bildern anlässlich der amerikanischen Zweihundertjahrfeier gehört, die er für seine im selben Jahr stattfindende Robert-Elkon-Ausstellung anfertigte. «Dieses eine entstand, glaube ich, aus dem Bild einer Turnerin.» Aber Wesley reagiert ebenso auf die Ereignisse selbst wie auf die Bilder, die die Geschichten begleiten. MISSOURI COMPROMISE, auch eines der Bilder zur Zweihundertjahrfeier, wurde von einem Zeitungsphoto und einem Artikel über einen Politiker aus dem mittleren Westen angeregt, der sich 1960 als Präsidentschaftskandidat nominieren lassen wollte und gegen John F. Kennedy antrat; eine Geschichte, die die meisten von uns gar nicht wahrgenommen haben. Aus nie geklärten Gründen wurde «soapy» Williams, dem Erben einer Seifenfabrikantendynastie, kurz nach Kennedys Nominierung ein Posten als Diplomat in Afrika angeboten. Das Photo zeigte, laut Wesley, Williams, wie er seinen Arm um einen andern Politiker legte. «Wahrscheinlich packte er den anderen auf dem Zeitungsphoto nicht wirklich am Kragen», fügte Wesley hinzu. «Ich habe sie wohl etwas näher zueinander gerückt.» (Man beachte die Widersprüchlichkeit der feissen umarmenden Pranke auf der Schulter und des zupackenden Griffs nach dem Kragen.) Wesley lässt zudem die Gesichtszüge von Williams leicht negroid erscheinen. Ich fragte ihn, ob er das berühmte Photo kenne, auf dem Ellington im Streit mit seinem Manager zu sehen ist. Er meinte, möglicherweise schon, deutete auf die Lippen des zukünftigen Botschafters in Afrika und meinte: «Ich hab seine Lippen vergrössert.»

Der Ursprung von BLUE BLANKET liegt laut Wesley in einem Bild des Sumo-Ringers, der 1998 die Olympischen Sommerspiele eröffnete. Wie manche seiner neueren Bilder, etwa UP DOGGY (Hoch, Hundchen, 2000) oder YOUNG ARTIST USING HIS WIFE AS A MODEL (Junger Künstler, der seine Frau als Modell verwendet, 2000), ist auch BLUE BLANKET versteckt autobiographisch. Es dürfte schwer fallen, einen anderen zeitgenössischen Künstler zu finden, der sich über seine weiblichen Modelle Gedanken macht oder sich so klug und ernsthaft bemüht zu verstehen, was die Frauen, die ihn so faszinieren, fühlen und denken. (Ähnliches haben offenbar nur Schriftsteller versucht: Henry James, Armistead Maupin, John Casey.) Wesleys Frauen wirken stets weniger verwirrt und mit sich selbst beschäftigt als seine Män-

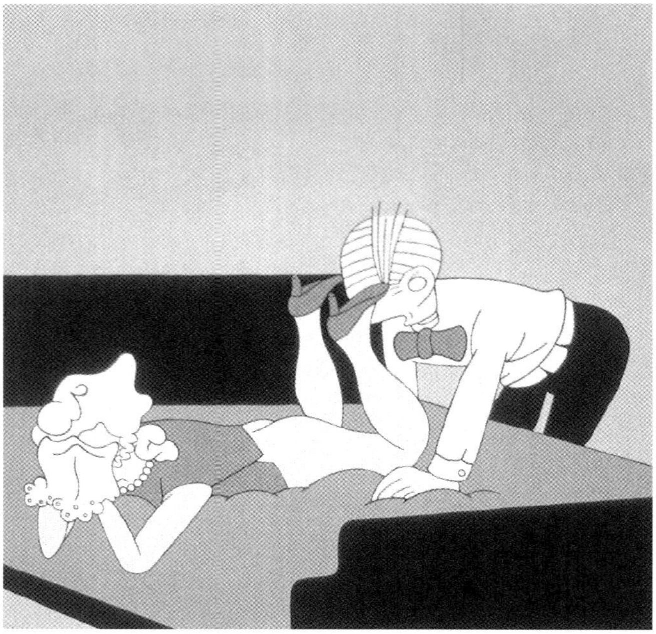

JOHN WESLEY, THE BUMSTEADS, 1974,
acrylic on canvas, 34 x 36" /
DIE BUMSTEADS,
Acryl auf Leinwand, 86,4 x 91,4 cm.

ner. Auch in BLUE BLANKET ist es die Frau, die unseren Blick sucht und die Situation abschätzt, während sie darüber, was sie offenbar zugelassen hat, etwas beunruhigt scheint. Der Ringer, verletzlich und splitternackt, ist voll und ganz mit seiner unbeholfenen Umarmung beschäftigt. Wesley kompliziert das Ganze noch, indem er seinem Ringer feminine Hände gibt und dadurch diese Allegorie des alten Lüstlings als eine Variation von *Die Schöne und das Tier* präsentiert, die in unser androgynes Zeitalter passt.

Wesleys Arbeitsweise ist ebenso vielschichtig und auf vieles bezogen wie die Assoziationen, die er weckt. Der zweite Teil der Fogg-Ausstellung sollte sowohl eine Atelier- und Archivatmosphäre vermitteln als auch einen Einblick in seinen Arbeitsprozess gestatten. In diesem Teil der Ausstellung wurden auch einige der Pausvorlagen gezeigt, die Wesley zur Komposition seiner Bilder verwendet, und obwohl er Motive aus Zeitschriften, Inseraten oder Zeitungsphotos direkt abpaust, wird schnell deutlich, wie wenig durch diese scheinbar mechanische Reproduktionsweise vorgegeben ist. Wesleys stilisierter Strich verwandelt die gefundene Vorlage durch ausdrucksstarke Details. Die Verwendung von Pauspapier erlaubt ihm auch, Figuren seitenverkehrt abzubilden und seine Kompositionen dadurch zu verdichten, dass er ihre Grösse beliebig variiert oder Figuren aus einem Bild ausspart und den Raum zwischen ihnen vergrössert oder verkleinert, um ihre expressive Qualität zu verändern, wie er das in MISSOURI COMPROMISE und kürzlich auch in LAUTREC'S BED (Lautrecs Bett, 2000) getan hat. Wesleys Pausen zu LAUTREC'S BED, zum Beispiel, geben einen Eindruck davon, wie sehr seine scheinbar so unbedeutenden Veränderungen die Ausdruckskraft der Vorlagen steigern. (Die Pausen geben das spätere Bild, abgesehen von den Farben, in allen Details vollständig wieder.) In diesem speziellen Fall kann man sowohl das Original von Lautrec zum Vergleich heranziehen – fein gezeichnet und in blassen Pastelltönen gehalten, aber nichts desto weniger von einer überwältigenden Erotik –, als auch zwei neuere Bilder von Laura Owens, die auf dasselbe Lautrec-Bild Bezug nehmen. Wo Owens die Harmonie von Farbe und Musterung übernimmt (sie ändert zwar die Farben, behält jedoch die Harmonie bei) und auch die kaum zu unterscheidenden, androgynen Liebenden in ihrer zerknüllten Trägheit beibehält, steigert Wesley das Ganze zu einem Bild härtester Gegensätze. Ohne die erotische Spannung des Androgynen aufzugeben, lässt er eines der beiden Mädchen die Augen schliessen, wodurch es ihm gelingt, sie männlich aussehen zu lassen, und zeichnet dann «seine» Locken in etwas ruhigeren Kurven als bei dem jungen Mädchen, das ihn mit weit aufgerissenen Augen und aus nur wenigen Zentimetern Entfernung, über die Kissen hinweg anschaut. «Ihr» Haar steht spitz empor, ein Hinweis auf ihre Wachsamkeit. Als Klaus Biesenbach den Künstler fragte, ob das tatsächlich ein Bild von Lautrecs Bett sei, antwortete Wesley: «Nein. Ich habe es von einem seiner Bilder abgepaust, seinen kleinen Mädchen im Bett. Ich hab sie in meinem Bild viel näher zueinander gerückt.»[7]

Im Lauf der letzten zehn Jahre hat Wesley in seinen Bildern einen neuen Weg eingeschlagen, er begann die Räume zwischen den Figuren zu öffnen, ersetzte die Wiederholung durch Distanz und vermittelte Persönlichkeit und Stimmung seiner Figuren weniger durch ihren Gesichtsausdruck als vielmehr durch einen verfeinerten, komplizierteren, abstrakten und manierierten Strich. Wesleys Zeichenweise war schon immer manieriert, aber sein Strich, am besten zu sehen bei Wellen und Haar, ist in letzter Zeit noch autonomer geworden. Die offenen Räume, etwa in BOYFRIENDS (1999) oder WIND (2000), werden oft durch nichts anderes zusammengehalten als einen unsichtbaren Blick oder einen Seufzer; wie die leeren Räume in Bumsteads Haus verstärken sie den Appell an unser Mitgefühl. Diese nunmehr leeren Räume erlauben es Wesley auch reichlich mit reinem Pigment auf grossen Flächen zu arbeiten und mit feinsten Farbabstufungen zu spielen, wie er das in BLUE BLANKET, BOYFRIENDS oder YOUNG ARTIST USING HIS WIFE AS A MODEL tut. Erstmals sind auch seine Pinselstriche erkennbar: nie triefend oder heftig bewegt, aber von überraschender Präsenz auf diesen beinah völlig plan wirkenden Oberflächen. «Überraschend», weil das Undurchdringliche von Wesleys Oberflächen zu einer Art Markenzeichen geworden ist: die Handlungen, die er inszeniert, scheinen sich immer direkt unter dieser Oberfläche abzuspielen.

Im Rückblick scheint es, als habe Wesley das Expressionistische nie aufgegeben, das seine Generation unbedingt über Bord werfen wollte. Vielmehr rettete er die Expressivität, die man mit fetter Farbe und gestischer Struktur in Verbindung brachte, heimlich in den sparsamen Farbauftrag und die Zeichnung hinüber. Die Distanz zwischen seinem präzis manierierten Strich und der aggressiven gestischen Gewalt, mit der Willem de Kooning seine Frauen heraufbeschwor, ist beinah unermesslich gross, genau wie die Verschiedenheit von Wesleys Pop-Ikonographie und de Koonings Urfrau. Aber Wesleys «passive» und vermittelte Ausdrucksweise ist nicht weniger intensiv gelebt.

«Warhols Arbeiten der frühen 60er Jahre», meinte kürzlich der Kritiker Peter Schjeldahl, «bezeichnen den Augenblick, in dem es nicht mehr möglich war, die Massenkultur als Sphäre des Kitsches zu betrachten, die meilenweit entfernt von den Werten ernst zu nehmender Leute war.»[8] Wesley, so könnte man sagen, dehnte Warhols Erkenntnis auf den häuslichen Bereich aus. Aber wo Warhol Ikonen vermenschlichte, indem er sie vereinfachte, vermenschlichte Wesley Karikaturen, indem er sie komplexer zeigte und uns vor Augen führte, dass Bumstead wie auch der Zinnsoldat ein Herz hatten und ein Verlangen und Launen. Wesley entdeckt den Appell, der vom Typus und vom Stereotypen ausgeht. Und uns Übrigen scheint es allmählich zu dämmern, dass auch wir irrsinnig, pervers und voller Schrecken, Lust und Staunen sind.

(Übersetzung: Wilma Parker)

1) Hannah Green, *Little Saint*, Random House, New York 2000, S. 27.
2) Peter Plagens, «John Wesley», *Artforum International*, Mai 1998, S. 140–141.
3) Donald Judd, «John Wesley», *Arts Magazine*, New York, April 1963, S. 50.
4) Vgl. Hannah Green, excerpts from «A Journal in Praise of John Wesley», *The Unmuzzled Ox*, New York, vol. II, No. 3, 1974, S. 46.
5) Donald Judd, op. cit.
6) Hannah Green, op.cit.
7) John Wesley zitiert von Klaus Biesenbach, in: Alanna Heiss, *John Wesley: Paintings 1961–2000*, Ausstellungskatalog, P.S.1 Contemporary Art Center, Long Island City, NY, 2000, S. 134. (Es handelt sich um Lautrecs Bild LE LIT von 1892.)
8) Peter Schjeldahl, «Barbarians at the Gate: the Triumph of Picabia and Warhol in Two New Shows», *The New Yorker*, 15. Mai 2000, S. 102–104.

KASPER KÖNIG & MARIANNE STOCKEBRAND sprechen am Telefon über JOHN WESLEY

Marianne Stockebrand: In der Chinati Foundation, hier in Marfa (Texas), arbeiten wir zurzeit an einer Dauerausstellung von John Wesley. Donald Judd hat eine Sammlung von Wesleys Arbeiten zusammengetragen, die nun die Basis für unsere zukünftige Präsentation sein wird, zu der John noch weitere Bilder, vor allem aus den frühen Jahren, beiträgt. Ausserdem möchte ich noch mehrere Gouachen erwerben, so dass wir eine repräsentative Auswahl seines Werks zeigen können. Wir haben dafür einen der ehemaligen Ställe draussen auf dem Feld ausgewählt, etwas entfernt von den Installationen Dan Flavins. Momentan planen wir die Renovierung dieses Gebäudes und treffen eine Auswahl von Wesleys Gemälden, um diese dann auf Dauer auszustellen. Ich hoffe, dass wir damit innerhalb der nächsten zwei Jahre fertig werden. Ich habe John durch Don (Donald Judd) kennen gelernt und war nach Dons Tod (1994) mit ihm und Hannah Green (Johns Frau seit 1979) recht eng befreundet. Dann ist Hannah gestorben und John und ich blieben gewissermassen übrig – wir haben immer noch eine sehr freundschaftliche Verbindung. Wie haben Sie John kennen gelernt?

Kasper König: Ich habe John indirekt durch Jo Baer kennen gelernt. Damals habe ich Jo bei einem Atelierbesuch darauf angesprochen, dass in ihren flachen monochromen Bildern das gleiche Babyblau und Babyrosa auftauchte, das ich in einer Ausstellung der Robert Elkon Gallery in den Bildern eines Malers gesehen hätte, dessen Namen mir entfallen sei. Es stellte sich heraus, dass dieser Maler, John Wesley, damals noch ihr Ehemann war. Jo war ein bisschen pikiert, dass ich Wesleys «Folklore» mit ihrer sehr dezidiert theoretischen Vorstellung in Verbindung brachte. Es gab zwar eine Art symbiotischer Beziehung zwischen den beiden, aber sie hatten trotzdem vollkommen verschiedene Einstellungen. Ich habe John daraufhin in seinem Atelier besucht und war sofort von seinen Arbeiten begeistert. Aus dieser Begeisterung heraus habe ich den Vorschlag gemacht, eine Ausstellung im Moderna Museet in Stockholm zu organisieren, für das ich als Repräsentant in New York war. Die Idee war, vier Künstler unter dem Titel «Jack, Dick, Bill und Cliff» zu zeigen, also ganz bewusst mit verkürzten, GI-mässigen, ame-

---

MARIANNE STOCKEBRAND ist Direktorin der Chinati Foundation in Marfa, Texas; *KASPER KÖNIG* ist Direktor des Kölner Museums Ludwig.

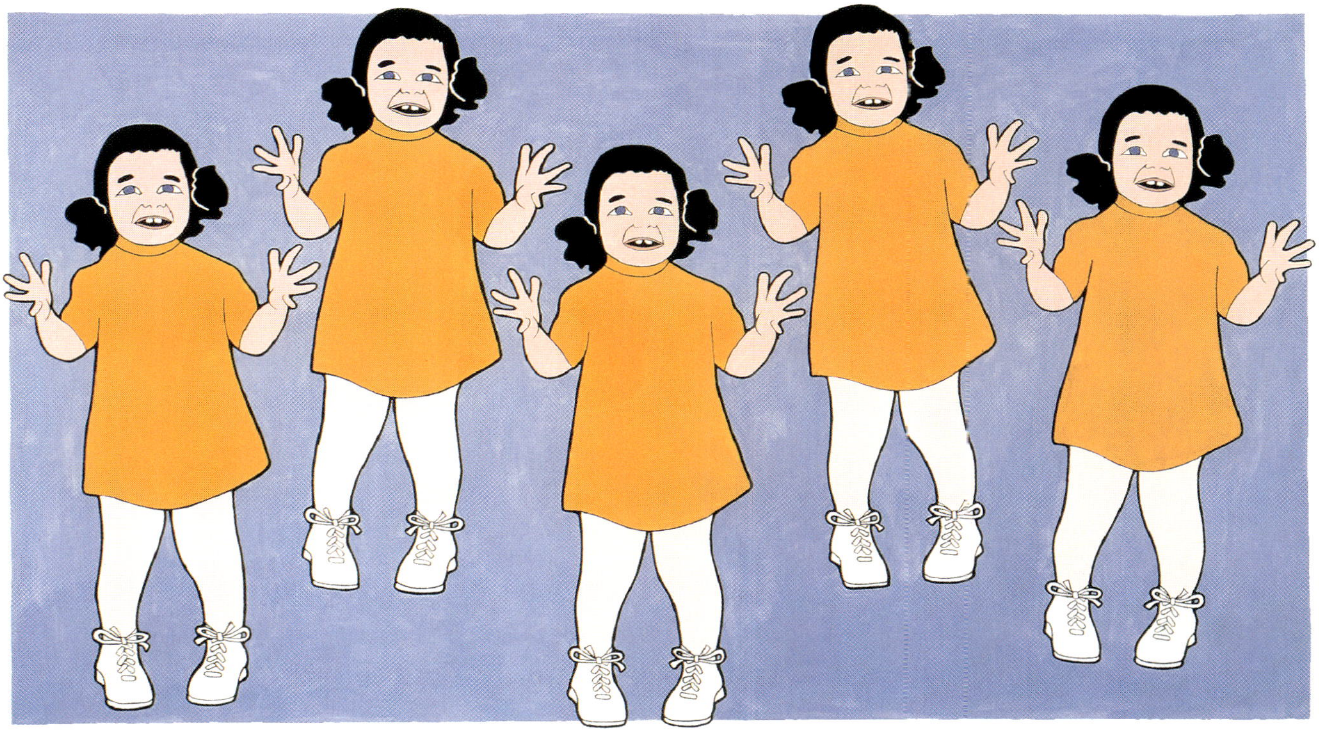

JOHN WESLEY, DADDY'S HOME, 1972, acrylic on canvas, 39 x 65" / PAPAS ZUHAUSE, Acryl auf Leinwand, 99 x 165,1 cm.

rikanischen Namen. Jack war John Wesley, Dick war Richard Artschwager, Bill war William Copley und Cliff war H. C. Westerman. Alle vier Künstler fanden die Idee wunderbar, dass ein junger Europäer amerikanische Colloquialisms aufspürte und sie nicht unter dem folkloristischen Aspekt, sondern auf einer rein ästhetischen Ebene zusammenbringen wollte. Leo Castelli hat daraufhin ein wahnsinniges Donnerwetter abgelassen und gesagt, ich könnte doch nicht wie ein wild gewordener Hund seine ganze kulturpolitische Strategie durcheinander bringen – Richard Artschwager könne man nicht mit Amateurmalern wie Bill Copley oder John Wesley zusammenbringen. Daran scheiterte der Plan. Das Interessante daran war, dass John diese Absage mit einem Achselzucken hingenommen hat und das Ganze überhaupt nicht persönlich nahm. Ich glaube, diese Gelassenheit zeichnet John aus.

Seine Werke wurden in den 60er Jahren in Bezug zur Pop-Art rezipiert, aber dann wurde diese Schublade nicht weiter benutzt, weil seine Arbeiten eben doch nicht Pop-Art sind. Wir haben gerade ein frühes Bild von John Wesley für das Museum Ludwig erworben. Für mich ist interessant, dass alles, was gut und teuer ist aus dieser Periode, hier in der Sammlung Ludwig vertreten ist, aber die sogenannten Aussenseiter, die im Kunsthandel wenig Berücksichtigung gefunden haben, wie zum Beispiel Georg Brecht, Robert Watts, aber auch Maler wie Patrick Caulfield, William Copley oder John Wesley, nicht anzutreffen sind. All diese Künstler haben doch in jedem Fall einen roten Faden gesponnen, der sich jetzt schon durch 40 Jahre zieht.

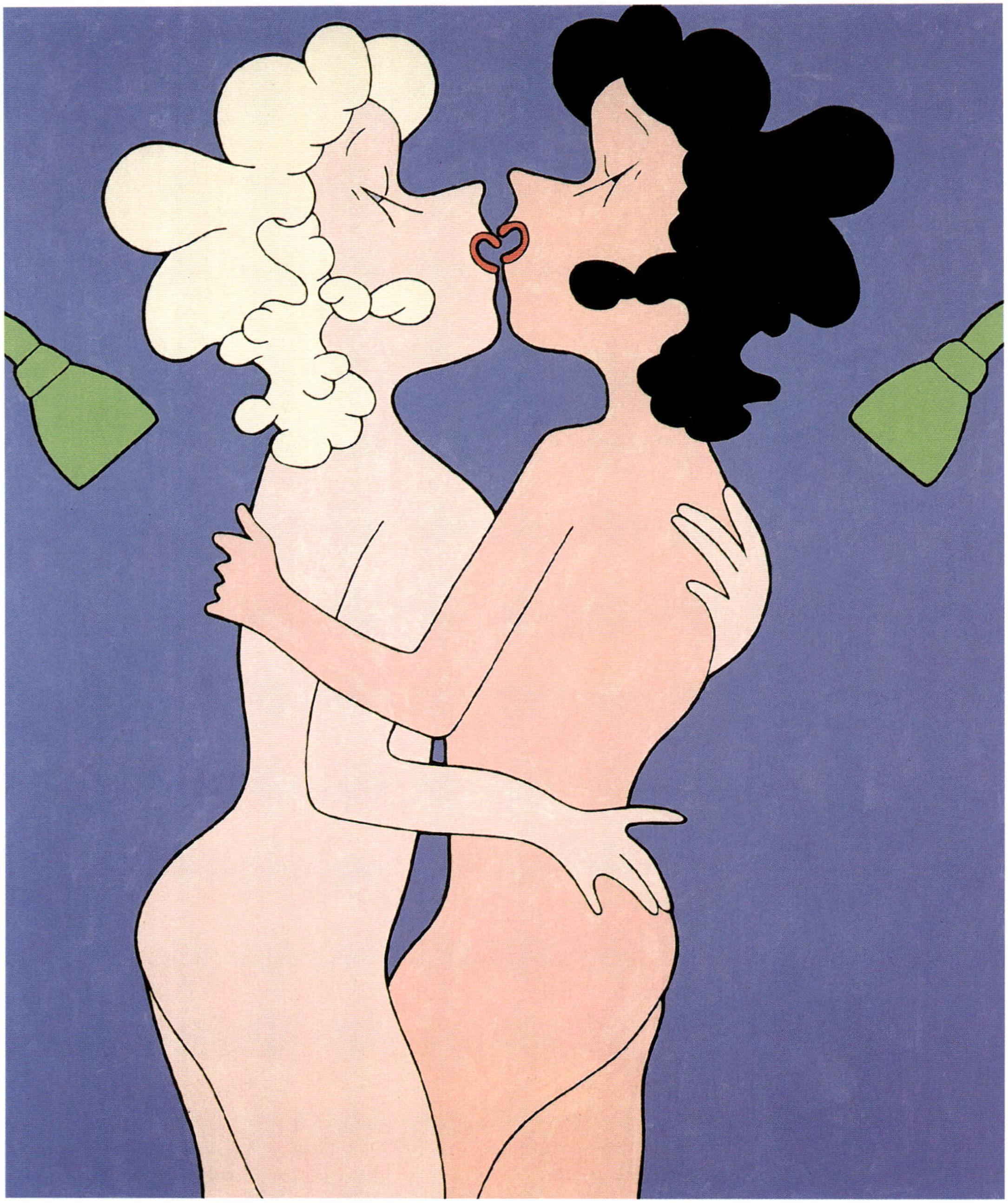

JOHN WESLEY, FIRST KISS: BLONDIE BUMSTEAD AND YNEZ SANCHEZ, 1991, acrylic on canvas, 54 x 44" /
DER ERSTE KUSS: BLONDIE BUMSTEAD UND YNEZ SANCHEZ, Acryl auf Leinwand, 137 x 111,8 cm.

MST: In der Literatur über John wird immer wieder unterstrichen, dass sein Werk einerseits in Verbindung zur Pop-Art steht und sich andererseits von ihr abhebt. Sie haben Recht, dass John auf Kommentare im Allgemeinen sehr gelassen reagiert; ich erinnere mich nicht daran, ihn schon einmal verärgert oder enttäuscht gesehen zu haben. Heutzutage wird er von jungen Künstlern, gerade hier in Amerika, sehr geschätzt und er ist an Kontakten zur jüngeren Generation interessiert. Allerdings hat sein Werk lange Zeit keine Breitenwirkung gehabt; es war hauptsächlich einer kleinen Gruppe von Insidern bekannt. In den letzten Jahren ist aber eine andere Aufmerksamkeit entstanden. So gab es voriges Jahr die Ausstellung im P. S. 1 in New York, die sicherlich noch Nachhall haben wird, und *Artforum* veröffentlichte einen Artikel von Dave Hickey, der ebenso auf grosses Interesse stiess. Ausserdem hat die Galerie Fredericks Freiser sich seit Jahren mit regelmässigen Ausstellungen für sein Werk eingesetzt. Gemessen an seiner künstlerischen Leistung kommt diese Anerkennung allerdings sehr spät und immer noch verhalten, wie an der spärlichen Präsenz in Ausstellungen und Sammlungen amerikanischer Museen zu erkennen ist. Dagegen wurde in Europa mehr für ihn getan, woran Sie selbst grossen Anteil haben. Ich erinnere hier nur an die Ausstellung 1993 im Portikus in Frankfurt, parallel zu der Präsentation in Ludwigsburg, die beide anschliessend im Stedelijk Museum in Amsterdam kombiniert gezeigt wurden.

KK: Das waren sehr verschiedene Ausstellungen. Udo Kittelmann hat damals in Ludwigsburg die Arbeiten auf Papier gezeigt und wir in Frankfurt die Bilder und einige Objekte. Die Arbeiten auf Papier waren eher kammermusikalisch, aber viel reicher im Programm. Insgesamt bekam das plötzlich die Wucht einer Retrospektive – fast sein ganzes Lebenswerk war präsent. Die Bilder machten auf jemand, der sie nicht kannte, fast den Eindruck, als kämen sie auf Umwegen aus dem Wien um 1902. Ein unentdecktes Potenzial also, das man vom ersten Eindruck her kulturell ganz woanders ansiedeln würde. So gibt es in Wesleys Arbeiten immer wieder diese seriellen Momente, die nicht im zeitgenössischen Sinne serielle sind, sondern ganz bewusst den Stil eines Frieses oder Dekors aufgreifen.

MST: Anfangs war dieses serielle Moment eher im Rahmen vorhanden, wenn beispielsweise kleine Bären das Bild wie eine Girlande umrahmen, während sich einer von ihnen in der Bildmitte einem nackten Mädchen nähert. Das Multiplizieren der Bären überführt sie einerseits ins Ornamentale, andrerseits wird das Sujet entschärft und spielerisch kindlich abgehandelt. Die Absurdität weicht einer gefühlvollen Komik. Spätere Bilder bestehen ganz aus Serien von Frauenkörpern, laufenden Männern, Tieren, Bäumen etc., was zwar den Gegenstand betont, ihn aber gleichzeitig unterläuft und ins Ironische verkehrt. John durchbricht solche Reihungen gelegentlich, indem er zum Beispiel einen Tierkopf unter vielen wie in einem Suchbild verkehrt herum platziert oder einen Radfahrer als einzigen einer Gruppe aufschauen lässt. Solche Momente können komisch und grotesk sein, aber sie sind selten ohne Ernst.

KK: Das Sehen ist grundsätzlich wichtig in seinen Arbeiten und wird oft sehr direkt thematisiert. So sieht man zum Beispiel in manchen Bildern ein leeres Möbelstück, dem gegenüber jemand sitzt, der auf das Möbelstück zu gucken scheint. Auf dem Bild ist ein Dialog impliziert, der gar nicht vorhanden ist, denn der eigentliche Dialog findet hier zwischen dem Betrachter und Wesleys Bild statt.

MST: Diese Leere ist ein wesentlicher Aspekt von Johns Werk und wird unterschiedlich thematisiert. So ist in vielen der Bumstead-Bilder die Leere zentraler Gegenstand des Bildes, oder, noch drastischer, in anderen Bildern, die Zimmer zeigen, denen der Fussboden oder ein anderes Raumteil fehlt. Diese Bilder zeichnet eine unglaubliche Melancholie aus.

KK: Ich finde, genau das widerspiegelt Johns Persönlichkeit. Als ich ihn einmal zur Freundschaft, die ihn mit Don verband, befragt habe, sagte er, er hätte Don unter anderem während langen Autofahrten eine Beziehung zur Country- und Westernmusik vermittelt, also ein Gefühl, das so eine Art Tennessee Blues oder Lonesome-Cowboy-Stimmung thematisiert.

MST: Diese und andere Amerikanismen hat er wiederholt aufgegriffen, am deutlichsten in der Verwendung von Cartoons, aber ebenso in der Stilisierung von Figuren, gleichgültig welchen Geschlechts.

KK: Das ist etwas, was Wesley auch ausmacht: Er greift auf eine sehr subtile Weise extreme Tabus auf und bricht sie ohne dabei vordergründig zu sein. So zeigt er zum Beispiel zwei Frauen unterschiedlicher Hautfarbe gemeinsam unter der Dusche oder eine Szene, die auf sehr technische Weise darstellt, wie Donald Duck geboren wird. Als Kind haben mich immer die Zeichnungen auf den Tampon-Packungen meiner Schwestern fasziniert, die auch auf sehr technische Art und Weise illustrierten, wie man einen Tampon einführt. Diesen objektiven Stil überträgt John auf eine ganze liegende Figur, die überhaupt nicht schwanger ist, aber trotzdem Donald Duck gebiert – das ist schon ziemlich böse.

Einerseits zeigen die Bilder diese Distanzierung und Objektivierung, die sicher damit zu tun hat, dass er zeitweilig als technischer Zeichner für die Flugzeugindustrie in Kalifornien gearbeitet hat. Andererseits haben die Arbeiten etwas Psychologisches – seine Bilder, die sich auf Comic-Mythen beziehen, scheint man (ähnlich wie bei vielen zeitgenössischen Arbeiten von Video-Künstlern, die mit einem Zeitbegriff von wenigen Minuten arbeiten) sogar in Sekundenbruchteilen aufzunehmen. Danach bildet sich so etwas wie ein Afterimage im Kopf, das einen dann psychisch beschäftigt, weil es etwas im Hinterkopf, im Unterbewusstsein wachruft. Und ich denke, da ist wiederum die Farbe ganz entscheidend.

MST: In unserer derzeitigen Ausstellung in der Chinati Foundation werden ein Dutzend Gemälde von John gezeigt, die insgesamt ungefähr neun Farben enthalten; seine Palette ist ausgesprochen reduziert. Es gibt ein Grün, drei Blautöne, ein Rosa und ein blasses Rot sowie Ocker, Schwarz und Weiss. Seit etwa 30 Jahren verwendet er fast ausschliesslich diese Farben. Zu Anfang, das heisst in den frühen 60er Jahren, wurden seine Bilder allerdings von einem dunklen Blau beherrscht, das meist mit Weiss und einem Beige-Ton kombiniert war, wodurch die Bilder ruhiger, verhaltener wirkten. Gegen Ende der 60er Jahre ging er dann zu den eben erwähnten Farben über. Es ist wunderbar, dass seine Bilder nie eindimensional wahrgenommen werden können, dass er liebend gern das Gewohnte auf den Kopf stellt und ironisiert. Am meisten fasziniert mich allerdings seine Phantasie. Wie kommt jemand darauf, einen nackten Mann mit Socken und Sockenhaltern hinter Leda, dem Schwan, herjagen zu lassen, oder eine Horde von kreischenden kleinen Mädchen zu Daddys Lieblingen zu nominieren? Dieser Aberwitz ist doch unglaublich. Als ich ihn fragte, wie er auf solche Dinge komme, antwortete er lakonisch, das wisse er auch nicht, er käme halt drauf. Meiner Ansicht nach liegt die Stärke seines Werks darin, dass es sich jeder Etikettierung entzieht und eine Freiheit der Vorstellungskraft verkörpert, die individualistisch ist – ein bisschen verschroben, aber gleichzeitig modern.

KK: Wie war denn die Freundschaft zwischen Don und John?

MST: Beide haben einander sehr geschätzt und viel Spass miteinander gehabt. In den 60er und 70er Jahren haben sie gemeinsam Reisen unternommen. Sie haben den gleichen Blick auf Leben und Politik gehabt.

KK: Ein ganz elementares, vielleicht sehr amerikanisches Gerechtigkeitsgefühl, oder?

MST: Ja, verbunden mit einem starken Sinn für das Individuum. Don war meist strenger als John, der zurückhaltender und gelassener war. Das heisst nicht, dass John nicht auch einen dezidierten Blick hätte, aber er behält ihn als persönlichen Blick für sich, während bei Don die Energie dahinter stand, Dinge durchzusetzen.

KK: Don hat die Dinge mehr reflektiert. Er war dogmatischer und hat seine Überzeugungen zum Programm gemacht.

MST: Don war ausserordentlich motiviert; deshalb konnte er so etwas wie die Chinati Foundation in Marfa realisieren. John ist stets privater gewesen und ist es auch heute noch. Er lebt seit dreissig Jahren in der gleichen Wohnung; es hat sich nicht viel verändert. Diese Kontinuität spiegelt sich in seinem Werk, das ebenso privat geblieben ist. Die Flächigkeit seiner Malweise, das Plakative ist zeitgenössisch und verständlich, die Inhalte sind sein persönlicher Blick auf etwas, das Allgemeingültigkeit hat.

KK: Und dieser Widerspruch führt dann zurück zur Malerei, zur Negation des Thematischen.

(Aufgezeichnet von Jutta Krautscheid)

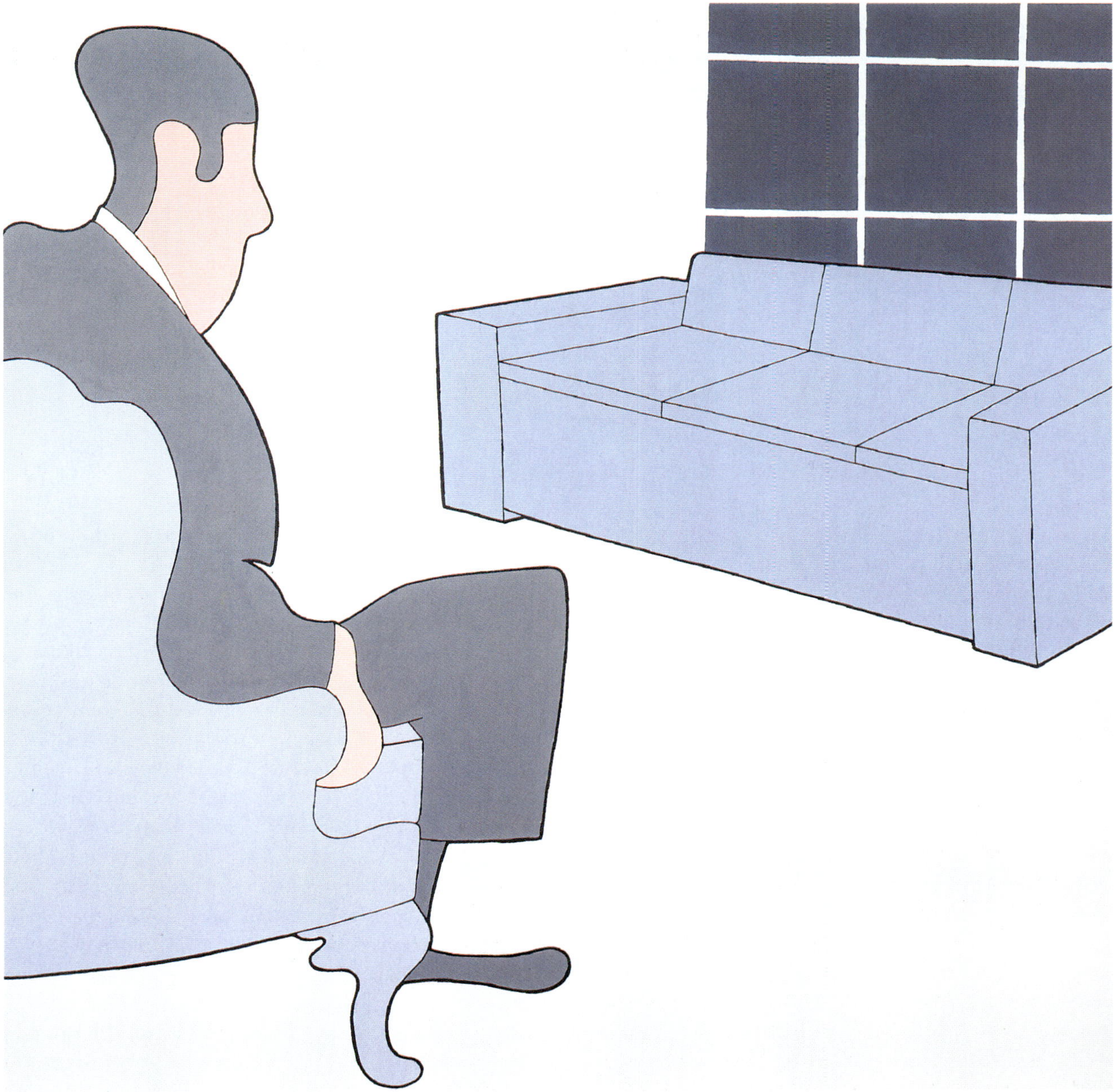

JOHN WESLEY, UNTITLED (MAN REGARDING COUCH), 1987, *acrylic on canvas, 66 x 66"* /
OHNE TITEL (MANN BETRACHTET SOFA), *Acryl auf Leinwand, 167,6 x 167,6 cm.*

KASPER KÖNIG & MARIANNE STOCKEBRAND talk on the telephone about JOHN WESLEY

Marianne Stockebrand: At the Chinati Foundation, here in Marfa, we are currently working on a permanent exhibition of John Wesley's work. Donald Judd had acquired a collection of works by Wesley, which will serve as the basis for our presentation, and John is going to contribute further works, especially early ones. In addition, I plan to acquire several gouaches so that we can show a representative selection. We've chosen one of the old stables not far from Dan Flavin's installations. We've plans to refurbish the building and are in the process of selecting the works that will be on permanent display. We hope to be ready for the public in two years. I met John and his wife, Hannah Green, through Don. We became pretty close friends after Don died in 1994. Then Hannah died and that somehow left the two of us—we're still close friends. How did you meet John?
Kasper König: Indirectly through Jo Baer, his first wife. I was visiting her studio and commented on the fact that I had seen the same baby blue and baby pink of her flat monochrome paintings in an exhibition at the Robert Elkon Gallery of work by an artist whose name I'd forgotten. It turned out that the artist, John Wesley, was her husband then. The idea that I could link Wesley's "folklore" with her decidedly theoretical approach didn't go over too well. There was a kind of symbiotic relationship between the two of them, although their approaches were diametrically opposed. Then when I visited Wesley at his studio, I was enthralled. I suggested organizing a show at the Moderna Museet in Stockholm, which I was then representing in New York. It was going to be called "Jack, Dick, Bill, and Cliff"—intentionally staccato, GI-like American names. Jack was John Wesley, Dick was Richard Artschwager, Bill was William Copley, and Cliff was H. C. Westerman. All four artists thought it was wonderful that a young European wanted to find out about American colloquialisms—not as a folkloristic phenomenon but on a purely aesthetic level. Leo Castelli had a fit. He said I couldn't run around like a mad dog, making a mess of an entire cultural strategy. There was no way Richard Artschwager could be related to amateur painters like Bill Copley or John Wesley. So the project fell through. John just shrugged his shoulders when it failed; he didn't take it personally. I think that's typical of him.

In the sixties his work was associated with Pop art but then the critics stopped using that pigeonhole because it obviously didn't fit. We've just acquired an early work for the Ludwig Museum. Interestingly you'll find everything that's good and expensive represented here in the Ludwig collection but nothing

---

MARIANNE STOCKEBRAND is the director of the Chinati Foundation in Marfa, Texas; *KASPER KÖNIG* is the director of the Museum Ludwig, Cologne.

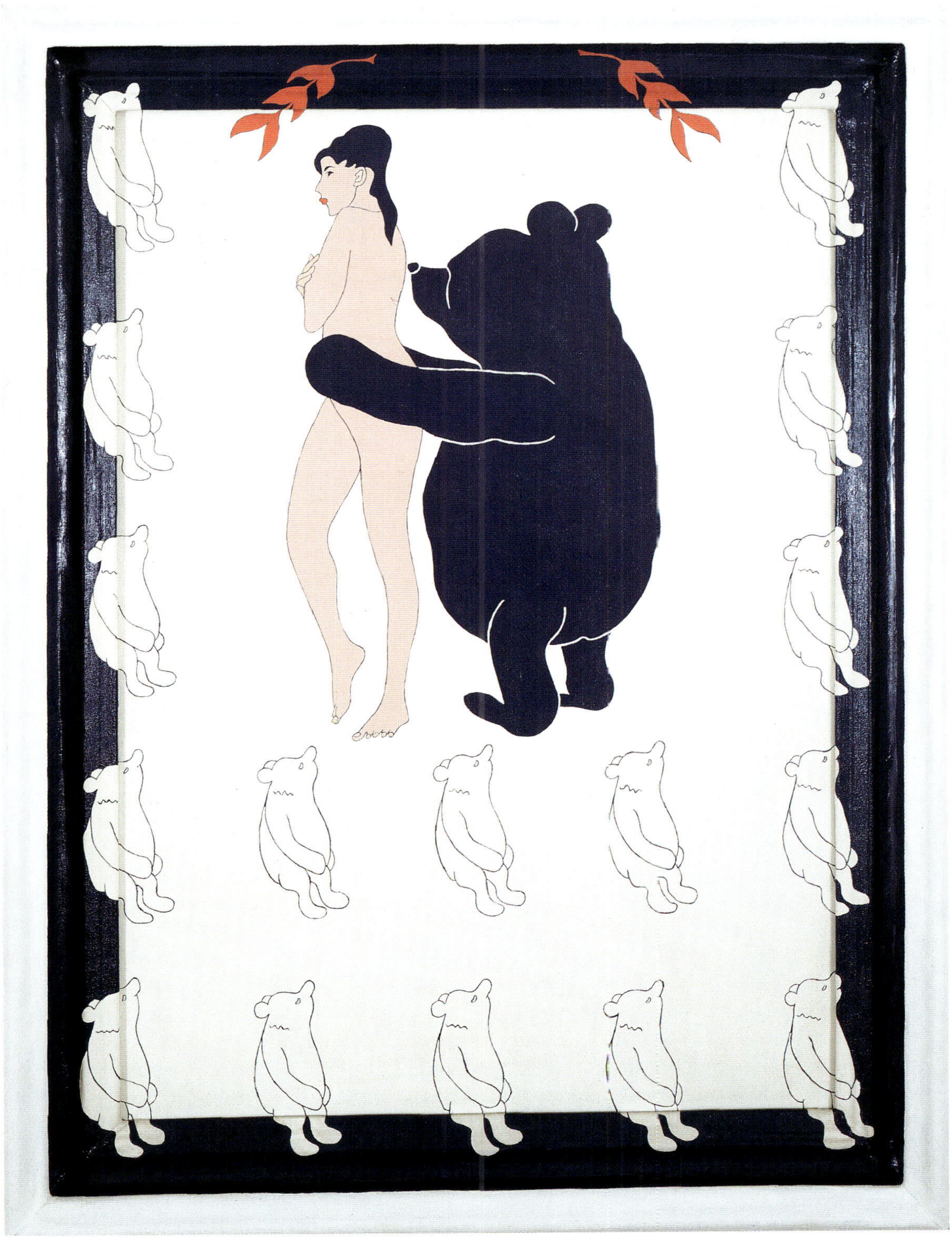

JOHN WESLEY, POOH, 1965, Duco and acrylic on canvas and frame, 36 x 48" /
PUH, Lackfarbe und Acryl auf Leinwand und Rahmen, 91,4 x 122 cm.

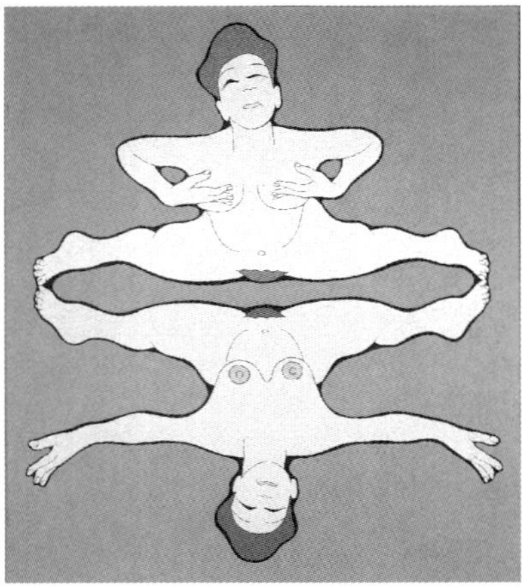

JOHN WESLEY, FLIGHT, 1968, acrylic on canvas, 39 x 33 1/2" / FLUG, Acryl auf Leinwand, 99 x 85 cm.

by the so-called outsiders, especially those who haven't attracted much attention in the art trade, people like Georg Brecht, Robert Watts, or painters like Patrick Caulfield, William Copley, and John Wesley. Yet all of these artists run like a red thread through the past 40 years.

MST: Critical writing on John emphasizes that his work is related to Pop art, yet also set apart from it. But you're right that John was unaffected by comments on his work. I can't ever remember him being angry or disappointed. Today he's highly appreciated by younger artists, especially here in the States, and he's interested in individual contact with the younger generation. But for a long time his work did not reach a broad public; it was appreciated mainly by a small group of insiders. Lately, it's begun to attract more attention. Last year there was the exhibition at P.S.1 in Queens, which will certainly have a long-term influence, and *Artforum* published an article by Dave Hickey, which also caught the public eye. In addition the Fredericks Freiser Gallery has been mounting exhibitions of his work for years. But compared to his artistic achievements, recognition of Wesley's contribution has come very late and is still sparing, as illustrated by his still modest presence in collections and exhibitions, at least in America. Europe has done more for him, and you've been instrumental in this. For instance, the 1993 exhibition at Portikus in Frankfurt that ran parallel to the presentation in Ludwigsburg, with both shows subsequently combined in the Stedelijk Museum in Amsterdam.

KK: They were two very different exhibitions. In Ludwigsburg Udo Kittelmann presented works on paper while here in Frankfurt we showed his paintings and a few objects. The works on paper were like chamber music but it was a much richer program. Suddenly, in combination, the whole thing acquired the thrust of a retrospective. Practically his entire lifework was on view. To someone who'd never seen them before, his paintings almost looked as if they might have detoured through Vienna around 1902. A great deal of unexplored potential lay in the fact that, at first sight, the work could be placed in an entirely different cultural context. There are always serial aspects in Wesley's art, but it's not a contemporary seriality because he intentionally adopts the style of a frieze or of ornamentation.

MST: Initially the serial aspect was restricted to the margins, for example little bears framing the picture like a garland, with one of them approaching a nude girl in the middle of the picture. The multiplication of the bears makes them ornamental, but it also tones down the subject matter and gives it a playfully childlike feel. Absurdity gives way to compassionate, kindhearted comedy. Later pictures consist completely of series of women's bodies, running men, animals, trees, etc., which emphasizes the subject matter but also undermines it and gives it an ironic twist. Occasionally John will interrupt a series by turning an animal's head the wrong way around like a mug shot or by having one cyclist in a group looking up from his bike. The effect may be comic and grotesque but there's almost always a serious undertone.

KK: Seeing is very important in his oeuvre. In fact, he often addresses it head on. For example, when he paints a piece of furniture with someone standing opposite, who seems to be looking at it. A dialogue is implied that isn't actually in the picture itself because it takes place between the viewer and Wesley's painting.

MST: This emptiness is an essential aspect and John deals with it in different ways. In a number of the Bumstead paintings, it's actually the main subject matter of the picture. It's even more drastic in other paintings that show rooms with something missing—the floor for instance. These paintings are filled with incredible melancholy.

KK: I think that's exactly what John's personality is like. Once, when I asked him about his friendship with Don, he told me that on long car rides together, he used to play Country and Western music, which conveys a feeling of Tennessee Blues or the Lonesome Cowboy.

MST: He keeps coming back to Americanisms of that kind—most conspicuously in the use of cartoons but also in his stylized figures, regardless of gender.

KK: That's also typical of Wesley: he tackles the most ingrained taboos with extreme subtlety and breaks them without being superficial about it. Like his painting of two women with different skin colors, taking a shower together, or his very technical rendition of how Donald Duck was born. As a child I was fascinated by the drawings on my sister's packages of tampons, with their extremely technical way of illustrating how they had to be inserted. John uses this pseudo-objective style in his painting of a reclining figure who does not look the least pregnant although she's giving birth to Donald Duck—that's going pretty far.

So, on one hand, a detachment and objectivity, which may well go back to the days when Wesley worked as an aeronautics draftsman in California. On the other hand, the pictures have a psychological impact. His images, indebted to the myths of comics, can be perceived in a fraction of a second (much like many contemporary video works that limit the time concept to just a few minutes). But then something like an afterimage sets in, that you keep thinking about because it stirs something in the back of your mind, in the subconscious. I think color probably plays a decisive role in this as well.

MST: In our current exhibition at the Chinati Foundation, a dozen of John's paintings are on view, presenting a total of about nine colors; his palette is extremely reduced. There's one green, three shades of blue, one pink and one pale red, as well as ochre, black, and white. His palette has basically been made up of these colors for the past 30 years, although at first, that is in the early sixties, a dark blue dominated his pictures, mostly in combination with white and a shade of beige, making the paintings quieter and more low-key. Then in the late sixties he started shifting to the colors I mentioned above. It's wonderful that his paintings can never be perceived one-dimensionally, that he loves upsetting and ironizing customary perception. But what fascinates me most is his imagination. What makes someone think of having a nude male wearing only socks, and sock suspenders, chase after Leda the swan, or of nominating a horde of screeching girls as Daddy's favorites? This madness is just incredible. When I asked him what makes him think of these things, he said laconically that he didn't know, they just came to him. To my mind the strength in John's work lies in the fact that he eludes classification, and in the freedom of his screwball imagination—so idiosyncratic and still so modern.

KK: What about the friendship between Don and John?

MST: They really appreciated each other and had a lot of fun, especially on trips together in the sixties and seventies. They had similar views on life and politics.

KK: Like a very elementary, American sense of justice, wouldn't you say?

MST: Yes, and linked with a strong respect for the individual. Don was usually stricter than John, who was more reserved and casual, relaxed. Which does not mean that John doesn't have a decided view but he keeps it to himself as a personal view while with Don there was an energy to push things.

KK: Don thought things through. He was more dogmatic and made a program out of his convictions.

MST: Don was extremely motivated, which enabled him to initiate a project like the Chinati Foundation in Marfa. John has always been a more private person and he still is. He's been living in the same apartment for thirty years; not much has changed. This continuity is mirrored in his work, which has remained equally personal. The flat, poster-like gesture of his painting is contemporary and accessible. And his content represents a personal take on universal issues.

KK: This contradiction leads back to painting, to the negation of subject matter.

*(Transcribed by Jutta Krautscheid/
Translation: Catherine Schelbert)*

Débordement de VIE

BRUCE HAINLEY

J'aime war eines der Dinge, die er mir beibrachte. Es war schwierig auszusprechen, aber nicht so schwierig wie je t'aime. Er sagte es leichthin, so wie er einen Fisch häutete. Er sagte es leichthin zu mir und all den übrigen Squaws, mit denen er verheiratet war. Mir blieb es im Hals stecken, bis Pomp kam. Pomp, der erstgeborene winzige Pomp, in weiche Windeln gewickelte Pomp, im Traggestell auf meinen Rücken gepackte Pomp. Je t'aime lernte ich mit Pomp. Kleiner Jean Baptiste Charbonneau. Zu ihm sagte ich immer wieder je t'aime auf dem Weg, dem langen Weg zum Pazifik. Pomp war die bessere Forschungsexpedition. Aber das kam später.

Je t'aime war eines der schwierigen Dinge, die ich auszusprechen lernte, und oui. Toussaints Widerstand mir beizubringen, wie man non sagt, nahm geradezu japanische Formen an. Es spielte keine Rolle. Ich sagte oui und machte einfach nicht, was immer es war, wozu ich oui sagen sollte. Er war gar nicht so schlimm. Er schlug mich manchmal, wenn er zu viel trank, aber ich hatte schon Schlimmeres erlebt. Er tat, was er tat. Er war ein Fallensteller und ich sass für einige Zeit in der Falle. Er kaufte mich oder gewann mich durch eine Wette, bei der es darum ging, ob er ein Ziel auf so und so viele Schritt Entfernung treffen könne oder nicht, und wenn er nicht betrunken war, konnte er das sehr wohl, tat es auch und gewann mich. Tant pis. Ich war ja schon einmal als Schoschonenprinzessin von einem gegnerischen Stamm entführt und als Leibeigene an einen anderen Stamm verkauft worden. Eine Leibeigene in North Dakota, Leibeigene mit zwölf. Aber ich habe auch noch Schlimmeres gesehen. Ich lernte viel, weil ich an einem Ort bleiben musste. Die Schoschonen zogen herum und ich vermisste das Herumziehen, aber weil ich bleiben musste, pflanzte ich alles Mögliche und beobachtete, wie es wuchs. Les fleurs jaunes der Kürbisse und die gelben Kürbisse selbst. J'aime les fleurs jaunes et les oiseaux. Alles war so unglaublich grün.

Ich kapierte es nie, wenn William Clark den unbesehenen Kauf von Louisiana zu erklären versuchte.[1)]

BRUCE HAINLEY ist redaktioneller Mitarbeiter von *Artforum* sowie freier Kurator.

Es war ein Übersetzungsproblem. Meriwether Lewis ignorierte mich, aber William Clark war nett. Er benannte einen Fluss nach mir. Sechzehn oder so, mit Pomp und als einzige Frau im Expeditionskorps, aber Clark war nett. Ich war hilfreich. Ich hatte dazugelernt. Als ich meinen Bruder nach so vielen Jahren und so vielen tant pis wiedersah, war das auch nett. Er war Häuptling; ich war schwesterliche Verwandtschaft. Keine Pferde und kein guter Führer durch die Bitterroot-Berge ohne mich. Es war hart, wäre aber noch härter gewesen ohne mich und den kleinen Pomp. Ich war bei den ersten, die die Riesenfische und das weite Wasser erblickten, den Pazifik. Man kann sich nicht vorstellen, was dieser Anblick bedeutete nach so viel Grün. Ich war stolz wie ein Rockstar, auf meinem Rücken der kleine Pomp und vor mir diese Weite, nichts als Wasser, so weit das Auge reichte.

Und dann. Wie versprochen zog William Clark den kleinen Pomp wie sein eigenes Kind auf. Ich entwischte. Dann starb ich entweder wenige Jahre später oder lebte noch lange. Wie das Datum meiner Geburt ist auch nicht bekannt, wann ich starb. Jahre später fertigte William Clark eine Liste über den Verbleib aller Expeditionsteilnehmer an und schrieb über mich: «Se car ja we au – Gestorben». An Sumpffieber, sagt man. Tant pis. Je t'aime.

Ich habe existiert. Dies ist ein Bild der Freude über meine Existenz. Es war mehr als nur existieren. Ich hatte Schlimmeres gesehen. Ich lebte. Oui. Sommernachmittag. So viel Grün. Der Himmel so hellblau wie je t'aime. Kein tant pis hier. Zwei Grün-, zwei Blautöne und ich in meinem schwarzen Einteiler in die Luft springend. Nicht aufgehoben, sondern in einem ekstatischen Schwebezustand festgehalten. Man beachte, dass nur mein Körper eine Umrisslinie hat. Sie ist das Einzige, was mein débordement de joie zu halten vermag. Viele Bilder des Künstlers verwenden diese Art von Eindämmung der Freude.

Eindämmung oui, mais dann auch die Tatsache, dass es noch viele ebenso seltsame Dinge gibt wie dieses plötzliche Entzücken. Da gab es einen jungen Mandan-Fährtensucher, der in mir dasselbe Gefühl auslöste. Er hatte einen wunderhübschen Körper. Es war das Entzücken über die Art, wie seine Hautsilhouette ihn umhüllte, das mich begreifen liess, dass niemand den Körper versteht und was in ihm steckt. Wie schön ist es, sich daran zu reiben, aber auch wie seltsam. Der Blick reibt sich an meiner springenden Silhouette, aber was sagt mir, dass dies ein Körper ist?

Ich mag die Art, wie der Künstler all diese Seltsamkeiten aufzeigt. Was tue ich? Wie bringe ich meinen Körper in diese Position? Wann hatte ich Zeit, solch akrobatische Kunststücke zu lernen? Vielleicht weniger aufzeigt als darstellt. Ich bin eine Darstellung. Nicht die historische *Se car ja we au*, die immer etwas Zufälliges bleiben wird, sondern die repräsentative Prinzessin. Ich überspringe den Snake River. Ich überspringe die Hecke. Ich springe, eine wirbelnde Chiffre überschäumender Lebensfreude. Chiffre, weil wie gesagt niemand den Körper, die Persönlichkeit wiederzugeben weiss. Es ist, wie wenn man den Pazifik zum ersten Mal erblickt. Überwältigend. Gigantische Fische. Schwindel erregend. Es gibt keine Worte dafür.

J'aime die Tatsache, dass der Künstler mich auswählte, um die berühmten Tricks rund um die Zweihundertjahrfeier zu repräsentieren. Man sieht meine Freude. Mein Springen. Ferner j'aime die Tatsache, dass weit und breit niemand sonst zu sehen ist. Es steht jedem und jeder frei, sich zu fragen, wie mein Name auszusprechen ist, wer ich war und wie wenig man eigentlich von mir weiss (wann ich geboren wurde, wann ich starb) und ob die Tatsache, dass niemand sonst zu sehen ist, vielleicht mit dem Völkermord zusammenhängt. Zu der Zeit, als das Bild entstand, lief im Fernsehen ein Werbespot, in welchem der Häuptling eines anderen Stammes über die Umweltzerstörung weinte. Man sieht nicht, ob ich weine oder nicht. Ob ich gar lächle beim Springen. Was hat mich zum Sprung veranlasst? Was geschieht, wenn und falls ich wieder auf die Erde zurückkehre? J'aime, dass man sich all diese Fragen stellen kann oder auch nicht. Es ist alles da, zum Greifen nah. Es ist da, ob man will oder nicht. Zweihundert Jahre sind keine sehr lange Zeit, aber es ist lange genug für so viel Freude und so viel Nichtfreude. Débordements. Das ist ein Teil der Bedeutung des Bildes, meiner Bedeutung. Man müsste schon geistig zurückgeblieben sein, um sich nicht zu fragen, was dieses Bild, oder jedes andere, bedeuten könnte. Und wie. J'aime die Grün- und Blautöne, mein Springen, aber j'aime aussi, was ich und mein Bild bedeuten und wie das geschieht. Vielleicht sogar noch mehr.

Sex ist ein Aspekt. Die Prinzessin ist wieder zurück. Hübsches Beutestück. Wie die kleinen Kontorsionistinnen im Zirkus vollführe ich Dinge mit meinem Körper, die euch Schweissperlen auf die Stirn treiben. Ich habe meine Zeit wie dieses Bild und jedes andere damit verbracht, ein konsumierbares Sexualobjekt zu sein. Tant pis. Jeder und jede fühlt sich von Zeit zu Zeit ganz gern mal als Objekt. Der Blick in den Augen jenes Fährtensuchers, als er bemerkte, dass ich ihn bemerkte. Le feu dans ses yeux. Il eut le feu sacré. Ihr solltet sehen, was ich jenseits der grünen Hecke erspähen kann. Zwei geile Krieger, die miteinander um die Wette keuchen wie geschmeidige Tiere, und noch mehr.

Die Überraschung besteht darin, dass die Überraschung, ist sie erst einmal vorbei, noch immer da ist. Sogar ich ertappe mich dabei, dass ich dieses Bild anschaue und nicht als Porträt meiner selbst erkenne. Der Perlmutterglanz in Muscheln oder in der Dämmerung hat mir immer eine ähnliche Freude bereitet, Überraschung. Das Blau des Himmels und das ungesäumte grüne Band unter der Hecke und auch das gesäumte Grün unterhalb des Flusses enthalten eine Spur solcher Perlmuttfreude. Die Überraschung besteht darin, dass das Gute noch existiert oder die Schönheit, trotz allem. Natürlich hat es nie einfach in und aus sich selbst existiert. Nichts tut das. William Clark sagte jeweils etwas über Gewalt und Veilchen. Und lachte dann. Stilles Herz der Finsternis. Es irritierte das Expeditionskorps immer, wenn ich lachte, wie wenn das nicht mit zu ihrem Entdeckungsauftrag gehörte. Aber es gehörte dazu. J'aime, dass das so war und immer noch ist.

Je suis ein Kompass der Freude.

(Übersetzung: Susanne Schmidt)

1) *Louisiana Purchase:* 1803 kauften die Vereinigten Staaten Napoleon das noch unerforschte Gebiet für 15 Mio. Dollar ab. Das damalige Louisiana war um einiges grösser als der heutige Bundesstaat. *Meriwether Lewis* und *William Clark* waren die Leiter der ersten Expedition durch dieses Gebiet, die bis zum Pazifik und wieder zurück nach St. Louis führte (Mai 1804 – September 1806).

JOHN WESLEY, *PRINCESS SACAJAWEA CROSSING THE SNAKE*, 1976, *acrylic on canvas, 42 x 50"* / PRINZESSIN SACAJAWEA ÜBERQUERT DEN SNAKE RIVER, *Acryl auf Leinwand, 106,7 x 127 cm.*
(ALL PHOTOS: FREDERICKS FREISER GALLERY, NEW YORK)

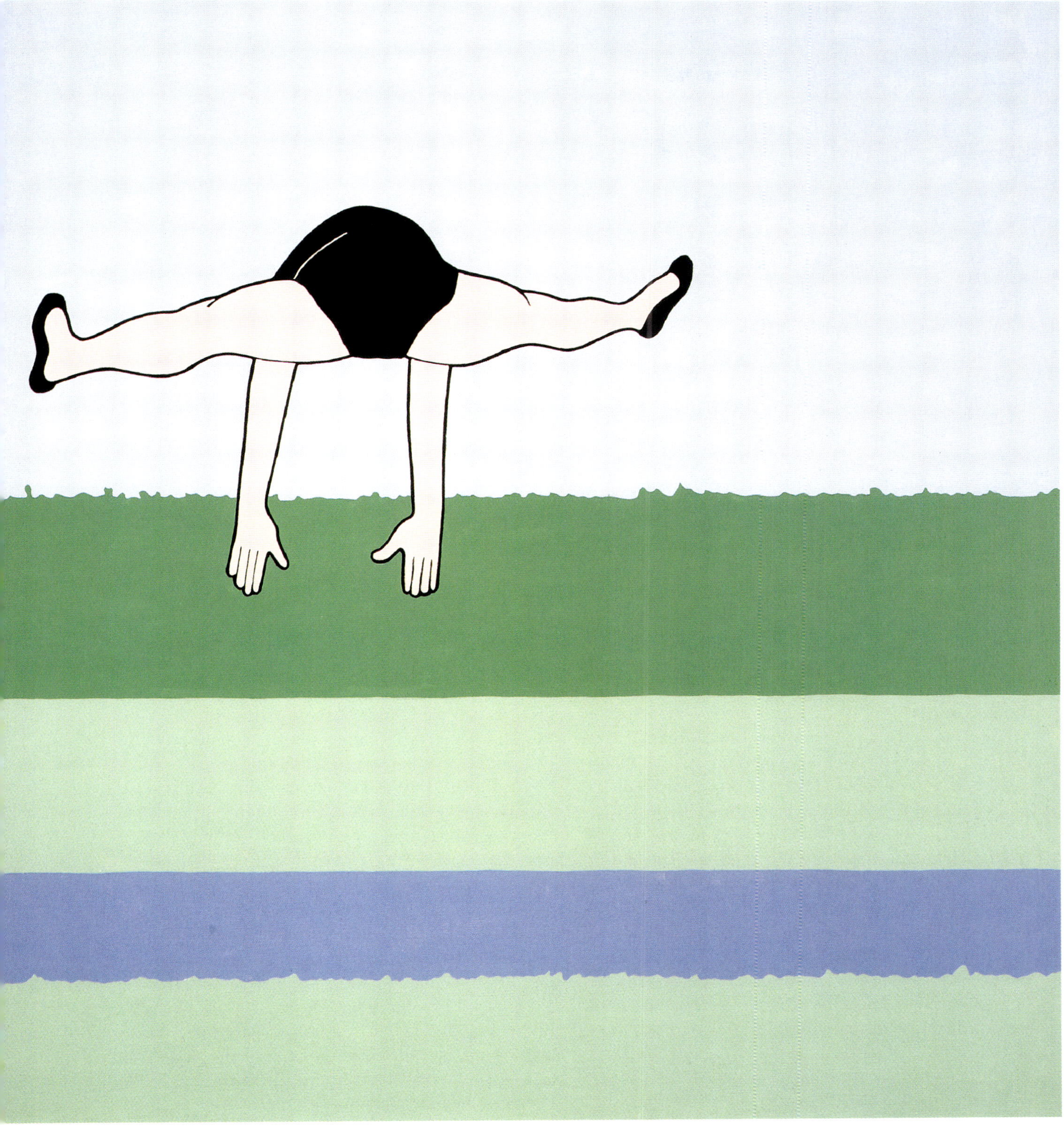

Débordement de VIE

BRUCE HAINLEY

J'aime was one of the things he taught me. It was hard to say, but not as hard as je t'aime. He said it easily, the way he skinned a fish. He said it easily to me and to the other squaws who were his wives. It stuck in my throat until Pomp arrived. Firstborn Pomp tiny Pomp wrapped in soft swaddling Pomp strapped on a cradle board to my back Pomp. Je t'aime I understood with Pomp. Petit Jean Baptiste Charbonneau. I said je t'aime to him so many times as we made the way the long way to the Pacific. Pomp was a better corps of discovery. But that was later.

Je t'aime was one of the hard things I learned to say and oui. Toussaint was almost Japanese in his resistance to teaching me a way to say non. It didn't matter. I said oui and just didn't do whatever it was I was supposed to say oui to. He wasn't that bad. He hit me sometimes when he drank too much but I've known worse. He did what he did. He was a trapper and I for some time was trapped. He bought me or won me in a bet as to whether or not he could shoot a mark at so many paces and when he wasn't drunk he could and did winning me. Tant pis. I'd already been a Shoshone princess captured by a rival tribe and sold as a slave to another. A slave in North Dakota slave by the time I was twelve. I've seen worse than that too. I learned much by having to stay in one place. The Shoshone moved and I missed moving, but staying I planted things and watched them grow. Les fleurs jaunes of the squash and the yellow squash themselves. J'aime les fleurs jaunes et les oiseaux. Everything was so incredibly green.

I never understood when William Clark tried to explain the Louisiana Purchase bought sight unseen. It was a translation problem. Meriwether Lewis ignored me, but William Clark was nice. He named a river for me. Sixteen or so with Pomp and the only woman amongst the Corps of Discovery, but Clark was nice. I helped. I'd learned. When I saw my brother again after so many years and so much tant pis it was nice too. He was chief; I was sororal liaison. No horses and no good guide without me across the Bitterroots. It was hard but would have been harder without me and little Pomp. I was in the first group to see the monstrous fish and the great waters, the Pacific. You can't imagine seeing it after so much

BRUCE HAINLEY is a contributing editor of *Artforum* and an independent curator.

green. I felt as proud as a rock star little Pomp on my back in front of so much space, waters until the eye couldn't see.

And then. William Clark as he promised raised little Pomp as his own. Escaped him. Then I either died not many years after or lived a long time. As with the date of my birth when I died isn't known. Years later William Clark made a list of all the Corps of Discovery's whereabouts and concerning me he wrote: "Se car ja we au—Dead." They say of putrid fever. Tant pis. Je t'aime.

I existed. This is a painting of the joy of my existence. It was more than just existing. I'd seen worse. I lived. Oui. Summer afternoon. So much green. The sky the bright blue of je t'aime. No tant pis here. Two greens, two blues, and me in my black unitard jumping. Not suspended but caught in ecstatic suspension. Notice how only my body has an outline. It's the only thing which contains my débordement de joie. Many of the artist's paintings deploy such joy containment.

Containment oui mais then the fact that so much is strange the way sudden delight can be. There was a young Mandan scout who gave me that feeling. He had such a pretty body. It was the delight at the way his skin outline hung on him that first taught me that no one understands the body and what it contains. How nice it is to rub up against but how strange. Looking rubs up against my outline jumping but tell me that's a body.

I like the way the artist signifies all this strangeness. What am I doing? How do I get my body into that position? When did I have time to learn such acrobatics? Perhaps not signifies but represents. I am a representation. Not the historical *Se car ja we au*, who will remain a contingency, but the representational Princess. I jump the Snake. I jump the hedge. I jump, a pinwheeled cipher of exuberance. Cipher because no one, as I said, no one knows how to convey the body, the personhood. It's like seeing the Pacific for the first time. Overwhelming. Monstrous fish. Dazzling. There are no words.

J'aime the fact that the artist chose me to represent the celebrated machinations of the Bicentennial. You have my joy. My jumping. Then j'aime the fact that no one else is to be seen anywhere. You are free to consider the invocation of my name and who I was and how little is actually known about me (when I was born, when I died) and that no one else's being seen in relation to genocide. Around the time the painting was painted there was a television commercial with a chief of another tribe crying about the environment. You can't see whether I'm crying or not. Whether I'm smiling as I'm jumping. What happened to cause me to jump? What happens when and if I ever return to earth? J'aime that you are free to consider any or all of this or not. It's there easily. It's there whether you want it to be or not. Two hundred years isn't a very long time but it's long enough for so much joy and so much not joy. Débordements. This is part of the painting's meaning, my meaning. You'd have to be a mental retard to not think about what this painting, like any other, means. And how. J'aime the greens and blues, my jumping, mais j'aime how and what I and my painting mean aussi. Perhaps more.

There is a sex part. Princess's got back. Fine booty. Like the little contortionists dans le cirque I do things with my body to explain the beads of sweat on your forehead. I've spent my time, like this painting, like any, being an erotic commodity. Tant pis. Everyone likes to feel like an object sometimes. The look in that scout's eyes when he noticed me noticing him. Le feu dans ses yeux. Il eut le feu sacré. You should see the goings-on I can see over the verdant hedge. Two braves in heat panting together like sleek beasts and more.

The surprise is that the surprise, once past, is always there. Even I catch myself looking at this painting not recognizing it as a portrait of myself. Pearlescence in shells or in the dawn has always given me a similar pleasure, surprise. The blue in the sky and the green band, unruched, below the hedge and the ruched green one below the river contain an admixture of such pearl pleasure. The surprise is that goodness still exists, or beauty, despite everything else. Of course it never existed just in and of itself. Nothing does. William Clark used to say something about the violence and the violets. And then he would laugh. Quiet heart of darkness. It always disconcerted the Corps of Discovery when I laughed as if it weren't part of what they were discovering. But it was. J'aime that it was and is still.

Je suis the joy compass.

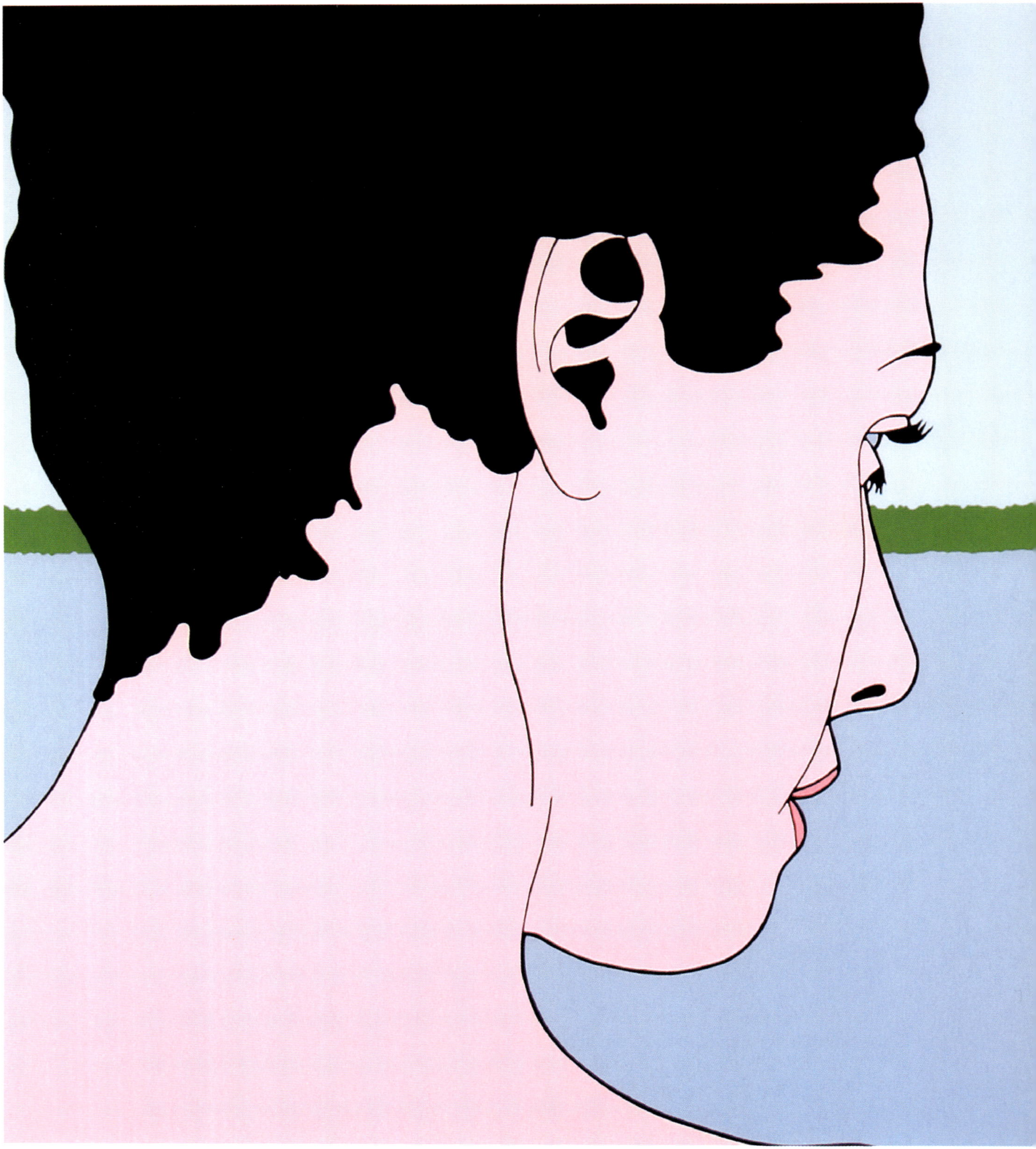

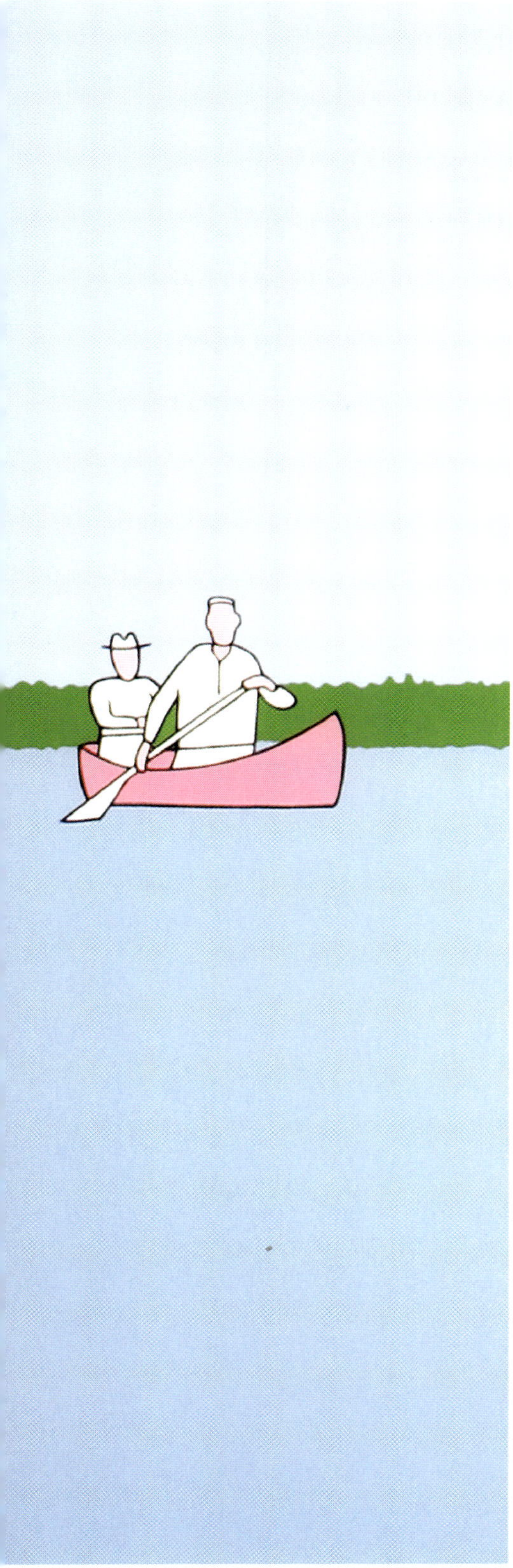

(PHOTO: MANCIA/BODMER, FBM STUDIO)

EDITION FOR PARKETT

JOHN WESLEY
BOYFRIENDS, 2001

6-color silkscreen on Coventry 290 gm^2

Image size 28 x 35"; paper size 31 x 38"

Printed by Bob Blanton, Brand X Editions, New York

Edition of 70, signed and numbered

Siebdruck (6 Farben) auf Coventry 290 gm^2

Bild 71 x 89 cm; Papierformat 87,7 x 96,5 cm

Gedruckt von Bob Blanton, Brand X Editions, New York

Auflage: 70, signiert und nummeriert

Thomas

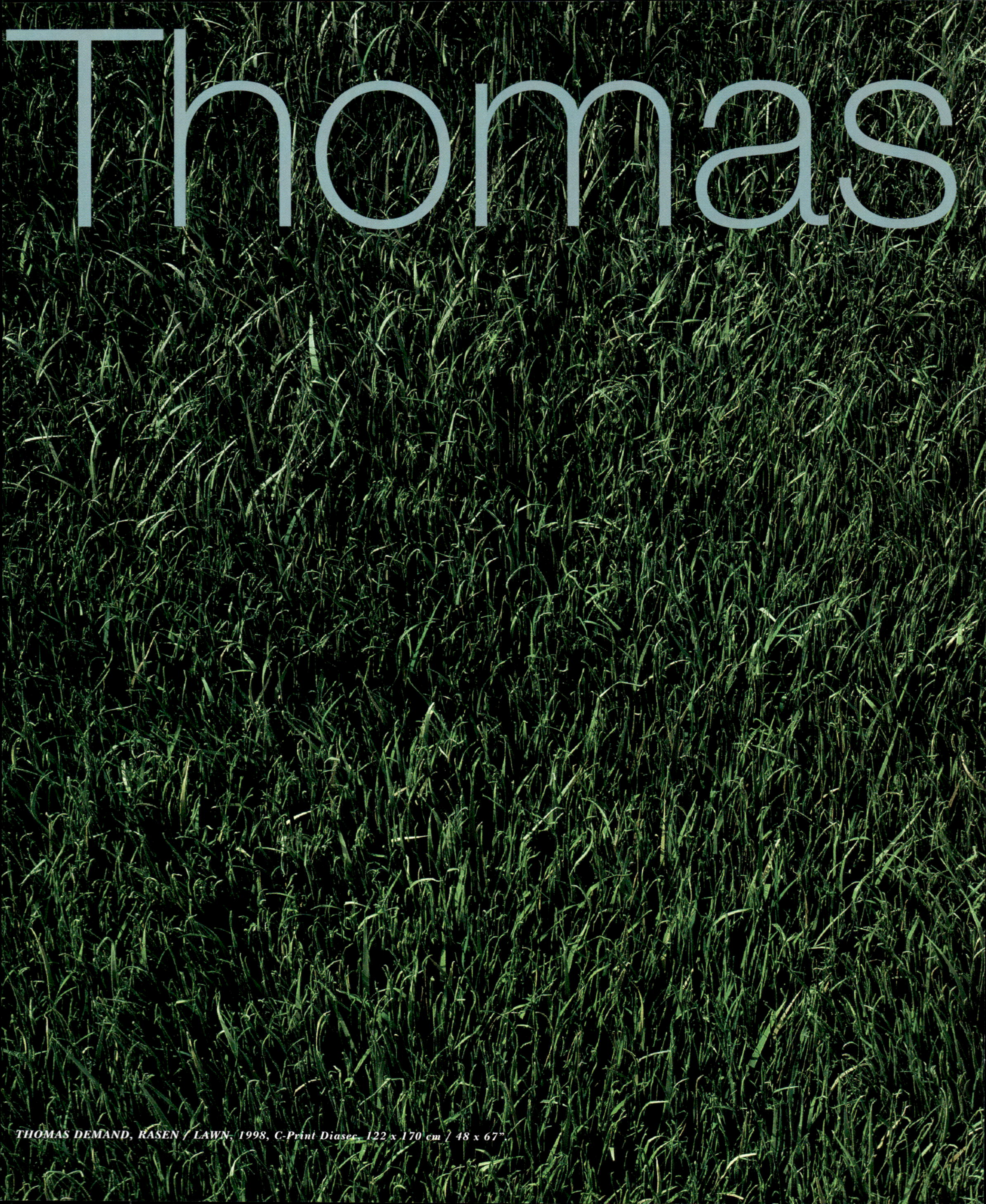

THOMAS DEMAND, RASEN / LAWN, 1998, C-Print Diasec, 122 x 170 cm / 48 x 67".

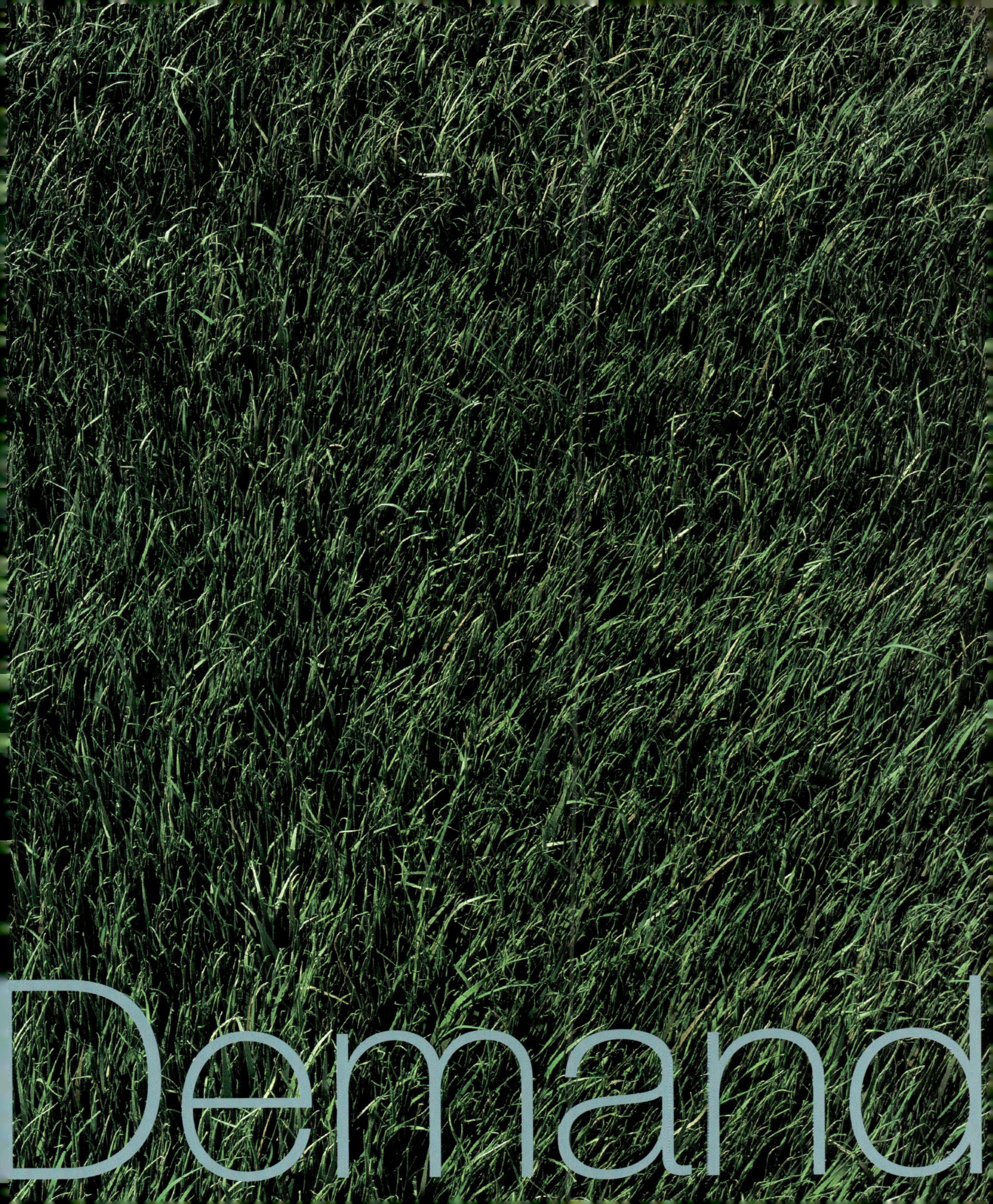
Demand

ADRIAN SEARLE

DOUBT THE DAY

Doubt the day, the view from the window, then the window then the room. The shadows are a test, bent and folded into place, measuring themselves against the walls. They at least seem real enough. But the unfurled blue of the sky, the grass underfoot, the near and distant buildings, the unpeopled balconies? Looking down into the yellow cone of lamplight, or at the papers strewn about, there is less to see the more one looks. Is this a disappointment? Only if you imagine, foolishly, that were you to peer closely enough at a Vermeer, with a magnifying glass, you'd find a darn in the woman's apron, grease spots fallen from the candle, skin pores and nostril hairs.

He thought he could describe what the mind's eye saw, set it down as clearly as it appeared to him. But memory is incandescent, burning things up even as it illuminates. It is all an abstraction.

Where are the ants and dead stems, the worm-casts in the grass, the dissolving vapor trails overhead, the smears of grime and fingerprints, the accidents and wear, the fly buzzing at the window? The images have a kind of exactitude, but some things are unnecessary, and some other things irretrievable. Who, in any case, would care if it was all made up? Telling stories is telling lies, the novelist B. S. Johnson said—the only line of his that's ever quoted, and even that an untruth. Johnson killed himself. How did he do it? Could someone please describe the room? What's left out is important. Omission in this case is no more a sin than the fatuous observation that either God or the Devil is in the details.

We all like a good story. The artist's job, as far as she or he has one, is surely to inform us in the ways of the world, through the manner of description, in the disclosure of a point of view. That's what stories are, even when they appear to amount to no more than a single unmoving image. That, in itself, can often be enough. And how fixed can an image be, anyhow? It is all re-description of one kind or another, more or less a partial view, one possible story amongst many. We are always in the middle, never knowing how anything will end, until we ourselves are overtaken.

When I looked at and wrote about Thomas Demand's 1999 film TUNNEL for a newspaper, I never thought for one moment about the underpass in Paris where Princess Diana crashed. Had I done my research, or had a journalistic nose for the salacious or the grim, I'd have made the bleak connection. I rarely think of the People's Princess, and saw something else instead, my own eye being dragged round the endless circuit, the pillars strobing past, the concrete light. When I look at Demand's photograph of his cardboard-box model of a barn, with the white light coming in through the blank windows and the slats, I do not think of the ramshackle outhouse where Jackson Pollock painted, though I know that's what provoked the model and the photograph that was taken of it. I can imagine Pollock in there well enough, zebra-striped in the narrow slits of sunlight with the dust motes floating, along with dozens of other details the photograph does not show, includ-

ADRIAN SEARLE is art critic for *The Guardian* newspaper. He also writes fiction, and is an occasional curator.

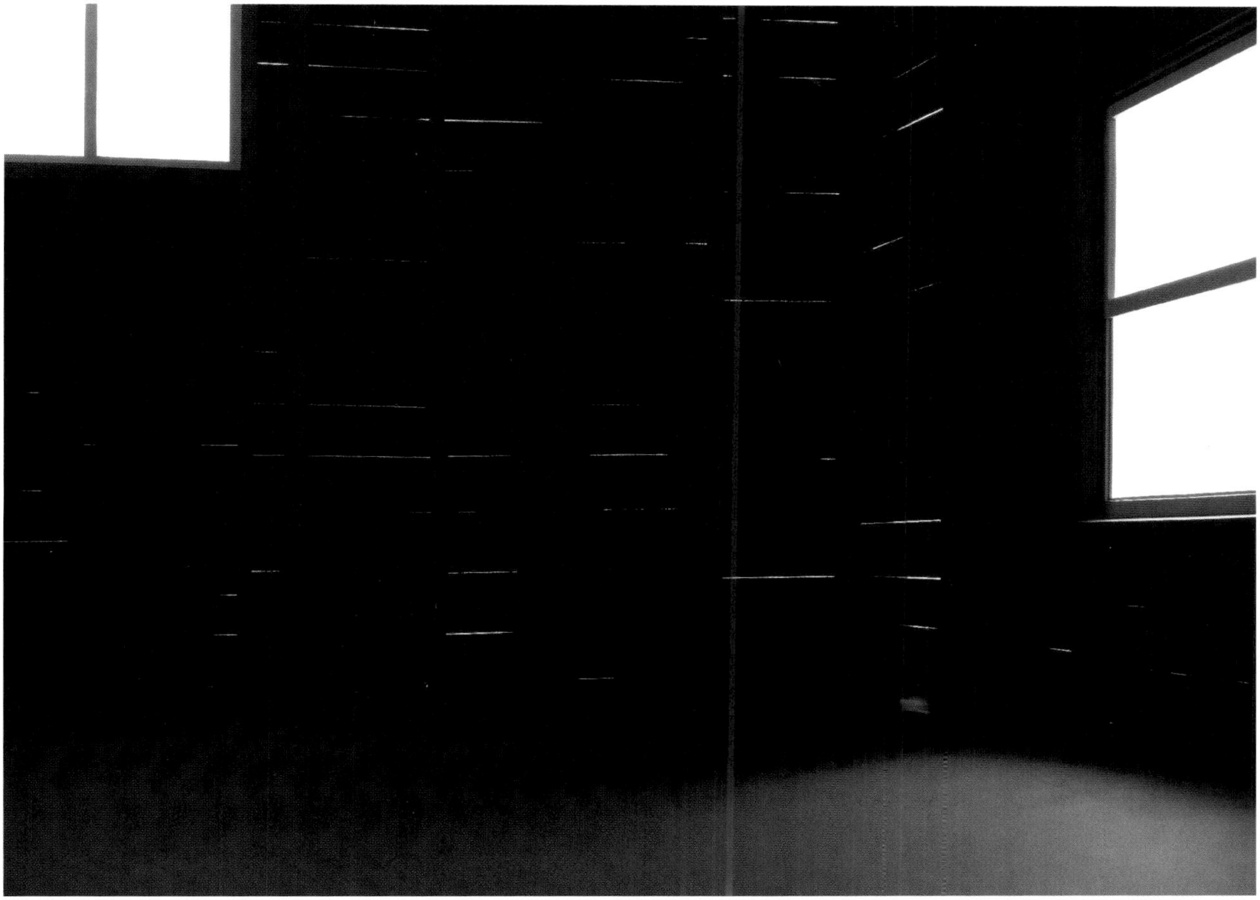

THOMAS DEMAND, SCHEUNE / BARN, 1997, C-Print Diasec, 183,5 x 254 cm / 72¼ x 100".

ing a frizzy halo of backlit hair on the painter's balding head. You can't keep this stuff at bay, though it is better to keep it mostly to yourself. If not, where would it end, we'd never get anything done. But there it is, sliding into the spaces in between, through the gaps.

I think of the Austrian novelist, Thomas Bernhard, already consumed in his descriptions when he first began writing. "Yeah, I was already writing novels then, endless, three-hundred pages long, impossible stuff," Bernhard recalls, "and one of them was called *Peter Goes into Town* and I was already on page one hundred and he hadn't even left the railroad station. So I gave up. The concept was all wrong. He hadn't even gotten on the streetcar by page a hundred and fifty. Zero sense of economy."[1]

A journey into town can take a lifetime. You mightn't make it even onto that tram. You might never take a step off the curb, or even get out of the door. Stalled for one reason or another, or for no reason at all. Do not leave the room, Kafka said, or something like it. The world will writhe before you.

Clear description, I realize, is all a matter of a certain kind of indifference. There's something hard and unyielding in Demand's vision, which isn't really photographic at all, but sculptural and filmic and almost literary, except that nothing ever moves or changes. It is a hard stare at something incomplete and disconnected, a corner of the world as yet unfinished. Or somewhere cropped or slyly paraphrased. It is somewhere immediate, like a space you have walked into for the first time, without yet taking in the scuff marks, the wretchedness of use, the inadvertent personality. Somewhere not quite here yet. We have not yet wholly arrived, are not yet bogged-down inside some nineteenth-century novel.

The absence of palpable human atmosphere sets the emotional tone, which remains flat and unchanging. Yet as well as the things in these spaces, and the places themselves, being already somehow familiar in themselves, so too is the way they come to us, with their reproduction sheen, the standard color, their knowing compositional rectitude. Everything is completely normal. These are normal views. You might even say that they have a kind of "objectivity," if only because they appear entirely indifferent towards their content.

We believe we have acquired our own kind of brevity and our own, modern and skeptical kind of realism, which knows the world cannot be rendered as it is, or as we remember it, with all the encumbrances memory brings, but only in terms of one kind of language or another. The more the world is pared away, the more it signals its persistence. You can still see the knife-cuts and the blood. Demand's images strike me as being like this. You could say they are husks: there is no one home. Everyone has left, is asleep, either gone off their shift or not arrived yet; they're down at the pub, getting on with their lives somewhere else, answering the telephone in another room, dead. It is like the *Marie Celeste* here.[2] It almost appears that Demand is more interested in space and light and objects and their conjunction than he is in people, but it seems to me his images are actually teeming with life. You and I are there, after all, and the someone who held the camera, the man who built the model (Demand, again, in one of his several guises), and there's also somewhere else beyond, cropped from the picture or back down the stairs or on the other side of the blinds, which may or may not be the world you and I actually inhabit. But here there's this flat disengaged emotional tone, places without empathies.

Yet there's something almost welcoming about all this emptiness, in the spaces between things, in the hovering imperturbable camera invitations. I look along these corridors, at the Louvre blinds, the sunlit walls, the gliding escalator, the swatch of lawn, the things stripped down to irreducibles and imagine that in my own abstracted way, I can walk around here, lean over a table, take a ride on the escalator, undress and wait on the paper sheet on the massage parlor bed. No one will know I've been here. I'll leave no trace. It is a still world, a solid state, as plainly described as it needs to be, to give a semblance of the real. Here, I am disembodied, weightless, I make no disturbance. It will always be like this, not so much deathly as suspended. I'll breathe my own life into it, and watch it burn.

1) Kurt Hoffmann, *Aus Gesprächen mit Thomas Bernhard* (Vienna: Löcker Verlag, 1988), p. 48.

2) The *Marie Celeste* was a famous "ghost ship" found adrift off the Azores on the 3rd of December 1872. There was no sign of life on board, either above or below decks. There were no clues to explain why the crew had disappeared. Indeed everything appeared to be quite normal. In the crew's quarters, clothing lay folded neatly on bunks and washing hung on lines. Breakfast had been prepared and some of it had been served. The captain's log showed entries up to the 25th of November and gave no hint of anything being wrong.

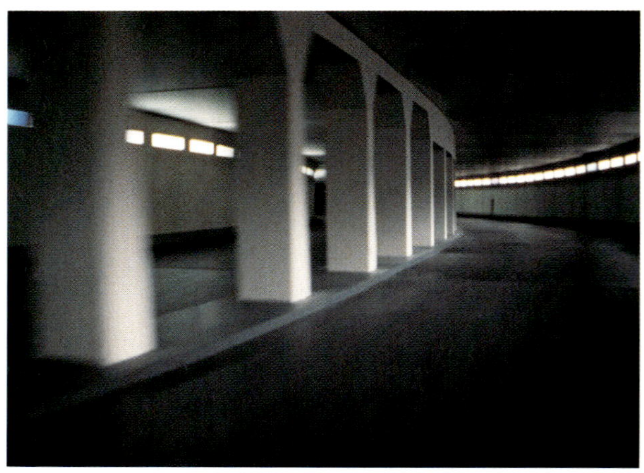

THOMAS DEMAND, TUNNEL, 1999, 35mm film / 35mm-Film.

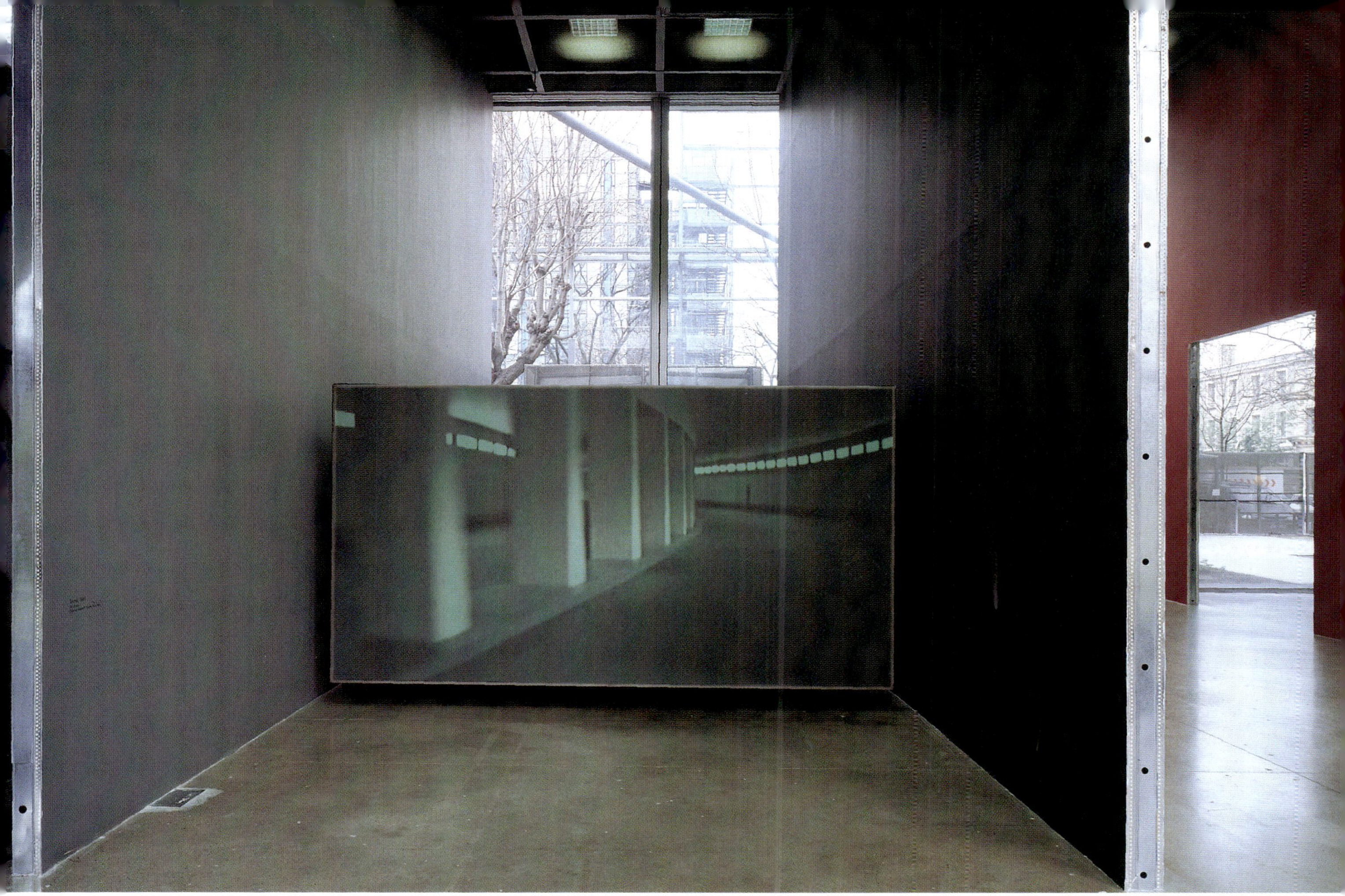

THOMAS DEMAND, TUNNEL, 1999, installation in collaboration with / in Zusammenarbeit mit CarusoSt.John Architects, Fondation Cartier, Paris, 2000/01.

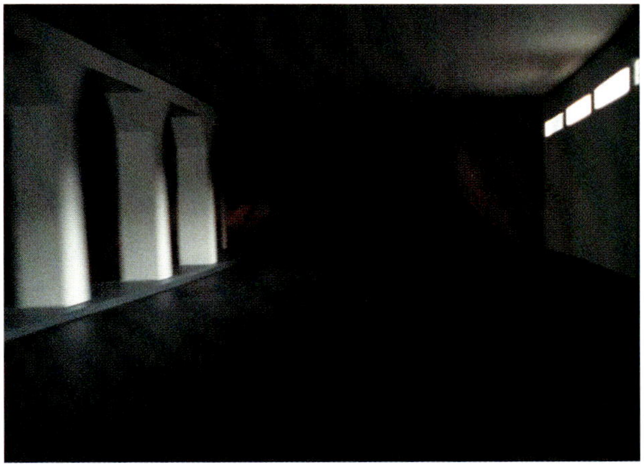

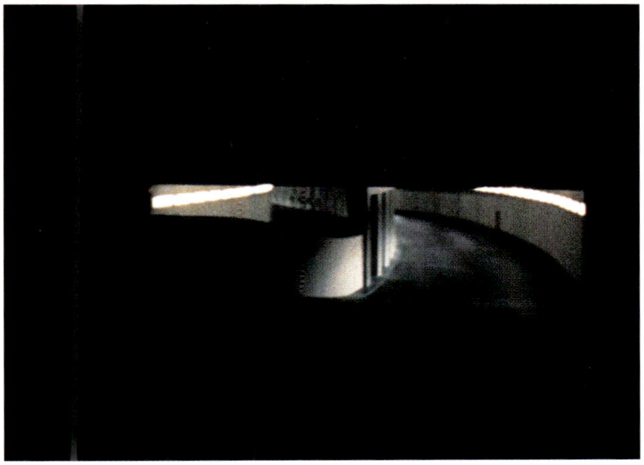

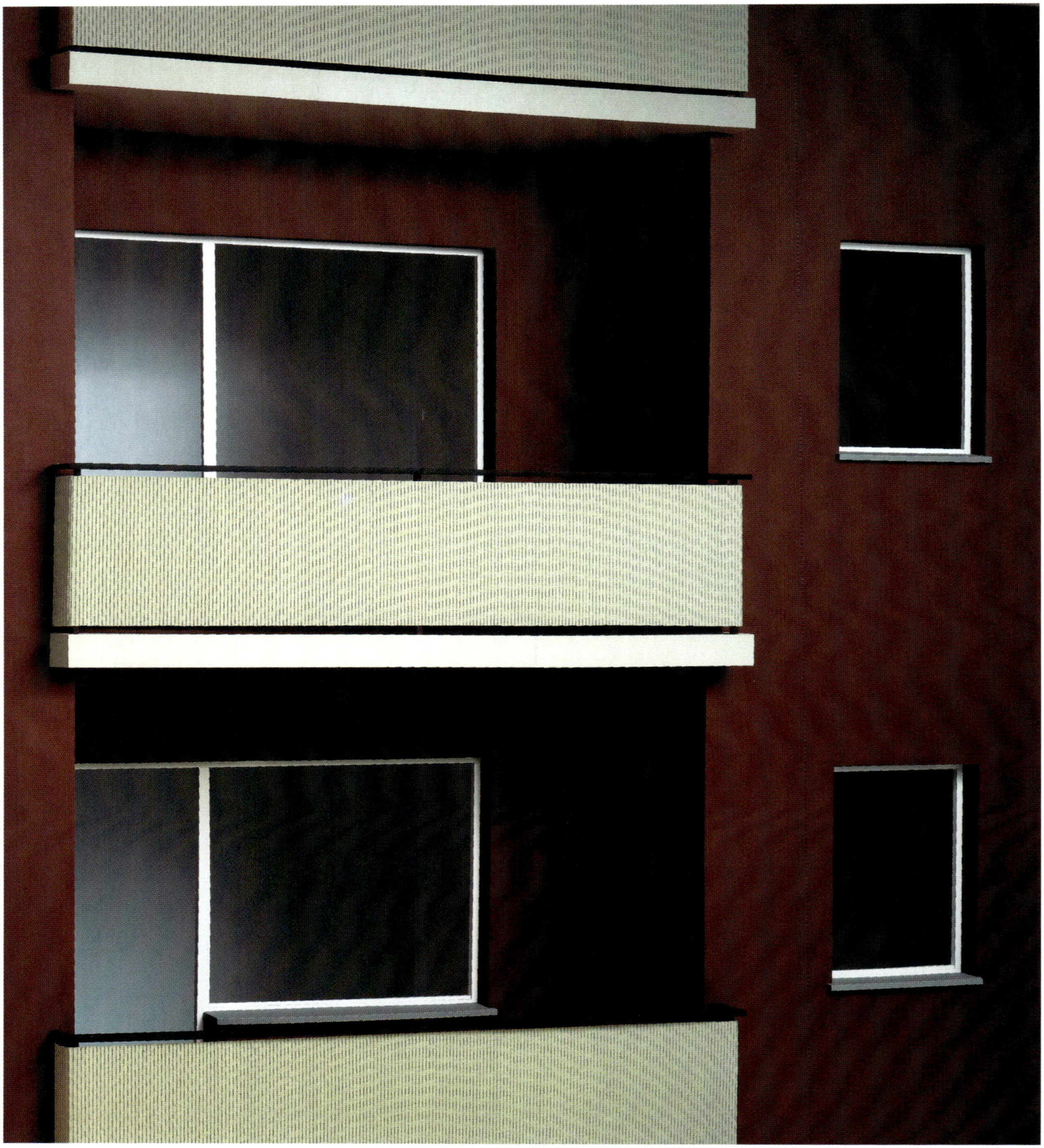

THOMAS DEMAND, BALKONE / BALCONIES, 1997, C-Print Diasec, 150 x 128 cm / 59 x 50⅜".

ADRIAN SEARLE

ZIEH DEN TAG IN ZWEIFEL

Zieh den Tag in Zweifel, die Sicht aus dem Fenster, dann auch das Fenster, das Zimmer. Die Schatten sind ein Prüfstein, geschmeidig legen sie sich in Falten, schmiegen sich an und messen sich mit den Wänden. Sie zumindest scheinen real zu sein. Aber das makellose Blau des Himmels, das Gras unter den Füssen, die nahen und fernen Gebäude, die menschenleeren Balkone? Sieht man hinunter in den gelben Kegel des Lichts einer Lampe oder auf die verstreuten Papiere, so sieht man immer weniger, je länger man hinschaut. Ist das eine Enttäuschung? Nur für jemanden, der sich naiver Weise einbildet, er würde bei genauer Untersuchung eines Vermeers mit der Lupe eine geflickte Stelle in der Schürze der Frau entdecken, aus der Kerze geflossene Talgtropfen, Hautporen und Nasenhaare.

Er dachte, er könnte beschreiben, was er vor seinem geistigen Auge sah, es in derselben Klarheit niederschreiben, mit der es ihm erschien. Aber die Erinnerung lodert und glüht und verzehrt die Dinge schon, während sie sie beleuchtet. Das Ganze ist eine Abstraktion.

Wo sind die Ameisen und die toten Halme, die Wurmspuren im Gras, die sich auflösenden Kondensstreifen über unseren Köpfen, die Schmutzschlieren und Fingerabdrücke, die Unfälle und Abnützungserscheinungen, die Fliege, die am Fenster brummt? Die Bilder haben eine gewisse Genauigkeit, aber einige Dinge sind unnötig und andere unmöglich wiederzugeben. Und wem würde es schon etwas ausmachen, wenn alles nur erfunden wäre? «Geschichten erzählen heisst Lügen erzählen», sagte der Schriftsteller B. S. Johnson – die einzige je zitierte Zeile von ihm, auch sie eine Unwahrheit. Johnson hat sich umgebracht. Wie hat er das getan? Könnte mir jemand bitte das Zimmer beschreiben? Die Auslassungen sind wichtig. In diesem Fall ist die Auslassung keine grössere Sünde als die idiotische Bemerkung, dass sowohl Gott wie der Teufel im Detail stecken.

Wir alle lieben gute Geschichten. Die Aufgabe des Künstlers oder der Künstlerin, falls sie überhaupt

ADRIAN SEARLE ist Kunstkritiker der britischen Zeitung *The Guardian* und Schriftsteller. Gelegentlich ist er auch als Kurator tätig.

eine Aufgabe haben, ist es, uns über die Welt aufzuklären – mit den Mitteln der Beschreibung, im Aufzeigen eines bestimmten Blickwinkels. Denn dies ist es, was eine Geschichte ausmacht, selbst wenn sie auf nicht mehr als ein einziges unbewegtes Bild hinauszulaufen scheint. Das allein genügt oft schon. Und überhaupt, wie definitiv feststehend kann ein Bild schon sein? Es ist immer wieder ein Beschreibungsversuch der einen oder anderen Art, mehr oder weniger ein Ausschnitt, eine mögliche Geschichte unter vielen. Wir stecken immer mitten drin und wissen nie, wie irgendwas ausgehen wird, bis wir selbst von den Ereignissen überrollt werden.

Als ich mir Thomas Demands Film TUNNEL (1999) anschaute und für eine Zeitung darüber schrieb, dachte ich keinen Moment an die Unterführung in Paris, wo Prinzessin Diana verunglückte. Hätte ich besser recherchiert oder eine bessere journalistische Nase für das Sensationelle oder Grausliche gehabt, hätte ich die traurige Verbindung herstellen können. Aber ich denke selten an die Königin der Herzen und sah stattdessen etwas anderes, nämlich, wie mein eigenes Auge allmählich in den endlosen Kreislauf hineingezerrt wurde, während die Stützpfeiler vorbeiglitten, der Beton hell erleuchtet. Betrachte ich Demands Photographie seines Kartonschachtel-Modells einer Scheune und wie das weisse Licht darin durch die leeren Fenster und zwischen den Latten einfällt, so denke ich nicht an den windschiefen Schuppen, in dem Jackson Pollock malte, obwohl ich weiss, dass er die Anregung für das Modell und die Photographie war. Ich kann mir Pollock sehr gut darin vorstellen, gestreift wie ein Zebra im Licht der schmalen Sonnenstreifen, die durch die Ritzen dringen, auch die darin schwebenden Staubpartikel und noch viele weitere Details, die auf der Photographie nicht zu sehen sind, einschliesslich des ausgefransten Haarkranzes, der im Gegenlicht den Kopf des Künstlers wie ein Heiligenschein krönt. Diese Dinge lassen sich kaum in Schach halten, aber man behält sie meist besser für sich. Wo kämen wir sonst hin? Wir brächten nichts mehr zu Ende. Aber sie sind da und schlüpfen durch die Spalten in die Zwischenräume.

Ich muss an Thomas Bernhard denken, der sich schon bei seinen ersten Romanversuchen mit sechzehn Jahren in endlosen Beschreibungen verlor. «Na, da hab' ich Romane g'schrieben schon, so lange, dreihundert Seiten lange, so unmögliche Sachen, nicht.», erinnert sich Bernhard: «Einer hat g'heissen *Peter geht in die Stadt*, und da war ich schon auf Seite hundert, und der war noch immer beim Bahnhof. Also, da hab' ich dann aufg'hört, das Konzept war falsch. Der ist noch nicht einmal in der Strassenbahn drin g'sessen, und es waren schon hundertfünfzig Seiten. Ökonomie gleich Null.»[1]

Eine Reise in die Stadt kann ein Leben lang dauern. Vielleicht schafft mans nicht einmal bis zur Strassenbahn. Vielleicht schafft man diesen Schritt über den Randstein hinaus nie oder scheitert schon an der Tür. Aufgehalten aus dem einen oder anderen Grund oder auch ohne Grund. Die Alternative wäre, den Bau gar nicht mehr zu verlassen und wie Kafka es formulierte: «die Dinge ihren Lauf nehmen zu lassen und sie durch unnütze Beobachtungen nicht aufzuhalten».[2]

Eine klare Beschreibung setzt, wie man sieht, eine gewisse Gleichgültigkeit voraus. Demands Sehweise hat etwas Hartes und Unnachgiebiges und ist eigentlich gar nicht wirklich photographisch, sondern plastisch, filmisch, ja beinah literarisch, einmal abgesehen davon, dass sich nie etwas bewegt oder verändert. Es ist ein unbarmherziger Blick auf etwas Unvollständiges und Isoliertes, wie auf einen noch nicht vollendeten Winkel der Welt. Oder auf einen Ort, der zurechtgestutzt ist oder eine raffinierte Paraphrase darstellt. Da ist etwas Unmittelbares, wie wenn man einen Raum zum ersten Mal betritt, noch ohne die Kratzspuren, das Elend der Abnützung und persönliche Schlampigkeiten wahrzunehmen. Ein Ort, der noch nicht ganz von dieser Welt ist. Wir sind noch nicht ganz angekommen, noch nicht im Treibsand eines Romans aus dem 19. Jahrhundert versunken.

Das Fehlen einer greifbaren menschlichen Atmosphäre gibt die Gefühlslage vor, die unspektakulär und unverändert bleibt. Aber ebenso wie die Dinge in diesen Räumen und die Örtlichkeiten selbst uns irgendwie vertraut sind, ist es auch die Art ihrer Präsentation: der Glanz der Reproduktion, die Standardfarben, die bewusste Richtigkeit ihrer Komposition. Alles ist völlig normal. Es handelt sich um

THOMAS DEMAND, PANEEL / PANEL, 1996, C-Print Diasec, 121 x 160 cm / 47 5/8 x 63".

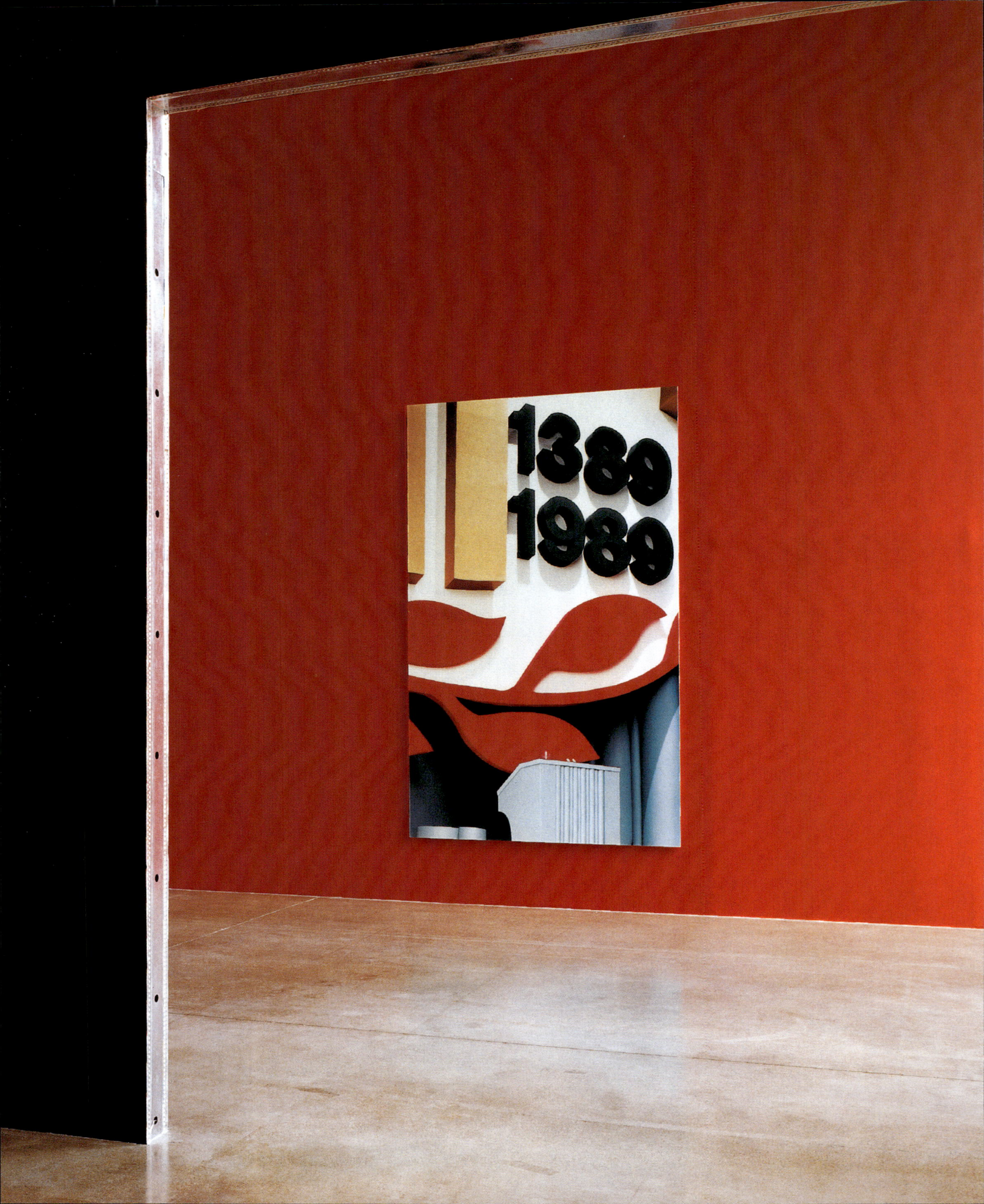
1389
1989

alltägliche Anblicke. Man könnte sogar sagen, dass sie in gewisser Weise «objektiv» sind, und sei es nur, weil sie ihrem Inhalt gegenüber vollkommen gleichgültig zu sein scheinen.

Wir glauben uns im Besitz einer eigenen Knappheit der Formulierung sowie eines eigenen, modernen und skeptischen Realismus, der darum weiss, dass die Welt nicht so wiedergegeben werden kann, wie sie ist oder wie wir sie in Erinnerung haben – mit allen Verwicklungen, die die Erinnerung mit sich bringt –, sondern nur unter den Bedingungen einer bestimmten Ausdrucksform. Je konsequenter die Welt ausgespart wird, desto dringender signalisiert sie ihr Fortbestehen. Noch sind die Schnitte und das Blut sichtbar. Demands Bilder führen dies besonders auffällig vor Augen. Man könnte sagen, es seien leere Hülsen: Es ist niemand zuhause. Alle sind gegangen, schlafen gerade, haben ihre Schicht beendet oder sind noch nicht angekommen; sie sitzen drunten in der Schenke, leben ihr Leben woanders weiter, telefonieren im Nebenraum oder sind tot. Es ist wie an Bord der *Marie Celeste*.[3] Man könnte fast meinen, Demand interessiere sich mehr für Raum- und Lichtverhältnisse oder für Gegenstände und ihre Kombination als für Menschen. Dennoch scheinen mir seine Bilder vor Leben zu strotzen. Sie und ich, immerhin, sind darin enthalten und derjenige, der die Kamera hielt, der Mensch, der das Modell baute (noch einmal Demand, in einer seiner zahlreichen Verkleidungen); und dann ist dahinter noch ein anderer Ort, der aus dem Bild geschnitten wurde, oder der Ort unten an der Treppe oder auf der anderen Seite der Jalousien, ein Ort, der vielleicht oder vielleicht auch nicht die Welt ist, in der wir leben. Aber hier im Bild herrscht diese emotionslose, neutrale Stimmung, da gibt es kein Erbarmen.

Und doch steckt in dieser Leere beinah ein Willkommensgruss, in den Zwischenräumen, in den schwebenden, unbeirrbaren Aufforderungen der Kamera. Ich schaue diese Gänge entlang, betrachte die Jalousien des Louvre, die sonnenbeschienenen Wände, die gleitende Rolltreppe, das Rasenstück, all die aufs Notwendigste reduzierten Dinge und stelle mir vor, ich könnte in meiner eigenen zerstreuten Art darin herumwandern, mich über den Tisch beugen, auf der Rolltreppe fahren, mich ausziehen und auf dem Papierlaken des Massagetischs liegend warten. Niemand wird je erfahren, dass ich hier war. Ich werde keine Spur hinterlassen. Es ist eine stille Welt, ein fester Zustand, so vollkommen beschrieben wie nötig um den Anschein von Realität zu erwecken. Hier bin ich vom Körper befreit, schwerelos, ich störe nicht. Und es wird immer so sein, nicht tot, aber im Zustand der Aufhebung. Ich hauche dem Bild mein eigenes Leben ein und schaue zu, wie es verbrennt.

(Übersetzung: Susanne Schmidt)

1) Vgl. Kurt Hoffmann, *Aus Gesprächen mit Thomas Bernhard*, Löcker Verlag, Wien 1988, S. 48.
2) Franz Kafka, *Der Bau*, in: *Sämtliche Erzählungen*, S. Fischer Verlag, Frankfurt am Main 1970, S. 368.
3) *Marie Celeste:* Berühmtes «Geisterschiff», das im Dezember 1872 vor den Azoren strandete. An Bord gab es keinerlei Lebenszeichen. Die Besatzung war auf unerklärliche Weise verschwunden. Aber sonst schien alles normal: In den Mannschaftsquartieren lagen die Kleider ordentlich zusammengefaltet, Wäsche hing an der Leine; das Frühstück stand bereit. Die letzten Einträge im Logbuch stammten vom 25. November ohne jeden Hinweis auf etwas Aussergewöhnliches.

THOMAS DEMAND, PODIUM, 2000, C-Print Diasec, 300 x 180 cm / 118⅛ x 70⅞". Installation in collaboration with/ in Zusammenarbeit mit Caruso St.John Architects, Fondation Cartier, Paris, 2000/01.

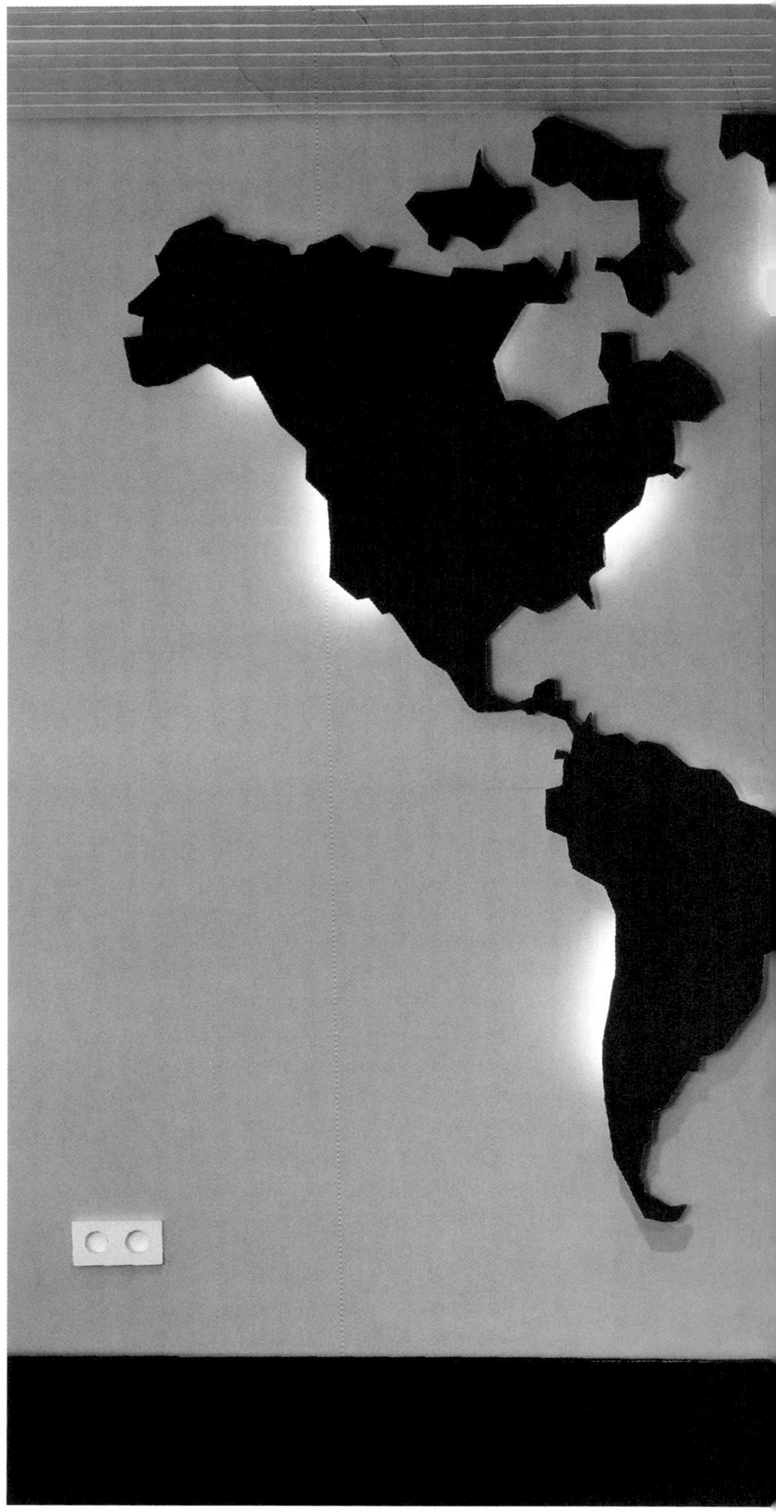

THOMAS DEMAND, WAND / MURAL, 1999, C-Print Diasec, 270 x 183,5 cm / 106¼ x 72¼".

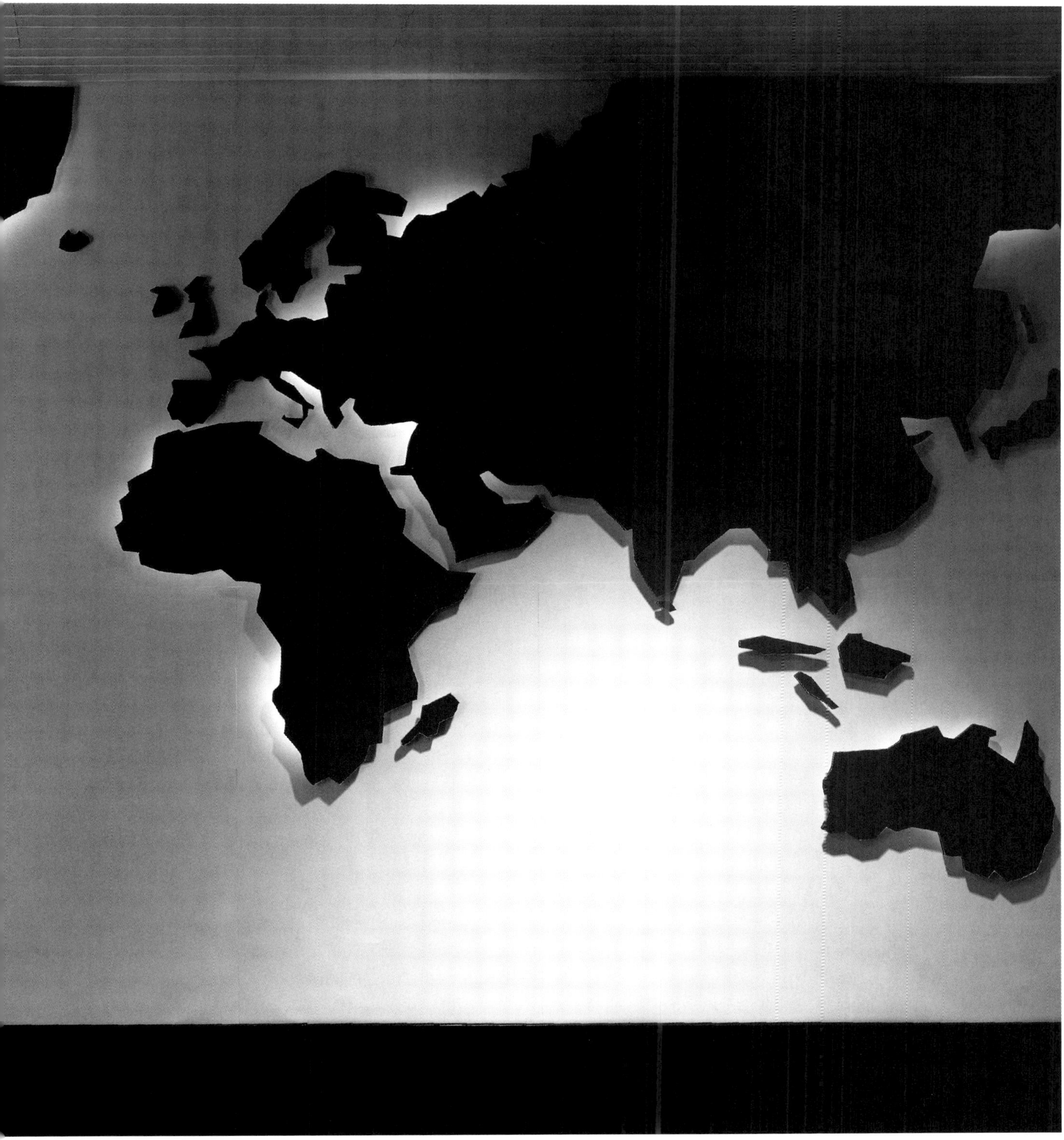

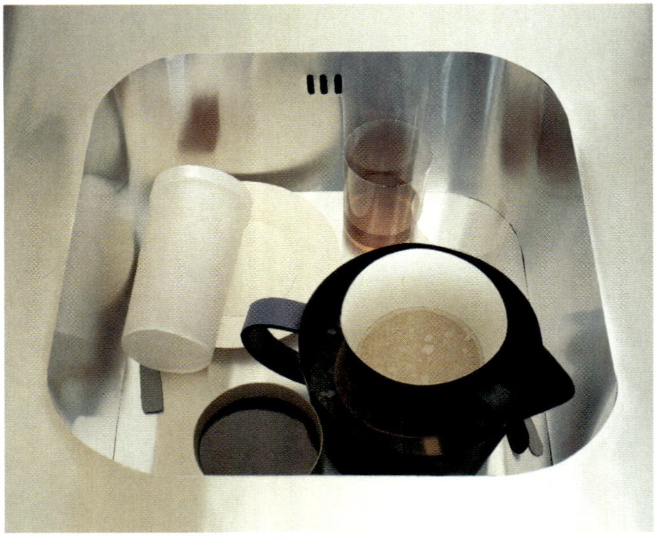

THOMAS DEMAND, SPÜLE / SINK, 1997, C-Print Diasec, 52 x 56,5 cm / 20½ x 22¼".

Memoryscapes

ANDREAS RUBY

Zu Beginn wirkt es wie eine ganz reale Szene, photographiert und an die Wand gehängt. Ein Motiv, das an Beiläufigkeit nicht zu übertreffen ist, wiegt den Blick in Sicherheit. Eine Spüle mit Abwasch drin, nichts Besonderes. Eigentlich will man schon nicht mehr hinschauen, weil es ja n i c h t m e h r zu sehen gibt. Aber man schaut doch wieder hin. Irgendwas scheint in dem Bild zu sein, was man nicht sehen kann. Es ist, als ob das Bild zurückschaut. Mit der Zeit wird der Blick aus dem Nichts unangenehm. Man beginnt sich gegen das Bild zu wehren, indem man es anschaut, es abhorcht und in ihm rumschnüffelt wie ein Spürhund. Irgendwo muss sich die Inszenierung verraten, wenn es denn eine ist. Seltsam, diese polierte Reinlichkeit der Edelstahlspüle. Ihre Oberflächen sind so blank, als seien sie noch nie von einem Tropfen Wasser benetzt worden. Stattdessen diese merkwürdig scharfen Kanten. Warum sie sich hier und da zu dunklen Fugen verdicken, ist unerklärlich. Sollte es etwa gar keine Spüle... aber die Tassen und Gläser sind doch ganz... nur dass der blaue Henkel so eckig ist... und alles andere so dünn...

Und dann ist es passiert. Wie ein Lauffeuer breitet sich der Zweifel im Bild aus, Stück für Stück entpuppt sich dessen Innenleben als mimetische Papierlandschaft. Eine riesige Ent-Täuschung lässt den Raum, der einem gerade vertraut zu werden begann, vor den eigenen Augen implodieren. Kuriose Verwirrung der Gefühle im Moment danach: eine Mischung aus Unverständnis (warum dieses Versteckspiel?), Enttäuschung (dass man sich an der Nase hat herumführen lassen), aber auch Bewunderung (für die Virtuosität der kunstvollen Illusion). Leicht benommen, die Initiation erfolgreich durchlaufen, wendet man sich an-

ANDREAS RUBY lebt in Köln und schreibt über zeitgenössische Kunst und Architektur.

deren Bildern zu, um die Verwandlung nun bewusst zu erleben. Ist die Manipulation der Vorstellung erst einmal abgestreift, richtet sich der Betrachter wieder in der souveränen Position des aktiv handelnden Subjekts ein. Auf einmal lässt sich das Schauspiel geniessen, wie eine Zeitlupenwiederholung im Fernsehen. Man möchte sich förmlich ausstrecken in diesem unmerklichen Gewahrwerden; sich selbst zu manipulieren macht Spass. An den Reglern des Realitätsmischpults stehend kontrolliert man wissend das Fading von Illusion zu Realität (und zurück). Als DJ der eigenen Erfahrung entscheidet man selbst, wie man von dem einen Track in den anderen überblendet. So kann man sich in STALL (2000) seelenruhig durch das Stroh wühlen ohne sich von der Illusion bedroht zu fühlen – schliesslich lässt sich der Prinz genauso leicht auch wieder in den Frosch zurückverwandeln: Ein Blick in die Ecke oben rechts auf das tapetenartig

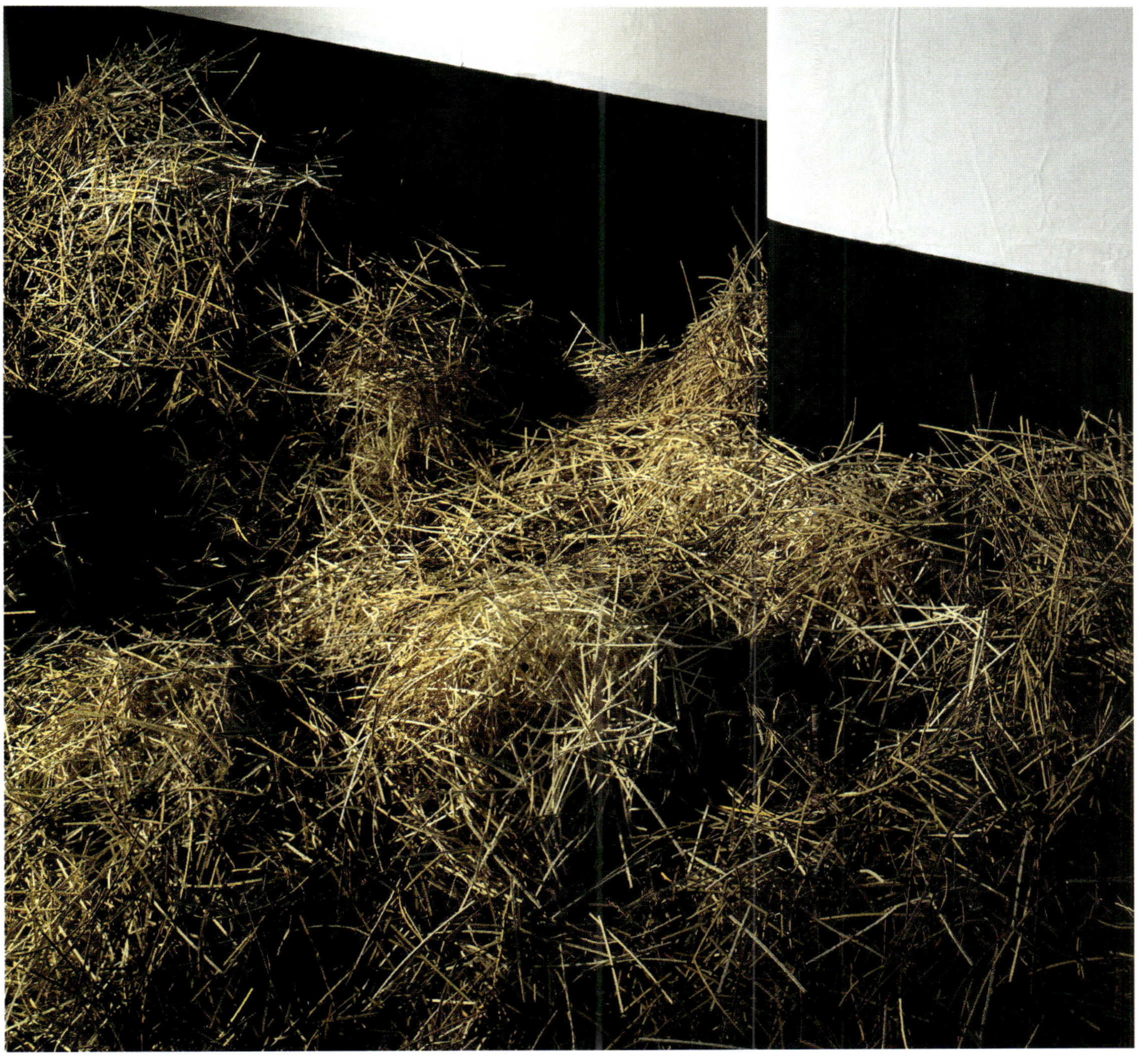

THOMAS DEMAND, STALL / STABLE, 2000, C-Print Diasec, 110 x 132 cm / 43 7/16 x 52".

an die Wand geklebte Papier genügt, um das Weltbild wieder gerade zu rücken.

Wie beim richtigen DJ-ing sind auch hier jene Phasen am faszinierendsten, in denen beide Tracks gleichzeitig hörbar sind, sich überlagern und Interferenzen schaffen. Der Beat gerät aus dem Takt, wird synkopisch; mehrere Tonarten färben aufeinander ab und erzeugen Zwischenräume. In diesem Sinn sind beispielsweise in ARCHIV (1995) beide Ebenen gleichzeitig präsent: Die Kistenstapel verströmen eine vollkommen glaubhafte Atmosphäre bürokratischer Ordnungsliebe und das fahle Licht versetzt den Betrachter unweigerlich in ein unterirdisches Aktenverlies. Andrerseits sind die Anzeichen der Papierwelt sensorisch nicht minder sichtbar: Der Papieransatz an der Wange der Leiter und die Klebestellen an den Stirnseiten der Regalkonstruktion haben gerade genug Präsenz, um die tatsächliche materielle Beschaffenheit des evozierten Interieurs anzudeuten.

Ambiguität

Diese Gleichzeitigkeit der Realitätsebenen verleiht den Bildern Thomas Demands jene Ambiguität, die dafür sorgt, dass das diskrete Spektakel ihrer Verwandlung nicht nach dem ersten Mal als Effekt verpufft. So lässt sich der Zweifel über den ontologischen Status der Bilder nie ganz ausräumen. Man schwankt zwischen den Interpretationen hin und her. Was, wenn sie doch real wären? Es bereitet Lust, sich der Verführung ihres Realitätsversprechens hinzugeben und die makellose Glätte ihrer Flächen für das zu halten, was sie vorzugeben scheinen: Putzwände, Aluminiumbleche, Plastikabdeckungen, Plüsch, Holz, Glas – und eben nicht Papier und Pappe. Nietzsche meint, wir ertrügen die Wahrheit nicht und zögen es deshalb vor, uns zu betrügen, indem wir uns die Welt solange zurechtfälschten, bis sie unserem Wunschbild entspräche.

Simulation / Spiel

Dabei geht es Demand um alles andere als eine Simulation der Realität. Seine Bilder zielen nicht darauf ab, den Betrachter zu betrügen; eher lassen sie ihm die Wahl, die Illusion an sich selbst zu vollziehen. Die Illusion aber ist keine Täuschung, wie der späte Baudrillard, nachdem er sich von der Theorie der Simulation verabschiedet hat, erkennt, sondern ein Spiel. Das lateinische Verb *illudere* bedeutet so viel wie «etwas ins Spiel setzen». Und das Spiel bringt die Wirklichkeit dazu, das Dogma ihrer unbedingten Gültigkeit abzulegen, um mit dem Möglichen zu flirten. Im Falle von Demands Bildern wird das Spiel dadurch abwechslungsreich, dass es ständig zwischen Nachahmung und Konstruktion von Wirklichkeit hin und her changiert. Man kann nie genau sagen, welche Wirklichkeit in diesen Bildern regiert: Ist es die des Dargestellten oder jene der Darstellung selbst? Oder beide gleichzeitig?

Rekonstruktion

In einem gewissen Sinn könnte man Demands Kunst als Rekonstruktion beschreiben. Sie zeigt räumliche Situationen, die als solche schon einmal existiert haben. Die Orte ihres Ursprungs sind dem Betrachter häufig unbekannt. Manchmal stammen sie aus der Erinnerung des Künstlers, häufig jedoch liegen ihnen Photographien zugrunde. Photographien, die oft in der Absicht gemacht wurden, eine Situation zu dokumentieren. Tatorte zum Beispiel. Indem Demand diese «Beweisphotos» in raumfüllenden Modellen aus Papier und Pappe «nachbaut», ergreift der photographische Impetus des «Zeugnis Ablegens» auch seine Bilder – jenes *ça a été* (das hat stattgefunden), das Roland Barthes als Grundaussage jeder Photographie herausstellt. Was den Willen zur Rekonstruktion anbelangt, übertreffen Demands Bilder die Photographie sogar noch, insofern sie sich nicht mit der flächigen Abbildung begnügen, sondern ihren Referenten dreidimensional wiederherstellen. Gleichzeitig entzieht Demand jedoch diese mühsam nachgebaute Wirklichkeit dem Betrachter wieder, indem er seine Modelle nur in Form von grossformatigen Photographien präsentiert (die ihnen allerdings massstäblich entsprechen). Diese Verkettung von Reproduktionen führt die Sehnsucht nach der Wiederherstellung von Wirklichkeit – wenn nicht d i e, so doch zumindest eine der populärsten Motivationen der Photographie – systematisch ad absurdum. So gesehen betreibt Demand nachgerade eine Dekonstruktion der Photographie als dominantes Bildmedium der Moderne. Dass er sich dabei der Photographie selbst bedient, ist kein Widerspruch, sondern die Bedingung dieser Dekonstruktion. Durch den Akt, den in einer Photographie abgebildeten Raum nachzubauen und von neuem zu photographieren, überdehnt Demand das Band zwischen Dargestelltem und Darstellung so weit, dass der Signalfluss der Zeichen zum Erliegen kommt. Was wofür steht, ist vollkommen unklar. Nur eines ist sicher: Beweisen tun diese Bilder nichts mehr.

Darstellung der Darstellung

Trotz Demands spürbarer Distanz zur traditionell mimetischen Funktion der Kunst kann man seine Bilder nicht als gegenstandslos bezeichnen. Diese Bilder haben jeweils schon einen Gegenstand, nur stellen sie diesen nicht direkt und als solchen dar, sondern als Ergebnis einer Verkettung von Darstellungen. Die Trennung von Signifikat und Signifikant wird dabei teilweise ähnlich auf die Spitze getrieben wie in den Hochzeiten der Zeichentheorie. Man denke an Jean-Luc Godards Film *Weekend* (1968), in welchem statt Blut rote Farbe eingesetzt wird – und zwar so, dass sie als rote Farbe erkennbar ist. Genauso kann man bei Demand sehen, dass Papier benutzt wird, um alles Mögliche darzustellen. Interessant ist, dass dieses Chamäleonspiel des Materials bei Demand das Papier derartig de-realisiert, dass es sogar dort, wo es tatsächlich als Papier eingesetzt ist, verfremdet und unglaubwürdig wirkt. Das gilt zum Beispiel für den ZEICHENSAAL (1996), obwohl die dort an der Wand aufgehängte blaue Planrolle ihre papierene Materialität mit betörender Sinnlichkeit in den Raum ausströmt.

Story / No Story

Angesichts der beobachteten Verflüchtigung der Rekonstruktion könnte man also Demands Thema in der Thematisierung der eigenen Darstellung vermuten. Dem widersprechen allerdings die vielfältigen zeitgeschichtlichen Bezüge, die sich aus den von Demand benutzten photographischen Primärquellen ergeben. Auch wenn der Künstler die Hintergründe der Geschichten in seinen Bildtiteln nicht preisgibt, kann er sicher sein, dass sie dem Publikum nicht verborgen bleiben werden. In einigen seiner Arbeiten zitiert Demand Ikonen der jüngeren Zeitgeschichte, etwa den Tunnel am Pont de l'Alma in Paris, in dem Prinzessin Diana verunglückt ist. Speziell deutsche Betrachter werden sich bei BADEZIMMER (BEAU RIVAGE) (1997) an das berühmte *Stern*-Photo erinnern, das den deutschen Politiker Barschel tot in der Badewanne zeigt. STUDIO (1997) wiederum lässt unzählige Fernsehabende der Sendung «Was bin ich?» auferstehen.

Viele von Demands Bildern weisen allerdings keine derartig prominente Ikonographie auf, sondern sind anonym. Deswegen stellt sich die Frage, welche Funktion die bildlichen Rekurse auf die erwähnten *fait divers* aus Tagespresse und Fernsehen haben. Dass es tatsächlich um die Inhalte der evozierten Anekdoten gehen könnte, ist unwahrscheinlich – dafür sind sie zu zurückhaltend eingesetzt (häufig kann man sie auch nur auf Umwegen, zum Beispiel über die Sekundärliteratur, erfahren). Ihre Bedeutung muss woanders liegen. Angesichts der von Demand betriebenen Dekonstruktion der Photographie spricht viel dafür, dass diese Bildthemen vornehmlich als Katalysatoren der Erinnerung eingesetzt sind. Erinnerung nicht an ein bestimmtes Ereignis, sondern als Technik zur Vergegenwärtigung der Welt, die eine Alternative zur erwähnten kulturellen Praxis der Photographie als Wirklichkeitsvergewisserung eröffnet («Ein Urlaub ohne Photos ist wie ein Erlebnis ohne Erinnerung» hiess vor einiger Zeit mal ein Photo-Werbespot). Das *ça a été* der photographischen Wirklichkeitsdefinition wandelt sich im Paradigma der Erinnerung in ein «das habe ich gesehen» (gehört, erlebt etc.): Nicht dass etwas stattgefunden hat, ist wesentlich, sondern dass man sich daran erinnert. Diese Praxis der Erinnerung beeinflusst den Umgang mit den Bildern erheblich, insbesondere mit jenen, die nicht mit einem ikonographischen Blickfang ausgestattet sind. Denn fast zwangsläufig projiziert man nun jenen Erinnerungseffekt aus den Bildern mit «prominenten» Motiven auch auf alle anderen. Auch diese Garagen, Hauswände und Rolltreppen könnten letztlich bedeutsame Orte sein, nur dass man es nicht weiss. Oft genug sind sie es tatsächlich, wie beispielsweise die SCHEUNE (1997), die auf ein Photo von Jackson Pollocks Atelier in Long Island zurückgeht. Doch geht es nicht darum, die Bilder zu dechiffrieren und ihnen ihr Geheimnis zu entreissen. Viel entscheidender ist es, diese andere Form von Erinnerung zu praktizieren, die sich aus dem Zusammentreffen der Bilder mit unserer Neugier ergibt. Eine Erinnerung, die Geschichten nicht rekonstruiert, sondern erst produziert (weil sie nicht mehr oder noch nicht da sind, im Gegensatz zum Raum des potenziellen Ereignisses). COPYSHOP (1999) ist deswegen ein Bild, das man nie zu Ende betrachten kann, weil es unserer Imagination endlos Spielraum und Stimulation bietet, jene Ereignisse zu (re)konstruieren, die in diesem Raum mit seiner mysteriösen Alltäglichkeit stattgefunden haben oder stattfinden könnten.

Memoryscapes

In einer anderen Reihe von Bildern erzeugt Demand diese Fiktionalisierung des Bildraums durch eine Abstraktion in der Darstellung. So gibt es vor allem in den Architekturbildern kaum Details. Die Häuser werden zu reinen Volumen, schemenhaft gezeichnet durch Licht und Schatten. Manche Bilder, wie LABOR (2000), PARKGARAGE (1996) oder BALKONE (1997), könnten deswegen fast gemalt sein. Man steht vor ihnen und möchte so sehr glauben, dass sie gebaute Modelle darstellen, und kann es einfach nicht. Aus dieser Unglaublichkeit erwächst den Bildern ein ganz eigener Realitätseffekt. Letztlich geht es Demand nicht um Photographie an sich, sondern er betreibt mit ihr gewissermassen ein mediales *cross-dressing*. Das Photo ist zwar das Endformat des Bildes, doch funktionieren die Arbeiten oft nach ganz anderen als photographischen Gesetzen. Häufig realisiert man das Photo als solches überhaupt nicht, weil man so mit dem Raum beschäftigt ist, den es realisiert. Spätestens jetzt wird nachvollziehbar, dass Demand als Plastiker angefangen hat. Photographie begann in seiner Arbeit erst eine Rolle zu spielen, als er die sich vermehrenden Rauminstallationen nicht mehr in seinen Räumlichkeiten unterbringen konnte.

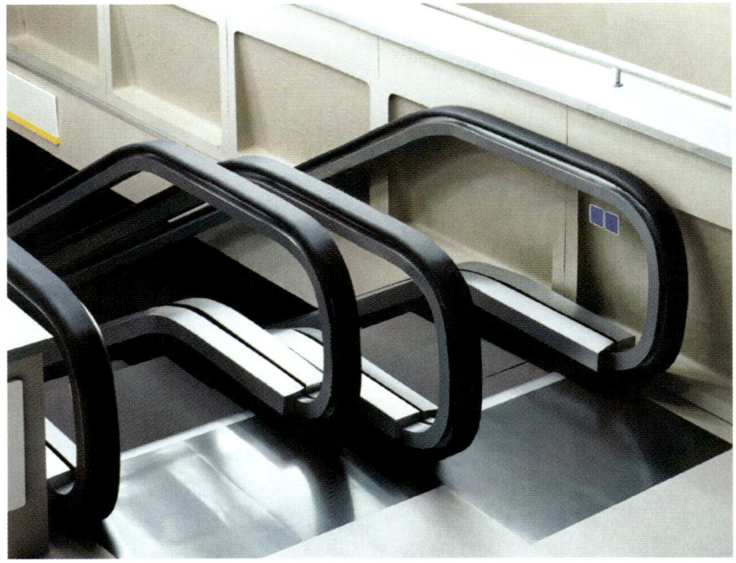

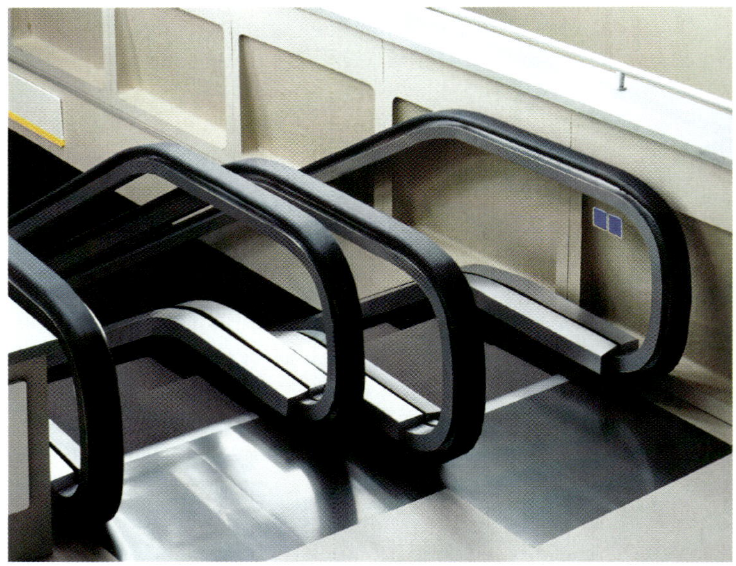

THOMAS DEMAND, ROLLTREPPE / ESCALATOR, 2000, 35mm-Film / 35mm film.

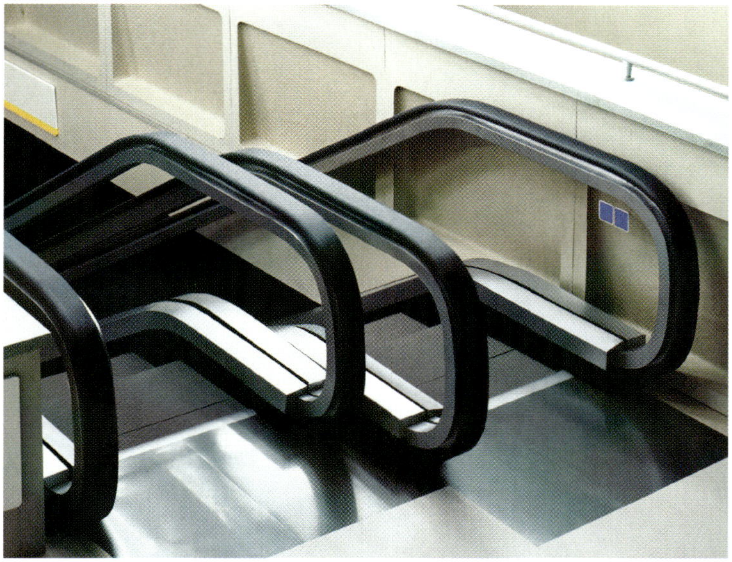

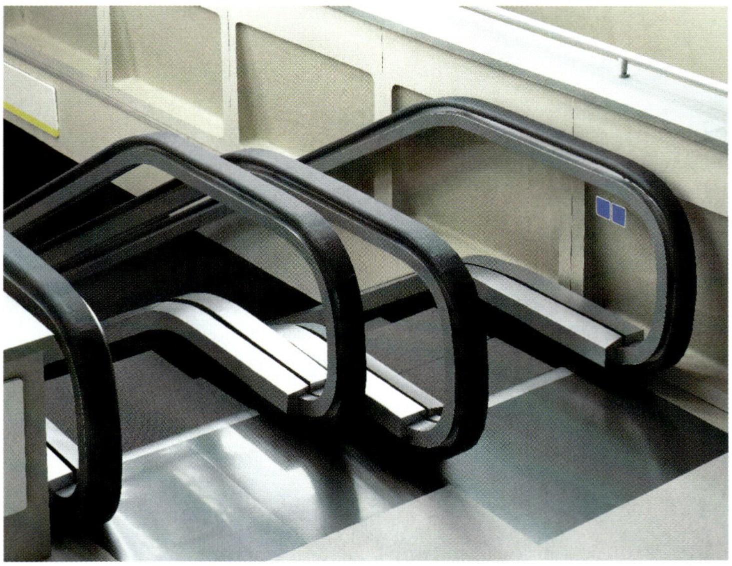

Diese Raumnot hat Demand schliesslich dazu geführt, die Photographie als Raummedium zu praktizieren. Dass er in seinen neueren Arbeiten wie TUNNEL (1999) oder ROLLTREPPE (2000) die Grenzen der Photographie überschreitet und sich des Films als Medium bedient, ist deswegen auch nicht als mediale Diskurswende in seiner Kunst zu verstehen; eher spitzt sie ihre Prinzipien noch zu. Auch hier geht es nicht um Kino an sich, sondern um die Stimulation einer Erinnerung, die in diesem Fall eben durch bewegte Bilder gespeist wird. Im Fall von TUNNEL wird Lady Dianas letzte Fahrt durch das unterirdische Paris zum TV-vermittelten Nacherleben präsentiert. Was die Vorlage für ROLLTREPPE gewesen sein mag, bleibt ebenso rätselhaft wie die merkwürdig gleichförmige Bewegung der filmischen Repräsentation. Der «Film» besteht in Wirklichkeit aus 24 Einzelbildern einer von Demand nachgebauten Rolltreppe, deren Stufenpositionen in jedem Bild leicht verschoben sind. Anschliessend wurden die einzelnen Bilder mit einem Computerprogramm zu einer filmischen Sequenz montiert, die für unseren Blick die Illusion einer Bewegung erzeugt – eine Technik, die sowohl im traditionellen Animationsfilm wie in modernsten Hollywoodstreifen zur Repräsentation des nicht naturalistisch verfügbaren Teils von Wirklichkeit angewendet wird. Das Fliessende der filmischen Bewegung, die ihrerseits ja völlig synthetisch ist, scheint den Realitätseffekt von Demands Konstruktionen auf eine noch höhere Ebene zu heben. Es ist, als umhülle die filmisch injizierte Bewegung das Bild automatisch mit einer Aura von Glaubwürdigkeit, die jeder Befragung seiner Wahrheit die Grundlage entzieht (zumindest solange man Poppers Prinzip folgt, dass wahr sei, was man nicht falsifizieren könne). Und so findet sich der Betrachter vor Demands Bildräumen in derselben Situation wie der Photograph am Ende von Michelangelo Antonionis *Blow up:* Soll er glauben, was er sieht, oder sehen, was er glaubt?

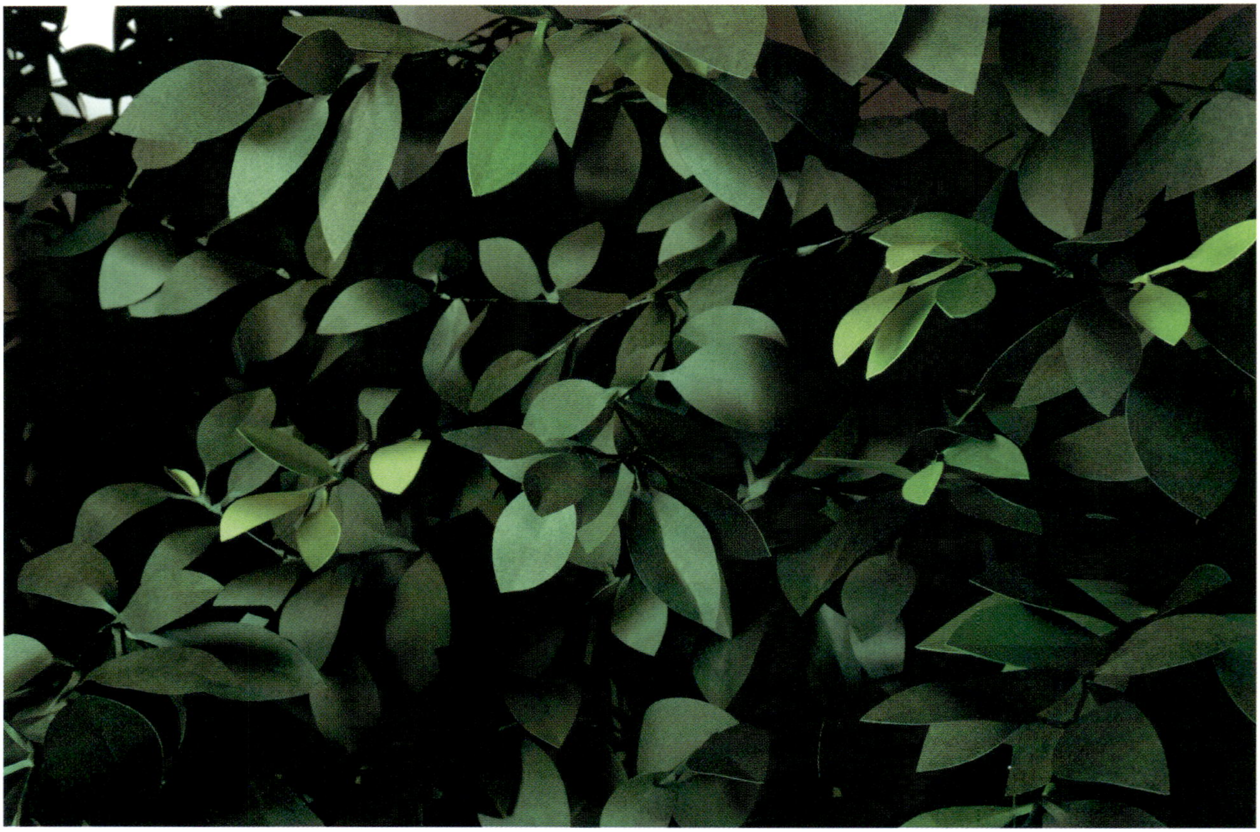

THOMAS DEMAND, HECKE / HEDGE, 1996, C-Print Diasec, 100 x 140 cm / 39 3/8 x 55 1/8".

THOMAS DEMAND, KONSTELLATION / CONSTELLATION, 2000, C-Print Diasec, 180 x 130 cm / 70⅞ x 51”.

Memoryscapes

ANDREAS RUBY

At first it looks like a perfectly real scene that has been photographed and hung on the wall. The gaze basks in the security of a motif that is casual to the extreme. A sink full of dishwater, nothing special. We are about to look away because there is n o t m o r e to see. But then we take another look after all. There seems to be something in the picture that we cannot see. It is as if it were looking back at us. After a while this gaze out of nothing is almost embarrassing. We begin to fight back—by studying the picture, listening to it, and sniffing it out like a bloodhound. There must be something somewhere that betrays the staged scene—if that's what it is. Odd, the polished cleanliness of the chrome sink. So clean, in fact, that it looks as if it had never seen a drop of water. Instead, these curiously sharp edges. Why they occasionally form these dark, thick joints is inexplicable. Maybe the sink isn't... but the cups and glasses are quite... except that the blue handle is so angular... and everything else so thin...

And then something clicks. Doubt spreads like wildfire as, piece by piece, the inner life of the picture proves to be a paper landscape. Immense disillusion, the room that was just beginning to feel familiar implodes before our very eyes. Oddly jumbled feelings ensue: a mixture of incomprehension (why this hide-and-seek?), disenchantment (because we've been tricked), and also admiration (for the superbly executed artifice). Slightly dazed after successfully surviving the initiation, we turn to the other pictures ready to take a now conscious look at their transformation. Having seen through the mental manipulation, the viewer has once again become the confident, active and acting subject, capable of enjoying the drama, like watching a slow-motion instant replay on TV. One is tempted to succumb to imperceptibly growing awareness, to indulge in the fun of self-manipulation. Standing at the levers of the reality mixing board, we knowingly check the fade from illusion to reality (and back again). As DJs of our own experience, we decide how to fade from one track to another. In STALL (Stable, 2000), we can poke around in the straw to our heart's content without feeling threatened by illusion. It's as easy as turning the prince back into a frog: we need only glance at the (wall)paper glued to the wall in the upper right-hand corner to realign our worldview.

As in real DJ-ing, the most fascinating bits are the ones in which both tracks are audible and superimposed, causing mutual interference. The beat gets out of kilter and becomes syncopated; different keys rub off on each other and generate spaces. For instance, in ARCHIV (Archive, 1995) both levels are present at once: emanating from a stack of boxes is a perfectly credible aura of bureaucratic order and the pallid lighting inevitably transports the viewer into deep underground archives. But signs of a paper world are equally visible: the papered edge on the cheek of the ladder and the glued patches on the front of the shelves have just enough presence to hint at the actual quality of the materials used to evoke the scene.

Ambiguity

These synchronous levels of reality lend Thomas Demand's pictures an ambiguity that prevents the discrete spectacle of their transformation from fizzling out after the first time. Since the effect of the pictures thus endures, doubts about their ontologi-

ANDREAS RUBY, based in Cologne, Germany, writes on contemporary art and architecture.

cal status are never fully allayed. We are buffeted back and forth between interpretations. What if they're actually real after all? It is a pleasure to surrender to their seductive promise of reality and to take the immaculate smoothness of their surfaces at face, or rather fake value, as plastered walls, sheet aluminum, plastic coating, plush, wood, glass—rather than paper and cardboard. Nietzsche thinks we cannot bear reality and therefore prefer to deceive ourselves by kneading and molding the world until it suits our fancy.

Simulation / Play

But the last thing Demand wants to do is simulate reality. His pictures have no intention of deceiving viewers; rather, they give them the choice of taking part in the illusion themselves. Illusion is not an act of deception; it is play, as Baudrillard realized late in life, having abandoned the theory of simulation. The Latin verb, *illudere*, means "to mock" or "to play on" something. Play compels reality to surrender the dogma of its unconditional validity in order to flirt with possibility. In the case of Demand's pictures, it acquires diversity by ceaselessly commuting between the imitation and the construction of reality. You can never quite tell what kind of reality prevails in these pictures: that of the represented? or the representation itself? or both at once?

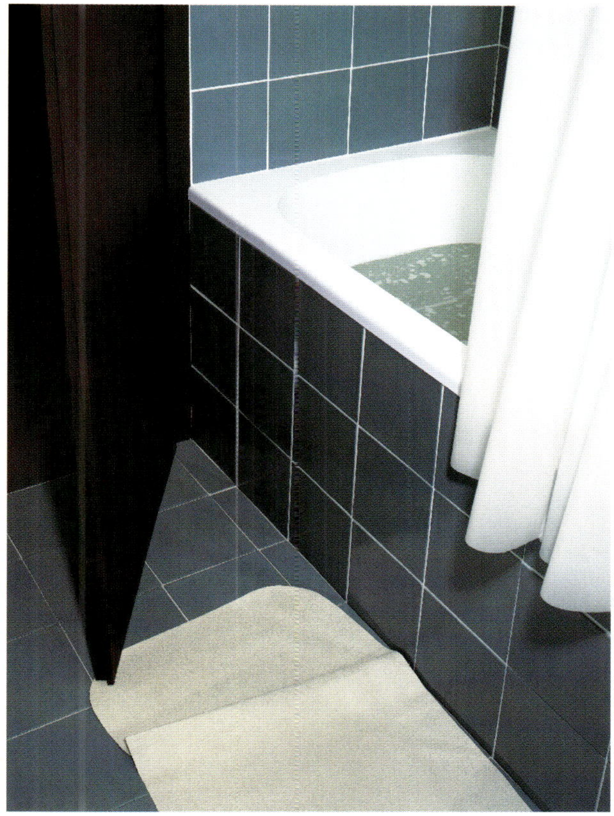

THOMAS DEMAND, BADEZIMMER / BATHROOM, 1997, C-Print Diasec, 160 x 122 cm / 63 x 48".

Reconstruction

To a certain extent Demand's art might be described as reconstruction. It shows spatial situations that once existed as such. We are often ignorant of their origin—geographical or otherwise. Sometimes they are a product of the artist's memory, but they are more frequently based on photographs. Photographs that were often taken to document a situation. The scene of a crime, for example. Through the "reconstruction" of this "photographic evidence" in large-scale models made of paper and cardboard, the photographic impetus of "testifying" spills over into Demand's pictures—the *ça a été* (that happened), declared by Roland Barthes to be the fundamental message of any photograph. Regarding the will to reconstruct, Demand's pictures even outdo the photograph inasmuch as they are not content to deal only in surface depiction but actually reconstruct their referent in three dimensions. At the same time Demand subverts this laboriously reconstructed reality by presenting his models only in large-format photographs (albeit in full scale). This concatenation of reproductions systematically leads the longing to restore reality *ad absurdum*—which is undoubtedly one of photography's most popular motivations. Demand has definitively deconstructed photography as the dominant visual medium of modernism. The fact that he does so by using the medium itself is not a contradiction but indeed a condition of deconstruction. The act of physically building a model of a room after a photograph and then re-photographing the reconstruction obstructs the link between represented and

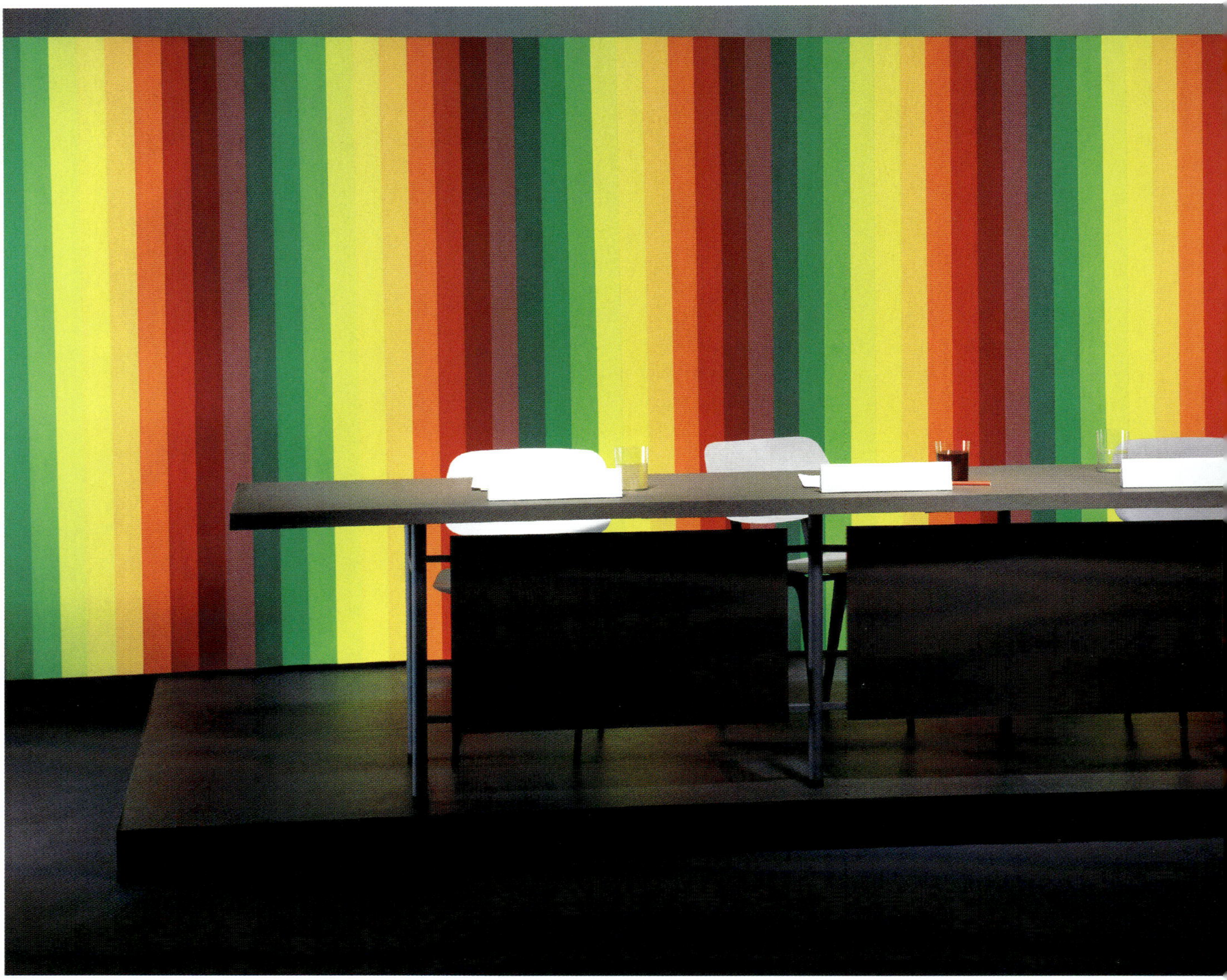

THOMAS DEMAND, STUDIO, 1997, C-Print Diasec, 183,5 x 349,5 cm / 72 1/4 x 137 5/8".

representation to the point of stopping the tide of signals that emanate from signs. Only one thing is certain: these pictures no longer prove anything.

Representation of Representation

Despite Demand's palpable distance from the traditionally mimetic function of art, his pictures cannot be described as having no subject matter. They do have one, only it is not represented directly and as such, but rather as the outcome of several linked representations. The distinction between signifier and signified is thus also driven to extremes, as in the heyday of semiotics. Think of Jean-Luc Godard's Film *Weekend* (1968), in which the red paint used for blood is intentionally shown to be red paint. Similarly Demand's use of paper to represent all manner of things is equally undisguised. Interestingly this chameleon-like exploitation of the material is so alienated in his work that even where it is meant to represent paper, it looks odd and implausible. This applies, for example, to ZEICHENSAAL (Drafting Room, 1996), although the blueprint hanging on the wall radiates its papery materiality with intoxicating sensuality.

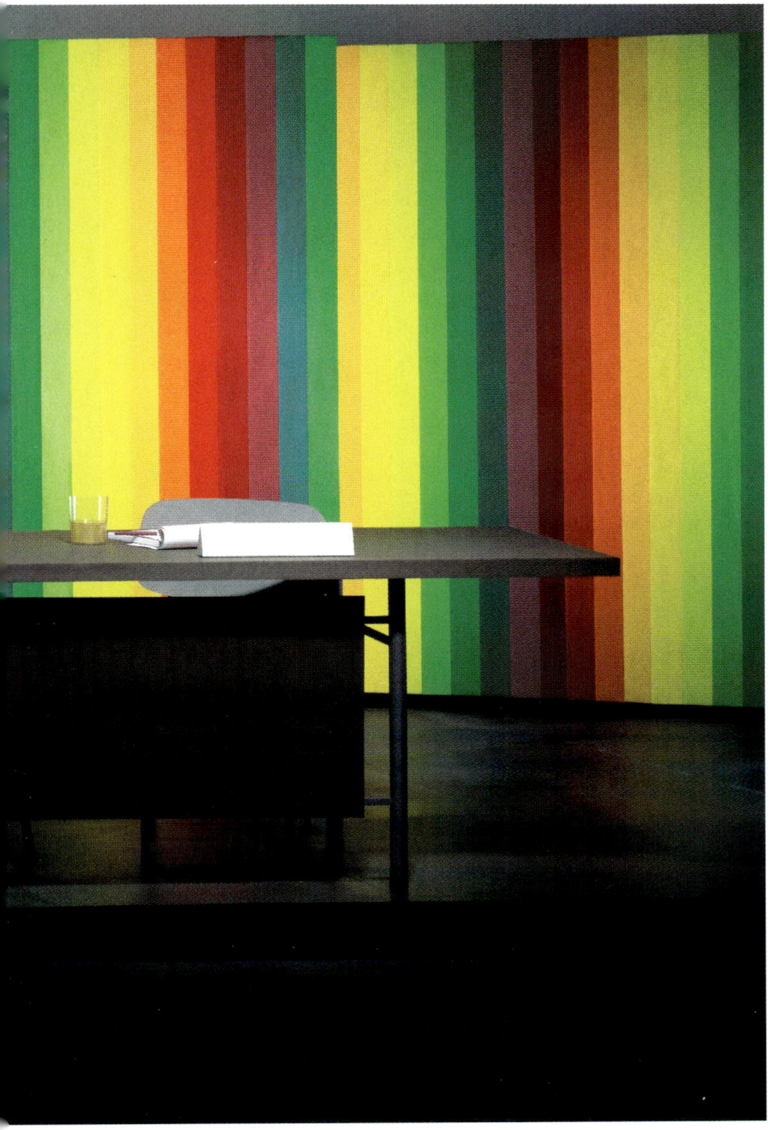

Story / No Story

Given the manner in which the reconstruction fades, Demand's agenda might also be found to address the question of the representation itself. However, the many historical references, resulting from the artist's choice of source photographs, contradict that hypothesis. Even though the titles do not reveal the stories behind the pictures, Demand can rest assured that his audience will not miss the point. In some of his works, he references icons of recent history such as the tunnel at Pont de l'Alma in Paris, the scene of Princess Diana's fatal accident. In BADEZIMMER (BEAU RIVAGE) / Bathroom (Beau Rivage), 1997, viewers from Germany will no doubt be reminded of the famous photograph in the magazine, *Stern*, of the German politician Barschel found dead in the bathtub, while STUDIO (1997) brings back to life countless showings of *Was bin ich?* (German version of *What's My Line?*).

Many of Demand's pictures do not entail such a prominent iconography; they are anonymous. What

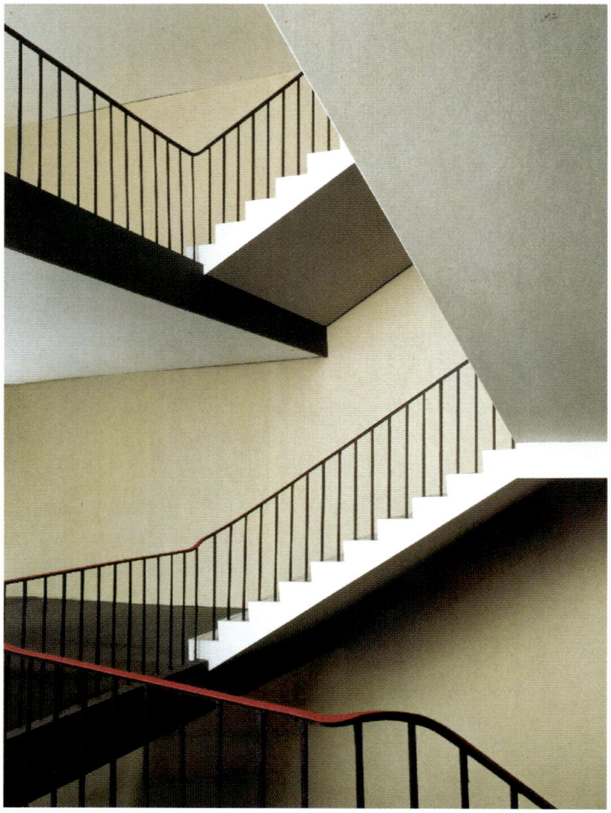

THOMAS DEMAND, TREPPENHAUS / STAIRCASE, 1995, C-Print Diasec, 150 x 118 cm / 59 x 46½".

then is the function of pictorial recourse to the *fait divers* from the daily press and television? The main concern is hardly the content of the evoked anecdotes; the use of them is too understated (and sometimes only discovered fortuitously, for example by reading secondary literature). Their significance must lie elsewhere. In view of Demand's deconstruction of photography, one might plausibly argue that the themes of his pictures primarily serve as catalysts of memory. Not the memory of a specific event but memory as a technique of conjuring world, which offers an alternative to the above-mentioned cultural practice of photography as a reality check. (As a recent commercial puts it, "a vacation without photos is like an event without a memory.") The paradigma of memory turns the *ça a été* of a photographically defined reality into "I saw that" (or heard it, experienced it, etc.). What matters is no longer that something happened but that I remember it. This aspect of memory substantially influences our approach to the pictures, especially those that are not furnished with an iconographic eye-catcher. We inevitably project the act of remembering inspired by the pictures with "prominent" motives onto the other pictures as well. These garages, walls of buildings, escalators could all be "important" places; we just don't have the necessary background information. Often enough they really are important as in SCHEUNE (Barn, 1997), which is derived from a photograph of Jackson Pollock's studio in Long Island. But deciphering the pictures and exposing their secrets is not the main concern. It is far more incisive to engage that other form of memory generated by the encounter between the pictures and our curiosity. A memory that does not reconstruct stories but actually produces them (because they are no longer or not yet there, in contrast to the room in which they potentially could have happened or will happen). This makes COPYSHOP (1999) a forever open-ended picture because it offers our imagination endless leeway and stimulation for reconstructing the events that have taken or might take place in this room with its enigmatic ordinariness.

Memoryscapes

In another series of pictures, Demand fictionalizes the pictorial space by adding an abstract aura to his representations. In the architectural pictures in particular there are hardly any details. The buildings become pure volume, schematically outlined by light and shadow. Some of the pictures, like LABOR (Laboratory, 2000), PARKGARAGE (Car Park, 1996), or BALKONE (Balconies, 1997), could almost be paintings. We stand in front of them, wanting so badly to believe that they represent built models, but simply unable to. This lack of belief lends the pictures a highly idiosyncratic sense of reality. Demand is not interested in photography as such; he is engaged in a kind of medial cross-dressing. The photograph is the final form the works take but they often obey laws entirely different from those of photography. Often we aren't even aware of the photograph as such because we are so involved in deciphering the room that it depicts. There is no denying that Demand started out as a sculptor. In fact, photography did not play a role in his work until he ran out of room for his proliferating installations. A shortage of space finally made him engage photography as a spatial medium. The fact that his more recent works, such as TUNNEL (1999) or ROLLTREPPE (Escalator, 2000), move on from photography to film does not mean that his artistic discourse has switched to another medium; rather, the principles underlying his endeavors have become even more focussed. Again, Demand is not primarily interested in the film medium as such, but in the stimulation of memory, which happens in this case to be activated by the moving picture. In TUNNEL, Lady Diana's last ride through subterranean Paris is presented as a televised re-enactment. The real-world source of ROLLTREPPE remains as enigmatic as the oddly monotone movement of the filmed representation. The "film" actually consists of 24 single pictures of an escalator that Demand built, with a slight shift in the position of the steps in each picture. The single pictures were then mounted as a moving sequence with a computer program that creates the illusion of movement—a technique that is used in both traditional animated films and in the latest Hollywood flicks to create those parts of reality that are not available in nature. The flowing movement of motion pictures, which is of course completely synthetic, serves to enhance the reality effect of Demand's work even more. The filmic injection of motion automatically seems to lend the images an aura of credibility and pulls the ground out from under any attempt to question their truth (at least if one embraces Popper's principle that truth is what cannot be falsified). Viewers of Demand's pictorial spaces ultimately find themselves facing the same situation as in the photograph at the end of Michelangelo Antonioni's *Blow up:* should they believe what they see, or do they see what they believe?

(Translation: Catherine Schelbert)

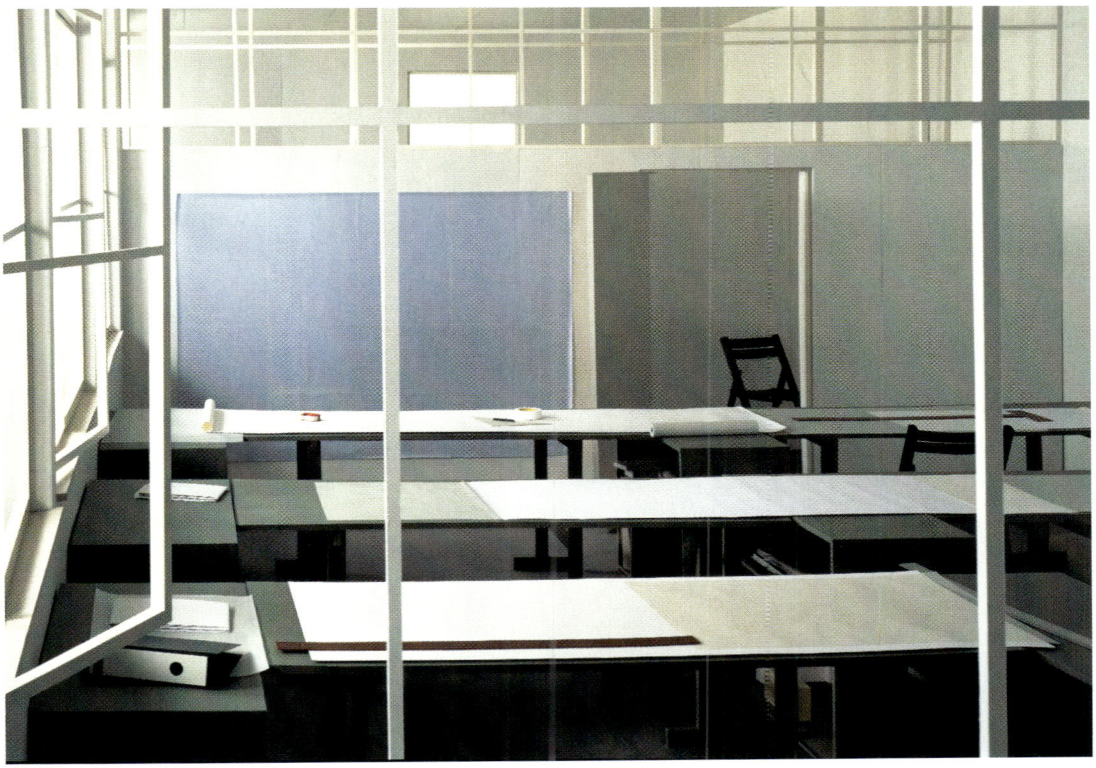

THOMAS DEMAND, ZEICHENSAAL / DRAFTING ROOM, 1996, C-Print Diasec, 183,5 x 285 cm / 72 1/4 x 112 1/5".

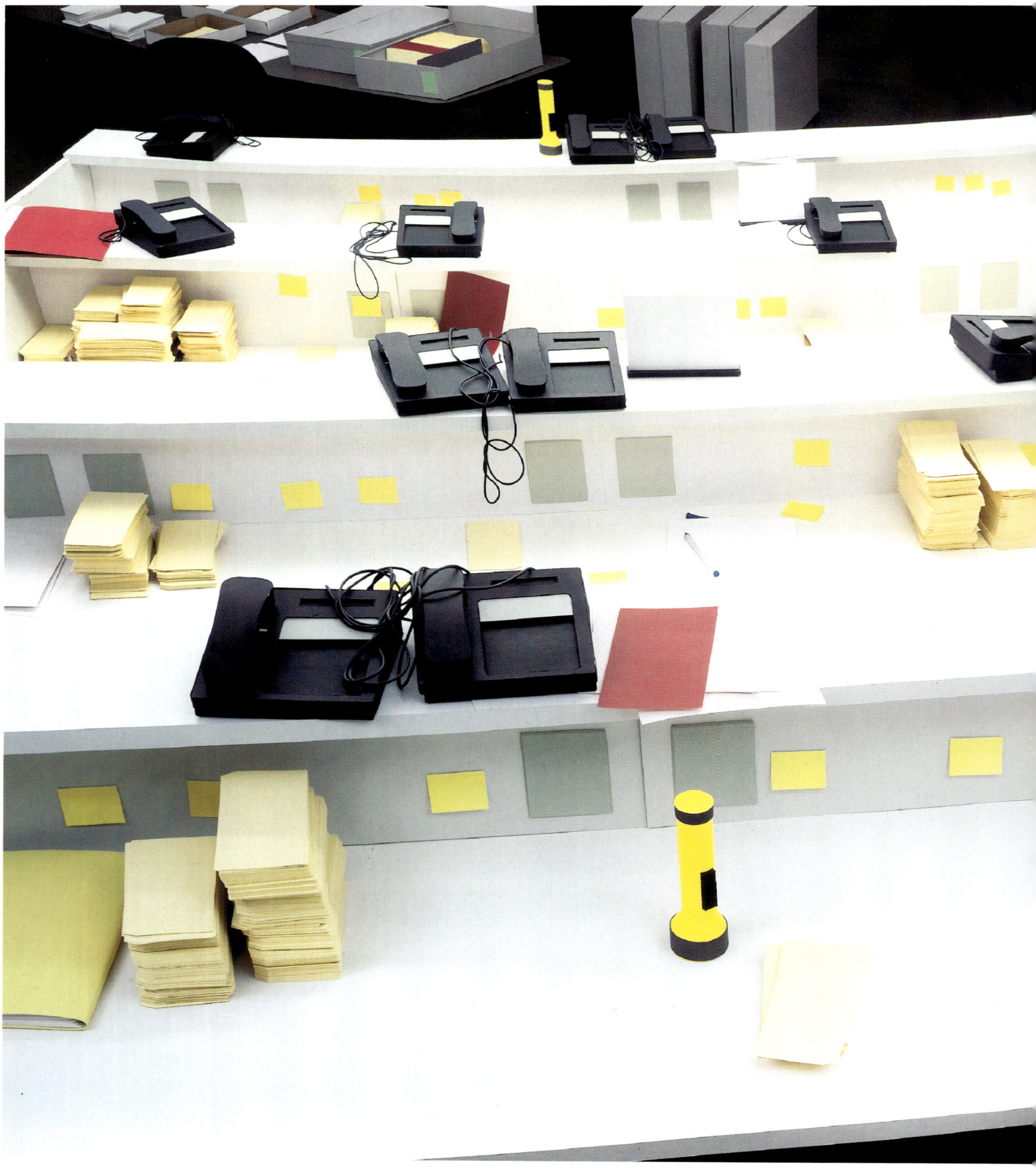

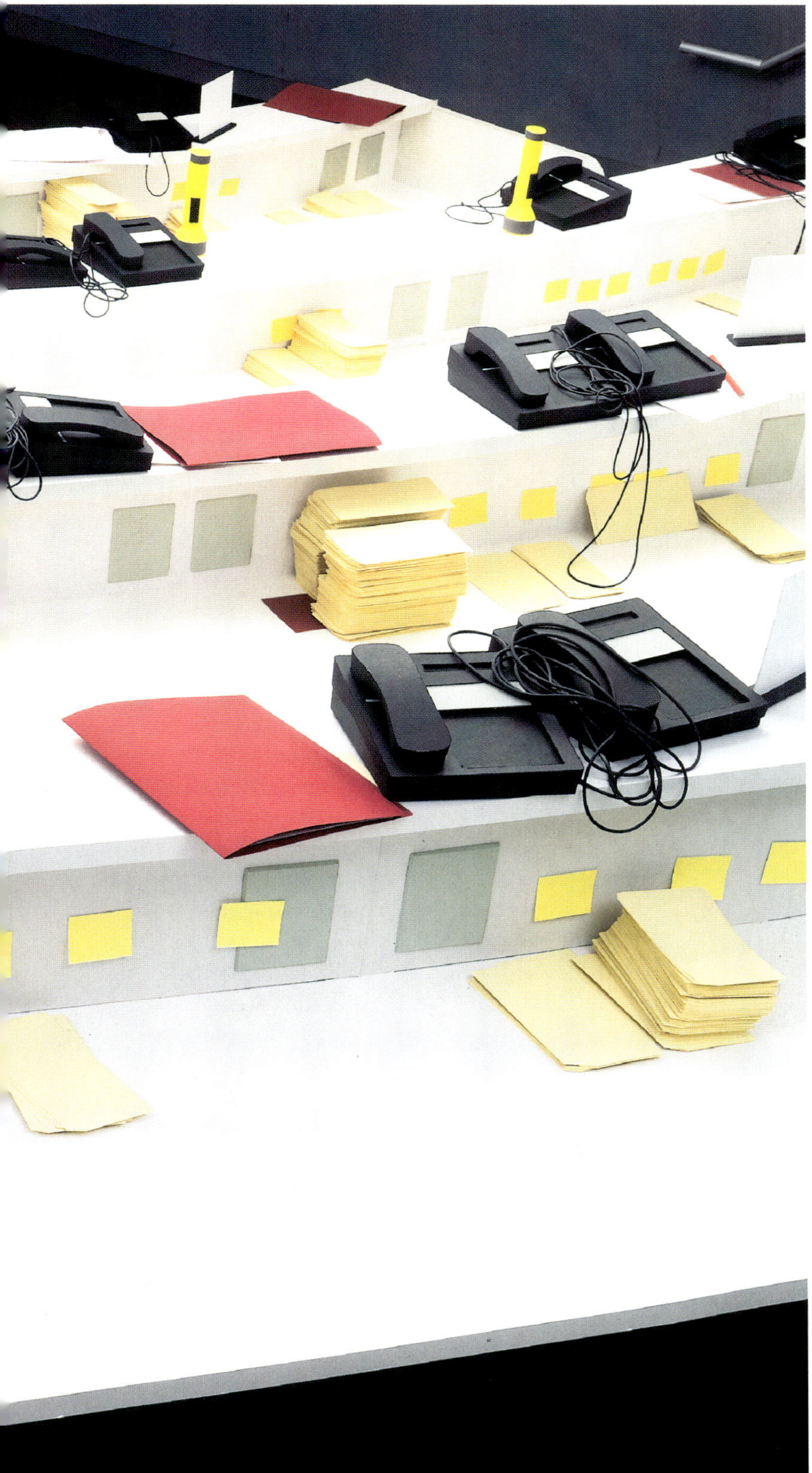

THOMAS DEMAND, POLL / AUSZÄHLUNG, 2001, C-Print Diasec, 165 x 275 cm / 65 x 108 1/4".

Der Neutronen-bomben-Effekt

JÖRG HEISER

Es ist niemand da, in diesem Raum, der aussieht wie eine Telefonzentrale oder der Arbeitsplatz eines Brokers. Vier lange Reihen weisser, zweistufiger Arbeitspulte, leicht von oben gesehen, als stünde man selbst vor der ersten Pultreihe; die Kanten der Pulte treten in dem in Büros üblichen Neonlicht scharf hervor. Irgendwie wirkt die Perspektive verkürzt, als wäre der Raum zwischen den Pultreihen zu schmal, um wirklich benutzt werden zu können. Mattschwarze, offenbar nicht angeschlossene Telefonapparate schlummern auf dem erhöhten Teil der Pulte. Warum sind sie nicht angeschlossen? Hat die Arbeit noch nicht begonnen oder wurde sie schon beendet? Gelbe unbeschriebene Post-It-Zettelchen sind allzu ordentlich befestigt. Ferner einige Stapel von ebenfalls gelben, genauso leeren Karteikarten. Vier gelbe Taschenlampen liegen über die Pulte verteilt. (Wozu braucht man an einem solchen Ort Taschenlampen?) Fünf rote Ordner setzen einen Akzent und ein einziger Kugelschreiber liegt auf einem makellos weissen Blatt Papier. Man sieht keine Stühle, keine gekritzelten Notizen, keine Kaffeeflecken, keinerlei Spuren menschlicher Aktivität. Dies ist kein Büro, sondern die leere Hülle eines Büros, aus dem jede Regung und jedes Anzeichen von Belebtsein getilgt wurden. Die Frage, ob die Arbeit noch nicht begonnen hat oder eben beendet wurde, ist sinnlos, da dieser Raum offensichtlich jedem zeitlichen Ablauf entrückt ist.

Dennoch entstand Thomas Demands POLL (Auszählung, 2001) aufgrund einer Reihe von Bildern, die zu Beginn des Jahres, wenige Wochen nach der Amtseinsetzung von Präsident George W. Bush, als das Werk in New York erstmals gezeigt wurde, allen geläufig waren. Wochenlang war sie Ende Jahr in den Medien präsent gewesen: die höchst umstrittene, manuelle Nachzählung von Stimmzetteln in Palm Beach, Florida, die der fragwürdigen Einsetzung Bushs vorausging. Die endlosen Analysen dieses absurden Vorgangs waren durchsetzt mit Bildern von Freiwilligen, die perforierte Stimmzettel unter die Lupe nahmen, als handle es sich um forensische Beweismittel, nur um herauszufinden, ob die Stimme an Bush oder Gore ging. Aber am häufigsten sah man jene Bilder, welche die mit diesem Vorgang verbundene, mühevolle Arbeit vor Augen führen sollten, und sie zeigten Nahaufnahmen ganzer Stapel von Stimmzetteln, im Fernsehen, in den Zeitungen und im Internet (wo Demand sie her hat). Dank der merkwürdigen Schlacht um die Präsidentschaft in Florida ist das Bild sich stapelnder Stimmzettel zu einem Sinnbild administrativen Versagens oder gar Verhinderns bei der Ermittlung des Volkswillens geworden.

Das Symbol des Papierstapels passt ausgezeichnet zur skulpturalen Seite von Demands Werk, ebenso wie der damit assoziierte mühevolle Arbeitsprozess. Denn wie alle Arbeiten Demands seit den frühen 90er Jahren ist POLL eine peinlich genaue, modell-

---

JÖRG HEISER ist Redaktor von *Frieze* und lebt in Berlin.

THOMAS DEMAND, STAPEL/ PILE (#5), 2001, C-Print Diasec, 36 x 55 cm / 14¼ x 21⅝".

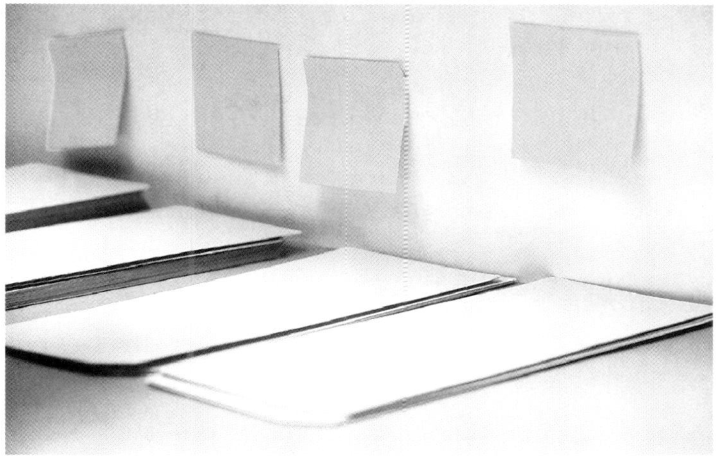

hafte Wiedergabe von Objekten an einem tatsächlich existierenden Ort – in diesem Fall des Büros, wo die Nachzählungen stattfanden –, handgefertigt aus Papier und Karton, genau oder doch nahezu im Originalmassstab. Und genauso unfassbar wie der «Wille des Volkes» bleibt auch dieses Modell, da es nicht selbst gezeigt wird, sondern nur vermittelt durch die exakte photographische Aufnahme mit einer Plattenkamera.

Die Täuschung ist zugleich versteckt und offenbar: versteckt, weil das Modell hinsichtlich Proportion und Oberfläche exakt ist. Dank der Verwendung einer industriell gefertigten, dichten, einfarbigen Papiersorte ist im Modell nichts Individuelles, nichts gestisch Geformtes zu entdecken. Aber zugleich offenbart es doch seinen abbildhaften Charakter, denn, egal wie präzis die Verarbeitung, Papier kann doch nie die unterschiedlichen Texturen aller anderen Materialien ersetzen. Wichtiger noch ist das bewusste Fehlen jeglicher Gebrauchs- und Verschleissspuren, was deutlich zeigt, dass eine Verschiebung stattgefunden hat. Im Grunde ist die «Arbeit», die im Originalraum geleistet wurde, ihres Körpers beraubt worden und hat die Gestalt von Demands aufwändiger Nachbildung angenommen.

Die Nachzählung in Florida machte einfache, alltägliche Dinge wie Papierstapel in einem Büro zu Symbolen einer gescheiterten Demokratie: Auf die Zählmaschinen konnte man nicht mehr zählen, was eine arbeitsintensive manuelle Überprüfung notwendig machte. Diese surreale historische Anekdote verdeutlicht eine allgemein gültige Wahrheit: Selbst die normiertesten Gegenstände und Räume können einzigartige Bedeutung erlangen. Demands Bilder halten die Zeit nicht an, um dem Ahistorischen zu huldigen, sondern um den – durch das Leben in standardisierter, industriell reproduzierter Umgebung verursachten – Verlust des historischen Gedächtnisses zu betrauern und zu bekämpfen. Was POLL von des Künstlers früheren Wiedergaben historischer Schauplätze abhebt – etwa von RAUM (1994), das Hitlers Hauptquartier nach dem Bombenattentat vom 20. Juli 1944 zeigt, oder der Pollocks Atelier nachempfundenen SCHEUNE (1997) –, ist, dass das Ereignis selbst zum Zeitpunkt der ersten Ausstellung noch nicht wirklich historisch war und sein Stellenwert noch nicht feststand, was aber das grausame, trocken pointierte Ignorieren einzelner Gebrauchsspuren nur umso deutlicher hervortreten lässt.

Demands Arbeit wirkt wie eine Neutronenbombe in belebten Räumen: Die Strukturen sind unversehrt, aber jedes Anzeichen von Gebrauch, Geschichte, Leben ist verschwunden. Aber gerade die Grausamkeit dieser Technik zeigt uns – *ex negativo* –, in welchem Mass technisch reproduzierte Räume und Gegenstände bereits geschichtslos sind, sowohl physisch wie medial, und dass sie nur durch das Hervorheben ihrer Mängel und Risse erträglich werden. Indem er sie zu an Dioramen erinnernden Schaubildern verarbeitet, die er in eigener Handarbeit herstellt, erzeugt Demand eine Art Oxymoron: Er entfernt einerseits diese Mängel aus den Bildern, versieht sie aber gleichzeitig mit neuen und macht sie so für unsere – und seine – Phantasien zugänglich.

Dieses Vorgehen ist fast eine Art ironische Verstärkung dessen, was wir im Leben täglich tun: Wir versuchen die moderne Welt bewohnbar zu machen, indem wir uns gerade ihre allgemeinsten Elemente persönlich anzueignen versuchen. Warhol hat einmal bemerkt, dass jedes McDonald's-Lokal der Welt ein Stück Zuhause sei, etwas Bekanntes, ja geradezu intim Vertrautes bezüglich Aussehen und Geschmack. In Douglas Couplands Roman *Miss Wyoming* (2000) läuft die gleichnamige Heldin nach einem Grenzerlebnis zwischen Leben und Tod – sie ist die einzige Überlebende eines Flugzeugabsturzes – weg, taucht für eine Weile unter und führt ein Obdachlosenleben. «Sie schlenderte durch das gehsteiglose Viertel, als sähe sie ihr Land zum ersten Mal – die Verkehrsschilder, die Autos, die Lichter und die Schaufenster waren grösser, heller und protziger als nötig. Der Geruch von Brathähnchen und Dieselabgasen stieg ihr in die Nase, aber da sie das bisschen Geld, das sie besass, bereits ausgegeben hatte, konnte sie sich nichts zu essen kaufen. Der Hunger war kaum noch auszuhalten. Sie lief stundenlang durch die Gegend. Sie kam an achtzig Wendy's, hundert Taco Bells, siebenhundert Exxon-Tankstellen vorbei, und dann gelangte sie zu ihrem neunhundertsten McDonald's...»[1] Miss Wyoming bemerkt einen Koch, der ein grosses Tablett voller nicht verkaufter Hamburger samt Verpackung in einen Müllcontainer kippt. Sie klettert hinein, um sie sich zu schnappen, und wird im Container eingeschlossen. «Es gab kein Licht, und in der Dunkelheit barsten die Konturen, die sie ertastete, wie kaputte Feuerwerkskörper unter ihren Fingerspitzen. Sie hatte Hunger, doch ihr Ekel vor den toten Lebensmitteln überwog. Sie versuchte sich ganz klein zu machen, wie ein Vogel, der in einem Haus gefangen ist. Und dann entspannte sie sich. Ein bisschen. (...) Aus gefalzter Pappe baute sie sich in der Ecke einen improvisierten Schlafplatz. Sie breitete zur Isolation eine Schicht aus trockenen Abfällen als Unterlage aus, und auf einer Seite errichtete sie sicherheitshal-

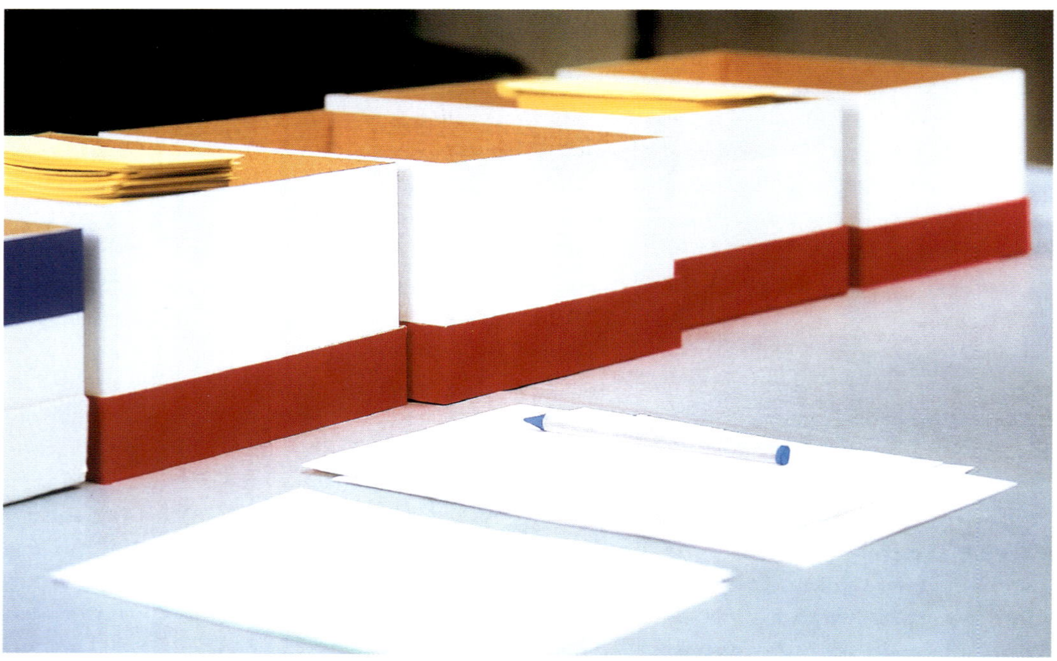

THOMAS DEMAND, STAPEL / PILE (#1),
C-Print Diasec, 53 x 84 cm / 20⅞ x 33".

ber ein Lawinendach, falls der Müll in der Nacht zusammenbrechen sollte. Als Kissen benutzte sie wiederum Pappe, auf die sie eine Tüte voller zerquetschter Pappbecher legte. Sie war selbst überrascht, wie gut sie sich in ihrer neuen Welt zurechtfand...»[2]

Eingeschlossen im wahllosen Durcheinander industriell erzeugter Produkte, macht die Heldin etwas Ähnliches wie Demand (der seine «Skulpturen» wegwirft, sobald sie photographiert sind): Sie verändert die Ordnung der Dinge, um sie sich anzueignen. Das traumatische Ereignis (der Flugzeugabsturz, das fehlgeschlagene Attentat auf Hitler) weckt die Kraft zur Aneignung, zur Rekonstruktion, zur Inbesitznahme. Das Trauma wird nicht neu g e s p i e l t, um es zu beherrschen und zu kontrollieren, sondern gewissermassen neu v e r r ä u m l i c h t, um eine Art Befreiung zu erlangen. Arbeiten wie ROLLTREPPE (2000), DREI GARAGEN (1995) oder BALKONE (1997) wenden dieses Nocheinmal-in-den-Raum-Stellen auf einförmigste Elemente unserer urbanen Umgebung an. Die Rolltreppe, zum Beispiel, mag Zeugin einander zugeworfener Blicke oder der Ausübung von Gewalt gewesen sein, aber in erster Linie ist sie halt doch nur eine Rolltreppe wie jede andere. Die Gleichgültigkeit des künstlerischen Blickwinkels wiederholt im Grunde die Gleichgültigkeit der modernen Architektur gegenüber den mit ihrem Funktionalismus einhergehenden Konsequenzen für das menschliche Individuum.

In der Mitte des fünfzehnten Jahrhunderts verglich der Architekturtheoretiker Filarete die Teile eines Bauwerks mit menschlichen Körperteilen, mit Augen, Ohren, Mund. Die natürliche Funktion und symmetrische Harmonie im Entwurf der Kinder Gottes galt als Mass aller Dinge. Mit dem Heraufdämmern des industriellen Zeitalters entwickelten die Romantiker eine skeptische Sicht auf diese angebliche Vollkommenheit und Harmonie, und nach E.T.A. Hoffmanns *Das öde Haus* (1817) läutete Edgar Allan Poe mit seinem *Fall des Hauses Ascher* (1839) die Totenglocke für die Verbindung von statischer und körperlicher Balance. Er verglich das Gebäude weniger mit dem Körper als solchem als vielmehr mit verschiedenen Seelenzuständen und den mit ihnen verbundenen Ausdrucksformen, von Freude und Schönheit bis zur Depression und dem blanken Schrecken des Untergangs.[3] In der Ballade «Das Geisterschloss», die in die Erzählung eingebettet ist, wird das Schloss eines Königs zunächst in der Phase des Ruhms und Wohlstands beschrieben: «Von Perlen und Rubinen glutend / war des Palastes Tor.» Es wird deutlich, dass die Perlen für Zähne stehen, die Rubine für die Lippen – es handelt sich um das Tor zur Seele. Später, im unaufhaltsamen Niedergang, fliehen die Geister durch dieses Tor und mit ihnen das Leben, die Gesundheit und die Inspiration: «und durch das fahle Tor stürzt schwellend / ein Spukhauf her, / auf und davon – sie lachen gellend – / doch lächeln nimmermehr.»[4]

Garagen, Rolltreppen, Balkone – architektonische Elemente, die auf der ganzen Welt technisch gleich hergestellt werden – waren noch nie von Geistern bewohnt, das hat etwas Beruhigendes und wirkt zugleich umso erschreckender. Es ist, als liesse Demands Kunst die romantische Furcht vor dem Verfall mit ihrem modernistischen Pendant kollidieren: der Furcht vor Konservierung. Bauwerke aus Metall, Glas und Beton mit ihren undurchdringlichen Oberflächen sind ohne weiteres völlig gleich reproduzierbar, sowohl virtuell wie physisch. Demand führt hier eine semiotische Spaltung ein, indem er sie in Karton nachahmt – und nebenbei auch gleich noch die Ablehnung «weicher» Materialien und der Raumillusion durch den Minimalismus unterläuft. Demand konzentriert sich auf die räumliche Grundstruktur und Oberflächenbeschaffenheit von so unscheinbaren Schauplätzen wie dem Stimmenzählbüro in Florida letztlich nicht, um die gelebte Erfahrung, mit denen sie aufgeladen sind, zu ignorieren, sondern gerade um sie heraufzubeschwören.

(Übersetzung: Wilma Parker)

1) Douglas Coupland, *Miss Wyoming*, übers. von Tina Hohl, Hoffmann und Campe, Hamburg 2001, S. 88.
2) Ebenda, S. 107–109.
3) Vergleiche dazu auch: Anthony Vidler, *The Architectural Uncanny*, MIT Press, Cambridge, MA, & London 1992, S. 17–20, sowie Jonathan Jones Artikel über Edgar Allan Poe und das zeitgenössische Kunstschaffen in *Frieze*, 55, November 2000.
4) Edgar Allan Poe, *Der Fall des Hauses Ascher*, übers. von Arno Schmidt und Hans Wollschläger, Haffmans Verlag, Zürich 1994, S. 46–47.

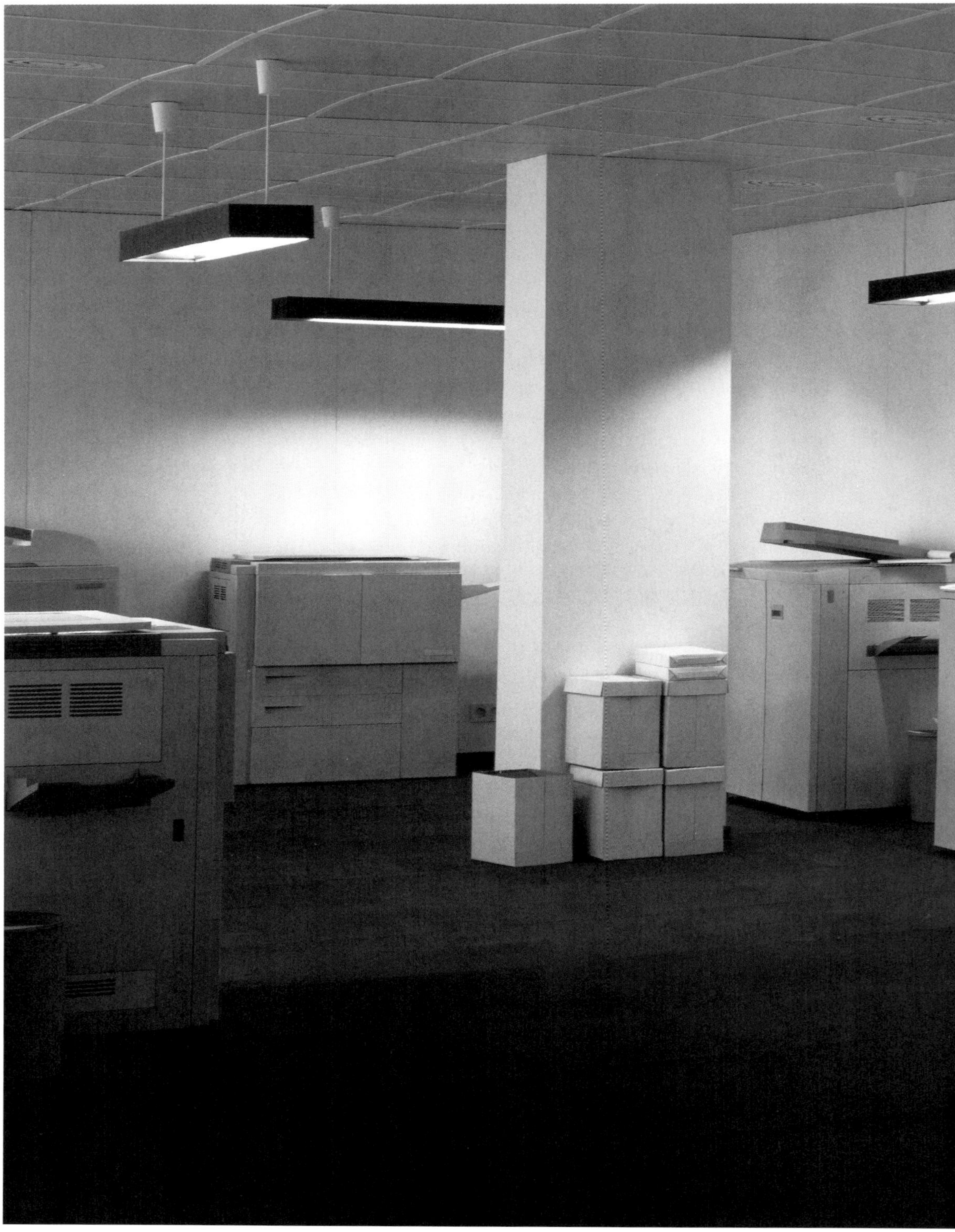

THOMAS DEMAND, COPYSHOP, 1999, C-Print Diasec, 183,5 x 300 cm / 72¼ x 118⅛".

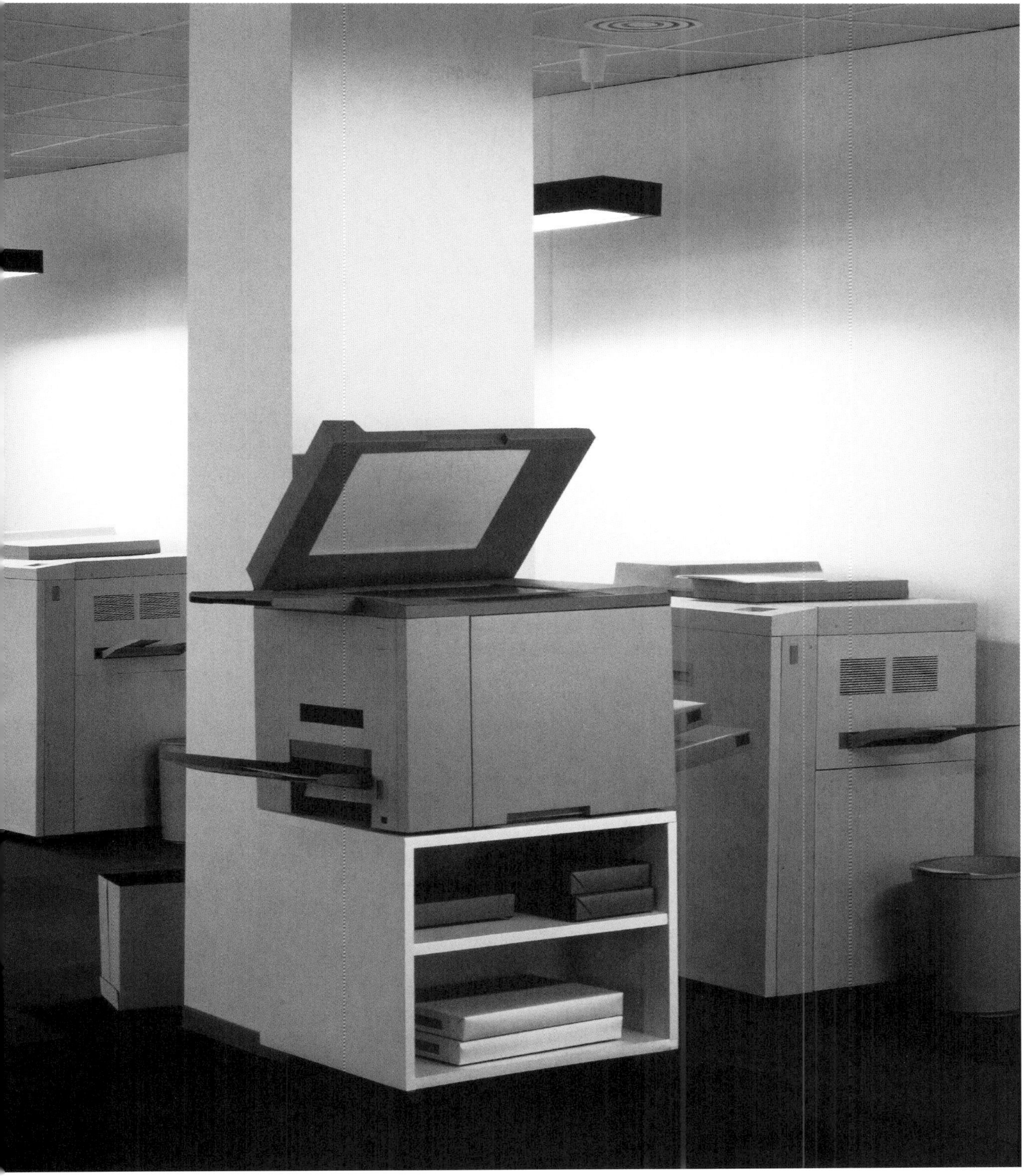

The Neutron Bomb Effect

JÖRG HEISER

No one is present in what looks like a calling center or a broker's boiler room. Four long rows of white, two-level working desks, the edges contoured by standard office neon lighting, are seen slightly from above, as if one were standing in front of the first row. Somehow the perspective seems contracted, as if the aisles between the rows of desks were too narrow to allow people to use them. Matte black telephones rest on the top level, cables seemingly unplugged. Why are they unplugged, has work not yet begun, or is it already finished? Yellow Post-It notes are attached all too neatly, completely blank. Stacks of equally yellow, equally blank filing cards. There are four yellow flashlights lying on the desks. (What do you need flashlights for in such a place?) Five red folders punctuate the scene, while a single pen rests on an immaculately white sheet of paper. There are no chairs visible, no scribbling, no coffee stains, no traces of human presence. This is not an office, this is the empty shell of an office, deprived of all gestures and signs of habitation. The question of whether work has begun or is already finished is pointless as it becomes apparent that this space is utterly isolated from the very passage of time.

Yet Thomas Demand's POLL (2001) is based on a series of images that were current when the work was first exhibited in New York in early 2001, just weeks after the inauguration of President George W. Bush. The highly contested manual recount of the ballots in Palm Beach, Florida, which preceded the controversial installation of Bush as president, had occupied the media for week after week in late 2000. The endless analyses of this absurd process were interspersed with images of volunteers peering at punched ballots, like forensic evidence, in order to find out whether the vote should go to Bush or Gore. But the repetitive visual bites, used to represent the painstaking labor involved in this process, were close-ups of ballot stacks shown on TV, in the papers, and on the internet (where Demand got them from). The memorable battle for the presidency in Florida has in fact established the image of stacked ballots as an emblem for the failed or obstructed administrational attempt to verify the People's will.

This emblem of the paper stack sits very well with the sculptural aspect of Demand's work, as does the laborious process it entails. For POLL, like all the work Demand has done since the early nineties, is a painstaking model rendition of objects in an actual site—in this case the office where the recounts took place—handmade of cardboard and paper, in near or absolute life size. And just as the "People's will" remains intangible, so does the model, as it is not shown itself, but only in and through the pristine photograph captured with a plate camera.

The illusion is concealed and revealed at the same time: concealed because the model is precise in proportion and surface. Employing the industrially

JÖRG HEISER is associate editor of *Frieze*, based in Berlin.

produced opaque quality of unicolored paper, the model lacks any signs of individuality, of gestural forming. Yet at the same time, it reveals its simulacral character because, no matter how precise the construction, paper cannot fully emulate the texture of all other materials. More important, the intentional lack of signs of wear and tear makes clear that a displacement has occurred. Basically, the "labor" that went on in the original space has been disembodied and shifted to (Demand's) labor of copying it.

The Florida recounts turned simple, everyday things like stacks of paper in an office into fetishes of failed democracy: the counting machines could not be counted on, necessitating labor-intensive manual inspection. This surreal anecdote of history thus highlights a general truth: even the most generic objects and spaces can be charged with a unique meaning. In Demand's pictures, time is frozen not in order to venerate the ahistoric, but to mourn and fight the loss of historic memory that life in a generic environment preempts. What sets POLL apart from the artist's earlier renditions of historic sites—RAUM (Room, 1994), which shows Hitler's headquarters after they had been bombed on 20 July 1944, or SCHEUNE (Barn, 1997), which is modeled after Pollock's studio—is that at the time of its first exhibition the event was not really historic yet, its status still undecided, which makes the cruel, deadpan indifference to details of use all the more apparent.

Demand's work acts like a neutron bomb on inhabited space: it leaves the structure intact while purging it of any sign of utilization, history, life. Yet the cruelty of this technique precisely indicates—*ex negativo*—how technically reproduced spaces and objects are actually already dehistoricized, both physically and medially, and how they can only be made bearable by pointing out their flaws and fissures. By turning them into dioramic simulacra, constructed by his own manual labor, Demand produces a kind of oxymoron: he both empties them of these flaws and charges them again with new ones, making them available for our—and his—phantasmic investments.

This approach is almost a kind of ironic amplification of what we do in everyday life: we try to make the modern world inhabitable by clinging to even its most generic elements, trying to make them our

THOMAS DEMAND, STAPEL / PILE (#2), C-Print Diasec, 53 x 50 cm / 20 7/8 x 19 5/8".

own. Warhol once remarked how every McDonald's around the world is a bit of home, something familiar, almost intimate in look and taste. In Douglas Coupland's *Miss Wyoming* (2000), the eponymous heroine, after a near-death experience—she is the sole survivor of a plane crash—walks off and vanishes for a while into a hobo life. "She strolled the sidewalk-free neighborhood as if seeing her country for the first time—the signs and cars and lights and shop fronts bigger and brighter and more powerful than they needed to be. She caught whiffs of fried chicken and diesel fumes, but having spent her only quarters, she couldn't buy food. She was starving. She walked for hours. She passed eighty Wendy's, a hundred Taco Bells, seven hundred Exxons, and then she came upon her nine hundredth McDonald's..."[1)] Miss Wyoming notices a crew chief who puts a large tray of fully wrapped, unsold burgers into a dumpster. She climbs in to get hold of them, but then gets locked inside. "There was no light, and in its absence, the shapes she touched burst forth on her fingertips like crippled fireworks. She was hungry, but her repulsion for the dead food overrode her hunger. She tried shrinking herself, like a bird caught inside a house. And then she relaxed. A bit. (...) Using folded cardboard, she built herself an impromptu shanty in the corner. For the shanty's floor she placed a buffer layer of dry garbage to insulate her from the dumpster's bottom, and on one side she built an avalanche shed, so as to be safe if the trash collapsed during the night. For a pillow she used folded cardboard, onto which she placed a bag full of crushed waxed paper cups. She was surprising herself with her adeptness at navigating inside her new world..."[2)]

Locked in the jumble of the generically produced, the heroine is doing something very similar to Demand (who throws away his "sculptures" after they are photographed): she slightly alters the structure to make it her own. The traumatic event (the plane crash, the failed attempt to assassinate Hitler) is a trigger for the power to adapt, to reconstruct, to inhabit. In a way, trauma is not re-e n a c t e d in order to master and control it, but "re-e n s p a c e d" to find release.

Pieces like ROLLTREPPE (Escalator, 2000), DREI GARAGEN (Three Garages, 1995) or BALKONE (Balconies, 1997) apply "re-enspacement" to some of the most uniform elements of the urban environment. The escalator, for instance, may have been witness to gazes exchanged or violence inflicted, but first and foremost it's just an escalator, like any other. The indifference of the artistic perspective basically mimics the indifference of modernist architecture's functionalist aftermath to the individual human being.

In the mid 15th century, Renaissance theorist Filarete compared the elements of a building to those of a human body, its eyes, ears, mouth. The natural function and symmetrical harmony in the design of god's children was supposed to set the scales. With the dawn of the industrial era, the Romantics became skeptical of this supposed perfect function and harmony and, after E.T.A. Hoffmann's *Deserted House* (1817), Edgar Allan Poe rang the death knell on the conjunction of static and bodily balance in *The Fall of the House of Usher* (1839). He likened the building not so much to the body as such but to the different psychic states and the appearance they create, from joy and beauty to depression and utter terror of decay.[3)] In the poem "The Haunted Palace," inserted into the story, a king's residence is first described as being in a state of glory and prosperity: "And all with pearl and ruby glowing / Was the fair palace door." It becomes apparent that "pearl" stands for teeth and "ruby" for lips—the door to the soul. Then, in decline, the spirits leave through it, and with them life,

THOMAS DEMAND, DREI GARAGEN / THREE GARAGES, 1995, C-Print Diasec, 108 x 223 cm / 42 1/2 x 87 4/5".

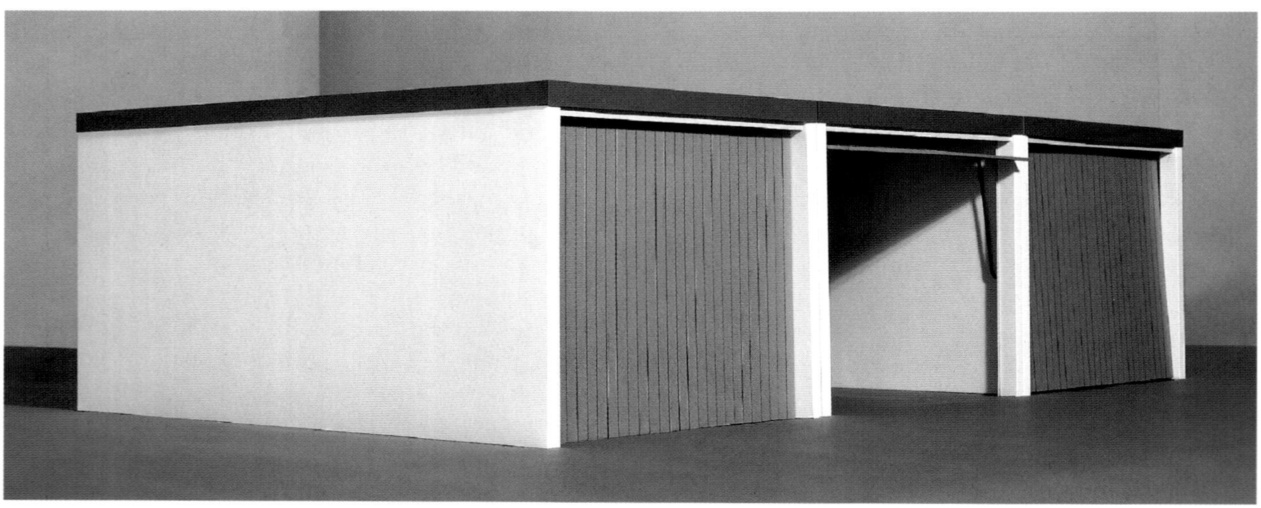

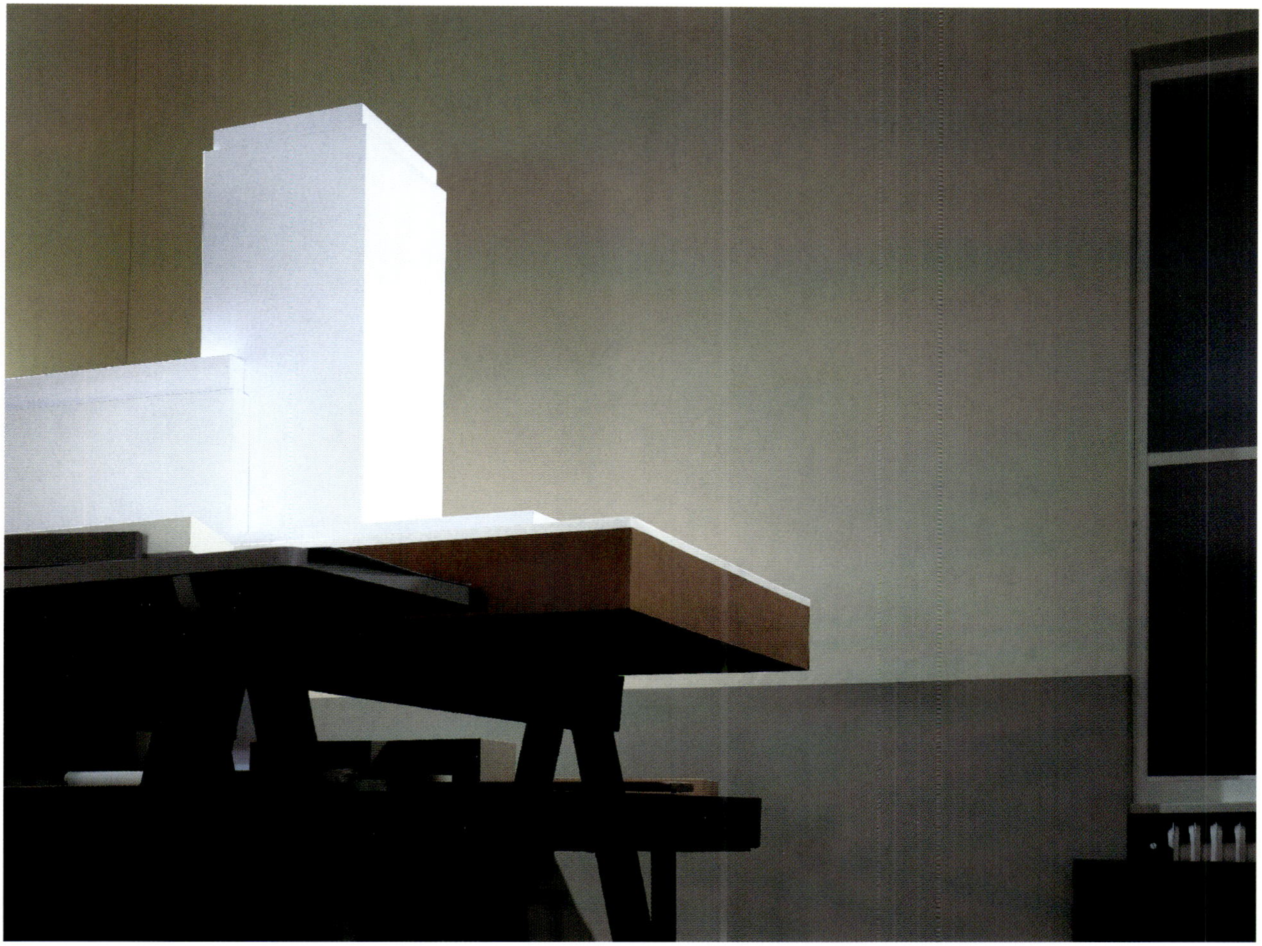

THOMAS DEMAND, MODELL / MODEL, 2000, C-Print Diasec, 210 x 164,5 cm / 82 11/16 x 64 3/4".

sanity and inspiration: "...like a rapid ghastly river, / Through the pale door, / A hideous throng rush out forever, / And laugh—but smile no more."[4]

Garages, escalators, balconies—architectural elements technically reproduced all over the world—were never really inhabited by spirits in the first place, which makes them comforting, and all the more terrifying at the same time. It's as if Demand's art lets the Romantic terror of decay collide with its Modernist sibling: terror of conservation. Architectures of metal, glass, and concrete with their opaque surfaces can be technically reproduced in complete sameness, both virtually and physically. Demand introduces a semiotic disjunction to this by mimicking them in cardboard—subverting Minimalism's rejection of "soft" materials and spatial illusionism on the way. Ultimately he concentrates on the basic spatial structure and surface quality of generic places like the Florida counting room not to ignore, but to conjure the lived experience with which they are loaded.

1) Douglas Coupland, *Miss Wyoming* (London: Flamingo, 2000), pp. 78f.
2) Ibid., pp. 96f.
3) See also: Anthony Vidler, *The Architectural Uncanny* (Cambridge, Mass. & London: MIT Press, 1992), pp. 17–20; and Jonathan Jones on Edgar Allan Poe and contemporary art practice in *Frieze*, 55, November 2000.
4) Edgar Allan Poe, *The Fall of the House of Usher and other Writings* (London: Penguin Books 1986), pp. 147f.

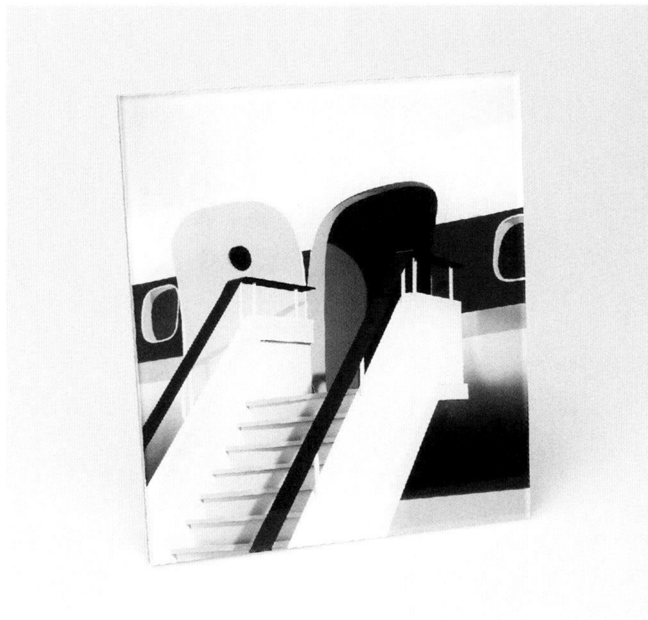

(PHOTO: MANCIA/BODMER, FBM STUDIO, ZÜRICH)

EDITION FOR PARKETT

THOMAS DEMAND

GANGWAY, 2001

Lambda-Print, Diasec auf schwarzem Acrylglas mit einschraubbarem verchromtem Standfuss, 21,0 x 25,5 x 0,5 cm.
Auflage: 75, signiert und nummeriert

Lamda print, Diasec on black acrylic glass with attachable chromium-plate stand, 8 1/4 x 10 x 1/5".
Edition of 75, signed and numbered

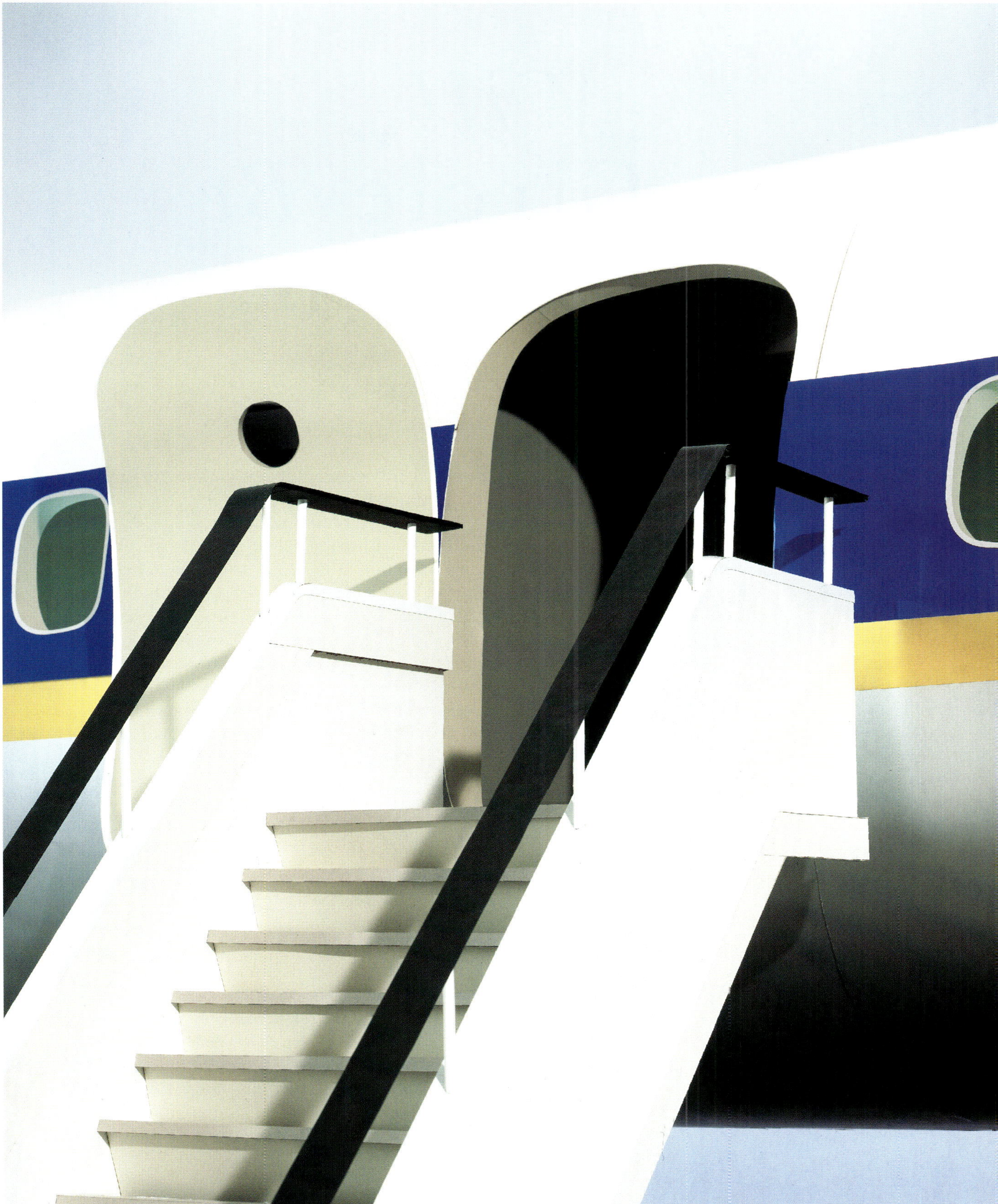

Will the Circle *Be* Unbroken?

RUSSELL FERGUSON

Glen Wilson has been out in the desert that stretches between San Diego and Tucson. He's been looking for some life in this apparently barren emptiness.

Inhospitable as it may seem, this landscape is deeply inscribed in the psychic structure of America. We know that it is there now, yet in many ways it is more present as a repository of historical myth, of childish Wild West fantasies. This is the territory that Huckleberry Finn was planning to light out for. Its presence today remains strangely undefined in the popular imagination. Most people who see it at all experience it only through the windshield of a car traveling at high speed down one of the endless highways that cut through it. Despite its vastness, it remains a transitional space.

In 1994, Wilson began taking photographs in this desert landscape. In particular, he began to make portraits of African-American men who live there. The portraits show them by the side of the road, often from behind. They appear to be traveling, though no specific destination is ever identified. These portraits evoke the mythic territory of America: the America of moving on, finding a better place, the endless cycle of re-invention and renewal. The solitary figures in Wilson's photographs acknowledge that this kind of travel can be lonely, but tell us too that it can offer a degree of freedom and independence.

They also evoke a particularly African-American tradition, of traveling on not just to get to somewhere new but to get away from somewhere bad. Some of them might remind us of Robert Johnson at the crossroads. We might think of the writer Joe Wood, standing "where the two roads crossed," searching for the essence of blackness. "I got there at 11 when the sun was near its hottest. Nothing moves when the air is that hot.... I leaned against my Chevy and waited for blackness to arrive. Nothing changed, so I shaded my eyes, looked further into the field, and tried to imagine it walking toward me: an old man strumming a blues."[1)]

Wilson himself is not out searching for any essential blackness. He is as aware as Wood that such essences are at least as problematic as they are empowering. He does deal with archetypes, but only as way stations on the road of his journey deeper into the nuances of community. He deals with them too as part of a journey of self-exploration, because his photographs are also, in a way, self-portraits. They represent part of Wilson's relationship to his own mixed-race heritage, and his own experiences in the process of trying to find a place for himself in the Southwest. "Even though I was drawn to the desert I didn't feel a presence there," he says. The photographs, then, are almost like a diary of his efforts to write himself into

RUSSELL FERGUSON is Deputy Director of Exhibitions and Programs, and Chief Curator, at the UCLA Hammer Museum in Los Angeles.

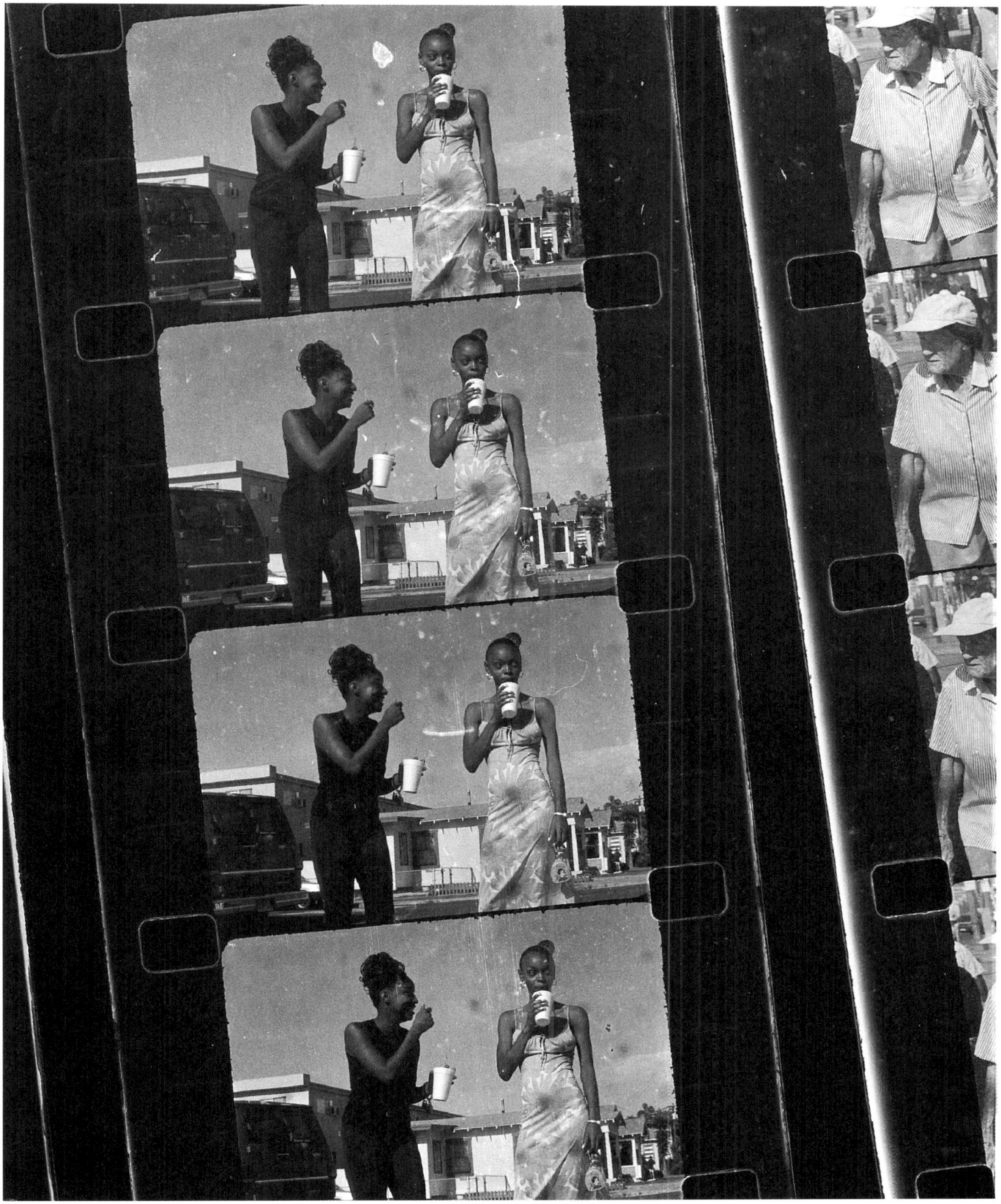

GLEN WILSON, untitled film stills from YOU ARE HERE/ESTAS AQUI, 1997, black-and-white silver gelatin print from 16mm film, 16 x 20" /
Filmstills aus DU BIST HIER/ESTAS AQUI, Schwarzweiss-Silbergelatin-Print ab 16mm-Film, 40,6 x 50,8 cm.

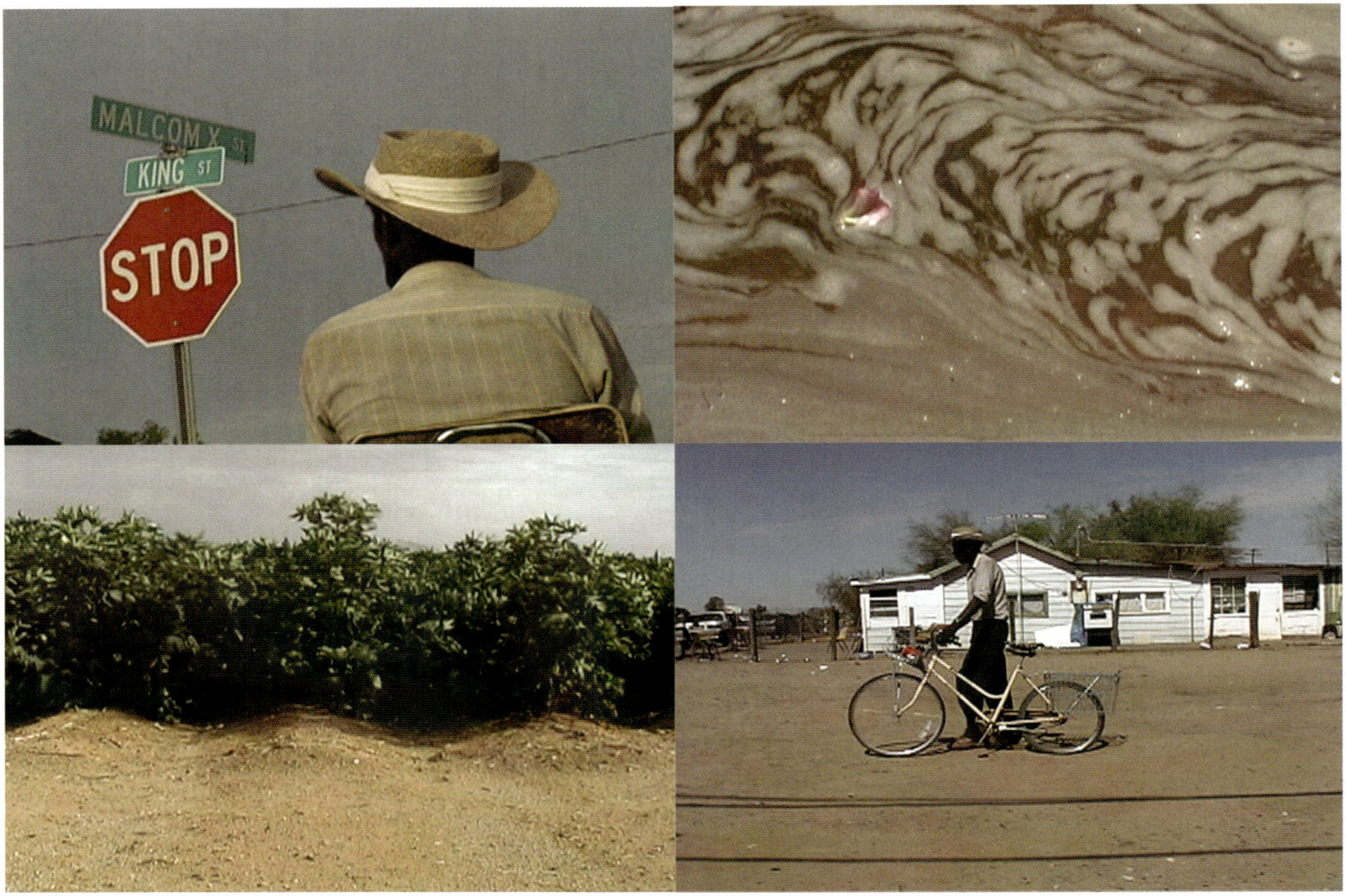

GLEN WILSON, DESERT FISHING, 2000, untitled digital stills / WÜSTENFISCHEN, digitale Standaufnahmen.

the picture, to find his own presence there. He is always, he says, "negotiating other people's desire to place me."[2] The result is a tenuous balance between the desire to establish a clear individual identity and the equally powerful desire to draw out the meaning of community, or communities.

Many of the men in his portraits are broken up into fragments. As Lorna Simpson has also sometimes done, Wilson has cut apart the figures he photographs. It is almost as if he were dissecting them, searching for the constituent elements that make them what they are. But the answers he's looking for cannot be found like that, and in the end the systematic fragmentation takes on another potential meaning. Wilson's subjects do hold together as whole people, but only just. There is a sense that, despite the pride that radiates from them, they could also fall apart, even disappear. That haunting possibility of disintegration is one of the factors that makes Wilson's most recent work so moving. Four years after the original portraits were made, he has gone back out into the desert and found resolution. He has found again one of his subjects. This man is no longer anonymous: his name is Elijah White. Besides his emergence as a named individual, he is also revealed to have a new context. Instead of (or in addition to) his earlier incarnation as the embodiment of solitary perseverance, we can see him now surrounded by a large and supportive family.

Wilson takes on just enough of the documentary tradition to give us that information, but he also resists the temptation to tell too much of the story, to

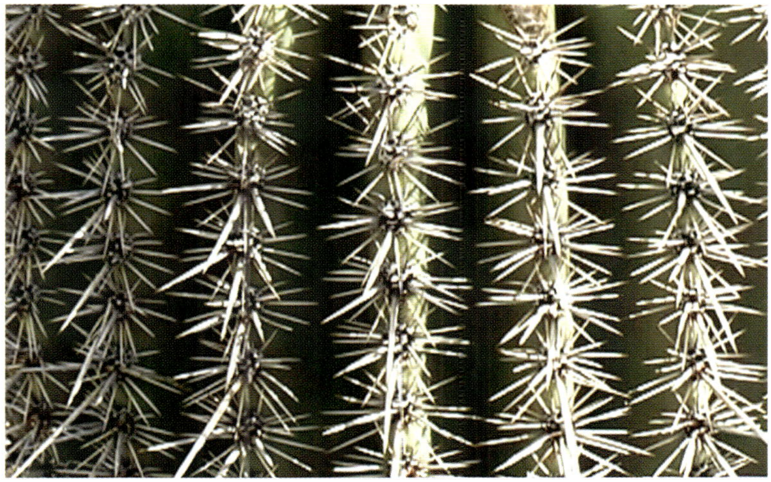

GLEN WILSON, DESERT FISHING, 2000, untitled digital still (saguaro spines) / WÜSTENFISCHEN, digitale Standaufnahme (Kaktusstacheln).

wrap everything up in a neat package. Elijah White is not turned into a parable. He retains a private quality even as we finally hear him speak for himself in the audiotapes that Wilson recorded.

One thing that is perfectly clear, however, is the enormous pleasure that White takes in the large portraits of himself that Wilson brought along. A photograph that in the inherently isolating context of a gallery can seem symbolic, even archetypal, can clearly also function in the same way as the most casual of old snapshots. "Can you believe how much hair I had on my head?" White says repeatedly. Yet White is also aware that the image will represent him in a much wider world than that marked by the dusty desert roads he has been down. "I've been to Africa. I've been to New York," he says, referring to the work's exhibition history. "Send me all over the world. Let me travel."

Most people, of course, do not have professional portraits made of themselves. It is part of Wilson's project to address the question of visibility and invisibility implicit in that reality. His 1997 project in the North Park district of San Diego, YOU ARE HERE/ESTAS ACQUI, consisted of a series of film portraits of people from the neighborhood. Working without any formal structure or any relationships with existing community groups, Wilson simply opened his own storefront workspace and over a period of six months gradually won the confidence of his neighbors. The resulting short films showed some of these people going about their routines. His goal, he has said, was "to reflect both the fleeting and sustained daily rhythms and rituals of North Park... I sought community within the constantly shifting boundaries of everyday public spaces."[3)]

YOU ARE HERE/ESTAS ACQUI was completed not by the making of the films themselves but by their return to the community in the form of impromptu screenings around the neighborhood. Although this project is clearly quite different from the work Wilson has done around his portraits of Elijah White, there are nevertheless elements in common. In both there is a process of self-imbrication into a particular community, with special attention given to the precise place of that community and then the later return to it with what he has made. It is a cyclical movement, in which Wilson begins by taking images from a place, but then brings them back as a kind of gift. "You return the work to where it came from," is how Wilson puts it.

The grainy black and white of his films gives them a vaguely historical quality, like records from long ago, although it is equally clear that they were shot recently. The past comes forward to meet the present in a single flickering space. "One night at 29th Street and University, a man on a bicycle stopped to look at the films," Wilson remembers. "As scenes unfolded he announced their locations. 'That house used to be right down here on Pershing... that was over near the park...' as if the locations no longer existed."[4)]

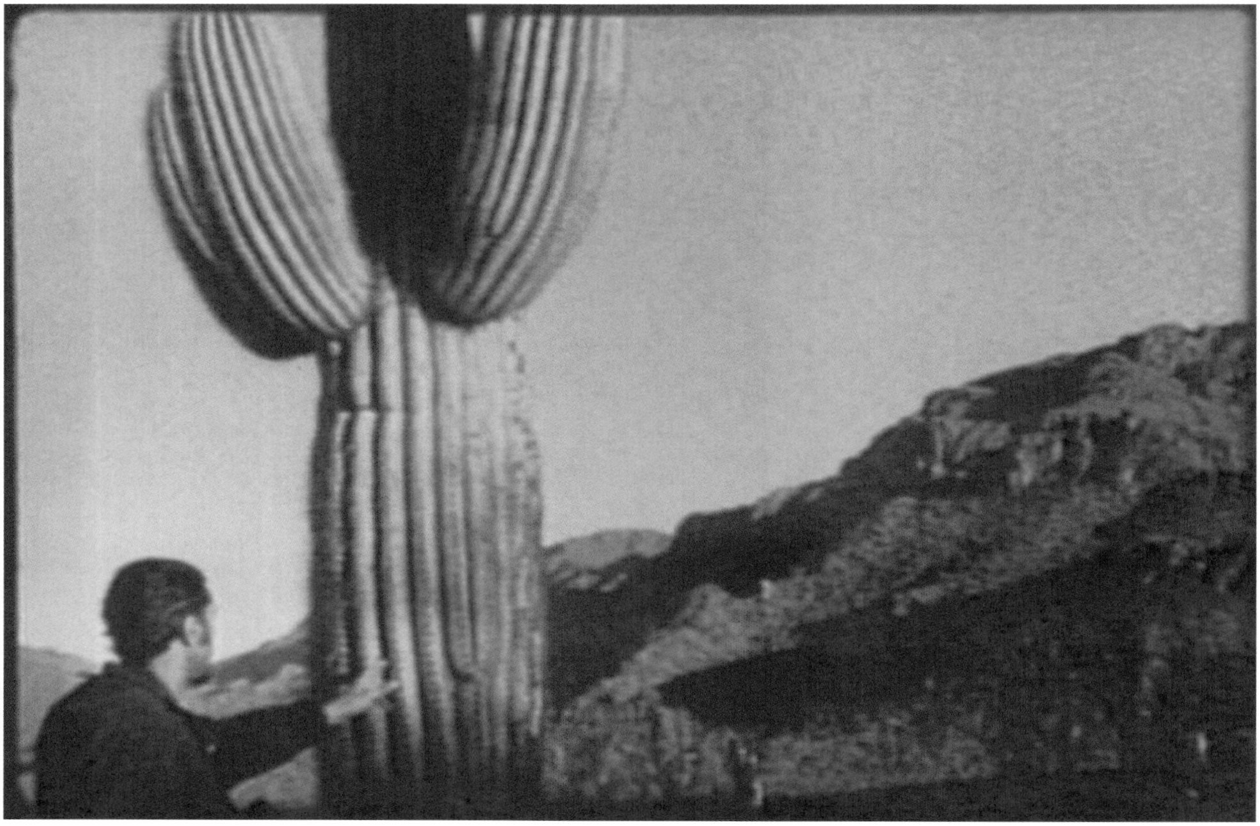

GLEN WILSON, DESERT FISHING, 2000, digital still from original super-8 film shot by MATTHEW MASCOTTE (1998).

Wilson's sense of the historical present is reflected in the title YOU ARE HERE. Within this apparently simple and descriptive statement is the slightly disturbing suggestion that you might perhaps not really be here. And will you be here tomorrow? North Park is a vibrant place, but many who live there are the potential victims of an economy that could easily find them expendable. YOU ARE HERE attempts to counter the instability of both community and individual identity through its simultaneous evocation of past and present. In its formal recognition of the people represented, it suggests too a possible extension of this community—and these people in particular—into the future. Each portrait becomes the focal point of an implied web of relationships that reach out in both space and time. As Michel de Certeau has written, "There is no place that is not haunted by many different spirits hidden there in silence, spirits one can 'invoke' or not. Haunted places are the only ones people live in."[5]

Wilson's practice as an artist is based on reciprocity. All portraiture is to a degree reciprocal, but Wilson's portraits are particularly dependent on trust. He must find some shared ground with his subjects. The exchange between the two is based on their overlapping relationships with particular places. There is then another exchange, this time between the work and the viewer. That too can take on a reciprocal quality. In his most recent experiments with installations that mix video and audio elements, Wilson is seeking to heighten that sense of exchange, "to draw out a cyclical sense of departures and arrivals."

1) Joe Wood, "It's a Trick" in: *Renée Green* (Los Angeles: Museum of Contemporary Art, 1993), p. C8.
2) Statements by Wilson are from a conversation on July 23, 1999, unless otherwise indicated.
3) Wilson in: *inSite 97* (San Diego: Installation, 1988), p. 207.
4) Wilson, unpublished text.
5) Michel de Certeau, *The Practice of Everyday Life* (1974) (Berkeley: University of California Press, 1988), p. 108.

Wird der Kreis *sich auch in* Zukunft *schliessen?*

RUSSELL FERGUSON

Glen Wilson war in der Wüste, die sich zwischen San Diego und Tucson ausbreitet. In dieser scheinbar unfruchtbaren Einöde hielt er Ausschau nach Leben.

So unwirtlich sie scheinen mag, diese Landschaft hat in der amerikanischen Psyche tiefe Spuren hinterlassen. Wir wissen zwar, dass das so ist, aber aus vielerlei Gründen ist sie uns eher als letzte Ruhestätte geschichtlicher Mythen und kindischer Wildwest-Phantasien präsent. Es ist die Gegend, in die Huckleberry Finn sich verdrücken wollte. Heute ist die allgemeine Vorstellung von ihr merkwürdig vage. Die meisten Leute bekommen sie, wenn überhaupt, durch die Windschutzscheibe eines Autos zu Gesicht, das mit hoher Geschwindigkeit auf einem der endlosen Highways unterwegs ist, die das Gebiet durchqueren. Trotz beachtlicher Ausdehnung bleibt es ein Ort der Durchreise.

1994 begann Wilson in dieser Wüstenlandschaft zu photographieren. Insbesondere begann er Porträts von den Afroamerikanern zu machen, die dort leben. Die Bilder zeigen sie neben der Strasse, oft von hinten. Und obwohl kein bestimmtes Ziel auszumachen ist, scheinen sie unterwegs zu sein. Die Porträts beschwören ein mythisches Amerika herauf: das Amerika des unermüdlichen Weiterziehens auf der Suche nach einem besseren Ort, den endlosen Zyklus von Neuerfindung und Erneuerung. Die solitären Gestalten in Wilsons Photos geben zu erkennen, dass diese Art des Reisens einsam sein kann, zeugen aber gleichzeitig von einer gewissen Freiheit und Unabhängigkeit.

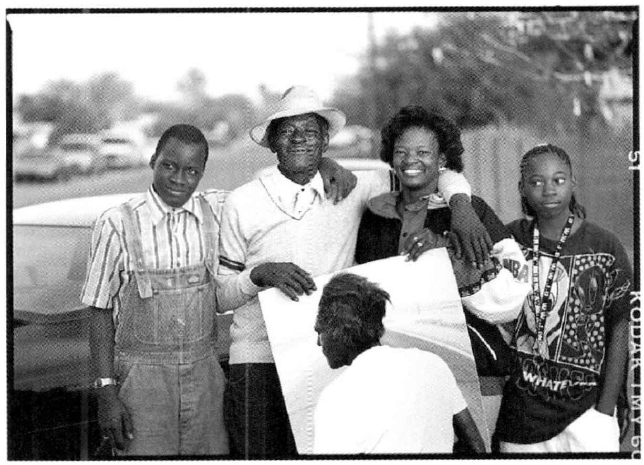

GLEN WILSON, ELIJAH WHITE (HOLDING PORTRAIT OF HIMSELF) WITH DAUGHTER SHERRY AND GRANDCHILDREN, 1998, black-and-white production still / ELIJAH WHITE (UND SEIN PORTRÄT) MIT TOCHTER SHERRY UND ENKELKINDERN, Schwarzweiss-Standaufnahme.

Sie erinnern auch an eine spezifisch afroamerikanische Tradition des Reisens, nämlich weniger um an ein neues Ziel zu gelangen, als vielmehr um von einem schlechten Ort wegzukommen. Manche mögen uns an Robert Johnson am Scheideweg erinnern. Man könnte auch an den Schriftsteller Joe Wood

RUSSELL FERGUSON ist *Deputy Director of Exhibitions and Programs* sowie Chefkurator des Hammer Museums der University of California in Los Angeles (UCLA).

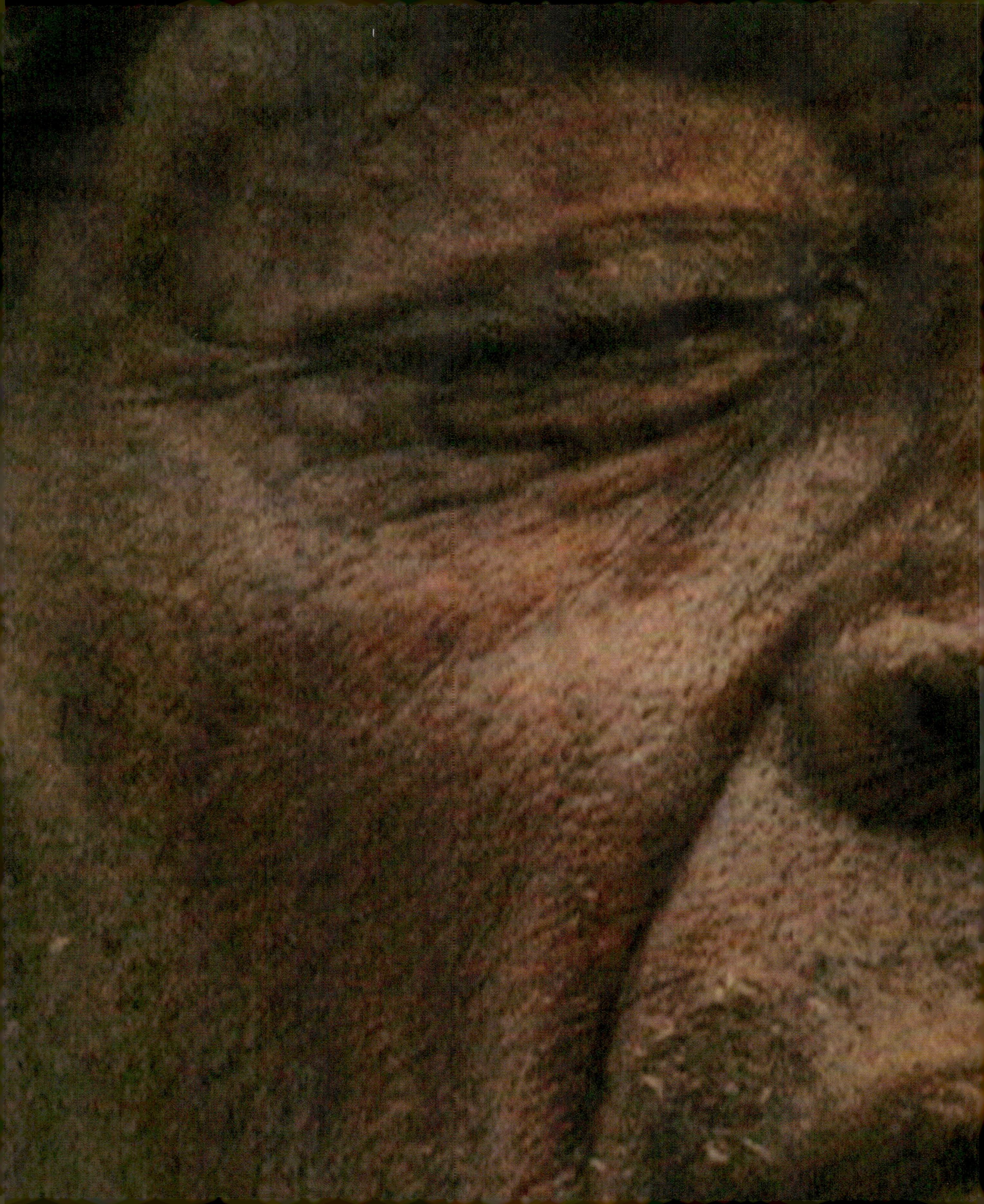

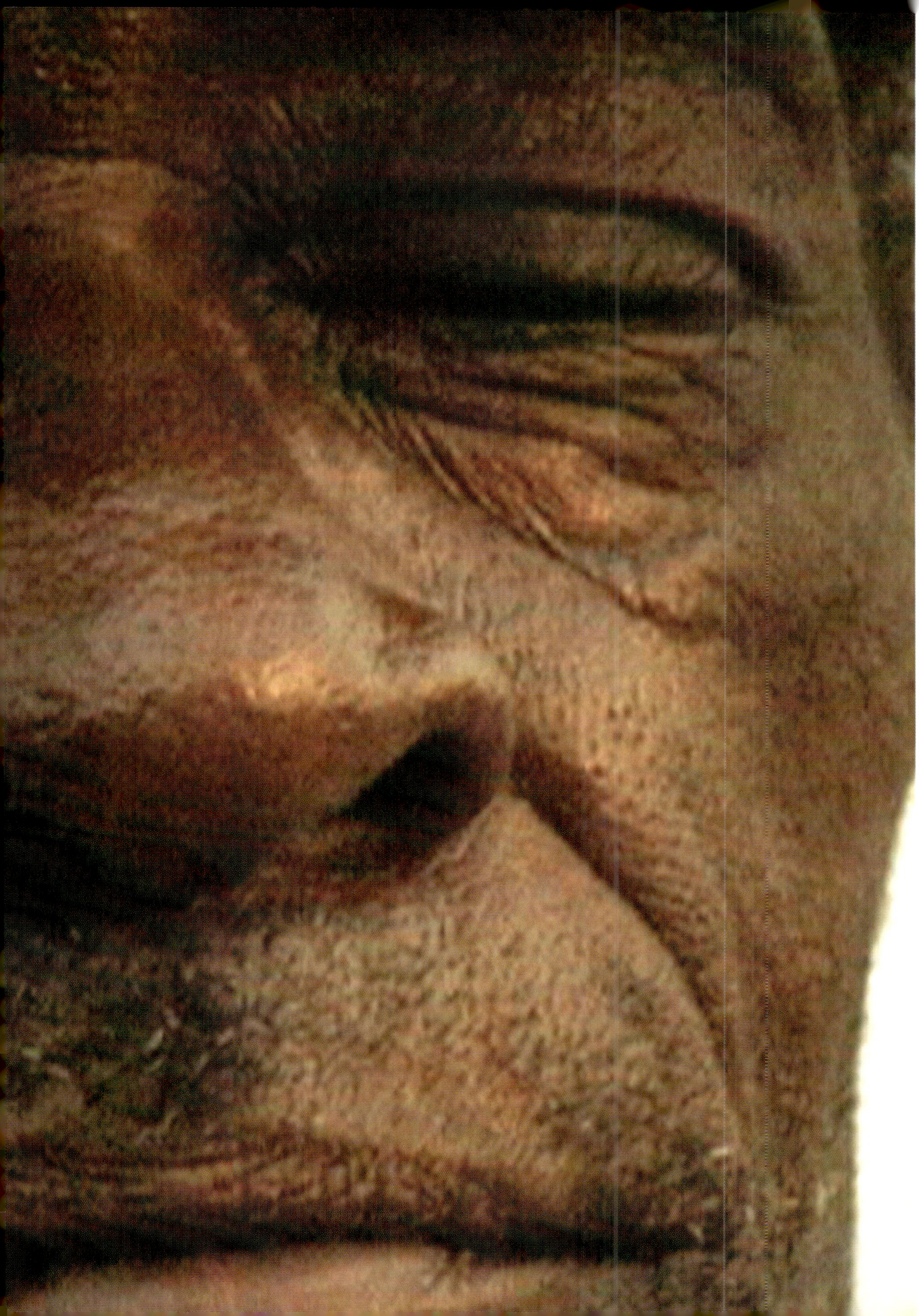

GLEN WILSON, *DESERT FISHING*, 2000, *untitled digital still* / *WÜSTENFISCHEN*, *digitale Standaufnahme.*

denken, wie er dort stand, «wo die beiden Strassen sich kreuzten», auf der Suche nach dem Wesen des Schwarzen an sich. «Ich kam um 11 Uhr dort an, als die Sonne fast schon am heissesten brannte. Nichts rührt sich, wenn die Luft so heiss ist... Ich lehnte gegen meinen Chevy und wartete auf das Schwarze. Nichts geschah, ich schirmte meine Augen, schaute weiter ins Feld hinein und versuchte mir vorzustellen, wie es auf mich zukam: ein alter Mann, der auf seiner Gitarre einen Blues spielte.»[1]

Wilson selbst ist nicht auf der Suche nach dem wahren Schwarzen. Er weiss ebenso gut wie Wood, dass solche Eigentlichkeitsideen mindestens ebenso problematisch wie kraftspendend sind. Er beschäftigt sich zwar mit Archetypen, aber nur als Stationen auf seinem Weg zu einem differenzierteren Verständnis von Gemeinschaft. Er betrachtet sie auch als Bestandteil einer Selbsterforschungsreise, denn in gewisser Weise sind seine Photographien auch Selbstporträts. Sie stellen zum Teil Wilsons Verhältnis zu seiner eigenen gemischtrassigen Herkunft dar und seine eigenen Erlebnisse beim Versuch seinen eigenen Platz im Südwesten zu finden. «Obwohl ich mich zur Wüste hingezogen fühlte, war mir dort nichts vertraut», meint er. Die Photographien sind also fast so etwas wie ein Tagebuch seiner Bemühungen seine eigene Spur im Bild zu hinterlassen, seinen eigenen Ort zu finden. Er befindet sich, wie er sagt, «in stetiger Auseinandersetzung mit dem Bedürfnis anderer Leute mich irgendwo einzuordnen».[2] Das Resultat ist ein gespanntes Gleichgewicht zwischen dem Bedürfnis eine klare individuelle Identität aufzubauen und dem ebenso mächtigen Bedürfnis die Bedeutung von Gemeinschaft oder Gemeinschaften hervorzuheben.

Viele Menschen in seinen Porträts sind in Fragmente aufgebrochen. Wie es auch Lorna Simpson manchmal tat, hat Wilson die von ihm photographierten Gestalten zerschnitten. Es ist beinahe, als würde er sie sezieren und nach jenen Bestandteilen suchen, die sie zu dem machen, was sie sind. Aber die Antworten, die er sucht, sind nicht so einfach zu finden, und am Ende gewinnt diese systematische Fragmentierung eine neue Bedeutungsmöglichkeit. Wilsons Sujets bleiben als ganze Menschen erhalten, aber nur haarscharf. Man hat das Gefühl, dass sie

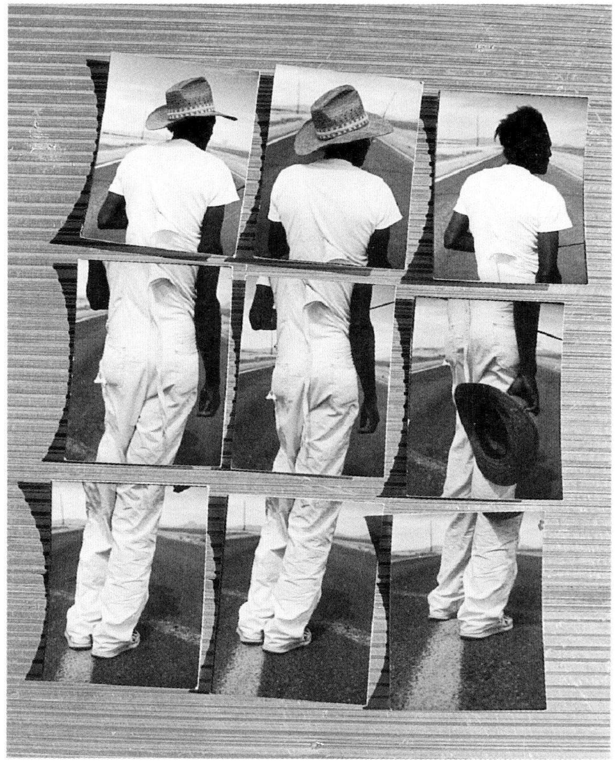

GLEN WILSON, DESERT CROSSROAD (CONTACT PRINTS ON HOT ALUMINUM TABLE), 1998, silver gelatin print, 16 x 20" / WÜSTENSTRASSENKREUZUNG (KONTAKTABZÜGE AUF HEISSEM ALU-TISCH), Silbergelatin-Print, 40,6 x 50,8 cm.

trotz des Stolzes, den sie ausstrahlen, jederzeit auseinander fallen oder sich sogar ganz in Luft auflösen könnten. Diese drohende Auflösung ist einer der Faktoren, die Wilsons jüngste Arbeiten so anrührend machen. Vier Jahre nach der Entstehung der ursprünglichen Porträts ging er zurück in die Wüste und wurde erlöst: Er traf eines seiner Sujets wieder, einen Mann, der nun nicht länger anonym ist. Sein Name ist Elijah White. Daneben, dass er zu einem Individuum mit Namen geworden ist, erfährt man auch, dass er ein neues Umfeld hat. Anstelle (oder in Ergänzung zu) seiner früheren Inkarnation, einer Verkörperung einsamer Unermüdlichkeit, sehen wir ihn nun im Kreis einer grossen Familie, die ihm Halt gibt.

Wilson übernimmt gerade so viel von der Tradition der Dokumentarphotographie, um uns diese

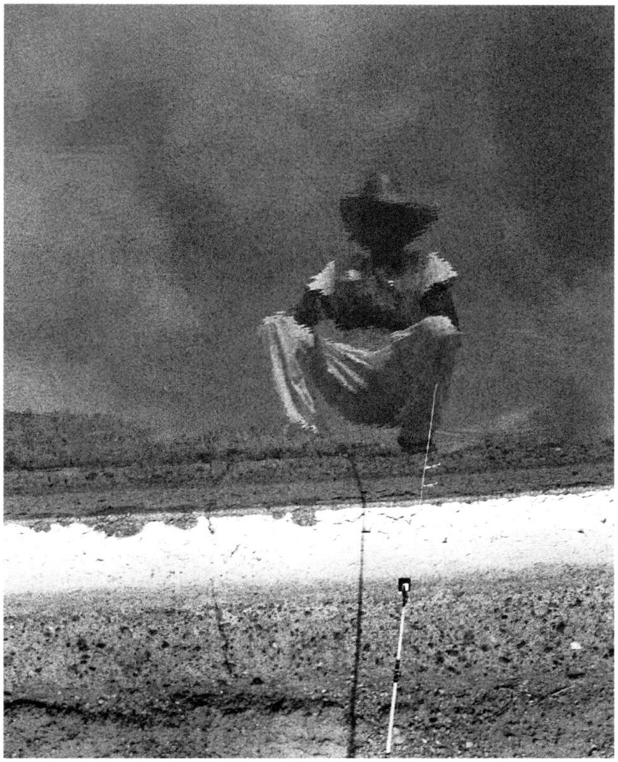

GLEN WILSON, DESERT FISHING (IRRIGATION DITCH, PAINTED ROCK ROAD, ARIZONA), 1995, silver gelatin print, 16 x 20" / WÜSTENFISCHEN (BEWÄSSERUNGSGRABEN, PAINTED ROCK ROAD, ARIZONA), Silbergelatin-Print, 40,6 x 50,8 cm.

Information zu vermitteln, aber er widersteht der Versuchung, die ganze Geschichte zu erzählen und alles zu einem wohlgefälligen Paket zu schnüren. Elijah White wird nicht zum Gleichnis. Auch in seinen eigenen, von Wilson auf Band aufgenommenen Aussagen bleibt der private Charakter gewahrt.

Etwas allerdings ist sonnenklar, nämlich Whites enorme Freude über die grossformatigen Porträts, die Wilson mitgebracht hat. Auch eine Photographie, die im zwangsläufig isolierenden Kontext einer Galerie oder eines Museums symbolisch, ja sogar archetypisch wirken mag, kann natürlich die Funktion eines ganz gewöhnlichen Schnappschusses übernehmen. «Kaum zu glauben, wie viele Haare ich auf dem Kopf hatte!», sagt White immer wieder. Aber White realisiert auch, dass sein Bild auch in einer anderen, weiteren Welt gezeigt wird als jener der staubigen Wüstenstrassen, auf denen er sich bewegt hat. Mit Bezug auf die Ausstellungsgeschichte des Bildes meint er: «Ich war in Afrika, ich war in New York. Schick mich rund um die Welt. Lass mich reisen!»

Natürlich lassen die meisten Leute keine professionellen Porträtaufnahmen von sich machen. Und es ist ein Bestandteil von Wilsons Arbeit, die mit dieser Tatsache zusammenhängende Problematik von Sichtbarkeit und Unsichtbarkeit anzusprechen. Das Projekt YOU ARE HERE / ESTAS ACQUI (Du bist hier), das er 1997 in North Park, einem Distrikt von San Diego, realisierte, bestand aus einer Serie von Filmporträts von Leuten aus diesem Stadtteil. Ohne sich auf formelle Strukturen oder Beziehungen mit bestehenden Gemeindegruppierungen abzustützen, machte Wilson dort einfach seinen eigenen Laden und Arbeitsraum auf und gewann im Lauf von sechs Monaten allmählich das Vertrauen der Nachbarn. Die entstandenen Kurzfilme zeigen einige dieser Leute bei ihren alltäglichen Verrichtungen. Sein Ziel war, wie er sagte: «ebenso die vorübergehenden wie die beständigen Tagesrhythmen und -rituale von North Park wiederzugeben... Ich suchte das Gemeinschaftliche innerhalb der sich ständig verschiebenden Grenzen öffentlicher Alltagsräume.»[3)]

YOU ARE HERE / ESTAS ACQUI erschöpfte sich nicht in den Filmen selbst, sondern wurde erst mit der Rückkehr in die Gemeinde – in Form von improvisierten Vorführungen an verschiedenen Orten des entsprechenden Stadtteils – vollständig. Obwohl sich dieses Projekt stark von Wilsons Arbeit rund um die Porträts von Elijah White unterscheidet, gibt es dennoch gemeinsame Elemente. In beiden Fällen fügt er sich in eine bestimmte Gemeinschaft ein und widmet seine Aufmerksamkeit speziell dem Ort dieser Gemeinschaft, um dann später mit dem Resultat seiner Arbeit dahin zurückzukehren. Es ist eine Kreisbewegung, in deren Verlauf Wilson zuerst Bilder von einem Ort macht und sie dann später als eine Art Geschenk wieder zurückbringt. Oder wie Wilson selbst sagt: «Man bringt das Werk dorthin zurück, wo es herkam.»

Das grobkörnige Schwarzweiss seiner Filme verleiht ihnen eine vage historische Qualität, als wären es alte Erinnerungen, obwohl gleichzeitig völlig klar

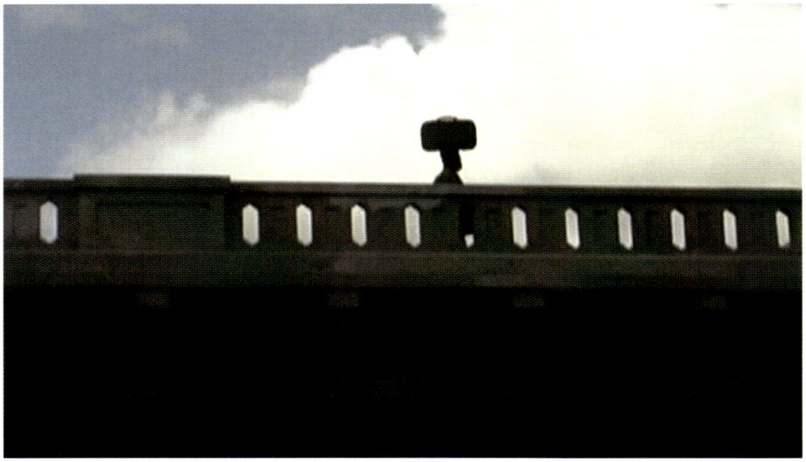

GLEN WILSON, THE NOMAD PROJECT, 2000, untitled digital still, part of "InSite" 2000/2001 / DAS NOMADENPROJEKT, digitale Standaufnahme ohne Titel.

ist, dass sie erst kürzlich entstanden sind. Die Vergangenheit tritt hervor und trifft sich mit der Gegenwart in ein und demselben flimmernden Raum. «Eines Abends an der Ecke 29th Street/University», erinnert sich Wilson, «hielt ein Mann auf einem Fahrrad an, um sich die Filmvorführung anzuschauen. Während die Szenen aufeinander folgten, nannte er die jeweiligen Örtlichkeiten. ‹Dieses Haus war doch gleich hier unten an der Pershing... das war drüben beim Park...›, so als ob diese Orte nicht mehr existierten.»[4)]

Wilsons Gefühl für das historische Präsens spiegelt sich auch im Titel YOU ARE HERE (Du bist hier). In dieser scheinbar einfachen deskriptiven Aussage steckt die leicht verstörende Andeutung, dass das angesprochene Du vielleicht nicht wirklich hier sein könnte. Und wirst du morgen da sein? North Park ist eine quicklebendige Gegend, aber viele, die dort wohnen, sind potenzielle Opfer einer Wirtschaft, die sie vielleicht morgen schon für entbehrlich hält. YOU ARE HERE versucht der Instabilität von Gemeinschaft und individueller Identität durch die gleichzeitige Beschwörung von Vergangenheit und Gegenwart zu begegnen. Durch die formelle Anerkennung der dargestellten Menschen wird auch ein Fortbestehen dieser Gemeinde – und insbesondere der dargestellten Personen – in der Zukunft nahe gelegt. Jedes Porträt wird zum Brennpunkt eines entsprechenden Beziehungsnetzes, das sich in Zeit und Raum ausdehnt. Oder wie Michel de Certeau schrieb: «Es gibt keinen Ort, der nicht von zahlreichen Geistern heimgesucht wäre, die dort schweigend lauern und die man ‹beschwören› kann oder nicht. Man bewohnt nur Orte, an denen es spukt.»[5)]

Wilsons künstlerische Praxis beruht auf Wechselseitigkeit. Jedes Porträt hat bis zu einem gewissen Grad reziproken Charakter, aber Wilsons Porträts sind besonders auf Vertrauen angewiesen. Er muss einen gemeinsamen Boden finden, der ihn mit seinen Sujets verbindet. Der Austausch zwischen beiden beruht auf ihren sich überschneidenden Beziehungen zu bestimmten Orten. Dann ist da noch ein anderer Austausch, diesmal zwischen dem Werk und dem Betrachter. Auch dieses Verhältnis kann reziproke Qualität annehmen. In seinen jüngsten Experimenten mit Installationen, die Video- und Audio-Elemente miteinander verbinden, versucht Wilson dieses Gefühl des Austauschs noch zu steigern und «das Gefühl eines Kreislaufs zwischen Abreisen und Ankommen zu vermitteln».

(Übersetzung: Susanne Schmidt)

1) Joe Wood, «It's a Trick», in: *Renée Green*, Ausstellungskatalog, Museum of Contemporary Art, *Los Angeles* 1993, S. C8.
2) Die Äusserungen von Wilson stammen sofern nicht anders vermerkt aus einem Gespräch mit dem Autor am 23. Juli 1999.
3) Glen Wilson, *inSite 97*, Installation, San Diego 1988, S. 207.
4) Glen Wilson in einem unveröffentlichten Text.
5) Michel de Certeau, *L'invention du quotidien I: Arts de faire*, Gallimard, Paris 1990, S. 162: «Il n'y a de lieu que hanté par des esprits multiples, tapis là en silence et qu'on peut ‹évoquer› ou non. On n'habite que des lieux hantés...»

THE VEIL OF THE LIMINAL

MIKE PARR'S BRIDES

EDWARD SCHEER

The bride was slowly freezing before our eyes. Lurching in and out of the frame, slipping and staggering, she walked across the frozen Baltic Sea until sunset. Luckily it sets early in the northern winter, around 2.30 p.m., so the bride, Australian artist Mike Parr, survived the ordeal. This performance on the 18th of February 1998, and entitled THE END OF NATURE, looks strange on video as the camera repeatedly cuts to images of the empty ice field. Parr explains that his camera operator was on skis with the camera attached to her back, skiing at the edge of the ice and not tracking the bride's increasingly bizarre locomotion. The bride in a flimsy white gown was clearly not dressed for the weather, but Parr is used to such extremes.

Previously the bride had spent days in freezing November rain on the grounds of the glass walled Fukui Museum of Fine Arts in Japan in 1997, in a piece called THE DELAY IN GLASS. In September 1996, for THE WHITE HYBRID (FADING), Parr walked the length of a huge derelict wharf in Sydney for 72 continuous hours, occasionally dropping from exhaustion and sleeping wherever he fell. These conditions force the body of the artist to respond authentically (i.e. beyond its everyday capacity) to the extremes of the environment. Parr has said that in such circumstances he has sometimes had to induce a lowering of his heart rate to endure the conditions. In these situations his body undergoes a genuine change in facing the crisis of its context in a manner which is both a function of will and necessity.

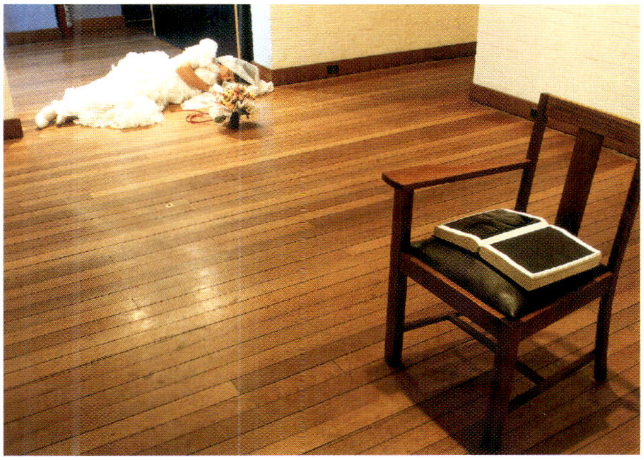

MIKE PARR, BLACK MIRROR/PALE FIRE, 1993, 8-hour performance, Ivan Dogherty Gallery, University of New South Wales College of Fine Art, Sydney, 21–23 October / SCHWARZER SPIEGEL / FAHLES FEUER 8-stündige Performance. (PHOTO: PAUL GREEN)

This raises questions about the extent of real visceral transformations in performance. If one can effect conscious changes in the autonomic nervous system, what is it in fact impossible for a body to do? Physical ritual events like these suggest that there are

EDWARD SCHEER is a freelance arts writer and lecturer in the School of Theatre, Film and Dance at the University of New South Wales in Sydney, Australia.

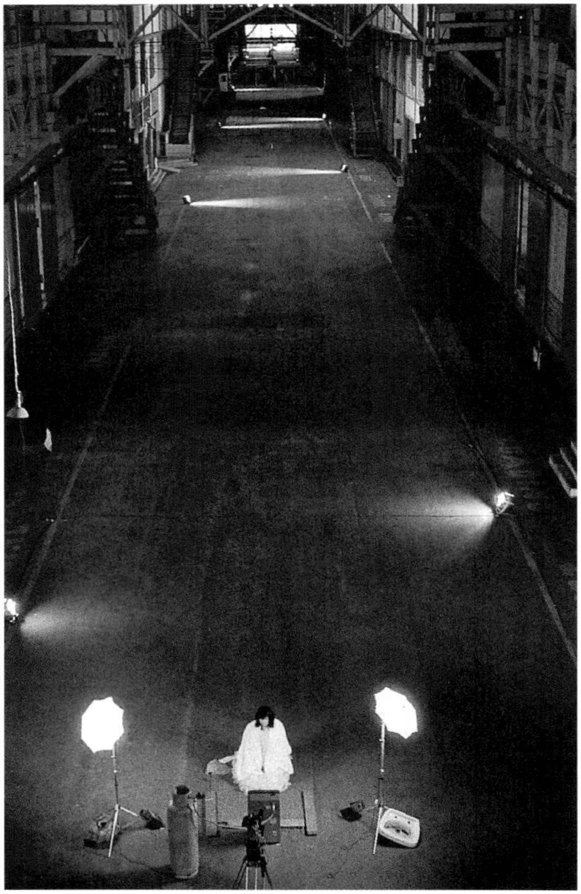

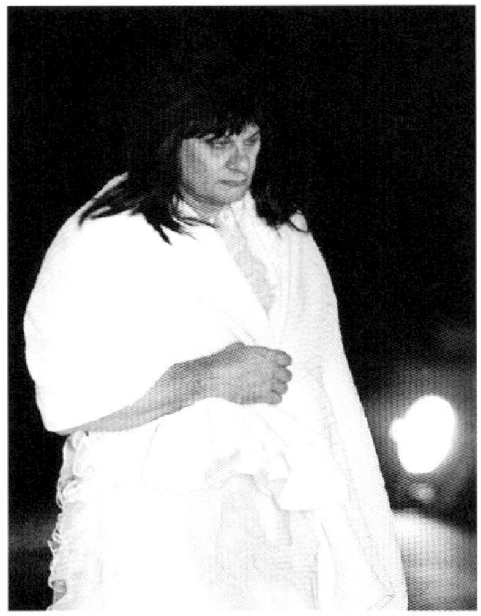

MIKE PARR, THE WHITE HYBRID (FADING), 1996, 3-day performance, Cowper Wharf, Artspace, Sydney, 13–15 September / DIE WEISSE HYBRIDE (SCHWINDEND), 3-tägige Performance.
(PHOTO: PAUL GREEN)

performances in which the experience of the body is not "staged" despite the circumstances of the event. Here the body is responding to a climate with "real"[1] effects in a necessary way which we might call the liminal corporeal.

The anthropologist Victor Turner located this concept of the "liminal" in the French folklorist Arnold van Gennep's division of rituals of passage into three stages: separation, liminality, and re-aggregation, where liminality refers to a "betwixt and between condition often involving segregation from the everyday scene."[2] He relates this concept to "life-crisis rituals" for individuals (e.g. birth, nuptial, or funerary rites) and for entire groups and cultures including "collective response to hazards such as war, famine, drought, plague, earthquake, volcanic eruption, and other natural or man-made disasters." The liminal phase is where these rituals, theater and performance art among them, are first imagined and dreamed into being.

Parr's twelve bridal performances (1993–2000) illustrate a shift in the notion of the liminal. While marriage is purely liminal, an "old fashioned ritual,"[3] the performance of the bride in the full nightmare of white chiffon by a male artist is anything but, yet Parr's performance contexts are often so extreme, his body is forced to respond out of necessity. The body thereby becomes the site of the liminal displacement. This is more than simply acting out a ritual or parodying it: in these works the very notion of 'body' enters a kind of suspended state, impersonal and intense, a field which encompasses the body but does not permit anything like an expression to emerge from it. It is the body of pure performance, iterative, citational, abreactive but recalling an intensive corporeal state. It is involved in a becoming rather than representing an identity. It enacts a necessary ritual in which identity itself is in crisis.

For Mike Parr the identity crisis concerns the compulsorily socialized performance of self, the pervasive and suffocating requirement on all individuals to perform the endless role of consumer, citizen, and subject. Parr has been responding to this crisis since 1972 when his IDEA DEMONSTRATIONS first brought him public notoriety and critical acclaim. These performances were experiments with identity and the relations between physical performance and language based on specific instructions, e.g. "Set fire to a portion of your clothing as you wear it. Extinguish the fire only after the heat has become unbearable." "Burn some hair from your body in a closed room."[4] Etc.

Throughout the seventies, Parr developed a unique approach to physical performance independent of developments in Vienna (Muehl, Brus, Nitsch) and in the U.S. (Oppenheim, Acconci). The best known performance of this period is his CATHARTIC ACTION SOCIAL GESTUS NUMBER 5 (THE ARMCHOP) performed at the Sydney Sculptural Centre on July 27, 1977. In this piece he engaged in a very personal life-crisis ritual. At birth Parr had suffered the mangling of his left arm in an accident at the hospital, resulting in the surgical removal of his arm just above the elbow. The 1977 performance was an abreaction of this traumatic event before an audience, some of whom were not aware that the prosthetic left arm he was wearing was made of latex and stuffed with meat and blood so that when he "abruptly hacked it off" the effect was startling, to say the least. The film of the event shows a stunned audience shocked into speechlessness and an equally stunned artist sitting at a podium with a bloodied tomahawk in his hand. He then explained his ideas to the audience. He talked about his family, ideas to do with abreaction, the desire for wholeness, the need to take control over his own "character structure"[5] without his disability determining everything in advance as it had once done. This event represented the culmination of his project of violent performance enacted against the socially imposed construction of a self, but his subsequent work has also dramatized concerns with identity transformation and the necessary responses of the body.

The first of the bride pieces was BLACK MIRROR/PALE FIRE in October 1993 (day one of a three-day event) at the Ivan Dougherty Gallery in Sydney. Parr had blacked out the pages of a copy of *The Australian National Dictionary, Australian Words and their Origins* (OUP, 1993) and displayed it on a table in the gallery with only the index words showing. On day one, all day, the index word "bride" was doubled by the presence in the doorway of the artist in complete bridal regalia: pearl necklace and bracelet, earrings, bouquet, heavy makeup, white dress and veil, lying with eyes closed across the threshold at the entrance to the gallery. Parr argues that this particular dictionary represents the "collective unconscious" of the nation,[6] as it collects Australia's linguistic self-representations. Blacking it out might therefore be seen as allowing a symbolic opening to occur in which the artist can dissociate from this national vocabulary and learn to think otherwise, no longer the bride of the people's imaginary. It is ironically a symbolic divorce in which the artist cuts himself loose from the collective image bank and invites the visitor to cross a similar threshold. Parr says that in this sense of threshold (the "limen" of the term "liminal") the bride became for him "the predominant theme" of his work throughout the nineties.[7]

In THE WHITE HYBRID (FADING)[8] Parr utilized a disused wharf in Woolloomooloo Bay as a corridor to mark out the route of a long intensive traversal, walking up and down in the glare of the spotlights for 72 hours. The unnatural hybrid bride figure was barely visible at the end of the wharf, slowly moving into focus and disappearing again. The hybrid in the title might represent the mutation that permits the new form to emerge, particularly significant in the conservative Australian context. It suggests uncertainty but also possibility. The hybrid bride is a nucleus of representations of identity, change, exchange and institutionality.

Mike Parr has described the bride variously as a "hinge figure" and a "parody of the symbolic."[9] "An absurd institution, of the feminine, of the notion of

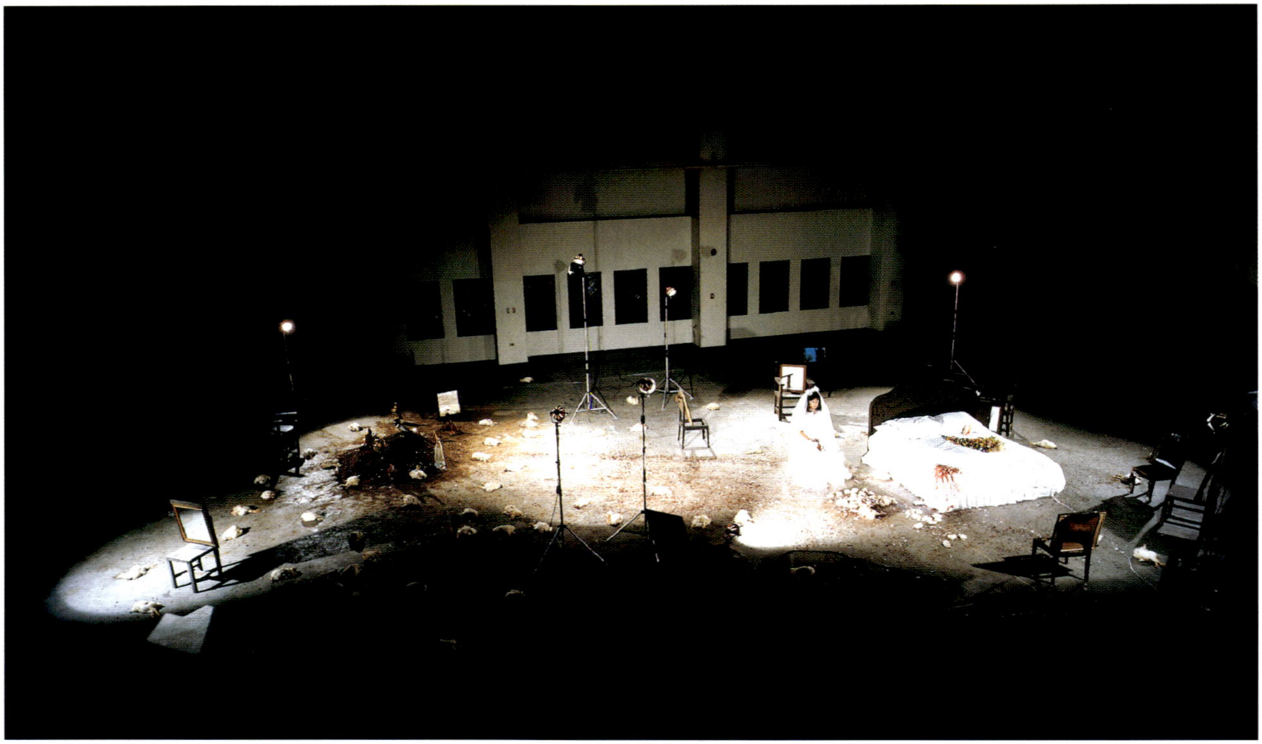

MIKE PARR, DAYBREAK, 1995, 24-hour performance, Scene Shop, Cultural Center of Manila, Philippines, 13–15 September / TAGESANBRUCH, 24-stündige Performance. (PHOTO: NEAL OSHIMA)

exchange and of sacrifice. The bride is a constructed image, a kind of screen or cosmetic overlay."[10] Inhabiting the bride is a way of doubling an image of the alienation of the body, an abreaction of this kind of disappearance of the self into an institution, turning the institution into a mirage. Parr's bride performances culminated in a 3-day event for the 12th Biennale of Sydney in July 2000, appropriately entitled SHALLOW GRAVE in which the bride slept by day in a room of classical statuary in the Art Gallery of New South Wales. Surrounded by 7000 photographs of the bride and in the midst of the statues, the bride literally occupied the space in between these registers of the symbolic: a liminal form in the graveyard of representations.

1) Real is intended in the Lacanian sense of unsymbolizable or beyond the signifying process.
2) Victor Turner, *The Anthropology of Performance* (New York: PAJ Publications, 1986), p. 101.
3) Richard Schechner and Victor Turner, *Between Theatre and Anthropology* (Philadelphia: University of Pennsylvania Press, 1985), p. 64.
4) These instructions, performed at the artist-run Inhibodress Gallery in Sydney's Woolloomooloo in 1972, were collected into two works both entitled 150 PROGRAMMES AND INVESTIGATIONS 1971–72, one a slide sequence and the other a black box containing the instructions printed on separate sheets of paper.
5) Mike Parr, transcript of Armchop discussion.
6) Interview with Mike Parr by the author on March 21, 2001.
7) Interview 2001.
8) Performed for the "100 Years of Cruelty" Artaud centenary event in Sydney in September 1996.
9) Interview 2001.
10) "Breaking through Language," interview with Mike Parr, Edward Scheer and Nick Tsoutas, 26 September 1997, in: Edward Scheer, ed., *100 Years of Cruelty: Essays on Artaud* (Sydney: Artspace and Power Publications, 2000), pp. 279–304.

IM SCHLEIER DES ÜBERGANGS: MIKE PARRS BRÄUTE

EDWARD SCHEER

Die Braut fror sich vor unseren Augen langsam zu Tode. Schlitternd und taumelnd stolperte sie über die zugefrorene Ostsee dem Sonnenuntergang entgegen und verschwand dabei immer mal wieder aus dem Bild. Glücklicherweise geht die Sonne im nordischen Winter schon gegen halb drei Uhr nachmittags unter, so dass die Braut, der australische Künstler Mike Parr, die Tortur überlebte. Die Performance mit dem Titel THE END OF NATURE (Das Ende der Natur), aufgenommen am 18. Februar 1998, nimmt sich auf Video seltsam aus, da die Kamera immer wieder auf die leere Eisfläche schwenkt. Parr erklärt, dass sich seine Kamerafrau, die Kamera auf den Rücken geschnallt, auf Skiern dem Rand der Eisfläche entlang bewegte und nicht die immer bizarrer werdenden Bewegungen der Braut verfolgte. Diese war in ihrem dünnen weissen Kleid eindeutig nicht wettergerecht angezogen, doch Parr ist solche Extreme gewohnt.

1997 hatte die Braut anlässlich der Performance THE DELAY IN GLASS (Der gläserne Aufschub) auf dem Gelände des mit Glaswänden versehenen japanischen Fukui Museum of Fine Arts tagelang im eisigen Novemberregen ausgeharrt. Im September 1996 wanderte Parr für seine Performance, THE WHITE HYBRID (FADING) / Die weisse Hybride (schwindend), 72 Stunden lang einem riesigen, verlassenen Quai entlang, wobei er manchmal vor Erschöpfung umkippte und auf der Stelle einschlief. In solchen Situationen ist der Körper des Künstlers gezwungen, authentisch auf die extremen Umweltbedingungen zu reagieren (und damit seine alltäglichen Fähigkeiten zu überschreiten). Parr sagt, dass er unter derartigen Umständen manchmal seine Herzfrequenz senken musste, um die Strapazen auszuhalten. Sein Körper macht in solchen Situationen eine echte Veränderung durch und begegnet den krisenhaften Umständen in einer Weise, die ebenso vom Willen wie von der Not diktiert ist.

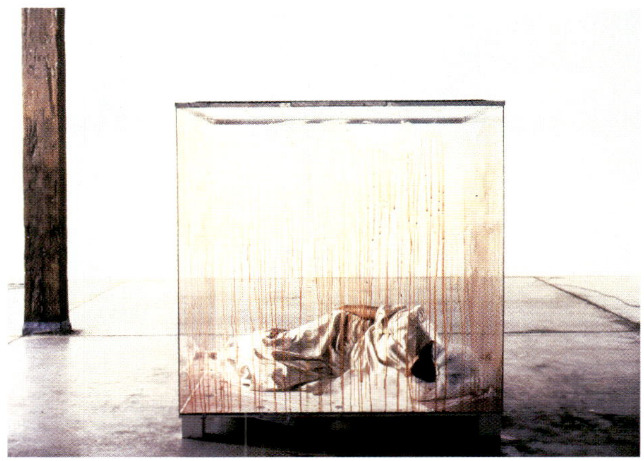

MIKE PARR, BLOOD BOX, 1998, 24-hour performance, Artspace, Sydney, 6–7 September / BLUTKASTEN, 24-stündige Performance.

EDWARD SCHEER ist freischaffender Kunstkritiker und Dozent am Institut für Theater, Film und Tanz der University of New South Wales in Sydney, Australien.

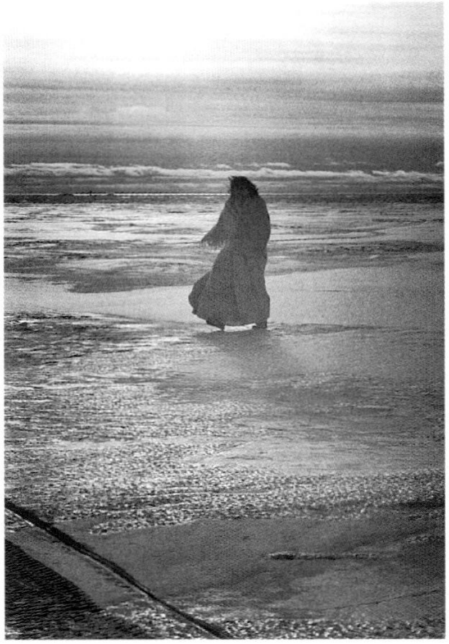

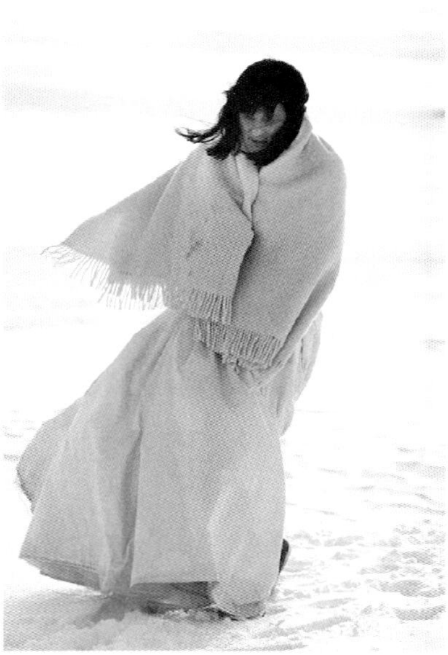

MIKE PARR, THE END OF NATURE, 1998, performance and video, Baltic Sea, Sweden, 18 February / DAS ENDE DER NATUR, Performance und Video an der Ostsee, Schweden. (PHOTO: FELIZITAS PARR)

Das wirft Fragen nach dem Ausmass echter körperinterner Veränderungen in der Performancekunst auf. Wenn es möglich ist, das vegetative Nervensystem bewusst zu beeinflussen, gibt es dann noch etwas, was der Körper nicht tun kann? Körperliche Rituale, wie Parr sie vollzieht, lassen vermuten, dass es Performances gibt, in denen die körperliche Erfahrung trotz vorgegebener Umstände nicht «inszeniert» ist. Der Körper reagiert dabei mit «realen» Auswirkungen auf ein bestimmtes Klima mit einer Notwendigkeit, die man als schwellenhafte Körperlichkeit bezeichnen könnte.[1]

Der Anthropologe Victor Turner fand den Begriff des «Schwellenhaften» beim französischen Ethnologen Arnold van Gennep, der die Übergangsriten in drei Phasen gliederte: Trennung, Schwellenphase und Wiedereingliederung, wobei die Schwellen- oder Übergangsphase ein «Zwischenstadium» bezeichnet, «das oft mit einer Loslösung aus dem alltäglichen Umfeld verbunden ist».[2] Er bezieht sich dabei auf «Lebenskrise-Rituale» von Individuen (z. B. Geburts-, Hochzeits- oder Bestattungsriten), ganzen Gruppen und Kulturen, einschliesslich «kollektiver Reaktionen auf Gefahren wie Kriege, Hungersnöte, Dürreperioden, Seuchen, Erdbeben, Vulkanausbrüche und andere von der Natur oder vom Menschen herbeigeführte Katastrophen». Die Schwellenphase ist das Stadium, in dem solche Rituale, wozu auch Theater und Performancekunst gehören, ausgedacht und erträumt werden.

Parrs zwölf *Braut-Performances* (1993–2000) illustrieren einen Wandel in der Vorstellung der Schwellenphase. Während die Hochzeit ein zutiefst schwellenhaftes «altmodisches Ritual»[3] darstellt, ist die Performance der von einem männlichen Künstler gespielten Braut in einem Alptraum aus weissem Chiffon das pure Gegenteil; doch das Umfeld, in dem sich Parrs Performances abspielen, ist häufig so extrem, dass seinem Körper gar nichts anderes übrig bleibt, als darauf zu reagieren. Der Körper wird dabei zum Schauplatz der schwellenhaften Verschiebung. Es geht dabei nicht einfach um das Durchspielen oder Parodieren eines Rituals: In diesen Aktionen gerät die Vorstellung des «Körpers» in eine Art Schwebezustand, unpersönlich und intensiv, ein Feld, das den Körper umgibt, ihm aber jede Art von Ausdruck verunmöglicht. Es ist der Körper der reinen Performance – iterativ, zitierend, abreaktiv –, der jedoch einen intensiven Körperzustand in Erinnerung ruft. Er ist eher an einem Werden beteiligt, als dass er eine Identität verkörpert. Er vollzieht ein notwendiges Ritual, in dem die Identität selbst in die Krise gerät.

Für Mike Parr hat die Identitätskrise mit der von der Gesellschaft zwangsweise verordneten Selbstdarstellung zu tun, mit der universellen und erstickenden, allen Menschen auferlegten Pflicht, die niemals endende Rolle des Konsumenten und Staatsbürgers zu spielen. Parr beschäftigt sich mit dieser Krise schon seit 1972, als er mit seinen IDEA DEMONSTRATIONS (Ideendemonstrationen) erstmals das Interesse der Öffentlichkeit auf sich zog und bei der Kritik Anerkennung fand. Bei diesen Performances wurde mit der Identität und dem Verhältnis zwischen Körperperformance und Sprache experimentiert, und zwar anhand von genauen Instruktionen wie: «Setzen Sie ein Kleidungsstück in Brand, das Sie gerade tragen. Löschen Sie das Feuer erst, wenn die Hitze unerträglich wird.» «Verbrennen Sie ein paar Körperhaare in einem geschlossenen Raum.»[4] Und so weiter.

Im Lauf der 70er Jahre entwickelte Parr unabhängig von den Tendenzen in Wien (Mühl, Brus, Nitsch) und in den USA (Oppenheim, Acconci) einen ganz persönlichen Ansatz zur Körperperformance. Seine bekannteste Performance aus dieser Zeit ist CATHARTIC ACTION SOCIAL GESTUS NUMBER 5 (THE ARM-CHOP) / Kathartische Aktion Sozialer Gestus Nummer 5 (Die Armamputation), die am 27. Juli 1977 im Sydney Sculptural Centre gezeigt wurde. In diesem Werk vollzog er ein sehr persönliches Lebenskrise-Ritual. Bei Parrs Geburt wurde sein linker Arm im Krankenhaus schwer verstümmelt und musste direkt oberhalb des Ellbogens amputiert werden. Die Performance von 1977 war ein Abreagieren dieses traumatischen Erlebnisses. Die Zuschauer wussten zum Teil nicht, dass er eine Armprothese aus Latex trug, die mit Fleisch und Blut gefüllt war, so dass die Wirkung gelinde gesagt bestürzend war, als er sie sich «plötzlich abhackte». Der Film über die Aktion zeigt ein sprachloses Publikum, das vor Schreck wie gelähmt ist, und einen ebenfalls bestürzten Künstler, der mit einem blutigen Tomahawk in der Hand auf einem Podest sitzt. Dann erläutert er dem Publikum seine Ideen. Er spricht über seine Familie, über Ideen im Zusammenhang mit Abreagieren, der Sehnsucht nach Ganzheit, dem Bedürfnis die Kontrolle über die eigene «Charakterstruktur»[5] zu übernehmen, ohne dass dabei seine Behinderung schon von vornherein alles bestimme, wie das früher der Fall gewesen sei. Diese Aktion war der Höhepunkt seiner Gewalt-Performances, die gegen die gesellschaftlich

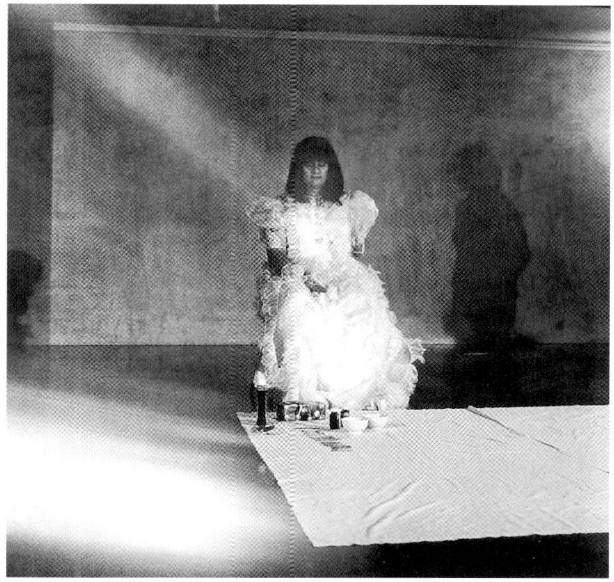

MIKE PARR, UNWORD, 1996, performance, University of Western Australia, Perth, September / UNWORT, Performance. (PHOTO: PAUL MOODIE)

verordnete Konstruktion eines Ichs gerichtet waren, doch das Thema des Identitätswandels und der notwendig damit verbundenen Körperreaktionen setzte er auch in späteren Werken szenisch um.

Die erste Braut-Performance war BLACK MIRROR/PALE FIRE (Schwarzer Spiegel/Fahles Feuer), die am ersten Tag einer dreitägigen Veranstaltung im Oktober 1993 in der Ivan Dougherty Gallery in Sydney gezeigt wurde. Parr hatte ein Exemplar des *Australian National Dictionary, Australian Words and their Origins* (OUP, 1993) so eingeschwärzt, dass nur noch die Stichwörter zu sehen waren, und stellte es auf einem Tisch in der Galerie zur Schau. Am ersten Tag erfuhr das Stichwort «Braut» eine Verdoppelung durch die Gegenwart des Künstlers, der in vollem Brautstaat – Perlenkette und -armband, Ohrringe, Blumenbukett, starkes Make-up, weisses Kleid und Schleier – mit geschlossenen Augen auf der Türschwelle der Galerie lag. Parr ist der Überzeugung, dass dieses Wörterbuch das «kollektive Unbewusste» der Nation darstellt,[6] da es Australiens sprachliche Selbstdarstellung aufzeichnet. Man kann das Einschwärzen daher als Schaffen einer symbolischen

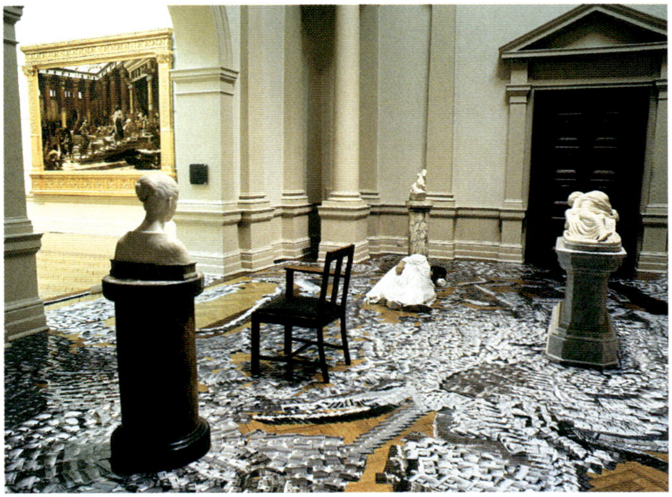

MIKE PARR, SHALLOW GRAVE, 2000, 3-day performance, Art Gallery of New South Wales, 12th Biennale of Sydney, 7–9 July / FLACHES GRAB, 3-tägige Performance. (PHOTO: PAUL GREEN)

Öffnung verstehen, durch welche der Künstler sich von diesem nationalen Vokabular abgrenzen und lernen kann, unabhängig zu denken, da er nicht länger die Braut ist, die das Volk sich vorstellt. Es ist ironischerweise eine symbolische Scheidung, durch die der Künstler sich aus dem kollektiven Bilderschatz löst und die Galeriebesucher auffordert eine ähnliche Schwelle zu überschreiten. Parr erklärt, dass in diesem Sinn des Überschreitens einer Schwelle die Braut für ihn «das beherrschende Thema» seiner Arbeiten der 90er Jahre wurde.[7]

In THE WHITE HYBRID (FADING)[8] verwendete Parr einen nicht mehr benutzten Quai in Woolloomooloo Bay als Korridor, den er während eines langen, harten Marsches im grellen Scheinwerferlicht 72 Stunden lang hinauf- und hinunterwanderte. Die unnatürliche, hybride Brautfigur war am Ende des Quais kaum zu erkennen, rückte langsam ins Blickfeld und verschwand dann wieder. Das Wort Hybride im Titel steht möglicherweise für den Verwandlungsprozess, der eine neue Form entstehen lässt, was im konservativen australischen Kontext von besonderer Bedeutung ist. Es bedeutet Ungewissheit, aber auch ein Potenzial. Die hybride Braut ist ein Nukleus, der verschiedene Ausdrucksformen von Identität, Wandel, Austausch und Institutionalisierung birgt.

Mike Parr hat die Braut verschiedentlich als «Schlüsselfigur» und «Parodie des Symbolischen» bezeichnet.[9] «Eine absurde Verkörperung des Weiblichen, der Vorstellung von Austausch und Opfer. Die Braut ist ein konstruiertes Bild, eine Art Maske oder kosmetische Hülle.»[10] In die Rolle der Braut zu schlüpfen ist eine Möglichkeit, ein Bild der körperlichen Entfremdung zu doubeln, ein Abreagieren dieser Art von Verschwinden des Ichs in der Institution, wobei Letztere als Trugbild entlarvt wird. Parrs Braut-Performances gipfelten im Juli 2000 an der 12. Biennale von Sydney in einer dreitägigen Aktion mit dem treffenden Titel SHALLOW GRAVE (Flaches Grab), bei der die Braut tagsüber in einem Raum mit klassischen Statuen in der Art Gallery of New South Wales schlief. Umgeben von den Statuen und 7000 Photographien ihrer selbst besetzte die Braut buchstäblich den Raum zwischen den verschiedenen Symbolebenen: ein Schwellenwesen auf dem Friedhof der Repräsentationsformen.

(Übersetzung: Irene Aeberli)

1) «Real» wird hier im Lacan'schen Sinne von nicht symbolisierbar oder ausserhalb des Signifizierungsprozesses gebraucht.
2) Victor Turner, *The Anthropology of Performance*, PAJ Publications, New York 1986, S. 101.
3) Richard Schechner und Victor Turner, *Between Theatre and Anthropology*, University of Pennsylvania Press, Philadelphia 1985, S. 64.
4) Diese Instruktionen, ausgeführt 1972 in der von Künstlern geleiteten Inhibodress Gallery im Woolloomooloo-Quartier in Sydney, wurden in zwei Werken mit dem Titel 150 PROGRAMMES AND INVESTIGATIONS 1971–72 zusammengefasst – einer Diareihe und einer schwarzen Schachtel, welche die auf einzelne Blätter geschriebenen Instruktionen enthielt.
5) Mike Parr, Transkript der Amputations-Diskussion.
6) Gespräch zwischen Mike Parr und dem Autor vom 21. März 2001.
7) Gespräch zwischen Mike Parr und dem Autor vom 21. März 2001.
8) Gezeigt im Rahmen der Veranstaltungsreihe zu Antonin Artauds 100. Geburtstag, «100 Years of Cruelty», im September 1996 in Sydney.
9) Gespräch zwischen Mike Parr und dem Autor vom 21. März 2001.
10) «Breaking through language», Gespräch zwischen Mike Parr, Edward Scheer und Nick Tsoutas vom 26. September 1997, in: *100 Years of Cruelty: Essays on Artaud*, hrsg. v. Edward Scheer, Artspace and Power Publications, Sydney 2000, S. 279–304.

GERDA STEINER & JÖRG LENZLINGER

LIFT-UP INSERT FOR PARKETT 2001

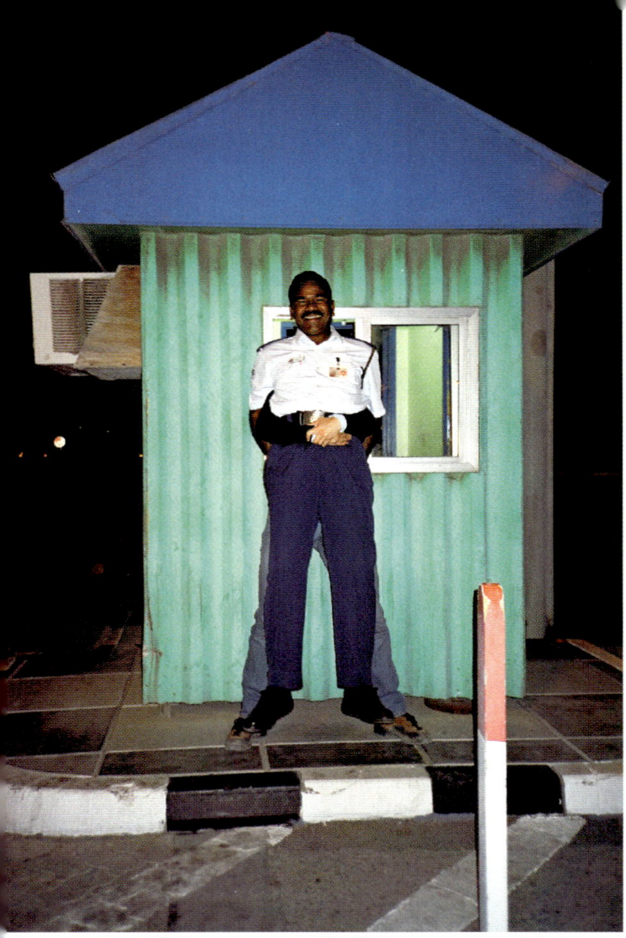
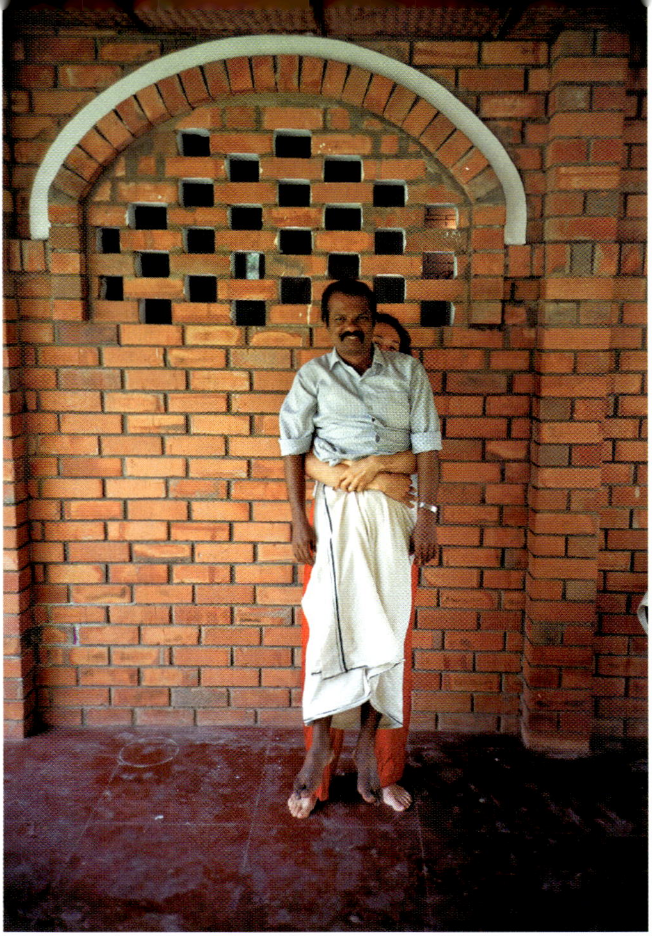
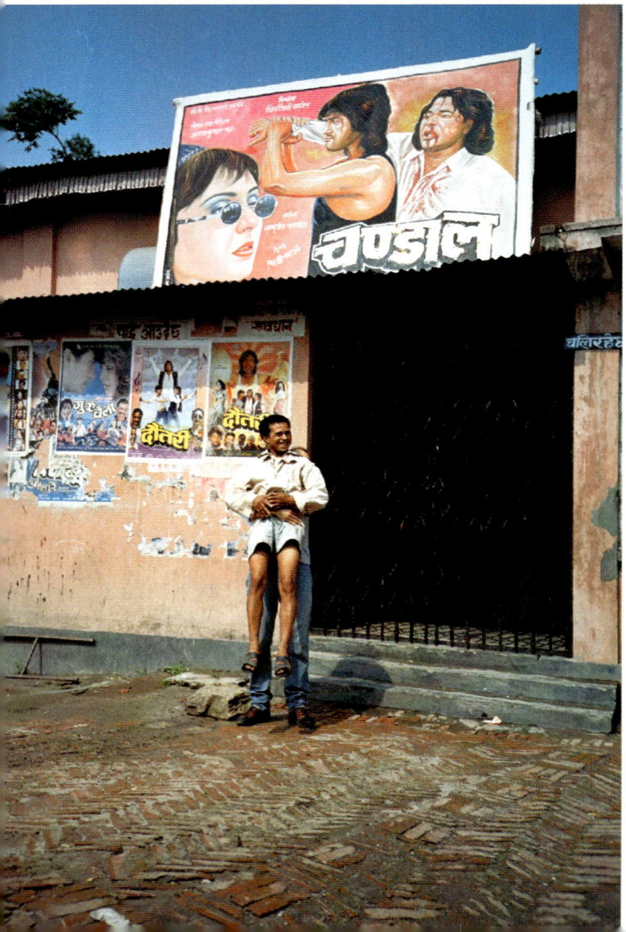
चण्डाल
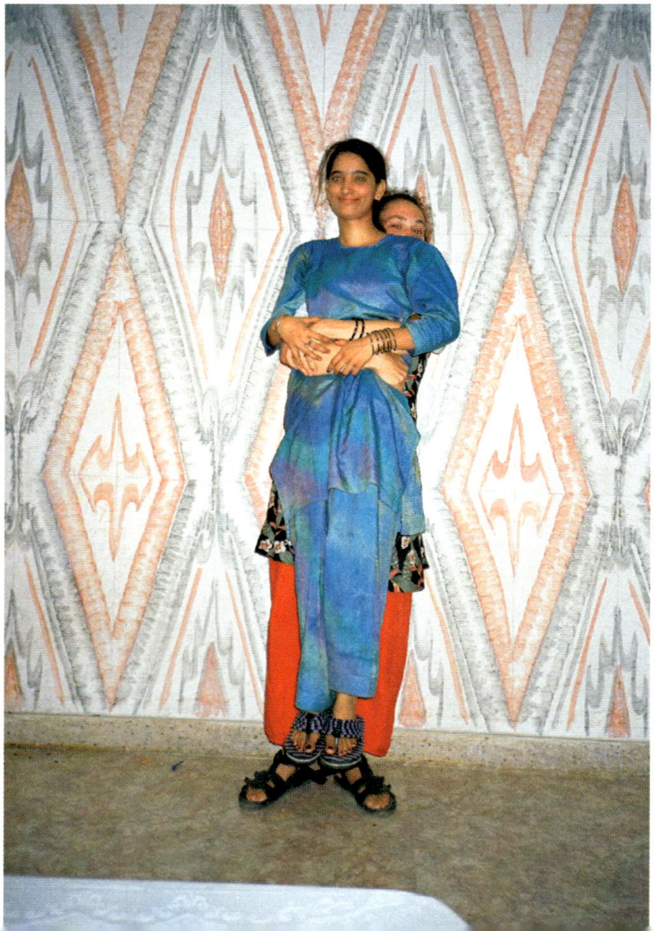

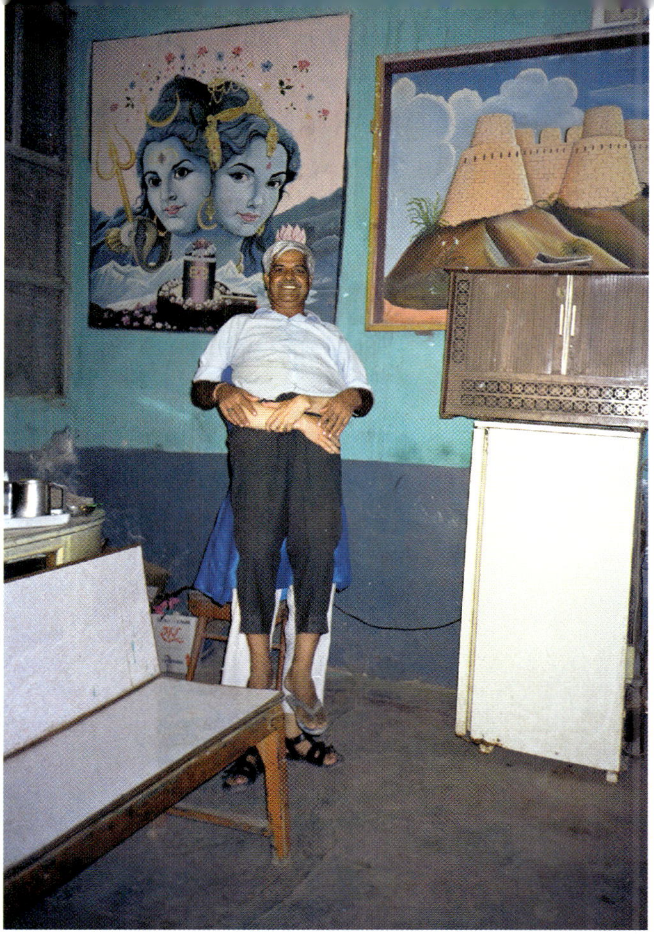

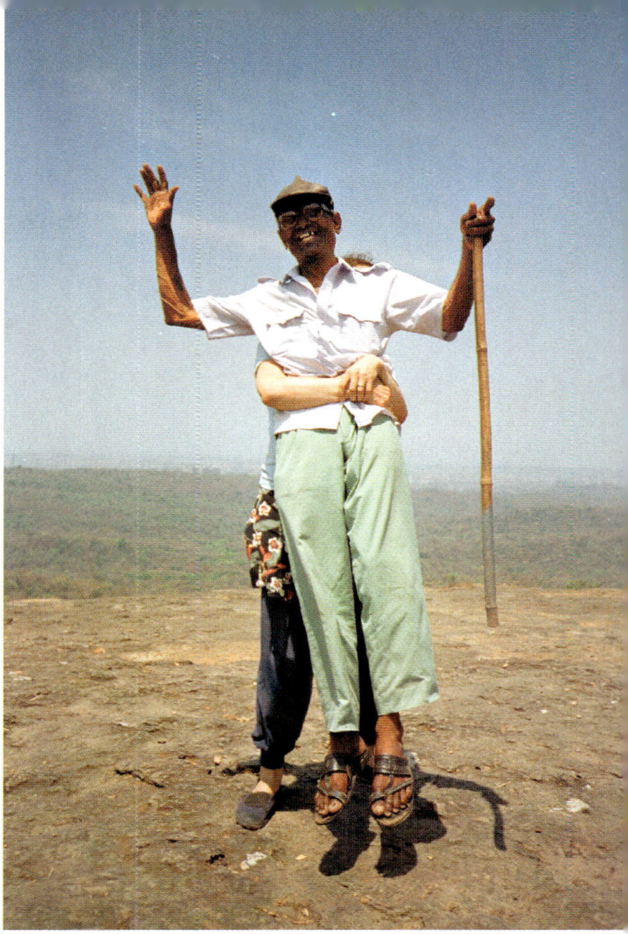

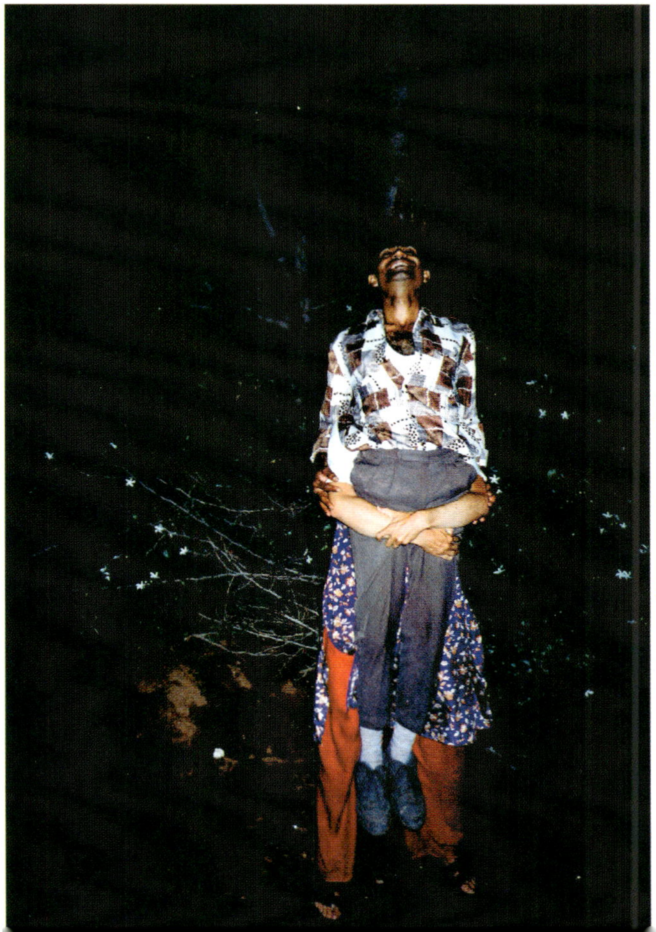

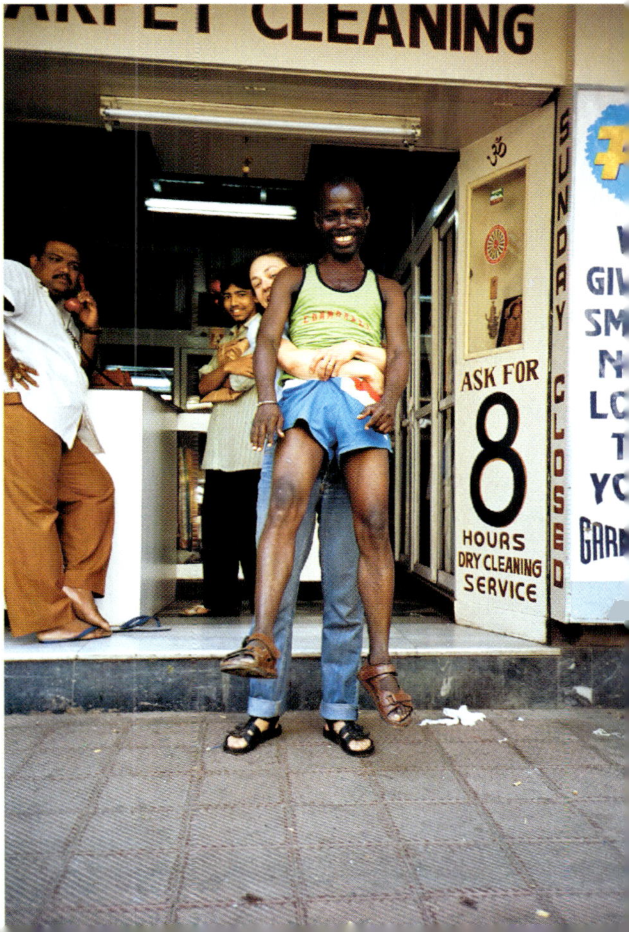
ARPET CLEANING
SUNDAY CLOSED
ASK FOR
8
HOURS
DRY CLEANING
SERVICE

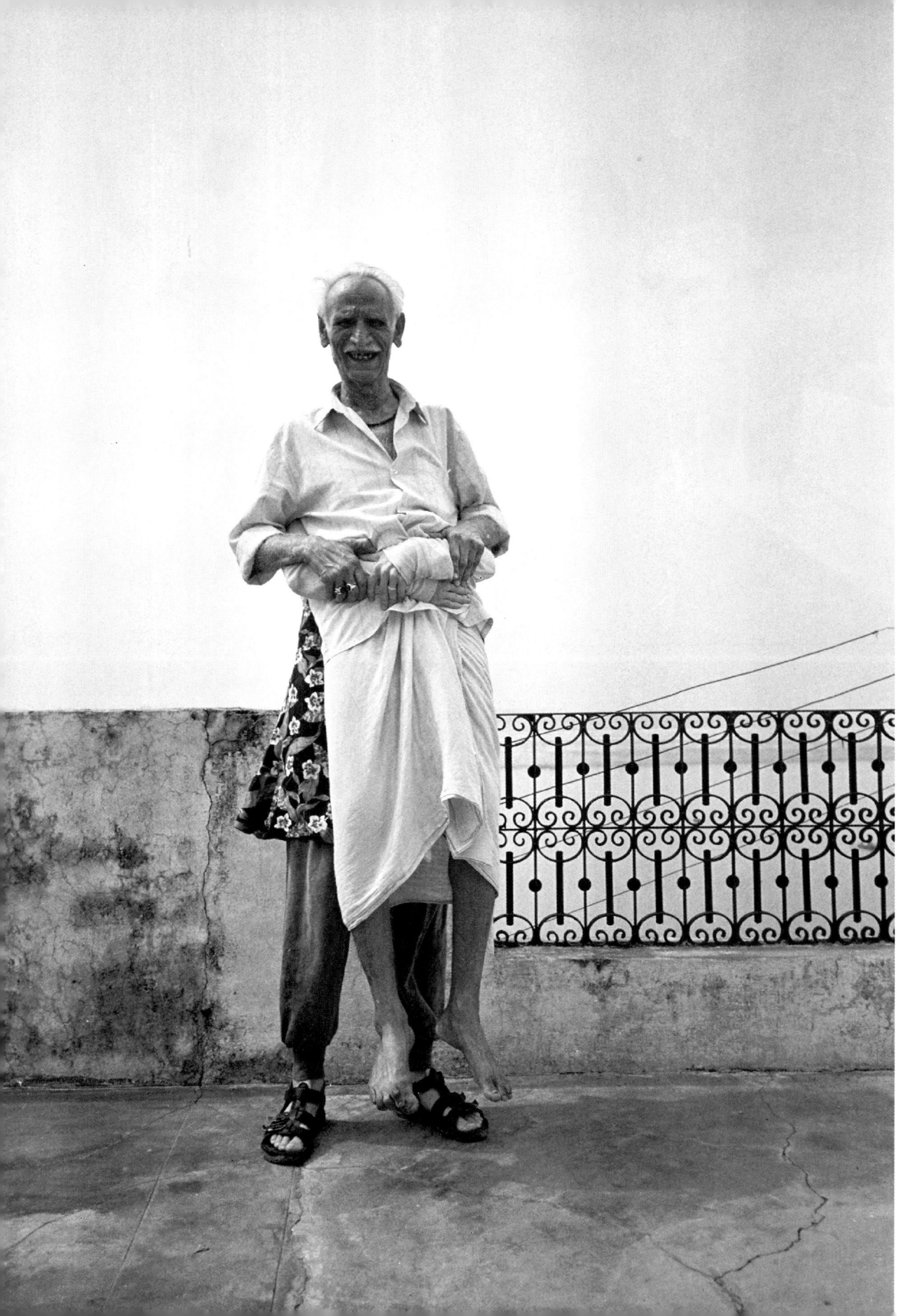

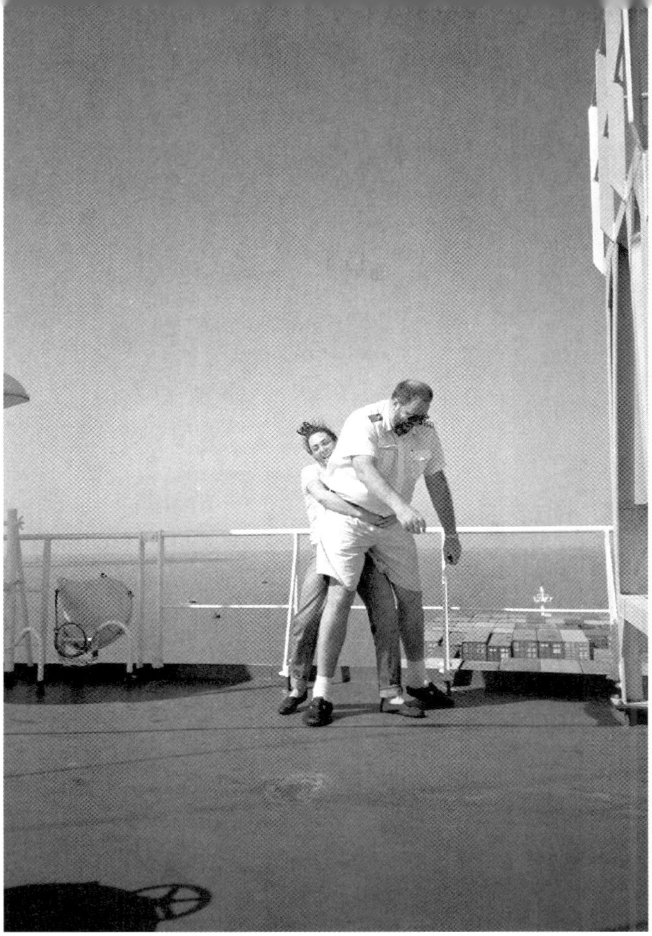
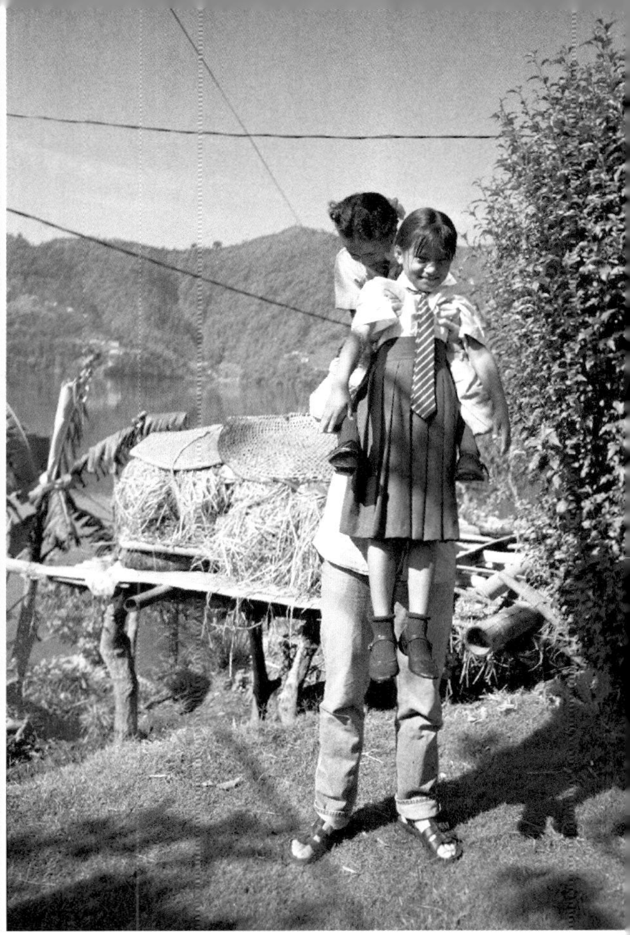
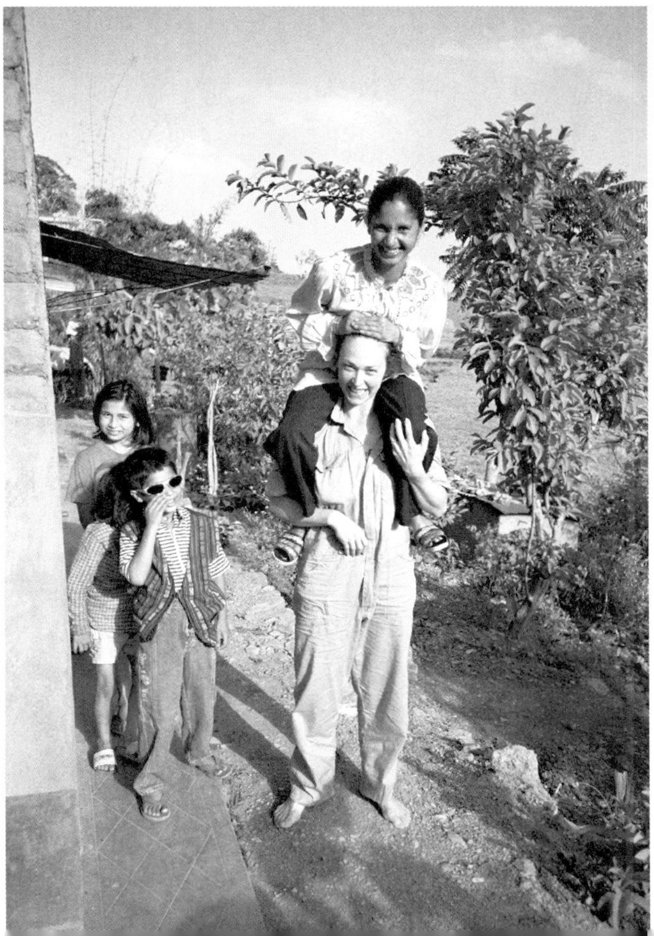
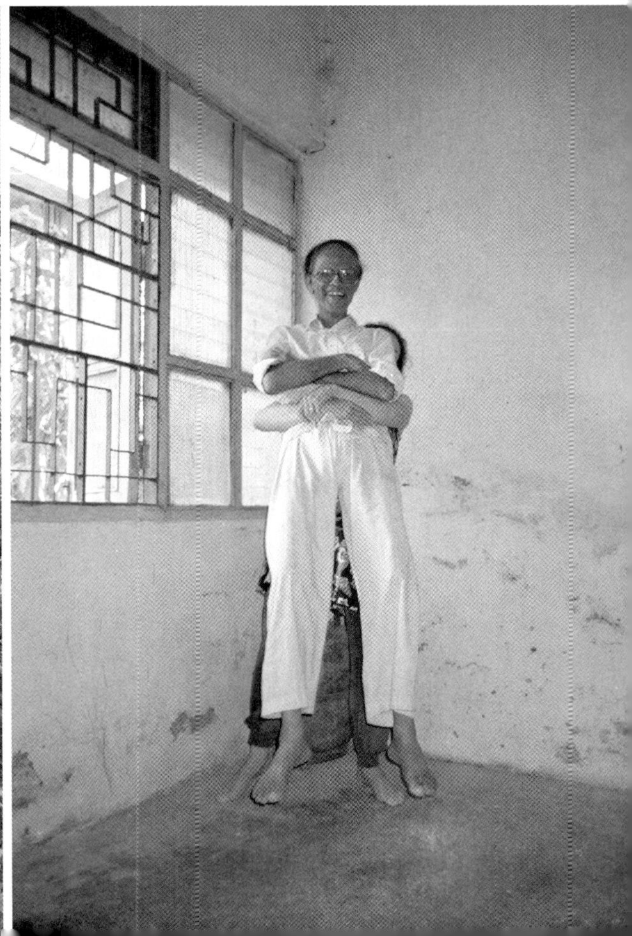

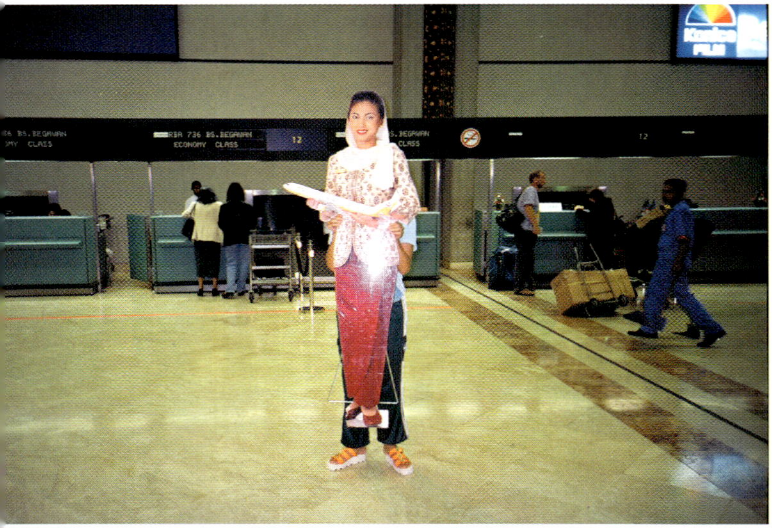
ECONOMY CLASS
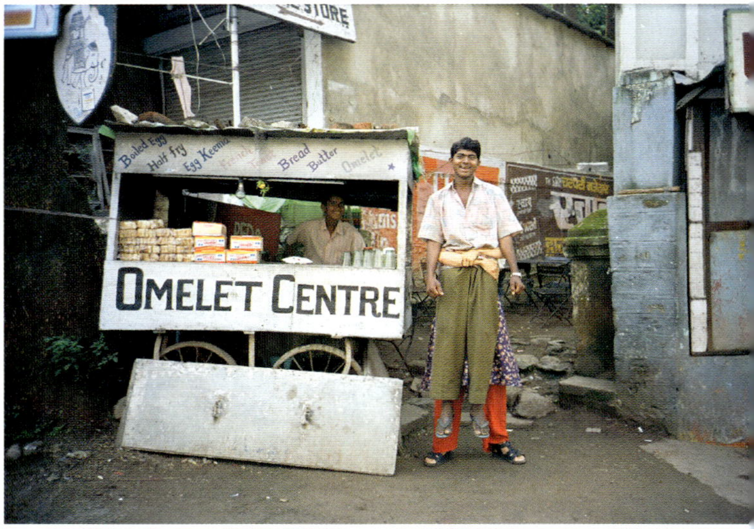
OMELET CENTRE
Bread
Butter
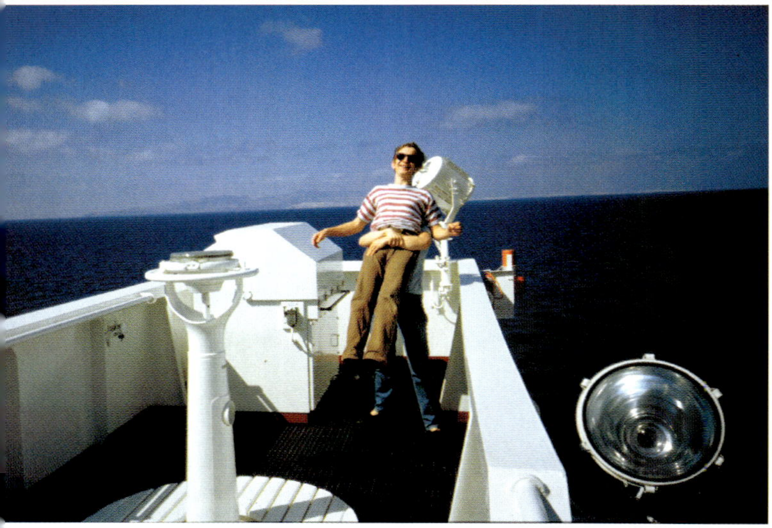
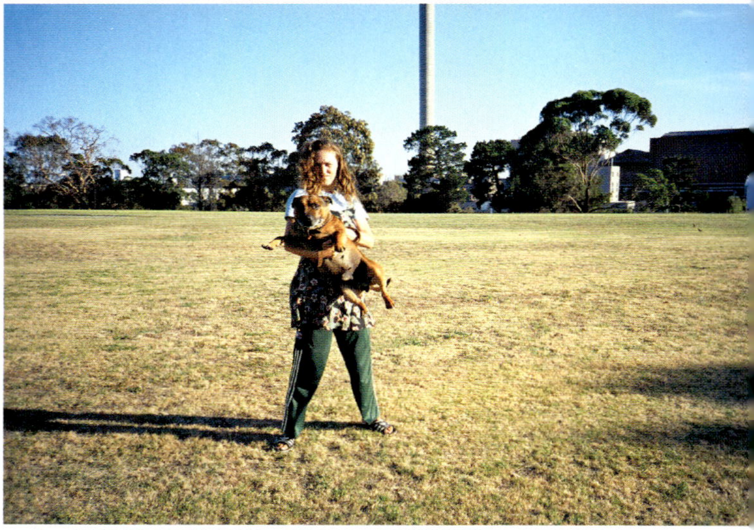
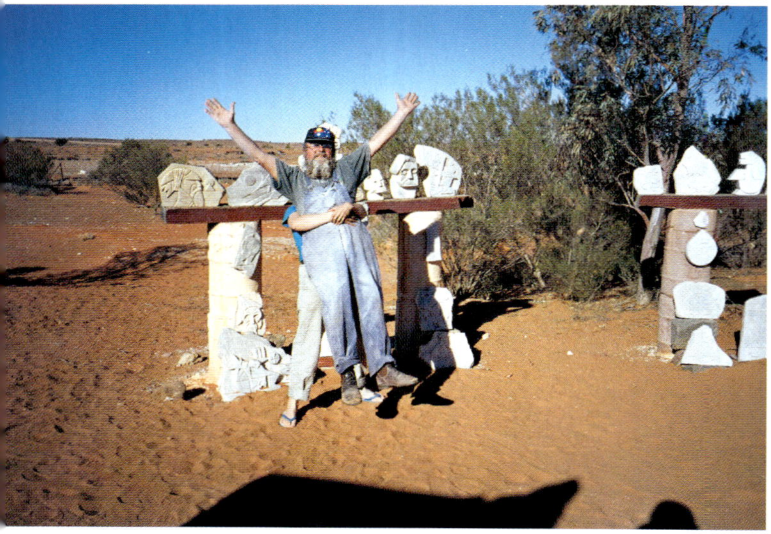
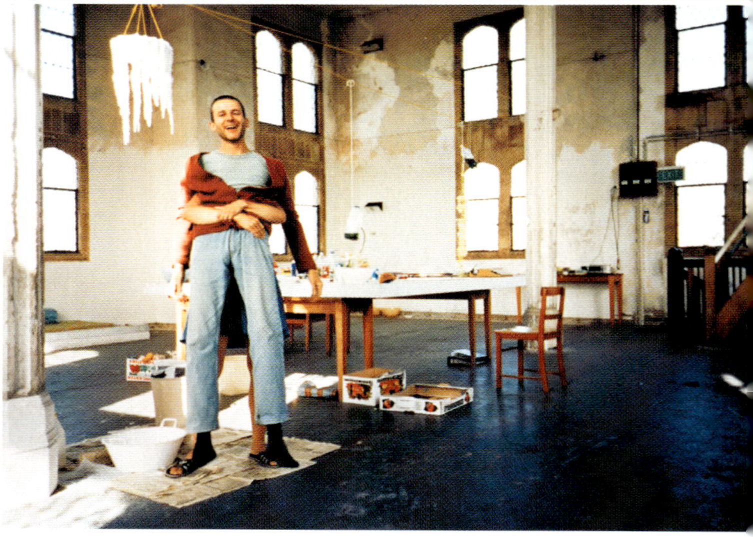

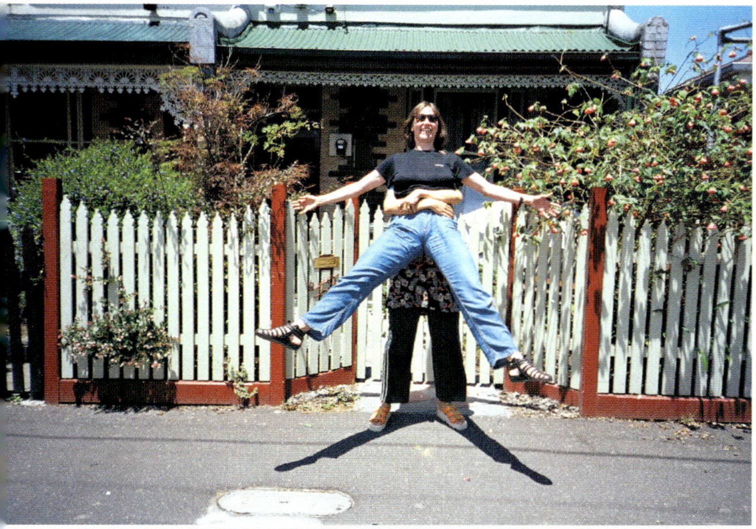
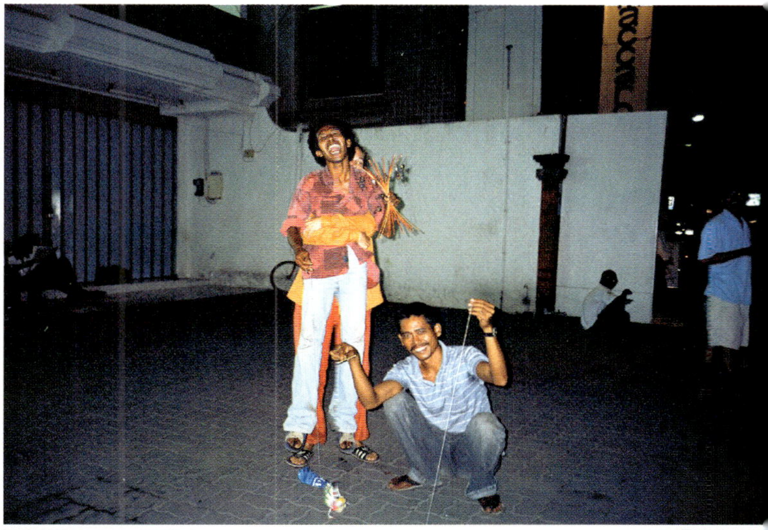
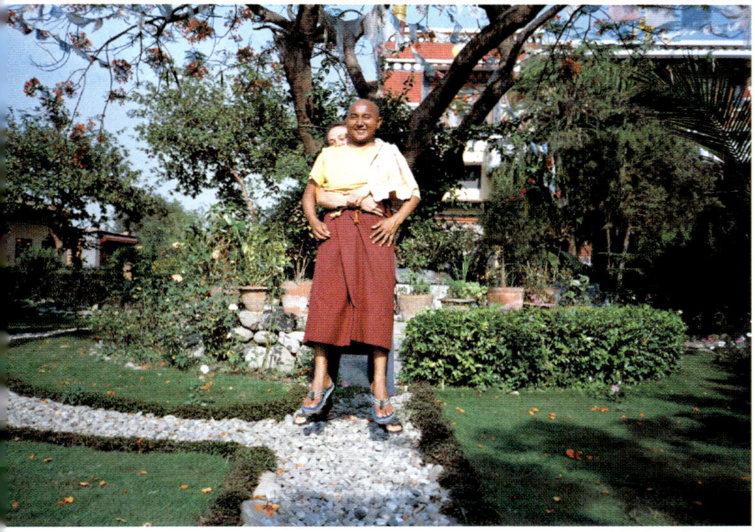
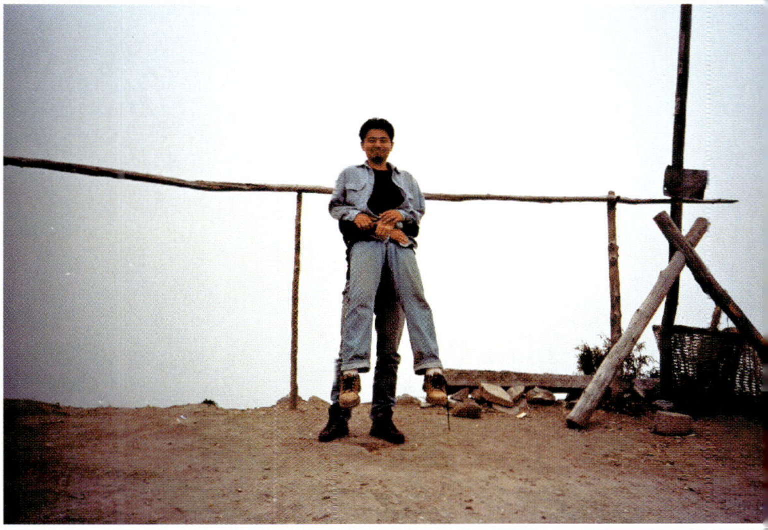
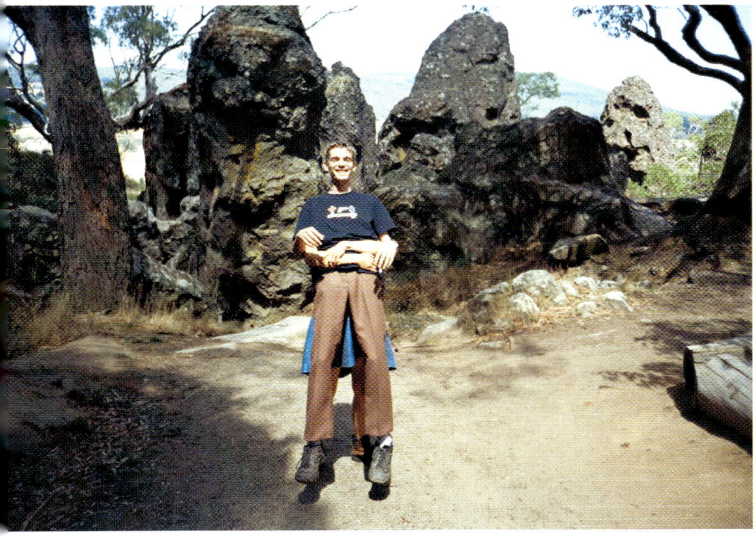
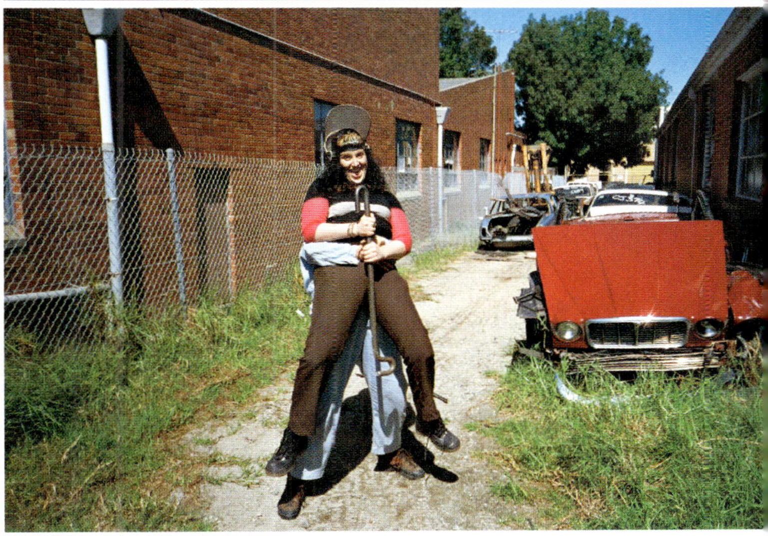

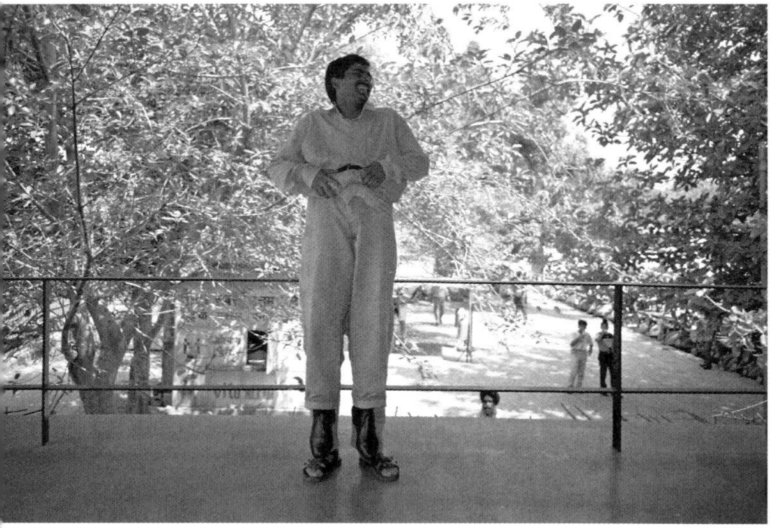

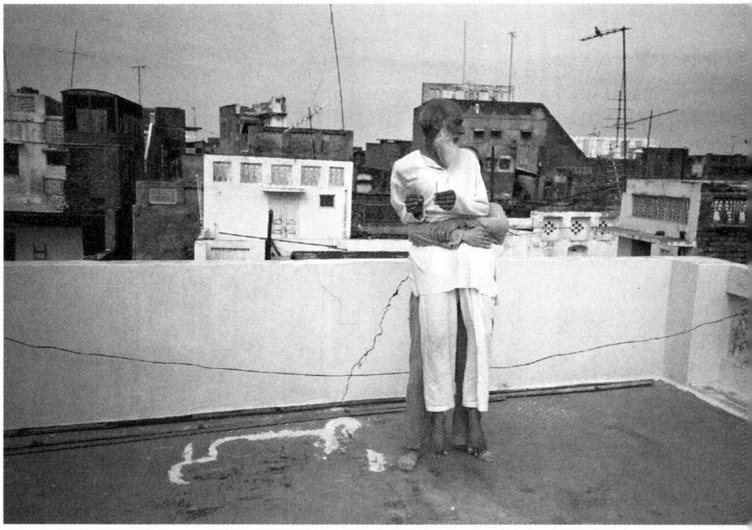

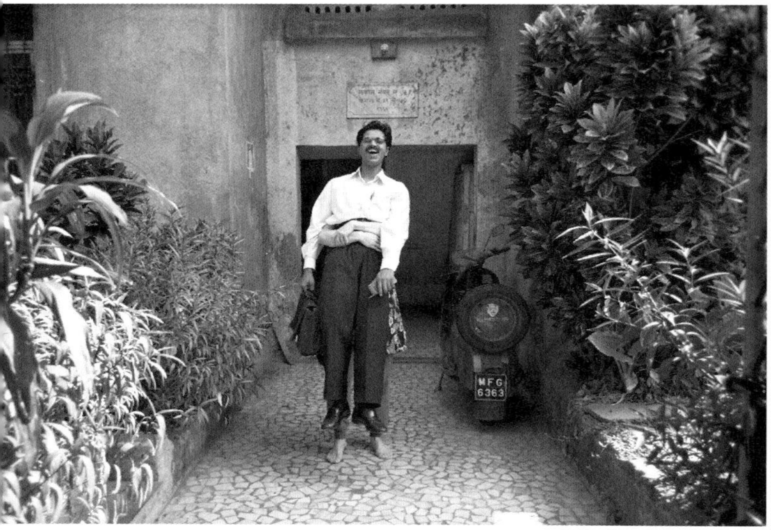
MFG
6363

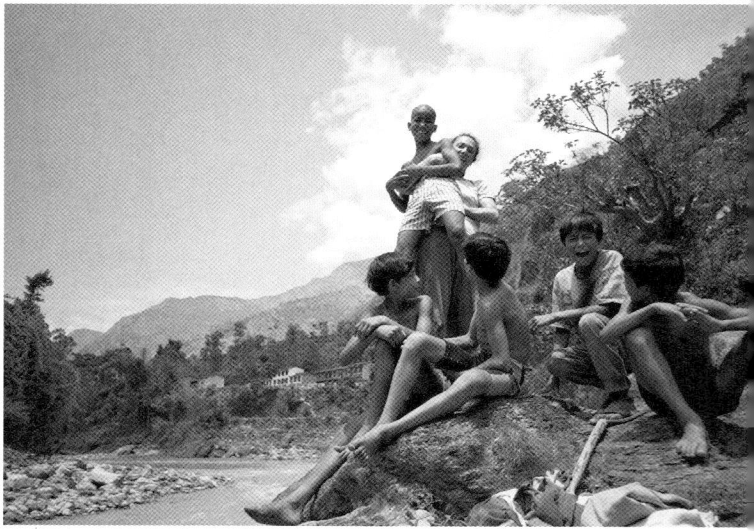

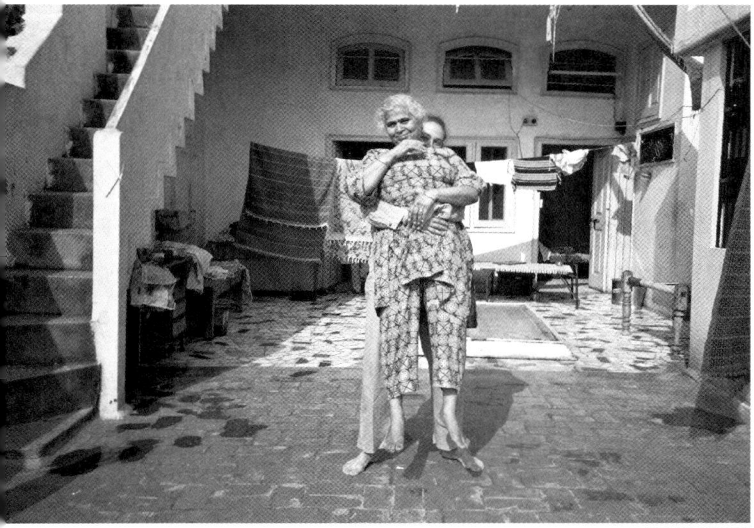
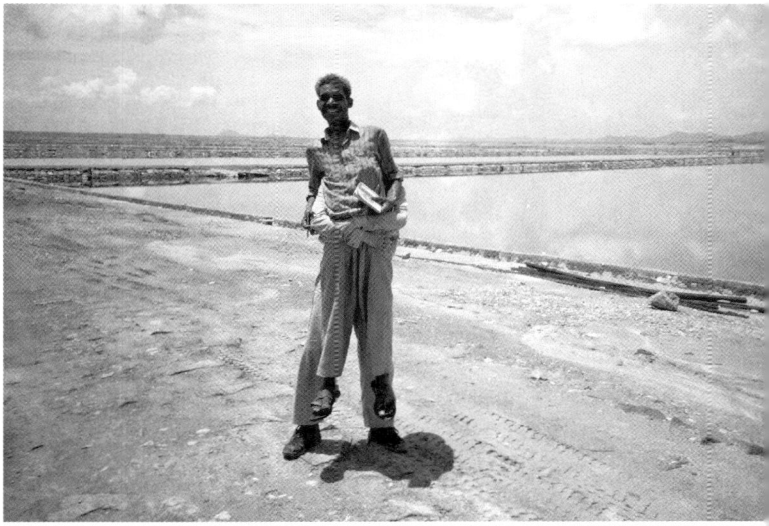
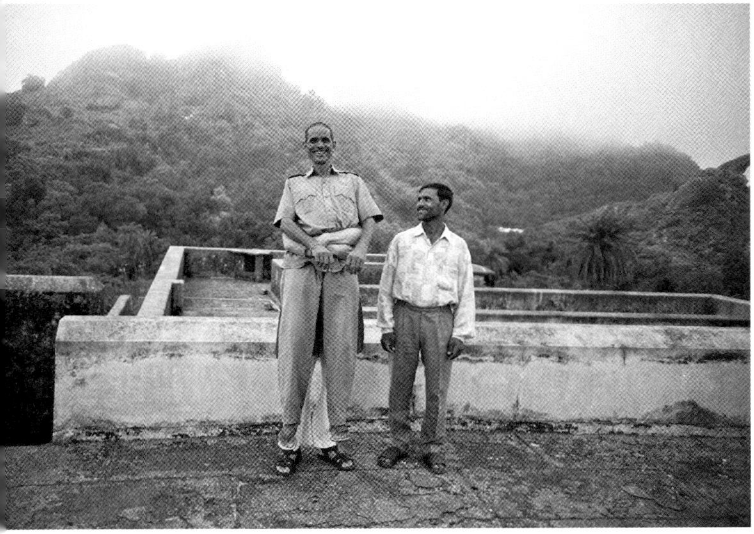
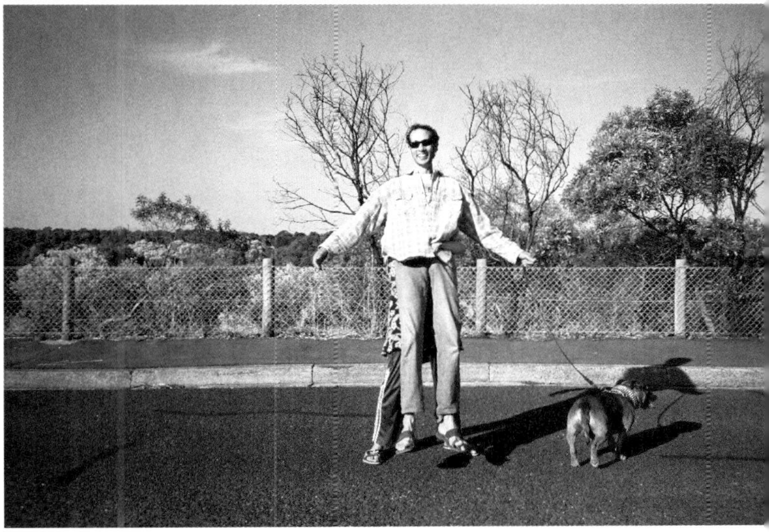

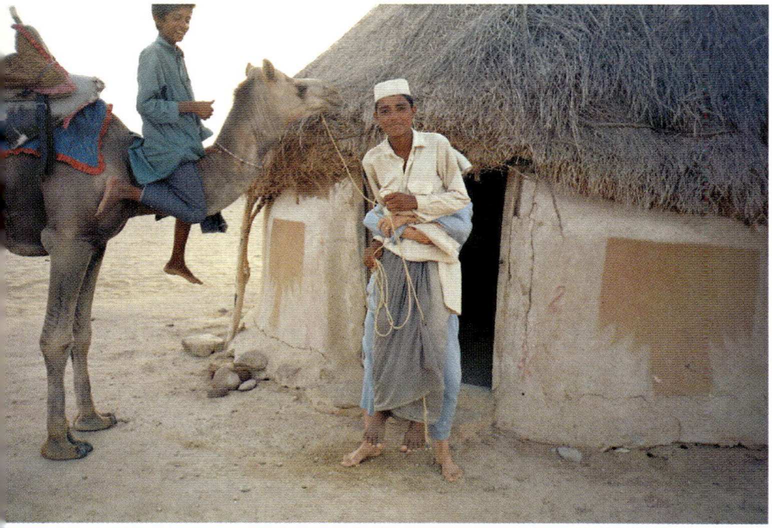
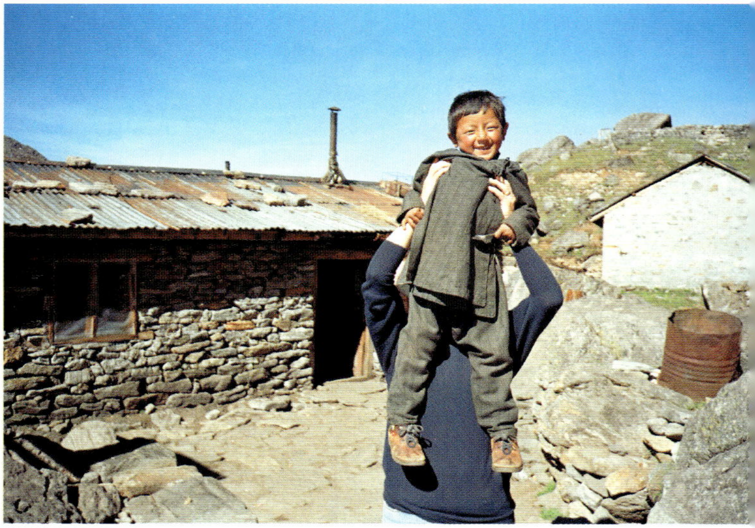
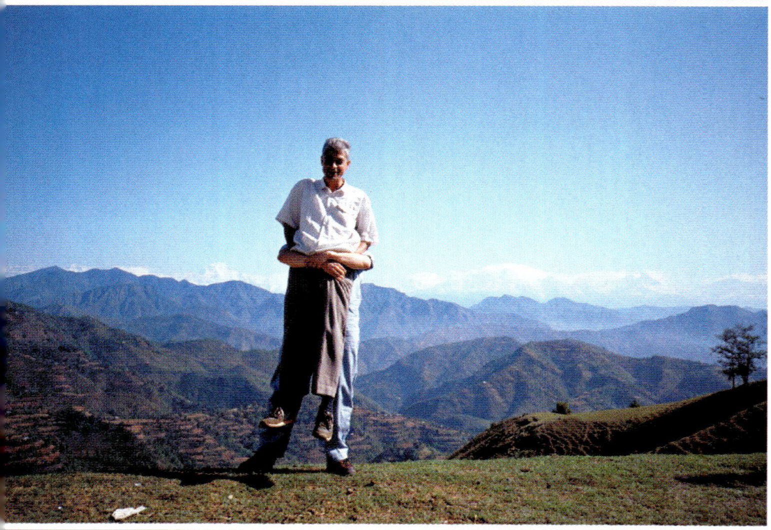
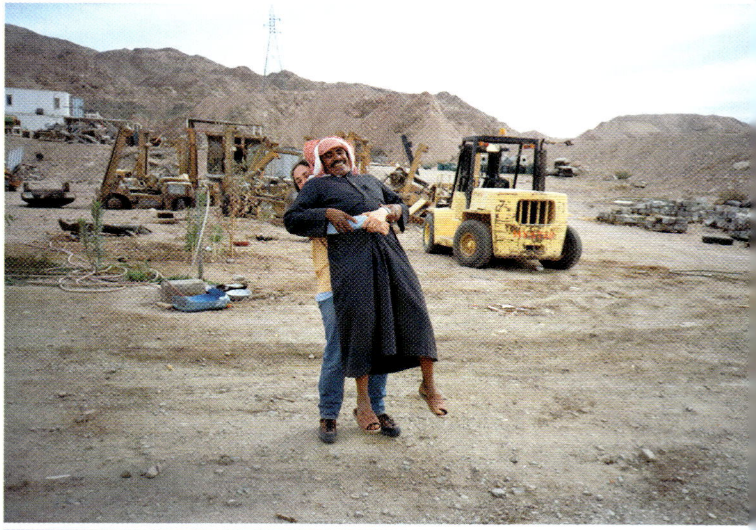
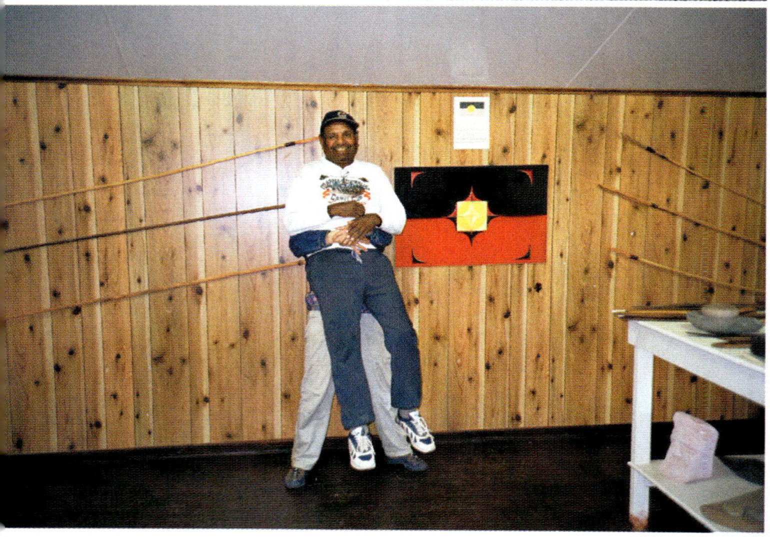
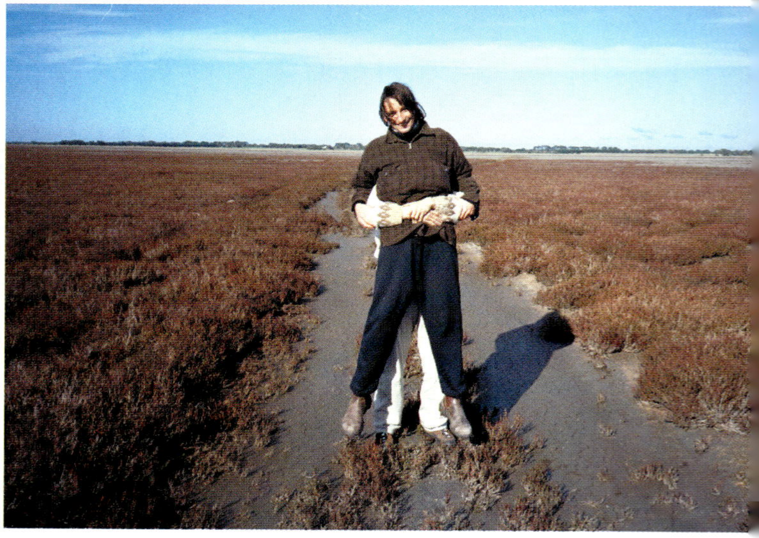

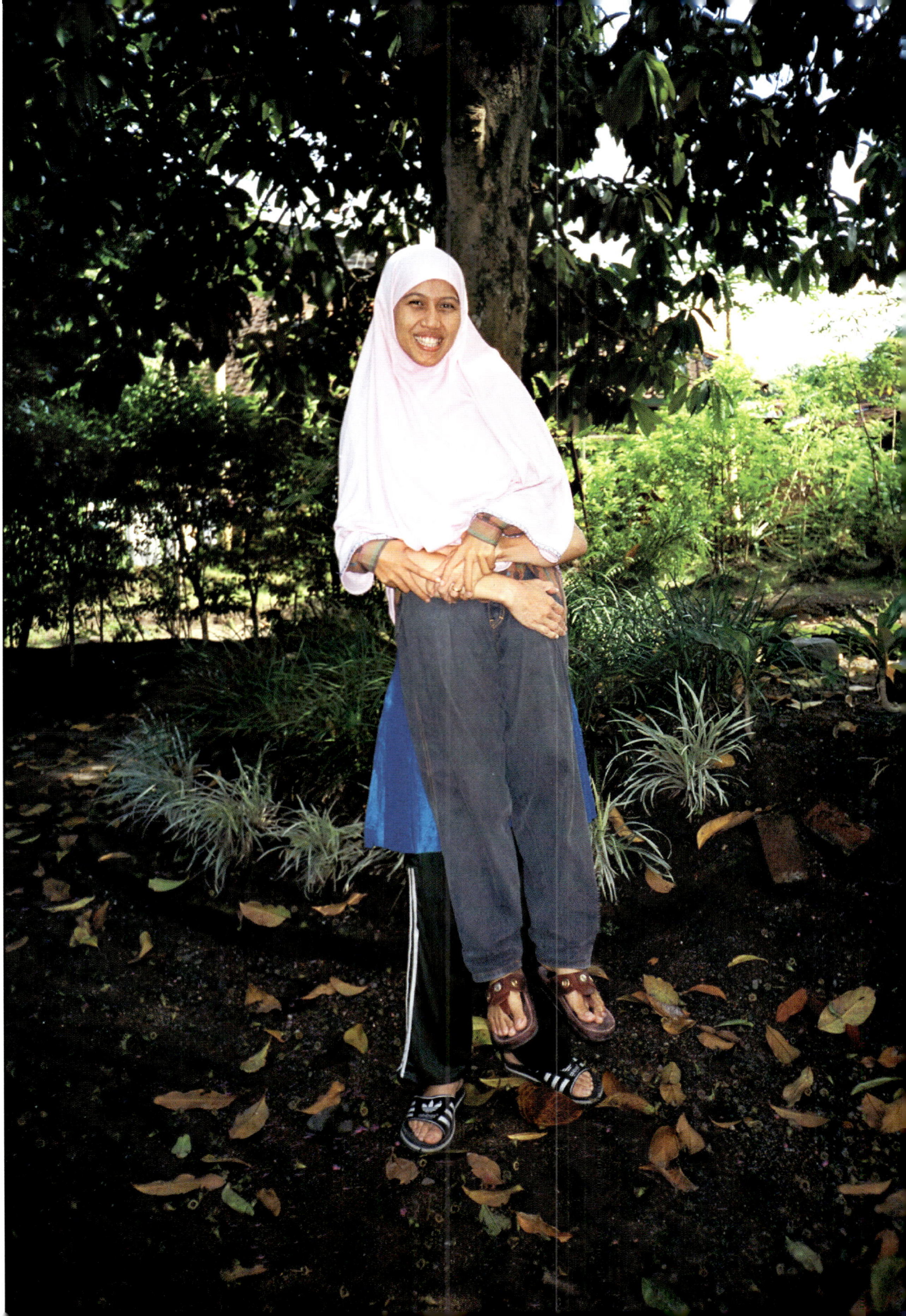

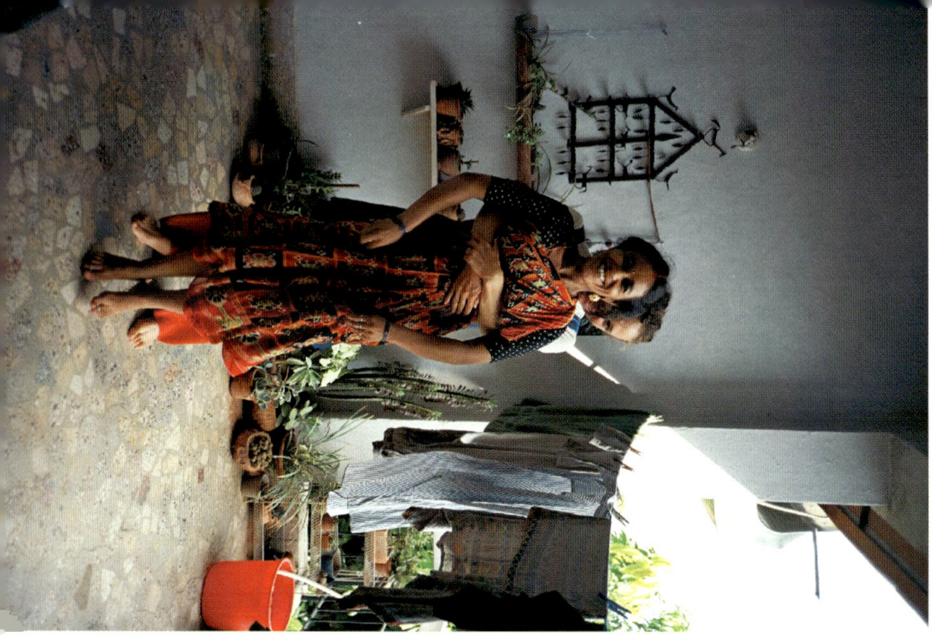

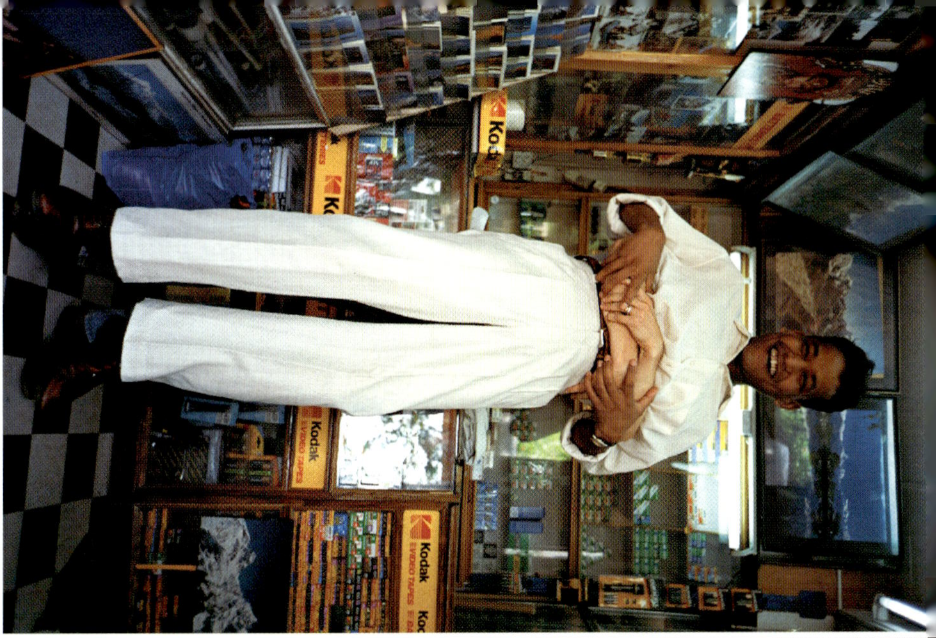

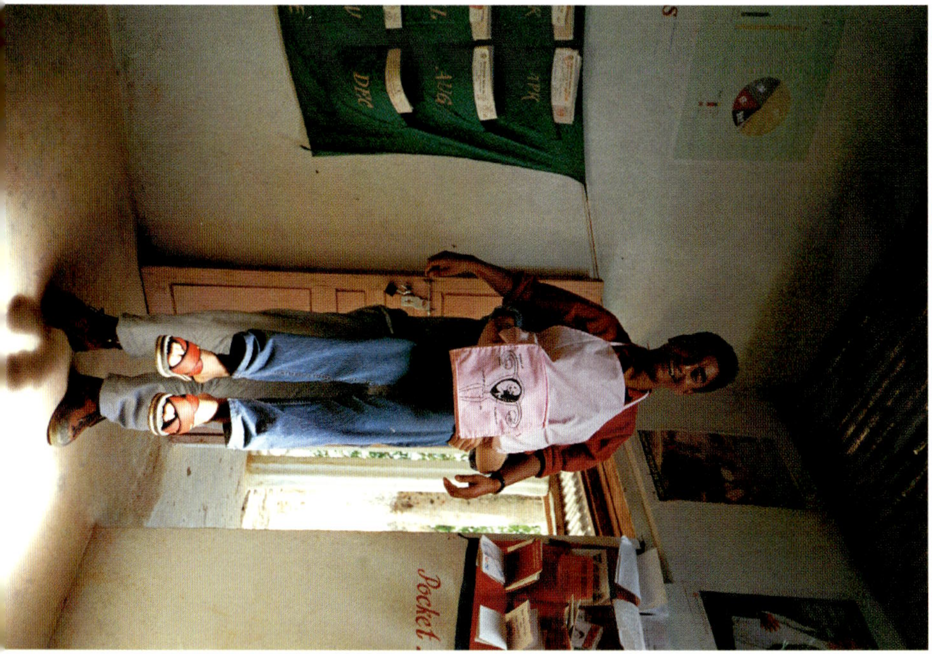

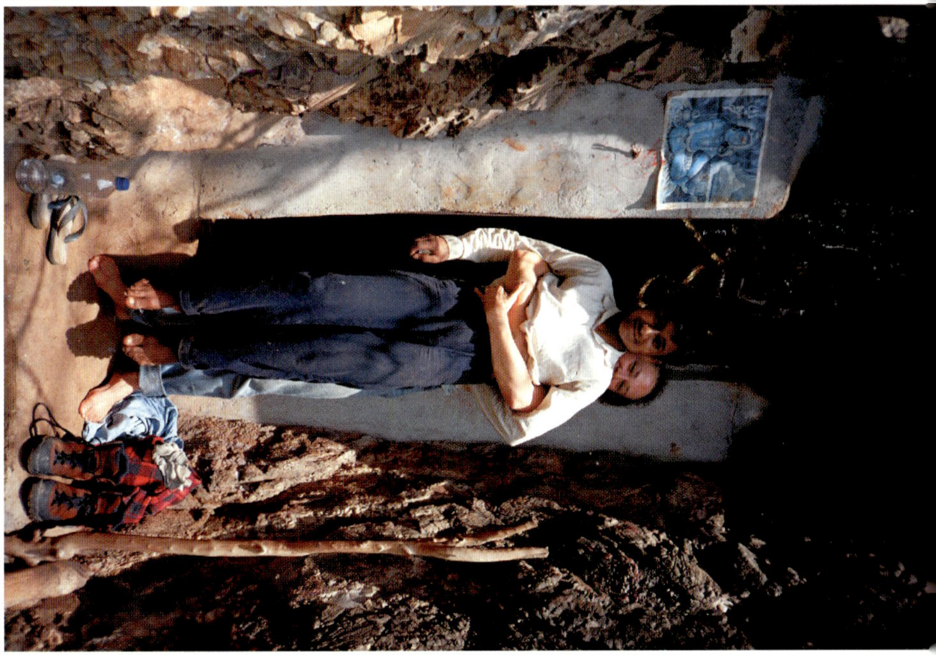

The project LIFT-UP was created during a world trip (1998–1999). Delighted at making new friends, Gerda lifts them up and Jörg takes pictures of them.
The complete series of LIFT-UP was published as a poster by "attitudes" and "CH Creatio Helvetica," Geneva, on the occasion of Gerda Steiner and Jörg Lenzlinger's exhibition at "attitudes, espace d'arts contemporains" in Geneva (20 May to 8 July 2000).

Das Projekt LIFT-UP ist in den Jahren 1998–1999 auf einer Weltreise entstanden: Aus Freude an neuen Bekanntschaften hebt Gerda diese in die Höhe und Jörg photographiert sie.
Die gesamte Serie von LIFT-UP ist als Poster (hrsg. von «attitudes» und «CH Creatio Helvetica», Genf) anlässlich einer Ausstellung der beiden Künstler bei «attitudes, espace d'arts contemporains» in Genf (20. Mai bis 8. Juli 2000) erschienen.

Illuminations The Drawings of Patti Smith

DAVID GREENBERG

everything is something else
a mouth is a wound
I violate with my pencil
the tip of my finger
the body of a canvas
the frescoes of florence
the porous skin of plaster saints
sweating bands and beads of love
all art seems pointless
one blurring photograph
an elusive face
– Patti Smith[1)]

The Whirling Dervish. The Shaman. The Preacher. The Rock'n'Roll Star. It seems that whenever an artist ventures into realms of mystical exploration, any number of these labels get tossed around with a certain air of resentment and sarcasm. Patti Smith has gracefully suffered these monikers, continuing down her ever-expanding path as a poet, singer, songwriter, and visual artist with the same intensity of spirit that first endeared her to audiences around the world in the seventies. Yet with all her success as a Rock'n'Roll Star, Patti Smith remains, to most in the art-world establishment, a curiosity at best. For many critics, artists are almost expected to transform themselves into one-trick ponies, find their riff, stick to it, and churn out slight variations on the same theme. But there is a deeper tradition that Smith labors in, which can be traced back to figures like William Blake—himself a poet, mystic, songwriter, and visual artist—Antonin Artaud, and Arthur Rimbaud. Within the context of this type of spiritual exploration, Smith moves through various disciplines with a fierce energy. She becomes an alchemist, merging the visual, written, and musical arts into a singular vision committed to what Rimbaud referred to as the process of becoming a "seer."

A portrait of Patti Smith as a young artist would inevitably begin with the physical nature of the written word. Handwriting, specifically calligraphy, held an alluring presence early on for Smith. Remembering a reproduction of The Declaration of Independence she acquired in a third grade class trip to the Franklin Institute in 1955, she explains: "The audacious grace of the script intrigued me and I spent hours as a child copying it out—the image of the word, the signatures—on long paper scrolls. I imagined that in mastering each bold, significant hand, I would capture some of the spirit of the author, of Independence itself."[2)] This early relationship with language re-

DAVID GREENBERG is a poet and musician living in New York. He wrote about the artist Donald Baechler for *Parkett 57.*

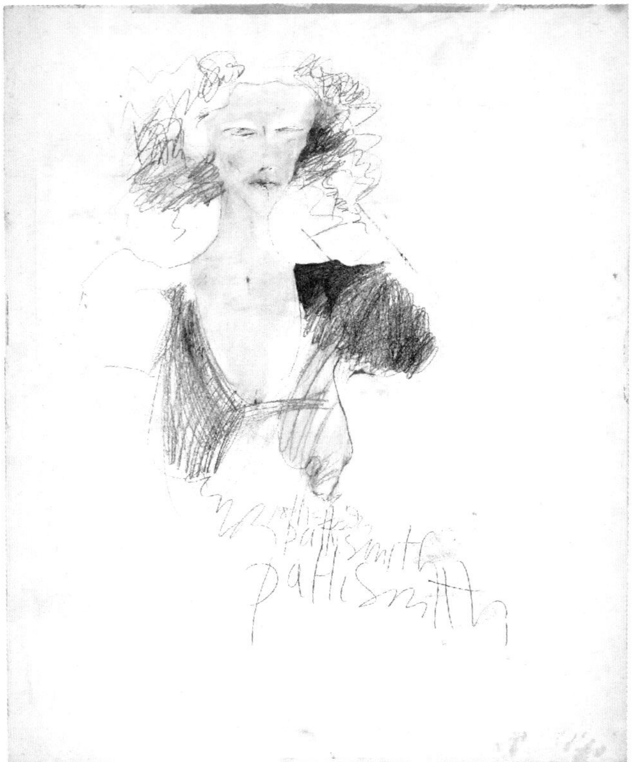

PATTI SMITH, PATTI SMITH, N.D., pencil, colored pencil and crayon on paper, 29 x 23 1/8" / Bleistift, Farbstift und Kreide auf Papier, 73,7 x 58,7 cm.
(ALL PHOTOS: ROBERT MILLER GALLERY, NEW YORK)

mains at the center of Smith's creative process. There is almost always a sense of channeling spirits in her poems, songs and, especially, in her drawings. The written word serves as a catalyst for creative energy. And more importantly, it is the physical image of language that both informs and inspires Smith's work.

Moving to New York City in the late sixties, Smith originally intended to become a painter. Her struggle in the visual arts would ultimately lead her to a more expansive creative process. "Standing before large sheets of paper tacked to a wall," Smith recounts, "frustrated with the image, I'd draw words instead—rhythms that ran off the page onto the plaster."[3] Her frustrations as a painter fueled a desire to expand the physical and psychic limitations of art. The drawings evolved into poems, the poems into songs. And all of this energy would eventually find its way onto the stage. The refinement of her process as a visual artist led Smith to performance. But she would always find her way back to drawing.

One of the earliest examples of Smith returning to drawing is SELF-PORTRAIT from 1971. This work contains a written commentary on the actual process of its creation. And again, the specter of frustration looms over the drawing. Scrawled beneath the actual image is perhaps an even more revealing self-portrait: "After not drawing for two years and attempting a first perfect comeback this ugly initial area roped off in ball point pen was an attempt at rebelling." The heightened awareness of process becomes integral to the overall impact of the drawing. It is a "comeback" and, by this association, something of an artifact, something other than simply art. Smith successfully casts an aura of the historical around the drawing. It becomes a self-portrait in image and spirit. Smith imbues the drawing with a sense of urgency and need. In one way it operates as a kind of illuminated manuscript, as in Blake, where the poet further evolves the metaphysical exploration of a poem with an image. In another way, this type of self-portrait seems to share an historical alliance with Antonin Artaud, who considered his drawings to be spells. Like Smith, Artaud used the written word as a springboard for his portraits, many times creating a new language which emblazoned the image with ritualistic markings. The physical execution of these "spells" was at times violent—he frequently burned holes into the drawings with lit cigarettes. And while his psychological motivation for drawing may have differed greatly from Smith's, Artaud's visual impact as an artist shares a unique kinship with Patti Smith. For like her best works, Artaud's drawings are also something other than just art.

With SELF-PORTRAIT, Smith also expresses her struggle with drawing in simple human terms. She opens up a whole other area of consciousness by giving voice to a child-like frustration. The scrawl continues: "I got pissed I gave up art yet here I am again." It is a sentiment that almost reads as a blueprint for Punk Rock, and in fact, it is this adolescent rebellious energy which spills forth in written form that was simultaneously evolving for Smith as a musician. Rock'n'Roll provided a new field for Smith's language to expand. It also provided another expanse for her growing pantheon of spirits. Smith derived a certain mystical energy from specific historical figures she had thrown together, re-contextualized, and re-mythologicalized—a kind of parallel universe where Jackson Pollock rubs shoulders with Brian Jones and Maria Callas. No figure was more prominent in this pantheon than Arthur Rimbaud. In language, style, and myth, Rimbaud had become the major hero for Smith. And she would again turn to drawing to try to capture some of his spirit, continuing the process, which began as a child copying the calligraphy of The Declaration of Independence. Now, she would attempt a form of spirit channeling through the image of language in the physical form of Rimbaud. And it all began with his face.

The discovery of Rimbaud has become infused with Patti Smith's own personal mythology. She has recounted the story numerous times. Recently she told Ingrid Sischy: "I found him in a Philadelphia bus depot when I was sixteen. I remember seeing a copy of *Illuminations* for sale on a table of used books. Of course, 'illuminations' is a great word, but what I was really taken by was the cover. It was a beautiful picture of Rimbaud. That's why I got the book."[4] Rimbaud's spirit forged its way into much of Smith's work in the early seventies. CAREFUL RIMBAUD (1973) is perhaps Smith's most realized visual representation of the young poet's disturbing presence. Her usually raw and frenzied draftsmanship is more refined and delicate in this portrait. The title suggests the precision and economy of line and, of course, the care involved, but it also serves as another commentary on the actual process. The hair, brow, lips, and nose all seem to be composed of script, painstakingly copied by Smith from some ancient text. And while the figure is clearly an image, the drawing seems to serve as a form of poem. The lines of the portrait spill out from the centralized image of the eyes—two pale blue ghosts executed in colored pencil. There is something both haunting and religious about the portrait. Something devotional. Smith comes close to creating a sort of relic. An icon of Rimbaud that seems to want to bleed or cry. An illuminated spirit.

While her career as a performer has ever evolved from underground legend to pop star to obscurity, retirement, cult figure, and back again, Patti Smith the artist has remained steadfast and committed. She has increasingly associated the process of making art to that of a ritual. In her essay "Drawing" Smith offers detailed accounts of her art-making process. The descriptions reflect a meditative, monk-like approach to her own idiosyncratic drawing methods from preparation to inspiration and execution. In one particular passage she calls upon the spirit of Robert Mapplethorpe—who was an integral part of her life as a collaborator, champion of her work, and great friend. Her ritual begins with the familiar process of copying a language: "I sat in the changing light in the center of the room, copying out the Lord's Prayer in Aramaic, hoping something would be revealed in the process... Inspired I pulled out my pencils and a pad of claycoat [and] made several small drawings in a manner I learned from Robert—a field composed of a single word—a simple phrase repeated, entwining. And then, as was my wont, more elaborate phrases snaking back to a single line."[5] Again we find Smith confronting the physicality of handwriting, the image of a language.

Over the years, she would create numerous variations on this type of field drawing. PEACE AND NOISE #1 (1997) is the most recent example. Composed of lyric fragments from her album *Peace and Noise*, the drawing has an expanding, organic feel, with words and phrases forming petal-like shapes that bloom out from a gestural center. Certain letters bend and elongate around the edge of each main cluster, leading to the appearance of some kind of magnetic pull. At first glance, this type of drawing seems to have some direct correlation to the work of Cy Twombly, though ultimately, the similarities are only superficial. While both artists employ a scribbled, gestural script in their compositions, the formal concerns are completely different. Twombly's focus is diffused. His main goal is to distribute gestural moments across a field in order to achieve an overall balanced state. Smith, however, tightens her focus. Her gestures are deliberately frenzied and awkward. The words themselves are part of an energy force field. New combinations of phrases and new

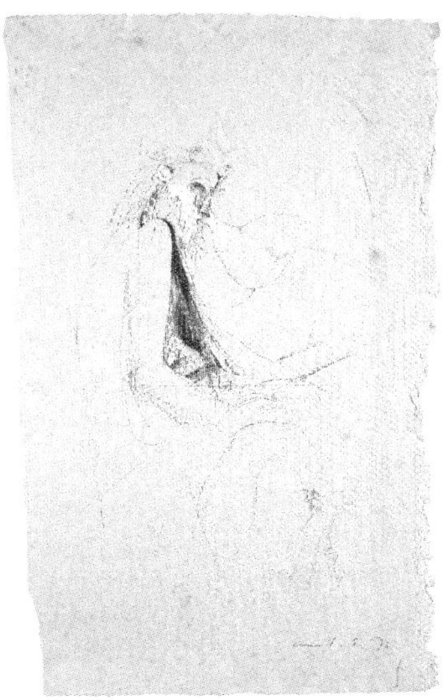

PATTI SMITH, UNTITLED, 1978, pencil and colored pencil on tan paper, 24 1/2 x 15 1/2" / OHNE TITEL, Bleistift und Farbstift auf getöntem Papier, 62,2 x 39,4 cm.

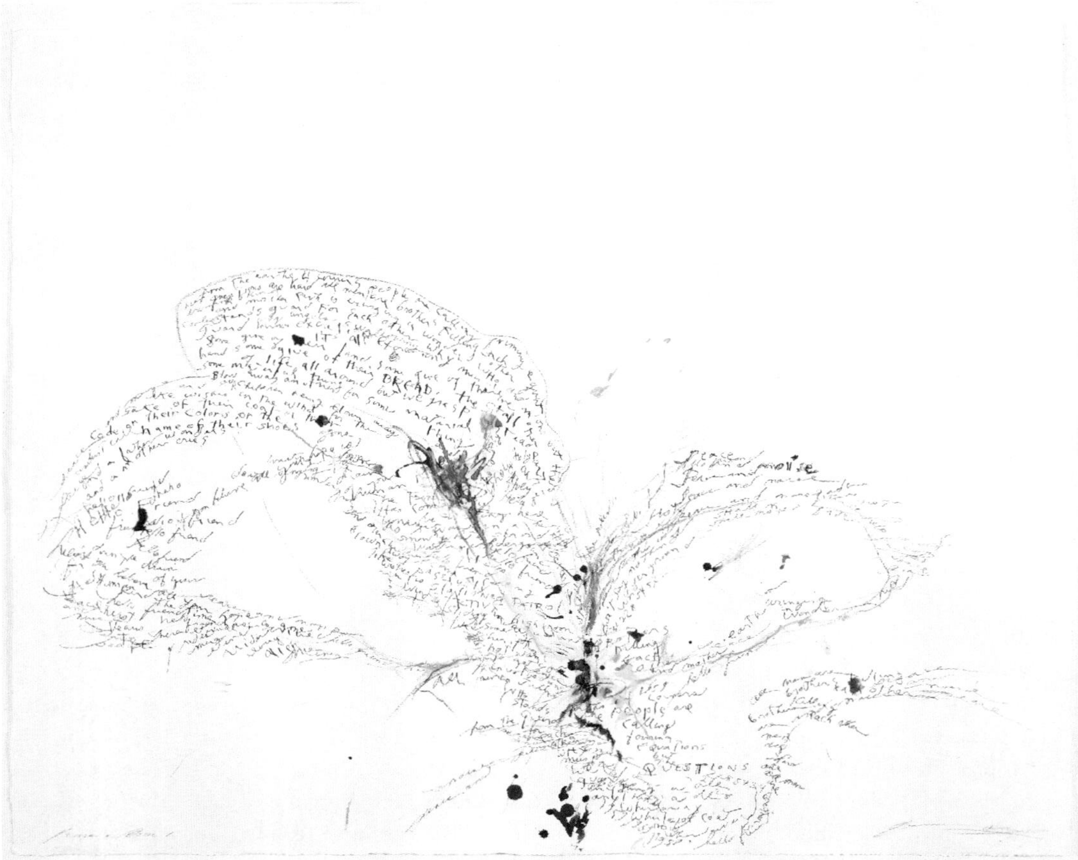

PATTI SMITH, PEACE AND NOISE I, 1997, pencil, colored pencil, ink and watercolor on paper, 20 x 24" / STILLE UND LÄRM I, Bleistift, Farbstift, Tusche und Aquarell auf Papier, 50,8 x 61 cm.

meanings are stretched out across the field. For Twombly, handwriting is a means to an end. For Smith, it is the process of manipulating the physical characteristics of the written language that serves her more spiritual and poetic goals. While she is concerned with aesthetics, the ultimate beauty of her drawings lies outside of form. She is not, like Twombly, aiming for a soft mood. Instead, she struggles to transform the written language itself, creating unforeseen permutations—an alchemy of word and gesture.

Patti Smith continues to approach drawing as a Buddhist would meditation: mindful of both prayer and practice. Her major focus as a visual artist takes on the air of the devotional. Her drawings are chants and mind-breaths. They are artifacts of a poetic process. Her own form of illumination. Nearing the end of her task, Smith writes: "...after a time the drawing itself took on a prominence relative to nothing. It became a work, a torture I soon abandoned. I placed the last of my tools—quills—in a box. I pressed my palms together and bowed, leaving my post in pursuit of life, noise."[6] The artist is acutely aware of the sanctity of her practice. And like a soldier, she is temporarily relieved of her duty. Leaving the spirit world for the material world, she bows, in acknowledgment and praise of a greater force, which has been ever so slightly revealed.

1) Patti Smith, "easter" in: *Early Work 1970–1999* (New York: W. W. Norton & Co., 1994).
2) Patti Smith, *Woolgathering* (New York: Hanuman Books, 1992), p. 42.
3) Patti Smith, *Patti Smith Complete: Lyrics, Reflections & Notes for the Future* (New York: Doubleday, 1998), p. xxi.
4) Ingrid Sischy, "Because The Light," *Interview* (New York: Brandt Publishers, June, 1996), p. 84.
5) Patti Smith, "Drawing" in: *Woolgathering*, pp. 44–46.
6) Ibid., p. 61.

Illuminationen

Die Zeichnungen von Patti Smith

DAVID GREENBERG

everything is something else
a mouth is a wound
I violate with my pencil
the tip of my finger
the body of a canvas
the frescoes of florence
the porous skin of plaster saints
sweating bands and beads of love
all art seems pointless
one blurring photograph
an elusive face
– Patti Smith[1]

Wirbelnder Derwisch. Schamane. Prediger. Rockstar. Sobald ein Künstler sich ins Reich mystischer Erfahrungen vorwagt, reagieren wir peinlich berührt bis sarkastisch und haben sofort jede Menge solcher Etiketten zur Hand. Patti Smith hat all diese Titulierungen gelassen ertragen und ist ihrem sich immer weiter verzweigenden Pfad als Dichterin, Sängerin, Liedtexterin und bildende Künstlerin unbeirrt gefolgt, mit derselben geistigen Intensität, die ihr Publikum weltweit von Anfang an gefesselt hatte. Doch trotz des Erfolgs als Rockstar ist Patti Smith für die meisten Leute des Kunstestablishments nach wie vor bestenfalls eine Kuriosität. Viele Kritiker erwarten ja von Künstlern geradezu, dass sie ihren einen speziellen Trick draufhaben, dass sie ihr Thema finden, dabei bleiben und es allenfalls noch leicht variieren. Aber es gibt eine tiefer reichende Tradition, auf die Smiths Arbeit Bezug nimmt und die sich zurückverfolgen lässt bis zu Gestalten wie William Blake – seinerseits Dichter, Mystiker, Liedermacher und bildender Künstler –, aber auch Antonin Artaud oder Arthur Rimbaud. Im Kontext dieser Art der spirituellen Suche durchmisst Smith mit ungeheurer Energie ganz unterschiedliche Disziplinen. Sie wird zur Alchemistin, indem sie Bild, Wort und Musik zu einer einzigen Vision verschmilzt in einem Prozess, den Rimbaud mit dem Ausdruck *se faire voyant* (sich sehend machen) bezeichnete.

Ein Porträt von Patti Smith als junger Künstlerin müsste unweigerlich mit dem Körperhaften des geschriebenen Wortes beginnen. Das Handschriftliche, insbesondere das Kalligraphische hatte für Smith schon früh eine verlockende Präsenz. In Erinnerung an eine Reproduktion der Unabhängigkeitserklärung, die sie 1955 auf einem Klassenausflug ins Franklin Institut erwarb, erklärt sie: «Die kühne Anmut der Schriftzüge fesselte mich, und ich verbrachte als Kind Stunden damit, sie auf lange Papierrollen zu kopieren – das Schriftbild, die Unterschriften. Ich stellte mir vor, dass ich durch das Beherrschen der kühnen charaktervollen Schriftzüge etwas vom Geist des Autors, ja der Unabhängigkeit selbst erfassen würde.»[2] Dieses frühe Verhältnis zur Sprache ist noch immer zentral für ihre Kreativität. In ihren Gedichten, Liedern und vor allem in ihren Zeichnungen weht fast immer ein Hauch von Geisterbeschwörung. Das geschriebene Wort dient ihr als Katalysator für die kreative Energie. Aber wichtiger noch: Es ist das physische Bild der Sprache, was Smiths Werk so sehr prägt und auszeichnet.

Als sie in den späten 60er Jahren nach New York zog, wollte sie eigentlich Malerin werden. Ihre Auseinandersetzung mit der bildenden Kunst

DAVID GREENBERG ist Dichter und Musiker und lebt in New York. In *Parkett* 57 schrieb er über den Künstler Donald Baechler.

führte sie schliesslich zu einer umfassenderen Kreativität. «Als ich vor den grossen, an die Wand gehefteten Papierbogen stand», erinnert sich Smith, «und mich das Bildliche nicht befriedigte, zeichnete ich stattdessen Worte – Rhythmen, die über die Seite hinaus auf dem Putz weiterliefen.»[3] Die Frustrationen, die sie als Malerin erlebte, erzeugten den Wunsch, die physischen und psychischen Grenzen der Kunst aufzubrechen. Die Zeichnungen entwickelten sich zu Gedichten, die Gedichte zu Liedern. Und all diese Energie fand schliesslich den Weg auf die Bühne. Der Differenzierungsprozess ihrer Arbeit als bildende Künstlerin führte Smith zur Performance. Aber sie fand immer wieder den Weg zurück zur Zeichnung.

PATTI SMITH, ROBERT WITH EYE OF PASOLINI, N.D., pencil and colored pencil on paper, 17 7/8 x 12" / ROBERT MIT DEM AUGE VON PASOLINI, Bleistift und Farbstift auf Papier, 45,4 x 30,5 cm.

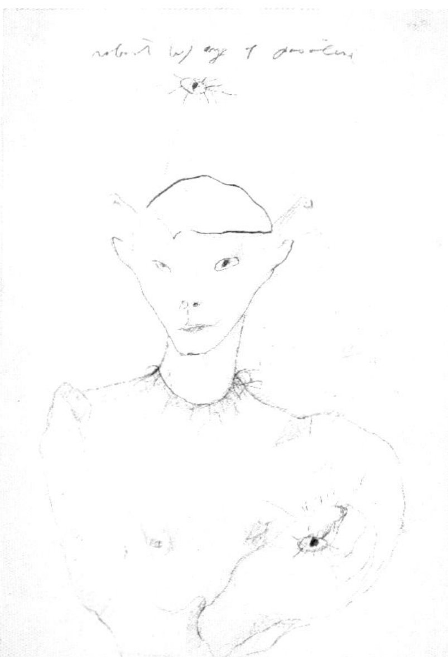

Ein ganz frühes Beispiel einer solchen Rückkehr ist SELF-PORTRAIT (Selbstporträt) aus dem Jahr 1971. Diese Arbeit schliesst einen schriftlichen Kommentar zu ihrem Entstehungsprozess mit ein. Und wiederum schwebt das Gespenst der Frustration drohend über der Zeichnung. Unter dem eigentlichen Bild ist ein womöglich noch aufschlussreicheres Selbstporträt hingekritzelt: «Nachdem ich zwei Jahre lang nicht gezeichnet hatte und ein erstes perfektes Comeback versuchte, zeigt diese hässliche, mit Kugelschreiber umrahmte Anfangsstelle einen Auflehnungsversuch.» Die erhöhte Sensibilität für das Prozessuale wird zum integralen Bestandteil des Gesamteindrucks der Zeichnung. Sie ist ein «Comeback» und wird durch diese Assoziation zu einem Artefakt, zu etwas anderem als nur Kunst. Es gelingt Smith, die Zeichnung mit einer historischen Aura auszustatten. Sie wird zum bildlichen und geistigen Selbstporträt. Smith verleiht der Zeichnung eine Atmosphäre von Dringlichkeit und Notwendigkeit. Einerseits funktioniert sie ähnlich wie eine illuminierte Handschrift, wo der Dichter, wie im Fall von Blake, die metaphysische Forschungsarbeit des Gedichts mit einem Bild weiter treibt. Andrerseits scheint diese Art Selbstporträt eine historische Verwandtschaft zu Antonin Artaud aufzuweisen, der seinen Zeichnungen magische Wirkung zuschrieb. Wie Smith verwendete auch Artaud das geschriebene Wort als Sprungbrett für seine Porträts, wobei er oft eine neue Sprache schuf, die das Bild mit rituellen Zeichen ausschmückte. Die physische Ausführung dieser magischen Formeln war manchmal gewalttätig; oft brannte er mit Zigaretten Löcher in die Zeichnungen. Aber auch wenn Artaud aus ganz anderen psychologischen Gründen zeichnen mochte als Smith, so besteht hinsichtlich des visuellen künstlerischen Eindrucks doch eine einzigartige Verwandtschaft zwischen den beiden. Denn wie Patti Smiths beste Arbeiten sind auch Artauds Zeichnungen noch etwas anderes als nur Kunst.

In SELF-PORTRAIT bringt Smith ihren Kampf mit dem Zeichnen auch auf eine allgemein menschliche Weise zum Ausdruck. Indem sie eine kindliche Enttäuschung in Worte fasst, betritt sie eine ganz andere Bewusstseinsebene. Das Gekritzel geht weiter: «Ich hatte die Nase voll, habe die Kunst aufgegeben, und dennoch bin ich wieder hier gelandet.» Dieser Gefühlszustand liest sich beinahe wie das Programm des Punk-Rock, und tatsächlich ist es diese in schriftlicher Form hervorbrechende jugendlich-rebellische Energie, die auch Smiths Entwicklung als Musikerin prägte. Der Rock and Roll eröffnete ihrer Sprache einen neuen Wirkungskreis. Er bot auch zusätzlichen Raum für ihre wachsende Geisterwelt. Smith zog mystische Energie aus bestimmten historischen Gestalten, die sie durcheinander mischte, in einen neuen Kontext stellte und denen sie eine neue Mythologie verpasste: eine Art Paralleluniversum, in welchem Jackson Pollock Seite an Seite mit Brian Jones und Maria Callas lebt. Niemand in diesem Götterhimmel überragt jedoch Arthur Rimbaud. In Sachen Sprache, Stil und Mythos war Rimbaud zu Smiths Lieblingsheld geworden. Und wieder wandte sie sich der Zeichnung zu, um etwas von seinem Geist zu erfassen, und setzte so den Prozess fort, der in ihrer Kindheit mit der kalligraphisch getreuen Abschrift der Unabhängigkeitserklärung

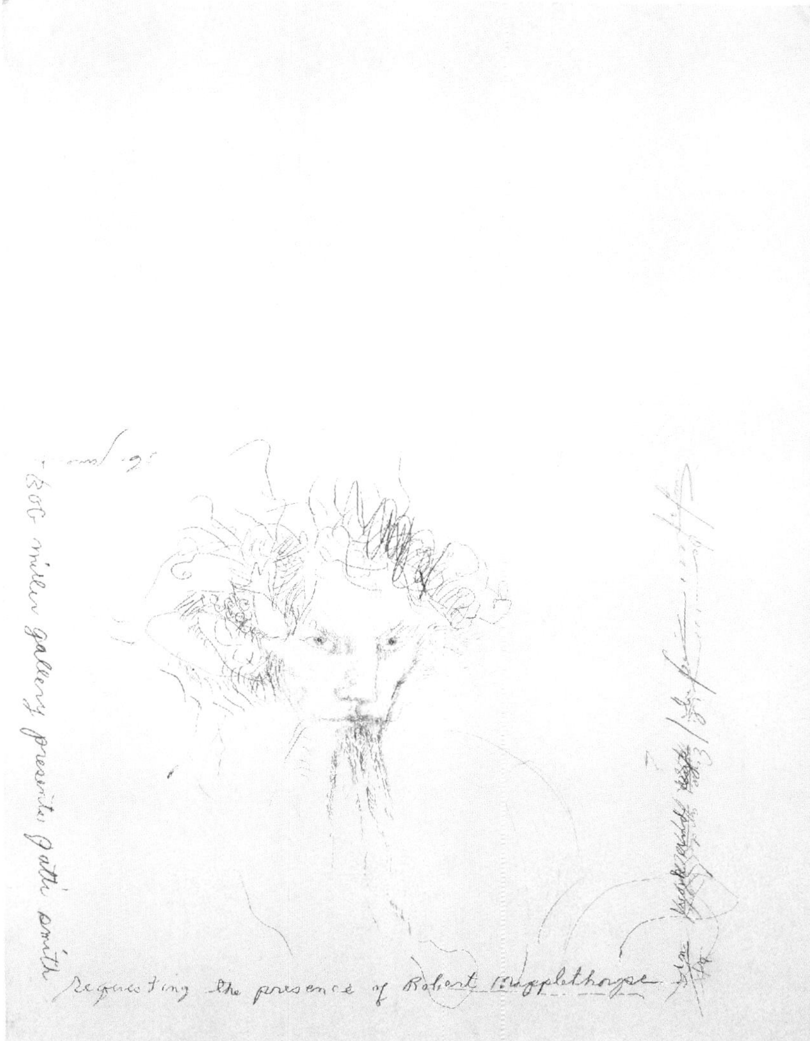

PATTI SMITH, ROBERT MAPPLETHORPE PORTRAIT FOR ROBERT MILLER, 1978, pencil on illustration board, 20 x 15" / PORTRÄT VON ROBERT MAPPLETHORPE FÜR ROBERT MILLER, Bleistift auf Zeichenkarton, 50,8 x 38,1 cm.

begonnen hatte. Nur versuchte sie jetzt eine Art Geisterbeschwörung durch ein Schriftbild in der physischen Gestalt von Rimbaud. Und alles hatte mit seinem Gesicht begonnen.

Die Entdeckung Rimbauds ist mit Patti Smiths eigener persönlicher Legende verflochten. Sie hat diese Geschichte schon oft erzählt. Kürzlich berichtete sie Ingrid Sischy: «Ich fand ihn mit sechzehn in einem Busdepot in Philadelphia. Ich weiss noch, wie ich ein Exemplar der *Illuminations* auf einem Tisch mit antiquarischen Büchern liegen sah. Natürlich ist ‹Illuminationen› ein grossartiges Wort, aber was mich wirklich umwarf, war der Umschlag. Es war ein wunderschönes Bild von Rimbaud. Deshalb habe ich das Buch gekauft.»[4] Rimbauds Geist ist in viele von Patti Smiths Arbeiten aus den frühen 70er Jahren eingeflossen. CAREFUL RIMBAUD (Sorgfältiger Rimbaud, 1973) ist vielleicht die am weitesten getriebene visuelle Darstellung der beunruhigenden Präsenz des jungen Dichters. Smiths normalerweise rüde wütender Zeichenstrich ist in diesem Porträt differenzierter und sensibler. Der Titel verweist auf die Präzision und Sparsamkeit der Linienführung und natürlich auf die damit verbundene Sorgfalt, aber er ist auch ein Kommentar zum Zeichenvorgang selbst. Haar, Brauen, Lippen und Nase scheinen aus peinlich genau aus einer alten Schrift kopierten Schriftzeichen zu bestehen. Und obwohl die Figur eindeutig ein Bild ist, scheint die Zeichnung auch eine Form von Gedicht zu sein. Die Linien des Porträts gehen alle aus dem zentralen Bild der Augen hervor – zwei blassblaue, in Farbstift ausgeführte Geister. Das Porträt hat etwas Unheimliches und Religiöses zugleich. Eine Art Heiligenbild. Smith macht beinah eine Reliquie daraus. Eine Ikone von Rimbaud, die, so scheint es, jeden Moment zu bluten oder weinen beginnen kann. Ein illuminierter Geist.

Während ihre Karriere immer in regem Wandel begriffen war – von der legendären Untergrundkünstlerin zum Popstar, in die Vergessenheit, den Rückzug, zur Kultfigur und wieder zurück –, blieb die Künstlerin Patti Smith ihrer Linie treu. Den Prozess des Kunstschaffens verstand sie immer mehr als Ritual. In ihrem Essay «Drawing» schildert Smith ausführlich, wie ihre Kunst entsteht. Von der Vorbereitung bis zum Moment der Inspiration und Ausführung vermitteln die Be-

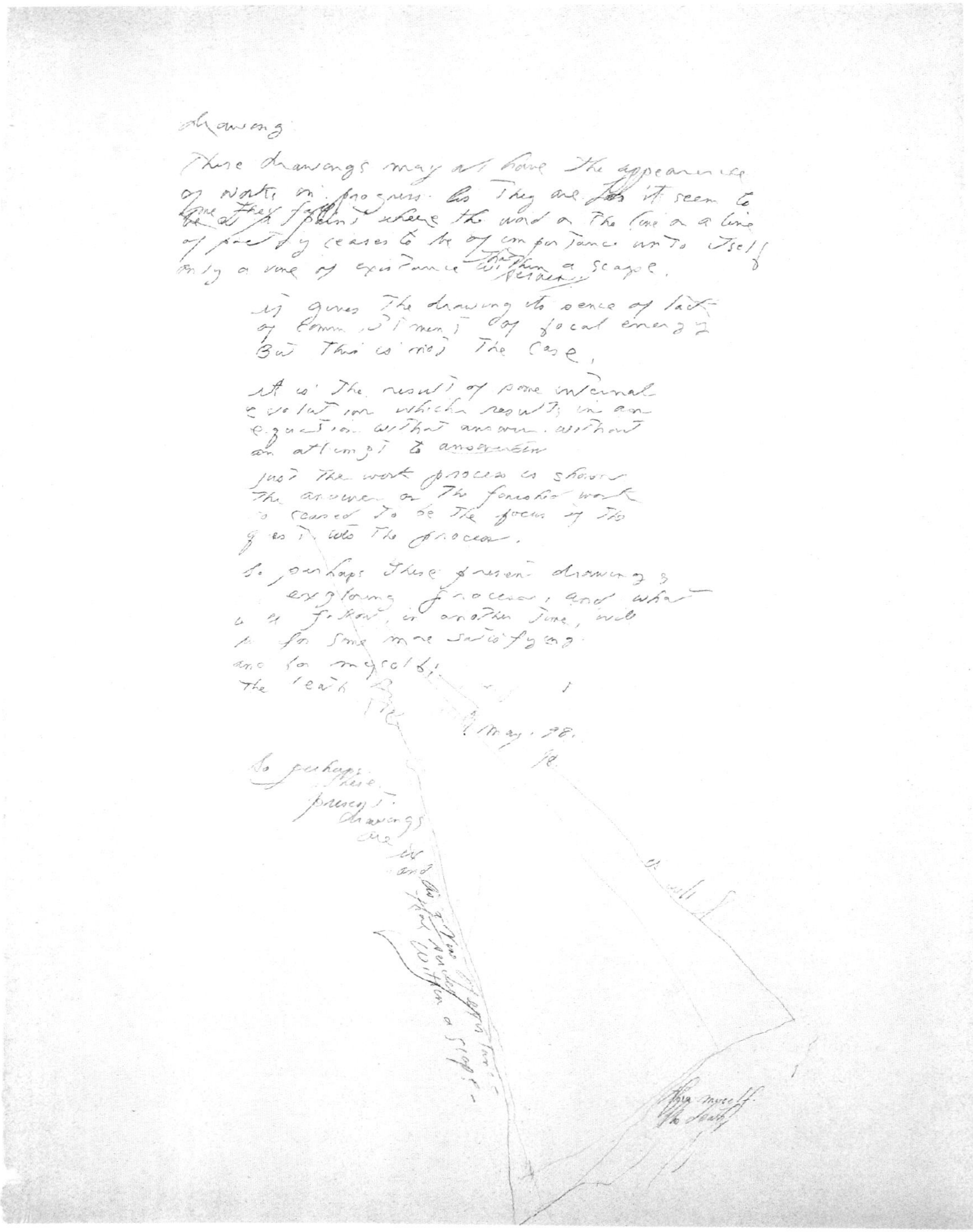

PATTI SMITH, DRAWING, 1998, pencil on paper, 12 3/8 x 9 1/2" / ZEICHNUNG, Bleistift auf Papier, 31,4 x 24,1 cm.
(ALL PHOTOS: ROBERT MILLER GALLERY, NEW YORK)

schreibungen das Bild eines meditativen, beinah mönchischen Umgangs mit ihren eigenen idiosynkratischen Zeichenmethoden. An einer Stelle beruft sie sich auf den Geist von Robert Mapplethorpe, der in ihrem Leben als Mitarbeiter, Verteidiger ihrer Kunst und guter Freund einen wichtigen Platz einnahm. Das Ritual beginnt jeweils mit dem vertrauten Kopieren eines Sprachgebildes: «Ich sass im wechselnden Licht in der Mitte des Zimmers, kopierte das Vaterunser in Aramäisch und hoffte, dass sich während dieses Prozesses etwas enthüllen würde... Inspiriert zog ich meine Stifte und einen Zeichenblock hervor und machte mehrere kleine Zeichnungen, so, wie ich es von Robert gelernt hatte: eine Fläche aus einem einzigen Wort bestehend, ein einfacher Ausdruck, so oft wiederholt, bis ein Geflecht entsteht. Und dann, wie es meiner Gewohnheit entsprach, kompliziertere Ausdrücke, die sich schlangenhaft zu einer einzigen Linie krümmten.»[5] Und wieder begegnen wir Patti Smith bei der Auseinandersetzung mit dem Körperhaften der Handschrift, dem Bildhaften der Sprache.

Über die Jahre hat sie zahlreiche Variationen dieser Art von flächendeckender Zeichnung geschaffen. PEACE AND NOISE NO. 1 (1997) ist das jüngste Beispiel. Die Zeichnung besteht aus lyrischen Fragmenten aus ihrem Album *Peace and Noise* (Frieden und Lärm). Sie wirkt raumgreifend und organisch mit ihren Worten und Ausdrücken, die wie Blütenblätter aus dem gestischen Zentrum herauswachsen. Einzelne Buchstaben biegen oder strecken sich dem Rand der Hauptformen entlang. Bei diesem Zeichnungstyp scheint es eine direkte Entsprechung zur Arbeit von Cy Twombly zu geben, obwohl die Ähnlichkeiten im Grunde nur oberflächlich sind. Zwar haben beide Künstler eine flüchtig hingeworfene, gestische Linienführung, aber ihre formalen Interessen sind völlig verschieden. Twomblys Fokus ist weit. Sein Hauptziel ist es, gestische Momente so über eine Fläche zu verteilen bis er insgesamt eine Balance erreicht. Smith dagegen verengt den Blickwinkel. Ihre Gesten sind mit Absicht nervös und ungelenk. Die Worte selbst sind Teil eines energetischen Kraftfeldes. Neue Kombinationen bestehender Ausdrücke und neue Bedeutungen durchmessen dieses Feld. Bei Twombly ist die Handschrift Mittel zum Zweck, während bei Smith die Manipulation der physischen Eigenschaften der geschriebenen Sprache mehr spirituellen und poetischen Zielen dient. Ästhetik ist ihr zwar wichtig, aber letztlich liegt die Schönheit ihrer Zeichnungen jenseits der Form. Sie versucht nicht wie Twombly eine sanfte Stimmung zu erzielen. Stattdessen gilt ihre Anstrengung der Verwandlung der geschriebenen Sprache selbst, wobei unerwartete Neubildungen entstehen – eine Alchemie von Wort und Gebärde.

Patti Smiths Einstellung zum Zeichnen gleicht derjenigen eines Buddhisten zur Meditation: Gebet und Übung sind gleich wichtig. Ihr Hauptinteresse als bildende Künstlerin hat religiöse Form angenommen. Ihre Zeichnungen sind Psalmen und Stossseufzer des Geistes. Sie sind das Resultat eines dichterischen Prozesses. Ihre eigene Form von Illumination. Über das Ende dieses Prozesses schreibt Smith: «... nach einer gewissen Zeit bekam die Zeichnung etwas unvergleichlich Beherrschendes. Sie wurde zu einem Werk, eine Tortur, der ich nicht lange standhielt. Ich legte mein letztes Werkzeug – Schreibfedern – in eine Schachtel. Ich presste meine Handflächen gegeneinander, verneigte mich und verliess meinen Posten um mich ins Leben, in den Lärm zu stürzen.»[6] Die Künstlerin weiss sehr wohl um das Heilige ihrer Aufgabe. Und wie ein Soldat wird sie vorübergehend von ihrer Pflicht entbunden. Im Begriff von der geistigen in die materielle Welt zu wechseln, verbeugt sie sich lobpreisend und demütig vor einer grösseren Macht, deren Schleier sich gerade eben ein bisschen gelüftet hat.

(Übersetzung: Susanne Schmidt)

1) aus Patti Smith, «easter», in: *Early Work 1970–1999*, W.W. Norton & Co, New York 1994.
Alles ist etwas anderes / ein Mund ist eine Wunde / mit dem Bleistift vergewaltige ich / meine Fingerspitze / den Körper einer Leinwand / die Fresken von Florenz / die poröse Haut von Heiligen aus Gips / Schweissbänder und Liebesperlen / alle Kunst scheint zwecklos / eine einzige verschwommene Photographie / ein flüchtiges Gesicht.

2) Patti Smith, *Woolgathering*, Hanuman Books, New York 1992, S. 42 (Zitat von der Redaktion übersetzt).

3) Patti Smith, *Patti Smith Complete: Lyrics, Reflections & Notes for the Future*, Doubleday, New York 1998, S. xxi.

4) Ingrid Sischy, «Because the Light», in: *Interview*, Juni 1996, Brandt Publishers, New York, S. 84.

5) Patti Smith, *Woolgathering*, S. 44–46.

6) Ebenda, S. 61.

CUMULUS

Aus Europa

IN JEDER AUSGABE VON PARKETT PEILT EINE CUMULUS-WOLKE AUS AMERIKA UND EINE AUS EUROPA DIE INTERESSIERTEN KUNSTFREUNDE AN. SIE TRÄGT PERSÖNLICHE RÜCKBLICKE, BEURTEILUNGEN UND DENKWÜRDIGE BEGEGNUNGEN MIT SICH – ALS JEWEILS GANZ EIGENE DARSTELLUNG EINER BERUFLICHEN AUSEINANDERSETZUNG.

IN DIESEM BAND ÄUSSERN SICH GIOVANNI CARMINE, FREIER KURATOR IN ZÜRICH, SOWIE STEVE DIETZ, KURATOR FÜR NEUE MEDIEN AM WALKER ART CENTER IN MINNEAPOLIS.

GIOVANNI CARMINE

San Keller: Kunst als «Service public»

Wie kann man die Komplexität eines künstlerischen Werks in Worte fassen, das doch von einfachen Gesten lebt? Die Aufgabe, eine geeignete Antwort auf dieses Problem zu finden, wird in meinem Fall noch zusätzlich erschwert, da ich, zumindest nach meinem Gefühl, persönlich in dieses Werk verwickelt bin und damit vielleicht die berühmte und – offenbar – notwendige «kritische Distanz» vermissen lasse. Aber vielleicht liegt der Schlüssel genau hier: San Keller gelingt es mit seinen Aktionen, die Distanzen durch Interaktion aufzuheben. So wird, wer auf eines seiner Angebote eingeht und an einer ersten Aktion teilnimmt, der Versuchung kaum widerstehen können, diese Erfahrung zu wiederholen. Man beginnt Teil eines Mechanismus oder besser gesagt einer Gruppendynamik zu werden, bei der die persönliche Beteiligung die Grundlage einer sozialen Struktur und in diesem besonderen Fall eines Kunstwerks bildet. In diesem Sinne bekenne ich hiermit, ein Opfer dieses Mechanismus zu sein, bin mir dessen jedoch voll bewusst und glücklich dabei.

Nicht jeder erhält die Gelegenheit, während der Direktausstrahlung der Abendnachrichten in einem Fernsehstudio zu schlafen. Nicht jeder würde es fertig bringen, eine Tanztruppe zusammenzustellen, die bereit ist, zur Feier des 125-jährigen Bestehens einer Kunsthochschule in einem öffentlichen Park 125 Stunden lang ohne Unterbruch zu tanzen. Nicht jedem würden wir erlauben, allein unter dem Vorwand uns beim Umzug zu helfen, sämtliche Gegenstände anzufassen, die wir besitzen. Doch San gelingt es. Und zweifellos reicht es als Erklärung nicht, dass diese Leistungen einfach zu «Kunst» erklärt werden. San Kellers grosse Stärke ist es, sich strategisch in einem bestimmten soziokulturellen Umfeld zu bewegen, und das in einer Stadt, in der die Kunst einen Status erreicht hat, der weit über ihre rein geistige oder intellektuelle Bedeutung hinausgeht. In Zürich, seiner und meiner Wahlheimat, ist die Kunst nämlich auch ein Lebensstil und nicht zuletzt ein wichtiger Wirtschaftsmotor. Und gerade hier, wo Kunst meist immer noch mit der Herstellung von wenn möglich verkäuflichen «Werken» in Verbindung gebracht wird, kommt meiner Meinung nach die Bedeutung von San Kellers Aktionen voll zum Tragen. Was sie so einzigartig macht, ist, dass der Akt der Beteiligung und das persönliche Mitwirken durch sie zu Kunst werden. Wir sind daher weit entfernt von einem statischen und sterilen Kunstbegriff, wie man ihn von Museen und Galerien her kennt: San bewegt sich unmittelbar im Alltagsleben. Die Aufmerksamkeit verschiebt sich so von einer objektbezogenen Kunstauffassung zu einer Auffassung, die den menschlichen Wert in den Mittelpunkt stellt. Es gibt nichts zu bewundern oder zu interpretieren. Man braucht bloss vom Angebot des Künstlers Kenntnis zu nehmen und sich allenfalls bereit zu erklären, an der Aktion teilzunehmen und sie gemeinsam zu realisieren.

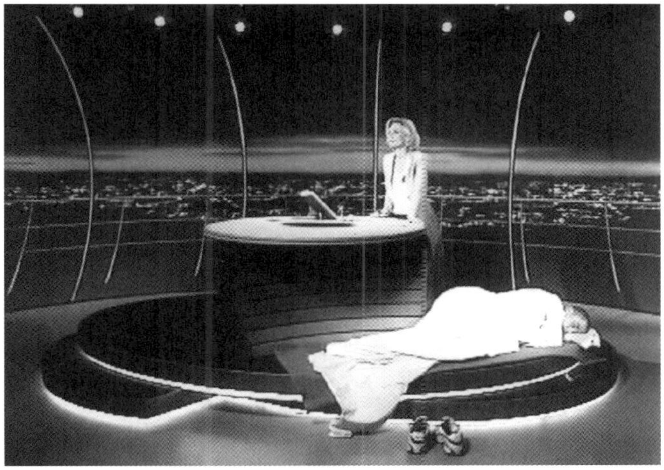

SAN KELLER SCHLÄFT AN IHREM ARBEITSORT, Zürich, 14.7.2000, Auftraggeber Schweizer Fernsehen DRS, Sendung «10 vor 10» / SAN KELLER WILL SLEEP AT YOUR WORK PLACE, commissioned by Swiss Television's newscast "10 to 10". (VIDEO STILL: SF DRS)

Zu diesem Zweck wirbt San auf äusserst verführerische und perfekt organisierte Weise erst einmal mit Flugblättern und Plakaten für seine Aktionen. Dabei wird zuerst mit Slogans wie «San Keller schläft an Ihrem Arbeitsort» oder «San Keller wartet auf Sie» das Interesse geweckt und dann das Angebot erläutert, das der Künstler dem Publikum macht. «Nutzen Sie die einmalige Chance und greifen Sie mit San Kellers Unterstützung temporär, aber nachhaltig in Ihren Arbeitsalltag ein. Sie werden sich durch den schlafenden San Keller an Ihrer Seite in einer überraschend neuen und ungewöhnlichen Arbeitssituation wiederfinden. Lassen Sie sich begeistert auf dieses Abenteuer ein!» Bei Interesse muss man nur die Instruktionen befolgen und sich mit dem Künstler in Verbindung setzen, um alle Einzelheiten zu vereinbaren, wie das auch die Redaktion des TV-Nachrichtenmagazins *10 vor 10* getan hat. Aber während San schläft, arbeitet er, und daher muss der Auftraggeber einen echten Anstellungsvertrag abschliessen, worin, wie bei jedem Arbeitnehmer üblich, ein Lohn festgelegt wird. Interessant ist dabei aber der Bezug zur Idee der Produktivität, der sich daraus ergibt: Wird hier ein Arbeitnehmer für das Schlafen bezahlt, oder erwirbt man ein vergängliches Kunstwerk?

San Keller verhält sich also wie ein Unternehmer seiner selbst, wie eine kleine Firma, die jedoch eine klar definierte, auf einem Grafik- und Kommunikationskonzept beruhende Corporate Identity besitzt. Als Einzelner wäre ihm dies nicht möglich: Das alles ist nur dank der Entwicklung von Kooperationsmodellen machbar, die auf dem Konzept der Gruppendynamik basieren. So ist die Idee der Zusammenarbeit von grundlegender Bedeutung: Ohne die Mitwirkung des Grafikers Schnittholz würde der Künstler San beim Publikum kaum dieselbe Wirkung erzielen. Ohne die fundamentale Mithilfe des Grafikers wäre es denn auch unmöglich, dass **«San Keller und die fette Helvetica unterstrichen ... inzwischen legendär und unzertrennlich»** sind, wie der Künstler selbst unbekümmert erklärt. Mit der Zeit ist so das «Label» San Keller mit seinen blinzelnden Sternchen und schlichten Farben entstanden, und die lineare Typographie hat eine Durchschlagskraft erlangt, die einer millionenschweren Werbekampagne würdig ist. Es ist bemerkenswert, dass San sich durch seine Aufrichtigkeit von vielen seiner Kollegen unterscheidet, die zwar für die Realisierung ihrer Arbeiten häufig Fachleute beiziehen, dies aber dem Publikum nicht mitteilen, da sie die alleinige Urheberschaft für ihr Werk in Anspruch nehmen (und dadurch höhere Preise erzielen wollen?). San Kellers künstlerische Strategie geht von einer gesellschaftlichen Kerngruppe aus, die man vielleicht auch als Stamm oder Familie bezeichnen könnte, die aber dank der Mechanismen, die ich erwähnt habe, keine geschlossene Einheit ist, sondern dynamisch und auf Erweiterung ausgerichtet. Obwohl in Zürich bereits eine «skeptische Vermischung» zwischen den verschiedenen Kunstmilieus stattfindet, bewegt sich San quer und frei zwischen einem Off-Space wie Esther Eppsteins «message salon», einer Institution mit Underground-Flair wie dem «migros museum» und den etablierten Seiten von *Parkett.* Und genau in diesem historischen Augenblick, da die Zürcher Kunstszene, oder zumindest deren institutioneller Teil, viel über ihre Rolle und ihre Zukunft nachzudenken scheint – u. a. wegen zahlreicher personeller Veränderungen an der Spitze der wichtigsten Institutionen –, präsentiert San Keller ein ganz anderes Ausstellungsmodell, indem er sich für Aktionen entscheidet, die direkt im öffentlichen Raum stattfinden. Besonders aktiv ist in dieser Hinsicht die «San Dance Company». Sie wurde gebildet, um an verschiedenen Orten in der Stadt Zürich eine «Live-Cover-Version» des Videoclips *Praise You* von Fatboy Slim darzubieten – eines Clips, in dem eine Amateurkamera eine Gruppe von Tänzern filmt, die in einem Einkaufszentrum vor erstauntem Publikum ein Ballett improvisiert – und bereitet sich, während ich dies schreibe, gerade auf die Aktion DANCIN' IN THE RAIN vor. Bei diesem einwöchigen Event bietet sich die Möglichkeit, mit der «San Dance Company» zu tanzen, aber nur, wenn es regnet. Angesiedelt zwischen dem Absurden und dem Hollywoodianischen, wird das Gebotene durch den Slogan «Regen, der Sie glücklich macht!» auf den Punkt gebracht. Einmal mehr entwickelt San in Form einer gebrauchsfertigen Struktur (DJ und Tänzer in steter Bereitschaft, eine rund um die Uhr geöffnete Bar, gedeckte Tribünen für die Zuschauer) einen Diskurs, bei dem die mit der sozialen Interaktion verbundenen Gefühle im Mittelpunkt stehen.

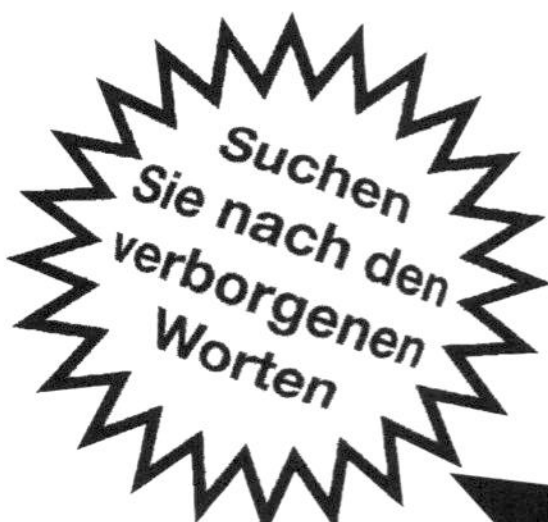

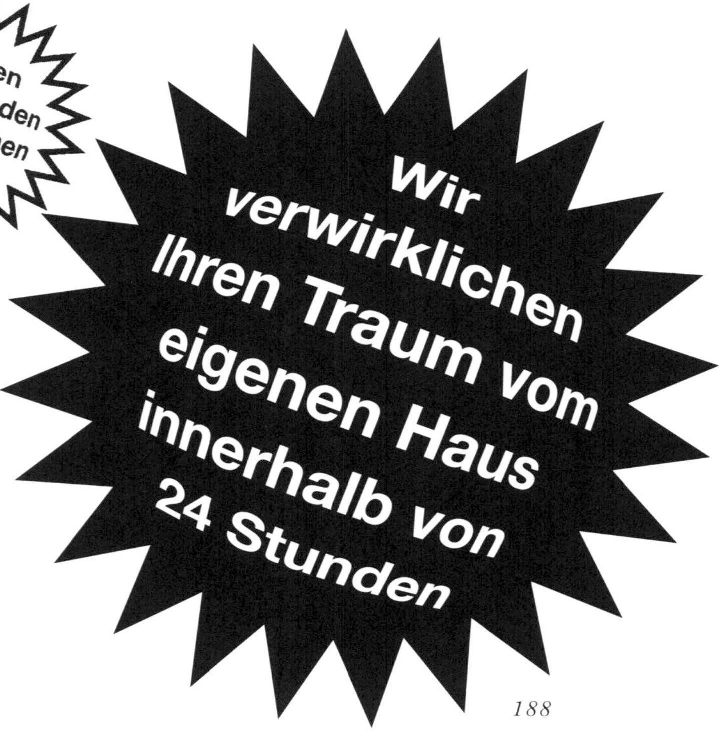

So denke ich gern an San Keller als einen Künstler, der sozial engagiert ist, und zwar weniger auf der politischen als auf der praktischen Ebene. Gleichsam als eine Art äusserst effizienter «Service public» nach reinster Schweizer Tradition. Unter dieser Optik können zum Beispiel die Aktionen SAN KELLER DEMONSTRIERT MIT DEINER BOTSCHAFT IN NEW YORK und SCHNITTHOLZ PRÄSENTIERT: SAN KELLER TANZT IN PARIS ZU IHRER MUSIK gesehen werden. San hat in diesen Städten im Auftrag von zahlreichen Leuten an einem ihm geeignet scheinenden Ort demonstriert oder getanzt. Nach seiner Rückkehr aus den beiden Metropolen hat er seinen Auftraggebern eine Videokassette zukommen lassen, die als Souvenir und Bestätigung für die Durchführung der Aktionen diente. *Customer Care* und *Follow-up:* Marketingprinzipien, die für erfolgreiche Unternehmen von fundamentaler Bedeutung sind.

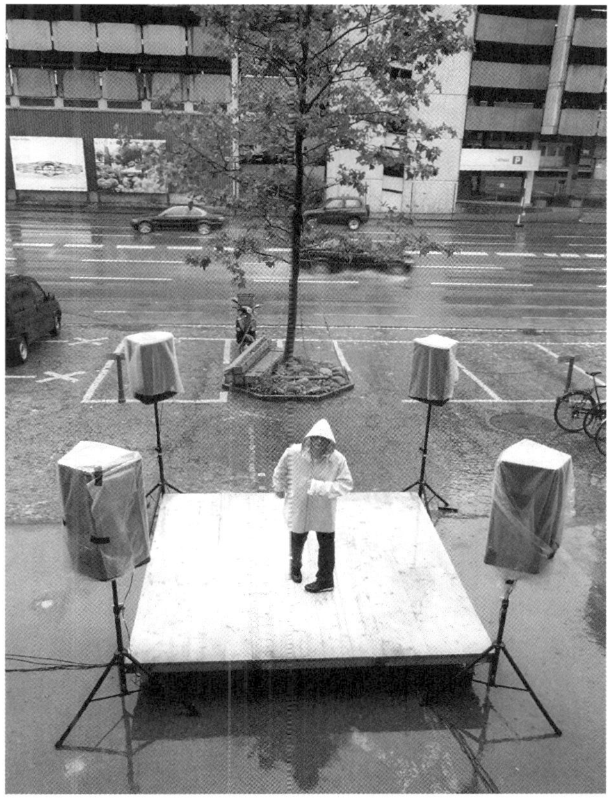

SAN DANCE COMPANY, *DANCIN' IN THE RAIN, Zürich, 5.–12. Juli 2001 / 5 – 12 July 2001. (PHOTO: MANCIA/BODMER, FBM STUDIO)*

Man könnte sagen, dass San Keller mit seinen Aktionen auf ironische, doch professionelle Weise darauf abzielt, Dienstleistungen anzubieten, welche die Mitwirkenden glücklich und zufrieden machen, aber auch dafür sorgen, dass sie sich des sozialen Netzes und des strukturellen Umfelds bewusst werden, in das sie sich hineinbegeben. Dies ermöglicht ihm, künstlerische Arbeiten nicht in einem Museum, sondern in einer flüchtigeren Umgebung zu realisieren: dem geistigen und menschlichen Raum. So hat San zum Beispiel in Alicia Framis' Projekt LONELINESS IN THE CITY (26. August bis 1. September 2000) im «migros museum» mit zwei ganz einfachen Aktionen das Problem der Einsamkeit in der Stadt perfekt umgesetzt. Unter dem Titel SAN KELLER SUCHT SIE und SAN KELLER WARTET AUF SIE machte er sich innerhalb eines festgesetzten Zeitraums und eines genau begrenzten Gebiets daran, die Personen zu suchen oder auf sie zu warten, die ihn auf einem Zettel mit wenigen kryptischen Angaben ausdrücklich darum gebeten hatten. Das Motiv ist einfach: Ist es für unser Ego vielleicht nicht beruhigend zu wissen, dass irgendwo, aber nicht allzu weit entfernt, jemand ist, der uns sucht oder auf uns wartet? Auf der Grundlage dieses «humanitären Geistes» gelingt es San mühelos, zahlreiche Kräfte zu mobilisieren. Seit ein paar Jahren veranstaltet er unter dem Label «winter-hilfe» jeden Winter Aktionen, die sich um das Thema der sozialen Auswirkungen der Jahreszeit drehen, in der das Haus eine wichtige Rolle spielt. Das Label nimmt direkten Bezug auf die gleichnamige Schweizer Wohltätigkeitsorganisation, für die San die Aufgabe übernimmt, ihren Aktionsradius von der rein materiellen auf die geistige und kulturelle Ebene auszuweiten. Im Winter 2000/2001 hiess das Projekt ZÜGELWANDERUNG MIT SAN KELLER und bestand darin, eine Gruppe von Leuten zu bilden, die sich bereit erklärten auf Anfrage anderen beim Umzug zu helfen. Es handelte sich darum, ohne Verwendung von motorisierten Transportmitteln innerhalb einer maximalen Entfernung von 50 Kilometern die gesamten Habseligkeiten einer Person von einem Ort zum anderen zu transportieren.

Und eben hier habe ich meine Objektivität in Bezug auf San verloren: Da ich selbst umziehen musste, habe ich mich mit ihm in Verbindung gesetzt. Meine neue Wohnung ist nur wenige Meter von meiner alten entfernt, praktisch direkt nebenan auf demselben Stockwerk. Für San war es daher ganz natürlich, eine Menschenkette zu organisieren. «So einfach wars noch nie und wirds nie wieder», las man auf den Flugblättern (doch es ist ihm auch gelungen, Freiwillige für eine ZÜGELWANDERUNG von Luzern nach Zürich zu finden...). Mit San am Anfang und mir am Ende der Kette und zahlreichen anderen Leuten dazwischen, in einem sozialen und gemeinschaftlichen Akt, geprägt von rhythmischem Geben und Nehmen, habe ich also meine neue Wohnung bezogen. Aber ausser mir hat nur ein einziger Mensch auf dieser Welt sämtliche Gegenstände, die ich besitze, angefasst und gesehen: San Keller. Ich glaube, dass er mich mittlerweile ganz gut kennt.

(Übersetzung aus dem Italienischen: Irene Aeberli)

GIOVANNI CARMINE

San Keller: Art as a Public Service

How does one translate into words the complexity of an artwork that is itself comprised of simple gestures? It becomes even more difficult to find a suitable answer to this question given that I am—or at least feel I am—personally involved in this same work and therefore run the risk of jeopardizing the much-vaunted critical distance. Perhaps the key lies in the very fact that San Keller's actions succeed in annulling distances, thanks to the force of the interaction. Anyone who accepts one of his proposals takes part in a first action and will find it difficult to avoid being tempted to repeat the experience. Consequently one participates in a mechanism, or better, a group dynamic, where personal involvement becomes the basis for social structure and, above all, a work of art. In this sense I hereby—happily and knowingly—declare myself a victim of this mechanism.

Not everyone is given the opportunity to sleep in a television studio during the live broadcast of a half-hour nightly newscast. Not everyone could put together a group of dancers, ready to break loose in a public park for 125 hours straight, to celebrate the 125th birthday of an art school. Not everyone would be allowed to touch each object in another's possession under the sole pretext of helping out on moving day. But San manages to do these things and his success cannot be explained by the mere fact of declaring his actions to be art. San Keller's great strength lies in his ability to move strategically within a precise social-cultural context in a city where art has achieved a status well beyond a purely spiritual or intellectual value.

In Zurich, which is both his and my adopted home, art is also a lifestyle and, not least, an important economic force. It is here, where the dominant concept of art remains tied to the production of works—preferably salable ones—that, in my opinion, the value of San's actions can be fully appreciated. What makes them unique is the way they render action participatory and involvement personal. This is a far cry from a static and sterile concept of art based on its appreciation in museums and galleries. San acts directly within the sphere of everyday life and thereby shifts attention from an idea of art restricted to objects to one that focuses on its total human value. There is nothing to admire or interpret. One need only take note of the artist's proposal and accept or refuse to participate in its creation.

In an extremely seductive and perfectly organized fashion, San first promotes his actions through leaflets and posters. He captures people's attention with such slogans as "San Keller will sleep at your work place" or "San Keller

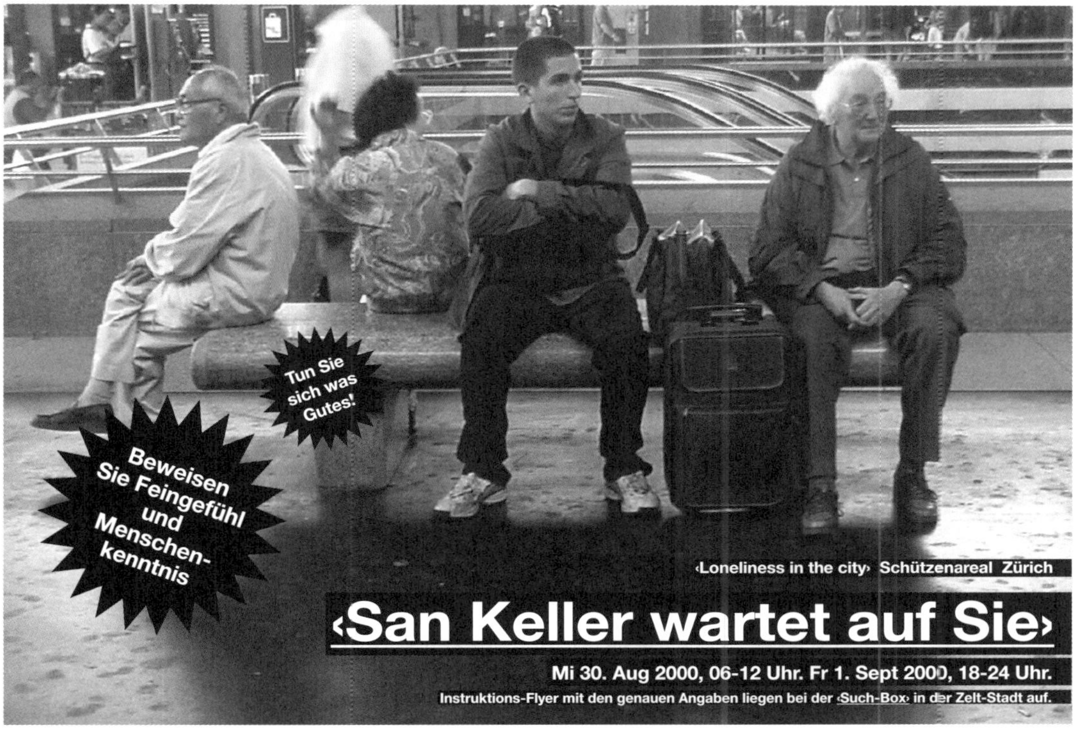

SAN KELLER IS WAITING FOR YOU, *Zurich, autumn 2000.*
(PLAKAT/POSTER: SCHNITTHOLZ)

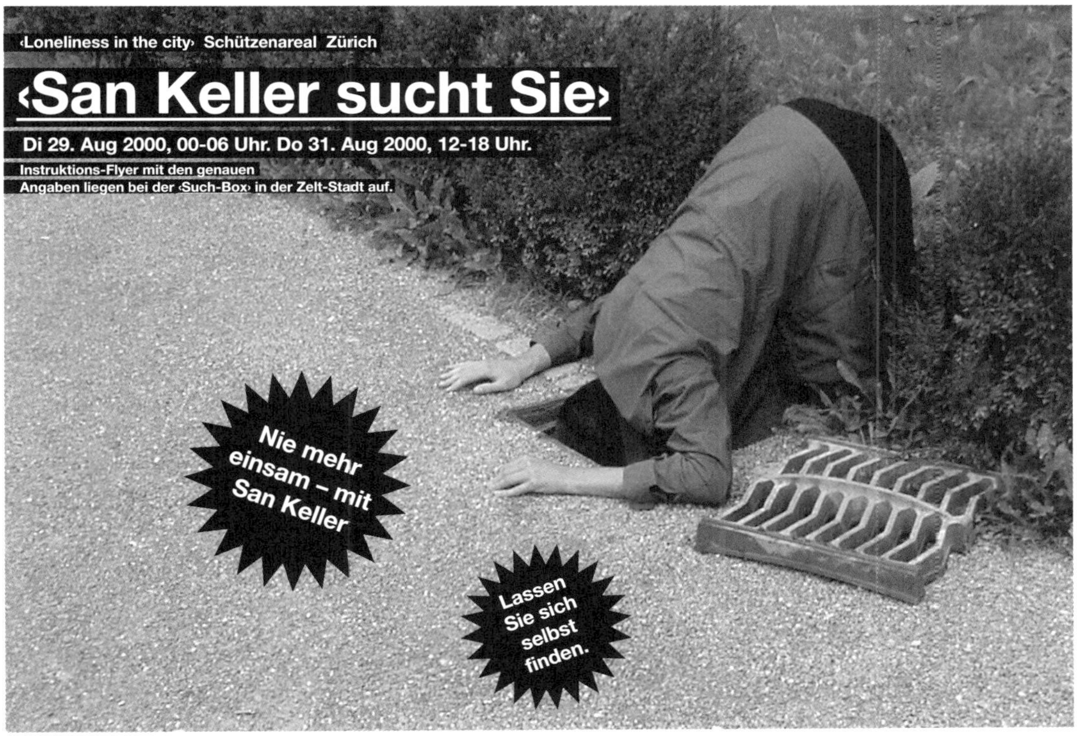

SAN KELLER IS LOOKING FOR YOU, *Zurich, autumn 2000.*
(PLAKAT/POSTER: SCHNITTHOLZ)

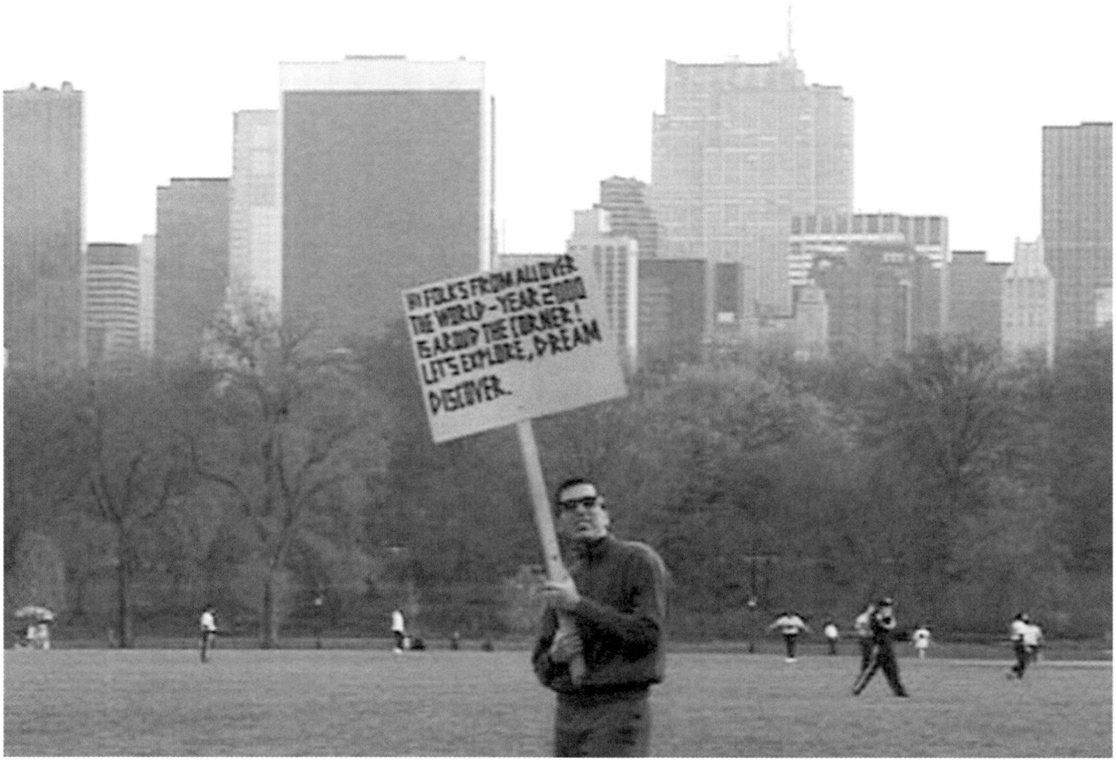

SAN KELLER DEMONSTRIERT MIT IHRER BOTSCHAFT IN NEW YORK, 16.–23. April 1999, Auftraggeber Sylvia Schönmann / SAN KELLER DEMONSTRATES WITH YOUR MESSAGE IN NEW YORK, commissioned by Sylvia Schönmann. (VIDEO STILL: SAN KELLER)

is waiting for you." Then the artist explains what he is offering. "Take this unique opportunity to enlist the support of San Keller and break the routine of your working day. With San Keller sleeping at your side, you will discover yourself in a startling new and unusual work situation. This is the chance of a lifetime! Grab it!" One need only follow the instructions and contact Keller to make the necessary arrangements, as did the editors of Switzerland's daily news program, *10 vor 10* (10 to 10). But while San sleeps, he is working. In fact, as with any employee/employer relationship, San and his client sign a contract establishing compensation. What is interesting about this, however, is the way the idea of productivity is subverted. Are we paying a worker to sleep, or are we buying an ephemeral work of art?

San Keller acts as his own entrepreneur; his is a small business with a well-defined "corporate identity," based on both a graphic concept and on communication. He would not succeed if he were to act alone; his "business" is possible solely thanks to the development of cooperative models which focus on the concept of group dynamics. Collaboration is vital. Without the intervention of Schnittholz the designer, San the artist would not have the same impact on the public. In fact, thanks to Schnittholz's mediation, **"San Keller and bold, underlined Helvetica lettering have become legendary and inseparable,"** as the artist himself casually notes. The San Keller "label," with its twinkling little stars, simple colors, and linear typography, has gradually acquired a level of public recognition that vies with million-dollar advertising campaigns.

I think it is interesting to stress how San's sincerity distinguishes him from many of his colleagues, who often resort to "specialists" in order to create their works but do not communicate this fact to the public in their desire to safeguard their exclusive authorship (and thus higher prices?). The core of Keller's art strategy is social, focused on what we might call tribe or family. Yet thanks to the mechanisms mentioned above, it is not closed, but rather dynamic and meant to expand. Even though a wary intercourse exists among the various art communities in Zurich, San moves crosswise through them all, freely roaming from an alternative venue such as Esther Eppstein's "message salon," to an institution with underground flair like the "migros museum," to the established pages of *Parkett*. Moreover, with the Zurich art community, or at least the institutional community, currently giving a great deal of thought to its role and future—due, among other reasons, to directorial changes in several major institutions—San Keller proposes an entirely different exhibition model, one based on actions that unfold directly in public space.

In this regard the San Dance Company is particularly active. It was established to present a "live cover version" of Fatboy Slim's *Praise You* music video in various places in the city, in which an amateur camera shoots a group that improvises a dance in a shopping center, before an astonished public. And while I am writing, another action is in preparation, DANCIN' IN THE RAIN. This weeklong event will offer the possibility for people to dance together with the San Dance Company, but only when it is raining. Part absurdity, part Hollywood, the project bears the slogan "Rain which makes you happy!" Once again, San, in the form of a ready-to-use structure (a DJ, dancers on duty, a bar open 24 hours a day, and covered stands for spectators), elaborates a discourse where the true center of interest is in the feelings tied to social interaction.

In this sense I like to think of San Keller as a socially committed artist, not so much on a political level, but rather in practical terms. He provides what is almost a form of extremely effective public service in the purest Swiss tradition. For example: SAN KELLER DEMONSTRATES WITH YOUR MESSAGE IN NEW YORK or SCHNITTHOLZ PRESENTS: SAN KELLER DANCES TO YOUR MUSIC IN PARIS. In these two cases San, working with numerous people, demonstrated and danced in spots in two cities chosen by him for their suitability to the assigned task. Upon his return from each city, he delivered a video cassette to his clients as a souvenir and to certify that he had completed the actions. Customer-care and follow-up: marketing principles that are fundamental to successful enterprises.

San Keller's ironic but professional services are designed to please and satisfy participants, but also to make them aware of the social fabric and the structural context in which they live. This gives him the near unlimited capability to create art outside of museums in a more transitory space, one that is both spiritual and human, as in his contribution to Alicia Framis's project LONELINESS IN THE CITY (26 August to 1 September 2000) at the migros museum. In two very simple actions, San pinpointed the problem of urban solitude. In SAN KELLER IS LOOKING FOR YOU and SAN KELLER IS WAITING FOR YOU, the artist would look or wait for a person who had expressly asked him to do so on the basis of a few enigmatic instructions within a specific timeframe and precisely defined area. The rationale is simple: isn't it perhaps reassuring for our ego to know that someone somewhere, not too far away, is looking or waiting for us?

By working in this "humanitarian spirit," San effortlessly succeeds in mobilizing considerable energy. For the past several years, under the label *winterhilfe* (winter relief), he has developed actions attuned to the social parameters of that season, when the home assumes an important role. The name is taken from a Swiss charitable organization, whose activities San has committed to expand from the strictly material to a more spiritual and cultural level. During the winter of 2000/2001 he offered a MOVING WALK WITH SAN KELLER, which consisted of organizing a group of people willing, on request, to help other people move. He would move all of the "client's" possessions without motorized means, but within a maximum distance of 50 kilometers.

At this point my critical objectivity went down the drain. Since I myself had to move, I got in touch with him. My new apartment was located a few meters away from my old one, practically next door, on the same landing. According to San's logic, what could be more natural than to organize a human chain? "It has never been that easy and never will be again," the leaflet read (though he even managed to find volunteers for a MOVING WALK from Lucerne to Zurich). With San at the beginning and me at the end of the chain and the helpers between us, I occupied my new home, through a social and communal act of giving and taking. But only one person in the world other than me touched and saw all the objects I possess: San Keller. Who I think at this point knows me well.

(Translated from Italian by Marguerite Shore)

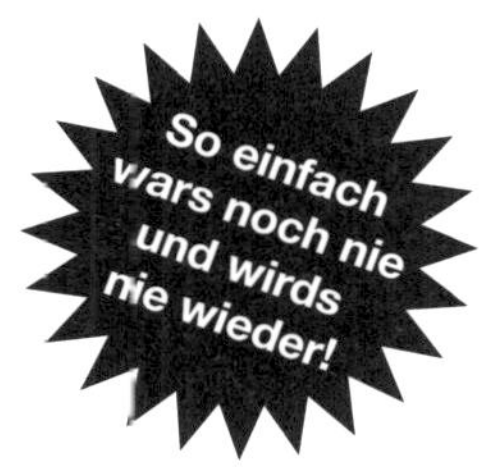

CUMULUS

From America

IN EVERY EDITION OF PARKETT, TWO CUMULUS CLOUDS, ONE FROM AMERICA, THE OTHER FROM EUROPE, FLOAT OUT TO AN INTERESTED PUBLIC. THEY CONVEY INDIVIDUAL OPINIONS, ASSESSMENTS, AND MEMORABLE ENCOUNTERS—AS ENTIRELY PERSONAL PRESENTATIONS OF PROFESSIONAL ISSUES.

OUR CONTRIBUTORS TO THIS ISSUE ARE STEVE DIETZ, CURATOR OF NEW MEDIA AT THE WALKER ART CENTER IN MINNEAPOLIS, AND GIOVANNI CARMINE, A FREE-LANCE CURATOR IN ZURICH.

STEVE DIETZ

Incunabula

"The future has already arrived. It's just unevenly distributed."

– William Gibson

Something is happening. Of this much I am certain. Reasonably. Although there are some that argue that net art is dead. If you read about it in *The New York Times*, it must be over and all that. But nevertheless there has been a moment of bicoastal technoglossolalia, which must signify. Something. Yes? We (who?) await our D.W. Griffith (how American); our Eisenstein to take us on a ride in something that is not a horseless carriage. If you know what I mean. Like, who really knew Robert Frank was not a Swiss tourist? At the time. Grainy Americans. OK, so the picture phone was a bust. We do not fly jetpacks to work. (Except Hans-Ulrich.) But still, remember when? More people were at Woodstock (online in 1992) than lived in New York City (there were computers). Dotcomboombust. Is it a cycle or a fad? Photography (medium) or Fluxus (movement)? Or future pre-post-neo-ist grad history thesis? Something is happening. Of this much I am certain. Reasonably.

Incunabula are books printed before 1501; before, as Janet Murray writes in *Hamlet on the Holodeck: …legible typefaces and proof sheet corrections; page numbering and paragraphing; and title pages, prefaces, and chapter divisions, which together made the published book a coherent means of communication.*[1)]

Murray suggests a parallel—a promise really—specifically for the "future of narrative in cyberspace" but also, arguably, for new media (incunabular) art in general.

The garish video games and tangled Web sites of the current digital environment are part of a similar period of technical evolution, part of a similar struggle for the conventions of coherent communication.[2)]

This is the thrust of an argument that countless commentators have made from the perspective of every medium. In the classic McLuhan rear-view mirror formulation, we can only imagine the future through the past.

The telephone: speech without walls. / The phonograph: music hall without walls. / The photograph: museum without walls. / The electric light: space without walls. / The movie, radio and TV: classroom without walls.[3)]

While the promise of future coherence is intended to be reassuring, even exhortatory, it also raises the specter of the commercialized and the conventional.

One of my photography teachers told the story of having a copy of *William Eggleston's Guide*, the 1976 New York Museum of Modern Art catalogue—the one with the hulking tricycle on the cover—next to his bed and looking at it every night, trying to understand.[4)] At the time, it was new. It was different. It didn't quite make sense according to what he already knew. But something about it was under his skin.

I don't think he was rereading John Szarkowski's essay each night. (Nor do I think he hadn't not read it.)

The net art duo, Jodi's work, functioned in a similar way for many people, including myself, early on. Yes, the question "Is it art?" was explicitly asked on the lists, but it was more like a global late night bull session than a museological bar that had to be passed. Besides being patently ridiculous—no museum had yet remotely considered integrating net art as part of its conventions for coherent communication—the point was somehow else.

In a funny way, the Wachowski brothers, with their dreamy cathode ray screenscapes of cascading ASCII on the monitors of the good ship Nebuchadnezzar, best capture that kind of sleepless intensity with which a community pored over the offerings of Heath Bunting and Rachel Baker's irational. org, Alexei Shulgin's easylife.org, Vuk Cosic's then-eponymous site, Olia Lialina's narratives, Natalie Bookchin's homework assignments, the latest posting on 7–11, Piotr Szyhalski's "The Spleen," Joe Squier's "The Place," äda'web, Stadiumweb, artnetweb, The Thing, backspace, Mongrel's hacks, and much more, including, discriminately, commercial sites, amateur pages, and new technologies. There was something there.

What did incunabula look like before 1501? Did people miss legible typefaces and proof sheet corrections; page numbering and paragraphing; and title pages, prefaces, and chapter divisions?

I do not doubt that what we are experiencing today on the net will be different next year, if not next week. I do not question the desirability for context to be expanded. Histories will emerge. Some consensual fantasy of clarity will be established. Nevertheless, this begs the question of what is an interesting role for the curator in a time of incunabular media. Is it simply to monitor from the sidelines until the "Bruce Nauman of the Net" can be

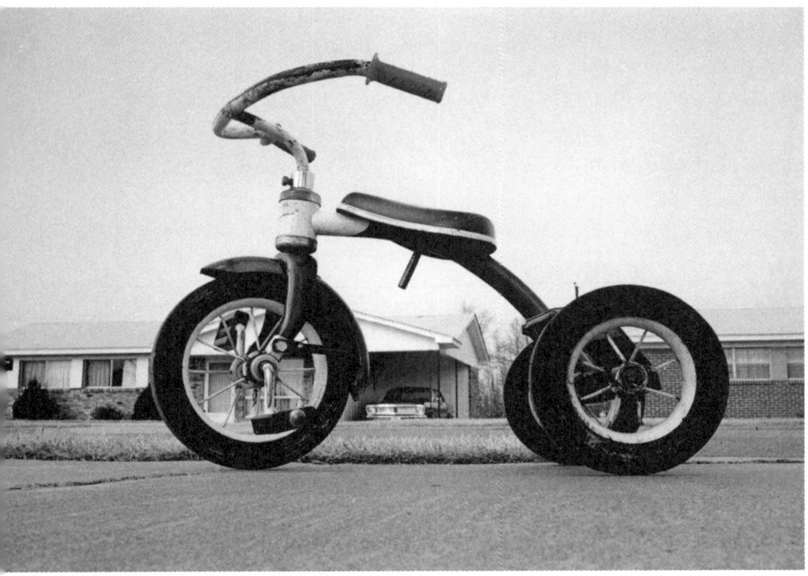

WILLIAM EGGLESTON, UNTITLED (TRICYCLE), ca. 1970 / OHNE TITEL (DREIRAD).

id-eified? Is it to hype-rlink net work into the same contexts as Gerhard Richter and Katharina Fritsch? What kind of a goal is coherence? What is the cost?

One way to cope with the provocations of novel art is to rest firm and maintain solid standards. ... A second way is more yielding. The critic interested in a novel manifestation holds his criteria and taste in reserve. Since they were formed upon yesterday's art, he does not assume that they are readymade for today. While he seeks to comprehend the objectives behind the new art produced, nothing is a priori excluded or judged irrelevant. Since he is not passing out grades, he suspends judgment until the work's intention has come into focus and his response to it is—in a literal sense of the word—sym-pathetic; not necessarily to approve, but to feel along with it as with a thing that is like no other.[5]

Like the photographer whose nightly meditation was *William Eggleston's Guide*?

Agnostic, omnivorous, obsessed, persistent, and ignorant. These seem to me like action items from Steinberg's admonition—laudable traits upon which to base one's study of incunabular as well as conventional media.

While I do not doubt the existence of net art, I am agnostic about its contours. To use David Antin's phrase, I am interested in the distinctive properties of net art—what makes it a thing that is like no other?—but more as possibilities than requirements; as permeable across boundaries rather than fixed; and as transient over time.

To be an obsessive omnivore is like trying to create the sleekest information architecture. It must be broad but not so broad that the map is coterminous with the territory. It must be deep, but not so deep as to end up solipsistic silos of unrelatable knowledge. Most important is the ratio. To be obsessively focused on the distinctive characteristics of incunabular media while omnivorously contextualizing across the fields of art, technology, and culture seems about right.

Persistence is a measure of commitment and a function of exploration. If one is exploring the distinctive properties of a medium, one exhibition is not a commitment. If one is exploring a particular cycle of themes in contemporary art, including "tech art" in only one of the exhibitions is not a commitment. Furthermore, persistence implies that, as with the scientific method, "failures" are as useful as "successes" if one is pursuing an ongoing commitment.

Finally ignorance, by which I mean the quality of "not knowing." It is commonplace, of course, for contemporary arts institutions, curators, and practitioners to assert that often what is important are not the answers given but the questions asked. But I mean ignorance a bit more pointedly. With incunabular media, mastery is a form of closure. Options are closed down. Coherence may not be the most beneficial goal.

Last year, Yoshi Sodeoka, the art director of the pioneering site Word threw in the towel. In an open letter, he (apparently) acknowledged that despite Word's award-winning and quirky art direction, in the realm of interactive (read incunabular) media, the form had cohered, and its name was Yahoo! Everyone knew that Yahoo! worked best and so from that point on, Word would appropriate the Yahoo! format. It was best for everyone. It was what the audience wanted. It was coherent. It was understood. He understood. And he was sorry for having troubled everyone for so long.

As the Art Director of Word, I have failed to carry out the duties of a competent designer. I have been creating art with the wrong medium. If I were a writer who published my work on the Web, I would want people to be able to actually read it. My lack of care for matters such as these has caused other people to suffer. ...What I do know is that Word's design team have begun to feel that we have fully exhausted the Web's potentials, and in turn, the Web has exhausted us. In short, it is finally time for us to settle down. ... The problem right now is, everything we try to do seems to backfire. That's why, in improving our site, we've decided not to invent a new interface of our own. We've simply borrowed from the best: Yahoo![6]

Ignorance is not bliss. It is hell not to know. But a rush to judgment now may only lead to the new media equivalent of TV wasteland; of earlier incunabular (utopian) media. Resist a productivist model of societal communications and expression based on overwhelming commercial interests.

1) Janet Murray, *Hamlet on the Holodeck: The Future of Narrative in Cyberspace* (New York: The Free Press, 1997), p. 28.
2) Ibid.
3) Marshall McLuhan, *Understanding Media: The Extensions of Man*, (New York: McGraw-Hill, 1964), p. 283.
4) *William Eggleston's Guide*, ex. cat. (New York: The Museum of Modern Art, 1976).
5) Leo Steinberg, "Other Criteria" in: *Other Criteria: Confrontations with Twentieth-Century Art* (New York: Oxford University Press, 1973), p. 63.
6) Sodeoka originally posted his open letter at http://www.word.com/yhome/artdirector.html, but the Word site is now defunct. These excerpts are from Alex Lash, "A Word-for-Word Imitation," *The Industry Standard Magazine*, Jan 21, 2000, 12:00 AM PST. (http://www.thestandard.com/article/0,1902,9061,00.html)

STEVE DIETZ

Inkunabeln

«Die Zukunft ist bereits da. Sie ist bloss ungleichmässig verteilt.»
– William Gibson

Es läuft etwas. Zumindest darüber bin ich mir sicher. Ziemlich sicher. Obschon es Leute gibt, die behaupten, die Netzkunst sei tot. Wenn schon die *New York Times* darüber schreibt, muss das Ganze ja ein alter Hut sein, klar. Dennoch hat es den Moment einer Technoglossolalie gegeben, die von der Ost- bis zur Westküste reichte. Das will etwas heissen. Was auch immer. Nicht? Wir (wer?) erwarten, dass uns unser D.W. Griffith (wie amerikanisch), unser Eisenstein in einem Vehikel ausführen, das keine Kutsche ohne Pferd ist. Sie verstehen, was ich meine. Wer wusste denn schon, dass Robert Frank kein Schweizer Tourist war? Damals. Körnige Amerikaner. O.K., das Bildtelefon war also ein Reinfall. Wir fliegen nicht mit Jetpacks zur Arbeit. (Ausser Hans-Ulrich.) Trotzdem, erinnern Sie sich noch? Es waren mehr Leute in Woodstock (online 1992), als New York City Einwohner hat (es gab schliesslich Computer). Dotcomboomfiasko. Ist es eine zyklische Bewegung oder ein vorübergehender Spleen? Photographie (Medium) oder Fluxus (Bewegung)? Oder eine zukünftige prä-post-neo-istische Geschichts-Dissertation? Es läuft etwas. Da bin ich mir sicher. Ziemlich sicher.

Inkunabeln sind Bücher, die vor 1501 gedruckt wurden; zu einer Zeit, als es, wie Janet Murray in *Hamlet on the Holodeck* schreibt, solche Dinge noch nicht gab: *...gut lesbare Druckschriften und Korrekturfahnen, Seitenzahlen und Absätze, Titelseiten, Vorwörter und die Unterteilung in Kapitel, die das gedruckte Buch insgesamt zu einem zusammenhängenden Kommunikationsmittel machten.*[1]

Murray glaubt darin eine viel versprechende Parallele in Bezug auf die «Zukunft der Literatur im Cyberspace» zu erkennen, aber möglicherweise auch in Bezug auf (inkunable) Kunst in den neuen Medien im Allgemeinen.

Die knallbunten Videospiele und verwirrenden Websites der heutigen digitalen Welt sind Bestandteile einer ähnlichen Phase der technischen Evolution, Teil eines ähnlichen Kampfes um die Konventionen einer zusammenhängenden Kommunikation.[2]

Dies ist der Tenor einer Argumentation, die man schon von unzähligen Kommentatoren und aus der Sicht aller möglichen Medien gehört hat. Laut McLuhans klassischer Rückspiegel-Formel können wir uns die Zukunft nur aufgrund der Vergangenheit vorstellen.

Das Telefon: Sprache ohne Wände. / Das Grammophon: Varieté ohne Wände. / Die Photographie: Museum ohne Wände. / Das elektrische Licht: Raum ohne Wände. / Film, Rundfunk und Fernsehen: Klassenzimmer ohne Wände.[3]

Das Versprechen zukünftiger Kohärenz soll uns zwar beruhigen oder sogar als Ermahnung dienen, doch wird damit auch das Gespenst des Kommerzialisierten und Konventionellen heraufbeschworen.

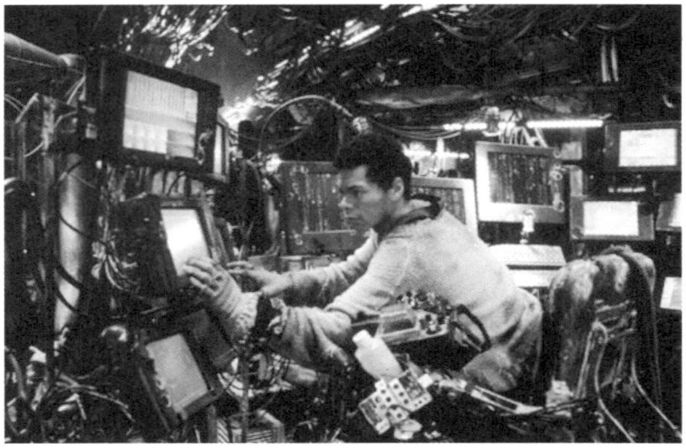

THE MATRIX, 1999, film still.

Einer meiner Photographiedozenten erzählte mir, er habe *William Eggleston's Guide*, einen 1976 veröffentlichten Katalog des Museum of Modern Art in New York – der mit dem riesigen Dreirad auf dem Einband –, neben dem Bett liegen und schaue ihn sich jeden Abend an und versuche etwas zu verstehen.[4] Damals war das neu. Es war anders. Aufgrund seines bisherigen Wissens ergab es nicht ohne weiteres einen Sinn. Doch irgendetwas daran hatte ihn berührt.

Ich glaube nicht, dass er jeden Abend John Szarkowskis Essay las. (Ebenso wenig glaube ich, dass er ihn gar nicht gelesen hat.)

Die Arbeit des Netzkunst-Duos Jordi spielte für viele Leute, mich eingeschlossen, zunächst eine ähnliche Rolle. Ja, die Frage «Ist das Kunst?» wurde explizit gestellt, aber es handelte sich dabei eher um eine zwanglose nächtliche Diskussionsrunde als um eine Überwindung musealer Schranken. Es war nicht nur offensichtlich lächerlich – kein Museum hatte bis anhin auch nur im Entferntesten daran gedacht, die Netzkunst in den Kreis der konventionellen Formen kohärenter Kommunikation aufzunehmen –, sondern es ging um etwas ganz anderes.

Lustigerweise gelingt es den Wachowski-Brüdern mit ihren verträumten, aus ASCII-Kaskaden bestehenden Kathodenstrahl-Landschaften auf den Monitoren des Mutterschiffs Nebukadnezar am besten, die rastlose Intensität einzufangen, mit der die Szene die Erzeugnisse von Heath Buntings und Rachel Bakers irational.org, Alexei Shulgins easylife.org, Vuk Cosics damals gleichnamiger Site, Olia Lialinas Erzählungen, Natalie Bookchins Aufgabenverteilung, das neuste Posting auf 7–11, Piotr Szyhalskis «The Spleen», Joe Squiers «The Place», äda'web, Stadiumweb, artnetweb, The Thing, backspace, Mongrel's hacks und eine Menge anderes studierte, einschliesslich ausgewählter kommerzieller Sites, Amateurseiten und neuer Technologien. Da tat sich was.

Wie sahen Inkunabeln vor 1501 aus? Vermissten die Leute leserliche Druckschriften und Korrekturfahnen, Seitenzahlen und Abschnitte, Titelseiten, Vorwörter und Kapitel?

Ich zweifle nicht daran, dass das, was wir heute im Netz finden, nächstes Jahr oder sogar nächste Woche bereits anders aussehen wird. Ich stelle nicht in Frage, dass es wünschenswert ist, den Kontext zu erweitern. Es werden Entwicklungen stattfinden. Man wird sich auf eine allgemein verbindliche Klarheitsphantasie einigen. Dennoch geht dies an der eigentlichen Frage vorbei, welche Rolle der Kurator in der Zeit der inkunablen Medien spielen soll. Soll er das Geschehen einfach von aussen beobachten, bis der «Bruce Nauman des Netzes» entdeckt wird? Soll er die Netzkunst in denselben Kontext «hyperlinken» wie Gerhard Richter und Katharina Fritsch? Was für ein Ziel ist Kohärenz? Was kostet es uns?

Eine Möglichkeit mit den Provokationen neuartiger Kunst umzugehen ist, unerschütterlich zu bleiben und feste Massstäbe aufrechtzuerhalten... Doch es gibt eine zweite, flexiblere Haltung. Der Kritiker, der sich für eine neue Kunstform interessiert, ist in Bezug auf seinen Geschmack und seine Kriterien zurückhaltend. Da sie sich anhand der Kunst von gestern gebildet haben, geht er nicht automatisch davon aus, dass sie auch heute geeignet sind. Während er versucht die Intentionen hinter der neuen Kunst zu begreifen, wird nichts a priori ausgeschlossen oder als irrelevant abgetan. Da er keine Noten verteilt, schiebt er seine Beurteilung auf, bis sich die Intention des Werks herauskristallisiert und seine Reaktion darauf – im wahrsten Sinn des Wortes – verständnisvoll ist: nicht unbedingt um es zu loben, sondern um es nachzuempfinden wie etwas ganz Einzigartiges.[5]

Wie der Photograph, der jede Nacht über William Eggleston's Guide meditierte?

Agnostisch, alles fressend, besessen, beharrlich und unwissend: Diese lobenswerten Eigenschaften scheinen sich als Verhaltensempfehlung aus Steinbergs mahnenden Worten herauszuschälen. Eigenschaften, auf die sich die Erforschung sowohl der inkunablen als auch der traditionellen Medien abstützen sollte.

Zwar zweifle ich nicht an der Existenz der Netzkunst, doch bin ich agnostisch, was ihre genauen Konturen angeht. Um mit David Antin zu sprechen: Mich interessieren die besonderen Eigenschaften der Netzkunst – was macht sie einzigartig? –, aber mehr im Sinn des Möglichen als des Notwendigen, als etwas, was nicht starr, sondern durchlässig, grenzüberschreitend und vorübergehend ist.

Ein besessener Allesfresser zu sein ist wie der Versuch, eine möglichst schnittige Informationsarchitektur zu schaffen. Sie muss umfassend sein, aber nicht so, dass die Karte sich mit dem Gelände deckt. Sie muss in die Tiefe gehen, aber nicht so weit, dass sich solipsistische Reservoirs unvermittelbaren Wissens bilden. Am wichtigsten ist die Verhältnismässigkeit. Die besonderen Eigenschaften der inkunablen Medien immer im Blick zu behalten und gleichzeitig mit der Gier des Allesfressers die Gebiete von Kunst, Kultur und Technik abzugrasen und Zusammenhänge herzustellen, scheint mehr oder weniger angemessen.

An der Beharrlichkeit zeigt sich das Engagement und die Intensität des Forschens. Erforscht man die besonderen Eigenschaften eines Mediums, so bedeutet eine einzelne Ausstellung noch kein Engagement. Untersucht man einen bestimmten Themenkreis zeitgenössischer Kunst und berücksichtigt die «Tech-Art» nur in einer einzigen Ausstellung, so ist auch das kein Engagement. Wie in der Wissenschaft gehört zur Beharrlichkeit auch, dass «Misserfolge» sich als ebenso nützlich erweisen können wie «Erfolge», vorausgesetzt man lässt sich auf ein dauerhaftes Engagement ein.

Schliesslich zur Unwissenheit, worunter ich «Nichtwissen» verstehe. Heute hört man von Kunstinstitutionen, Kuratoren und Fachleuten natürlich häufig, dass nicht die Antworten wichtig seien, sondern die gestellten Fragen. Doch mir geht es um Unwissen in einem expliziteren Sinn. Bei allen inkunablen Medien hat Meisterschaft etwas Abschliessendes: Möglichkeiten fallen weg. Vielleicht ist Kohärenz wirklich nicht das ergiebigste Ziel.

Yoshi Sodeoka, Art Director der Pioniersite Word, warf letztes Jahr das Handtuch. In einem offenen Brief gestand er (offensichtlich) ein, dass sich ungeachtet der preisgekrönten, schrägen Gestaltung von Word die Form im Bereich der interaktiven (lies inkunablen) Medien vereinheitlicht habe, und ihr Name sei Yahoo! Alle wüssten, dass Yahoo! am besten funktioniere, und daher werde Word nun das Yahoo!-Format übernehmen. Dies sei für alle das Beste. Es sei das, was das Publikum wünsche. Es sei kohärent. Es sei verständlich. Er verstehe das. Und es tue ihm Leid, dass er alle so lange belästigt habe.

Als Art Director von Word habe ich meine Pflichten als zuständiger Designer nicht erfüllt. Ich habe mit dem falschen Medium Kunst geschaffen. Wäre ich ein Schriftsteller, der seine Werke im Netz veröffentlicht, so wäre es mir ein Anliegen, dass die Leute sie tatsächlich lesen können. Da ich solchen Dingen nicht die nötige Aufmerksamkeit geschenkt habe, mussten andere darunter leiden... Ich weiss allerdings, dass wir im Design-Team von Word allmählich das Gefühl bekamen, wir hätten das Potenzial des Webs vollständig ausgeschöpft und im Gegenzug hat das Web uns erschöpft. Kurz gesagt, es ist endlich Zeit, dass hier etwas Ruhe einkehrt... Im Moment haben wir das Problem, dass bei allem, was wir versuchen, der Schuss nach hinten losgeht. Deshalb beschlossen wir, kein neues Interface zu erfinden um unsere Site zu verbessern. Wir haben einfach das Beste übernommen. von Yahoo![6]

Unwissenheit macht nicht selig. Nicht wissen ist die Hölle. Aber ein überstürztes Urteil würde jetzt wohl nur dazu führen, dass sich die Ödnis des Fernsehens und älterer inkunabler (utopischer) Medien auch auf die neuen Medien ausbreitet. Widersetzen Sie sich dem Modell einer gesellschaftlichen Kommunikation und Ausdrucksweise, die auf Produktivität ausgerichtet ist und überwiegend auf kommerziellen Interessen beruht!

(Übersetzung: Irene Aeberli)

1) Janet Murray, *Hamlet on the Holodeck: The Future of Narrative in Cyberspace*, The Free Press, New York 1997, S. 28.
2) Ebenda.
3) Marshall McLuhan, *Die magischen Kanäle: Understanding Media*, Verlag der Kunst, Dresden 1994, S. 430.
4) *William Eggleston's Guide*, Ausstellungskatalog, Museum of Modern Art, New York 1976.
5) Leo Steinberg, «Other Criteria», in: *Other Criteria: Confrontations with Twentieth-Century Art*, Oxford University Press, New York 1973, S. 63.
6) Sodeoka publizierte seinen offenen Brief ursprünglich unter http://www.word.com/yhome/artdirector.html, doch die Word-Site wurde mittlerweile aufgehoben. Diese Ausschnitte stammen aus Alex Lash, «A Word-for-Word Imitation», *The Industry Standard Magazine*, 21.1.2000, 12.00 mittags, pazifische Zeit. (http://www.thestandard.com/article/0,1902,9061,00.html)

tautological circular dot
Times critic dumbstruck
tender corpse dissolves
thoroughly calcified dinosaur
terrible Cardiff drunkenness
the clumsy dentist
traffickers carry doughnuts
thirteen Celtic doppelgangers
Timotei clears dandruff
topless Catherine Deneuve
too cool, dammit
tampons can disappear
towels conspicuously don't
thespians crave drama
traditional Cumbrian Druids
tenderly caressing Dorothy
Texans create dogmas
terrible circular dreams
trice circumcised dick
Titanic crushes DiCaprio
Timothy counts days
throttle Chris Deburgh
test crash dummies
try Chilean dictator
twins chat dually
Tchaikovsky's creative drive
Tuymans' casual daubs
total compulsive disorder
Tolstoy's clever dialogue
telegram caused dyspepsia
Toblerone chocolate dream
tremendously creamy discharge
toffee coloured diarrhoea
Tarkovksky's celluloid dreams
the communist defector
titillating chicks disrobe
the cervix dilates
tailor creases dufflecoats
Tracy's cocaine detox
tiny cock droops

torturing Cruella's Dalmatians
trash collecting dustmen
The Celebration (Denmark)
tackle Colombian drug-running
the CD
thawing cryogenic Diana
Tampax: Charles' discovery
tortilla con dip
Tichborne Claimant's disfigurement
trench coat delinquent
take care, darling
Tories continually defect
try com dot
Theban's cross-road death
tulip clogged Dutchmen
try cultivating daffodils
today's curry dish
tomorrow's casserole dish
Thomas' catalogue delay
two curators drown
ten clear days
terrible cattle devastation
Turkish Cypriots demonstrate
turning causes disorientation
the country doctor
Teignmouth, Crowhurst's destination
trimaran's circumnavigation deceit
Thomas' cardboard desk
the Catholic doctrine
throw cupid's dart
torture causes discomfort
tangerine cream dream
truly cruelly deeply
Tony Cragg's disappointing
toothy cold Dracula
the chronic dipsomaniac
theatre cast drama
tobacco causes dizziness
tortoises can't delay
twats can't dick

tense cunt drama
teleological communist dialectics
trust creates dilemmas
they cancelled dessert
tomatoes contaminate Daiquiris
thick cucumber dildo
try copying Douglas
Tom Cruise divorces
Tony Curtis drags
things change daily
taraa, cheeky devil
travel Calais-Dover
tartan causes division
thin condoms dissolve
Tippex covers disclosures
Tottenham challenge Düsseldorf
to crucify Deus
to cuddle daddy
the comfortable divan
towards controlled development
thirty cherished demoiselles
thunder clouds darken
Thomas Cook delay
trustworthy Cologne dealers
Thomas calms down
touch clitoris daily
thoroughly clever dame
today Christ died
Thomas can decide
try crocheting dungarees
three cunts dribbling
turgid convoluted discourse
Thornton's chocolate dicks
twelve Christ disciples
tropical cyclone depression
Thursday's child's depressed
the collapsed democracy
Tinkerbell can dance
Thumbelina can't dance
Transylvanian crypt dawn

Garderobe

'gär-ˌdrōb

the company director
the common denominator
try changing Deutschmarks
Tieopolo's clouds delight
tai chi dilettante
the culture destroyers
ticking clocks detonate
twelve Christian democrats
two cantankerous dipsticks
three cannibals debauch
twenty criminologists dig
Thomas Carlisle dictated
tycoon counts dollars
three course dinner
threadbare clothes disintegrate
tantric crop dance
the Cuban dictator
tennis coach's daughter
troops conquer Deutschland
tick/cross dialectic
transvestite's convincing drag
too co-dependent
things coincide dramatically
three-leaf clover disappointment
tits can delight
Trollop's courteous delivery
terrific cunt, darling
torpedoes creep deep
Tempelhof crash disaster
they celebrated Doomsday
titillation cleverly disguised
therapy compounds depression
Thursday constitutes Donnerstag
three called drei
two called duo
top class drugs
Turin crowd dispersal
the candle died
two copulating dogs
the cathedral diocese

they cancelled dinner
theoreticians conform dutifully
taste Canada Dry
tantrums conceal dyslexia
transcontinental drift
Travolta's cute dimple
theologian contemplates death
Trimble craves decommissioning
Texan's Christian duty
Turner can't draw
Twist copies Dodger
the Chinese dragon
troglodytic Charles Darwin
tarantula consumes dog
tobacco chewing dykes
the crystal decanter
traditional charcoal drawings
trice cloned Dolly
"that's called disembowelling"
taxi cab driver
tarot card destiny
thumb creates dog-ears
Taiwan/China dispute
Telepathic Communication Day
Tirpitz crew drowns
train crushes driver
tomorrow's Christmas Day
Top Cat, disputable
The Chambers Dictionary
to cure disease
thyroid calcium deficiency
The Castafiore Diamond
Terpsichorean contemporary dance
tooth cavity decay
teetotallers could drink
the country diary
the childish dreamer
travel card discount
that clever Duchamp
Tarzan's chimp duplicate

the class divide
tiptoe carefully downstairs
test card dissemination
tough cookie's disfavour
telephone Camp David
testicular cancer diagnosed
Tate Centenary dinner
two college dons
the cocked dice
the coal-miner's dispute
Thatcher concedes defeat
terrier chews dachshund
the crippled detective
the cylindrical drum
taffeta cocktail dress
trinkets collect dust
time consuming debate
the chairman dies
tired cliched derivative
terminal clinical depression
teenage cheerleader develops
toddler's crappy diaper
true confessions divulged
traditional country dancing
trust counteracts distrust
their collective decision
totally crap documentation
Thomas Charlotte discrepancy
Tacita Cyrillus ditto

COMPLETE YOUR PARKETT LIBRARY
VERVOLLSTÄNDIGEN SIE IHRE PARKETT-BIBLIOTHEK

OUT OF PRINT / VERGRIFFEN: **NO. 1** ENZO CUCCHI, **2** SIGMAR POLKE, **3** MARTIN DISLER, **4** MERET OPPENHEIM, **5** ERIC FISCHL, **6** JANNIS KOUNELLIS, **7** BRICE MARDEN, **8** MARKUS RAETZ, **9** FRANCESCO CLEMENTE, **10** BRUCE NAUMAN, **12** ANDY WARHOL, **13** REBECCA HORN, **16** ROBERT WILSON, **17** FISCHLI/WEISS, **19** JEFF KOONS, MARTIN KIPPENBERGER, **22** CHRISTIAN BOLTANSKI, JEFF WALL, **25** KATHARINA FRITSCH, **26** GÜNTHER FÖRG, PHILIP TAAFFE, JAMES TURRELL, **27** LOUISE BOURGEOIS, ROBERT GOBER, **29** CINDY SHERMAN, JOHN BALDESSARI, **30** SIGMAR POLKE, **31** DAVID HAMMONS, MIKE KELLEY, **35** GERHARD RICHTER, **38** ROSS BLECKNER, MARLENE DUMAS

For out-of-print issues you can register your name and address with Parkett and you will be notified, if your issue(s) become(s) available on the secondary market / Für vergriffene Bände nimmt der Verlag gerne Ihren Suchauftrag entgegen und macht Ihnen bei allfälliger Verfügbarkeit im Handel ein Angebot.

COLLABORATIONS

JOHN WESLEY
TACITA DEAN
THOMAS DEMAND
MILLAR, CARABELL, SCHWARZ
NORDEN, KÖNIG/STOCKEBRAND
HAINLEY, SEARLE, RUBY, HEISER
INSERT: **G. STEINER & J. LENZLINGER**
PHILIP URSPRUNG: **ALLAN KAPROW**
RUSSELL FERGUSON: **GLEN WILSON**
EDWARD A. SCHEER: **MIKE PARR**
LES INFOS: DAVID GREENBERG
CUMULUS: GIOVANNI CARMINE, STEVE DIETZ

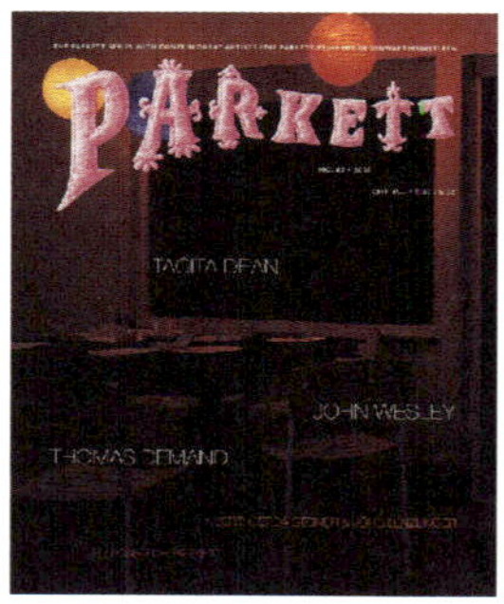

No. 62 - ISBN 3-907582-12-8

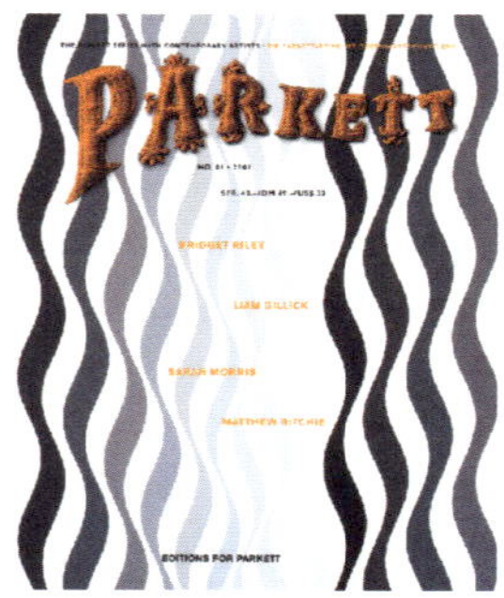

No. 61 - ISBN 3-907582-11-X

BRIDGET RILEY
LIAM GILLICK
SARAH MORRIS
MATTHEW RITCHIE
KUDIELKA, HICKEY
GILLICK, STEMMRICH, WOLLEN
NICHOLS GOODEVE, KLEIN, PRINZHORN
RABINOWITZ, GALISON/JONES, MARCUS
ELISABETH KLEY: **PAUL LINCOLN**
CUMULUS: OKWUI ENWEZOR, MARINA WARNER
BALKON: STELLA ROLLIG

CHUCK CLOSE
DIANA THATER
LUC TUYMANS
PROSE, CLOSE/PEYTON, SHIFF, CLOSE/CURIGER,
ARRHENIUS, HASLINGER, GILBERT-ROLFE,
HOPTMAN, MOSQUERA, REUST
INSERT: **SHIRANA SHAHBAZI**
GREG HILTY: **JEREMY DELLER**
HOWARD SINGERMAN: **DAVID BUNN**
LES INFOS: THIERRY DE DUVE—INTERVIEW
CUMULUS: FRAZER WARD, HANS ULRICH RECK

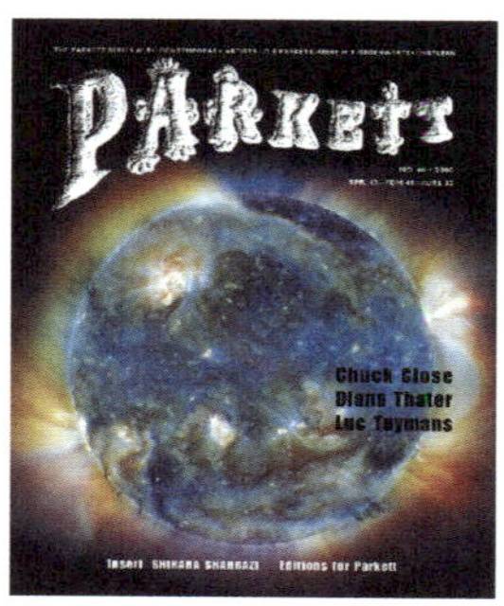

No. 60 - ISBN 3-907582-10-1

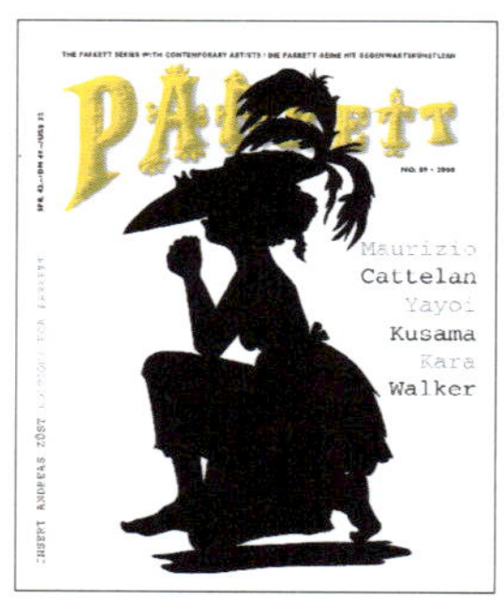

No. 59 - ISBN 3-907582-09-8

MAURIZIO CATTELAN
YAYOI KUSAMA
KARA WALKER
BOURRIAUD, GINGERAS, BONAMI
PANHANS-BÜHLER, MATSUI, POLLOCK
DUBOIS SHAW, JANUS, WALKER
INSERT: **ANDREAS ZÜST**
VINCENT KATZ,
ELISABETH BRONFEN: **ANNETTE MESSAGER**
JAN AVGIKOS: **ANNA GASKELL**
LES INFOS: ALI SUBOTNICK
CUMULUS: MARGIT ROWELL, LASZLO FÖLDENY
BALKON: MICHELLE NICOL

JAMES ROSENQUIST
SYLVIE FLEURY
JASON RHOADES
RUSSELL, KOONS/ROSENQUIST, HULTEN, FELIX
GLENN, LOBEL, DANNATT, RUF, KOETHER
FERGUSON, ORTH, SCHEIDEMANN/HERMANN
INSERT: **HENRY BOND**
GILDA WILLIAMS: **JANE & LOUISE WILSON**
SLAVOJ ZIZEK, PAUL D. MILLER & CHRIS OFILI
LES INFOS: ANNA HELWING
CUMULUS: DAVID ROBBINS, HILDE TEERLINCK
BALKON: KNUT EBELING

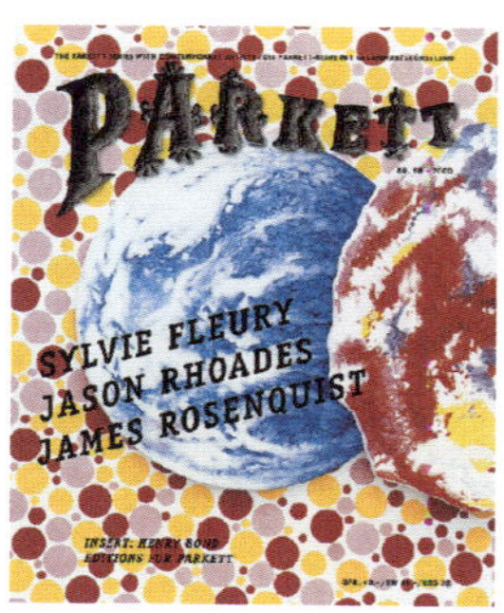

No. 58 - ISBN 3-907582-08-X

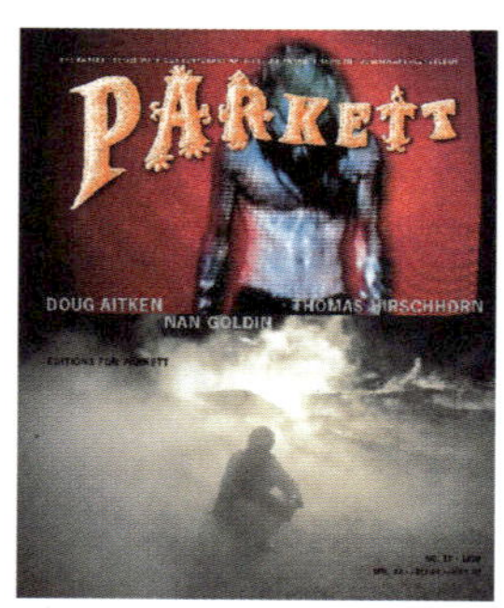

No. 57 - ISBN 3-907582-07-1

DOUG AITKEN
NAN GOLDIN
THOMAS HIRSCHHORN
ROBERTS, BONAMI, VAN ASSCHE, LEBOVICI
DANTO, LIEBMANN, FRIIS-HANSEN, HAKERT,
EISENBERG, FLECK, GINGERAS, VERGNE, STEINWE
DAVID GREENBERG: **DONALD BAECHLER**
ANDREA KROKSNES: **LOUISE LAWLER**
LIONEL BOVIER: **JOHN MILLER**
LES INFOS: RUDOLF SCHMITZ
CUMULUS: H.U. OBRIST, CONNIE BUTLER
BALKON: JURI STEINER & ANNELISE COSTE

ELLSWORTH KELLY
VANESSA BEECROFT
JORGE PARDO
KELLEIN, FER, MAURER, RIMANELLI
BRYSON, TAZZI, SEWARD, AVGIKOS
FERGUSON, VÉGH, VAN WINKEL
FRANGENBERG, BUSH
GREG HILTY: **CERITH WYN EVANS**
THOMAS Y. LEVIN: **CHRISTIAN MARCLAY**
LYNNE COOKE: **DIANA THATER**
LES INFOS: DIANE LEWIS
CUMULUS: ADRIAN DANNATT, PETR NEDOMA

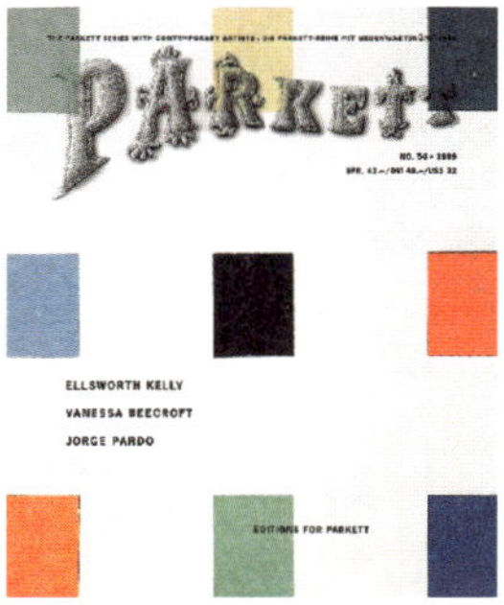

No. 56 - ISBN 3-907582-06-3

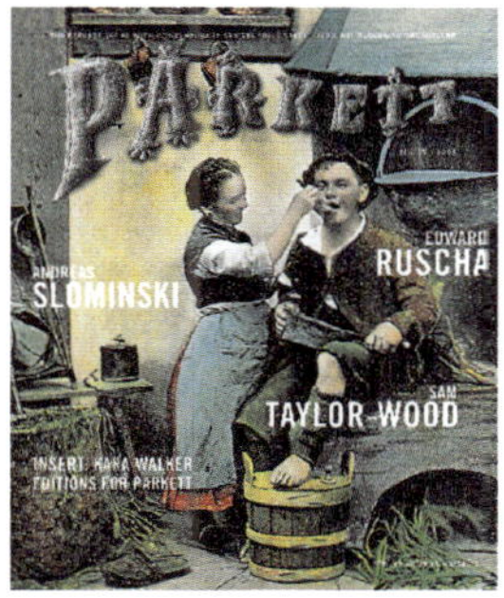

No. 55 - ISBN 3-907582-05-5

EDWARD RUSCHA
ANDREAS SLOMINSKI
SAM TAYLOR-WOOD
PERRONE, HIGGIE, SINGERMAN, SCHENKER
SCANLAN, SPECTOR, FREY, HEYNEN
GROYS/FUNCKE/HOFFMANN, BRONFEN
BONAMI, LAJER-BURCHARTH
INSERT: **KARA WALKER**
BORIS GROYS: **PAVEL PEPPERSTEIN**
RUDOLF SCHMITZ: **ALEXANDER KLUGE**
BEATRIX RUF: **EIJA-LIISA AHTILA**
CUMULUS: MICHELLE NICOL, SUELY ROLNIK

RONI HORN
MARIKO MORI
BEAT STREULI
SCHORR, GUNNARSSON, GOROVOY, LEWIS
SPECTOR, BRYSON, NAKAZAWA, NICHOLS
GOODEVE, STALS, DANTO, AMANO, SMITH
INSERT: **MATTHEW RITCHIE**
VINCENT KATZ: **ALEX KATZ**
HORST BREDEKAMP: **STEPHAN VON HUENE**
PAUL D. MILLER: **SHIRIN NESHAT**
LES INFOS:
OKWUI ENWEZOR & WILLIAM KENTRIDGE
CUMULUS: VALÉRIA PICCOLI, MARIA LIND

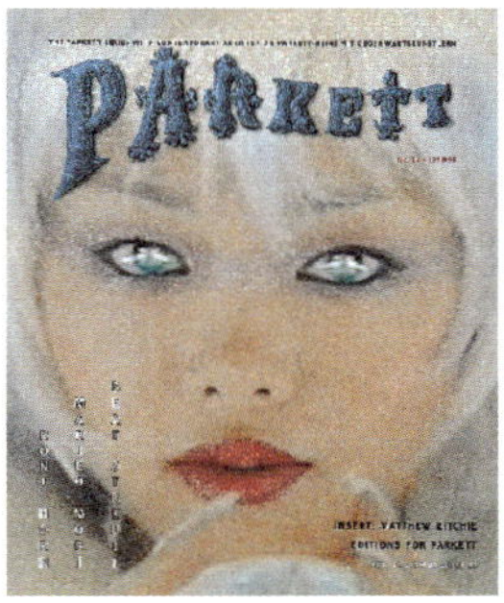

No. 54 - ISBN 3-907582-04-7

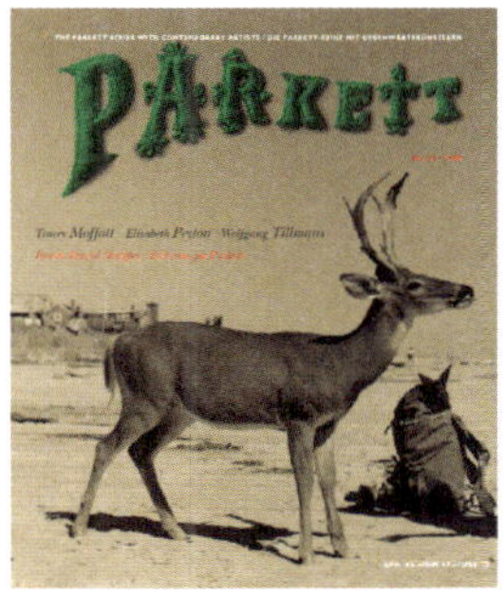

No. 53 - ISBN 3-907582-03-9

TRACEY MOFFATT
ELIZABETH PEYTON
WOLFGANG TILLMANS
MARTIN, LAJER-BURCHARTH, RIMANELLI
PILGRIM, URSPRUNG, LIEBMANN, MATSUI
WAKEFIELD, BUDNEY, NESBITT, ZIEGLER
INSERT: **DAVID SHRIGLEY**
CATHERINE BERNARD: **JOHAN GRIMONPREZ**
BERNARD MARCADÉ: **ROBERT GOBER**
LES INFOS DE L'ENFER: VALERIA LIEBERMANN
CUMULUS: BLESSING, AUPETITALLOT
BALKON: STEINER/MAGNAGUAGNO

KAREN KILIMNIK
MALCOLM MORLEY
UGO RONDINONE
SCHORR, BÜRGI, JUNCOSA, MORLEY,
LEBENSZTEJN, BONAMI, VERWOERT, HOPTMAN,
INSERT: **THOMAS BAYRLE**
ED WHITE: **JEAN MICHEL OTHONIEL**
NEVILLE WAKEFIELD: **RICHARD SERRA**
GILDA WILLIAMS: **GILLIAN WEARING**
ROBERT GRESKOVIC: **MERCE CUNNINGHAM**
CUMULUS: WALKER, KURZMEYER
BALKON: CECILIA VICUÑA

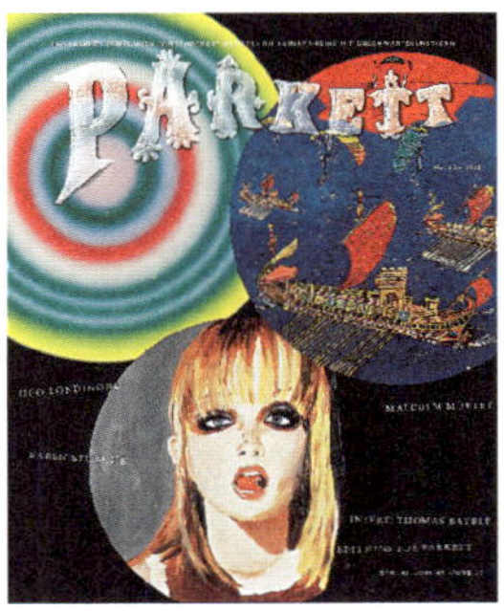

No. 52 - ISBN 3-907582-02-0

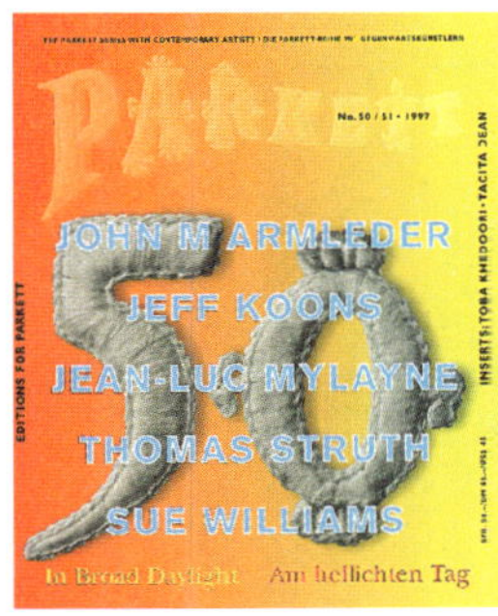

50/51 - ISBN 3-907582-00-4

JOHN M ARMLEDER, JEFF KOONS
JEAN-LUC MYLAYNE
THOMAS STRUTH, SUE WILLIAMS
DI PIETRANTONIO, BOVIER, MUNIZ,
SEWARD, LOERS, NICHOLS GOODEVE,
COOKE, DION, ARNAUDET, MYLAYNE,
CURIGER, LINGWOOD, OKUTSU, BRYSON,
SCHJELDAHL, NESBIT, DANNATT, CAMHI
INSERTS: **TOBA KHEDOORI, TACITA DEAN**
ONFRAY: **HYACINTHE RIGAUD,** NICOL: **SAM SAMORE**
MURPHY, VAN DER WALLE, STEINER,
KURT W. FORSTER: **FRANK GEHRY**
CUMULUS: COLEMAN, BIRNBAUM

LAURIE ANDERSON
DOUGLAS GORDON
JEFF WALL
FLOOD, BEZZOLA, FERGUSON
GILLICK/GORDON, BRYSON, PONTBRIAND
SCHORR, ANDERSON, BURCKHARDT, BUDNEY
INSERT: **SILVIA BÄCHLI**
COLIN DE LAND: **JOHN WATERS**
ROBERT STORR: **SEYDOU KEITA**
DANIELA SALVIONI: **CLEGG & GUTTMANN**
CUMULUS: KITTELMANN, MEYER

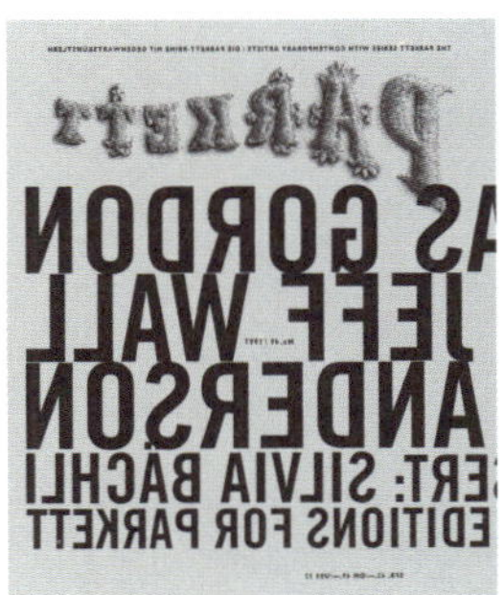

No. 49 - ISBN 3-907509-99-4

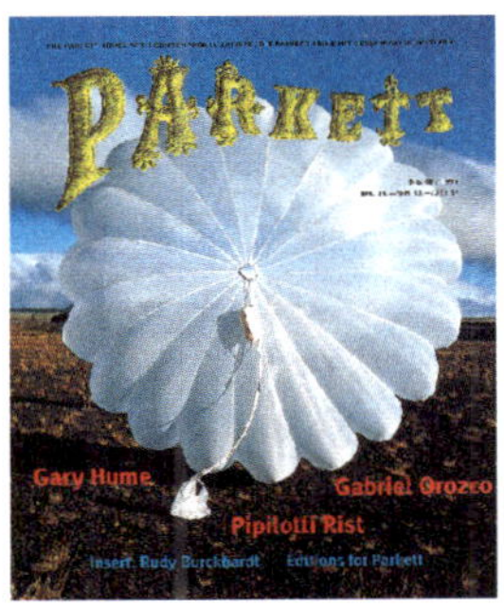

No. 48 - ISBN 3-907509-98-6

GARY HUME
GABRIEL OROZCO
PIPILOTTI RIST
BOVIER, MUIR, FOGLE, BONAMI
DE ZEGHER, SPECTOR, URSPRUNG
BABIAS, COLOMBO, ANDERSON
INSERT: **RUDY BURCKHARDT**
VINCENT KATZ: **RUDY BURCKHARDT**
VAN DER WALLE: **CHARLES LONG**
& STEREOLAB
FAYE HIRSCH: **BRUCE CONNER**
CHRISTOPH DOSWALD: **IAN ANÜLL**
CUMULUS: LEGGAT, SCHNEIDER

TONY OURSLER
RAYMOND PETTIBON
THOMAS SCHÜTTE
COOKE, RICHARD, NERI,
LEWIS, GROYS, ALS, RUGOFF,
GOODEVE, SEARLE, MARI, REUST,
WAKEFIELD, LOOCK, JANUS
INSERT: **ZOE LEONARD & CHERYL DUNYE**
JURI STEINER: **EMMA KUNZ**
MAX WECHSLER: **CHRISTOPH RÜTIMANN**
SUSAN MORGAN: **DIANE ARBUS**
CUMULUS: PRINCENTHAL, BOVIER/CHERIX

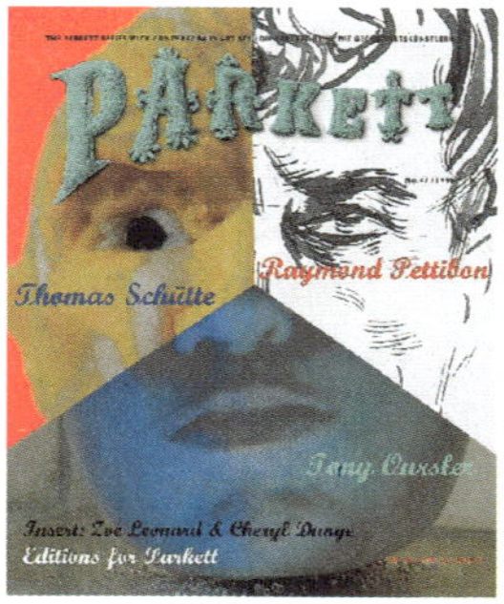

No. 47 - ISBN 3-907509-97-8

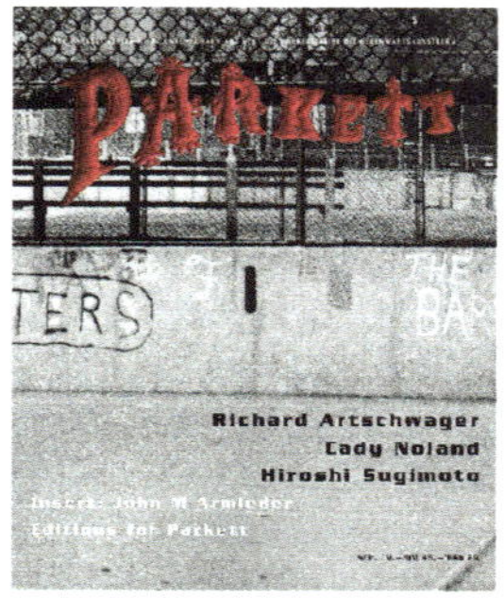

No. 46 - ISBN 3-907509-96-X

RICHARD ARTSCHWAGER
CADY NOLAND
HIROSHI SUGIMOTO
DEITCHER, SCHAFFNER, FORSTER, MUNIZ
ARMSTRONG, RELYEA, BOGDAN, GOODEVE
NICKAS, BRYSON, RUGOFF, DENSON
INSERT: **JOHN M ARMLEDER**
ROLAND WÄSPE: **ERWIN WURM**
DANIEL BIRNBAUM: **ÖYVIND FAHLSTRÖM**
LES INFOS DU PARADIS: ROBERT FLECK
CUMULUS: MILLER, VETTESE
BALKON: MARTIN HELLER

MATTHEW BARNEY
SARAH LUCAS
ROMAN SIGNER
BRYSON, ONFRAY, SEWARD, GOODEVE,
SALTZ, VAN ADRICHEM, SCHORR, FREEDMAN,
JOUANNAIS, BITTERLI, DOSWALD,
VIEWING, WECHSLER, DELAND
INSERT: **ELLIOTT PUCKETTE**
HEIDI GILPIN: **WILLIAM FORSYTHE**
ROBYN McKENZIE: **GEOFF LOWE**
MICHAEL TARANTINO: **CHANTAL AKERMAN**
CUMULUS: McEVILLEY, WAKEFIELD

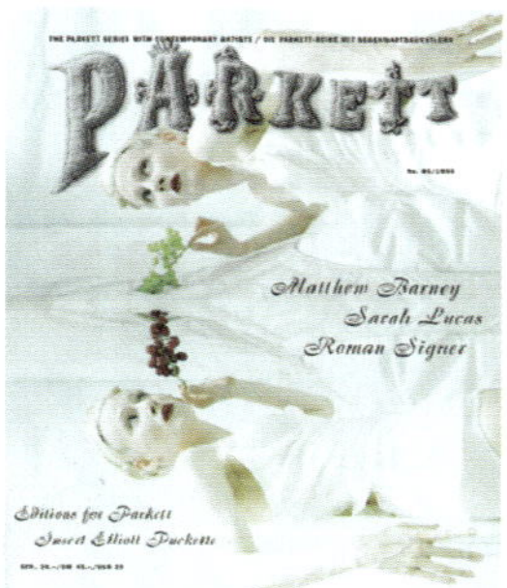

No. 45 - ISBN 3-907509-95-1

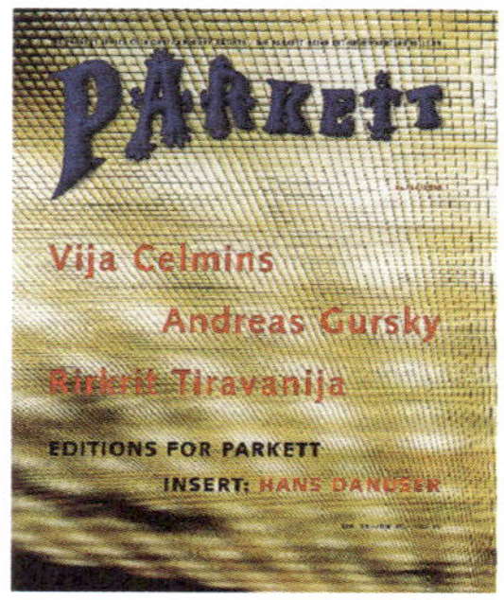

No. 44 - ISBN 3-907509-94-3

VIJA CELMINS
ANDREAS GURSKY
RIRKRIT TIRAVANIJA
PRINCENTHAL, LEWIS, SILVERTHORNE
SHIFF, CRIQUI, BURCKHARDT, WAKEFIELD
SCHORR, MELO, GILLICK, FLOOD, STEINER
INSERT: **HANS DANUSER**
LES INFOS: LIAM GILLICK & DOUGLAS GORDON
LYNNE COOKE, DAVID DEITCHER
DANIEL KURJAKOVIC: **MARIE JOSÉ BURKI**
NAN GOLDIN: **PETER HUJAR**
NOEMI SMOLIK: **ANDREAS SLOMINSKI**
JASON SIMON: **MARK DION**
LUK LAMBRECHT: **MARK LUYTEN**

JUAN MUÑOZ
SUSAN ROTHENBERG
LYNNE COOKE, ALEXANDRE MELO
JAMES LINGWOOD, GAVIN BRYARS
ROBERT CREELEY, INGRID SCHAFFNER
JEAN-CHRISTOPHE AMMANN
MARK STEVENS, JOAN SIMON
INSERT: **ROBERT SMITHSON**
NEVILLE WAKEFIELD
MICHELLE NICOL: **CARSTEN HÖLLER**
HANS-ULRICH OBRIST: **FABRICE HYBERT**

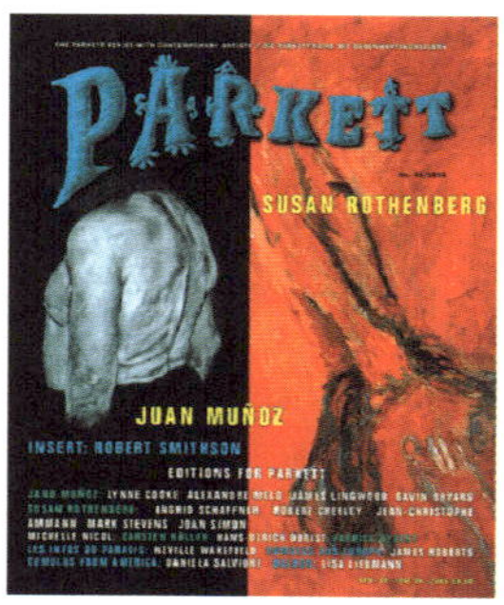

No. 43 - ISBN 3-907509-93-5

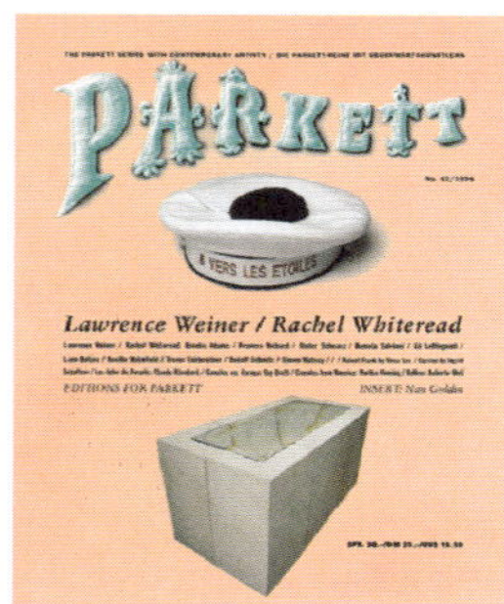

No. 42 - ISBN 3-907509-92-7

LAWRENCE WEINER
RACHEL WHITEREAD
BROOKS ADAMS, FRANCES RICHARD
DIETER SCHWARZ, DANIELA SALVIONI
ED LEFFINGWELL, LANE RELYEA
NEVILLE WAKEFIELD, RUDOLF SCHMITZ
TREVOR FAIRBROTHER, SIMON WATNEY
INSERT: **NAN GOLDIN**
VINCE LEO: **ROBERT FRANK**
CLAUDE RITSCHARD: **MARKUS RAETZ**

FRANCESCO CLEMENTE
GÜNTHER FÖRG
PETER FISCHLI/DAVID WEISS
DAMIEN HIRST
JENNY HOLZER
REBECCA HORN
SIGMAR POLKE
HOLLAND COTTER, BORIS GROYS
MAX WECHSLER, DAVID RIMANELLI
JOAN SIMON, GORDON BURN
GILBERT LASCAULT, WERNER SPIES
BICE CURIGER, JEFF PERRONE
G. ROGER DENSON, VIK MUNIZ
DAVE HICKEY

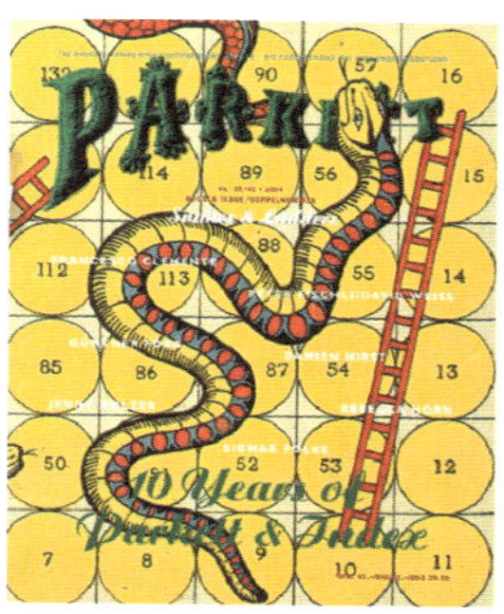

40/41 - ISBN 3-907509-90-0

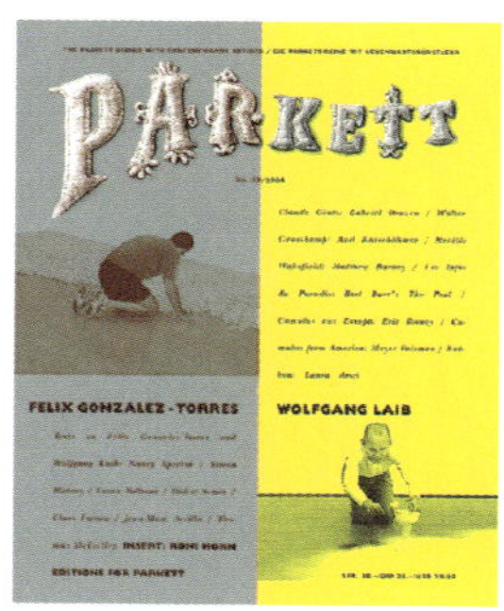

No. 39 - ISBN 3-907509-89-7

FELIX GONZALEZ-TORRES
WOLFGANG LAIB
NANCY SPECTOR, SIMON WATNEY,
SUSAN TALLMAN, DIDIER SEMIN,
CLARE FARROW, JEAN-MARC AVRILLA,
THOMAS McEVILLEY
CLAUDE GINTZ: **GABRIEL OROZCO**
WALTER GRASSKAMP: **AXEL KASSEBÖHMER**
NEVILLE WAKEFIELD: **MATTHEW BARNEY**
INSERT: **RONI HORN**
LES INFOS DU PARADIS: **BURT BARR**
CUMULUS: **MEYER VAISMAN**

CHARLES RAY
FRANZ WEST
KLAUS KERTESS, CHRISTOPHER KNIGHT
PETER SCHJELDAHL, ROBERT STORR
JAN AVGIKOS, AXEL HUBER
MARTIN PRINZHORN, ELISABETH
SCHLEBRÜGGE, HARALD SZEEMANN,
DENYS ZACHAROPOULOS
INSERT: **PIPILOTTI RIST**
JEAN BAUDRILLARD
HANS RUDOLF REUST: **LUC TUYMANS**
PARKETT INQUIRY:
CHERCHEZ LA FEMME PEINTRE!

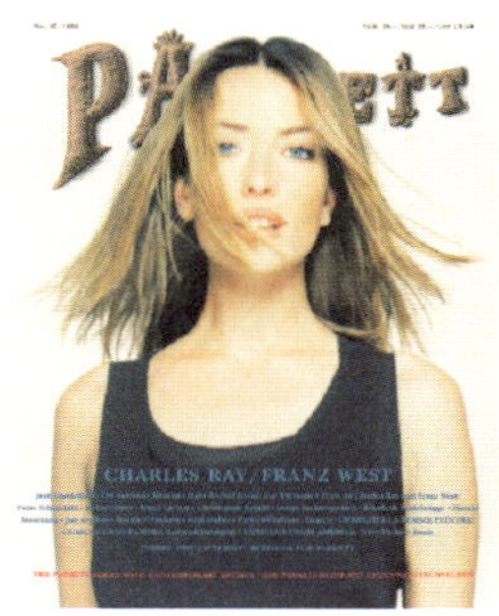

No. 37 - ISBN 3-907509-87-0

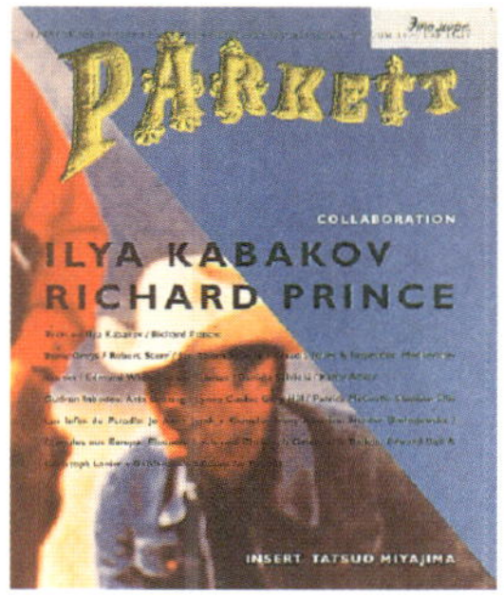

No. 34 - ISBN 3-907509-84-6

ILYA KABAKOV
RICHARD PRINCE
BORIS GROYS, ROBERT STORR
JAN THORN-PRIKKER
CLAUDIA JOLLES, EDMUND WHITE
SUSAN TALLMAN, DANIELA
SALVIONI, KATHY ACKER
INSERT: **TATSUO MIYAJIMA**
GUDRUN INBODEN: **ASTA GRÖTING**
LYNNE COOKE: **GARY HILL**
PATRICK McGRATH: **STEPHEN ELLIS**

ROSEMARIE TROCKEL
CHRISTOPHER WOOL
VERONIQUE BACCHETTA,
BARRETT WATTEN,
ANNE WAGNER, JIM LEWIS,
GREIL MARCUS, JEFF PERRONE,
DIEDRICH DIEDERICHSEN
INSERT: **ADRIAN SCHIESS**
MARINA WARNER: **PENIS PLENTY**
G. ROGER DENSON:
DENNIS OPPENHEIM
CAMIEL VAN WINKEL

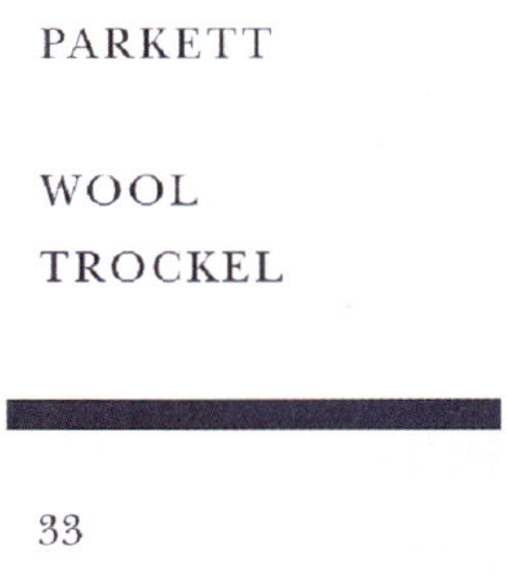

No. 33 - ISBN 3-907509-83-3

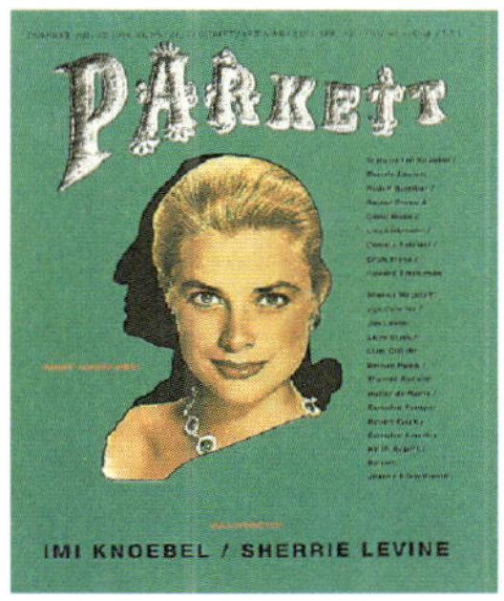

No. 32 - ISBN 3-907509-82-X

IMI KNOEBEL
SHERRIE LEVINE
RUDOLF BUMILLER
RAINER CRONE/DAVID MOOS
LISA LIEBMANN, DANIELA SALVIONI
ERICH FRANZ, HOWARD SINGERMANN
INSERT: **DAMIEN HIRST**
SHEENA WAGSTAFF: **VIJA CELMINS**
JIM LEWIS: **LARRY CLARK**
LIAM GILLICK: **BETHAN HUWS**
THOMAS KELLEIN: **WALTER DE MARIA**

FRANZ GERTSCH
THOMAS RUFF
HELMUT FRIEDEL, ULRICH LOOCK
I. MICHAEL DANOFF, AMEI WALLACH
RAINER MICHAEL MASON
MARC FREIDUS, JÖRG JOHNEN
TREVOR FAIRBROTHER/NORMAN BRYSON
INSERT: **LIZ LARNER**
JAMES LEWIS: **RICHARD PRINCE**
DAVID HICKEY:
THE INVISIBLE DRAGON/
DER UNSICHTBARE DRACHEN
PAUL TAYLOR: **JAMES ROSENQUIST**

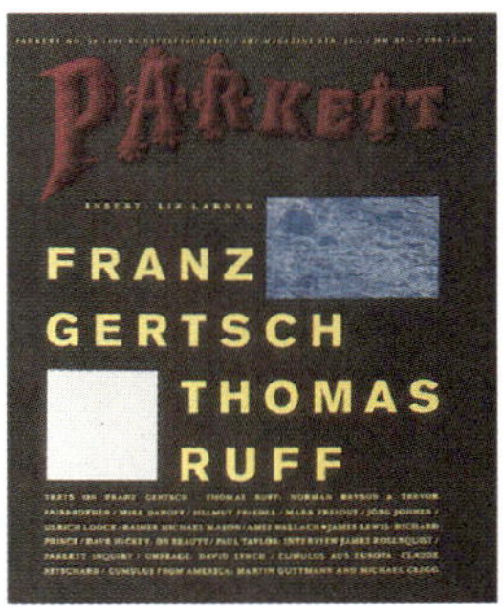

No. 28 - ISBN 3-907509-78-1

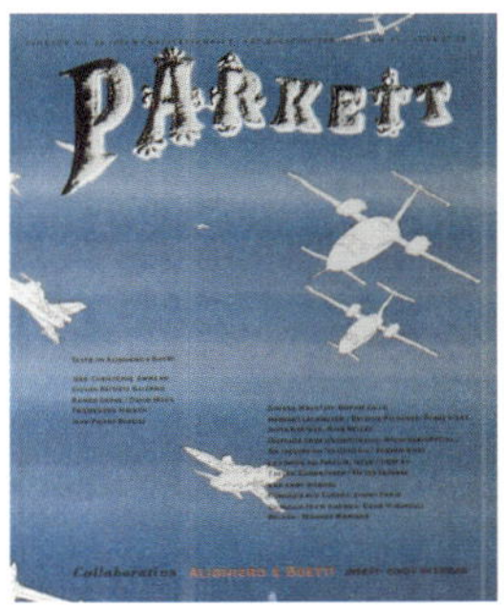

No. 24 - ISBN 3-907509-74-9

ALIGHIERO E BOETTI
JEAN-CHRISTOPHE AMMANN
GIOVAN BATTISTA SALERNO
RAINER CRONE & DAVID MOOS
FRIEDEMANN MALSCH
JEAN-PIERRE BORDAZ
ALAIN CUEFF
INSERT: **CINDY SHERMAN**
SHEENA WAGSTAFF:
SOPHIE CALLE
HERBERT LACHMEYER/
BRIGITTE FELDERER: **FRANZ WEST**
JUTTA KOETHER: **MIKE KELLEY**

RICHARD ARTSCHWAGER
ARTHUR C. DANTO, GEORG KOHLER,
MARIO A. ORLANDO, JOYCE
CAROL OATES, WERNER OECHSLIN,
ALAN LIGHTMAN, PATRICK
McGRATH, DANIEL SOUTIF,
LASZLO F. FÖLDENYI, JEAN STROUSE
INSERT: **DAVID BYRNE**
RENATE PUVOGEL: **ANDRÉ THOMKINS**
ULRICH LOOCK: **THOMAS STRUTH**
NANCY SPECTOR: **MEREDITH MONK**

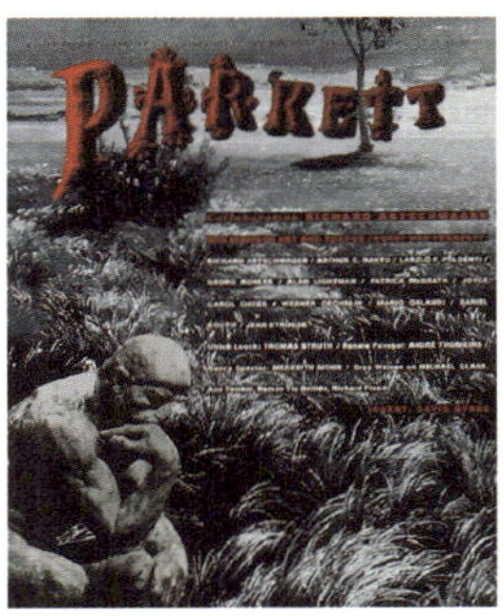

No. 23 - ISBN 3-907509-73-0

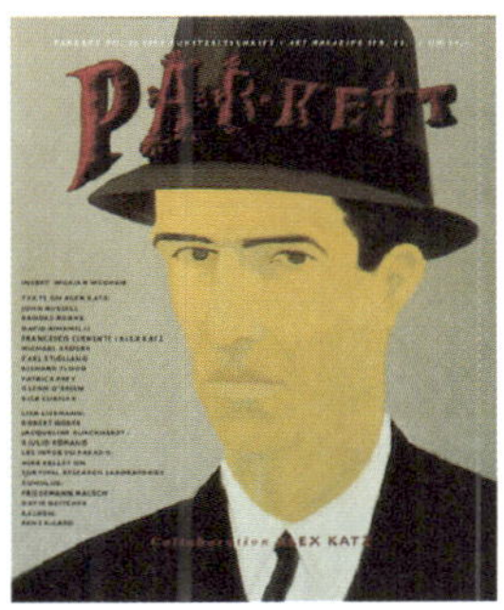

No. 21 - ISBN 3-907509-71-4

ALEX KATZ
JOHN RUSSELL, BROOKS ADAMS,
DAVID RIMANELLI, FRANCESCO
CLEMENTE, MICHAEL KRÜGER,
RICHARD FLOOD, PATRICK FREY,
CARL STIGLIANO, BICE CURIGER,
GLENN O'BRIEN
INSERT: **WILLIAM WEGMAN**
LISA LIEBMAN: **ROBERT GOBER**
JACQUELINE BURCKHARDT:
GIULIO ROMANO

TIM ROLLINS + K.O.S.
MARSHALL BERMAN
TREVOR FAIRBROTHER
STATEMENTS, DIALOGUE 5
INSERT: **ANDREAS GURSKY**
MICHAEL NASH: **BILL VIOLA**
STEPHEN ELLIS: **ROSS BLECKNER**
KLAUS KERTESS: **TRISHA BROWN**

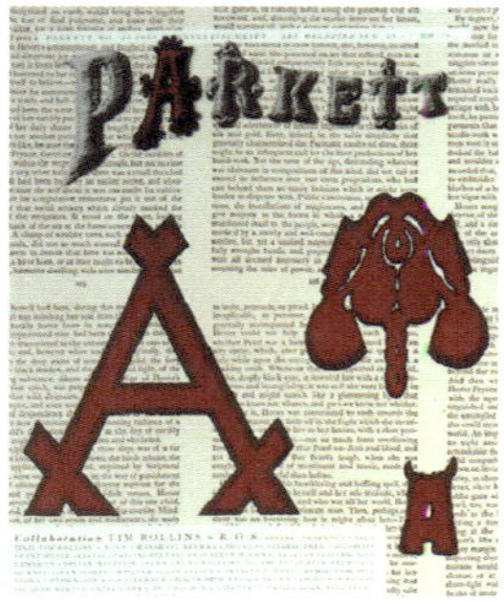

No. 20 - ISBN 3-907509-70-6

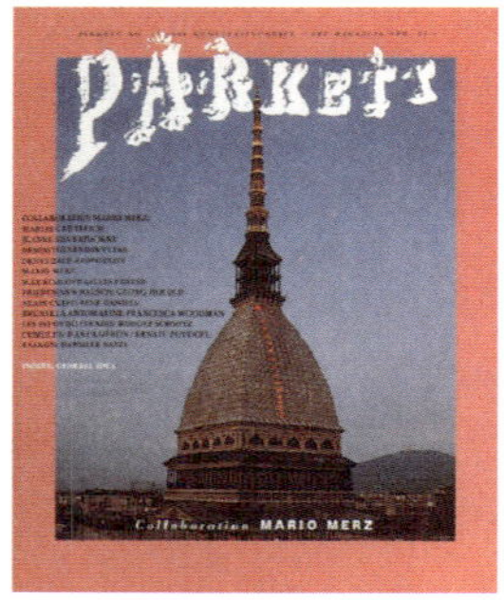

No. 15 - ISBN 3-907509-65-X

MARIO MERZ
MARLIS GRÜTERICH, JEANNE SILVERTHORNE, DEMOSTHENES DAVVETAS, HARALD SZEEMANN, DENYS ZACHAROPOULOS
INSERT: **GENERAL IDEA**
MAX KOZLOFF: **GILLES PERESS**
FRIEDEMANN MALSCH:
GEORG HEROLD
BRUNELLA ANTOMARINI:
FRANCESCA WOODMAN

GILBERT & GEORGE
DUNCAN FALLOWELL, MARIO CODOGNATO, JEREMY COOPER, DEMOSTHENES DAVVETAS, WOLF JAHN
INSERT: **ROSEMARIE TROCKEL**
ROBERT STORR: **NANCY SPERO**
HAIM STEINBACH: **MANIFESTO**
JÖRG ZUTTER: **THOMAS HUBER**

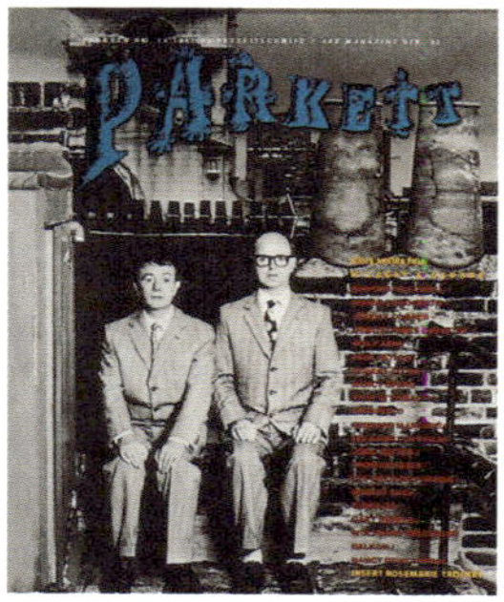

No. 14 - ISBN 3-907509-64-1

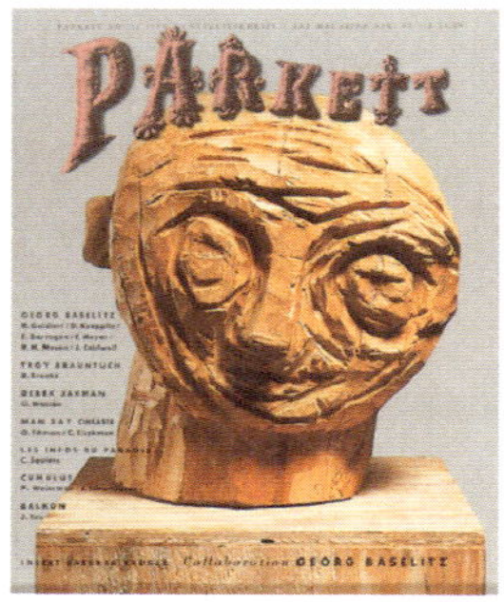

No. 11 - ISBN 3-907509-61-7

GEORG BASELITZ
REMO GUIDIERI, DIETER KOEPPLIN, ERIC DARRAGON, RAINER MICHAEL MASON, FRANZ MEYER, JOHN CALDWELL
INSERT: **BARBARA KRUGER**
GRAY WATSON: **DEREK JARMAN**
CAROL SQUIERS:
PHOTO OPPORTUNITY
ROSETTA BROOKS:
TROY BRAUNTUCH

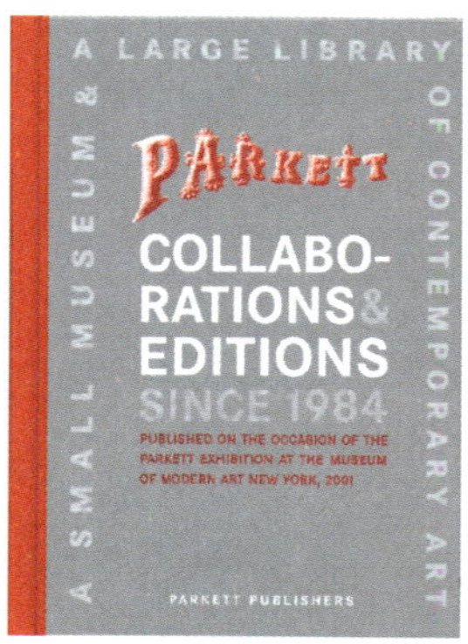

PARKETT COLLABORATIONS & EDITIONS SINCE 1984
CATALOGUE RAISONNÉ OF ALL ARTISTS' EDITIONS
from No. 1 – 61, hardcover, 6 x $4^{1}/_{4}$", 346 pages, 120 full-page color reproductions, 60 color reproductions of all Parkett covers, authors' index.

WERKVERZEICHNIS ALLER PARKETT-KÜNSTLER-EDITIONEN
von Nr. 1 – 61 in englischer Sprache, Hardcover, 15 x 11 cm, 346 Seiten, 120 ganzseitige Farbabbildungen, 60 farbige Abbildungen aller Parkett-Cover, Autorenindex.

CHF 32.– / $ 20 / € 22
ISBN 3-907582-22-5

NEW PARKETT POSTCARD SET
featuring 120 artists' editions made for Parkett

DAS NEUE PARKETT-POSTKARTEN-SET
mit 120 Editionen, die von Künstlern für Parkett geschaffen wurden.

CHF 39.– / $ 25 / € 27
ISBN 3-907582-21-7

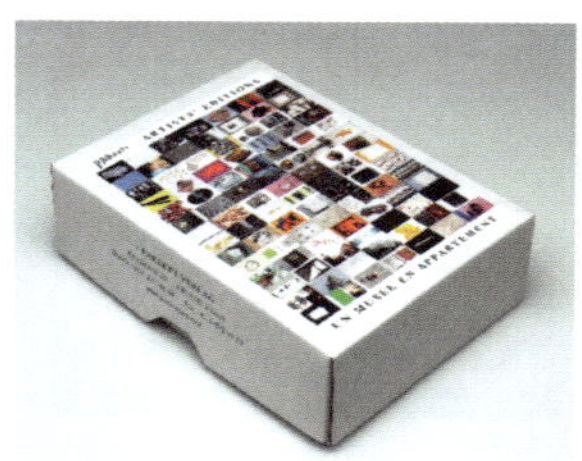

PARKETT

ARTISTS' MONOGRAPHS & EDITIONS / KÜNSTLERMONOGRAPHIEN & EDITIONEN

FOR AVAILABILITY SEE NEXT PAGE / LIEFERBARKEIT SIEHE FOLGENDE SEITE

vol.	Collaboration		
63	Tracey Emin		
	William Kentridge		
	Gregor Schneider		
62	Tacita Dean	m	e
	Thomas Demand	m	e
	John Wesley	m	e
61	Liam Gillick	m	
	Sarah Morris	m	e
	Bridget Riley	m	e
	Matthew Ritchie	m	e
60	Chuck Close	m	
	Diana Thater	m	e
	Luc Tuymans	m	e
59	Maurizio Cattelan	m	
	Yayoi Kusama	m	e
	Kara Walker	m	
58	Sylvie Fleury	m	e
	Jason Rhoades	m	e
	James Rosenquist	m	e
57	Doug Aitken	m	e
	Nan Goldin	m	
	Thomas Hirschhorn	m	
56	Vanessa Beecroft	m	
	Ellsworth Kelly	m	
	Jorge Pardo	m	e
55	Edward Ruscha	m	
	Andreas Slominski	m	
	Sam Taylor-Wood	m	
54	Roni Horn	m	e
	Mariko Mori	m	
	Beat Streuli	m	e
53	Tracey Moffatt	m	
	Elizabeth Peyton	m	
	Wolfgang Tillmans	m	
52	Karen Kilimnik	m	e
	Malcolm Morley	m	e
	Ugo Rondinone	m	e
50/51	John Armleder	m	
	Jeff Koons	m	e
	Jean-Luc Mylayne	m	
	Thomas Struth	m	
	Sue Williams	m	
49	Laurie Anderson	m	e
	Douglas Gordon	m	
	Jeff Wall	m	
48	Gary Hume	m	
	Gabriel Orozco	m	
	Pipilotti Rist	m	
47	Tony Oursler	m	
	Raymond Pettibon	m	
	Thomas Schütte	m	e
46	Richard Artschwager	m	
	Cady Noland	m	
	Hiroshi Sugimoto	m	
45	Matthew Barney		
	Sarah Lucas	m	
	Roman Signer	m	e
44	Vija Celmins	m	
	Andreas Gursky	m	
	Rirkrit Tiravanija	m	e
43	Juan Muñoz	m	e
	Susan Rothenberg	m	e
42	Lawrence Weiner	m	e
	Rachel Whiteread	m	
40/41	Francesco Clemente	m	
	Fischli/Weiss	m	
	Günther Förg	m	
	Damien Hirst	m	
	Jenny Holzer	m	
	Rebecca Horn	m	
	Sigmar Polke	m	
39	Felix Gonzalez-Torres	m	
	Wolfgang Laib	m	e
38	Ross Bleckner		
	Marlene Dumas		
37	Charles Ray	m	
	Franz West	m	e
36	Stephan Balkenhol		
	Sophie Calle		
35	Gerhard Richter		
34	Ilya Kabakov	m	
	Richard Prince	m	e
33	Rosemarie Trockel	m	
	Christopher Wool	m	
32	Imi Knoebel	m	
	Sherrie Levine	m	
31	David Hammons		
	Mike Kelley		
30	Sigmar Polke		
29	John Baldessari		
29	Cindy Sherman		
28	Franz Gertsch	m	e
	Thomas Ruff	m	
27	Louise Bourgeois		
	Robert Gober		
26	Günther Förg		
	Philip Taaffe		
25	Katharina Fritsch	m	e
	James Turrell	m	e
24	Alighiero e Boetti	m	e
23	Richard Artschwager	m	
22	Christian Boltanski		
	Jeff Wall		
21	Alex Katz	m	e
20	Tim Rollins + K.O.S.	m	
19	Martin Kippenberger		
	Jeff Koons		
18	Ed Ruscha	m	
17	Fischli/Weiss		
16	Robert Wilson		
15	Mario Merz	m	
14	Gilbert & George	m	
13	Rebecca Horn		
12	Andy Warhol		
11	Georg Baselitz	m	
10	Bruce Nauman		
9	Francesco Clemente		
8	Markus Raetz		
7	Brice Marden		
6	Jannis Kounellis		
5	Eric Fischl		
4	Meret Oppenheim		
3	Martin Disler		
2	Sigmar Polke		
1	Enzo Cucchi		

m = available monograph / erhältliche Monographie, e = available edition / erhältliche Edition
Delivery subject to availability at time of order / Lieferung solange Vorrat

ARTISTS' EDITIONS FOR PARKETT SUBSCRIBERS
WWW.PARKETTART.COM

The PARKETT Series is created in collaboration with artists, who contribute an original work available exclusively to the subscribers in the form of a signed limited SPECIAL EDITION. The available works are also reproduced in each PARKETT issue.

Each SPECIAL EDITION is available by order from any one of our offices in New York or Zurich. Just fill in the details below and send this card to the office nearest you. Once your order has been processed, you will be issued with an invoice and your personal edition number. Upon receipt of payment, you will receive the SPECIAL EDITION. (Please note that supply is subject to availability. PARKETT does not assume responsibility for any delays in production of SPECIAL EDITIONS. Postage is not included.)

☐ As a subscriber to PARKETT, I would like to order the following Special Edition(s), signed and numbered by the artist.

PARKETT No.	ARTIST	NAME:
PARKETT No.	ARTIST	ADDRESS:
PARKETT No.	ARTIST	CITY:
PARKETT No.	ARTIST	STATE/ZIP:
PARKETT No.	ARTIST	COUNTRY:
PARKETT No.	ARTIST	PHONE:

☐ I have indicated my way of payment on the reverse side of this form.

Send this form to the PARKETT office nearest you:

PARKETT PUBLISHERS 155 AV. OF THE AMERICAS NEW YORK, NY 10013 PHONE (212) 673-2660 FAX (212) 271-0704
PARKETT VERLAG QUELLENSTRASSE 27 CH-8031 ZÜRICH TELEFON +41-1-271 81 40 FAX +41-1-272 43 01
PARKETT VERLAG TANNENWALDALLEE 17 D-61348 BAD HOMBURG FAX 06172-937 444 www.parkettart.com

KÜNSTLEREDITIONEN FÜR PARKETT-ABONNENTEN
WWW.PARKETTART.COM

Die PARKETT-Buchreihe entsteht in Zusammenarbeit mit Künstlern, die eigens für die Abonnenten einen Originalbeitrag in Form einer limitierten und signierten EDITION gestalten. Diese Editionen sind auch in der Zeitschrift abgebildet und können mit dieser Bestellkarte in jedem unserer Büros in Zürich, Frankfurt oder New York bestellt werden. Sie erhalten dann Ihre persönliche Editionsnummer und eine Rechnung. Sobald wir Ihre Zahlung erhalten haben, schicken wir Ihnen Ihre Edition(en). (Lieferung nur solange vorrätig. PARKETT übernimmt keine Verantwortung für allfällige Verzögerungen bei der Herstellung der Vorzugsausgaben. Versandkosten zuzüglich.)

☐ Ich bin PARKETT-Abonnent(in) und bestelle folgende EDITION(EN), nummeriert und vom Künstler signiert:

PARKETT Nr.	KÜNSTLER/IN	NAME:
PARKETT Nr.	KÜNSTLER/IN	STRASSE:
PARKETT Nr.	KÜNSTLER/IN	PLZ/STADT:
PARKETT Nr.	KÜNSTLER/IN	LAND:
PARKETT Nr.	KÜNSTLER/IN	TEL.:

☐ Meine Zahlungsweise habe ich auf der Rückseite angegeben.

Senden Sie die Bestellkarte an das PARKETT-Büro in Ihrer Nähe:

PARKETT VERLAG QUELLENSTRASSE 27 CH-8031 ZÜRICH TELEFON +41-1-271 81 40 FAX +41-1-272 43 01
PARKETT VERLAG TANNENWALDALLEE 17 D-61348 BAD HOMBURG FAX 06172-937 444 www.parkettart.com
PARKETT PUBLISHERS 155 AV. OF THE AMERICAS NEW YORK, NY 10013 PHONE (212) 673-2660 FAX (212) 271-0704

PARKETT

SUBSCRIBE, COMPLETE OR SEND A GIFT SUBSCRIPTION TO THE BEST BOOK SERIES ON CONTEMPORARY ARTISTS – WWW.PARKETTART.COM

62

☐ I wish to subscribe to the PARKETT Series, starting with issue no. ______

☐ I wish to send a gift subscription, starting with issue no. ______ (a gift card in my name will be sent to the recipient):

- ☐ for 1 year (3 issues) at US $ 80 (USA/Canada), € 82 (Europe), € 98 (Rest of the World)
- ☐ for 2 years (6 issues) at US $ 145 (USA/Canada), € 150 (Europe), € 188 (Rest of the World)
- ☐ for 3 years (9 issues) at US $ 205 (USA/Canada), € 212 (Europe), € 278 (Rest of the World)
- ☐ for 1 year (3 issues) at the special student discount (US $ 65 for USA/Canada, € 67 for Europe). A copy of my student ID is enclosed.
  Postage included. All prices subject to change.

☐ I wish to complete my PARKETT library and order the following issue(s):

No. ______

at € 30 each (up to no. 43: € 20; no. 44–48: € 28), postage not included. Within the USA & Canada $ 32 (up to no. 43: $ 22.50; no. 44–48: $ 29), add postage: $ 5 (USA), $ 10 (Canada). (Sold out: No. 1–10, 12, 13, 16, 17, 19, 22, 26, 27, 29–31, 35, 36, 38).

☐ I wish to order ________ copies of the new catalogue raisonné of all PARKETT Artists' Editions since 1984 (346 pages, 140 in color, published on the occasion of the PARKETT exhibition at MoMA, New York) for € 22 (USA: $ 20) excl. postage.

☐ I wish to order ________ copies of the new set of 120 postcards featuring PARKETT Artists' Editions for € 27 (USA: $ 25) per set, excl. postage.

NAME:

ADDRESS:

CITY:

STATE/ZIP/COUNTRY:

TEL.: FAX:

E-MAIL:

GIFT RECIPIENT:

ADDRESS:

CITY:

STATE/ZIP:

COUNTRY:

☐ Charge my Visa Card ☐ Mastercard ☐ AMEX

Card No. ______ Expiration date ______

☐ Payment enclosed (US check or money order) ☐ Bill me

DATE

SIGNATURE

end this
orm to the
ARKETT office
earest you:

PARKETT PUBLISHERS 155 AV. OF THE AMERICAS NEW YORK, NY 10013 PHONE (212) 673-2660 FAX (212) 271-0704

PARKETT VERLAG QUELLENSTRASSE 27 CH-8031 ZÜRICH TELEFON +41-1-271 81 40 FAX +41-1-272 43 01

PARKETT VERLAG TANNENWALDALLEE 17 D-61348 BAD HOMBURG FAX 06172-937 444 www.parkettart.com

PARKETT

ABONNIEREN, VERVOLLSTÄNDIGEN ODER VERSCHENKEN SIE DIE UMFASSENDSTE BUCHREIHE ÜBER GEGENWARTSKÜNSTLER – WWW.PARKETTART.COM

62

☐ Ich abonniere die PARKETT-Reihe ab Nr. ______

☐ Ich verschenke ein PARKETT-Abonnement ab Nr. ______ (Der/die Beschenkte erhält eine Geschenkkarte in meinem Namen)

- ☐ für 1 Jahr (3 Bände) zu: € 78 (Deutschland), CHF 116.– (Schweiz), € 82 (übriges Europa)
- ☐ für 2 Jahre (6 Bände) zu: € 140 (Deutschland), CHF 216.– (Schweiz), € 150 (übriges Europa)
- ☐ für 3 Jahre (9 Bände) zu: € 200 (Deutschland), CHF 312.– (Schweiz), € 212 (übriges Europa)
- ☐ für 1 Jahr (3 Bände) zum Studenten-Sonderpreis (Deutschland: € 65 /Schweiz: CHF 96.– / übriges Europa: € 67). Eine Kopie meines gültigen Studentenausweises lege ich bei.
  Preise einschliesslich Versandkosten. Preisänderungen vorbehalten.

☐ Ich möchte meine PARKETT-Bibliothek vervollständigen und bestelle die folgenden noch erhältliche(n) Ausgabe(n):

Nr. ______

zu je € 30 / CHF 45.– (bis Nr. 43: € 20 / CHF 30.–; Nr. 44–48: € 28 / CHF 39.–, zzgl. Versandkosten (vergriffen: Nr. 1–10, 12, 13, 16, 17, 19, 22, 26, 27, 29–31, 35, 36, 38).

☐ Ich bestelle ______ Ex. des neuen Werkverzeichnisses der PARKETT-Künstlereditionen seit 1984 (346 S., 140 farbig, erschienen zur PARKETT-Ausstellung im MoMA, New York) für € 22 / CHF 32.– pro Ex. zzgl. Versandkosten.

☐ Ich bestelle ______ Ex. des neuen Postkarten-Sets mit 120 PARKETT-Künstlereditionen zum Preis von € 27 / CHF 39.– pro Set, zzgl. Versandkosten.

NAME:

STRASSE:

PLZ/STADT:

LAND:

TEL.: FAX:

E-MAIL:

BESCHENKTE(R):

STRASSE:

PLZ/STADT:

LAND:

☐ Ich zahle mit Visa ☐ Eurocard/Mastercard ☐ AMEX

Karten Nr. ______ Gültig bis ______

☐ Mein Scheck über CHF/€ ______ liegt bei.

☐ Bitte senden Sie mir eine Rechnung.

DATUM

UNTERSCHRIFT

enden Sie die
estellkarte an
as PARKETT-Büro
ı Ihrer Nähe:

PARKETT VERLAG QUELLENSTRASSE 27 CH-8031 ZÜRICH TELEFON +41-1-271 81 40 FAX +41-1-272 43 01

PARKETT VERLAG TANNENWALDALLEE 17 D-61348 BAD HOMBURG FAX 06172-937 444 www.parkettart.com

PARKETT PUBLISHERS 155 AV. OF THE AMERICAS NEW YORK, NY 10013 PHONE (212) 673-2660 FAX (212) 271-0704

Each volume of PARKETT is created in collaboration with artists, who contribute an original work specially made for the readers of PARKETT. The works are available in a signed and numbered Special Edition. Prices are subject to change. Postage is not included.

EDITIONS FOR PARKETT

Jeder PARKETT-Band entsteht in Collaboration mit Künstlern, die eigens für die Leser von PARKETT Originalbeiträge gestalten. Diese Vorzugsausgaben sind als nummerierte und signierte Editionen erhältlich. Preisänderungen vorbehalten. Versandkosten und MwSt. (Schweiz) nicht inbegriffen.

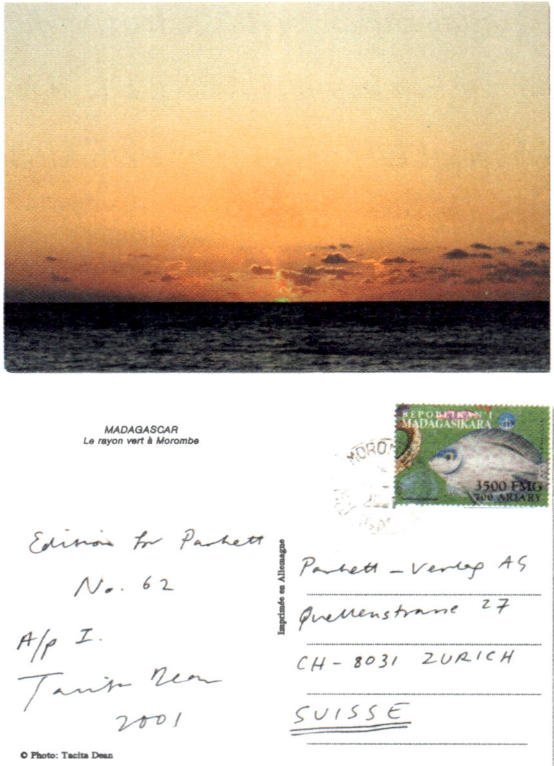

The enchantment of the green ray has captured the imagination of Jules Verne, Marcel Duchamp, and now Tacita Dean.

Das grüne Leuchten am Horizont verzauberte Jules Verne, Marcel Duchamp und auch Tacita Dean.

PARKETT 62

TACITA DEAN

THE GREEN RAY, 2001

Color postcard, 105 x 148,5 mm.
Printed by Steidl Verlag, Göttingen, Germany.
Edition of 100, signed, numbered, stamped, and posted in Morombe, Western Madagascar, **$ 350 / € 390**

Farbpostkarte, 105 x 148,5 mm.
Gedruckt bei Steidl Verlag, Göttingen.
Auflage: 100, signiert, nummeriert, mit Poststempel aufgegeben in Morombe, West-Madagaskar, **CHF 580.–**

Hairline, coastline: a mental and physical topography.

Jordan, Styx oder harmloser Weekendplausch am See?

PARKETT 62

JOHN WESLEY

BOYFRIENDS, 2001

6-color silkscreen on Coventry 290 gm^2;
paper size 31 x 38", image 28 x 35".
Printed by Bob Blanton, Brand X Editions, New York.
Edition of 70, signed and numbered, **$ 920 / € 990**

Siebdruck (6 Farben) auf Coventry 290 gm^2
Papierformat 87,7 x 96,5 cm; Bild 71 x 89 cm.
Gedruckt durch Bob Blanton, Brand X Editions, New York.
Auflage: 70, signiert und nummeriert, **CHF 1500.–**

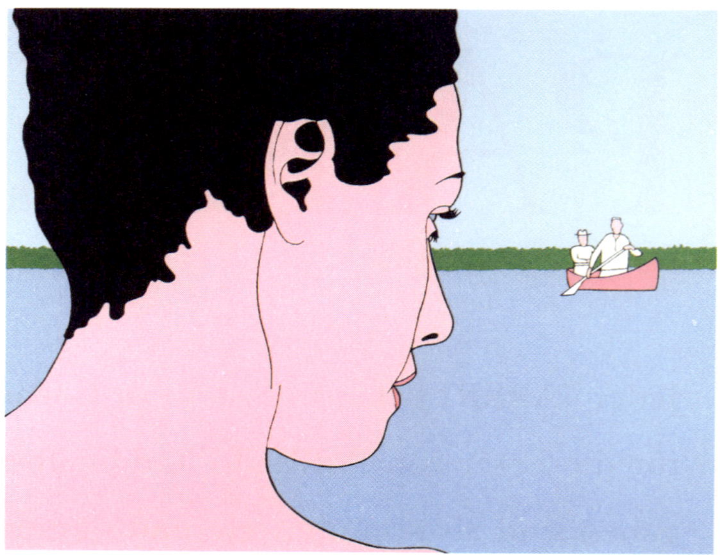

Sag mir, wo die Menschen sind,
wo sind sie geblieben?

Where have all the travelers gone?
Long time passing.

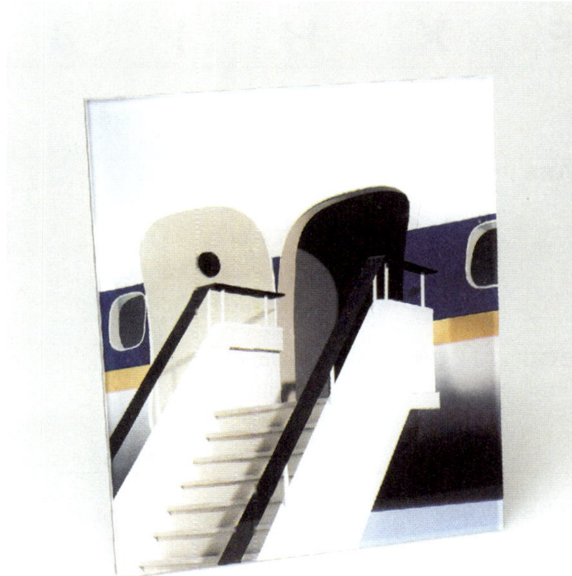

PARKETT 62

THOMAS DEMAND

GANGWAY, 2001

Lamda print, Diasec on black acrylic glass with attachable chromium-plate stand, $8^{1}/_{4}$ x 10 x $^{1}/_{5}$".
Edition of 75, signed and numbered, **$ 880 / € 950**

Lambda-Print, Diasec auf schwarzem Acrylglas mit einschraubbarem verchromtem Standfuss, 21,0 x 25,5 x 0,5 cm.
Auflage: 75, signiert und nummeriert, **CHF 1400.–**

E X H I B I T I O N S

ZÜRICH

ARS FUTURA	Bleicherweg 45 8002 Zürich Tel. 01 201 88 10 www.arsfutura.ch arsfutura@bluewin.ch	ALEXANDRA VOGT – "dreams are my reality"	**31.8.–6.10.2001**
		ERWIN WURM – "one minute sculptures"	**12.10.–17.11.2001**
BOB VAN ORSOUW	Limmatstrasse 270 8005 Zürich Tel. 01 273 11 00 bobvanorsouw@access.ch	FIONA RAE – New Paintings	**25.8.–29.9.2001**
		TERESA HUBBARD AND ALEXANDER BIRCHLER – Videoinstallation	**6.10.–17.11.2001**
		KARIN KNEFFEL – New Works	**24.11.01–29.9.2002**
BOB GYSIN	Ausstellungsstrasse 24 8005 Zürich Tel. 01 278 40 60 www.bg-galerie.ch info@bg-galerie.ch	MATTHIAS BOSSHART	**23.8.–13.10.2001**
		FAIRY TALES – Internat. Gruppenausstellung	**26.10.–8.12.2001**
		ART COLOGNE	**31.10.–4.11.2001**
GALERIE LELONG	Utoquai 31 8006 Zürich Tel. 01 251 11 20 galerie.lelong@dplanet.ch	DAVID NASH – Sculptures	**15.9.–3.11.2001**
MAI 36 GALERIE	Rämistrasse 37 8001 Zürich Tel. 01 261 68 80 www.artgalleries/mai36 mai36@artgalleries.ch	HARALD F. MÜLLER	**24.8.–6.10.2001**
		AMERIKANISCHE FOTOGRAFIE CA. 1970 Robert Adams – Walker Evans – William Egglestone Robert Frank – Joel Meyerowitz – Steven Shore Joel Sternfeld	**24.8.–6.10.2001**
		Art Forum Berlin	**2.10.–7.10.2001**
MARK MÜLLER	Gessnerallee 36 8001 Zürich Tel. 01 211 81 55 www.markmueller.ch mark.muller@dplanet.ch	KARIM NOURELDIN – Unknown Zone	
		im Guestroom: AGATHA ZOBRIST, THERESE WAECKERLIN	**23.8.–13.10.2001**
		ART FORUM BERLIN – KünstlerInnen der Galerie	**3.10.–7.10.2001**
		STEFAN GRITSCH – Weniger und mehr INGO MELLER – Sinn und Verstand	**20.10.–15.12.2001**
		ART COLOGNE – KünstlerInnen der Galerie	**31.10.–4.11.2001**
SEMINA RERUM IRÈNE PREISWERK	Cäcilienstrasse 3 8032 Zürich Tel. 01 251 26 39 ipreiswerk@bluewin.ch	UTE LANGANKY	**bis 6. Oktober 2001**
		CHRISTIAN DENZLER	**12.10.–24.11.2001**
		ANNELIES ŠTRBA	**30.11.01– Januar 2002**

E X H I B I T I O N S

GALERIE SCHEDLER	Josefstrasse 53	CHRISTOPH HÄNSLI – Malerei	**bis 29. September 2001**
	8005 Zürich	ALLEN FRAME, DETOUR	
	Tel. 01 440 61 20	(Photography 1990–2000)	**5.10.–3.11.2001**
	www.schedler.ch	PHILIPP SPÄTI – Malerei	**9.11.–9.12.2001**
	zurich@schedler.ch	MAX GRÜTER	**14.12.01–19.1.2002**
ANNEMARIE VERNA	Neptunstrasse 45	ROBERT MANGOLD – Recent Works	**2.10.–17.11.2001**
	8032 Zürich	ANDREAS CHRISTEN	**20.11.01–19.1.2002**
	Tel. 01 262 38 20		
	office@annemarie-verna.ch		
JAMILEH WEBER	Waldmannstrasse 6	REBECCA HORN	**22.9.–10.11.2001**
	8001 Zürich	BASELITZ, HORN, JAHANGUIR, JUDD, LICHTSTEINER	
	Tel. 01 252 10 66	MANGOLD, MARDEN, POTTORF, RAUSCHENBERG	
	www.jamilehweber.com	SCULLY, SERRA – Selected works	**Nov.–Dez. 2001**
	jamilehweber@access.ch		
BRIGITTE WEISS	Müllerstrasse 67	GRAEME TODD	**22.8.–20.10.2001**
	8004 Zürich	ART FORUM BERLIN, Halle/Stand 21a/4a	**3.10.–7.10.2001**
	Tel. 01 241 83 35	CHRISTIAN VETTER	
	brigitteweiss@bluewin.ch	ANDRO WEKUA	**Nov.–Dez. 2001**
	www.likeyou.com/brigitteweiss		
		BASEL	
NICOLAS KRUPP	Erlenstr. 15	"LADIES TALK" – Sonja Feldmeier, Franziska Furter	
	4058 Basel	Marica Gojević, Rachel Mahler, Edit Oberbolz	**9.8.–15.9.2001**
	Tel. 061 683 32 65	ALBRECHT FUCHS – Kippenberger-Portraits	
	www.nicolaskrupp.com	MARKUS SCHWANDER	**20.9.–3.11.2001**
	nic@nicolaskrupp.com	ALEXIA WALTHER	**8.11.01–5.1.2002**
		GENÈVE	
DANIEL VARENNE	8, rue Toepffer	PAINTINGS AND DRAWINGS	
	1206 Genève	19TH AND 20TH CENTURY	
	Tel. 022 789 16 75		
		ST. GALLEN	
WILMA LOCK	Schmiedgasse 15	BERNARD FRIZE – Nouvelles Peintures	**1.9.–11.11.2001**
	9001 St. Gallen	JÜRGEN PARTENHEIMER	**17.11.01–19.1.2002**
	Tel. 071 222 62 52	GESCHLOSSEN	**24.12.01–5.1.2002**
		LUISA LAMBRI – Photos	**2.2.–6.4.2002**
		ZUG	
KUNSTHAUS ZUG	Dorfstrasse 27	Projekt Sammlung (4) – ILYA KABAKOV,	
	6300 Zug	BORIS GROYS, PAVEL PEPPERSTEIN –	
	Tel. 041 725 33 44	Die Ausstellung eines Gesprächs	**2.9.–4.11.2001**
	www.museenzug.ch	EGON SCHIELE – der Zeichner und die Wiener Moderne	
	info@kunsthauszug.ch	(KLIMT, GERSTL, HOFFMANN, KOKOSCHKA u.a.)	
		Werke der Albertina, Wien	
		und eigene Bestände	**18.11.01.–17.2.2002**

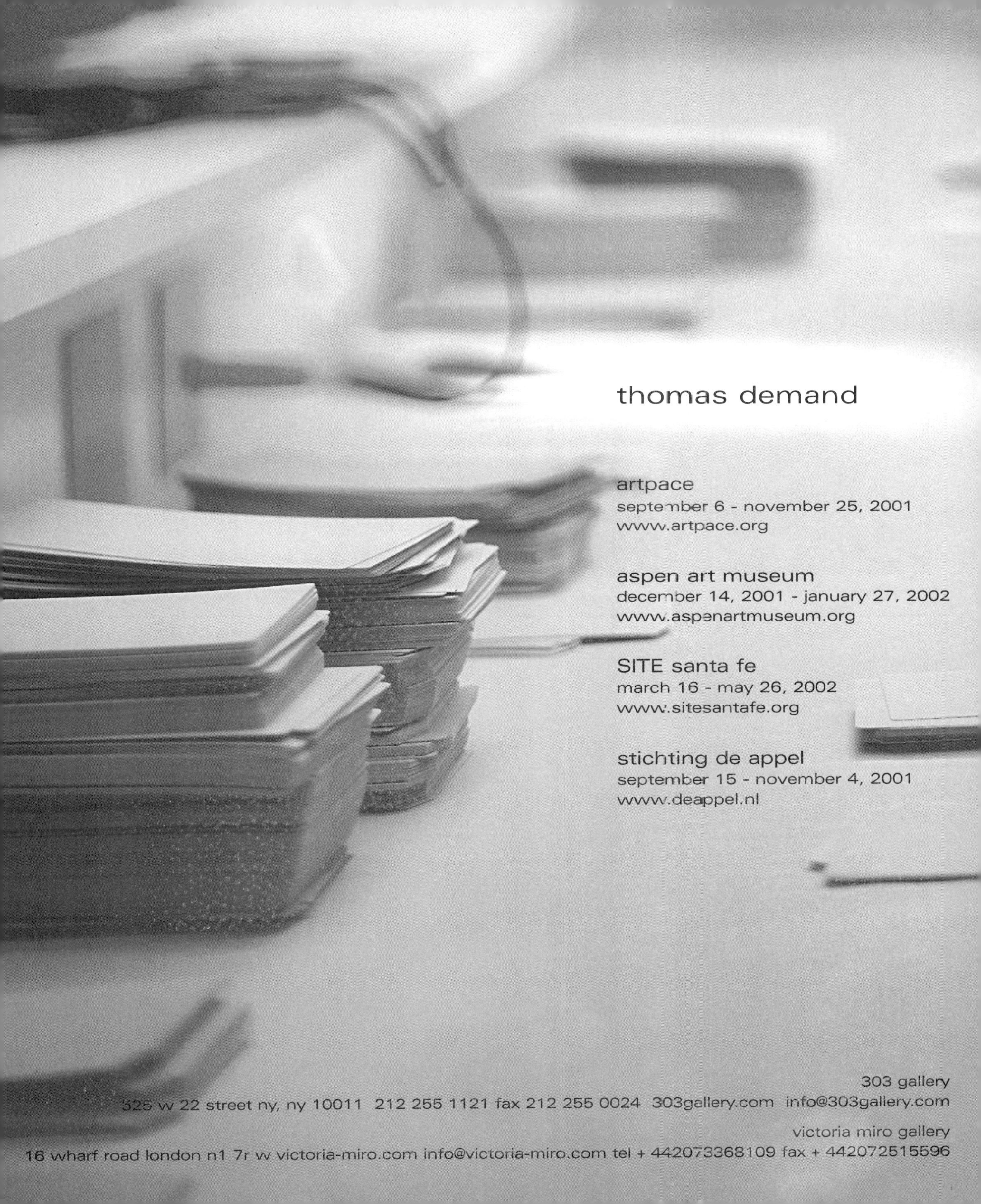
thomas demand
artpace
september 6 - november 25, 2001
www.artpace.org
aspen art museum
december 14, 2001 - january 27, 2002
www.aspenartmuseum.org
SITE santa fe
march 16 - may 26, 2002
www.sitesantafe.org
stichting de appel
september 15 - november 4, 2001
www.deappel.nl
303 gallery
525 w 22 street ny, ny 10011 212 255 1121 fax 212 255 0024 303gallery.com info@303gallery.com
victoria miro gallery
16 wharf road london n1 7r w victoria-miro.com info@victoria-miro.com tel + 442073368109 fax + 442072515596

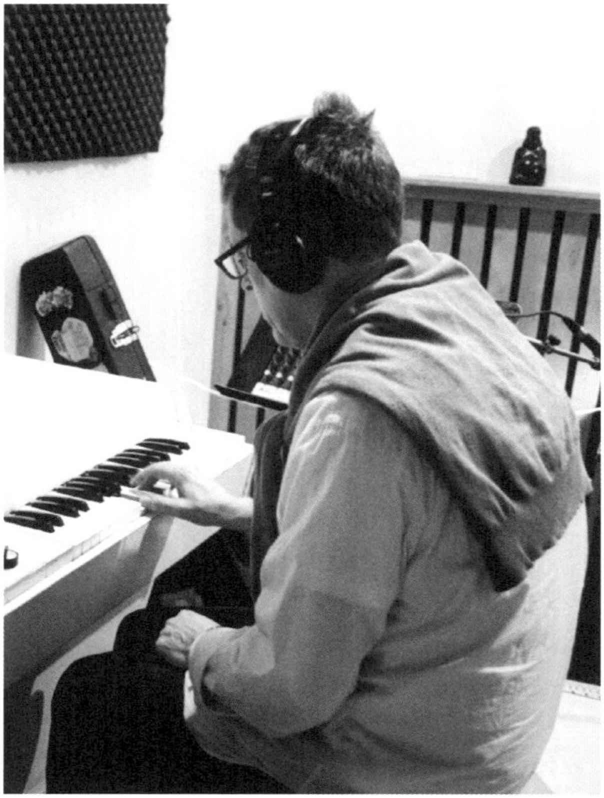

rodney graham

the phonokinetoscope
september 15- october 27, 2001

303 gallery
525 w 22 street
new york, ny 10011
tel 212 255 1121
fax 212 255 0024
www.303gallery.com
info@303gallery.com

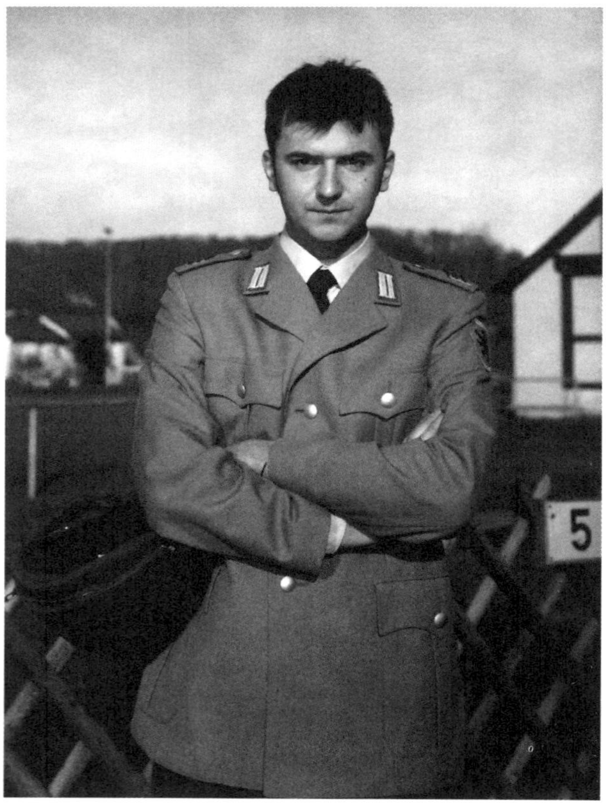

collier schorr

november 3 - december 22, 2001

303 gallery
525 w 22 street
new york, ny 10011
tel 212 255 1121
fax 212 255 0024
www.303gallery.com
info@303gallery.com

25. AUGUST BIS 13. OKTOBER 2001

PAUL MCCARTHY

15. SEPTEMBER BIS 13. OKTOBER 2001

GUILLERMO KUITCA

27. OKTOBER BIS 22. DEZEMBER 2001

MARY HEILMANN

27. OKTOBER BIS 22. DEZEMBER 2001

DAN GRAHAM

LOUISE BOURGEOIS - PAUL MCCARTHY - JOHN MCCRACKEN - DAN GRAHAM - MARY HEILMANN
THE ESTATE OF EVA HESSE - RICHARD JACKSON - ON KAWARA - RACHEL KHEDOORI - RAYMOND PETTIBON
JASON RHOADES - PIPILOTTI RIST - ROMAN SIGNER - DIANA THATER

GALERIE HAUSER & WIRTH
Limmatstrasse 270, 8005 Zürich / Tel: +41 1 446 80 50, Fax: +41 1 446 80 55 / www.ghw.ch / Öffnungszeiten: Di-Fr 12-18, Sa 11-16 Uhr

25. AUGUST BIS 17. OKTOBER 2001

URS FISCHER

27. OKTOBER BIS 22. DEZEMBER 2001

CANDIDA HÖFER

DOUG AITKEN - EMMANUELLE ANTILLE - ANGELA BULLOCH - MARIA EICHHORN - URS FISCHER - PETER FISCHLI / DAVID WEISS
SYLVIE FLEURY - URS FREI - LIAM GILLICK - DOUGLAS GORDON - CANDIDA HÖFER - RONI HORN - KAREN KILIMNIK
GERWALD ROCKENSCHAUB - UGO RONDINONE - DIETER ROTH - JEAN-FRÉDÉRIC SCHNYDER - BEAT STREULI - FRANZ WEST - SUE WILLIAMS

GALERIE HAUSER & WIRTH & PRESENHUBER
Limmatstrasse 270, 8005 Zürich / Tel: +41 1 446 80 60, Fax: +41 1 446 80 65 / www.ghwp.ch / Öffnungszeiten: Di-Fr 12-18, Sa 11-16 Uhr

BERNIER/ELIADES
11, EPTACHALKOU, GR-118 51 ATHENS, GREECE
TEL.: +30 01 0341 39 35-7 FAX: +30 01 0341 39 38
E-Mail: bernier_eliades@attglobal.net

GILBERT & GEORGE

NINE DARK PICTURES
2001

OCTOBER 6–NOVEMBER 25, 2001

THE ART OF GILBERT & GEORGE

ATHINA 2001

FREE ART EXHIBITION

ATHENS SCHOOL OF FINE ARTS
«THE FACTORY»
PIREOS 256, RENTIS

OCTOBER 5 – NOVEMBER 25, 2001

OPENING HOURS: TUE-FRI 12-8 PM SAT-SUN 12-4 PM

FRANK GERRITZ

SEPTEMBER · NOVEMBER

CLAY KETTER

DECEMBER · FEBRUARY

vera munro

GALERIE VERA MUNRO

HEILWIGSTRASSE 64

20249 HAMBURG

TELEFON 040 - 47 47 46

TELEFAX 040 - 47 25 50

GALLERY@VERAMUNRO.DE

WWW.VERAMUNRO.DE

William Eggleston

Recent Photographs

13 SEPTEMBER – 3 NOVEMBER 2001

FIAC Paris

10 – 15 OCTOBER 2001

Roni Horn

8 NOVEMBER 2001 – 5 JANUARY 2002

Xavier Hufkens

Sint-Jorisstraat 6–8 rue Saint-Georges

Brussel 1050 Bruxelles

TEL. +32 (0)2 639 67 30 – FAX +32 (0)2 639 67 38

info@xavierhufkens.com
http://www.xavierhufkens.com

Open Tuesday to Saturday, noon to 6 pm

GALERIE LELONG ZÜRICH

Utoquai 31 • 8008 Zürich • Telefon 01/251 11 20 • Fax 01/262 52 85

DAVID NASH • SCULPTURES • 15 September – 3 November, 2001

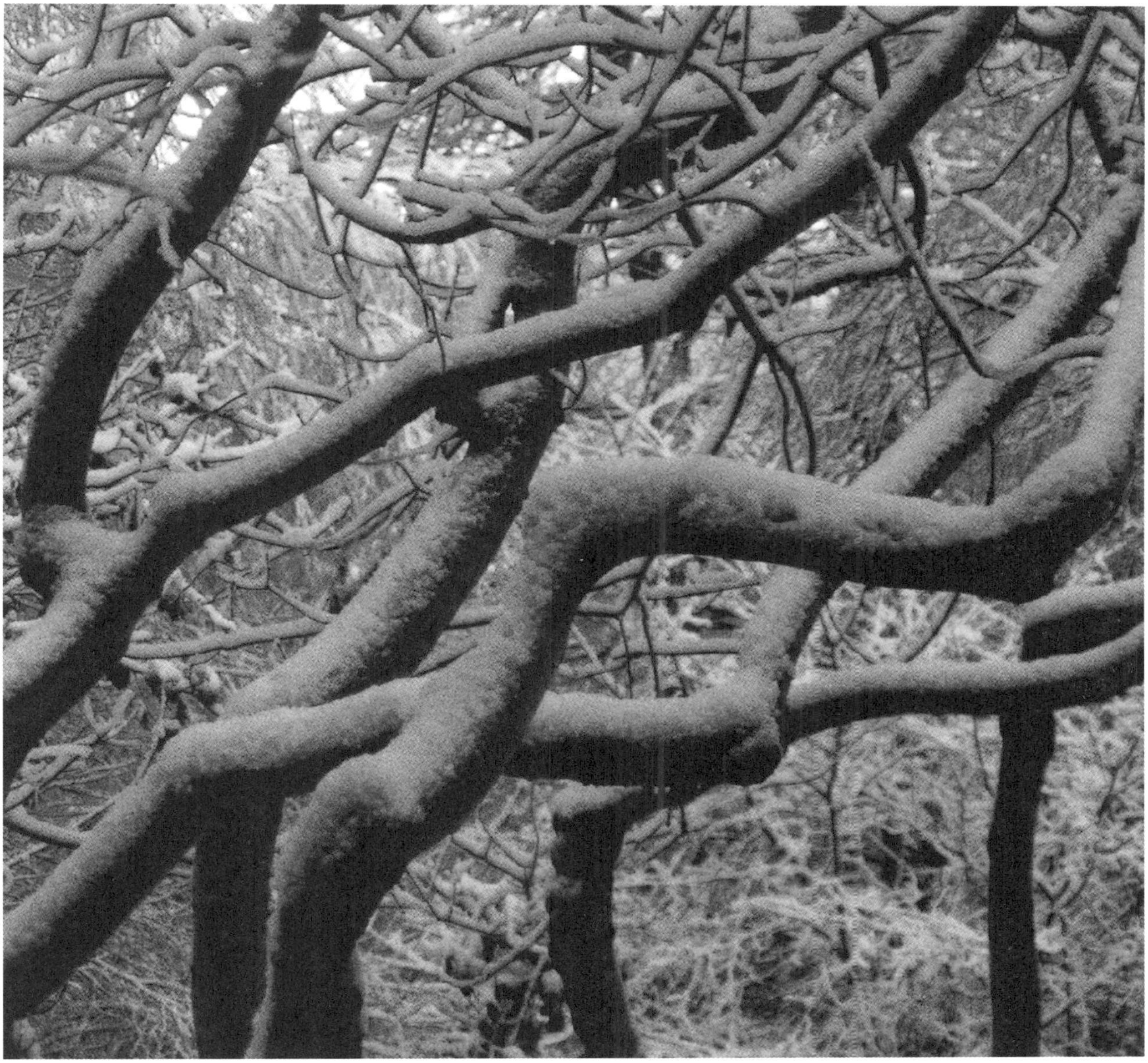

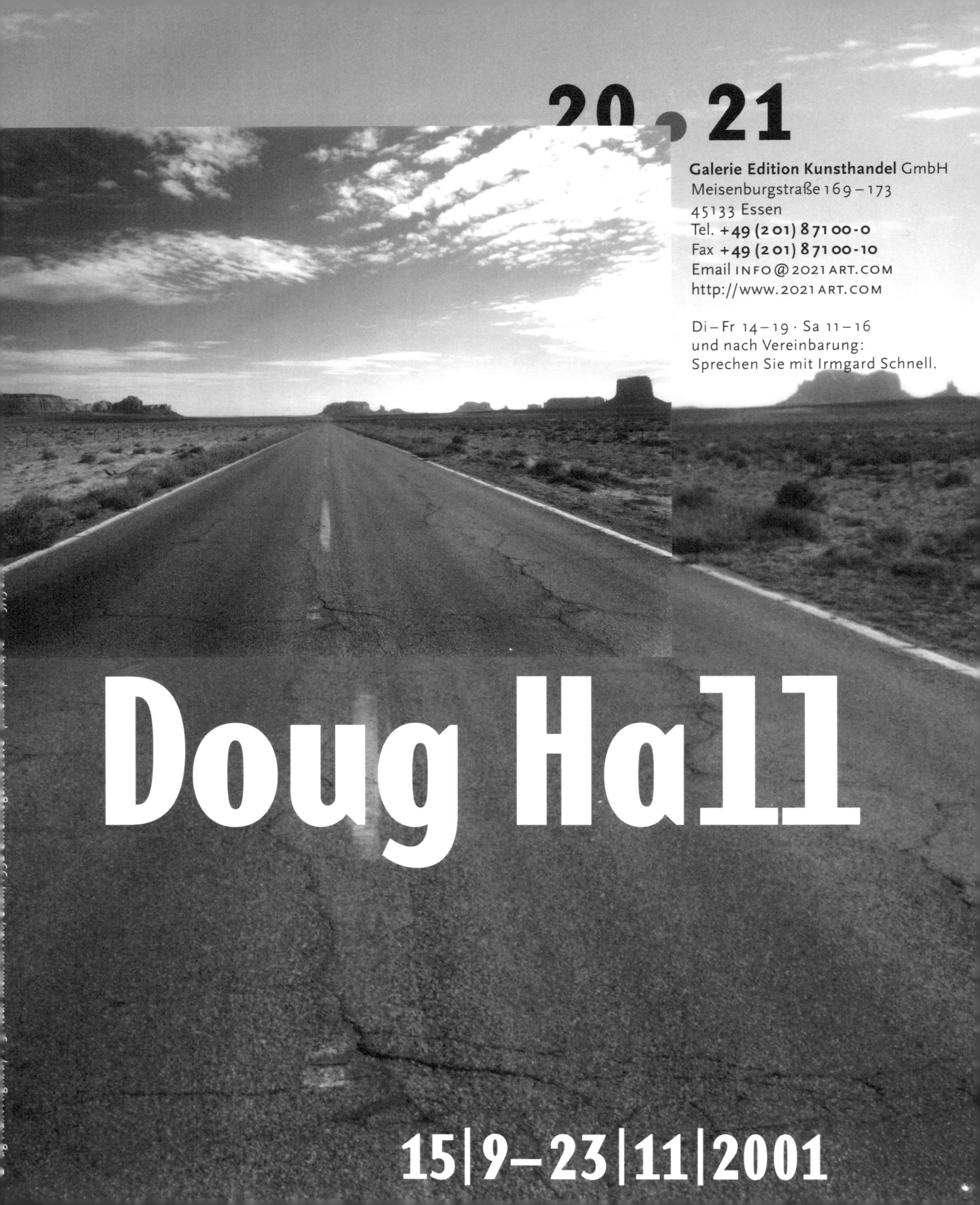
20 21
Galerie Edition Kunsthandel GmbH
Meisenburgstraße 169 – 173
45133 Essen
Tel. +49 (201) 87100-0
Fax +49 (201) 87100-10
Email INFO@2021ART.COM
http://www.2021ART.COM
Di – Fr 14 – 19 · Sa 11 – 16
und nach Vereinbarung:
Sprechen Sie mit Irmgard Schnell.
Doug Hall
15|9–23|11|2001

GALERIE MEERT RIHOUX

CARLA ACCARDI
ROBERT ADAMS
JOHN BALDESSARI
ROBERT BARRY
ENRICO CASTELLANI
HANNE DARBOVEN
MARIA ANNA DEWES
PAUL DRISSEN
SYLVIE EYBERG
ISA GENZKEN
JEF GEYS
MIMMO JODICE
PETER JOSEPH
DONALD JUDD
BRANDT JUNCEAU
LOUISE LAWLER
SOL LEWITT
KEN LUM
ROBERT MANGOLD
EVA MARISALDI > OCT. - NOV.
LILIANA MORO
FRED SANDBACK
THOMAS STRUTH > NOV.- DEC.
GRAZIA TODERI
RICHARD TUTTLE
MICHAEL VENEZIA
IAN WALLACE
JEFF WALL

RUE DU CANAL 13
1000 BRUXELLES
VAARTSTRAAT 13
1000 BRUSSEL
TEL 32(0)2 219 14 22
FAX 32(0)2 219 37 21
GRETA.MEERT@SKYNET.BE

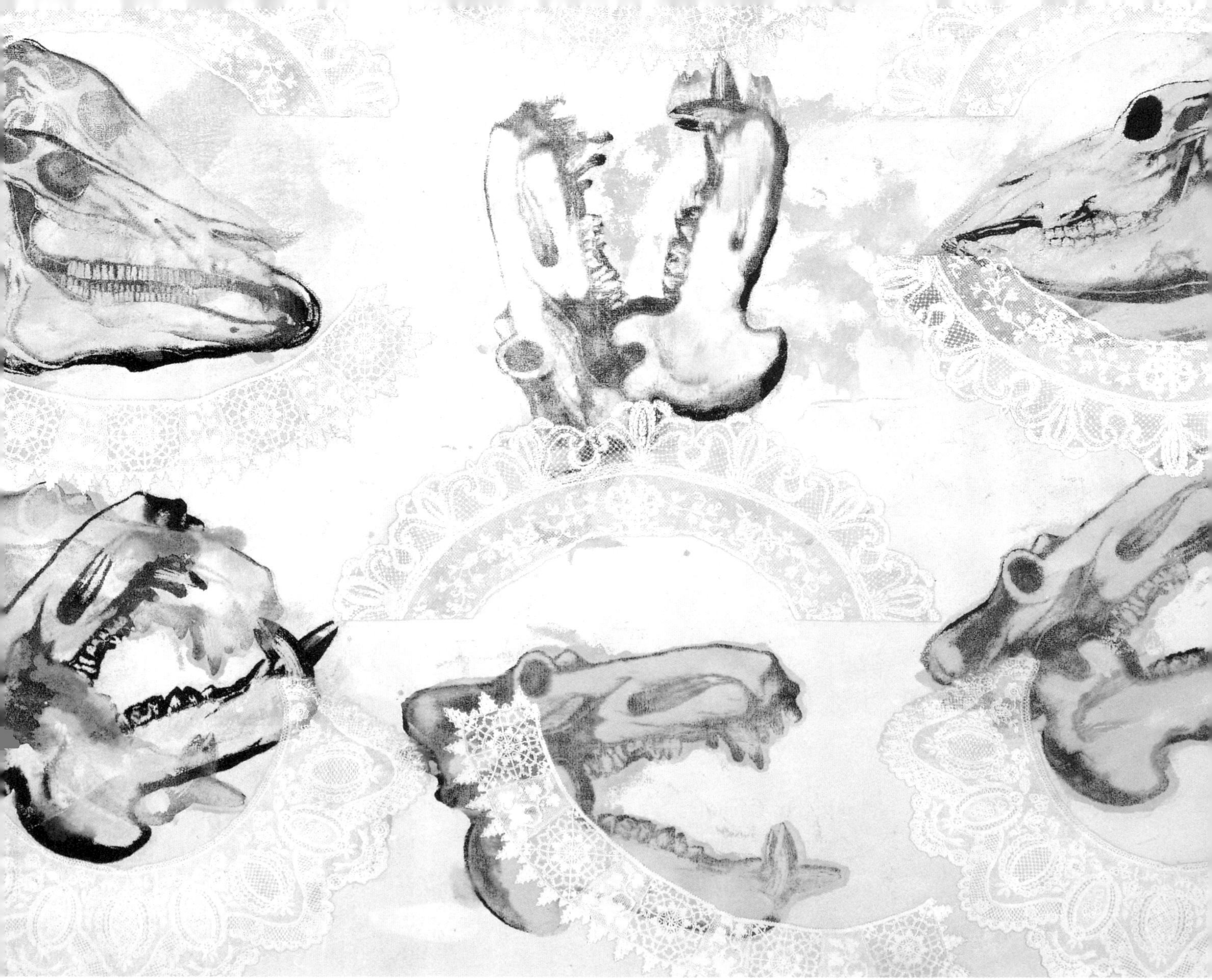

PHILIP TAAFFE

NOVEMBER / DECEMBER 2001

GALERIE THADDAEUS ROPAC

7 RUE DEBELLEYME 75003 PARIS TEL 33 1 42 72 99 00 FAX 33 1 42 72 61 66 www.ropac.net

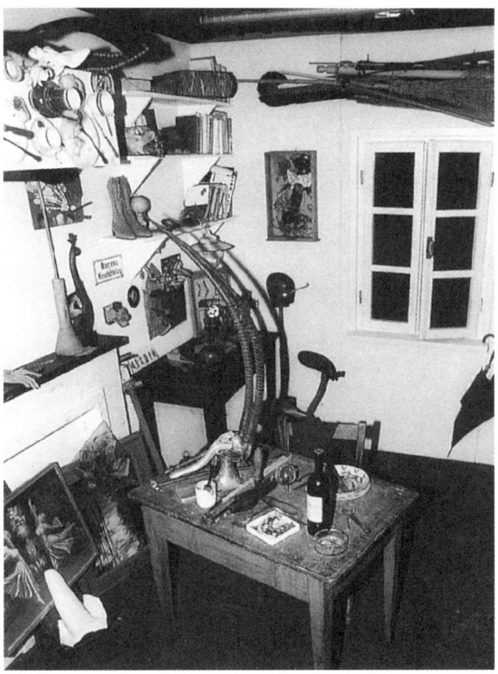

OCTOBER - NOVEMBER 2001

GRAHAM GILLMORE

GALLERIA CARDI

PIAZZA S. ERASMO, 3 I- 20121 MILANO TEL. +39 02 29003235 FAX +39 02 29003382

GALLERIA.CARDI@ALL.IT

TOM SACHS

GALLERIA CARDI & CO.

CORSO DI PORTA NUOVA, 38 I-20121 MILANO TEL +39 02 62690945 FAX +39 02 62694016

WWW.GALLEERIACARDI.COM

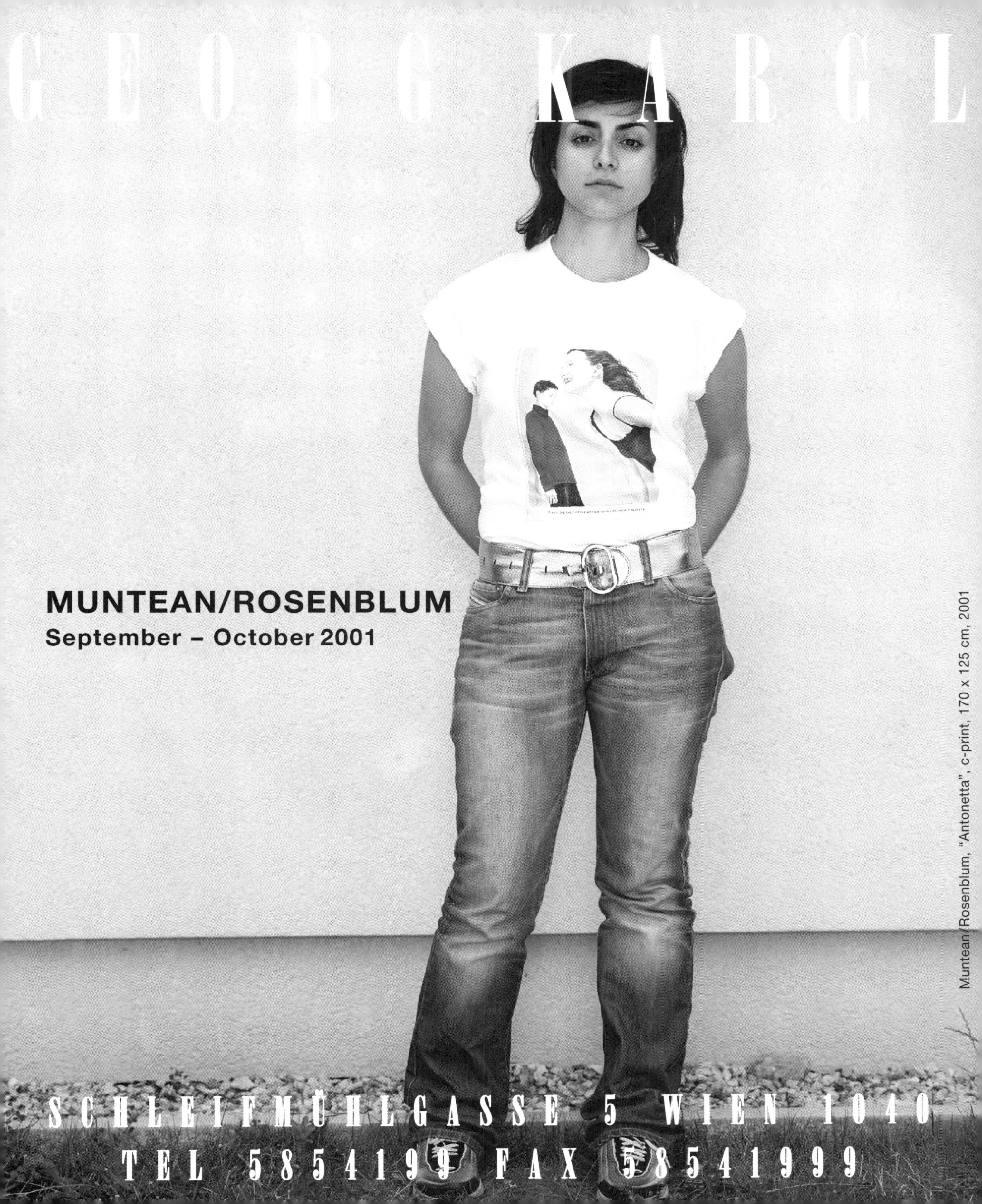

Muntean/Rosenblum, "Antonetta", c-print, 170 x 125 cm, 2001

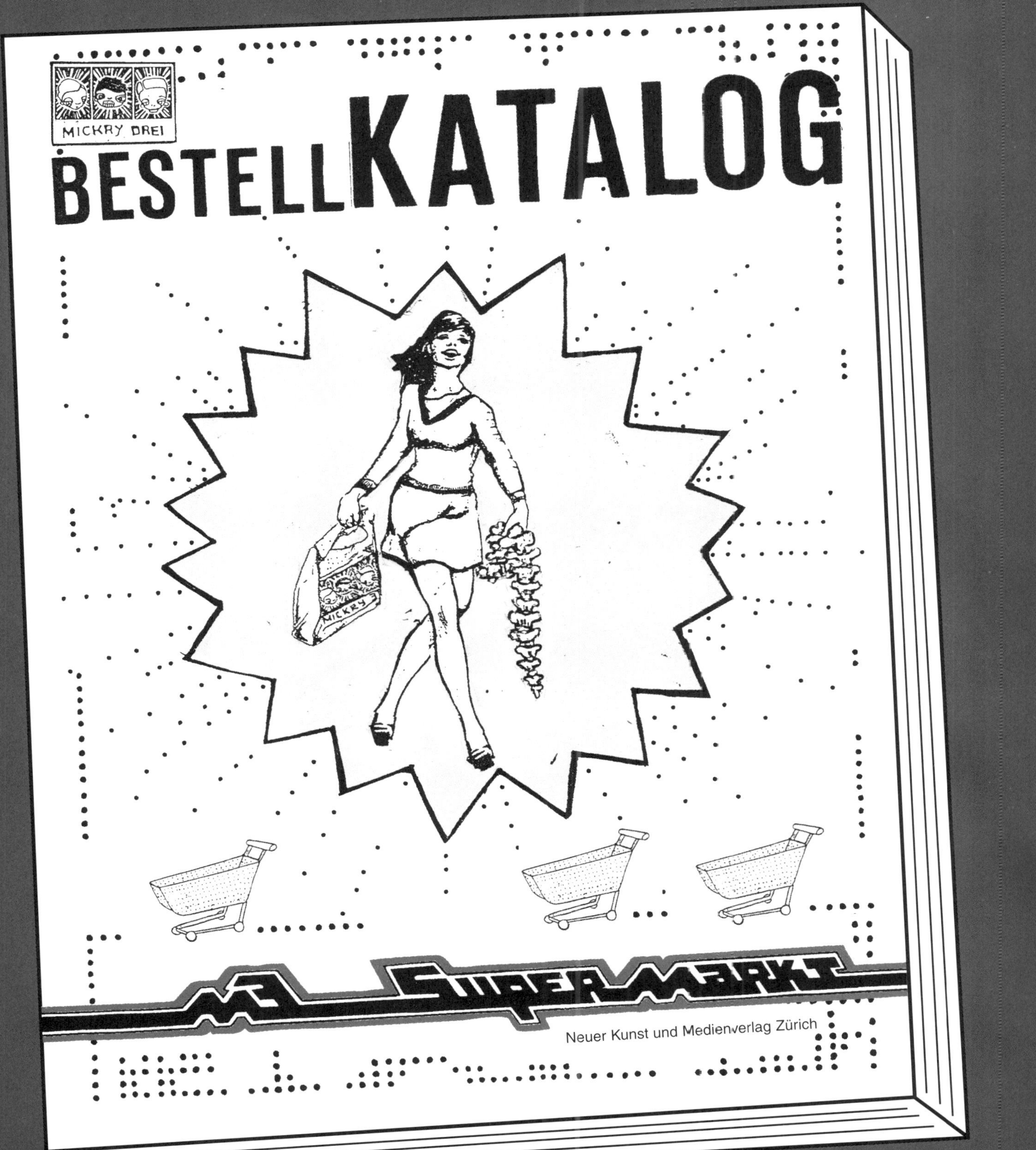

kunstraum walcheturm, walchestrasse 6, 8005 zürich, info@walcheturm.ch
mickry 3 «supermarkt» gäste: mark divo und ingo giezendanner
vernissage: 12. september 2001, finissage: 17. oktober 2001, ausstellung: 13. september – 17. oktober
mittwoch: 17 – 22 uhr, donnerstag und freitag: 17 – 20 uhr, samstag: 16 – 19 uhr
das buch zur ausstellung «supermarkt» erscheint mitte september bei neuer kunst und medienverlag zürich
[info@neuerkunst-medienverlag.ch] und ist ebenfalls der bestellkatalog für sämtliche mickry 3 produkte.

GALERIE PATRIK FRÖHLICH

GALERIE BOB GYSIN

WWW.BG-GALERIE.CH

AUSSTELLUNGSSTRASSE 24, 8005 ZÜRICH
T 01 278 40 60—F 01 278 40 50—INFO@BG-GALERIE.CH

Matthias Bosshart
23. August–13. Oktober

DONNERSTAG, 4. OKTOBER 2001, 19 UHR: PROJEKTION VON MATTHIAS BOSSHARTS FILMEN. ANSCHLIESSEND GESPRÄCH ZUM THEMA <KUNST UND FILM> MIT KATHLEEN BÜHLER

Fairy Tales—internationale Gruppenausstellung
26. Oktober–8. Dezember

DI–FR 12–18—SA 11–16

ART COLOGNE
31. OKTOBER–4. NOVEMBER

Zurich's New Museum presents

James Turrell
September 30, 2001 to January 27, 2002

Schweiz konkret
September 30, 2001 to May 26, 2002

Wednesday–Friday 12 am–6 pm
Saturday/Sunday 11 am–6 pm
Closed Monday/Tuesday

haus konstruktiv

Haus Konstruktiv
Selnaustrasse 25, CH-8001 Zürich
Phone +41 1 217 70 80, Fax +41 1 217 70 90
info@hauskonstruktiv.ch
www.hauskonstruktiv.ch

Open: Wed - Sun 10 - 17
Tuesday 10 - 19

Kunsthalle Bern
Helvetiaplatz 1
CH-3005 Bern
Phone +41 31. 351 00 31
Fax +41 31. 352 53 85
E-mail: kunsthalle@bluewin.ch
www.kunsthallebern.ch

Richard Wright
Gregor Zivić

**August 24 -
October 14, 2001**

Maria Eichhorn

**October 27 -
December 9, 2001**

Inforaum
Meschac Gaba

Kunsthalle Bern

Inflatable Balloon Flower (yellow)

Edition for Parkett 50/51
by Jeff Koons

manufactured by

schultes.wien

p.michael schultes, mollardgasse 85A/1/30, A-1060 wien
fon & fax +43-1-596 5961
www.schulteswien.com
schultes@schulteswien.com

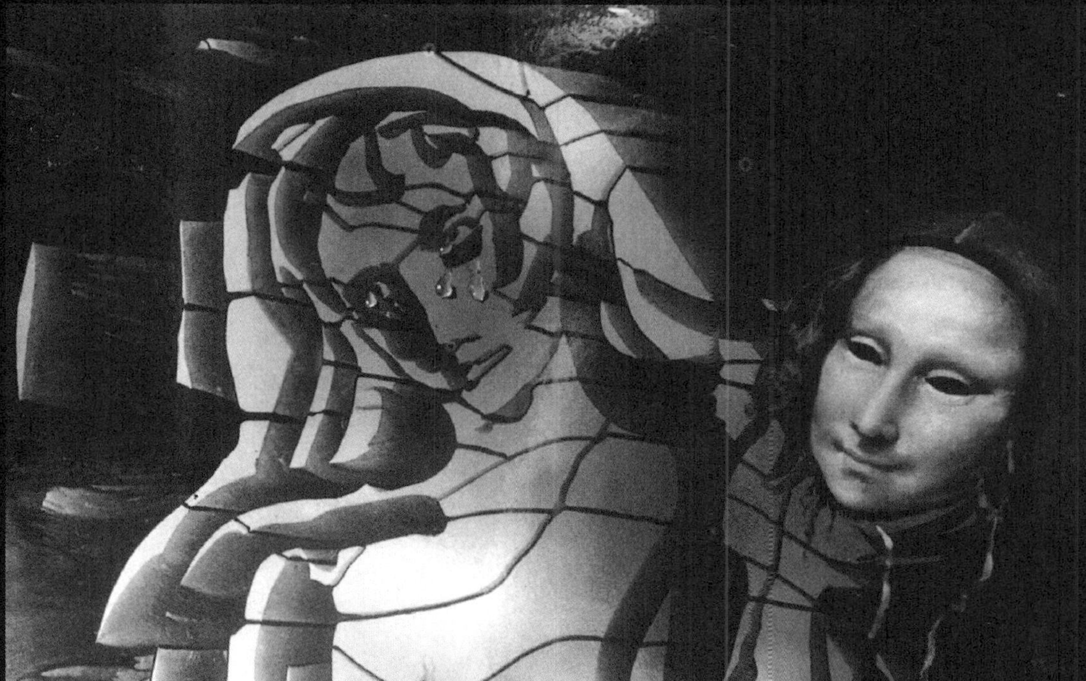

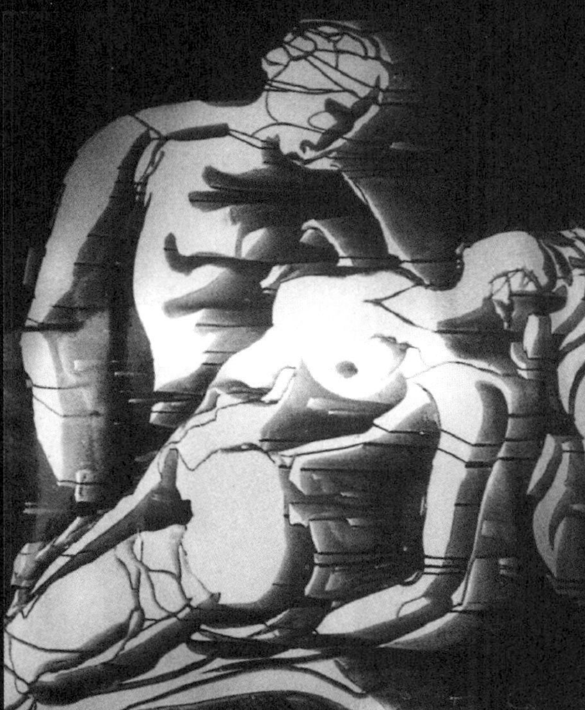

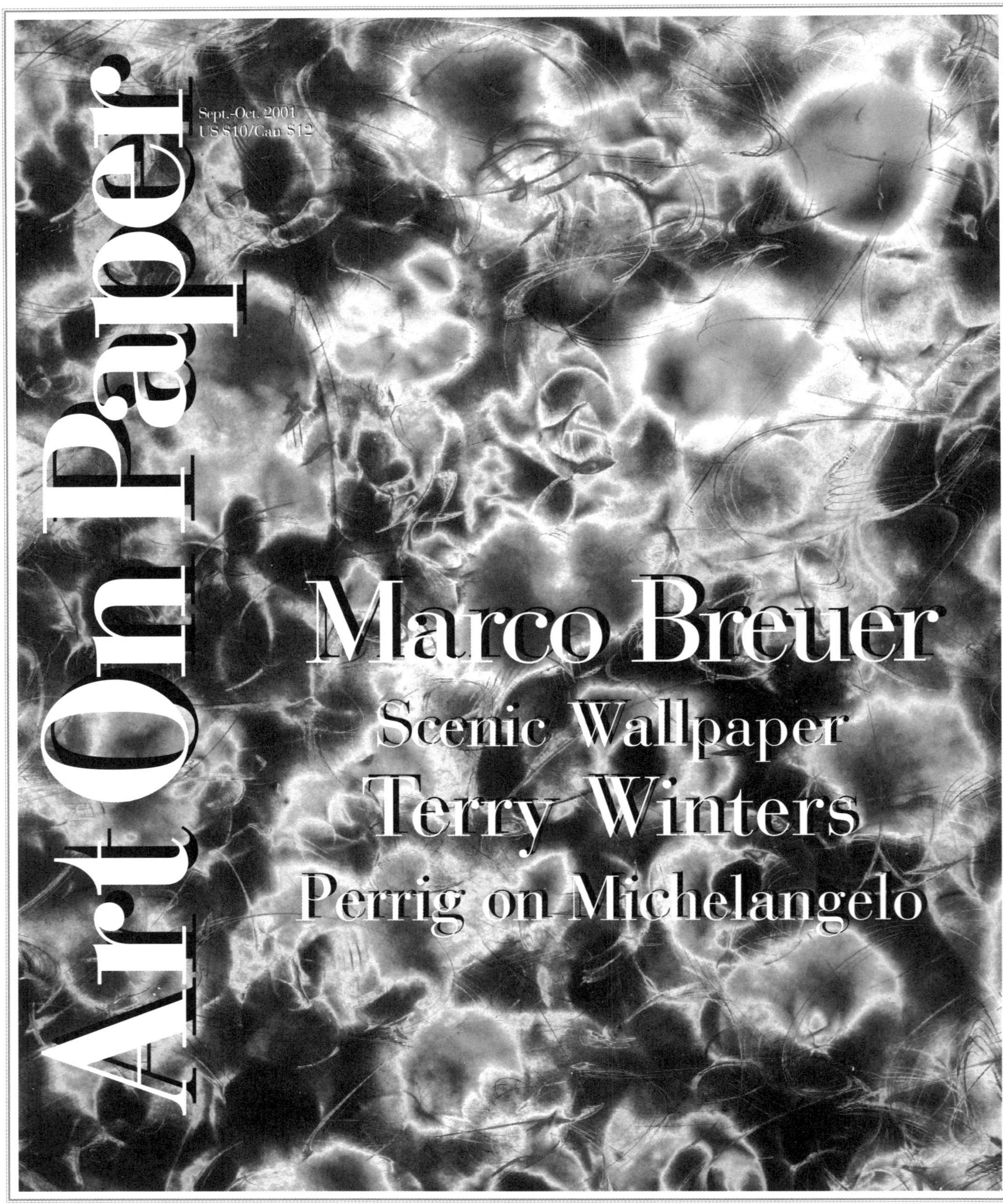
Art On Paper
Sept.-Oct. 2001
US $10/Can $12
Marco Breuer
Scenic Wallpaper
Terry Winters
Perrig on Michelangelo

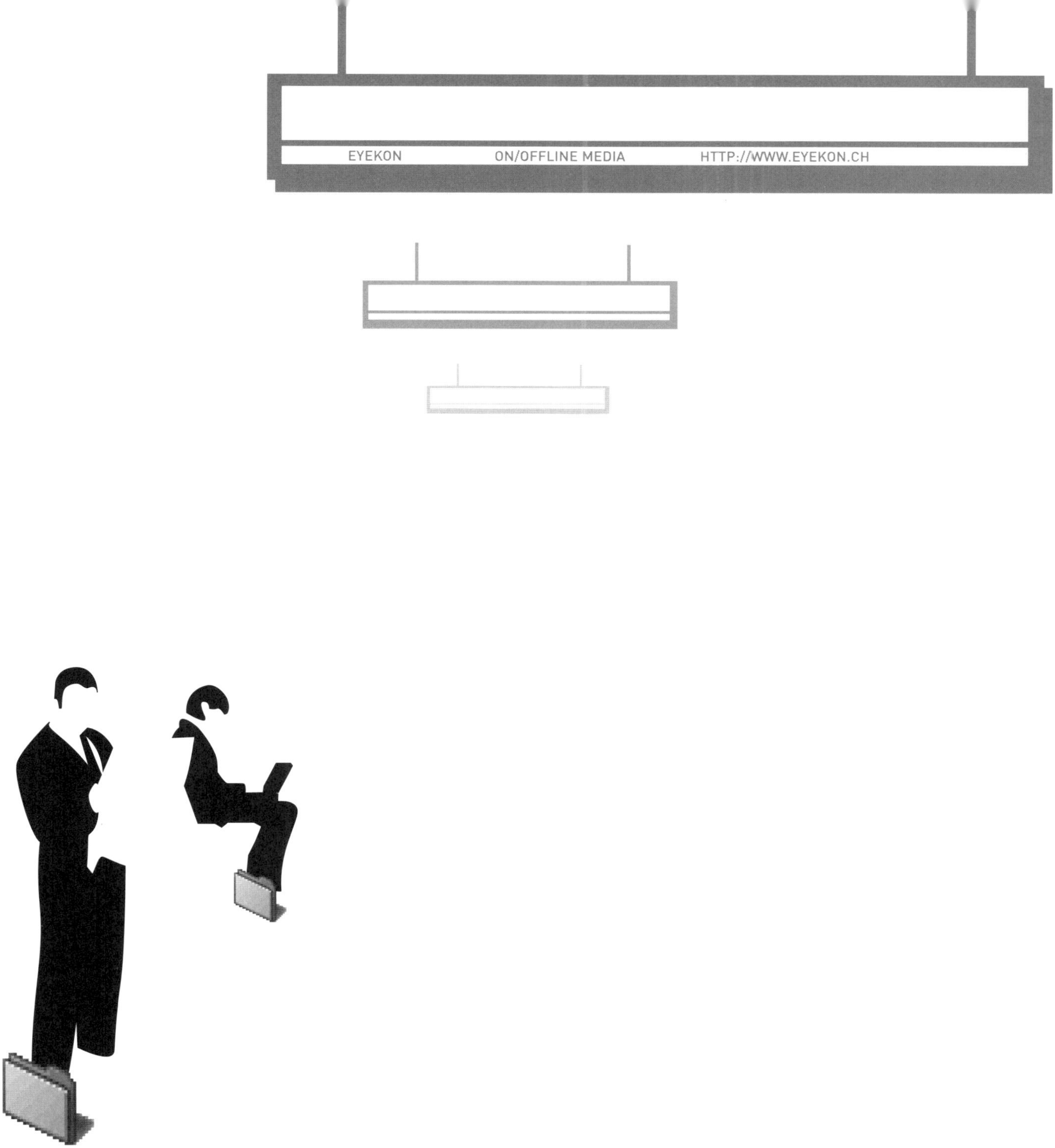
EYEKON
ON/OFFLINE MEDIA
HTTP://WWW.EYEKON.CH

FIAC2001

10-15 OCTOBER / PORTE DE VERSAILLES / PARIS EXPO - FRANCE

ONE PERSON SHOWS • AIR DE PARIS, Paris • ART: CONCEPT, Paris • ALFONSO ARTIACO, Pozzuoli-Napoli • RAMIS BARQUET, New York • GUY BARTSCHI, Geneva • CLAUDE BERNARD, Paris • BERNARD BOUCHE, Paris • JEANNE BUCHER, Paris • EVELYNE CANUS, Paris • LOUIS CARRÉ & CIE, Paris • CHARIMGALERIE, Wien • M. & T. DE LA CHÂTRE, Paris • DEWEER ART GALLERY, Otegem • SALVADOR DIAZ, Madrid • EL MUSEO, Bogota • FAGGIONATO, London • BARBARA FARBER / LA SERRE, Trets • FRANK, Paris • ALAIN LE GAILLARD, Paris • ALAIN GUTHARC, Paris • HACHMEISTER, Munster • MARWAN HOSS, Paris • HUE-WILLIAMS, London • HUSSENOT, Paris • CATHERINE ISSERT, Saint Paul de Vence • JACOBSON, London • CRANE KALMAN, London • KRINZINGER, Wien • ANNE LAHUMIÈRE, Paris • FRED LANZENBERG, Brussels • LAROCK GRANOFF, Paris • THOMAS LEVY, Hamburg-Madrid • MARIA MARTIN, Madrid • MEIER FINE ARTS, San Francisco NINA MENOCAL, Mexico • ALAIN NOIRHOMME, Brussels • NOTHELFER, Berlin • ONIRIS, Rennes • ROGER PAILHAS, Marseille • ALICE PAULI, Lausanne • GIORGIO PERSANO, Torino • PIÈCE UNIQUE, Paris • GUY PIETERS, Knokke le Zoute • PRAZ-DELAVALLADE, Paris • PUNTO, Valencia • RABOUAN MOUSSION, Paris • SAN CARLO, Milano • SAPONE, Nice • MICHAEL SCHULTZ, Berlin • SENDA, Barcelona • STEINEK, Wien • TENDANCES, Paris • THE BOX ASSOCIATI, Torino • ALINE VIDAL, Paris • VIDAL SAINT PHALLE, Paris • DINA VIERNY, Paris • WETTERLING GALLERY, Stockholm • ZABRISKIE, New York • ZANNETTACCI, Geneva • **GROUP SHOWS** • LUIS ADELANTADO, Valencia • APPLICAT-PRAZAN, Paris • BARONIAN, Brussels • ANNE BARRAULT, Paris • BEAUBOURG, Vence • BOGHICI, Rio • BORZO, Hertogenbosch • DE BROCK, Knokke • FERRAN CANO, Barcelona • CATS, Brussels • CENT8, Paris • CHINESE CONTEMPORARY, London • CHOBOT, Wien • CONTINI, Venice • CONTINUA, San Gemignano • CROUSEL, Paris • DI MEO, Paris • ERIC DUPONT, Paris • LES FILLES DU CALVAIRE, Paris • GALERIE DE FRANCE, Paris • GAN, Tokyo • GMURZYNSKA, Koln • THESSA HEROLD, Paris • HILGER, Wien • XAVIER HUFKENS, Brussels • RODOLPHE JANSSEN, Brussels • JAY JOPLING / WHITE CUBE, London • JGM, Paris • JORDAN, Paris • DU JOUR AGNÈS B, Paris • JOUSSE ENTREPRISE, Paris • KETEILMAN, Brussels • YVON LAMBERT, Paris • BAUDOIN LEBON, Paris • LELONG, New York • LISSON GALLERY, London • DIANA LOWENSTEIN, Miami • MALBOROUGH, New York • THE MAYOR GALLERY, London • KAMEL MENNOUR, Paris • METRO PICTURES, New York • METTA, Madrid • GALERIE 1900-2000, Paris • HELLY NAHMAD, London • NO CODE, Bologna • MARCO NOIRE, Torino • DE NOIRMONT, Paris • NATHALIE OBADIA, Paris • DE OSMA, Madrid • PAPILLON FIAT, Paris • YVONAMOR PALIX, Paris • NATHALIE PARIENTE, Paris • FRANÇOISE PAVIOT, Paris • EMMANUEL PERROTIN, Paris • POLARIS, Paris • RAAB, Berlin • ALMINE RECH, Paris • MICHEL REIN, Paris • DENISE RENÉ, Paris • LE RÉVERBÈRE, Lyon • THADDAEUS ROPPAC, Paris • AUREL SCHEIBLER, Koln • NATHALIE SÉROUSSI, Paris • SUSAN SHEEHAN, New York • SIMOENS, Knokke • SOLLERTIS, Toulouse • PIETRO SPARTA, Chagny • GIAN ENZO SPERONE, Rome • MICHELINE SZWAJCER, Antwerpen • TEGA, Milano • DANIEL TEMPLON, Paris • TRIGANO, Paris • TORNABUONI, Firenze • G-P. & N. VALLOIS, Paris • VEDOVI, Brussels • DE VILLEPOIX, Paris • WADDINGTON GALLERIES, London • ANTON WELLER, Paris • XIPPAS, Paris • ZONCA & ZONCA, Milano • ZURCHER, Paris • **PERSPECTIVES** • ARNDT & PARTNER, Berlin • ART ATTITUDE HERVÉ BIZE, Nancy • DAMASQUINE & AEROPLASTICS, Brussels • ESPAI 292, Barcelona • GANDY GALLERY, Praha • OLIVIER HOUG, Lyon • IN SITU, Paris • LA FERRONNERIE / BRIGITTE NÉGRIER, Paris • MAZE, Torino • SHANGART, Shangaï • SHINE GALLERY, London • LE SOUS-SOL, Paris • SPENCER BROWNSTONE, New York • CHEZ VALENTIN, Paris • **EDITION** • ART OF THIS CENTURY, New York • FRANCK BORDAS, Paris • HERVÉ BORDAS, Venice • CLOT, BRAMSEN & GEORGES, Paris • FANAL, Basel • ITEMS, Paris • PASNIC, Paris • CATHERINE PUTMAN, Paris • ERIC SEYDOUX, Paris • WOOLWORTH, Paris • Liste au 26/06 • **NEW SECTOR: VIDEO CUBE**

SPECIAL EVENTS FOR ART COLLECTORS:

Throughout FIAC, "Parcours Privé" tour is giving art collectors the opportunity of exclusive viewings of the fair as well as the most prestigious cultural institutions of Paris.

To find out more about FIAC special collector's events, visit our web site:

www.fiac-online.com

TRAVEL AGENCY USA: Turon Travel
Phone: +1 /212- 925 5453 - Fax: +1 /212- 219 18 65

AIRLINE:
Agreement N° SS8069
Validity from Oct.7 to 17, 2001
Preferential fares on international routes.
For information contact your nearest Air France office
www.airfrance.com

For exhibition information : Reed-OIP - 11, rue du colonel Pierre Avia - BP 571 - 75726 Paris Cedex 15 - Tel: +33 (0)1 41 90 47 80 - Fax: + 33 (0)1 41 90 47 89 - Email: fiac@reed-oip.fr

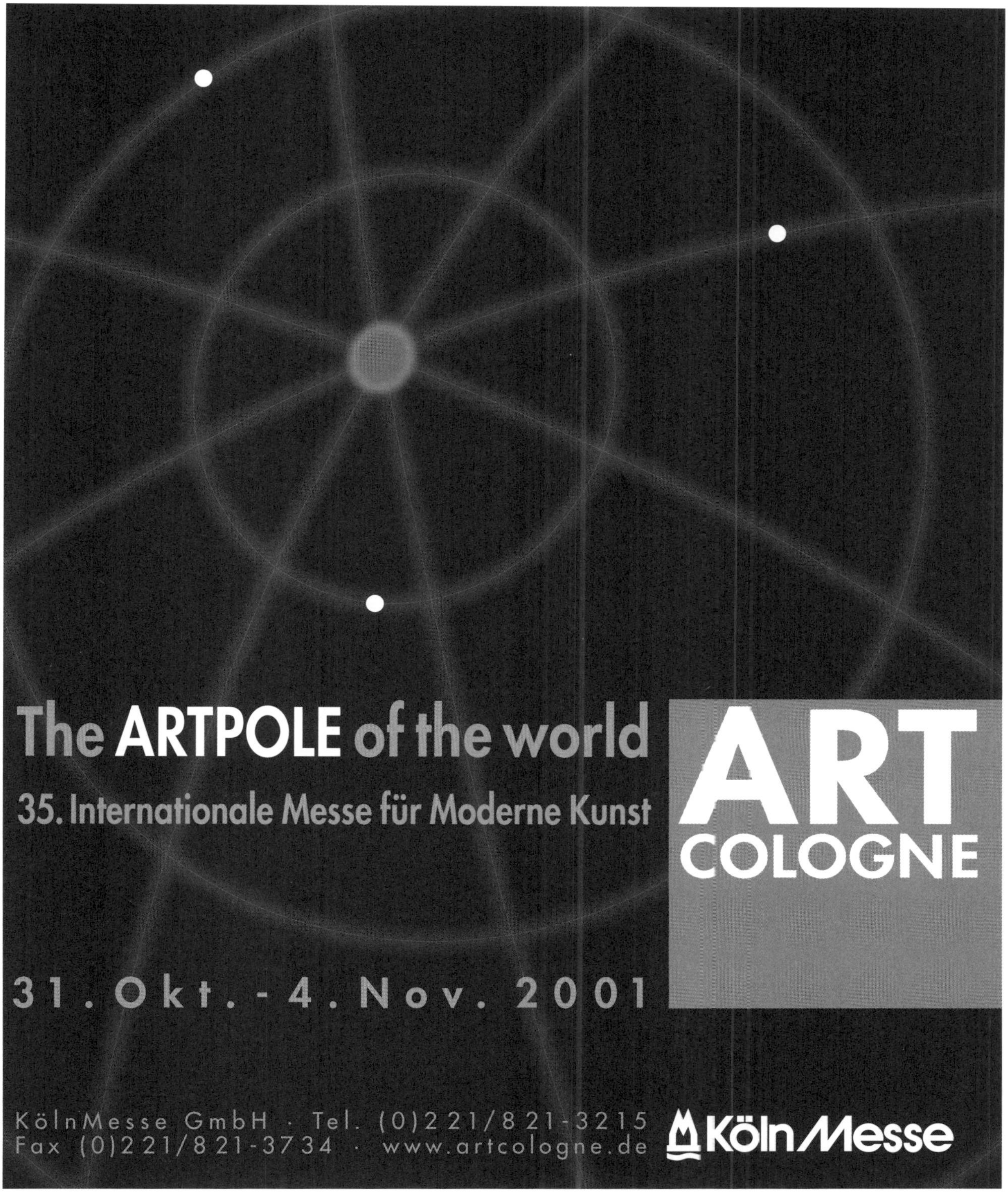
The ARTPOLE of the world
35. Internationale Messe für Moderne Kunst
ART
COLOGNE
31. Okt. - 4. Nov. 2001
KölnMesse GmbH · Tel. (0)221/821-3215
Fax (0)221/821-3734 · www.artcologne.de
KölnMesse

26.–30. Mai 2002

art frankfurt

Die europäische Messe für junge Kunst: New Attitudes, Kunst ab 1960, Editions District. Für Fachbesucher und Publikum. Messe Frankfurt. Infoline +49 (0)69 75 75 66 94
www.artfrankfurt.de

buy art!

Heine/Lenz/Zizka

Messe Frankfurt

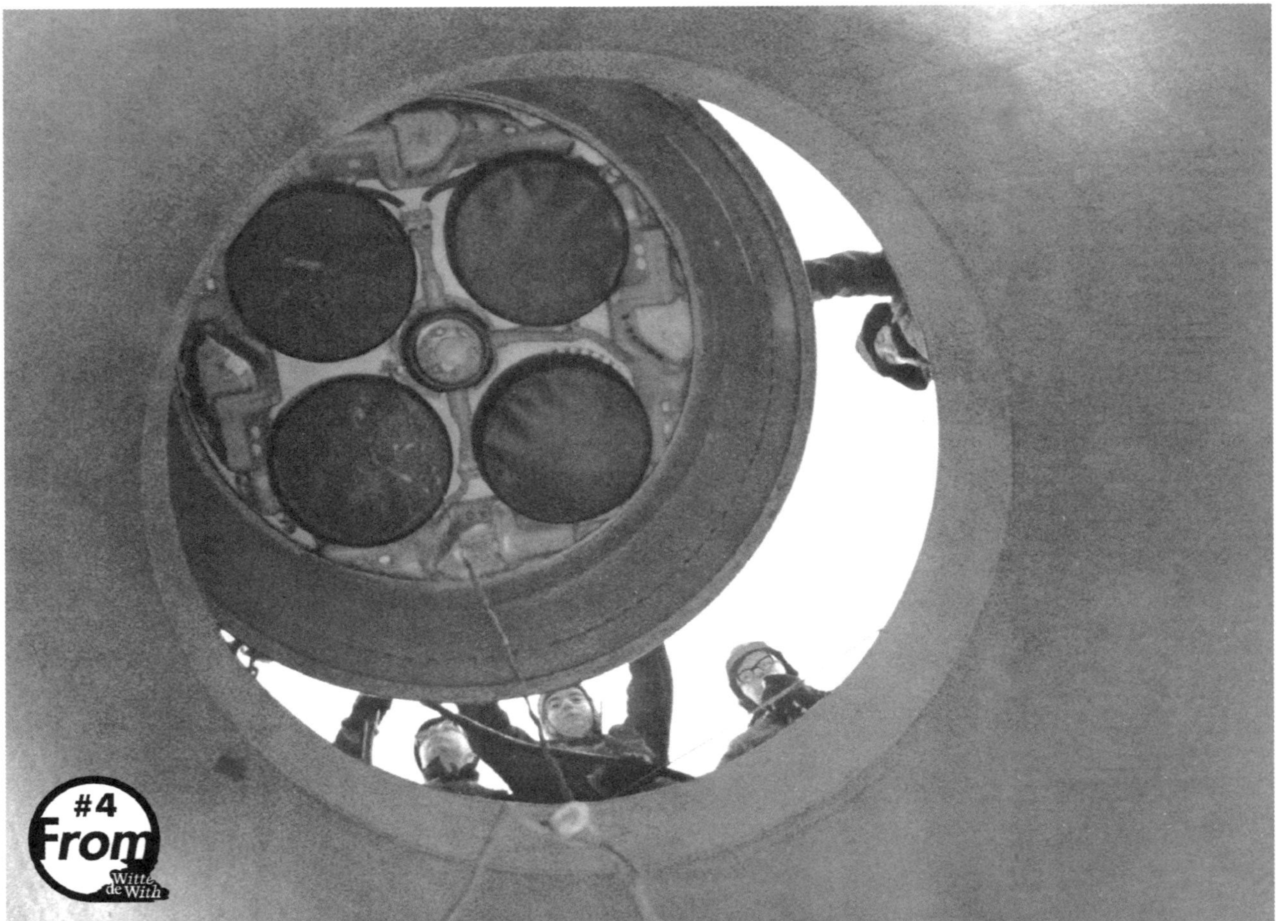
#4
From
Witte de With

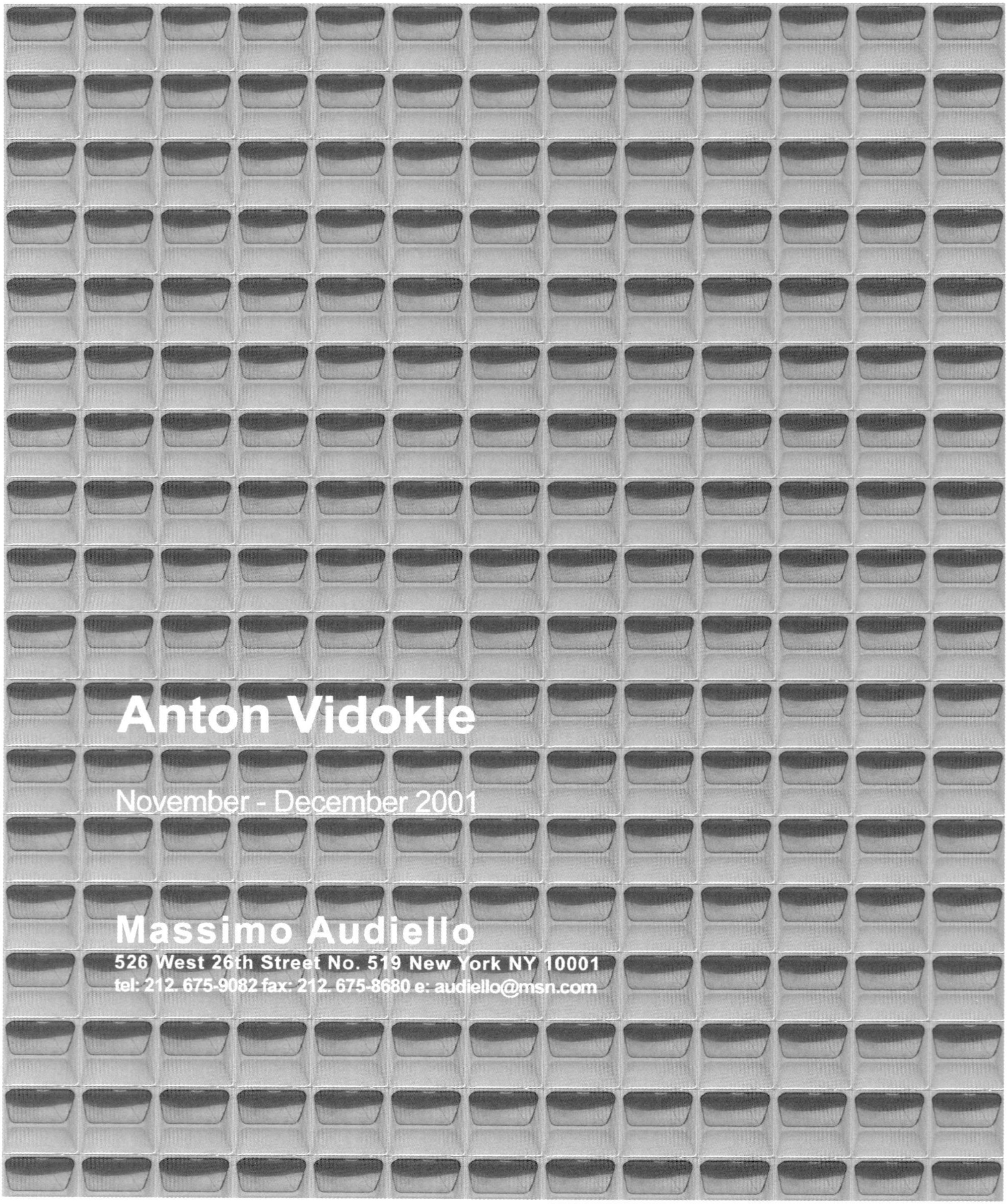
Anton Vidokle
November - December 2001
Massimo Audiello
526 West 26th Street No. 519 New York NY 10001
tel: 212. 675-9082 fax: 212. 675-8680 e: audiello@msn.com

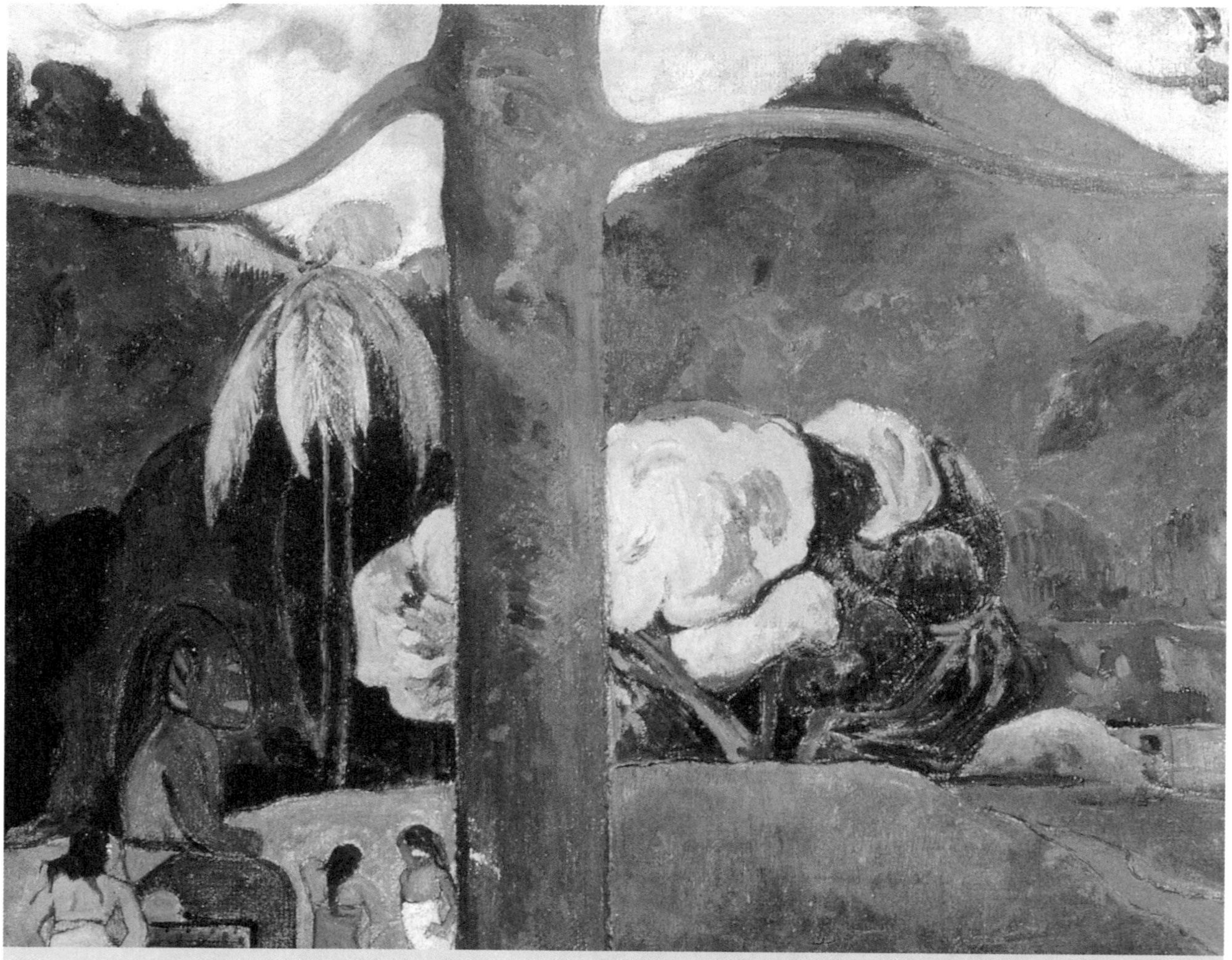

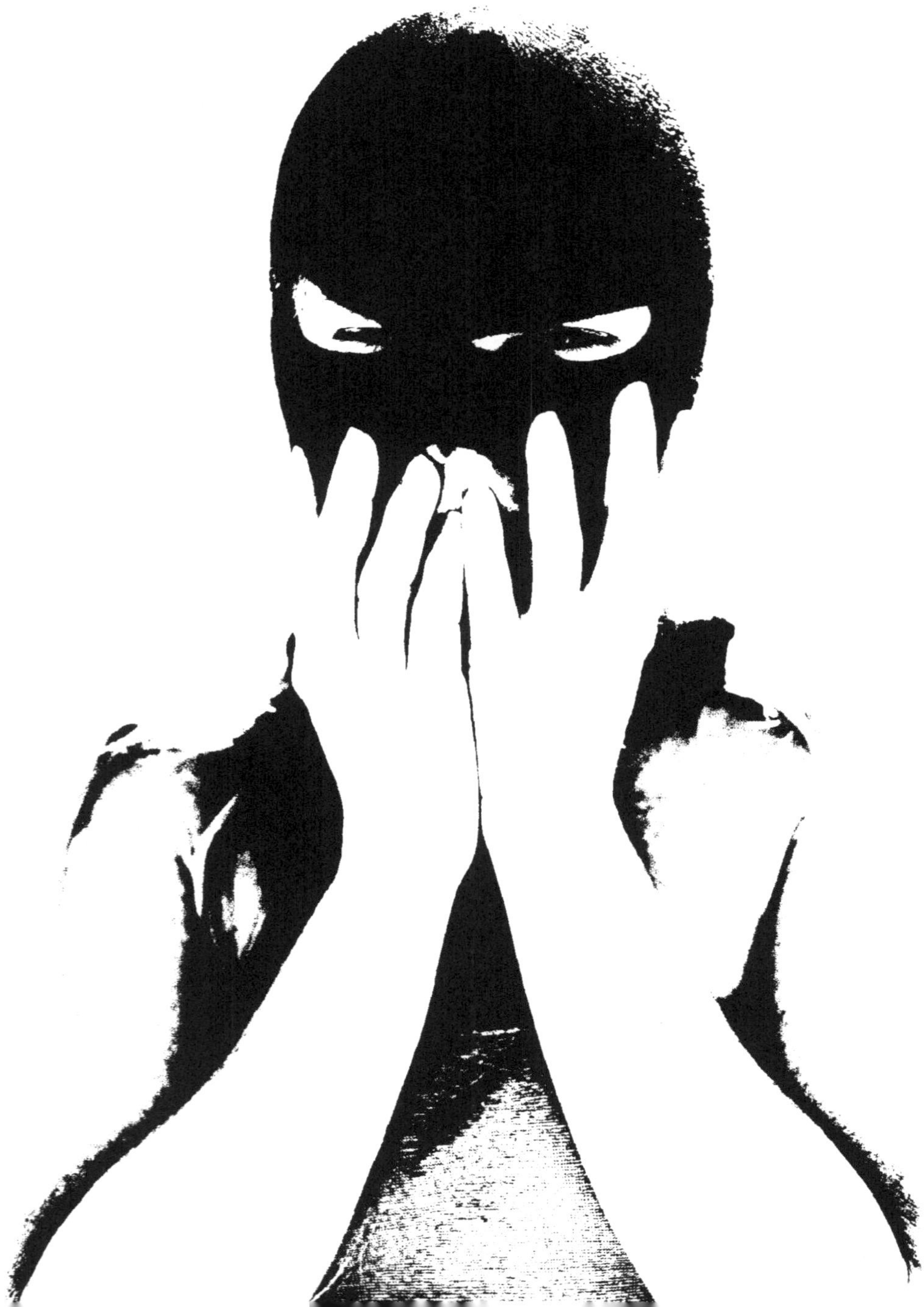

doug aitken

NEW OCEAN

serpentine gallery
12 october - 25 november 2001
kensington gardens
london
W2 3XA
T: 020 72 98 15 15

produced by the
fondazione sandretto
re rebaudengo per l'arte,
presented in association with
the serpentine gallery

Serpentine Gallery

7. September – 20. Dezember 2001

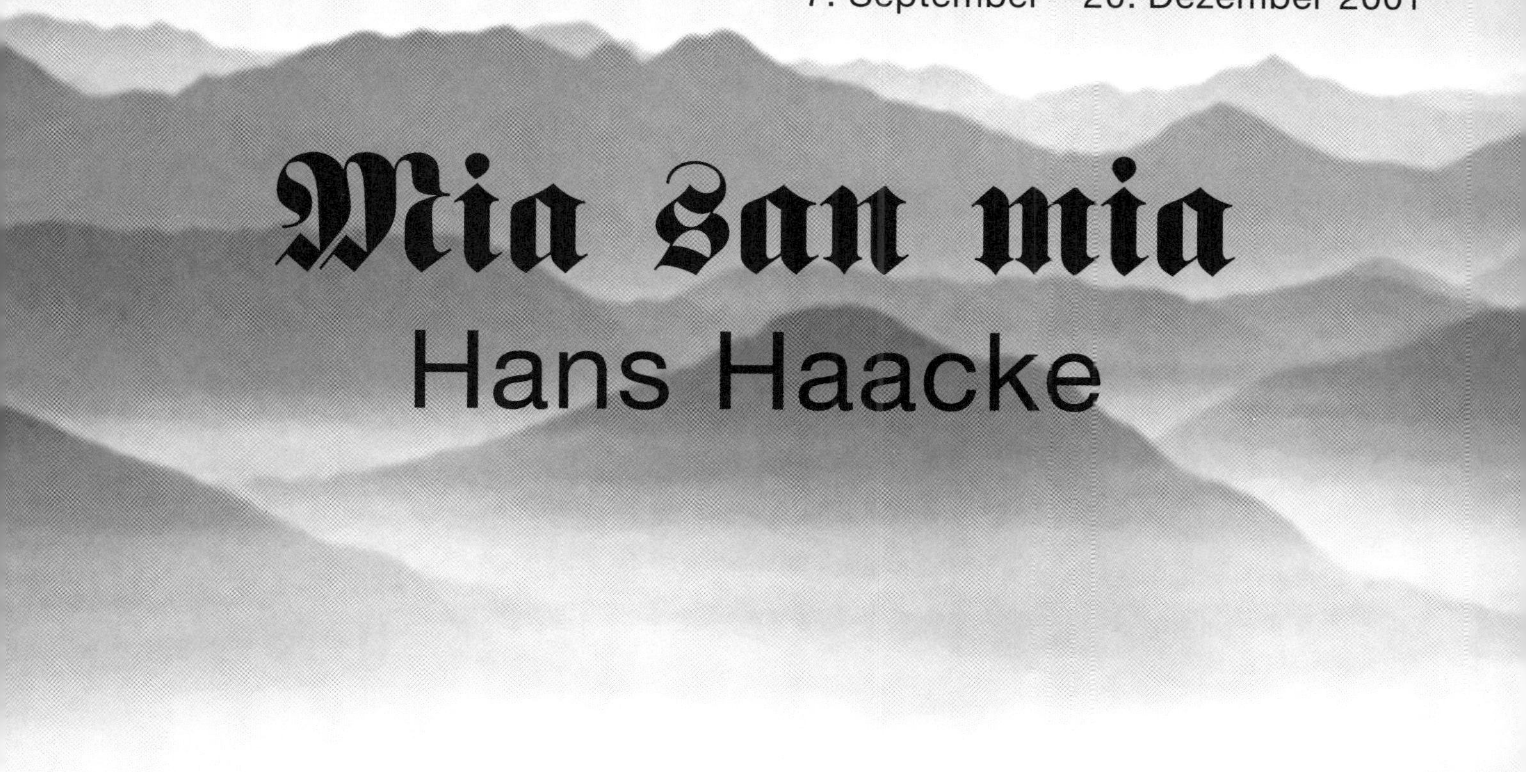

Mia san mia

Hans Haacke

7. September – 20. Dezember 2001

Werke aus der Sammlung

Generali Foundation
Wiedner Hauptstraße 15
1040 Wien, Austria

Tel. (+43 1) 504 98 80
Fax (+43 1) 504 98 83

http://foundation.generali.at

Publikation

GERHARD RICHTER

PAINTINGS 1996–2001

SEPTEMBER 14 THROUGH OCTOBER 27, 2001

MARIAN GOODMAN GALLERY

24 WEST 57TH STREET NEW YORK NY 10019 TEL 212 977-7160
FAX 212 581-5187 GOODMAN@MARIANGOODMAN.COM

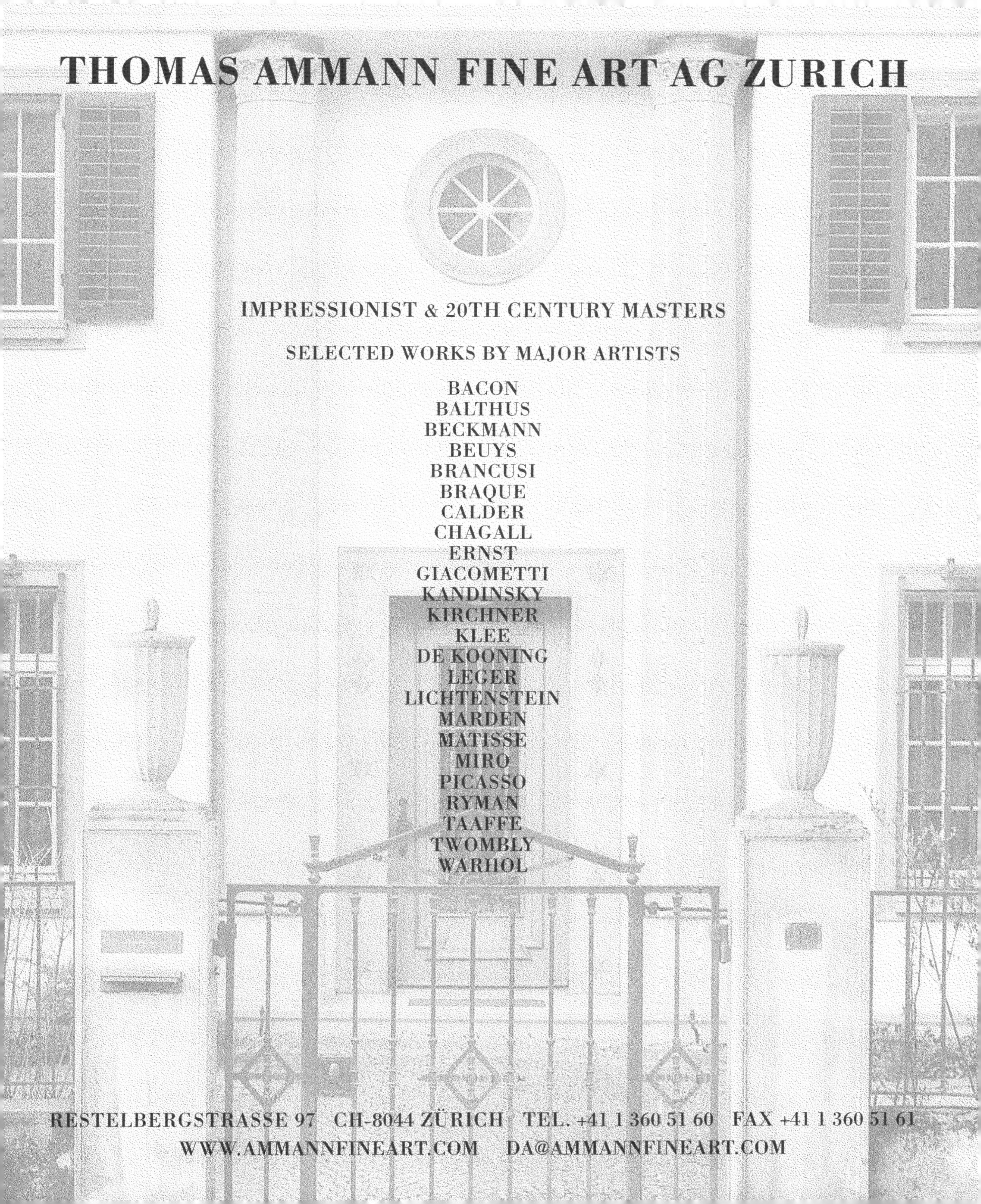
THOMAS AMMANN FINE ART AG ZURICH
IMPRESSIONIST & 20TH CENTURY MASTERS
SELECTED WORKS BY MAJOR ARTISTS
BACON
BALTHUS
BECKMANN
BEUYS
BRANCUSI
BRAQUE
CALDER
CHAGALL
ERNST
GIACOMETTI
KANDINSKY
KIRCHNER
KLEE
DE KOONING
LEGER
LICHTENSTEIN
MARDEN
MATISSE
MIRO
PICASSO
RYMAN
TAAFFE
TWOMBLY
WARHOL
RESTELBERGSTRASSE 97 CH-8044 ZÜRICH TEL. +41 1 360 51 60 FAX +41 1 360 51 61
WWW.AMMANNFINEART.COM DA@AMMANNFINEART.COM